BOARD OF EDITORS

RICHARD J. CONVISER
Professor of Law, IIT/Kent
Editorial Director

MICHAEL R. ASIMOW
Professor of Law, U.C.L.A.

JOHN A. BAUMAN
Professor of Law, U.C.L.A.

PAUL D. CARRINGTON
Dean and Professor of Law, Duke University

JESSE H. CHOPER
Professor of Law, U.C. Berkeley

GEORGE E. DIX
Professor of Law, University of Texas

JESSE DUKEMINIER
Professor of Law, U.C.L.A.

MELVIN A. EISENBERG
Professor of Law, U.C. Berkeley

WILLIAM A. FLETCHER
Professor of Law, U.C. Berkeley

MARC A. FRANKLIN
Professor of Law, Stanford University

JACK H. FRIEDENTHAL
Dean and Professor of Law, George Washington University

EDWARD C. HALBACH, JR.
Professor of Law, U.C. Berkeley

GEOFFREY C. HAZARD, JR.
Professor of Law, Yale University

STANLEY M. JOHANSON
Professor of Law, University of Texas

THOMAS M. JORDE
Professor of Law, U.C. Berkeley

HERMA HILL KAY
Dean and Professor of Law, U.C. Berkeley

JOHN H. McCORD
Professor of Law, University of Illinois

PAUL MARCUS
Professor of Law, College of William and Mary

RICHARD L. MARCUS
Professor of Law, U.C. Hastings

ARTHUR R. MILLER
Professor of Law, Harvard University

ROBERT H. MNOOKIN
Professor of Law, Harvard University

THOMAS D. MORGAN
Professor of Law, George Washington University

JARRET C. OELTJEN
Professor of Law, Florida State University

JAMES C. OLDHAM
Professor of Law, Georgetown University

WILLIAM A. REPPY, JR.
Professor of Law, Duke University

THOMAS D. ROWE, JR.
Professor of Law, Duke University

JON R. WALTZ
Professor of Law, Northwestern University

DOUGLAS J. WHALEY
Professor of Law, Ohio State University

CHARLES H. WHITEBREAD
Professor of Law, U.S.C.

KENNETH H. YORK
Professor of Law, Pepperdine University

gilbert
LAW SUMMARIES

CIVIL PROCEDURE

Fifteenth Edition—1995

Richard L. Marcus
Professor of Law
University of California, Hastings

Thomas D. Rowe, Jr.
Professor of Law
Duke University

HARCOURT BRACE LEGAL AND PROFESSIONAL PUBLICATIONS, INC.
EDITORIAL OFFICES: 176 W. Adams, Suite 2100, Chicago, IL 60603

REGIONAL OFFICES: New York, Chicago, Los Angeles, Washington, D.C.
Distributed by: **Harcourt Brace & Company** 6277 Sea Harbor Drive, Orlando, FL 32887 (800)787-8717

PROJECT EDITOR
Steven J. Levin, B.A., J.D.

SERIES EDITOR
Elizabeth L. Snyder, B.A., J.D.

QUALITY CONTROL EDITOR
Megan Knowles, B.A.

Copyright © 1994 by Harcourt Brace Legal and Professional Publications, Inc. All rights reserved. No part of this publication may be reproduced or transmitted in any form or by any means, electronic or mechanical, including photocopy, recording, or any information storage and retrieval system, without permission in writing from the publisher. Printed in the United States of America.

gilbert
LAW SUMMARIES

Titles Available

Administrative Law
Agency & Partnership
Antitrust
Bankruptcy
Basic Accounting for Lawyers
Business Law
California Bar Performance Test Skills
Civil Procedure
Civil Procedure & Practice
Commercial Paper & Payment Law
Community Property
Conflict of Laws
Constitutional Law
Contracts
Corporations
Criminal Law
Criminal Procedure
Dictionary of Legal Terms
Estate and Gift Tax
Evidence

Family Law
Federal Courts
First Year Questions & Answers
Future Interests
Income Tax I (Individual)
Income Tax II (Corporate)
Labor Law
Legal Ethics
Legal Research & Writing
Multistate Bar Exam
Personal Property
Property
Remedies
Sales & Lease of Goods
Securities Regulation
Secured Transactions
Torts
Trusts
Wills

Also Available:
First Year Program
Pocket Size Law Dictionary
Success in Law School Handbook

Gilbert Law Audio Tapes
"The Law School Legends Series"

Bankruptcy
Civil Procedure
Commercial Paper
Constitutional Law
Contracts
Corporations
Criminal Law

Criminal Procedure
Evidence
Family Law
Federal Income Taxation
Future Interests
Law School ABC's
Law School Exam Writing

Professional Responsibility
Real Property
Remedies
Sales & Lease of Goods
Secured Transactions
Torts
Wills & Trusts

**All Titles Available at Your Law School Bookstore,
or Call to Order: 1-800-787-8717**

Harcourt Brace Legal and Professional Publications, Inc.
176 West Adams, Suite 2100
Chicago, IL 60603

Also Available from Harcourt Brace...

Legalines™

**Features Detailed Case Briefs of Every Major Case,
Plus Summaries of the Black Letter Law.**

Titles Available

Administrative Law	Keyed to Breyer
Administrative Law	Keyed to Gellhorn
Administrative Law	Keyed to Schwartz
Antitrust	Keyed to Handler
Antitrust	Keyed to Areeda
Civil Procedure	Keyed to Cound
Civil Procedure	Keyed to Field
Civil Procedure	Keyed to Louisell
Civil Procedure	Keyed to Rosenberg
Civil Procedure	Keyed to Yeazell
Commercial Law	Keyed to Farnsworth
Commercial Law	Keyed to Speidel
Conflict of Laws	Keyed to Cramton
Conflict of Laws	Keyed to Reese
Constitutional Law	Keyed to Brest
Constitutional Law	Keyed to Cohen
Constitutional Law	Keyed to Gunther
Constitutional Law	Keyed to Lockhart
Constitutional Law	Keyed to Rotunda
Constitutional Law	Keyed to Stone
Contracts	Keyed to Calamari
Contracts	Keyed to Dawson
Contracts	Keyed to Farnsworth
Contracts	Keyed to Fuller
Contracts	Keyed to Kessler
Contracts	Keyed to Knapp/Crystal
Contracts	Keyed to Murphy
Corporations	Keyed to Cary
Corporations	Keyed to Choper
Corporations	Keyed to Hamilton
Corporations	Keyed to Vagts
Criminal Law	Keyed to Boyce
Criminal Law	Keyed to Dix
Criminal Law	Keyed to Johnson
Criminal Law	Keyed to Kadish
Criminal Law	Keyed to La Fave
Criminal Procedure	Keyed to Kamisar
Decedents Estates	Keyed to Ritchie
Domestic Relations	Keyed to Clark
Domestic Relations	Keyed to Wadlington
Enterprise Organizations	Keyed to Conard
Estate & Gift Tax	Keyed to Surrey
Evidence	Keyed to Kaplan
Evidence	Keyed to McCormick
Evidence	Keyed to Weinstein
Family Law	Keyed to Areen
Federal Courts	Keyed to McCormick
Income Taxation	Keyed to Andrews
Income Taxation	Keyed to Freeland
Income Taxation	Keyed to Klein
Labor Law	Keyed to Cox
Labor Law	Keyed to Merrifield
Partnership & Corporate Tax	Keyed to Surrey
Property	Keyed to Browder
Property	Keyed to Casner
Property	Keyed to Cribbet
Property	Keyed to Dukeminier
Real Property	Keyed to Rabin
Remedies	Keyed to Re
Remedies	Keyed to York
Securities Regulation	Keyed to Jennings
Torts	Keyed to Dobbs
Torts	Keyed to Epstein
Torts	Keyed to Franklin
Torts	Keyed to Henderson
Torts	Keyed to Keeton
Torts	Keyed to Prosser
Wills, Trusts & Estates	Keyed to Dukeminier

Other Titles Available:
Accounting For Lawyers
Criminal Law Questions & Answers
Excelling on Exams/How to Study
Torts Questions & Answers

*All Titles Available at Your Law School Bookstore,
or Call to Order: 1-800-787-8717*

Harcourt Brace Legal and Professional Publications, Inc.
176 West Adams, Suite 2100
Chicago, IL 60603

SUMMARY OF CONTENTS

Page

CIVIL PROCEDURE CAPSULE SUMMARY I

TEXT CORRELATION CHART i

APPROACH TO EXAMS .... (i)

I. **TERRITORIAL JURISDICTION AND RELATED MATTERS** 1
   Chapter Approach 1
   A. **Introduction** 1
   B. **Contemporary Constitutional Grounds for State Court Jurisdiction** 6
      1. Contacts with Forum 6
      2. Presence of Defendant's Property in Forum 13
      3. General Jurisdiction 16
      4. Consent 18
      5. Service Within the Jurisdiction 19
      6. Territorial Jurisdiction of Federal Courts 20
   C. **Statutory Authorization for Jurisdiction** 21
   D. **Litigating Jurisdiction** 23
   E. **Venue** 24
   F. **Forum Non Conveniens** 31
   G. **Notice** 34

II. **SUBJECT MATTER JURISDICTION OF THE FEDERAL COURTS** 41
    Chapter Approach 41
    A. **Introduction** 42
    B. **Diversity Jurisdiction** 45
    C. **Federal Question Jurisdiction** 53
    D. **Supplemental Jurisdiction** 59
    E. **Removal** 66

III. **RELATION BETWEEN STATE AND FEDERAL LAW** 72
     Chapter Approach 72
     A. **State Law in the Federal Courts** 73
     B. **Federal Common Law** 88

IV. **PLEADING** 90
    Chapter Approach 90
    A. **Introduction** 91
    B. **History of Pleading** 91
    C. **Complaint** 95
    D. **Challenges to Complaint** 111
    E. **Attorney's Duty to Investigate Claims and Defenses** 123
    F. **Answer** 127
    G. **Counterclaims and Cross-Claims** 134
    H. **Amended and Supplemental Pleadings** 140
    I. **Default Procedure** 147
    J. **Judgment on the Pleadings** 147
    K. **Voluntary Dismissal By Plaintiff** 148

Civil Procedure

V.	**PARTIES**	151
	Chapter Approach	151
	A. Real Party in Interest Rule	152
	B. Capacity of Party to Sue or Be Sued	156
	C. Joinder of Parties	158
	D. Class Actions	176
VI.	**DISCOVERY**	196
	Chapter Approach	196
	A. Introduction	196
	B. Basic Discovery Devices	198
	1. Prediscovery Disclosure	198
	2. Depositions	200
	3. Interrogatories	205
	4. Requests for Admission	207
	5. Requests for Inspection of Documents and Other Things	209
	6. Medical Examinations	211
	7. Duty to Supplement Responses	212
	C. Scope of Discovery	213
	D. Protective Orders	226
	E. Failure to Disclose or to Comply with Discovery	230
	F. Appellate Review of Discovery Orders	233
	G. Use of Discovery at Trial	234
	H. Private Investigation	235
VII.	**SUMMARY JUDGMENT**	236
	Chapter Approach	236
	A. Introduction	236
	B. Standard for Grant of Summary Judgment	238
	C. Procedure	240
VIII.	**MANAGERIAL JUDGING, PRETRIAL CONFERENCE, AND SETTLEMENT PROMOTION**	247
	Chapter Approach	247
	A. Pretrial Conferences and Managerial Judging	247
	B. Court-Annexed Settlement Devices	252
IX.	**TRIAL**	256
	Chapter Approach	256
	A. Right to Trial By Jury	256
	B. Selection of the Jury	262
	C. Disqualification of Judge	266
	D. Order of Trial	267
	E. Presentation of Evidence	268
	F. Motions at Close of Proof	269
	G. Argument to Jury	273
	H. Instructions to Jury	274
	I. Jury Deliberation and Verdict	276
	J. Motions After Verdict or Judgment	282
X.	**APPEAL**	294
	Chapter Approach	294

	A.	Introduction	294
	B.	Right to Appeal	295
	C.	Courts of Review	295
	D.	Appellate Procedure	298
	E.	Rulings Subject to Appeal	299
	F.	Scope of Appellate Review	304
	G.	Appellate Review By Extraordinary Writ	309
XI.		**PRECLUSIVE EFFECT OF JUDGMENTS**	312
		Chapter Approach	312
	A.	Introduction	313
	B.	Claim Preclusion	313
	C.	Issue Preclusion	319
	D.	Persons Precluded By Judgments	322

REVIEW QUESTIONS AND ANSWERS 327

SAMPLE EXAM QUESTIONS AND ANSWERS 361

TABLE OF CITATIONS TO FEDERAL RULES OF CIVIL PROCEDURE 377

TABLE OF CASES 381

INDEX 391

gilbert
capsule summary
civil procedure

Text Section

I. TERRITORIAL JURISDICTION AND RELATED MATTERS

A. INTRODUCTION

1. **Types of Territorial Jurisdiction**
   a. **In personam jurisdiction:** In personam jurisdiction permits a court to enter a judgment that is **personally binding** on defendant .... [1]
   b. **In rem jurisdiction:** In rem jurisdiction permits a court to adjudicate the rights of **all the world in a specific piece of property** .... [2]
   c. **Quasi in rem jurisdiction:** There are two types of quasi in rem jurisdiction. The first type permits a court to determine rights of **particular parties** in property under its control. The second type permits a court having jurisdiction over defendant's property, but not over defendant personally, to use the property to satisfy plaintiff's personal claim against defendant. Use of this latter type as a basis for jurisdiction over nonresident defendants has been severely limited .... [3]

2. **Shift to Minimum Contacts:** With *International Shoe,* the Court shifted from an emphasis on in-state service to requirement of **minimum contacts** with the forum state "such that the maintenance of the suit does not offend traditional notions of fair play and substantial justice" .... [21]

B. CONTEMPORARY CONSTITUTIONAL GROUNDS FOR STATE COURT JURISDICTION

1. **Contacts with Forum:** *International Shoe* generated a two-stage approach to jurisdiction problems, looking first at the **purposeful availment** requirement and then at the **reasonableness** of permitting jurisdiction .... [26]

   a. **Minimum contacts—purposeful availment:** Purposeful availment inquiry focuses solely on activities of defendant, looking for some voluntary action by defendant establishing a **beneficial relationship** with forum state .... [27]

      (1) **Foreseeability:** Mere foreseeability of contact with the forum is important but insufficient; defendant's conduct with respect to the forum state must be such that he should reasonably **anticipate being haled into court there** (*e.g.,* long-term relationship with forum or seeking to serve forum market) .... [28]

      (2) **Relation to claim:** The Court assumes jurisdiction is proper with regard to claims that are related to forum contacts that satisfy purposeful availment, but it may also be proper where the claim is related to contacts not satisfying purposeful availment requirement. This might be rationalized by focusing on foreseeability .... [39]

      (3) **Commercial vs. noncommercial:** Purposeful availment is more easily found with regard to defendant's commercial activity ...... [41]

      (4) **Choice of law distinguished:** Fact that particular state's law may apply under choice-of-law "center of gravity" principles does not alone satisfy purposeful availment requirement as to that state ... [42]

      (5) **Reasonableness insufficient to satisfy purposeful availment requirement:** Factors such as a lack of inconvenience to defendant cannot outweigh requirement of purposeful availment .... [45]

			Text Section

      b. **Fair play and substantial justice—reasonableness:** In the reasonableness inquiry, consideration of plaintiff's interests is proper .... [46]

         (1) **Factors:** Reasonableness factors include *state's interests* in providing a forum and regulating the activity, *relative burdens* on plaintiff and defendant, *nature of defendant's activities* in forum, and desirability of *avoiding multiple suits* .... [47]

2. **Presence of Defendant's Property in Forum:** Presence of defendant's property in the forum will often establish a constitutionally sufficient contact between defendant and the forum, ordinarily because it establishes relevant contact between defendant and forum .... [53]

      a. **Location of property:** Tangible property is located in a state if it is physically present there. Intangible property may be considered located in a jurisdiction if some transaction related to the property occurred there, but if embodied in an instrument, it is usually said to be located where the instrument is .... [54]

      b. **Presence of property supports jurisdiction:** Presence of property in state may support jurisdiction by providing contacts among forum, defendant, and litigation .... [58]

         (1) **True in rem:** States continue to have power to exercise true in rem jurisdiction, as in condemnation proceedings .... [59]

         (2) **Claim related to rights and duties arising from ownership:** Property provides sufficient contact where the claim is related to rights or duties related to the property (*e.g.,* absentee owner might be sued for injuries sustained on property located in the forum) .... [61]

         (3) **Absence of other forum:** The Court has not ruled on the scope of jurisdiction by necessity, which may exist in cases where defendant's property is located in the forum and no other forum is available to plaintiff .... [63]

      c. **Presence of property insufficient for jurisdiction:** When property is completely unrelated to plaintiff's cause of action, its presence alone will not support jurisdiction .... [66]

3. **General Jurisdiction:** Some courts distinguish between *general jurisdiction*, which subjects defendant to suit on any claim in the forum; and *specific jurisdiction*, which confers jurisdiction only for claims arising from defendant's contact with the forum .... [69]

      a. **Natural persons:** General jurisdiction is available in the state of a natural person's domicile .... [70]

      b. **Corporations:** A corporation is subject to general jurisdiction in the state of incorporation, the state in which its headquarters are located if different from state of incorporation, and in states in which it conducts "substantial activity" .... [71]

      c. **Relation to claim:** General jurisdiction analysis becomes important when defendant's contacts with the forum are not sufficiently related to the claim sued upon .... [74]

4. **Consent:** Defendant may consent to jurisdiction in a forum .... [75]

      a. **Express consent:** Defendant may expressly consent to jurisdiction, either before or after suit is filed .... [76]

      b. **Implied consent:** By filing suit in a forum, plaintiff consents to jurisdiction as to any related counterclaim by defendant .... [81]

      c. **Appearance:** Depending on prevailing rules, jurisdiction may be supported by a party's voluntary appearance in court to contest issues other than jurisdiction .... [83]

5. **Service Within Jurisdiction:** Traditionally, service within the jurisdiction was *presumptively sufficient* to support jurisdiction .... [91]

      a. **Possible minimum contacts requirement:** After *Shaffer v. Heitner*, many thought that transient jurisdiction (jurisdiction obtained solely on

	Text Section

the basis of service in the forum) was invalid absent minimum contacts, but the Supreme Court has since upheld transient jurisdiction. *Note:* The Court has left open the question whether service would be sufficient if defendant is not present voluntarily .... [92]

    b. **Fraudulent inducement:** If defendant is served with process after being fraudulently induced to enter the state, the court will not exercise jurisdiction .... [93]

  6. **Territorial Jurisdiction of the Federal Courts:** In most cases, the territorial jurisdiction of a federal court is no broader than that of the state where it is located .... [96]

    a. **Constitutional limitations on nationwide service:** Subject to possible due process limitations, Congress could constitutionally give federal courts nationwide personal jurisdiction .... [97]

    b. **National contacts:** The Court has not decided whether an alien defendant's contacts with this country may be aggregated to support jurisdiction .... [98]

C. STATUTORY AUTHORIZATION FOR JURISDICTION

1. **Long Arm Statutes:** It is not enough that an exercise of jurisdiction is constitutionally authorized; there must also be a statute authorizing jurisdiction. After *International Shoe,* state legislatures began to enact long arm statutes extending the reach of their courts' jurisdiction. Some long arm statutes authorize jurisdiction whenever it would not violate the Constitution, but most long arm statutes list specific acts that will warrant the exercise of jurisdiction . [100]

2. **Federal Court Jurisdiction:** In general, federal courts exercise jurisdiction no broader than that authorized by the long arm statute of the state where the court is located .... [107]

D. LITIGATING JURISDICTION

1. **Default:** If a party believes the court lacks personal jurisdiction, she may default and later argue that the judgment should not be given full faith and credit because the court did not have jurisdiction .... [116]

2. **Appearance to Litigate Jurisdiction:** In federal court and in most states, defendant may raise lack of personal jurisdiction along with other defenses in her answer or preanswer motion. A few states require a special appearance . [117]

E. VENUE

1. **Introduction:** Venue is a statutory limitation on the *geographic location* of litigation to prevent a plaintiff from suing where it would be burdensome for the defendant to appear and defend .... [121]

2. **Federal Venue Limitations:** Where *any defendant resides*, if all defendants reside in the same state; or where a *substantial part* of the events or omissions giving rise to the claim occurred or a substantial part of the property that is subject to the litigation is situated. If no other district is available, venue is proper: (i) in diversity cases, where any defendant is subject to personal jurisdiction and (ii) in federal question cases, where defendant is found .... [122]

3. **Litigating Venue:** Improper venue may be *waived* unless the issue is properly raised (*e.g.,* by timely motion) .... [160]

4. **Federal Transfer Provisions:** A federal case may be transferred to another federal court in the following cases .... [162]

    a. **Venue or jurisdiction improper in original court:** If venue or jurisdiction is improper, court may transfer case to proper court .... [163]

    b. **Transfer for convenience:** Court will respect plaintiff's choice of forum, but may, for convenience in the interests of justice, transfer case to another district where it might have been brought .... [166]

			Text Section

F. FORUM NON CONVENIENS
Even when jurisdiction and venue are proper, a court may decline to exercise jurisdiction if the venue selected by the plaintiff is *grossly inconvenient* .... [182]

G. NOTICE
1. **Constitutional Requirements:** Due process requires that *reasonable efforts to provide notice* be made with regard to persons whose interests are to be determined .... [200]
2. **Service of Process:** Usual method of giving notice is service of a summons and complaint on defendant, directing that he file an answer or suffer a default .... [212]
   a. **Methods of service:** Depending on the rules of the jurisdiction, service of process may be made by personal delivery, by mail (waiver of service), or by leaving it at defendant's home or office .... [214]
   b. **Immunity from service:** In some jurisdictions, rules immunize from service those persons who are present in the state only to participate in a legal proceeding .... [226]
3. **Timing of Notice—Prejudgment Seizures:** At common law, defendant's property could be seized, even before defendant had notice of the action, to provide security for any judgment plaintiff might obtain .... [227]
   a. **State law requirements:** States have placed various limits on prejudgment seizures .... [228]
   b. **Procedural due process requirements for prejudgment seizure:** Supreme Court decisions on prejudgment seizures without notice or advance hearing where the claimant's interest in the property does not antedate the suit seem to require proof of exigent circumstances and a factual setting where claims can reliably be evaluated on documentary proof .... [230]

II. SUBJECT MATTER JURISDICTION OF THE FEDERAL COURTS

A. INTRODUCTION
1. **Nature of Subject Matter Jurisdiction:** Subject matter jurisdiction involves a court's *authority* to rule on a particular type of case .... [255]
2. **Defect Not Waivable:** Lack of subject matter jurisdiction is not waivable ... [257]
   a. **Defendant may raise at any time:** Lack of subject matter jurisdiction may be raised at any time, even after final judgment .... [259]
   b. **Court to raise sua sponte:** If the parties do not raise lack of subject matter jurisdiction, the court will raise it on its own motion .... [260]

B. DIVERSITY JURISDICTION
1. **Constitutional Authorization:** Article III, Section 2 authorizes diversity jurisdiction to provide a forum for persons who might be victims of *local prejudice*. The Constitution requires only *minimal diversity* (*i.e.*, that diversity exist between one plaintiff and one defendant) .... [281]
2. **Diversity Statute**
   a. **Complete diversity requirement:** The diversity statute requires complete diversity (*i.e.*, that *no defendant have the same citizenship as any plaintiff*) .... [286]
   b. **How citizenship determined:** For natural persons, including permanent resident aliens, citizenship is generally the same as *domicile*. A corporation is a citizen of any state in which it is incorporated and of the state of its *principal place of business*. Unincorporated associations are citizens of *each state of which any member is a citizen* .... [287]
      (1) **Class actions:** Only the citizenship of the *named representatives* is considered .... [301]

				Text Section
		(2)	**Fictitious defendants:** Citizenship of fictitious defendants is ***disregarded*** in considering whether a case is removable	[302]
		(3)	**Executors, guardians, and trustees:** Legal representatives of decedents or incompetents are deemed citizens of the ***same state as the person represented***	[304]
	c.	**Time for determination:** Diversity need exist only at the ***commencement of the action***		[305]
		(1)	**Removal:** For removed cases, diversity must exist both at the time of filing the suit and at the time the removal notice is filed	[308]
	d.	**Realigning parties:** In considering diversity, the court looks to the ***real interests*** of the parties and may realign them accordingly as plaintiffs or defendants		[310]
	e.	**Efforts to create diversity:** Diversity cannot be created by collusively or improperly joining a party or by assigning a claim without sufficient consideration		[312]
	f.	**Efforts to defeat diversity:** Plaintiffs are allowed some latitude in taking steps to defeat diversity (*e.g.,* adding bona fide claims against nondiverse defendants)		[316]
	g.	**Effect of lack of diversity:** A plaintiff may sometimes preserve diversity by dismissing a nondiverse defendant, but may not proceed in federal court without a necessary party, *infra*		[321]
	h.	**Jurisdictional amount:** ***More than $50,000*** must be in controversy in a diversity case		[324]
		(1)	**Legal certainty test:** The amount claimed by plaintiff is determinative unless defendant shows to a legal certainty that the minimum cannot be met	[326]
		(2)	**Aggregation of claims to satisfy requirement:** Single plaintiff may aggregate all claims against a single defendant to meet the minimum. Single plaintiff may aggregate claims against several defendants ***only if*** all defendants are jointly liable. Multiple plaintiffs may aggregate claims against single defendant ***only if*** they have a common undivided interest in the claims. Defendant's counterclaim may not be aggregated with plaintiff's claim to meet minimum	[334]
C.	**FEDERAL QUESTION JURISDICTION**			
	1.	**Constitutional Grant:** Article III, Section 2 extends the federal judicial power to cases ***arising under*** the Constitution, the laws of the U.S., and treaties; cases affecting ambassadors, consuls, etc.; admiralty cases; and cases to which the U.S. is a party		[347]
	2.	**Federal Question Statute**		
		a.	**Statute interpreted more narrowly than Constitution:** The language of the federal question statute is very similar to that in Article III, but has been interpreted more narrowly	[352]
			(1) **State court jurisdiction over cases raising federal questions:** State courts have ***concurrent*** jurisdiction over most federal question issues	[353]
		b.	**Standards for determining whether federal question is raised:** A federal question may be raised when federal law has created the claim sued upon or when a right under state law turns on construction of federal law.	[355]
		c.	**Well-pleaded complaint rule:** The federal question must appear in the properly pleaded allegations in the complaint	[364]
			(1) **Anticipation of defense insufficient:** A federal question is not sufficiently raised by plaintiff's allegation that defendant will rely on a defense based on federal law	[366]
			(2) **Plaintiff's election not to assert federal claim:** Plaintiff may, within limits, elect not to assert a federal claim and thus avoid federal question jurisdiction	[369]

	Text Section

    d. **Plausible assertion of federal right sufficient:** A federal question is sufficient to vest the court with jurisdiction unless it is frivolous or made solely to bring about jurisdiction .... [371]

    e. **Jurisdictional amount:** In most federal question cases, there is **no required minimum** amount in controversy .... [375]

D. SUPPLEMENTAL JURISDICTION

  1. **Introduction:** Where jurisdiction is proper, federal courts have jurisdiction over **all issues in the case**, not just federal questions .... [376]

  2. **Background—Pendent and Ancillary Jurisdiction:** The supplemental jurisdiction statute arises from the common law concepts of ancillary jurisdiction and pendent jurisdiction .... [380]

    a. **Ancillary jurisdiction:** The doctrine of ancillary jurisdiction gave federal courts the power to hear claims brought by parties other than the plaintiff related to the plaintiff's claim, such as counterclaims, cross-claims, interpleader claims, and claims by intervenors .... [381]

    b. **Pendent jurisdiction:** The doctrine of pendent jurisdiction gave federal courts the power to hear nonfederal claims against a nondiverse defendant as long as such claims arose from the same event as the federal claim .... [390]

    c. **Lack of statutory basis:** In 1989, the Supreme Court called the validity of ancillary and pendent jurisdiction into doubt, at least with regard to claims against added parties, because there was no statutory basis for such jurisdiction and all exercises of federal court jurisdiction have been said to require a statutory basis .... [397]

  3. **Supplemental Jurisdiction Statute:** In response to Supreme Court cases, Congress adopted the Supplemental Jurisdiction Statute, which grants federal courts that have original jurisdiction over a claim supplemental jurisdiction over all other claims that form **part of the same case or controversy** under Article III. Thus, any claim that is part of the same constitutional case may be added, including claims that involve the joinder or intervention of additional parties .... [398]

    a. **Standard:** In determining whether supplemental jurisdiction is proper the Court will ask whether: .... [400]
      (i) The **federal claim is sufficiently substantial**;
      (ii) The federal and nonfederal claims arise from a **common nucleus of operative fact**; and
      (iii) The federal and nonfederal claims are such that they would ordinarily be tried in **one judicial proceeding**.

    b. **Limitation on diversity cases:** When federal subject matter jurisdiction is founded solely on diversity there is no supplemental jurisdiction over claims by plaintiffs against persons made parties under Rule 14, Rule 19, or Rule 24, nor over claims by persons proposed to be joined under Rule 19 or Rule 24 .... [409]

    c. **Discretionary decline of jurisdiction:** A federal court can decline to exercise supplemental jurisdiction where: (i) a novel or complex issue of state law is involved; (ii) the nonfederal claim predominates; (iii) all original jurisdiction claims are dismissed; or (iv) in other extraordinary circumstances .... [416]

E. REMOVAL

  1. **Grounds for Removal:** In general, an action that plaintiff **could originally have filed in federal court** can be removed there by defendant .... [427]

    a. **Local defendant:** Removal on grounds of diversity is not permitted if any defendant is a citizen of the state in which the action is brought ...... [436]

    b. **Separate and independent federal claim:** Defendant may remove if

			Text Section
		sued on a removable separate and independent federal claim, even if plaintiff has joined nonremovable claims	[440]
	2.	**Procedure for Removal:** Defendant removes by filing a notice of removal in the appropriate federal district court and notifying the other parties and the state court	[448]
		a. **Only defendants can remove:** Plaintiff may not remove on the basis of defendant's assertion of a counterclaim	[449]
		b. **All defendants must join:** Unless an individual defendant has a separate and independent claim against him, all defendants who have been served must join in filing for removal	[450]
	3.	**Remand:** The federal court should remand an improperly removed case to state court	[455]

III. RELATION BETWEEN STATE AND FEDERAL LAW

A. STATE LAW IN THE FEDERAL COURTS

1. **Rules of Decision Act:** Under the Act, the *laws of the states* are the rules of decision in federal courts, except where the Constitution or federal laws or treaties provide otherwise . . . . [462]

2. *Swift v. Tyson*: Under *Swift v. Tyson,* "laws" in the Rules of Decision Act was held not to include state common law. Thus federal courts followed their own view of what the "general" common law was or should be . . . . [463]

3. **Overruling of *Swift* by *Erie*:** *Erie* held that state common law principles should govern where Congress had not provided otherwise . . . . [470]

   a. **Reasoning of *Erie*:** The Court **found** that the Rules of Decision Act was not intended to exclude all state general common law and that *Swift* had led to a lack of uniformity and resulting discrimination. But more importantly, the Court **held** that the Constitution did not give the courts the power to declare the substantive common law that would apply in a state . . . . [471]

   b. **Principal cases developing *Erie*:** Cases after Erie have attempted to develop the general guideline that *state substantive law* and *federal procedural law* should govern state law actions in the federal courts . . [482]

      (1) *Guaranty Trust Co. v. York*: *York,* in holding that a state statute of limitations took precedence over a more flexible federal laches approach, articulated an "***outcome determination***" test; *i.e.,* a federal law is substantive if application of the federal law instead of the state law will **significantly affect the outcome of the litigation**. It was hard to know where to stop in applying this rule, since almost any rule could qualify as substantive under the test, especially if disobeyed . . . . [483]

      (2) ***Byrd* and the "interest balancing" approach:** *Byrd* adopted a balancing test that considered (i) the relation between the state rule and the underlying state right; (ii) the interests of the federal judicial system; and (iii) the outcome determination effect of each choice. This approach suffers from difficulties of weighing nonequivalent interest . . . . [488]

4. **Approach Under *Hanna v. Plumer*:** *Hanna* gave preference to the Federal Rules in a conflict between a state requirement of personal service and the federal allowance of substituted service . . . . [496]

   a. ***Erie* dictum in *Hanna*:** In dicta, *Hanna* confirmed the scaling back of the *York* test, but suggested that the test be applied in light of the **twin aims** of the *Erie* rule: "discouragement of forum shopping and avoidance of inequitable administration of the laws." The Court found, however, that this approach should be applied only to unguided *Erie* choice problems and not to cases such as the one here, where Congress had established guidelines by statute . . . . [499]

				Text Section
		b.	**Holding with respect to validity of Federal Rules:** The Court held that the standard established by Congress under the Rules Enabling Act, under which the Federal Rules are promulgated, is the standard to apply in determining whether to apply a Federal Rule, because Congress has broad constitutional authority to regulate the federal courts. Federal Rules are to be applied if they regard practice or procedure and do not abridge, enlarge, or modify a substantive right	[500]

5. **Modern Approach Under *Erie* and *Hanna***
    a. **Conflict determination stage:** It should first be determined whether there is any direct conflict between the federal and state rules .... [507]
    b. **Conflict resolution stage:** If a true conflict is found, the *source* of the federal rule should be considered .... [509]
        (1) **Federal Constitution:** Rules that derive from the Constitution always govern state law actions in federal courts .... [510]
        (2) **Acts of Congress:** Statutes governing federal courts prevail over state law if the federal statute is "arguably procedural" .... [511]
        (3) **Federal Rules:** Federal Rules are judged according to the standards of the Rules Enabling Act. Incidental effects on state substantive law are disregarded .... [512]
        (4) **Judge-made federal procedural rules:** Decisional rules are judged according to whether they meet *Erie's* twin aims of discouraging forum shopping and avoiding inequitable administration of the laws .. [516]
6. **Which State's Law Applies?** Under *Klaxon Co. v. Stentor Manufacturing Co.*, in diversity cases requiring application of state law, the court will apply ***the law of the state in which it sits, including that state's choice-of-law rules*** .... [519]
7. **Determining Applicable State Law:** A problem may arise if a state's highest court has not recently ruled on the point of law in question .... [524]
    a. **General guideline—"proper regard" to state court rulings:** The federal court must give "proper regard" to state court precedents, but is not necessarily bound by rulings of intermediate state courts .... [525]
    b. **Implementation in light of *Erie* aims:** Unclear state law should be approached with *Erie's* twin aims in mind, and not with simplistic or rigid tests .... [526]

B. **FEDERAL COMMON LAW**
Although there is ***no federal general common law***, federal courts have authority to create common law in particular areas of federal authority or interest .... [529]

IV. PLEADING

A. **INTRODUCTION**
The basic purpose of pleading is to give notice of the general character of the controversy between the parties. Under ***code pleading*** (used in California, New York, Illinois, and other states), pleadings are also intended to narrow and frame the issues .... [537]

B. **HISTORY OF PLEADING**
1. **Common Law Pleading:** Pleadings at common law had to fit within one of the recognized forms of action (*e.g.,* case, trespass, assumpsit, etc.). A plaintiff was thus forced to shape the out-of-court transaction into the mold of a theory of substantive law expressed in one of the forms. Amendments to change a form were not permitted .... [539]
    a. **Compare—equity pleading:** Equity courts were governed by different procedures. Equitable relief was available only where there was no right to recover under any forms of action at law, *i.e.,* no adequate remedy at law. In equity, a plaintiff went outside the forms of action and recited

facts showing his grievance. This ***fact pleading*** was the basis of code pleading . . . . [542]

2. **Code Pleading:** The New York Code of 1848 (Field Code) originated code pleadings. It was later adopted or adapted by a majority of the states and is still used in several today. Code pleading departed from common law pleading rules in several important ways . . . . [543]

    a. **Single form of action:** The fundamental principle of code pleading is that plaintiff's claim is a statement of facts showing a right to a remedy. Code pleading abolished forms of action; a plaintiff could recover under any legal theory applicable to the facts he pleaded and proved . . . . [544]

    b. **Limited number of pleadings:** Far fewer pleadings are allowed under code pleading than under the common law, and no attempt is made to reduce a case to a single issue . . . . [548]

    c. **Fact pleading:** A pleading under the codes must set forth the ***ultimate facts*** constituting the ***cause of action*** in ordinary and concise language . [550]

3. **Pleading Under the Federal Rules:** The Federal Rules, now adopted by most states, ***further liberalize*** pleading rules and eliminate the technicalities of the Field Code . . . . [553]

    a. **Pleadings permitted:** Fewer pleadings are permitted under the Federal Rules than in code states. A ***motion to dismiss*** is used instead of demurrer . . . . [554]

    b. **Notice pleading:** The Federal Rules eliminate the requirement of "facts constituting a cause of action." Now, all that is needed is a ***short and plain statement of the claim showing the pleader is entitled to relief*** . . . . . . [555]

C. **COMPLAINT**

1. **Form:** The essential parts of the complaint are as follows . . . . [557]

    a. **Caption:** The complaint must set forth the name of the court, the number assigned to the action, a designation of the pleading (*e.g.,* Complaint for Damages), and the names of the parties . . . . [558]

    b. **Jurisdictional allegations:** In ***federal court***, the complaint must allege the ground(s) upon which federal jurisdiction is invoked. Failure to do so results in a dismissal if the complaint is not amended to supply the ground(s). (This is not normally required in state courts because they are usually courts of general jurisdiction) . . . . [561]

    c. **Body:** There must also be a statement of ultimate facts constituting the cause of action (code pleading) or a short and plain statement of the claim showing pleader is entitled to relief (Federal Rules). Each claim or cause of action should be set forth in a separate group of paragraphs, and each paragraph should be limited to a single set of facts . . . . [563]

        (1) **Allegations:** The allegations should be simple, concise, and ***direct***. A plaintiff who lacks personal knowledge as to some element of the claim may plead that "to the best of his knowledge, information, and belief," the claim is "well-grounded in fact," but in federal court, reasonable inquiry must first be made pursuant to Rule 11 . . . . [565]

        (2) **Alternative and inconsistent allegations:** A plaintiff may plead in the alternative by alleging facts based on ***inconsistent legal theories***; he may also allege ***inconsistent facts*** if he has reason for not knowing which version is true . . . . [573]

        (3) **Defenses need not be anticipated:** Ordinarily, plaintiff's complaint need not anticipate defendant's defenses . . . . [578]

    d. **Prayer for relief:** The pleading must set forth a prayer for relief. If a defendant ***defaults*** by failing to defend, the relief granted cannot exceed what is requested. In ***contested*** cases, the relief is ***not*** limited to that which is requested, with a few exceptions. In ***federal court***, a prayer determines the ***amount in controversy*** for jurisdictional purposes. In ***state***

		court (and state law actions in federal court), the prayer may determine the nature of the action (legal vs. equitable) on which the ***right to jury trial*** depends	[580]
	e.	**Subscription:** The complaint must be signed by the attorney. In federal practice, the signature certifies that: (i) to the best of the attorney's knowledge formed after reasonable inquiry the evidentiary contentions have evidentiary support or are likely to have support after discovery, (ii) the claims or defenses are warranted by existing law or a good faith argument for existing law, and (iii) the complaint is not imposed for any improper purpose	[587]
2.		**Pleading Specific Claims:** The elements of the claim are specified by the applicable substantive law, *e.g.,* torts, contracts, etc. The responsibility to plead and prove various issues relevant to liability may be allocated to plaintiff or defendant. If plaintiff must plead an element, it is essential to stating a claim. Otherwise it is an affirmative defense, which must be raised by defendant	[595]
3.		**Joinder of Claims:** There is ***no compulsory*** joinder of claims. Practically, plaintiffs usually join related claims because of the danger of collateral estoppel, *infra*	[636]
	a.	**Permissive joinder:** At common law, joinder was permitted only if all claims were in the same form of action and there was complete identity of parties to each claim. Under the ***Federal Rules***, adopted by most states, a single plaintiff may join ***as many claims*** as he has against a single defendant, ***regardless of the subject matter***. However, in ***multi-party*** cases, ***at least one*** of the claims by or against each party must arise out of the same transaction ***and*** must involve a common question of law or fact	[637]

D. **CHALLENGES TO THE COMPLAINT**

1.		**Common Law:** Defects in the pleadings could be raised by two kinds of demurrer	[647]
	a.	**General demurrer:** This challenged the ***substantive sufficiency*** of the causes in the complaint	[649]
	b.	**Special demurrer:** This demurrer challenged ***specific matters of form***	[650]
2.		**State Practice:** In the Field Code, the demurrer was preserved. Elsewhere, a motion to dismiss or a motion to make more definite and certain is used	[651]
	a.	**General vs. special demurrer:** A general demurrer is used for a failure to plead facts sufficient to constitute a cause of action. A demurrer on any other ground is a special demurrer	[655]
	b.	**Effect of failure to raise:** Grounds for demurrer are ***waived*** unless raised in the defendant's ***initial pleading*** (demurrer or answer). *Exceptions:* Failure to state facts sufficient to constitute a cause of action and the court's lack of subject matter jurisdiction are ***never*** waived	[664]
	c.	**Motion to strike:** A motion to strike reaches defects not subject to demurrer (*e.g.,* irrelevant or redundant matter in the complaint)	[668]
3.		**Federal Practice**	
	a.	**Motion to dismiss:** A motion to dismiss is the basic challenge to the legal sufficiency of adversary pleadings and is ***always optional*** with the defendant. It can be made on grounds such as lack of subject matter or personal jurisdiction, improper venue, or a failure to state a claim. If the motion is ***granted***, a court has discretion to allow the plaintiff to ***amend*** the complaint [Fed. R. Civ. P. 12(b)]	[672]
		(1) **Test for sufficiency of complaint:** The standard for sufficiency of the complaint is more liberal than under code pleading: the plaintiff need only set out facts sufficient to outline his cause of action or claim. However, fraud and mistake must be pleaded with particularity	[675]

	Text Section
b. **Motion for more definite statement:** This motion permits a very limited attack on the form of pleadings. It is granted when a pleading is so ***vague*** that it would be ***unreasonable*** to require the moving party to reply to it [Fed. R. Civ. P. 12(e)]	[687]
c. **Motion to strike:** Either party may move to strike any insufficient defense or any redundant immaterial, impertinent or scandalous material from the other's pleadings. [Fed. R. Civ. P. 12(f)] A motion to strike may also be used to attack separate ***portions*** of the complaint that are insufficient as a matter of ***law***	[689]
d. **Waiver of defenses:** A failure to file a Rule 12 motion waives objections to the ***form*** of the complaint and ***defenses*** of lack of venue, personal jurisdiction, or sufficiency of process. However, the defenses of lack of ***subject matter jurisdiction***, failure to join an ***indispensable party***, and ***failure to state a claim*** are ***not*** waived	[695]
4. **Additional Rules of Pleading:** The following apply in both state and federal practice	[699]
a. **Pleading considered on its face:** A challenge by demurrer or motion to dismiss usually considers only the sufficiency of a complaint itself. Reference to other matters will ***not*** be made (with a few exceptions)	[700]
(1) **Conversion to summary judgment:** If a motion to dismiss is accompanied by supporting evidentiary materials, the court may treat it as a motion for summary judgment, *infra*	[701]
b. **Anticipatory defenses:** A complaint need ***not*** anticipate affirmative defenses that might be raised. However, if it does so, it must plead facts to avoid the defenses	[708]

E. **ATTORNEY'S DUTY TO INVESTIGATE CLAIMS AND DEFENSES**

1. **Certification Requirement:** Federal Rule 11 requires that every paper filed in court be signed by an attorney, or by the party himself if unrepresented	[710]
2. **Matter Certified by Signature:** By signing, a person certifies that:	[714]
(i) She has made an ***inquiry reasonable under the circumstances*** to support the factual and legal positions taken;	
(ii) The ***factual assertions have evidentiary support***; and	
(iii) The paper was ***not filed for an improper purpose***.	
3. **Sanctions:** Imposition of sanctions for violation of Rule 11 is ***discretionary***. Sanctions can be monetary or nonmonetary, but in any event are to be limited to what is necessary to deter repetition of such conduct. Law firms should be held jointly liable for sanctions along with the firm members who violate Rule 11	[735]
4. **Procedure:** A party may move for sanctions, but must give the nonmoving party notice and 21 days to withdraw or correct the sanctionable paper. The court also has power to impose sanctions on its own initiative	[744]

F. **ANSWER**

1. **Denials:** A defendant's answer must contain ***effective*** denials to put plaintiff's allegations at issue. Material allegations ***not denied*** are ***deemed admitted***.	[750]
a. **General denials:** A defendant may deny all the allegations of a complaint in a single denial. ***Federal practice*** requires a basic pleading requirement of ***good faith***; thus, a general denial is ***rarely proper*** since there is usually something in a complaint that defendant should admit.	[752]
b. **Specific denials:** Anything less than a general denial is a specific denial *e.g.*, denial by ***parts*** (paragraphs or sentences in complaint); merely ***negating*** an allegation ("defendant was not drunk"); or alleging a ***lack of sufficient information*** to respond	[756]
2. **Affirmative Defenses:** Any defense or objections constituting new matter or an affirmative defense must be pleaded in the answer; a simple denial is not	

	Text Section
sufficient. New matter is anything that the defendant must prove to **avoid** plaintiff's claim. The test usually is whether defendant would bear the **burden of proof** on the issue at trial; if so, it is new matter	[770]
a. **Application:** The following new matter must be specially pleaded in most states and in federal practice	[773]
(1) **Tort cases:** New matter includes the defenses of self-defense, consent, justification or other privilege, contributory negligence and assumption of risk, privilege or license (defense to trespass), and consent (defense to conversion). **Lack of proximate cause** is **not** new matter	[774]
(2) **Contract cases:** Fraud, mistake, duress, incapacity, release, waiver, estoppel, condition subsequent, payment, Statute of Frauds (federal and most states), statute of limitations, and pleas in abatement (assert a reason why action should be put off or not heard) must usually be specially pleaded	[775]
b. **Effect of failure to plead new matter:** If new matter is not pleaded in the answer, defendant **may not offer evidence** of such defenses **unless** plaintiff fails to object to the introduction of the evidence or the court allows leave to **amend**	[790]
3. **Allegations of Answer Deemed Controverted:** In federal practice, **no reply** to an answer is permitted unless the answer contains a counterclaim. Plaintiff may avoid any new matter in defendant's answer by the introduction of evidence without further pleading	[797]
4. **Challenges to Answer:** Plaintiff may challenge the legal sufficiency of an affirmative defense by **demurrer** (state practice) or **motion to strike** (federal practice). A motion for summary judgment or judgment on the pleadings may also be used	[798]
G. **COUNTERCLAIMS AND CROSS-CLAIMS**	
1. **Federal Practice**	
a. **Counterclaims:** In her answer, a defendant may set forth as counterclaims any claims she has against plaintiff, even if **not related** to plaintiff's claims in the complaint	[799]
(1) **Pleading:** The sufficiency of a counterclaim is tested by the same rules used to test the sufficiency of a complaint	[803]
(2) **Joinder of other parties:** A counterclaim lies only against the **plaintiff**. But a court may order joinder where needed to facilitate a complete determination of the counterclaim	[807]
b. **Cross-claims in federal practice:** A defendant may set forth in the answer any claims that she has against a **co-defendant** that relate to the **transaction or occurrence** (or to any property) that is the subject of plaintiff's complaint	[821]
2. **State Practice—Cross-Complaint:** Most state rules follow the Federal Rules. A few states provide that a defendant's claims against **any** party (plaintiff, co-defendant, or a third person) may be asserted in a cross-complaint	[829]
H. **AMENDED AND SUPPLEMENTAL PLEADINGS**	
1. **Amendments Prior to Trial**	
a. **As a matter of right:** Either party may amend his pleading **once** as a matter of right, either before the other party serves a responsive pleading or, if no responsive pleading is permitted and the action is not yet on the trial calendar, within 20 days after the pleading is served	[842]
b. **By permission of court:** In any other situation, amendment may be made only by leave of court, however, such permission is usually granted freely before trial	[843]
c. **Permissible scope of amendment**	

	Text Section

        (1) **State practice:** Today, an amendment is permitted if it is based on the ***same general set of facts*** as were set forth in the original pleading .... [847]

        (2) **Federal practice:** Under the Federal Rules, the determinative question is whether the amendment results in ***prejudice*** to the opposing party .... [849]

    d. **"Relation back doctrine"—statute of limitations problems:** When a plaintiff seeks to amend the complaint after the applicable statute of limitations would otherwise have run, the question arises whether the amendment relates back to the date of filing the original complaint. In most jurisdictions, it relates back if the cause of action asserted in the amended pleading arose out of the ***same conduct, transaction, or occurrence*** as in the original complaint. In ***diversity cases***, the question is procedural and is governed by the Federal Rules, *supra* .... [851]

    e. **Amendment supersedes original pleading:** An amended pleading supersedes the original, so the original has no further effect as a pleading. It may, however, still be used ***in evidence*** against the pleader (*e.g.,* as an admission) .... [859]

  2. **Amendments at Trial**

    a. **Background—doctrine of variance:** At common law, the slightest variance between the facts pleaded and those proved was often fatal to recovery .... [861]

    b. **Code pleading practice:** Pleading rules today are usually more relaxed. When the evidence offered at trial is only a ***partial*** variance from the pleadings, leave to amend is usually granted if no prejudice will result .. [862]

    c. **Federal practice:** Since pleadings are now less important, amendments are liberally allowed; doctrine of variance is effectively ***abolished*** ..... [866]

  3. **Amendments After Trial:** In federal practice, pleadings can be amended to conform to the proof at any time, even after entry of judgment or on appeal ... [873]

  4. **Supplemental Pleadings:** The function of these is to call attention of the court to material facts that have occurred ***subsequent*** to the filing of the complaint. The right to file a supplemental pleading is at the court's ***discretion***, but is liberally given. A supplemental pleading ***adds to***, but does not modify, the original pleading .... [874]

I. DEFAULT PROCEDURE

  1. **In General:** If a defendant fails to answer or otherwise timely plead, a default is entered .... [879]

  2. **Effect of Default Entry:** Defendant's failure to plead is considered an ***admission*** of the claim against her .... [880]

  3. **Obtaining Judgment:** After entry of a default, plaintiff must proceed to obtain a default judgment. ***Relief is limited*** to the amount or type that was sought in the prayer. The defendant is ***not*** entitled to appear in the proceeding ...... [881]

  4. **Setting Aside Default:** Once a default is entered, defendant's remedy is to move the court to set it (and any judgment entered pursuant to it) aside. In ***federal practice***, the motion can be made at any time before judgment is entered. Thereafter, the motion must be made within ***one year*** after entry of the judgment or order. The defendant must show that she has a ***valid excuse*** for the default ***and*** a ***meritorious defense*** to the action and that ***plaintiff will not be prejudiced*** .... [884]

J. JUDGMENT ON THE PLEADINGS

  1. **Purpose:** A motion for judgment on the pleadings is analogous to a demurrer or motion to dismiss, and challenges the adversary's pleadings on the ground that they are insufficient to establish any valid claim or defense .... [888]

  2. **Making the Motion:** Either party may move for judgment on the pleadings at any time after the pleadings have closed, but not so late as to delay trial ... [889]

				Text Section

        3. **Issues Raised:** Originally, the motion raised only sufficiency of the pleadings. Under modern practice, if the moving party presents matters beyond the pleadings, the motion is treated as a motion for summary judgment .... [890]

  K. **VOLUNTARY DISMISSAL BY PLAINTIFF**
      1. **Common Law:** At common law, plaintiff could dismiss his own case without prejudice at any time before verdict .... [894]
      2. **Code Practice:** Code pleading states provided that plaintiff could only dismiss his own case before trial began, otherwise it was with prejudice ...... [895]
      3. **Federal Practice:** Plaintiff may voluntarily dismiss his case once without prejudice by giving notice, if he does so before defendant has filed an answer or motion for summary judgment. Thereafter, plaintiff may dismiss only with defendant's consent or court permission .... [896]

V. PARTIES

  A. **REAL PARTY IN INTEREST RULE**
      1. **Background:** At common law, the party having the legal right was the proper party to bring suit at law. Modern procedure requires that a civil action be prosecuted only by the "real party in interest" .... [906]
      2. **Definition:** The person bringing suit (i) must use his own name as plaintiff, **and** (ii) must have a legal right to enforce the claim under the applicable substantive law .... [907]
         a. **Under Federal Rules and state rules:** The following parties have a right to sue as representatives even though they may have no beneficial interest in the claim: an executor, administrator, guardian, or trustee of an estate; a party to a contract made for the benefit of another; and a private claimant suing in the name of the federal government if such a claim is expressly authorized by statute .... [909]
         b. **In other cases:** In **all** other cases, the real party in interest is determined by reference to the applicable substantive law. In diversity actions, it is determined by reference to the applicable state law .... [910]
      3. **Determination of Real Party in Interest**
         a. **Assignments:** Whether the assignee is the real party in interest depends on the nature of the assignment. If the assignment is of the **entire** interest, the assignee is the real party in interest; this is so even for gratuitous assignments. If the assignment is of a **partial** interest, at common law the assignee could not enforce a claim; the modern rule is that partial assignees and the assignor are **necessary parties** .... [912]
         b. **Subrogation:** Subrogation is equitable and results in an assignment by operation of law so that one who pays another for loss or injury caused by an act of a third person becomes entitled to enforce (as subrogee) the claim that the injured person (subrogor) had against the third party .... [919]
         c. **Trusts:** The trustee, as holder of legal title, is the real party for redress of any wrong to the **trust estate**. But a beneficiary may sue the trustee to protect her beneficial rights .... [921]
         d. **Executors and administrators:** These are the proper parties to sue on behalf of decedents' estates .... [923]
         e. **Principal and agent:** If the obligation is owed to the **principal alone**, he is the only proper plaintiff. If the obligation is owed to both the agent and the principal, either may sue .... [926]

  B. **CAPACITY OF PARTY TO SUE OR BE SUED**
      1. **Definition:** "Capacity" is the legal competence of a party to sue or be sued .. [934]
      2. **Individuals:** A person's capacity is determined by the law of his domicile. If he lacks capacity (*e.g.,* is a minor), suit must be filed by a guardian or conservator .... [935]

	Text Section

3. **Corporations:** The capacity of a corporation to sue (or be sued) is determined by the law of the state in which it is organized .... [938]
4. **Partnerships**
   a. **Federal practice:** In federal court, a partnership can always sue or be sued as an *entity* if the litigation involves a federal question .... [940]
   b. **State law varies:** Some states permit a partnership to sue *or* be sued as an entity. Many states permit a partnership to be sued, but *not* to sue, as an entity (in the partnership name). In those states, an action on behalf of the partnership must be brought in the names of the individual partners .... [941]
5. **Unincorporated Associations:** At common law, unincorporated associations were treated like partnerships and thus lacked capacity to sue or be sued as entities .... [942]
   a. **State practice:** Many states now treat unincorporated associations like corporations .... [943]
   b. **Federal practice:** An unincorporated association has capacity to sue or be sued when a *federal right* is being enforced by or against the association. But when a *state* law is being enforced (*e.g.,* in a diversity action), the capacity of the unincorporated association is determined by the law of the state in which the action is brought .... [944]

C. **JOINDER OF PARTIES**
   1. **Permissive Joinder**
      a. **Early approach:** Under the original codes, a plaintiff could join plaintiffs or defendants only if they *all* had an interest in the subject of the action *and* the relief sought .... [951]
      b. **Modern approach:** Today, a person may join or be joined if: .... [952]
         (i) A right to relief is asserted by (or against) her *jointly, severally, or in the alternative*;
         (ii) The right to relief *arises out of the same transaction or series of transactions*; *and*
         (iii) There is *at least one question of law or fact common to all parties* sought to be joined.
         (1) **Additional claims:** As long as the above requirements are met, a party may assert as many claims as she has against an opposing party, but the court has discretion to sever .... [957]
      c. **Subject matter jurisdiction:** In addition to the requirement of personal jurisdiction, federal subject matter jurisdiction requirements must be satisfied as to *all* parties .... [960]
   2. **Compulsory Joinder:** Joinder is required for any person who has a *material interest* in the case and whose absence would result in *substantial* prejudice to him or to other parties .... [961]
      a. **Traditional approach:** Traditionally, a distinction was made between *necessary* parties (those who ought to be joined *if possible*; interests are *severable*) and *indispensable* parties (interests are *nonseverable*; action would have to be dismissed without them) .... [962]
      b. **Modern approach:** The focus now is on the *practical consequences* of an interested person's absence. Any interested person should be joined if his absence would prevent *complete relief* from being given to other parties *or* if his absence would *substantially prejudice* his or other parties' interests. If a person who should be joined cannot be made a party, the court has discretion to determine whether to proceed or dismiss ... [965]
      c. **Procedure for compelling joinder:** Defendant can raise the existence of unjoined necessary parties in a motion to dismiss or in the answer. The court will order joinder *unless* this would destroy subject matter jurisdiction or the court lacks personal Jurisdiction over the necessary

parties. If an added party objects to venue, she **must** be dismissed. Whenever joinder of necessary parties is not feasible, the court may dismiss the action .... [980]
    d. **Waiver of right to compel joinder:** An objection to nonjoinder must be raised at the first opportunity or it is waived. However, objection to nonjoinder of an *indispensable* party may be raised at any time ..... [987]
3. **Impleader:** Impleader is a procedure that permits the defendant to bring into the lawsuit a third person who is or *may be* liable for all or part of plaintiff's claim against the defendant. Impleader is *limited* to situations in which the defendant has a *right to indemnity* against the impleaded third party. Whether such a right exists is determined by applicable *substantive law* ... [990]
    a. **Pleadings and procedure:** Leave of court is not required for impleader if the defendant (third party plaintiff) files a third party complaint of impleader no later than *10 days* after he serves his original answer. Thereafter, leave of court is required. The impleaded party may also file a *counterclaim or cross-claim* against existing parties, or may implead any person who may be liable over to him .... [1002]
    b. **Effect on jurisdiction and venue:** An impleader claim usually is considered ancillary and thus has no effect on jurisdictional and venue requirements .... [1006]
    c. **Compare—cross-claim:** *Impleader* can be asserted only against a person *not yet a party*; a *cross-claim* is by one party against *another party*. Also, impleader must be based on a claim for *indemnification* while a cross-claim need not be .... [1007]
4. **Intervention:** By intervening, a nonparty becomes a party to protect his interest from being adversely affected by a judgment in the action. Whether intervention is allowed depends on a balancing of two conflicting policies: (i) plaintiff alone should generally be allowed to join parties, with or against him, as he wishes; and (ii) other interested parties and the court have an interest in avoiding multiplicity of litigation or inconsistency of results .... [1009]
    a. **Types of intervention in federal cases**
        (1) **Intervention of right:** Intervention is granted as a matter of right where the unconditional right to intervene is conferred by a federal statute, *or* where the *disposition* of the action without the would be intervenor would likely *impair or impede* his ability to protect an interest relating to the subject of the action .... [1011]
        (2) **Permissive intervention:** This is granted at a court's broad discretion where a *federal statute* gives a conditional right to intervene or where the would-be intervenor's claim or defense has a *question of law or fact in common* with the action .... [1024]
    b. **Effect of intervention in federal cases**
        (1) **Subject matter jurisdiction:** In actions based solely on diversity, there is no supplemental jurisdiction over claims by plaintiff against persons who intervene. When jurisdiction is not based solely on diversity, there usually is supplemental jurisdiction over claims by or against intervenors of right .... [1029]
        (2) **Judgment:** Judgment rendered after intervention is binding on the intervenor as though she had been an original party .... [1031]
5. **Consolidation of Separate Actions:** Even where joinder rules do not permit addition of new parties, the same result may be achieved by consolidating suits pending in the same court. The court has broad discretion to consolidate actions with common issues .... [1035]
6. **Interpleader:** This enables a party against whom conflicting claims to the same debt or property are asserted (the "stakeholder") to join all adverse claimants in one action and to require them to litigate among themselves to determine who, if anyone, has a valid claim to the involved property. Once the

	Text Section

stakeholder deposits the funds or property in the court, he can be discharged from the litigation, unless he also claims the asset . . . . [1036]

    a. **Procedure:** The party against whom claims are made may: (i) institute an interpleader action, naming all claimants as defendants, or (ii) interplead in any action pending between the adverse claimants. If he is named as a defendant in such an action, he may interplead by filing a *counterclaim*, infra . . . . [1038]

        (1) **Deposit with court:** In a statutory interpleader action, the stakeholder must *deposit with the court* or give security for the entire disputed amount in his possession. Rule 22 interpleader does not require deposit . . . . [1039]

    b. **Types of federal interpleader actions**

        (1) **Statutory:** Interpleader is permitted by 28 U.S.C. section 1335 if two or more *claimants of diverse citizenship* (minimal diversity) are making adverse claims to the same property, debt, or instrument, and it has a *value of at least $500* . . . . [1044]

        (2) **Rule 22 interpleader:** Rule 22 permits interpleader in an action that meets the normal jurisdictional requirements in federal court. Unlike statutory interpleader, there must be *complete diversity* between the stakeholder and *all* of the adverse claimants and the jurisdictional amount must be in excess of $50,000 . . . . [1045]

        (3) **Limits of process:** In *statutory* interpleader, the reach of process is nationwide. Under *Rule 22*, service of process is the same as in other civil actions . . . . [1052]

        (4) **Cross-claims and counterclaims:** Interpleaded claimants often cross-claim against each other, counterclaim against plaintiff, and implead third parties. Such additional claims must have an independent basis of jurisdiction unless they relate to the original impleaded claim (and thus fall within supplemental jurisdiction) . . . . [1053]

        (5) **Venue:** In statutory interpleader, proper venue is the district where *any* claimant resides. Under Rule 22, venue is the same as in any other civil action . . . . [1056]

D. CLASS ACTIONS

  1. **In General:** One or more members of a class of persons similarly situated may sue or be sued on behalf of all members of that class, where such action is justified by considerations of *necessity or convenience* . . . . [1058]

  2. **Background:** Class actions were originally permitted *only in equity*, and then only if it was shown that joinder of all parties was *impractical* and a few members could fairly represent all of the class. Later, under *code pleading*, class actions were allowed when there were "questions of common or general interest of many persons," or when the parties were so numerous as to make it impractical to join all of them . . . . [1059]

  3. **Prerequisites to Class Action:** Under Fed. R. Civ. P. 23(a), *all four* of the following conditions must be met: . . . . [1064]

    a. **Numerous parties requirement:** The trial court has considerable discretion in this issue since there is *no fixed minimum* needed to make a class. However, the class must be definitely *ascertainable* and it must be *manageable*. In some cases, all members must be given *individual notice* of the action . . . . [1065]

    b. **Common question:** There must be "questions of law or fact common to the class" . . . . [1070]

    c. **Typical claim requirement:** The representative's claim must be typical of those of the class so that she will be motivated to protect the class interests . . . . [1075]

    d. **Adequate representation:** Similar to the typical claim requirement, this

		Text Section
	condition also focuses on whether there is any *actual or potential conflict of interest* between the representative and the class	[1079]
4.	**Three Grounds for Class Actions:** If the above *four conditions are met*, a class action may be based on *any one* of the following grounds	[1084]
	a. **Prejudice from separate actions:** A class suit is permitted if the prosecution of separate actions would create the risk of *establishing incompatible standards of conduct* for defendant through inconsistent adjudications, or of *substantially impairing the interests* of other class members	[1085]
	b. **Equitable relief:** A class action is also proper where the basis on which the opponent has acted is generally applicable to the class and *declaratory or injunctive* relief would benefit the class as a whole	[1089]
	c. **Common predominant question:** The most common basis for a class suit occurs when common questions of law or fact *predominate* over questions affecting only individual members, and, *on balance*, *a class action is superior* to other available methods for adjudication	[1091]
5.	**Jurisdictional Requirements in Diversity Jurisdiction Class Suits**	
	a. **Diversity of citizenship:** Only the citizenship of the *representative* is considered	[1100]
	b. **Jurisdictional amount:** In a class action in which members would be entitled to separate recoveries and the amount in controversy requirement is applicable, *each member* must have an *individual claim in excess of $50,000*; *i.e.*, usually no aggregation of claims is permitted .	[1101]
6.	**Procedure in Conducting Class Suits**	
	a. **Certification hearing:** As soon as possible after the action is commenced, a hearing is held on whether a class action is proper. If the requirements are met, the action is certified as such. The certification is subject to *later modification*. At this time, the court may *not consider the merits*	[1108]
	b. **Statute of limitations:** The filing of a suit as a class action suspends the running of the statute of limitations for all putative members of the class until class certification is decided. The period begins to run again if certification is denied or members opt out	[1116]
	c. **Notice requirements:** Individual notice is *mandatory* in a *damages class* action based on a predominant question common to the class, and also before any type of class action may be *settled or dismissed*. In most other class actions, notice to individual members is *discretionary*, and no specific form for notice is required, but it must advise the member of the suit's existence, the nature of the claim and the relief requested, provisions for costs of suit, and the identity of the class representative .	[1121]
	(1) **Costs of notice:** The *plaintiff* must pay the costs of notification, but can recover them from defendant if plaintiff wins	[1129]
	d. **Opting out by class members:** Under Rule 23(b)(3), unnamed members of the class may opt out, and thus avoid the binding effects of the class action. There is no mandatory opt-out right in other Rule 23 class actions. Class members who have opted out may not use the collateral estoppel effects of a successful class action in their individual actions . .	[1131]
	e. **Intervention:** Intervention by class members in a class action is allowed on the same terms that govern intervention otherwise	[1137]
	f. **Discovery:** Class members are "quasi-parties" for discovery purposes. An opponent cannot depose each member, but may use interrogatories and depositions to assess such issues as the typicality of claims, individual damages, etc.	[1141]
	g. **Communications with class members:** To prevent overreaching, the court may regulate communications between litigants or their counsel and unnamed class members	[1142]

	Text Section

  h. **Dismissal and compromise:** No dismissal or compromise may be made without *notice* to all members and *court approval* .... [1148]
  i. **Distribution of settlement proceeds:** Usually, a judgment settlement fund is held intact with members being notified to file claims to establish their shares .... [1153]
  j. **Attorneys' fees:** Federal and state courts routinely allow awards of attorneys' fees out of any class recovery, but the basis and amount of the fee is closely scrutinized by the court .... [1155]
 7. **Effect of Judgment in Class Action:** The central issue is whether the judgment binds members of the class who were not before the court .... [1156]
  a. **State rules:** In states retaining the distinctions between the three types of class (as per old Federal Rules) the "nature" of the action determines whether all members are bound .... [1157]
  b. **Federal Rule:** In federal courts, a valid judgment in any class action ***binds all*** class members ***who do not request exclusion*** ("opt out") ... [1158]

VI. DISCOVERY

A. PURPOSE OF DISCOVERY
1. **Obtaining Factual Information:** A party who has effectively used discovery can go to trial with the best evidence for his contentions and knowledge of his adversary's case, thus avoiding delay or surprise, and the chance of a judgment resting on an accurate finding of fact is enhanced .... [1174]
2. **Narrowing and Simplifying:** Discovery eliminates fictitious issues, claims, and defenses. Additionally, since pleadings are no longer the sole source of information, pleadings are simplified .... [1175]

B. BASIC DISCOVERY DEVICES
1. **Prediscovery Disclosure:** Federal Rule 26(a) requires certain disclosures to be made *before* formal discovery begins .... [1183]
 a. **Early meeting of counsel:** Counsel are required to meet as soon as practicable to develop a proposed discovery plan, and generally formal discovery cannot commence until after this meeting .... [1184]
 b. **Material to be disclosed:** Each party is required to disclose: .... [1190]
  (i) The names and, if known, addresses and phone numbers of persons with discoverable information relevant to disputed facts pleaded with particularity;
  (ii) Copies or descriptions of all documents that the party possesses relevant to disputed facts pleaded with particularity;
  (iii) A computation of damages and the documents on which the computation is based; and
  (iv) Any insurance agreement that might cover the claim.
 c. **Timing:** These disclosures are to be made at or within 10 days after the early meeting of counsel .... [1194]
 d. **Sanctions:** A party failing to disclose is subject to sanctions, such as a prohibition against using the undisclosed material as evidence .... [1197]
 e. **Opt-out:** The Federal Rule allows local district courts to opt out of the above provisions by general rule or in a particular case .... [1201]
2. **Depositions:** A deposition is an examination of a witness under oath in the presence of a court reporter. Parties have the right to be represented by counsel who may examine and cross-examine the witness. Subject to deferral until a discovery plan is discussed, a party may take a deposition ***at any stage*** of a pending action after the parties meet and confer on a discovery plan, but ***before*** an action is filed (or while an appeal is pending) a deposition may be taken only by leave of court ***to perpetuate testimony*** .... [1202]
 a. **Numerical cap:** Under the Federal Rules, each side may take only 10 depositions and a witness may be deposed only once .... [1207]

	Text Section

- b. **Compulsory appearance of witness:** Witnesses *must* appear at a deposition when served with a *subpoena*. However, no subpoena is needed for an *adverse party* .... [1211]
- c. **Notice to parties:** Before taking a deposition, the party must give written notice to *every other party*, including the deponent. The notice must include the time and place of the deposition and must do so *reasonably* in advance of the deposition .... [1217]
- d. **Production of documents:** The notice or subpoena may direct the witness to bring specified documents to the deposition .... [1219]
- e. **Questioning of deponent:** Examination of deponents is usually *oral*, but the questions may be *written*. If a witness *objects* to a question and refuses to answer it, the examining party may seek a court order compelling an answer .... [1221]
- f. **Transcription:** If requested before completion of the deposition, a deponent is entitled to review and correct the transcript of his testimony. In federal court, other means of transcription (*e.g.,* videotape) may be used if the party noticing the deposition so chooses .... [1233]
- g. **Use of deposition testimony at trial:** Statements in depositions are hearsay and thus are usually inadmissible *except* when used: (i) by one party against an adverse party as an *admission*; (ii) for *impeachment purposes*; or (iii) where the *deponent is unavailable* .... [1235]
3. **Interrogatories:** Interrogatories are written questions from one party to another requiring written responses .... [1241]
    - a. **Who must answer:** Co-parties and corporate parties are obliged to answer; a nonparty witness is not subject to interrogatories .... [1243]
    - b. **Numerical limit:** Interrogatories are limited to 25 per party, including subparts .... [1248]
    - c. **Duty to respond:** A party must respond (or object) with all the information under her control (*i.e.,* in her files or by questioning employees) ... [1249]
4. **Requests for Admissions:** This is a device that imposes a duty on the party served to acknowledge facts not in doubt which thus need not be proved at trial. A request for admission may be served by any party *on any other party* ..... [1256]
    - a. **Subject of request:** A request may ask for the admission of the *genuineness* of a document, the truth of factual allegations, or the applicability of legal concepts to facts. The admissions requested may include *conclusions of law*, *ultimate facts* (under Federal Rules), matters of opinion, or facts that are outside the responding party's knowledge .... [1258]
    - b. **Appropriate responses:** A requested admission, if made, binds the responding party in the present action. A party may always *deny*, but may be liable for full costs of proof if the denial is unjustified. Refusal to respond at all is rarely justified. If *no* timely response is made, the matter is deemed *admitted* .... [1265]
    - c. **Withdrawal or amendment:** A withdrawal or amendment of an admission is allowed when it would promote presentation of the merits ..... [1275]
5. **Requests for Inspection of Documents and Other Things:** A party may inspect and copy real evidence in the possession of any other party (*e.g.,* documents, maps, records). Inspection may include testing and sampling of materials .... [1276]
    - a. **Making request for inspection:** A party may serve a request without prior court order or a showing of good cause unless the other party objects. In federal practice, a request may be served at any time after the Rule 26(f) conference; some states are more restrictive .... [1279]
    - b. **Designation of items:** The description of the items to be produced must be clear enough to allow a person of ordinary intelligence to know what is sought. The request must also specify the *time, place, and manner* of making the inspection .... [1282]

	Text Section

    c. **Objection to requests:** Objections to requests must be filed within 30 days after service of a request .... [1286]

    d. **Organization of produced materials:** In federal court and some state courts, the responding party is required to produce requested materials either as they are normally kept or organized to correspond to the request .... [1289]

    e. **Failure to respond:** A failure to respond exposes a party to sanctions, including the striking of pleadings and a determination of the facts on the assumption that inspection would have provided the requesting party with persuasive evidence .... [1290]

    f. **Materials in possession of nonparty:** Under the Federal Rules and in some states, a subpoena can order a nonparty to permit inspection and copying of documents in its control or inspection of premises. Some states require a showing of good cause as a condition precedent to issuance of the subpoena .... [1291]

  6. **Medical Examinations:** A court order is required to examine a party whose physical or mental condition is in issue. The *condition in issue* must be raised directly by the pleadings or in discovery. A showing of *good cause* is required and *only parties* (or persons in the custody or control of parties) are subject to examination .... [1293]

    a. **Examination procedures:** The examining physician whom the court orders a party to see will usually be the doctor the examining party requested; however, courts often appoint an impartial examiner. The *place of examination* is normally the place selected by the examining party. The examination may be novel and even painful, as long as it is reasonably safe and the information it will reveal is necessary .... [1299]

    b. **Copies of reports:** An examinee has the right to receive a copy of the examiner's report. However, if such a request is made, the examinee *waives* the doctor-patient privilege as to any previous examination of the same condition by the patient's own physician .... [1300]

  7. **Duty to Supplement Discovery Responses**

    a. **Federal practice:** Prior discovery disclosures or responses must be supplemented if in some material respect they are incomplete or incorrect or if additional or corrective information has been obtained since the disclosure or response was made .... [1302]

    b. **State practice compared:** In states not following the Federal Rules, *supplemental interrogatories* or other procedures may be used to obtain the same information .... [1306]

C. SCOPE OF DISCOVERY

  1. **Relation of Discovery to Proof:** Usually, discovery may inquire into all nonprivileged information *relevant* to the subject matter of the action (whether or not admissible as proof) that is reasonably calculated to lead to discovery of admissible evidence .... [1309]

    a. **Judicial limitations on discovery:** The court may hold discovery conferences, and will limit discovery that it finds to be unreasonably *cumulative, delayed,* or *burdensome* .... [1310]

  2. **Scope of Relevant Material**

    a. **Meaning of relevance:** Information is relevant if it tends to make the existence of any fact that is of consequence to the determination of the action more probable or less probable than it would be without the evidence .... [1315]

    b. **Relation to subject matter:** The requirement that the information sought be relevant to the subject matter of the action is interpreted broadly ... [1320]

    c. **Information about witnesses:** The identity and location of witnesses is discoverable, as is information relating to a witness's *credibility* ...... [1322]

			Text Section

- d. **Insurance coverage:** Although not admissible, such coverage is discoverable in most jurisdictions .... [1323]
- e. **Financial status:** A defendant's ability to satisfy a judgment is usually not discoverable. However, in some cases, both a defendant's and plaintiff's financial conditions are pertinent and thus discoverable ..... [1324]

3. **Privilege:** Privileged material is excluded from obligatory disclosure through discovery. The attorney-client privilege is the most frequently invoked ..... [1329]
   - a. **Requirements for attorney-client privilege:** The privilege applies only to communications made *in confidence while seeking legal advice from a lawyer*, and it is waivable .... [1330]
   - b. **Federal vs. state law:** In federal court, when a federal claim or defense is involved, the federal courts may make rules governing privileges; where a state law claim or defense is involved, privilege issues are determined in accordance with state law .... [1347]
   - c. **Corporate clients:** Questions as to which corporate employees the attorney-client privilege covers may be determined, depending on the jurisdiction, by the older *control group test* or by the newer *Upjohn test*, which potentially extends coverage to *any* employee if certain requirements are met .... [1349]
   - d. **Other communicational privileges:** Other privileges protect certain communications between spouses, doctors and patients, and priests and penitents .... [1356]

4. **Trial Preparation Materials**
   - a. **"Work product"—*Hickman v. Taylor* rule:** Materials prepared by or under the direction of a party or her attorney in anticipation of litigation are subject to discovery *only if* the seeker can show substantial need and an inability to obtain equivalent material by other means; *i.e.*, it is a *qualified privilege* .... [1364]
     - (1) **Matters protected:** Materials such as accident reports might not be protected if they are regularly made and usable for purposes other than litigation .... [1366]
     - (2) **Special protection for mental impressions of an attorney:** Federal Rule 26(b) and similar state provisions protect against disclosure of the mental impressions and legal theories of an attorney .... [1372]
     - (3) **Other applications:** The work product privilege also applies to the work product of claims agents, insurers, sureties, indemnitors, and some statements of witnesses to lawyers .... [1381]
   - b. **Expert reports:** Experts may help the lawyer prepare for trial, or may testify at trial to support the party's case .... [1390]
     - (1) **Nontestifying experts:** Facts known to and opinions held by nontestifying experts are discoverable only in exceptional circumstances. Where discovery is ordered, the discovering party must pay a portion of the expert's fee .... [1391]
     - (2) **Testifying experts:** At least 90 days before trial, each party must identify each person that the party will call as an expert witness and must provide a detailed report of the witness's testimony and the basis therefor, qualifications, and compensation .... [1397]
     - (3) **Unaffiliated experts:** On occasion, experts who have not consented to assist either side may be compelled by subpoena to testify, although they probably must be paid a fee .... [1413]

D. **PROTECTIVE ORDERS**
   1. **Purpose:** The purpose of a protective order is to avoid undue burdens due to discovery .... [1416]
   2. **Requirement of Good Cause:** A protective order should be granted only on a showing of good cause by the party seeking protection .... [1417]

	Text Section

- a. **Confidential information:** A protective order may be entered to protect trade secrets or other confidential research, development, or commercial information . . . . [1418]
    - (1) **Showing required:** The party seeking protection must show that the information has in fact been held in confidence and that a specific harm is likely to flow from discovery of the information . . . . [1419]
    - (2) **Format—umbrella orders:** A common type of order allows the producing party to designate material as confidential, and requires the other party to hold it in confidence and use it only for trial preparation . . . . [1424]
- b. **Other uses of protective orders:** Protective orders may be issued if a deposition has been scheduled at an inconvenient place; to prevent a litigant from conducting a deposition that is annoying, embarrassing, or oppressive; and to limit discovery that is burdensome in relation to the importance of the case . . . . [1432]

E. **SANCTIONS FOR FAILURE TO DISCLOSE OR TO COMPLY WITH DISCOVERY**
  1. **Order Compelling Response—Necessary Prerequisite:** Before discovery sanctions can be imposed, a party seeking discovery must usually obtain an order compelling it . . . . [1451]
      - a. **Exception—failure to make required disclosure:** If a party fails to make the disclosures required by Rule 26 or to supplement them, the court should usually *exclude* the undisclosed materials . . . . [1454]
  2. **Sanctions for Failure to Comply with Order:** The court has a variety of options available as sanctions, including orders that establish facts in favor of the party seeking discovery, disallowance of claims or defenses, grant of dismissal or default, or a finding that a party is in contempt . . . . [1457]
  3. **Culpability Necessary for Sanctions:** Due process limits the power of the court to impose sanctions that affect the merits of a case. The court will ordinarily consider whether the party was guilty of willfulness, bad faith, or other fault. Where a lawyer's misconduct is involved, most courts will consider the extent of the client's involvement in the litigation before imposing harsh sanctions on the client . . . . [1465]
  4. **Contempt Power:** Contempt is an appropriate sanction only where the party or witness refuses to make disclosure in defiance of a *prior court order*. The contempt sanction may be *civil* (party may purge himself of the contempt by providing the information) or *criminal*. *No* contempt sanction of either kind may be used to compel a medical examination . . . . [1475]
  5. **Compare—Sanctions for Improper Certification:** Federal Rule 26(f) makes the attorney's signature on a discovery paper a certification that the material in it *is supported by law, has a proper purpose,* and *is reasonable*. If a paper is signed in violation of the Rule, the court is to sanction the offending person . . . . [1479]

F. **APPELLATE REVIEW OF DISCOVERY ORDERS**
  1. **Orders Usually Not Appealable:** Most discovery orders are not final, and thus in most jurisdictions are not appealable. Neither are discovery orders considered collateral to the main action, nor are they injunctions . . . . [1483]
  2. **Modes of Review**
      - a. **Certified appeal:** In federal practice, a trial court may certify an important discovery question to the appellate court . . . . [1487]
      - b. **Mandamus or prohibition:** These writs may be issued by an appellate court (in both state and federal practice) to correct or prevent a trial judge's *abuse of discretion* in discovery . . . . [1488]
      - c. **Review after judgment:** Failure of the trial court to compel effective disclosure *may* be the basis for reversal if the ruling was *prejudicial* . . . . . [1489]

Civil Procedure—XXIII

			Text Section

    d. **Review of contempt order:** A civil contempt order against a party is not final and appealable; a conviction of criminal contempt ***is*** final and appealable .... [1491]

G. USE OF DISCOVERY AT TRIAL
1. **Statements of Adversary:** ***Admissions*** by a party in a deposition or in response to interrogatories are admissible and, in some cases, are conclusive proof of facts admitted. The ***right to object*** is retained at all times by the party whose statement is used at trial .... [1492]
2. **Statements of Other Witnesses:** ***Prior inconsistent statements*** of a witness may be shown by a deposition admitted at trial. A ***deponent's unavailability*** also permits a deposition to be admitted. A ***party's own deposition*** may be used by the party if he is ***genuinely*** unavailable for trial ..... [1494]

H. PRIVATE INVESTIGATIONS
Civil litigants may conduct their own private investigation of the facts; *i.e.,* they are ***not*** required to use formal discovery procedures. Such litigants may use proof obtained, even by tortious means, since they are not subject to Fourth Amendment limits on searches .... [1497]

VII. SUMMARY JUDGMENT

A. INTRODUCTION
1. **Purpose:** Summary judgment enables a court to look behind the pleadings to determine whether some ***contentions are so lacking in substance*** that judgment can be rendered against the party making them without the expense and delay of a full trial .... [1500]
2. **Impact on Right to Trial:** Although the traditional belief is that a litigant has a right to test her claims at trial, there is no such right where there is no genuine factual dispute .... [1511]
3. **Trend Favoring Use of Summary Judgment:** The advent of notice pleading has helped the motion for summary judgment supplant the motion to dismiss . [1512]

B. STANDARD FOR GRANT OF SUMMARY JUDGMENT
1. **In General:** The court is to grant summary judgment if there is ***no genuine issue as to any material fact*** .... [1513]
2. **Relation to Standard for Judgment as a Matter of Law:** The Supreme Court has stated that in federal court the standard is the same at the summary judgment stage as at the judgment as a matter of law stage .... [1514]
    a. **Moving party with burden of proof:** If the moving party has the burden on the issue, summary judgment should be granted only if the jury could not reasonably disbelieve the moving party's evidence .... [1515]
    b. **Opposing party with burden:** If the moving party does not have the burden, summary judgment should be granted only if the opposing party does not present sufficient evidence to permit a jury reasonably to find for him .... [1516]
3. **Case-by-Case Determination:** The evaluation of motions for summary judgment is done case-by-case, based not on specific rules but rather on general principles .... [1517]
    a. **All reasonable inferences indulged in favor of opposing party:** The court makes all reasonable inferences in favor of the opposing party, and views evidence in the light most favorable to that party .... [1518]
    b. **Court may not "weigh" evidence:** The court may not judge the relative persuasiveness of conflicting versions of events .... [1519]
    c. **Role of higher burden of proof:** The Supreme Court has held that when a party will bear a higher burden of proof at trial, that standard should be used in deciding the motion for summary judgment .... [1520]

				Text Section
		d.	**Witness credibility:** Witness credibility is not ordinarily assessed in deciding a motion for summary judgment	[1521]
			(1) **Uncontradicted interested witness:** Even if uncontradicted, an *interested* witness's testimony will usually not be sufficient to support summary judgment because it might not be believed by the jury	[1522]
			(2) **Disinterested witness:** Some courts have held that an uncontradicted affidavit of a *disinterested* witness will support summary judgment for the party with the burden of proof	[1523]
		e.	**Motive, intent, and state of mind:** When mental state is at issue, summary judgment is usually *inappropriate*	[1526]
		f.	**"Slightest doubt" standard contrasted:** The notion that summary judgment should be avoided whenever there was the "slightest doubt" about the outcome at trial has been *repudiated*	[1529]
C.	**PROCEDURE**			
	1.	**Initial Showing:** The court must first evaluate the moving party's showing to determine whether it justifies pretrial scrutiny of the evidence		[1530]
		a.	**Moving party's burden:** The moving party must show that there is no factual issue and that he is entitled to judgment	[1531]
			(1) **Moving party with burden of proof:** If the moving party has the burden of proof, he must produce evidence such that no reasonable jury could find for the opponent	[1532]
			(2) **Moving party without burden of proof:** The Supreme Court has rejected the early view that a moving party without the burden of proof must make a showing of the same strength as a party with the burden. The exact requirements are not clear, but a bald assertion that the opposing party lacks sufficient evidence is not enough; and the moving party should at least point to portions of the record showing the absence of factual issues	[1533]
		b.	**Opposing party's burden:** If the moving party has not made the required initial showing, the opposing party technically need not make any showing in response. If the moving party has made an initial showing, the opponent has the burden of coming forward with sufficient evidence to support a jury verdict in his favor	[1541]
	2.	**Materials Considered on Motion:** A court deciding a motion for summary judgment may consider *admissions* contained in the pleadings, *affidavits* made on personal knowledge, and *discovery materials*. Oral testimony is rarely used		[1550]
		a.	**Admissibility:** Materials considered in deciding a motion for summary judgment must generally be capable of admission as evidence, and the court will entertain objections to admissibility before considering the materials	[1554]
			(1) **Possible relaxation for opposing party:** The opposing party might not be held to the requirement of admissibility if it can show that it will have admissible evidence at trial	[1555]
	3.	**Partial Summary Judgment:** The court can grant summary judgment as to some but not all of the claims or defenses before it		[1559]
	4.	**Inability to Provide Responsive Materials:** The court may *continue* the hearing on the motion for summary judgment to allow time for the opposing party to obtain evidence. The evidence with respect to which the continuance is sought must be *material* to the motion and reasonably *obtainable*		[1562]
	5.	**Appellate Review:** The appellate court uses a *plenary standard* of review, giving no deference to the trial court decision		[1568]
		a.	**Timing:** Where full summary judgment is not granted, review may be delayed until the final decision of the case	[1569]
		b.	**Order denying motion:** If summary judgment is mistakenly denied, the	

	Text Section
order is not reviewable until after trial, at which time it may be *harmless error* if the trial was properly conducted	[1570]

VIII. MANAGERIAL JUDGING, PRETRIAL CONFERENCES, AND SETTLEMENT PROMOTION

A. PRETRIAL CONFERENCES AND MANAGERIAL JUDGING

1. **Historical Background:** The original Federal Rule 16 authorized a pretrial conference to be held shortly before trial for the purpose of organizing it. Amendments in the 1980s and 1990s provided for mandatory meet-and-confer sessions among the parties, more numerous pretrial conferences, discovery conferences, and a final pretrial conference .... [1571]
2. **Scheduling:** Federal district courts are required, after consulting the parties, to enter a *scheduling order* within 90 days after a defendant's appearance and within 120 days after service of the complaint. This order sets time limits for joinder, amendments, discovery, and motions .... [1573]
3. **Discovery Control:** Judges are required to limit discovery that is unduly cumulative, delayed, or burdensome .... [1578]
   a. **Meet and confer sessions:** At least 14 days before the Rule 16 scheduling conference or order, the parties are to meet and confer regarding the nature and basis of their claims and defenses and to develop a discovery plan. Within 10 days after the meeting, they are to submit a written report to the court .... [1579]
   b. **Court's pretrial order:** Based on the parties' submission, the court is to enter an order limiting the time to complete discovery .... [1580]
4. **Issue Simplification:** By the time a pretrial conference is held, the parties know more about their case and are in a better position to simplify the issues for trial. The court may not compel admissions, but may pressure parties to abandon unsupportable positions .... [1581]
5. **Settlement Promotion:** Judges were once reluctant to become involved in settlement discussions, but Rule 16 now explicitly authorizes it .... [1583]
   a. **No power to dictate terms of settlement:** The court may suggest but not dictate the terms of settlement .... [1586]
   b. **Ambiguity of judicial role:** It is unclear how the judge's role in settlement comports with her usual role of deciding disputed matters according to legal standards. It is also unclear what role her pretrial opinion of the relative strengths of the cases should play .... [1587]
   c. **Promotion of alternative dispute resolution:** The judge may discuss special procedures to assist in resolving the dispute at a pretrial conference .... [1590]
6. **Final Pretrial Conference:** The final pretrial conference seeks to resolve as much as possible before trial and to give notice of the subjects to be covered at trial .... [1591]
   a. **Required pretrial disclosures:** At least 30 days before trial, each party is to disclose: (i) *the names of witnesses* the party expects to present, (ii) *designate witnesses whose testimony will be presented by deposition*, and (iii) *identify documents and other exhibits* the party expects to offer .... [1592]
   b. **Topics covered:** The final pretrial order encompasses the matters covered at the pretrial conference. It controls at trial and can be modified only to prevent manifest injustice .... [1599]

B. COURT-ANNEXED SETTLEMENT DEVICES

1. **Court-Annexed Arbitration:** Some federal court districts and some states have experimented with *mandatory nonbinding arbitration* for many types

	of cases where only money damages of less than a specified amount are involved. Where arbitration is not mandatory, the court may direct it if the parties consent	[1614]

      a. **Hearing:** The arbitration decision is based on a trial-like hearing, at which the rules of evidence and other procedural rules may be relaxed . [1626]

      b. **Trial de novo:** The arbitrator's decision becomes the judgment of the court unless a party demands a trial de novo. The party who demands a trial may be required to reimburse its opponent for certain expenses if the trial does not produce a more favorable result for the demanding party than the arbitration did [1628]

   2. **Summary Jury Trial:** The summary jury trial is a ***nonbinding abbreviated trial*** conducted after pretrial matters are concluded and held before a jury summoned in the usual manner. The bulk of the case is presented by lawyers who summarize evidence. The nonbinding verdict is intended to provide information to encourage settlement [1631]

      a. **Compulsory participation:** Courts have split as to whether a summary judgment trial can be compulsory, but under revised Rule 16, courts probably have such power [1644]

IX. TRIAL

A. RIGHT TO TRIAL BY JURY

1. **Source of Right:** In federal courts, the right to a jury trial in civil actions at law is derived from the ***Seventh Amendment*** and, if that does not apply, the right may be provided by ***Congress***. In ***state courts***, the right to a jury trial in civil cases is ***not*** a due process right protected by the Fourteenth Amendment. However, there may be a federal statutory right to jury trial in state court actions that are governed by federal law. Note that most ***state constitutions*** have provisions similar to the Seventh Amendment of the U.S. Constitution . [1645]

2. **Cases Where Right Exists**

      a. **Basic historical test:** The historical test used to determine whether a right to jury trial exists in civil cases in federal court is whether the claim involved is ***legal or equitable*** as those terms were understood in 1791 (when the Seventh Amendment became effective) [1650]

      b. **Present standards for right to jury trial:** The right was observed in English law courts but not in Chancery (equity). Modern actions that are ***counterparts to actions at law*** (e.g., personal injury claims) are triable to a jury. Actions that are ***counterparts to equity suits*** (e.g., injunctions) do ***not*** give rise to a jury trial [1653]

      c. **Declaratory relief:** A declaratory judgment action is jury triable if the claim in issue would have been so if sued upon in an action for coercive relief [1660]

3. **Proceedings in Which Right to Jury Applies in Part**

      a. **Actions joining legal and equitable claims:** In federal court, actions involving both legal and equitable claims are to be structured to preserve a jury trial on issues common to the legal and equitable aspects of the case, even if the equitable aspects predominate. Some states are contra and allow nonjury disposition of minor legal matters under the equitable "clean-up" doctrine [1661]

      b. **Priority of issues at trial:** The order in which issues are tried can be important because it may determine the outcome. In ***federal*** court, issues respecting a claim for legal relief ordinarily must be tried ***first***. In ***state*** courts, the order is often within the ***discretion*** of the trial judge [1662]

4. **Right to Jury Trial Depends on Timely Demand**

      a. **State practice:** The right to jury trial usually must be exercised by a written demand at the time the case is set for trial; if demand is not timely made, the right is waived [1669]

			Text Section

- b. **Federal practice:** In federal court, a jury must be demanded in writing not later than 10 days after service of the last pleading directed to the issue for which the jury is demanded .... [1671]
- 5. **Jury Trials Discretionary with Court:** A court may order a jury trial on any or all issues where the right has been waived, where a claim is not jury triable (with both parties' consent), and for the purpose of taking an advisory verdict . [1673]

B. SELECTION OF JURY
1. **Summons of the Venire:** Prospective jurors ("veniremen") are summoned by the court. The venire must be selected by a method that does not systematically exclude any religious, ethnic, or political group .... [1676]
2. **Number of Jurors Required:** The venire is usually two to three times larger than the number of jurors needed. Common law required a jury of 12. However, today *12 is not required* by either due process or the Seventh Amendment. Due process *does* require at least six jurors in a *criminal* case, and some local district rules also require six jurors in *state civil trials*, but this depends entirely on state law .... [1694]
3. **Voir Dire Examination of Jurors:** The examination of prospective jurors as to possible biases is known as voir dire .... [1701]
    - a. **Challenge for cause:** A prospective juror may be challenged if it appears that he or a member of his family has a financial interest in the litigation, or for other reasons indicating he will not be an impartial juror. There is *no limit* to the number of challenges for cause .... [1702]
    - b. **Peremptory challenge:** Each party is entitled to a limited number of challenges *without* a showing of cause, but peremptory challenges cannot be based on the juror's race or sex .... [1703]

C. DISQUALIFICATION OF JUDGE
1. **Grounds for Disqualification:** Grounds include any basis that may affect a judge's impartiality; *e.g.,* personal bias, personal knowledge of facts, previous involvement as a lawyer, financial interest, or family relationship. The disqualifying reason must be based on *matters outside the courtroom* .... [1713]
2. **Procedure for Disqualification**
    - a. **Federal practice:** A party seeking disqualification files an affidavit of bias setting forth the necessary facts. If the facts are legally sufficient to disqualify the judge, she *must* excuse herself and reassign the case .. [1721]
    - b. **State practice:** Most states require an actual showing by affidavit on grounds for disqualification. In some states, each party has an absolute right to disqualify *one* judge by simply stating in an affidavit that a fair trial cannot be obtained before that judge .... [1722]

D. ORDER OF TRIAL
1. **Right to Speak First and Last:** The general rule is that the party that has the *burden of proof* as to the principal issues (usually plaintiff) speaks first and last. However, the trial judge usually has the discretion whether to accord that right .... [1725]
2. **Stages of Jury Trial:** The normal sequence in a civil trial is plaintiff's opening statement; defendant's opening statement; presentation of direct evidence by plaintiff, with cross-examination of each witness by defendant, followed by redirect and re-cross, whereupon *plaintiff rests*; presentation of direct evidence by defendant, with cross-examination, re-direct, and re-cross and then *defendant rests*; rebuttal evidence by plaintiff, and then by defendant; plaintiff's argument to jury; defendant's argument to jury; plaintiff's closing argument: instructions to jury by judge; and the jury verdict .... [1727]
3. **Nonjury Trial:** The order is usually the same as above until the evidence has been presented, whereupon the parties may propose specific findings of facts and conclusions of law to the court .... [1728]

		Text Section

E. **PRESENTATION OF EVIDENCE**
   1. **Control Over Presentation:** The presentation of evidence is usually the responsibility of the parties and their counsel, although most courts give a judge discretion to call his own witness .... [1729]
   2. **Rules of Evidence:** Federal court proceedings are governed by the Federal Rules of Evidence. Some states have their own evidence codes, while others rely on common law rules .... [1730]
   3. **Objections and Exceptions:** Failure to object to admission of evidence waives the objection. If no objection is made to evidence that raises new evidence, the pleadings (or pretrial order) are treated as if amended to include those issues (*amendment by proof*) .... [1731]

F. **MOTIONS AT CLOSE OF PROOF**
   1. **In General:** At the close of proof, motions may be used to determine whether a party has carried the burden of producing evidence .... [1736]
   2. **Jury Trial—Motion for Judgment as a Matter of Law (Directed Verdict):** Either party may make such a motion after the adversary has been fully heard with respect to the issue in question .... [1737]
      a. **Standard for grant:** The standard looks to whether *the jury could reasonably find for the nonmoving party*. If the moving party has the burden of proof, the evidence favoring him must be of *such compelling strength* that the jury could not reasonably find for the opponent. If the party opposing the motion has the burden, that party must have *no substantial evidence* (no "scintilla" of evidence in some states) that would permit a jury to find in her favor .... [1739]
      b. **Case-by-case determination:** Evaluation is case-by-case, using general principles rather than fixed rules .... [1744]
         (1) **Attitude toward evidence:** The court is to view evidence in the *light most favorable to the opposing party*, and is to make all reasonable inferences in that party's favor .... [1745]
         (2) **Court may not "weigh" evidence:** The court may not "weigh" conflicting versions of events as to persuasiveness .... [1746]
         (3) **Demeanor evidence:** Where the moving party has the burden of proof and relies on witnesses whom the jury could disbelieve, it is generally not entitled to a directed verdict, even if there is no conflicting evidence. There is a possible exception for occasions when the witness is *disinterested* and *unimpeached* .... [1751]
      c. **Compare—renewed motion for judgment as a matter of law:** Whether resolved before or after the verdict, the same standard is used. Practical considerations related to potential appeals may favor the use of the post-verdict motion .... [1755]
   3. **Jury Trial—Motion for Nonsuit:** In some states, the defendant may move for a nonsuit at the close of plaintiff's opening statement (or at close of plaintiff's proof) if the statement of proof reveals that plaintiff's case is *legally insufficient* .... [1763]
   4. **Nonjury Trial—Motion for Judgment as a Matter of Law:** In a nonjury trial, after a party has been fully heard with respect to an issue, the court may enter a judgment as a matter of law. The motion is analogous to the common law *demurrer* to the evidence. Today, some states call it a *motion to dismiss*, while in others it is a *motion for judgment* .... [1766]
      a. **Test applied:** A court may grant the motion if it finds plaintiff's proof is *unpersuasive* on issues on which plaintiff had the burden of proof .... [1769]

G. **ARGUMENT TO JURY**
   1. **Time for Argument:** In federal practice and most state courts, counsels' arguments take place at the close of the evidence and *before* the jury receives the judge's instructions .... [1770]

		Text Section

2. **Right to Argue:** Counsel have an absolute right to argument in a jury trial. However, the trial judge has discretion to control the duration and manner of argument ... [1771]

3. **Limitations on Argument:** Counsels' comments must be *based on the evidence*, the argument must be within the limits of the *governing substantive law*, and counsel may *not appeal to the passions or prejudices* of the jurors ... [1773]

H. INSTRUCTIONS TO THE JURY

1. **In General:** Before a jury deliberates, the judge instructs it on certain relevant matters ... [1775]

2. **Issues of Fact:** A *judge* determines issues of *law* (*e.g.*, interpretation of statute), while a *jury* decides disputed issues of *fact*. Questions of fact are specific and pertain to past events ... [1776]

3. **Burden of Persuasion**
   a. **Assigning the burden:** The judge must explain to the jury which party has the burden of persuasion concerning each issue of fact the jury must decide ... [1781]
   b. **Degree of persuasion:** In a civil case, the usual burden of persuasion is by *preponderance of the evidence*. However, issues of fraud, duress, or undue influence must be shown by *clear and convincing proof* ... [1782]

4. **Comment on the Evidence:** Generally, a judge is allowed to comment to the jury on the quality of the evidence presented ... [1785]

5. **Instructions Requested by Counsel:** Although the responsibility for instructions rests with the judge, counsel has a duty to propose instructions that present the theory of the case. Proposed instructions must be *written* and served on opposing counsel and filed by the close of evidence. Each party must be given the *opportunity to object* to an adversary's proposed instructions ... [1786]

6. **Appellate Review of Jury Instructions:** Generally, errors in instructions are waived unless objections are timely made. However, egregious ("*plain*") error may be reversible even without a timely objection ... [1792]

I. JURY DELIBERATION AND VERDICT

1. **Types of Verdicts**
   a. **General verdict:** The most common form of verdict, a general verdict is simply a decision in favor of one party or the other ... [1794]
   b. **Special verdict:** This consists of the jury's *answers to specific factual* questions that it is instructed to decide; it is not a direct decision as to which party should prevail on the law ... [1796]
   c. **General verdict with special interrogatories:** This verdict *combines the two forms* above. The jury makes a general decision as to which party should prevail on the law while simultaneously answering specific questions of fact. If there is an *inconsistency* between the *special finding and the general verdict*, a judge may ignore the verdict and enter judgment based on the special findings. However, inconsistency among *the special findings* usually requires a new trial ... [1802]

2. **Requirement of Unanimity:** The general rule in federal and most state courts is that the jury must render a unanimous verdict unless the parties otherwise agree ... [1809]

3. **Jury Deliberation and Impeachment of Verdict**
   a. **Standards of jury conduct:** Only information presented at trial may be considered by the jury; any communication from the judge must be received in the *presence of counsel*. Each juror must make up his own mind; there can be no verdict of the average or by lots. *No coercion* by the judge is allowed ... [1814]

b. **Juror misconduct:** At *common law*, juror misconduct had to be established by the testimony of a person *other than* a juror. The federal rule today is that a juror may testify to any "extraneous prejudicial information" or "outside influence." Some states allow jurors to testify to *any* improper influence, either inside or outside the jury room .... [1820]
c. **Impeachment of verdict:** Impeachment can result from a juror's having concealed a ground for disqualification on voir dire examination, as well as from misconduct during jury deliberations .... [1823]
d. **Announcement of verdict:** The verdict must be announced in open court. At the request of either party, the jury may be *polled*. If the verdict is incomplete, the court may direct the jury to continue its deliberations . [1826]

J. **MOTIONS AFTER VERDICT OR JUDGMENT**
1. **Renewed Motion for Judgment as a Matter of Law (Judgment n.o.v.):** A renewed motion for judgment as a matter of law is granted after a verdict when the trial judge concludes that there is no substantial evidence supporting the decision .... [1830]
   a. **Procedural requirements:** In federal practice, a renewed motion can be entered *only* on motion of a *party*; in some states it can be entered *by the court* sua sponte. The federal rule requires the motion to be made within 10 days after judgment was entered on the verdict; state requirements vary .... [1832]
      (1) **Prior motion:** In federal court, a renewed motion cannot be considered unless the moving party made a motion for judgment as a matter of law at the close of all the evidence .... [1836]
2. **Motion for New Trial:** A trial judge has the power to order a new trial on all or some of the contested factual issues .... [1842]
   a. **Grounds for motions—jury trial:** A federal court may order a new trial in a jury case "for any of the reasons for which new trials have heretofore been granted in actions at law in the courts of the United States." Some state statutes are more explicit in specifying when a new trial is appropriate, *e.g.,* where counsel's argument to jury was improper or where there is newly discovered evidence. A judge may also order a new trial if the verdict is contrary to the *weight* of the evidence .... [1843]
   b. **Grounds for motion—nonjury trial:** Such a motion may be granted on grounds of newly discovered evidence, erroneous findings of fact, and/or error in the conduct of the trial .... [1865]
   c. **Procedural requirements:** A federal court may order a new trial on its own motion; some states require a party to make the motion. In federal practice, the motion must be served not later than 10 days after the entry of judgment; state time limits vary .... [1866]
   d. **Order:** In nonjury cases, a court may order a full or partial new trial; in jury cases, the court must grant or deny the motion but may do so in parts or on conditions. In federal court, a judge need not specify grounds on which the new trial is granted; in some states, grounds must be stated. Grounds include *excessive or inadequate damages and insufficiency of proof* .. [1876]
      (1) **Conditional new trial:** A *remittitur* is an order for a new trial unless plaintiff consents to a *reduction* of the damage award. An *additur* (not allowed in federal court) orders a new trial unless defendant consents to an *increase* in the verdict amount .... [1883]
3. **Motion to Alter or Amend Judgment:** This is used to reopen judgments in both jury and nonjury cases and is used to correct *errors of law only*. Such a motion is subject to the same time limits as a motion for a new trial .... [1894]
4. **Motion for Relief from Judgment:** Such a motion may be used to correct a clerical error (no time limit); or on the grounds of mistake, inadvertence, or surprise; excusable neglect; newly discovered evidence; fraud; void judgment;

	Text Section
change of circumstances; and under federal rules, for any other reason justifying relief. In federal court, the motion must be made within reasonable time; state rules vary	[1897]
a. **Distinguish independent suit to set aside judgment:** This is an equitable proceeding usually based on *jurisdictional defects* or *fraud*. The independent suit may be addressed to a different court while a motion for relief from a judgment is made to the court that rendered the judgment. Grounds for an independent suit are more narrow and more strictly applied	[1912]
5. **Coram Nobis:** *Abolished in federal courts*, the common law writ of coram nobis is still available in some states. It is *cautiously applied* and is granted only where it is absolutely clear that a fact previously determined to be true is false and that the fact was crucial to the outcome of the case	[1916]

X. APPEAL

A. RIGHT TO APPEAL

1. **Status as Right:** At *common law*, there was no right to appeal; a writ of error was discretionary with the court. Also, the Due Process Clause does not guarantee a right of appeal, at least in civil cases. However, the right to appeal is *statutorily created* in every state, and federal courts have a general right of appeal	[1920]
2. **Waiver of Right:** The right of appeal may be lost through an express waiver, an untimely assertion, or the voluntary compliance with a judgment	[1925]

B. APPELLATE PROCEDURE

1. **Filing of Appeal:** In the federal system, an appeal is commenced by filing a *notice of appeal* in the appellate or trial court within 30 days after entry of judgment (60 days if U.S. is a party). State rules vary. In any case, time limits are jurisdictional and usually *cannot be waived*	[1944]
2. **Appeal Bonds:** An appeal bond must generally be filed to secure the adversary's costs if the judgment is affirmed. Assurance that a judgment will be satisfied if affirmed may also have to be given by posting *supersedeas bond*, which keeps the judgment from taking effect pending appeal	[1950]
3. **Record on Appeal:** Review on appeal is usually limited to the trial record	[1953]
4. **Stay of Proceedings Below:** While an appeal from a final judgment is pending, the trial court generally has *no power* to alter or vacate its judgment, and very limited power to make any other order affecting the rights of the parties with respect to the case on appeal	[1956]

C. RULINGS SUBJECT TO APPEAL

1. **Final Decision Requirement**

a. **General rule:** At *common law*, a writ of error could be taken only from a final judgment—*i.e.,* judgment that stated the outcome of the proceedings and manifested that the proceedings were complete. Now, the final decision rule is the basic rule, but it is subject to exceptions	[1958]
b. **Jurisdictional character of rule:** The final decision rule is jurisdictional in that it *cannot be waived*	[1971]

2. **Exceptions to Final Decision Requirement**

a. **Partial final decisions:** If multiple claims or parties are involved in an action, an order disposing of fewer than all claims is usually not a final judgment unless the trial court enters a partial final judgment (when that is authorized)	[1972]
b. **Review of equitable remedies:** In early equity practice, the rule was not applied because personal orders (*e.g.,* injunctions), if erroneous, might result in irreversible consequences. Thus immediate appellate review	

	Text Section

was permitted. Modern practice preserves the right to interlocutory review from orders that might result in irreparable consequences .... [1975]

    c. **Discretionary review:** Interlocutory appeals are also permitted in the federal system when the ***trial court certifies*** that determination of a controlling question of law would speed the ultimate resolution of the case, ***and*** the court appeals ***grants leave*** to appeal .... [1977]

    d. **Collateral orders:** In federal court, an immediate appeal is permitted from orders as to collateral matters if (i) the issue the order concerns is an important one that is completely separate from the merits of the underlying case; (ii) deferred review would effectively destroy appellant's rights; and (iii) the trial court has made its final decision on the challenged issue .... [1980]

    e. **Practical construction of "finality":** The U.S. Supreme Court has held that the final decision rule should be construed practically, not technically . [1985]

D. **SCOPE OF APPELLATE REVIEW**
  1. **In General:** Appellate review does not extend to retrying facts or supplanting the trial judge's decision in discretionary matters .... [1986]
  2. **Findings of Fact Subject to Limited Review**
    a. **Jury verdicts:** The role of the appellate court is to oversee the jury's adherence to the law. Verdicts must be supported by ***substantial evidence*** [1988]
    b. **Judicial findings in nonjury trials:** A judge's findings in a nonjury trial may be set aside if in ***clear error***. Note that this is a less restrictive test, permitting reversal more often than the test for jury verdicts .... [1991]
    c. **"Fact" and "law" distinguished:** Only findings of fact are entitled to deference. ***Errors of law*** (*e.g.,* improper jury instructions, erroneous conclusions of law by judge) are reviewed de novo and, if not harmless, result in reversal. The distinction between law and fact can be difficult, and there is no satisfactory test .... [1994]
  3. **Review of Discretionary Rulings:** A trial judge is entrusted by law with discretion as to certain matters, especially procedural questions. An appellate court will not reverse such decisions absent a clear ***abuse of discretion*** ... [2003]
  4. **"Harmless Error" Standard:** The general rule is that an appellate court will not reverse any judgment unless the trial court's error was ***prejudicial*** (*i.e.,* affected substantial rights of the parties) or the error was ***egregious*** ...... [2005]
  5. **Waiver of Objections in Lower Court**
    a. **General rule:** An appellate court will not reverse a judgment to correct any error that might have been avoided or corrected if the appellant had made a timely objection .... [2009]
    b. **Exceptions:** An appellate court may review despite the lack of a timely objection if: (i) the trial court lacked ***subject matter jurisdiction*** or (ii) error is so clear and fundamental that it would be ***unjust*** to let the judgment stand .... [2014]
  6. **Trial de Novo:** Sometimes legislatively authorized, this is, in effect, a new trial in a court of general jurisdiction .... [2017]

E. **APPELLATE REVIEW BY EXTRAORDINARY WRIT**
  1. **Prerogative Writs:** The available writs, depending on the court system, are: [2018]
    (i) ***Mandamus***—order directing a judge to perform her legal duty; and
    (ii) ***Prohibition***—an order enjoining a judge from conduct exceeding her lawful authority.
  2. **Source of Power to Issue Writs:** State court writs are usually based on common law practice. Federal courts are statutorily empowered to issue prerogative writs .... [2019]
  3. **Discretionary Character of Writ:** The issuance of a prerogative writ is always discretionary with the appellate court. There is ***no right*** to a hearing .... [2021]

	Text Section

  4. **Grounds for Issuance:** A writ may issue for abuse of discretion, excess of jurisdiction, or refusal to exercise jurisdiction. There must be a ***need for immediate review***, *i.e.,* when petitioner has no right to a present appeal and would suffer undue hardship or substantial prejudice if review was delayed until after a final judgment .... [2022]

  5. **Common Uses of Writs:** The courts of appeals use discretionary writs to correct erroneous denials of jury trial and to prevent the improper delegation of judicial power .... [2024]

  6. **Supervisory Mandamus:** In rare circumstances, mandamus may be used to resolve ***issues of first impression*** that may be important in a significant number of cases .... [2025]

  7. **Availability:** The increased availability of these writs in some states makes them equivalent to a device for seeking an interlocutory order .... [2026]

XI. PRECLUSIVE EFFECTS OF JUDGMENTS

A. INTRODUCTION

  1. **In General:** Res judicata has two components: claim preclusion and issue preclusion .... [2027]

  2. **Claim Preclusion (Also Called Res Judicata):** A final judgment on a claim or cause of action ***precludes reassertion of that claim*** or cause of action in a subsequent suit. If the judgment was for plaintiff, there is a ***merger*** of the claim in the judgment; if judgment was for defendant, it is a ***bar*** against plaintiff's suing again on the same claim .... [2028]

  3. **Issue Preclusion (Also Called Estoppel):** A decision regarding an ***issue of fact*** may be binding in later litigation between the same parties, or sometimes against a prior party (but usually not against a prior nonparty) .... [2031]

  4. **Rationale:** The purpose of the res judicata doctrine is to avoid the time and expense of multiple litigation on the same matter, and it stabilizes the result of adjudication by preventing inconsistent outcomes .... [2032]

  5. **Interjurisdictional Effect:** Under the Full Faith and Credit Clause, with respect to res judicata, courts of other states generally must give a judgment the same effect it would have in courts of the state where it was rendered. Federal courts follow the same rule with respect to state court judgments ... [2033]

B. CLAIM PRECLUSION

  1. **In General:** Before any judgment can have claim preclusion effect it must be final, on the merits, and valid .... [2034]

  2. **Policy Basis:** Litigants should be compelled to litigate their entire claim their first time in court, for policy reasons related to judicial efficiency, prevention of vexation of defendants, and consistency .... [2036]

    a. **Effect:** The effect of claim preclusion may be to foreclose matters that were never litigated because they were never raised in the first litigation .. [2039]

  3. **Meaning of "Claim"—Breadth of Preclusion:** Unless the claim in the second suit is the *"same,"* claim preclusion does not apply (although collateral estoppel might) .... [2040]

    a. **Traditional tests:** Traditionally, the courts applied preclusion when the second claim involved the ***same primary right and duty***, turned on essentially the ***same evidence***, or ***merely changed the legal theory*** ... [2041]

    b. **Modern approach—transactional test:** Under the Restatement, claim preclusion applies to all or part of the transaction or series of connected transactions out of which the action arose .... [2045]

  4. **"Final"**

    a. **Effect of appeal:** Whether a judgment on appeal is final for res judicata purposes is determined by the ***law of the state*** where the judgment was rendered .... [2048]

		Text Section

- b. **Modifiable judgments:** Such judgments (*e.g.,* alimony awards, child custody) are res judicata ***until modified*** ... [2051]
- c. **Conflicting judgments:** Where two judgments conflict, the ***last in time*** controls ... [2052]
5. **"On the Merits":** A judgment is on the merits where the claim has been tried and determined, and includes dispositions such as summary judgment, directed verdict, nonsuit, etc. Note that a ***dismissal*** that does ***not*** relate to the merits (*e.g.,* for lack of jurisdiction) does not bar subsequent action, although dismissals for misconduct in litigation (*e.g.,* as a sanction for discovery abuse) can have claim preclusion effect ... [2053]
6. **"Valid":** A judgment is valid ***unless*** the court lacked subject matter or territorial ***jurisdiction***, or notice to defendant did not conform to ***due process*** requirements. However, if the question of validity was ***litigated*** in the original action, that determination is usually res judicata ... [2059]
7. **Attachment Jurisdiction:** Attachment jurisdiction (restricted, but not eliminated, by *Shaffer v. Heitner*) is gained by seizing local property as a basis for collecting an obligation unrelated to the property. A judgment based on attachment jurisdiction does ***not*** extinguish the claim except to the extent of the property seized. However, ***issues*** actually litigated are ***conclusive*** on the parties if the amount of the attached property gave them a fair incentive to litigate ... [2065]
8. **Exceptions to Claim Preclusion:** Exceptions to the doctrine are recognized only under ***extraordinary*** circumstances (*e.g.,* fraud on the court). There is a ***very strong policy*** against relitigation ... [2069]
9. **Defenses and Counterclaims**
   - a. **Effect of compulsory counterclaim statutes and rules:** A defendant must set up any counterclaim she has against plaintiff that arises from the same transaction as plaintiff's claim. If defendant fails to do so, she is barred from later asserting it, either as a defense or as a basis for relief in an independent action ... [2070]
   - b. **Where no compulsory counterclaim involved:** In such cases, res judicata does not prevent a defendant from asserting the same matter first as a defense, and later as a basis for independent relief against the former plaintiff (although issue preclusion may apply) ... [2071]

C. ISSUE PRECLUSION
1. **Direct Estoppel:** Issues actually litigated ***between the parties*** are binding on them in subsequent actions concerning the ***same claim*** ... [2073]
2. **Collateral Estoppel:** Where a second suit involves a different claim (thus no merger, bar, or direct estoppel), the first judgment may be invoked as to all matters ***actually litigated and decided in the first action and essential to its determination*** ... [2074]
   - a. **Identical issue:** The issue in the first adjudication must be identical to the one presented in the subsequent action ... [2087]
   - b. **Exceptions:** Issue preclusion might not be applied if, in the second suit, the stakes are much higher, the burden of proof is different, the issue arises in a substantially different context, or other reasons justify relitigation ... [2088]

D. PERSONS PRECLUDED BY JUDGMENTS
1. **Parties and Privies:** A party to a judgment is bound by claim preclusion ***and*** issue preclusion; a privy is usually bound to the ***same extent***. Privity with a party is a legal conclusion, encompasses a number of relationships, and may be substantive or procedural ... [2089]
2. **Nonparties Not Bound:** Generally, a nonparty is not bound by a judgment because to do so would violate due process ... [2099]

a. **Nonparty may benefit:** A nonparty to an action may benefit from the judgment	[2100]
(1) **Claim preclusion:** Where a relationship of ***vicarious liability*** (but ***not*** joint liability) exists, a judgment exonerating either potential defendant precludes an action on the same claim against the other	[2101]
(2) **Issue preclusion:** Generally, a person who litigates an issue against one party and loses may not relitigate that issue with another party, but this estoppel may be limited in cases where the issue would not be conclusive between the parties to the original action or where unjust under the circumstances	[2103]

TEXT CORRELATION CHART

Gilbert Law Summary Civil Procedure	Cound, Friedenthal, Miller, Sexton Civil Procedure: Cases and Materials 1993 (6th ed.)	Field, Kaplan, Clermont Materials for a Basic Course in Civil Procedure 1993 (6th ed.) 1994 Supp.	Hazard, Tait, Fletcher Pleading and Procedure Cases and Materials 1994 (7th ed.)	Marcus, Redish, Sherman Civil Procedure: A Modern Approach 1989 (1st ed.) 1994 Supp.	Rosenberg, Smit Dreyfuss Elements of Civil Procedure: Cases and Materials 1990 (5th ed.) 1994 Supp.	Yeazell, Landers, Martin Civil Procedure 1992 (3d ed.) 1994 Supp.
I. TERRITORIAL JURISDICTION AND RELATED MATTERS						
A. Introduction	65-77	885-905	180-202	572-592	178-179, 222-225	61-74
B. Contemporary Constitutional Grounds for State Court Jurisdiction	77-137	909-944, 956-1003; Supp. 67, 69-85	202-268, 307-351	592-603, 612-688; Supp. 126-149	225-248, 259-325; Supp. 35-36, 38	76-159; Supp. 357-369
C. Statutory Authorization for Jurisdiction	85-137	945-956	287-306	603-612; Supp. 124-125	248-258, 325-329; Supp. 37-41	172-180; Supp. 374
D. Litigating Jurisdiction	191-195	1192-1199	351-361	688-690	325	146-159
E. Venue	339-360	1016-1025	446-468	700-706; Supp. 150-156	335-350; Supp. 42-43	180-185, 238-239; Supp. 375-377
F. Forum Non Conveniens	360-371	1025-1045; Supp. 94 1046-1067; Supp. 95-103	469-480	706-718; Supp. 156-157	335-350; Supp. 42-43	185-193; Supp. 377
G. Notice	196-260		269-287	690-700; Supp. 149-150	330-335; Supp. 41-42	159-172; Supp. 369-374
II. SUBJECT MATTER JURISDICTION OF THE FEDERAL COURTS						
A. Introduction	261-265	824-827	380-392	718	178-181	193-196
B. Diversity Jurisdiction	265-282	188-196, 853-867	407-418	718-728; Supp. 157-160	181-189, 200-205; Supp. 18-22	204-212; Supp. 378-386
C. Federal Question Jurisdiction	282-304	185-188, 827-834	392-407, 445-446	728-748; Supp. 161	189-200; Supp. 23-25	196-204
D. Supplemental Jurisdiction	304-323	834-853; Supp. 50-57	418-434	748-775; Supp. 161-184	206-219; Supp. 25-35	212-219; Supp. 386
E. Removal	323-333	867-872; Supp. 57-66	434-444	775-785; Supp. 184-198	219-222; Supp. 34-35	220-228; Supp. 386
III. RELATION BETWEEN STATE AND FEDERAL LAW						
A. State Law in the Federal Courts	373-429	218-267	481-551	786-848; Supp. 199-204	351-389, 395-398; Supp. 44-56	229-282; Supp. 391
B. Federal Common Law	429-447	267-272	551-556	848-871; Supp. 205-207	389-395; Supp. 56-57	240-241
IV. PLEADING						
A. Introduction	455-458	484-486	557-558	109	543-545	345-346
B. History of Pleading	458-503	409-415	565-570	109-118	546-562	346-375

TEXT CORRELATION CHART (continued)

Gilbert Law Summary Civil Procedure	Cound, Friedenthal, Miller, Sexton Civil Procedure: Cases and Materials 1993 (6th ed.)	Field, Kaplan, Clermont Materials for a Basic Course in Civil Procedure 1993 (6th ed.) 1994 Supp.	Hazard, Tait, Fletcher Pleading and Procedure Cases and Materials 1994 (7th ed.)	Marcus, Redish, Sherman Civil Procedure: A Modern Approach 1989 (1st ed.) 1994 Supp.	Rosenberg, Smit, Dreyfuss Elements of Civil Procedure: Cases and Materials 1990 (5th ed.) 1994 Supp.	Yeazell, Landers, Martin Civil Procedure 1992 (3d ed.) 1994 Supp.
C. Complaint	505-541	35-42, 502-522; Supp. 21-23	570-592	118-129	575-588	375-386
D. Challenges to Complaint	541-552	46-55, 532-540; Supp. 2	592-621	137-160; Supp. 32-39	589-614; Supp. 80-81	423-439, 405-414
E. Attorney's Duty to Investigate Claims and Defenses	581-598	42-45, 522-531, 537-538; Supp. 1, 23-38	646-660	129-137, 177-178; Supp. 29-32	563-574; Supp. 66-80	12-14, 387-404; Supp. 395-402
F. Answer	553-566	47-50, 537-540; Supp. 2	622-628	167-178; Supp. 40	32-33, 604-611	17-19, 427-438
G. Counterclaims and Cross-Claims	602-625	56-61, 540-546, 1104-1108	751-762	178-183, 230-231; Supp. 44	417-426, 435-437; Supp. 58-59	19-20, 455-464, 469-491
H. Amended and Supplemental Pleadings	566-581	62-66, 257-260, 480-481, 490-495; Supp. 19	628-646	188-197; Supp. 41	614-629; Supp. 81	21-22, 439-452
I. Default Procedure	914-920	46, 1054	1015-1022	160-167; Supp. 39-40	630-631, 941-942	642-649, 902-904
J. Judgment on the Pleadings	550-552	99, 107	1013-1015	176-177	558-562	17-18, 424-427
K. Voluntary Dismissal by Plaintiff	911-914	673-674, 1100; Supp. 48	1014-1015	183-187; Supp. 41	650-654	387-405, 649-653; Supp. 395-402
V. PARTIES						
A. Real Party in Interest Rule	625-628	1218-1220	840-842	198-207; Supp. 42	400-405; Supp. 58	501-503
B. Capacity of Party to Sue or Be Sued	628-629	1218-1220	842-848	206-207	406-412	503-504
C. Joinder of Parties	629-702	204-213, 1200-1220	765-840	207-261; Supp. 42-45	412-483; Supp. 58-60	22-27, 464-504; Supp. 409
D. Class Actions	703-760	213-216, 1221-1306	848-922	261-286; Supp. 45-48	483-542; Supp. 60-65	533-571
VI. DISCOVERY						
A. Introduction	9-10	66-67; Supp. 2-14	922-929	287-296; Supp. 49	658-665; Supp. 82-89	28-32, 573-576; Supp. 411-415
B. Basic Discovery Devices	785-816	68-82	929-942	296-311; Supp. 49-51	719-729	577-589; Supp. 416-422
C. Scope of Discovery	761-784, 831-844	68-69, 549-576; Supp. 39	942-989	311-324; Supp. 51-52	665-719	589-619; Supp. 422-424
D. Protective Orders	819-840	576-585	932, 987-990	324-352; Supp. 52-61	729-748	587-588, 621-623

TEXT CORRELATION CHART (continued)

Gilbert Law Summary Civil Procedure	Cound, Friedenthal, Miller, Sexton Civil Procedure: Cases and Materials 1993 (6th ed.)	Field, Kaplan, Clermont Materials for a Basic Course in Civil Procedure 1993 (6th ed.) 1994 Supp.	Hazard, Tait, Fletcher Pleading and Procedure Cases and Materials 1994 (7th ed.)	Marcus, Redish, Sherman Civil Procedure: A Modern Approach 1989 (1st ed.) 1994 Supp.	Rosenberg, Smit Dreyfuss Elements of Civil Procedure: Cases and Materials 1990 (5th ed.) 1994 Supp.	Yeazell, Landers, Martin Civil Procedure 1992 (3d ed.) 1994 Supp.
E. Sanctions for Failure to Disclose or to Comply with Discovery	844-854	82-83, 586-590	932-935, 938-940, 990-995	355-363	729-748	623-637
F. Appellate Review of Discovery Orders	1122-1169	590-592, 1363-1366	942, 990-992	896-897	1068-1070	843-868
G. Use of Discovery at Trial	816-819	87-89, 150	936-940	349-352; Supp. 53-61 352-355; Supp. 161-162	719-735	600-601; Supp. 422
H. Private Investigations		66-67	928-929		660-663	582
VII. SUMMARY JUDGMENT						
A. Introduction	881	99-107	1056-1057	364-365	631-634	33-38
B. Standard for Grant of Summary Judgment	881-910	99-107, 621-638	1031-1056	387-407; Supp. 74-76	634-644	653-667
C. Procedure	881-910	621-638	1056-1060	365-387; Supp. 72-74	644-650	33-38, 653-667
VIII. MANAGERIAL JUDGING, PRE-TRIAL CONFERENCE, AND SETTLEMENT PROMOTION						
A. Pretrial Conference and Managerial Judging	855-880	91-98, 593-620; Supp. 15, 40-46	995-1012, 1273-1311	3-24, 408-414; Supp. 77	781-827; Supp. 90-98	685-698; Supp. 437-438
B. Court-Annexed Settlement Devices	1305-1331	98-107, 330-353	1022-1030, 1331-1352	414-424; Supp. 78-80	1111-1135	668-686; Supp. 427-436
IX. TRIAL						
A. Right to Trial by Jury	921-982	116-117, 775-823; Supp. 49	1060-1121	433-480; Supp. 80-120	753-754, 760-773	699-734; Supp. 439-440
B. Selection of the Jury	983-999	117-130; Supp. 15	1121-1152	479-483; Supp. 121-122	829-836; Supp. 99	734-753; Supp. 440
C. Disqualification of Judge		129	1152-1167	15-18		753-764; Supp. 440-441
D. Order of Trial	1000-1004	130-133; Supp. 15 133-155	10-12, 1060-1064	425-433	837-842	38-42
E. Presentation of Evidence	1004-1006	155-156, 673-697; Supp. 48	10-12, 1060-1064	426-429	838-851; 895-918; Supp. 99-100	765-774
F. Motions at Close of Proof	1008-1031		1182-1205	429		765-786
G. Argument to Jury	1006-1008	156-157, 728-731	11, 1205-1213	429-430	41, 837	40-41
H. Instructions to the Jury	1033-1042	156-159, 700-705; Supp. 16	11, 1213-1226	430-432	41-42, 838-842	40-41, 787-792

TEXT CORRELATION CHART (continued)

Gilbert Law Summary Civil Procedure	Cound, Friedenthal, Miller, Sexton Civil Procedure: Cases and Materials 1993 (6th ed.)	Field, Kaplan, Clermont Materials for a Basic Course in Civil Procedure 1993 (6th ed.) 1994 Supp.	Hazard, Tait, Fletcher Pleading and Procedure Cases and Materials 1994 (7th ed.)	Marcus, Redish, Sherman Civil Procedure: A Modern Approach 1989 (1st ed.) 1994 Supp.	Rosenberg, Smit Dreyfuss Elements of Civil Procedure: Cases and Materials 1990 (5th ed.) 1994 Supp.	Yeazell, Landers, Martin Civil Procedure 1992 (3d ed.) 1994 Supp.
I. Jury Deliberation and Verdict	1042-1049	156-159, 705-723; Supp. 16	11-12, 1226-1228	432-433	42-43, 851-872	792-803; Supp. 441-442
J. Motions after Verdict or Judgment	1020-1033, 1053-1092	159-161; Supp. 16	12, 1228-1267	433	43, 872-895, 911-915	42-45, 804-826; Supp. 442
X. APPEAL						
A. Introduction	16-17		12-13, 1353-1354	872-875	1031-1034	52-58
B. Right to Appeal	1122-1130	176-182	1353-1355	875	1040-1045	833-843
C. Courts of Review	1131-1149	176-182	16-18	923-924	1031-1034, 1081-1092	52-53, 833-834, 886
D. Appellate Procedure	1131-1149	179-181	1355-1368	935-946; Supp. 210	43-45, 1034-1040	878-886; Supp. 443-445
E. Rulings Subject to Appeal	1131-1169	1352-1380; Supp. 107-108	1368-1399	875-902, 908-923; Supp. 208-210	1046-1081	52-53, 834-865; Supp. 443
F. Scope of Appellate Review	1176-1200	1349-1355, 1363-1369; Supp. 107-108	1354-1355	924-935	1092-1101	54-58, 868-878
G. Appellate Review by Extraordinary Writ	1150-1156	1381-1392	1401-1413	902-908	1107-1110	857-868
XI. PRECLUSIVE EFFECTS OF JUDGMENTS						
A. Introduction	1208-1209	1068-1072	663-666	947-950	955-958; Supp. 101-107	45-52, 887-888
B. Claim Preclusion	1210-1228	1073-1108; Supp. 104	666-745	950-981; Supp. 211	958-964, 974-977	887-920; Supp. 447
C. Issue Preclusion	1228-1247	1109-1134	666-745	981-999; Supp. 211-213 999-1019; Supp. 213-218	978-986, 1001-1021; Supp. 107-109	920-949
D. Persons Precluded by Judgments	1258-1289	1135-1174	666-745		964-974, 986-1001	932-967

approach to exams

Examination questions on civil procedure can concern a wide range of issues. The issues that you are most likely to encounter are discussed below and can be analyzed in the following sequence. (Note that these issues are discussed in greater detail in the chapter approach sections at the beginning of the appropriate chapters.)

1. **Jurisdiction:** Does the court have *authority* to render judgment in the present action, consistent with constitutional requirements of due process?

    a. Does the court have jurisdiction *over the parties* (territorial jurisdiction of the state)?

    b. Does the court have jurisdiction *over the subject matter* (over the particular type of action)?

    c. Has *adequate notice* been given to all parties?

2. **Venue:** Assuming the court does have jurisdiction, is it the *proper place* for trial of the action under the rules governing venue?

    a. If the action was originally filed in a court having proper venue, are there grounds for *transfer* or change of venue to another court?

3. **State and Federal Law**

    a. If the action is in federal court, does it concern a state law matter (usually this means it is a diversity case)? If so, the court will generally follow *state substantive law* and *federal procedural law.*

    b. Is there an *Erie* problem—*i.e.*, is there a *true conflict* between federal and state rules of law? (Only if there is a true conflict do you need to consider which rule, state or federal, applies.)

4. **Pleadings**

    a. Does the complaint contain a *valid substantive legal claim*?

    b. Does the complaint state the elements of a *prima facie case*?

    c. Is the complaint *sufficiently specific* so as to give fair notice of the basis of the claim(s) made?

    d. Does the answer properly admit or deny the complaint's allegations? Does it properly raise any applicable defenses?

5. **Parties**

    a. Are the named parties proper (*real party in interest* and *capacity to sue or be sued*)?

    b. Are the named parties *properly joined*?

c. Are there *other parties* who should be joined under the necessary party rule or who may become parties by intervention or impleader?

d. Can the parties assert *claims against each other* in addition to those in the complaint—*i.e.*, counterclaims or cross-claims? Can the parties *implead* other parties?

e. Is a *class action* appropriate?

6. **Discovery:** Is there a controversy as to either party's right to obtain pretrial discovery from the other party or from some third person? If so, consider:

   a. Is there a requirement of *disclosure*?

   b. Is the information sought within the *permissible scope* of discovery (*i.e.*, does it relate to the "subject matter of the action")?

   c. Is the information protected by a *privilege* or as *work product*?

   d. Is the *proper mechanism* used (*e.g.*, deposition, interrogatory, etc.)?

   e. What limitations by *protective order* are needed to prevent abuse?

7. **Trial**

   a. Is there a *right to a jury trial*?

   b. Are the issues before the court within the *scope* of the pleadings or pretrial order, or properly in issue because evidence on them was received without valid objection?

   c. Who has the *burden of proof* as to a particular issue, and has the burden been met?

   d. Were *instructions* properly given to the jury, and were they substantially correct?

   e. Was there *improper conduct* by the judge, a counsel, party, witness, or juror?

   f. Did plaintiff put on sufficient evidence to survive a *motion for judgment as a matter of law*?

8. **Post-Trial**

   a. Is there relief that the *trial court* can give?

      (1) Motion for a *new trial* (to overcome procedural error or if the verdict is against the weight of the evidence).

      (2) *Renewed motion for judgment as a matter of law* (if the verdict is unsupported by sufficient evidence).

      (3) *Extraordinary relief* (*e.g.*, if newly discovered evidence, fraud).

   b. Can the *appellate court* provide relief?

      (1) Is there a *final judgment* or other appealable order?

    (2) Is *discretionary appeal* available?

    (3) May review be obtained by *extraordinary writ*?

c. Does *res judicata* (claim preclusion) or *direct or collateral estoppel* (issue preclusion) bar relitigation of this matter in later trials?

I. TERRITORIAL JURISDICTION AND RELATED MATTERS

chapter approach

Almost all civil procedure examinations will include some question regarding the legal limitations on the geographic location of litigation. Such problems raise issues of personal jurisdiction and related matters, such as venue. (Note that problems of subject matter jurisdiction are covered in Chapter II.) When faced with a question raising issues of geographic location, ask yourself:

1. *Is there a statutory or rule basis for the exercise of jurisdiction?* There must be some "enabling legislation" by which the court obtains authority to exercise jurisdiction in the case. Often you must analyze the specific wording of the statute or rule involved.

2. *Is this exercise of jurisdiction constitutional?* This analysis may look to one of a number of grounds for constitutional assertion of jurisdiction:

    a. Does the defendant have **minimum contacts** with the forum that support the exercise of jurisdiction?

    b. Are the defendant's contacts with the forum so substantial that it can be subjected to jurisdiction on unrelated claims on a theory of *general jurisdiction*?

    c. Has **property** of the defendant been seized within the state? If so, is this a sufficient ground for exercise of jurisdiction?

    d. Has the defendant **consented** to jurisdiction in the forum?

    e. Was the defendant **personally served** within the forum?

3. *Is venue proper?* This inquiry may include consideration of the possibility of transfer of the case to a location that is a proper venue.

4. *Was proper notice given?* This looks to the constitutionality of the underlying statutory requirement for notice and the sufficiency of **service of process** in this case.

A. INTRODUCTION

1. **Types of Territorial Jurisdiction**

    a. **In personam jurisdiction:** [§1] In personam jurisdiction permits a court to enter a judgment that is personally binding on the defendant, either ordering her to do or refrain from doing a certain act (equitable or injunctive relief) or decreeing that the plaintiff may collect a certain amount of damages from the defendant (legal relief).

    b. **In rem jurisdiction:** [§2] In rem jurisdiction permits a court to adjudicate the rights of all claimants to a specific piece of property, as in a condemnation proceeding. This authority originated from a state's power to determine controversies regarding real property within its borders: "The well-being of every community requires that the title to real estate therein shall be secure, and that there be convenient and certain methods of determining any unsettled questions respecting it." [Arndt v. Griggs, 134 U.S. 316 (1890)]

    c. **Quasi in rem jurisdiction:** [§3] Quasi in rem jurisdiction formerly included cases of two types. The first category included cases involving disputes related to property under the court's control (such as actions for specific performance of a contract to purchase land). This type of quasi in rem jurisdiction continues to provide a constitutional basis for exercise of jurisdiction. The second category of cases involved essentially personal disputes where the court lacked personal jurisdiction over the defendant, but had jurisdiction over property belonging to the defendant. That property would be seized by the plaintiff and used to satisfy the claim if the plaintiff prevailed. The use of this second category of quasi in rem jurisdiction to provide a basis for exercise of jurisdiction over nonresident defendants has been severely limited on constitutional grounds. (*See infra*, §§53-68.)

2. ***Pennoyer v. Neff* and the Traditional Power Theory:** [§4] In *Pennoyer v. Neff,* 95 U.S. 714 (1878), the Court adopted a rigid power-based approach to state court jurisdiction that was later applied to determine the constitutional limits of jurisdiction under the Due Process Clause of the Fourteenth Amendment. Although this approach has been substantially eroded by more modern decisions, it is important to understand its operation and limitations.

    a. **The *Pennoyer* decision:** [§5] In 1865, attorney Mitchell sued Neff in an Oregon state court, alleging that Neff owed him about $250 for legal work performed. Neff was not personally served; rather service was by publication based on Mitchell's assertion that Neff owned property in Oregon. When Neff did not appear in the action, Mitchell obtained a default judgment. A month later, Neff acquired title to a tract of land in Oregon, and Mitchell had the sheriff seize and sell the land to satisfy the judgment. Mitchell bought the land at the sheriff's sale and sold it to Pennoyer shortly thereafter. Many years later, Neff sued Pennoyer in federal court, arguing that the sale was invalid because the Oregon court lacked jurisdiction to enter the judgment against him. The Supreme Court agreed. It held that the Oregon court lacked jurisdiction in Mitchell's suit because there was no personal service of process on Neff in Oregon. It relied on two "principles of public law":

        (i) Every state has *"exclusive jurisdiction" over persons and property within the state*; and

        (ii) As a corollary, states may not exercise *"direct" authority over persons or property outside the state*.

        (1) **Criticism:** This analysis is highly formalistic and disregards the significance of "indirect" effects of the exercise of state jurisdiction. For example, a valid in personam judgment against Neff in favor of Mitchell in Oregon would be entitled to full faith and credit in California, and California would therefore be required to satisfy the judgment out of Neff's California property. In this manner, California's "exclusive" jurisdiction over property within California would be impaired.

(2) **Relation to due process:** Because the Fourteenth Amendment did not become effective until after Mitchell had Neff's property sold, the Fourteenth Amendment Due Process Clause was not involved in the case. However, the Court made it clear in dictum that in the future, *due process would apply the same limitations on exercise of jurisdiction*.

b. **Territorial limits on process:** [§6] *Pennoyer* also stated that "[p]rocess from the tribunals of one State cannot run into another State." This basic limitation on the power of state courts to exercise in personam jurisdiction has been weakened by the modern shift to a contacts analysis. (*See infra*, §§21-25.)

c. **Service within state sufficient:** [§7] *Pennoyer* also said that service of process within the state was sufficient for jurisdiction. This conclusion is implicit from *Pennoyer's* reasoning, and is the basis for what has come to be known as *transient jurisdiction* (*i.e.*, obtaining jurisdiction by serving a defendant when he was temporarily physically present in the state). It has been carried to great lengths.

  (1) **Example—service in airplane:** Service on a passenger on a nonstop scheduled airline flight from Memphis, Tennessee, to Dallas, Texas, while the plane was over Pine Bluff, Arkansas, was held to be sufficient to establish jurisdiction in Arkansas. [Grace v. McArthur, 170 F. Supp. 442 (E.D. Ark. 1959)]

  (2) **Limitation—fraudulent inducement into forum:** [§8] Courts decline transient jurisdiction where the defendant was fraudulently lured into the jurisdiction. (*See infra*, §93.)

  (3) **Constitutional validity:** [§9] A number of legal authorities questioned the constitutional validity of transient jurisdiction in the wake of *Shaffer v. Heitner* (*see infra*, §92), but the Supreme Court has upheld the practice in *Burnham v. Superior Court*, 495 U.S. 604 (1990).

d. **Seizure of defendant's property:** [§10] *Pennoyer* indicated in dictum that prejudgment seizure of a defendant's property was sufficient to permit a state to dispose of that property to satisfy unrelated claims. Where such seizure was accomplished, the absence of service within the jurisdiction did not limit the court's power to proceed with regard to disposition of the property. This is an application of the second category of *quasi in rem jurisdiction* discussed above. (*See supra*, §3.)

  (1) **Need for prejudgment seizure:** [§11] Quasi in rem jurisdiction was not available in *Pennoyer* itself because in the first action, the plaintiff, Mitchell, did not attach defendant Neff's property *before* entry of the judgment. The Court held that seizure after judgment was insufficient to support jurisdiction.

  (2) **Scope of "property"**

    (a) **Debt as property:** [§12] In *Harris v. Balk*, 198 U.S. 215 (1905), the Court upheld assertion of quasi in rem jurisdiction over a debt owed to the defendant by a temporary visitor to the state. The Court reasoned that "[t]he obligation of the debtor to pay his debt clings to and accompanies him wherever he goes." Therefore, the debt was sufficiently "present" to permit its seizure to provide a basis for exercise of jurisdiction to the extent of the debt.

    (b) **Insurance policies:** [§13] Some states extended this idea to justify the seizure of an insurer's obligation to defend and indemnify its insured. The obligation was said to be property of the insured, present wherever the insurer could be served, thereby justifying jurisdiction. [*See* Seider v. Roth, 17 N.Y.2d 111 (1966)] The Supreme Court invalidated this practice in *Rush v. Savchuk* (*see infra*, §67).

e. **Exceptions:** [§14] In *Pennoyer,* the Court recognized some exceptions to its rigorous rules:

  (1) **Status:** [§15] Even absent service within the state, the *Pennoyer* Court acknowledged that a state court could determine the status of one of its citizens toward a nonresident. This exception bore principally on divorce cases and gave rise to the "Nevada divorce," in which one spouse would move to Nevada for the period required to establish residency and obtain a divorce there. Jurisprudentially, it led to the concept of the ***divisible divorce***, under which the marital status was treated as a res that could be the subject of adjudication by the state in which either spouse resided, but alimony, child support, and other financial matters were viewed as in personam and beyond the authority of a state that had not obtained jurisdiction by personal service.

  (2) **Consent:** [§16] *Pennoyer* suggested that states could require noncitizens to consent to suit as a condition for conducting activities in the state. As explained in *Pennoyer,* this depended on the state's right to forbid or exclude the activity. However, there were limitations on the power of a state to exclude noncitizens, and there gradually arose a doctrine of ***implied consent***, which holds that a defendant's in-state activities are sufficient to justify service for suits related to the activities, despite doubts about the power to forbid them.

    (a) **Example—nonresident motorist statutes:** [§17] In *Hess v. Pawloski,* 274 U.S. 352 (1927), the Court upheld jurisdiction based on a statute that treated driving within the state as implied consent to suit there on claims arising from that driving. It stressed that "[m]otor vehicles are dangerous machines, even when skillfully and carefully operated."

    (b) **Example:** In *Henry L. Doherty & Co. v. Goodman,* 294 U.S. 623 (1935), the Court upheld the state's authority to adjudicate claims against a nonresident individual who had, through agents, established an office in the state for dealing in corporate securities. It observed that the state "treats the business of dealing in corporate securities as exceptional."

f. **Notice:** [§18] *Pennoyer* had an ambivalent attitude toward the need for notice to the defendant of the pendency of the action.

(1) **Notice not sufficient:** [§19]   Because process could not run into another state, notice to Neff in California of the suit filed by Mitchell in Oregon would not have had any effect on the power of the Oregon court to enter a binding judgment.

(2) **Notice not required:** [§20]   *Pennoyer* similarly did not indicate that notice was required for entry of a valid judgment. Instead, it indicated that prejudgment seizure of the defendant's property would be sufficient. The Court observed that the law presumes that property is always in the possession of its owner, and therefore its seizure will inform the owner "that he must look to any proceedings authorized by law upon such seizure for its condemnation and sale." For examination of the current requirement that notice be given, *see infra*, §§201 *et seq.*

3. **Shift to Minimum Contacts:** [§21]   In *International Shoe Co. v. Washington*, 326 U.S. 310 (1945), the Court shifted away from *Pennoyer's* insistence on service within the state to support in personam jurisdiction. Instead, it held that to subject a defendant to a judgment in personam, due process requires only that "he have certain minimum contacts with [the forum] such that the maintenance of the suit does not offend 'traditional notions of fair play and substantial justice.'"

   a. **Systematic and continuous activity:** [§22]   The Court has upheld in personam jurisdiction over a nonresident defendant based on systematic and continuous contacts with the state. In *International Shoe*, the defendant was a Delaware corporation headquartered in St. Louis, Missouri. It employed 11 to 13 salespeople in Washington, who were authorized only to solicit orders. The orders could be accepted or rejected only by the home office. Although it had no permanent office in Washington, the sales efforts there generated commissions of at least $31,000 per year. The state claimed that *International Shoe* was obligated to contribute to the state's unemployment compensation fund in amounts proportional to the activities there of its salespeople. The Court upheld Washington's jurisdiction, an easy decision given the volume and systematic and continuous nature of the contacts with the state, as well as the fact that the amount of the claim was directly related to the level of activities in the state.

   b. **Single contact:** [§23]   The Court has also upheld jurisdiction over a nonresident (Texas) defendant based on a single contact with the forum (California)—sending a contract for reinsurance to an insured in California. [McGee v. International Life Insurance Co., 355 U.S. 220 (1957)] The Court emphasized that there was a trend toward expanding the permissible scope of state jurisdiction, based on a fundamental change in the national economy to a more nationalized form of commerce. This reduced the burden on a defendant of defending in any state in which it engages in economic activity. The Court indicated that it was sufficient that the contract sued on in *McGee* had "a substantial connection with the State." This conclusion was based in part on the presence in California of witnesses to the company's defense of suicide, and also on the existence of pervasive regulation of insurance companies in California. *McGee* is regarded by many as a high-water mark for extended state court jurisdiction.

   c. **Purposeful availment limitation:** [§24]   The Court cautioned, however, that "it is a mistake to assume that this trend heralds the eventual demise of all restrictions on the personal jurisdiction of state courts." [Hanson v. Denckla, 357 U.S. 235 (1958)] In *Hanson,* the Court said that there must be "some act by which the defendant ***purposefully avails*** itself of the privilege of conducting activities within the forum state, thus invoking the benefits and protections of its laws."

d. **Post-*International Shoe* trend:** [§25]   For 30 years after *International Shoe* was decided, state courts and legislatures expanded state court jurisdiction. The usual impetus behind such expansions was to provide a forum for local plaintiffs claiming injury due to products or services provided by distant defendants. Given elastic limitations on jurisdiction, there were strong pressures to open the doors of the local courts to such plaintiffs.

B. CONTEMPORARY CONSTITUTIONAL GROUNDS FOR STATE COURT JURISDICTION

1. **Contacts with Forum:** [§26]   *International Shoe's* approach has generated a two-stage analysis for determining whether the exercise of jurisdiction over a nonresident defendant is proper. The first stage looks to the purposeful availment requirement introduced in *Hanson v. Denckla, supra,* which is usually the harder requirement to satisfy. If that is satisfied, the analysis turns to questions of reasonableness.

    a. **Minimum contacts—purposeful availment:** [§27]   This criterion is the requirement on which the Supreme Court has usually relied in overturning overbroad extensions of jurisdiction by the lower courts. Usually the lower courts justified extensions of jurisdiction on grounds of reasonableness, lack of burden to the defendant, state interest in local adjudication, and convenience to the plaintiff. It is important to keep in mind that, unlike the reasonableness inquiry (*see infra,* §§46-52), the purposeful availment inquiry ***focuses solely on the activities of the defendant*** and not on the interests of the plaintiff.

        (1) **Definition:** Although far from absolutely clear, the purposeful availment inquiry looks to some voluntary action by the defendant establishing a relationship with the forum, usually one in which the defendant seeks to benefit from the relationship with the forum state.

        (2) **Rationale:** This requirement gives defendants "fair warning that a particular activity may subject [them] to the jurisdiction of a foreign sovereign." [Burger King Corp. v. Rudzewicz, 471 U.S. 462 (1985)] It thereby "gives a degree of predictability to the legal system that allows potential defendants to structure their primary conduct with some minimum assurance as to where that conduct will and will not render them liable to suit." [World-Wide Volkswagen Corp. v. Woodson, 444 U.S. 286 (1980)]

        (3) **Foreseeability:** [§28]   Standing alone, the reasonable foreseeability that a suit might be filed in a forum is not sufficient. "[T]he foreseeability that is critical to due process analysis . . . is that the defendant's conduct and connection with the forum State are such that he should reasonably anticipate being haled into court there." [World-Wide Volkswagen v. Woodson, *supra*]

(a) **Unilateral act of plaintiff:** [§29] It is said that the unilateral act of the plaintiff in bringing a product to the forum or relocating in the forum is insufficient to establish the requisite connection.

   1) **Example—relocation to forum:** Where the donor under a trust moved to Florida after setting up the trust in Delaware, that unilateral act did not justify Florida's assertion of jurisdiction over the Delaware trustee even though the move was foreseeable. [Hanson v. Denckla, *supra*, §26]

   2) **Example—taking product to forum:** Where plaintiffs bought a car in New York and drove it to Oklahoma, this action by plaintiffs did not establish a contact between the retail seller and Oklahoma. [World-Wide Volkswagen v. Woodson, *supra*]

(b) **Long-term relationship with forum:** [§30] Where the defendant has established a long-term relationship with a forum resident, that may suffice. In *Burger King Corp. v. Rudzewicz, supra,* the Court stated that Florida jurisdiction was proper where the defendant reached "out beyond Michigan and negotiated with a Florida corporation for the purchase of a long-term franchise and the manifold benefits that would derive from affiliation with a nationwide organization."

   1) **Example—franchise agreement:** Where a Michigan defendant entered into a 20-year franchise agreement with a Florida fast-food corporation that required defendant to adhere to a detailed set of specifications in operation of his franchised restaurant, Florida jurisdiction was proper in litigation over a dispute under the agreement. [Burger King Corp. v. Rudzewicz, *supra*]

   2) **Compare—acceptance of corporate directorship:** When defendants have accepted directorships in a corporation incorporated in the forum state, they may be subject to jurisdiction in that state. [*See* Armstrong v. Pomerance, 423 A.2d 174 (Del. 1980)] The rationale is that the defendants' status as directors and their power to act in that capacity arise exclusively under the forum state's laws. The Delaware court held that the directors accepted their directorships with explicit statutory notice that they could be haled into the forum state's courts "to answer for alleged breaches of the duties imposed on them by the very laws which empowered them to act in their corporate capacities."

(c) **Seeking to serve:** [§31] In *World-Wide Volkswagen v. Woodson, supra,* the Court indicated that Oklahoma contacts would have been sufficient to support jurisdiction on a showing that the defendants "regularly sell cars at wholesale or retail to Oklahoma customers or residents or that they indirectly, through others, ***serve or seek to serve*** the Oklahoma market."

   1) **Single act:** [§32] A single act seeking to serve the forum market has been held to suffice to support jurisdiction in an action

asserting a claim growing out of the act. [*See* McGee v. International Life Insurance Co., *supra*, §23]

(d) **Stream of commerce:** [§33]   The Court has also said that a forum state may assert personal jurisdiction over a corporation that "delivers its products into the stream of commerce with the expectation that they will be purchased by consumers in the forum State." [World-Wide Volkswagen v. Woodson, *supra*]

   1) **Retail seller:** [§34]   In W*orld-Wide Volkswagen,* the Court held that the stream of commerce ends with the retail sale of the product, even if it is foreseeable that the purchaser will take the product to another state. (Note that a retail seller who regularly serves customers from a given state would be said to "seek to serve" that state's market even if located in another state.)

   2) **Manufacturer or component supplier:** [§35]   In *World-Wide Volkswagen* the Court cited with seeming approval *Gray v. American Radiator & Standard Sanitary Corp.,* 176 N.E.2d 761 (Ill. 1961), which upheld jurisdiction over a component supplier whose product was sent into the forum state as part of a product manufactured by its customer. However, the Court more recently failed to resolve a similar issue involving a Japanese component manufacturer and a Taiwanese tire manufacturer whose product failed in California. [Asahi Metal Industry Co. v. Superior Court, 480 U.S. 102 (1987)] Justice O'Connor's opinion (not for a majority of the Court) indicated that placing a product in the stream of commerce is not sufficient, and that some "additional conduct" by which the defendant indicates "an intent or purpose to serve the forum state" is essential. The circumstances under which a manufacturer will be found subject to jurisdiction in a state because its product is sold there remain unclear.

(e) **Targeted or intended effects in forum:** [§36]   The Court has indicated that, at least for ***intentional torts***, jurisdiction can be obtained over a nonresident defendant in a forum where the defendant has targeted its action. [Calder v. Jones, 465 U.S. 783 (1984)—Court indicated that the editor and author of an allegedly libelous story about a California plaintiff were subject to jurisdiction in California because "California is the focal point, both of the story and of the harm suffered"]

   1) **Limited to wrongful or commercial activity:** [§37]   The Court has stated that the effects test "was intended to reach wrongful activity outside of the State causing injury within the State or commercial activity affecting State residents." [Kulko v. Superior Court, 436 U.S. 84 (1978)] In *Kulko,* an ex-wife who moved from New York to California sued her New Yorker ex-husband in California to modify child custody and child support arrangements. (*See supra,* §15, regarding divisible divorce.) The Court held that the ex-husband's act of buying the couple's daughter a ticket to move to California, at her

request, was not sufficient to support California jurisdiction, even though the ex-husband could have foreseen effects there.

    2) **Not applicable to all intentional torts:** [§38] The test may not apply to all intentional torts. [*See* Wallace v. Herron, 778 F.2d 391 (7th Cir. 1985)—alleged abuse of process by California lawyer in filing suit against Indiana resident in California court did not subject California lawyer to jurisdiction in Indiana]

(4) **Relation to claim:** [§39] The Court assumes that jurisdiction is proper with regard to claims that are related to the forum contacts that satisfy the purposeful availment requirement. This involves what has been called *specific jurisdiction*. [*See* Burger King Corp. v. Rudzewicz, 471 U.S. at 473 n.15] (For discussion of the concept of general jurisdiction, *see infra,* §§69-74.) Some cases, however, present difficult problems that are often raised on examinations:

    (a) **Example:** In *World-Wide Volkswagen v. Woodson, supra,* it seemed to be assumed that jurisdiction was proper over Audi, the German manufacturer, and Volkswagen of America, the importer for the entire country, because both "seek to serve" the Oklahoma market. But it is difficult to see how the claim by the plaintiffs, who bought their car in New York, arose out of or was related to the efforts to serve Oklahoma.

    (b) **Example:** In *Buckeye Boiler Co. v. Superior Court,* 71 Cal. 2d 893 (1969), the plaintiff was injured in California by the explosion of a boiler manufactured by the defendant. The defendant regularly supplied boilers to a California purchaser, but these were of a different type from the one that injured the plaintiff, and nobody could explain how that boiler got to California. The California court upheld jurisdiction because "plaintiff's cause of action appears to arise from Buckeye's economic activity in California, the totality of its sales of pressure tanks to California customers or to other customers for foreseeable resale or use in California."

    (c) **Possible resolution:** [§40] One resolution of this problem of similar claims not evidently connected with the forum contacts is to focus on the foreseeability elements mentioned above. (*See supra,* §§27-28.) If the claim actually asserted is of the type the defendant should have foreseen in the forum, it is not unfair to subject the defendant to jurisdiction even if this particular claim does not arise from the defendant's contacts. [*See* Twitchell, *The Myth of General Jurisdiction,* 101 Harv. L. Rev. 610, 661-62 (1988)] However, consider the "tricky problem of what constitutes adequate similarity. Must it be the identical product that is distributed? A similar make or model? . . . Would assertion of specific jurisdiction require that a similar product sent into the forum state have an identical defect?" [Brilmayer, *Related Contacts and Personal Jurisdiction,* 101 Harv. L. Rev. 1444 (1988)]

(5) **Commercial vs. noncommercial:** [§41] Purposeful availment may be found more easily with regard to a defendant's commercial activity than with regard to noncommercial activity.

   (a) **Example—franchising agreement:** In *Burger King Corp. v. Rudzewicz, supra,* the defendant, a Michigan citizen, dealt face-to-face with the Michigan office of Burger King regarding opening a Burger King franchise in Michigan. However, he also negotiated via telephone with the Florida headquarters and agreed to send payments and notices there. Noting that the defendant was a "*commercial actor,*" the Court held that the Florida contacts constituted purposeful availment and thus upheld jurisdiction at Burger King's home in Florida.

   (b) **Compare—suits against consumers:** In *Burger King,* the Court indicated that suits against consumers to collect payments due on personal purchases would not be permitted at the distant sellers' locations.

   (c) **Compare—family law:** It is significant whether a defendant seeks "commercial benefit from solicitation of business" from a resident of the forum state in assessing his contacts with the state. Thus, the Court held that a divorced father who sent his daughter to live with his ex-wife did not thereby become subject to California jurisdiction in an action to modify support and child custody arrangements. The Court reasoned that "[a] father who agrees, in the interests of family harmony and his children's preferences, to allow them to spend more time in California than was required under a separation agreement can hardly be said to have 'purposefully availed himself' of the 'benefits and protections' of California's laws." [*Kulko v. Superior Court, supra*]

(6) **Choice of law distinguished:** [§42] The Court has repeatedly emphasized that the fact that a given state's law may apply does not bear on satisfying the purposeful availment requirement. [*Kulko v. Superior Court, supra*—fact that California may be "center of gravity" for choice-of-law purposes does not mean that California has personal jurisdiction over the defendant]

   (a) **Choice of law clause:** [§43] The parties' election that a certain state's law will govern their relations may, however, support jurisdiction in that state. In *Burger King Corp. v. Rudzewicz, supra,* the Court stated that the inclusion of a provision selecting Florida law in the parties' contract, although not sufficient of itself to support jurisdiction, "reinforced [defendant's] deliberate affiliation" with Florida.

(7) **Relation to federalism:** [§44] The Supreme Court has sometimes suggested that the limitations on personal jurisdiction are related to principles of interstate federalism in terms of state sovereignty vis-a-vis other states. [*See* World-Wide Volkswagen Corp. v. Woodson, *supra,* §39] However, the Court has since stated that the requirement of personal jurisdiction ultimately arises from the Due Process Clause and is unaffected by notions of federalism. If it were otherwise, it would not be

possible for a defendant to waive the personal jurisdiction requirement, because this would interfere with state sovereignty. [*See* Insurance Corp. of Ireland, Ltd. v. Compagnie des Bauxites de Guinee, 456 U.S. 694 (1982)]

(8) **Reasonableness insufficient to satisfy purposeful availment requirement:** [§45] The Court has rejected the idea that other factors can outweigh the importance of the purposeful availment requirement: "Even if the defendant would suffer minimal or no inconvenience from being forced to litigate before the tribunals of another State; even if the forum State has a strong interest in applying its law to the controversy; even if the forum State is the most convenient location for litigation, the Due Process Clause . . . may sometimes act to divest the State of its power to render a valid judgment." [World-Wide Volkswagen Corp. v. Woodson, *supra*]

b. **Fair play and substantial justice—reasonableness:** [§46] Besides focusing on the defendant's contacts with the forum, the jurisdictional inquiry takes account of a number of other factors that bear together on whether the exercise of jurisdiction in the state is reasonable. Under this heading, unlike the purposeful availment inquiry, above, ***consideration of the plaintiff's interests is proper***.

(1) **Factors:** [§47] A variety of factors can be considered:

(a) The interest of the state in providing a forum to the plaintiff;

(b) The interest of the state in regulating the activity involved;

(c) The burden of defense in the forum on the defendant;

(d) The relative burden of prosecution elsewhere on the plaintiff;

(e) Whether the defendant's activity in the forum is systematic and continuous;

(f) The extent to which the claim is related to the defendant's local activities; and

(g) Avoidance of multiplicity of suits and conflicting adjudications.

(2) **Overlap:** [§48] The same facts may be used in connection with more than one of the above factors. For example, if the action arises out of an injury to the plaintiff in the forum, that may bear on the state's interest in opening its courts to the plaintiff, on the state's interest in regulating the allegedly injury-producing activity, and on the ease with which the plaintiff can sue elsewhere given the supposed presence in the forum of important witnesses to the event.

(3) **None critical:** [§49] The fact that certain factors do not point toward forum jurisdiction is not fatal to jurisdiction. Thus, the plaintiff need not be local for jurisdiction to be valid. [Keeton v. Hustler Magazine, Inc.,

465 U.S. 770 (1984)] Similarly, the fact that the defendant has conducted only one piece of business in the state does not by itself defeat jurisdiction over a claim arising out of that business. [McGee v. International Life Insurance Co., *supra*, §32]

(4) **Easy to satisfy:** [§50] "[W]here a defendant who purposefully has directed his activities at forum residents seeks to defeat jurisdiction, he must present a compelling case that the presence of some other considerations would render jurisdiction unreasonable." [Burger King v. Rudzewicz, *supra*, §43]

 (a) **Example:** In *Keeton v. Hustler Magazine, Inc., supra,* plaintiff sued in New Hampshire after her first suit in Ohio was dismissed. She had no prior contact with New Hampshire, and sued there only because the limitations period had expired in all other states. The Court found that the defendant's regular sale of 10,000 to 15,000 magazines in the state constituted purposeful availment and upheld jurisdiction as reasonable even though the plaintiff sought to recover damages for defamation worldwide under the "single publication rule." (*See* Torts Summary.)

(5) **Greater concern with foreign defendants:** [§51] The Court has indicated that it may be relevant that the defendant is a foreigner, recognizing the "unique burdens placed upon one who must defend oneself in a foreign legal system." [Asahi Metal Industry v. Superior Court, *supra*, §35]

 (a) **Example:** In *Asahi,* the Court held that it was unreasonable for California to exercise jurisdiction over a cross-complaint for indemnity by a Taiwanese manufacturer against a Japanese component manufacturer. In addition to the extra burdens placed on foreign defendants, the Court placed weight on the fact that the California plaintiff had settled his claim, leaving only the indemnification claim to be decided, and that it could be decided equally conveniently in Japan or Taiwan, where the dealings between the parties occurred.

 (b) **Caution:** It is not clear whether *Asahi* indicates that as a general matter there is greater concern with foreign defendants. It may be that the Court would have viewed things differently had the California plaintiff been pursuing a claim against the Japanese component manufacturer who objected to jurisdiction.

(6) **First Amendment concerns:** [§52] Some lower courts felt that in certain defamation cases the risk of chilling the exercise of First Amendment rights warranted more demanding scrutiny of the reasonableness of jurisdiction. However, in *Calder v. Jones, supra,* §36, the Court rejected this reasoning: "[T]he potential chill on protected First Amendment activity stemming from libel and defamation actions is already taken into account in the constitutional limitations on the substantive law governing such suits. To reintroduce those concerns at the jurisdictional stage would be a form of double counting."

2. **Presence of Defendant's Property in Forum:** [§53] Quasi in rem and in rem jurisdiction have been curtailed since *Harris v. Balk, supra,* §12. Nevertheless, the presence of the defendant's property in the jurisdiction may often suffice to make jurisdiction constitutional, but ordinarily only because it establishes a relevant contact between the defendant and the forum.

   a. **Location of property**

      (1) **Tangible property:** [§54] Tangible property (*e.g.,* real estate, chattels) is located in a state if it is physically present therein.

      (2) **Intangible property:** [§55] Generally, states may declare that intangible property is located within their jurisdiction if some transaction related to the property occurred within the state. Where intangible property is embodied in an instrument (*e.g.,* negotiable paper), however, it is usually said to be located in the state where the instrument is located.

         (a) **Examples:** A *debt* (such as a bank account) may be deemed located where the debtor (the bank) is located, but generally shares of stock are said to be located where the certificate is located.

         (b) **Absence of constitutional limitations:** [§56] The Court has placed no constitutional limitations on the power of a state to declare intangible property present within its borders. It has upheld multiple death taxation of property by different states that all claim the property is within their jurisdiction [Blackstone v. Miller, 188 U.S. 189 (1903)], but has held that when a debt may be located in more than one state, due process forbids a state from declaring the property escheated unless it can guarantee that no other state would make a conflicting and duplicative claim [Western Union Telegraph Co. v. Pennsylvania, 368 U.S. 71 (1961)].

            1) **Example—corporate stock:** In *Shaffer v. Heitner,* 433 U.S. 186 (1977), Delaware, unique among the 50 states, declared that shares of stock in corporations it chartered were located in that state rather than where the certificate was located. The Court did not question this.

            2) **Example—insurer's duty to defend and indemnify:** In *Rush v. Savchuk,* 444 U.S. 320 (1980), the Court did not question the state's conclusion that the insurer's obligation to defend and indemnify the insured constituted property in the state, while holding that contact insufficient to support jurisdiction.

   b. **Contacts test:** [§57] *Shaffer v. Heitner, supra,* held that the minimum contacts analysis of *International Shoe* should be applied to jurisdiction over property. *Rationale:* Jurisdiction over a thing "is a customary elliptical way of referring to jurisdiction over the interests of persons in a thing" and should therefore be viewed as analogous to personal jurisdiction in terms of protection of those interests.

      (1) **Caution:** In *Burnham v. Superior Court, supra,* §9, Justice Scalia indicated doubts about the continuing validity of the reasoning in *Shaffer v.*

Heitner, stating that, "while our holding today does not contradict *Shaffer,* our basic approach to the due process issue is different." Although Justice Scalia's opinion announced the Court's judgment, it was not joined by a majority. Nevertheless, it has been suggested that this view may lead to curtailing *Shaffer.* [*See* Weintraub, An Objective Basis for Rejecting Transient Jurisdiction, 20 Rutgers L.J. 611, 621-23 (1991)]

c. **Presence of property supports jurisdiction:** [§58] In *Shaffer,* the Court recognized that "the presence of property in a State may bear on the existence of jurisdiction by providing contacts among the forum State, the defendant, and the litigation."

   (1) **True in rem:** [§59] The Court appeared to leave untouched the state's power to exercise true in rem jurisdiction, which "affects the interests of all persons in designated property." Therefore, the **state would have jurisdiction** based on the presence of the property in true in rem cases (*e.g.,* condemnation).

   (2) **Preexisting claim to property:** [§60] Actions for specific performance or otherwise to perfect a claim to the property (such as actions to remove a cloud on title) *should also still be permissible* in the state where the property is located.

      (a) **Compare:** This reasoning would not necessarily apply to an action by the owner of local property to force a nonresident to perform an alleged contract to purchase the property, as the presence of the property may not imply any connection between the defendant and the state.

   (3) **Claim related to rights and duties arising from ownership:** [§61] The Court also noted that jurisdiction could be sustained on the basis of presence of the property where the claim relates to the duties of the owner.

      (a) **Example:** In *Dubin v. Philadelphia,* 32 Pa. D. & C. 61 (1938), jurisdiction was upheld in a suit against an absentee owner of property for injuries sustained on the property. The court reasoned that "[i]t is just as important that nonresident owners of Philadelphia real estate should keep their property in such shape as not to injure our citizens as it is that nonresident owners of cars should drive about our streets with equal care. It is only a short step beyond this to assert that defendants in both classes of cases should be answerable in this forum."

      (b) **Compare:** In *Rush v. Savchuk, supra,* the Court held that the presence of "property" (the insurer's obligation to defend and indemnify the insured) was jurisdictionally insignificant since "[t]he insurance policy is not the subject matter of the case, . . . nor is it related to the operative facts of the negligence action."

   (4) **Real property:** [§62] Justices Powell and Stevens argued in concurring opinions that *Shaffer v. Heitner, supra,* should not invalidate jurisdiction in actions against nonresident owners of real property in the state.

[§§63-68]

(5) **Absence of other forum:** [§63] In a footnote in *Shaffer v. Heitner, supra,* the Court noted that "[t]his case does not raise, and we therefore do not consider, the question whether the presence of a defendant's property in a State is a sufficient basis for jurisdiction when no other forum is available to the plaintiff." [*See* Shaffer v. Heitner, 433 U.S. at 211 n.37] This may sanction *jurisdiction by necessity*.

    (a) **Example:** In *Mullane v. Central Hanover Bank & Trust Co.,* 339 U.S. 306 (1950), the Court upheld New York jurisdiction to determine the interests of all beneficiaries (including claims of mismanagement by the trustee) in trusts established in New York without examining the beneficiaries' personal affiliation with New York. Eschewing an attempt to categorize this jurisdiction as in rem or in personam, the Court reasoned that "the interest of each state in providing means to close trusts that exist by the grace of its laws and are administered under the supervision of its courts is so insistent and rooted in custom as to establish beyond doubt the right of its courts to determine the interests of all claimants, resident or nonresident, provided its procedure affords full opportunity to appear and be heard." The *scope* of this "jurisdiction by necessity" is *unclear*.

(6) **Securing judgment in another forum:** [§64] In *Shaffer,* the Court rejected the argument that quasi in rem jurisdiction is necessary to prevent a defendant from moving his assets to a state in which he is not subject to suit. The Court suggested that in such a situation it might be proper for the plaintiff to attach the property as security for a judgment being pursued in a state that has in personam jurisdiction over the defendant. (For an example upholding jurisdiction to attach defendant's assets pending judgment in a jurisdiction that has personal jurisdiction over defendant, *see Carolina Power & Light Co. v. Uranex,* 451 F. Supp. 1044 (N.D. Cal. 1977).)

(7) **Enforcing valid judgment:** [§65] Similarly, the Court noted that once a judgment is entered by a court with in personam jurisdiction, it is proper for another state to enforce the judgment, even if it did not have jurisdiction to decide the case as an original matter. [*See* Shaffer v. Heitner, 433 U.S. at 211 n.36]

d. **Presence of property insufficient for jurisdiction:** [§66] *Shaffer* holds that when property is *"completely unrelated to the plaintiff's cause of action"* its presence alone will not suffice to support jurisdiction. This *overrules Harris v. Balk, supra,* §53.

e. **Insurance obligations:** [§67] States cannot obtain jurisdiction over nonresident defendants in automobile tort actions by treating the defendant's insurer's obligation to defend and indemnify as property in the state and garnishing the insurer. [Rush v. Savchuk, *supra,* §61]

f. **In personam alternative:** [§68] Whenever the defendant may be subject to in rem jurisdiction, it is important to consider in personam jurisdiction as well.

Civil Procedure—15

(1) **Example:** In *Shaffer,* Justice Brennan, while agreeing that *International Shoe* should be applied to quasi in rem jurisdiction, argued that the defendants' acceptance of positions as officers or directors in Delaware corporations should support jurisdiction over them in Delaware. After the decision in *Shaffer,* the Delaware legislature promptly enacted a statute so providing, and such exercise of in personam jurisdiction was upheld. [Armstrong v. Pomerance, *supra,* §30]

3. **General Jurisdiction**

   a. **Introduction:** [§69] Recently, courts have begun to distinguish between ***specific*** and ***general*** personal jurisdiction. If general jurisdiction is justified, the defendant is subject to suit on ***any claim*** in the forum. Specific jurisdiction, on the other hand, gives rise to jurisdiction only for claims related to the jurisdictional contact with the state. The Supreme Court has now taken to using this dichotomy. [*See* Burger King Corp. v. Rudzewicz, 471 U.S. at 473 n.15]

   b. **Rationale:** Since *International Shoe* forbids jurisdiction only where it would violate fair play and substantial justice for the state to exercise jurisdiction, one might well question the need for general jurisdiction in other cases. The general idea is to provide a **"safe harbor"** where the defendant is amenable to suit without the worry that a court might later question the existence of sufficient contacts under *International Shoe.*

   c. **Natural persons:** [§70] General jurisdiction is available in the state of a person's ***domicile***. [Milliken v. Meyer, 311 U.S. 457 (1940)] One acquires a domicile by being present in a state and intending to make it one's home for an indefinite period.

   (1) **Compare—diversity of citizenship subject matter jurisdiction:** Domicile is also important for determining diversity of citizenship in connection with the subject matter jurisdiction of federal courts. (*See infra,* §287.) Be sure to keep the concepts of personal jurisdiction and subject matter jurisdiction separate.

   d. **Corporations**

   (1) **State of incorporation:** [§71] A corporation is subject to general jurisdiction in its state of incorporation.

   (2) **Headquarters:** [§72] A corporation is also subject to general jurisdiction in the state in which its headquarters are located, if different from its state of incorporation. This may produce problems if the executive offices are in one state and the manufacturing headquarters are in another. (*See infra,* §§290 *et seq.,* regarding citizenship of corporation for diversity purposes.)

   (3) **Substantial contacts:** [§73] Corporations have been held subject to suits on unrelated claims in states in which they conduct "substantial activity." The level of activity that is sufficient for this purpose is ambiguous. Although one could argue that only a very large volume of activity

should suffice, some courts have seemingly lowered the threshold. A number of examples provide touchstones:

(a) **Temporary headquarters:** In *Perkins v. Benguet Consolidated Mining Co.,* 342 U.S. 437 (1952), a Philippine corporation was unable to operate due to the Japanese occupation of the Philippines during World War II. Its president and general manager maintained an office in Ohio that seems to have been a substitute head office. The Court stated that defendant had been "carrying on in Ohio a continuous and systematic, but limited, part of its general business." Jurisdiction in Ohio was upheld.

(b) **Purchase of equipment and execution of contract:** In *Helicopteros Nacionales de Colombia v. Hall,* 466 U.S. 408 (1984), defendant, a Colombian corporation, had contracted to provide transportation services in Peru, in connection with a project being built there by a Texas-based joint venture, and had been paid over $5 million for its services under the contract. Defendant had also purchased most of its helicopter fleet from a Texas manufacturer and sent its pilots to Texas for training. The Court held the defendant's contacts with Texas to be insufficient as a basis for general jurisdiction over the defendant.

(c) **Ongoing operation of office:** In *Bryant v. Finnish National Airline,* 15 N.Y.2d 426 (1965), the New York Court of Appeals upheld jurisdiction over a claim for injuries sustained in Europe based on the defendant's operation of a one-and-a-half room office in New York, staffed by three full-time and four part-time employees, and maintenance of a bank account in New York. *Caution:* This case may lower the standard ***too low***.

(d) **Regular purchases in forum:** In *Rosenburg Bros. & Co. v. Curtis Brown Co.,* 260 U.S. 516 (1923), an Oklahoma retailer's purchase of a large portion of its merchandise in New York was held not to be sufficient for jurisdiction, even when coupled with regular visits to New York in connection with the purchases. The Supreme Court cited this case with approval in *Helicopteros Nacionales de Colombia v. Hall, supra.*

e. **Relation to claim:** [§74] The general jurisdiction analysis usually becomes important when the relation between the defendant's contacts with the jurisdiction and the claim sued upon is not sufficient. (*See supra,* §39, regarding purposeful availment focus on relation between contacts and claim.) Where there is not a sufficient relation to the claim, one may fall back on general jurisdiction reasoning.

(1) **Example:** In *Helicopteros Nacionales de Colombia v. Hall, supra,* plaintiffs sued in Texas to recover for the deaths of workers killed in a crash in Peru of a helicopter operated by defendant, a Colombian company. The Court looked only to general jurisdiction because the parties conceded that the claims did not arise out of defendant's contacts with Texas. Justice

Brennan dissented, arguing that the claims sufficiently related to defendant's Texas contacts to permit specific jurisdiction because defendant negotiated the contract it was performing in Texas, bought in Texas the helicopter that crashed, and sent its pilots to Texas for training.

4. **Consent:** [§75]   A defendant may consent to jurisdiction in the forum. This consent may be *express, implied,* or due to the making of a *general appearance* in the minority of states that do not follow federal practice.

   a. **Express consent:** [§76]   Express consent can be made either before or after suit is filed, and suffices to support jurisdiction without reference to other contacts with the forum.

      (1) **Example:** In *National Equipment Rental, Ltd. v. Szukhent,* 375 U.S. 311 (1964), defendant Michigan farmers signed the plaintiff's form lease for farm equipment providing that one Florence Weinberg of Long Island would be their agent for service of process in New York. Defendants did not know Weinberg, who was the wife of an officer of the plaintiff, but the Court upheld the effectiveness of service on her to establish jurisdiction in New York.

      (2) **Registration by corporation:** [§77]   In many states, foreign corporations that engage in business in the state are required to register and appoint an agent for service of process in the state, thereby consenting to suit there.

         (a) **Commerce Clause limitations:** [§78]   The power of a state to insist on consent to general jurisdiction may be questionable to the extent that it unreasonably burdens interstate commerce. [*Compare* Pennsylvania Fire Insurance Co. v. Gold Issue Mining & Milling Co., 243 U.S. 93 (1917)—state could require corporations wishing to do business to consent to jurisdiction on unrelated claims—*with* Bendix Autolite Corp. v. Midwesco Enterprises, Inc., 486 U.S. 888 (1988)—state may not deny protection of statute of limitations to foreign corporation that refuses to consent to jurisdiction on unrelated suits]

         (b) **Implied consent contrasted:** [§79]   As an adjunct to the registration requirements, states often treat conduct of business in the state to be impliedly appointing a state official, often the secretary of state, as agent for service of process. This is not based on a true consent theory, but on the constitutionality of exercise of state jurisdiction over claims arising from the corporation's activities in the state.

      (3) **Limitation—local actions:** [§80]   In cases involving title to land, courts will proceed only if the land is located in the jurisdiction. (*See infra,* §150.) In such cases *consent of the parties is insufficient*.

   b. **Implied consent:** [§81]   By filing suit, the plaintiff is deemed to have consented to the jurisdiction of the forum for the purpose of a counterclaim by the defendant. [Adam v. Saenger, 303 U.S. 59 (1938)] However, this implied consent does not extend to a counterclaim unrelated to the subject matter of plaintiff's claim against the defendant.

- (1) **Consent in class actions:** [§82] In class actions, the failure of unnamed *plaintiff* class members to opt out of the class action constitutes consent to adjudication of their claims in the forum. [Phillips Petroleum Co. v. Shutts, 472 U.S. 797 (1985)] The Court has not resolved the question of whether the same reasoning would apply to a defendant class.

c. **Appearance:** [§83] A party's voluntary appearance in an action is sufficient by itself to support jurisdiction.

- (1) **What constitutes an appearance?** [§84] In general, an appearance occurs when the defendant defends litigation on the merits. Depending on the prevailing rules in the jurisdiction, the issue turns on the extent to which the defendant raises issues other than jurisdiction.

  - (a) **State courts:** [§85] In many states, a defendant who wishes to preserve objections to personal jurisdiction must make a *special appearance* raising only jurisdictional issues. Raising other matters subjects the defendant to the risk of having made a general appearance and thereby consenting to jurisdiction.

  - (b) **Federal courts:** [§86] In federal courts and in most state courts, a defendant need not make a special appearance; all grounds of defense, including lack of personal jurisdiction, can be asserted in a motion or answer. [*See* Fed. R. Civ. P. 12(b)]

    - 1) **Waiver:** [§87] If the defendant fails to raise personal jurisdiction in her initial motion or answer, that objection is waived. [Fed. R. Civ. P. 12(h)(1)]

    - 2) **Consent to jurisdiction to decide jurisdiction:** [§88] By moving to dismiss for lack of personal jurisdiction, the defendant consents to the power of the court to decide that question, *including the power to order discovery pertinent to the jurisdictional question*. [Insurance Corp. of Ireland, Ltd. v. Compagnie des Bauxites de Guinee, *supra*, §44]

  - (c) **Extent of jurisdiction conferred:** [§89] A general appearance may be limited to the claims made or issues raised in the action at the time of the appearance.

  - (d) **Alternative of default:** [§90] A defendant who believes that jurisdiction in the forum is improper may disregard the suit and permit a default to be taken. When the plaintiff later attempts to enforce the judgment in another jurisdiction under the Full Faith and Credit Clause, the defendant can then challenge on the ground that the rendering court lacked jurisdiction. If the enforcing court finds jurisdiction was proper, however, there will be no further opportunity to defend on the merits. (*See infra*, §116.)

5. **Service Within the Jurisdiction:** [§91] Under *Pennoyer v. Neff, supra,* §21, service within the jurisdiction was *presumptively sufficient* to support jurisdiction.

a. **Possible minimum contacts requirement:** [§92]   In *Shaffer v. Heitner, supra,* §65, the Court stated that "all assertions of state court jurisdiction must be evaluated according to the standards set forth in *International Shoe.*" However, in *Burnham v. Superior Court,* 495 U.S. 604 (1990), the Supreme Court, without a majority opinion but with no dissents, **upheld** the constitutionality of *"transient jurisdiction,"* obtained by service on a nonresident temporarily within the state, even though the suit was unrelated to the defendant's activities in the state. *Caution:* This ground for jurisdiction may not suffice, according to some Justices' opinions, where the defendant's presence in the state was not intentional or voluntary.

b. **Fraudulent inducement:** [§93]   Where the defendant is personally served in the forum state, the court will *not* exercise jurisdiction on that ground if the defendant was lured into the jurisdiction by the plaintiff's *false statements*. [*See* Wyman v. Newhouse, 93 F.2d 313 (2d Cir. 1937)]

   (1) **Compare—trickery to effect service:** [§94]   Although fraudulently inducing a defendant into the jurisdiction is generally a defense to service, using trickery to effect service on a defendant already in the jurisdiction generally *does not interfere with the effectiveness of service*.

   (2) **In rem cases:** [§95]   When the plaintiff relies on seizure of the defendant's moveable property to establish jurisdiction, the seizure should be disregarded if the *property is moved* to the forum as the result of some *trickery by the plaintiff.* [*See* Commercial Air Charters v. Sundorph, 57 F.R.D. 84 (D. Conn. 1972)—jurisdiction refused because plaintiff's friend "rented" defendant's airplane, misrepresenting his intentions, and took it into forum so that plaintiff could levy attachment]

6. **Territorial Jurisdiction of Federal Courts:** [§96]   In most cases, federal courts *do not exercise nationwide jurisdiction*. Except in the few situations where such powers are conferred by rule or statute, the territorial jurisdiction of a federal court is usually no broader than that of the state in which the federal court is located. (*See infra,* §§107 *et seq.*)

   a. **Constitutional limitations on nationwide service:** [§97]   It appears that Congress *could* constitutionally create nationwide personal jurisdiction for the federal courts. [*See* United States v. Union Pacific Railroad, 98 U.S. 569 (1878)—asserting that Congress could have created a single federal district court with nationwide jurisdiction] There may, however, be *limitations under the Due Process Clause* of the Fifth Amendment on extremely inconvenient exercises of jurisdiction. [*Compare* Oxford First Corp. v. PNC Liquidating Corp., 372 F. Supp. 191 (E.D. Pa. 1974)—finding nationwide jurisdiction limited by fundamental notions of fairness—*with* FTC v. Jim Walter Corp., 651 F.2d 251 (5th Cir. 1981)—rejecting Fifth Amendment limitation on federal court jurisdiction]

   b. **National contacts:** [§98]   Some have argued that in actions against aliens, contacts with the United States should be aggregated in order to determine whether together they would support jurisdiction in this country, even though no state has sufficient contacts to justify jurisdiction. The Supreme Court has not passed on this argument. [*See* Omni Capital International v. Rudolf Wolff & Co., Ltd., 484 U.S. 97 (1988)]

C. STATUTORY AUTHORIZATION FOR JURISDICTION

1. **Introduction:** [§99] Constitutionally permissible extraterritorial jurisdiction is not self-executing; a court needs authority granted by some statute or rule to exercise it. In state court, such authority is usually in the form of a *long arm statute*, which operates as *enabling legislation*. Thus, the *first step* in a jurisdictional analysis is to examine this legislation and determine whether it covers the case presented. This often involves a problem of *statutory interpretation*—deciding what the legislators or rule-makers meant by the words selected for the statute or rule.

2. **Long Arm Statutes:** [§100] In the wake of *International Shoe*, legislatures began to enact statutes extending the reach of their courts' jurisdiction (the long arm of the law).

    a. **Full power:** [§101] Long arm statutes in a few states explicitly authorize exercise of jurisdiction whenever it would not violate the Constitution. [*See, e.g.,* Cal. Civ. Proc. Code §410.10] In such states, the only question that need be considered is the constitutionality of jurisdiction. Note that some courts have interpreted statutes that do not expressly provide this broad jurisdiction to nevertheless have this effect. (*See infra,* §106.)

    b. **Specific acts:** [§102] Most long arm statutes designate specific acts as warranting the exercise of jurisdiction. Common examples include: the transaction of any business within the state; the commission of a tortious act within the state; ownership, use, or possession of real property within the state; contracting to insure any person, property, or risk located in the state at the time of contracting; and the maintenance of a marital domicile in the state in an action for divorce. With such a statute, one must consider (i) whether the defendant's activities fall within the terms of the statute and (ii), if so, whether the exercise of jurisdiction in this case is constitutional.

        (1) **Common-sense reading:** In general, courts say that they will give the words of the rule or statute their ordinary meaning. In some instances, however, they seem to overextend that reading. Thus, in *Gray v. American Radiator & Standard Sanitary Corp., supra,* §35, the court read the Illinois statute's provision of jurisdiction for "the commission of a tortious act within this State" to cover the manufacture in Ohio of an allegedly defective valve that was shipped to a manufacturer in Pennsylvania and incorporated into a boiler made there. [*Compare* Feathers v. McLucas, 15 N.Y.2d 443 (1965)—language "tortious act within the state" too clear to include tortious act outside the state that causes an injury within the state]

        (2) **Different legal theory:** [§103] If the defendant's specific act is within the statute, claims based on the same act but a different legal theory can also be asserted in the action. [Mack Trucks, Inc. v. Arrow Aluminum Castings Co., 510 F.2d 1029 (5th Cir. 1975)—products liability suit based on "tortious act" long arm provision can assert both negligence and breach of contract theories]

        (3) **"Arising out of" requirement:** [§104] Usually, long arm statutes that designate specific acts require that claims arise out of that act. This presents

a problem similar to that in determining whether there is a relationship between the claim and the contacts on a minimum contacts analysis (*supra*, §39) and whether specific or general jurisdiction is being invoked (*supra*, §74). However, in this instance, the analysis made is of the relationship between the contacts and the claim as a matter of state law, rather than as a matter of federal constitutional law.

(4) **"Tortious act":** [§105] The tortious act requirement is generally held to be satisfied when the ***act as alleged would be tortious***. [Nelson v. Miller, 143 N.E.2d 673 (Ill. 1957)] If the ground were actual commission of a tort, a finding that the defendant did not commit a tort would mean that the court lacked jurisdiction.

(5) **Full power through interpretation:** [§106] In some states that have specific act statutes, the courts have interpreted the statutes to extend jurisdiction to the constitutional limit. [*See* World-Wide Volkswagen Corp. v. Woodson, *supra*, §45—Oklahoma statute interpreted as conferring jurisdiction to the limits permitted by constitution; Nelson v. Miller, *supra*—same with regard to Illinois statute]

(a) **Rationale:** Often the reasoning behind such extensions is that the legislature had no reason to deny residents access to the courts in cases in which jurisdiction would be constitutional.

(b) **Caution:** States that have taken this approach sometimes balk at pursuing. Thus, after *Nelson v. Miller, supra,* the Illinois Supreme Court cautioned that "[a] statute worded in the way ours is should have a fixed meaning without regard to changing concepts of due process." [Green v. Advance Ross Electronics Corp., 427 N.E.2d 1203 (Ill. 1981)]

3. **Federal Court Jurisdiction:** [§107] In general, federal courts exercise jurisdiction no broader than that authorized by state long arm statutes.

   a. **In personam jurisdiction**

   (1) **Subject to jurisdiction of state court:** [§108] Process from a federal court is effective to confer jurisdiction over a defendant if the defendant would be subject to jurisdiction of a court of general jurisdiction in the state in which the federal court is located. [Fed. R. Civ. P. 4(k)(1)(A)]

   (a) **Constitutionality:** Where this is the ground for exercise of personal jurisdiction, the constitutionality of that exercise is the same as if the case were in state court.

   (2) **Rule 14 or Rule 19 joinder:** [§109] A party who is served within a judicial district and within 100 miles of the place from which the summons was issued is subject to jurisdiction if joined under Rule 14 (impleader, *see infra,* §§990 *et seq.*) or Rule 19 (necessary parties, *see infra,* §§961 *et seq.*). [Fed. R. Civ. P. 4(k)(1)(B)]

(3) **Interpleader or other federal statutory basis:** [§110] Where a federal statute authorizes *nationwide jurisdiction*, federal courts can exercise jurisdiction even though state courts could not. Examples include interpleader [28 U.S.C. §2361] and securities fraud actions [15 U.S.C. §78aa]. [Fed. R. Civ. P. 4(k)(1)(C), (D)]

(4) **Minimum contacts with United States:** [§111] For *claims arising under federal law*, federal courts can exercise jurisdiction even though the defendant is *not subject* to the jurisdiction of the courts of general jurisdiction in any state, if this would be consistent with the Constitution. [Fed. R. Civ. P. 4(k)(2)]

   (a) **National v. state contacts:** [§112] This provision could apply if defendant's national contacts permit exercise of jurisdiction although no state has sufficient contacts to support it. [*See, e.g.,* Go-Video, Inc. v. Akai Electric Co., 885 F.2d 1406 (9th Cir. 1989)]

   (b) **Narrow long arm statute:** [§113] Alternatively, this provision could apply if the state in which the court is located has a narrow long arm statute that does not apply to the circumstances presented in the case although there are constitutionally sufficient grounds for exercise of jurisdiction.

b. **In rem jurisdiction:** [§114] The federal court may assert jurisdiction by seizing a defendant's assets found within the district only if *defendant cannot be served by means otherwise authorized*, and then only in the *manner provided by the law of the state* in which the district court is located. [Fed. R. Civ. P. 4(n)(2)] It may still be possible to challenge the seizure under *Shaffer v. Heitner*. (*See supra,* §§53 *et seq.*)

c. **No court-created authority:** [§115] In *Omni Capital International v. Rudolf Wolff & Co., supra,* §98, the Court rejected arguments that it should authorize nationwide service of summons in connection with a federal claim for which Congress had not provided for such service. The Court found it "likely that Congress has been acting on the assumption that federal courts cannot add to the scope of service of summons Congress has authorized."

D. **LITIGATING JURISDICTION**

1. **Introduction:** Implicit in the idea of consent (*supra,* §§75-90) is the need for the defendant to raise personal jurisdictional objections in a timely fashion. In reality, the defendant faces a variety of options.

2. **Default:** [§116] A party served with summons who believes that the court lacks personal jurisdiction or authority to serve process on her may disregard the process and allow her default to be taken. If an effort is later made to enforce the resulting default judgment, she can argue that full faith and credit should not be given to it because it was entered by a court without jurisdiction. If this argument is rejected, however, the defendant may not then defend on the merits.

3. **Appearance to Litigate Jurisdiction:** [§117] The defendant can appear in the action and litigate jurisdiction in the court in which the suit was filed. In federal

court and in most state courts, the jurisdictional objection can be raised along with other defenses (*see supra*, §86), but in a few states, the defendant would have to enter a special appearance (*see supra*, §85).

4. **Discovery:** [§118]   Where factual issues (*e.g.,* defendant's level of contacts with the forum) are pertinent to resolution of a personal jurisdiction objection, the court may order discovery regarding those issues. By making a *personal jurisdiction objection*, the defendant *consents to the court's jurisdiction with respect to such discovery*. [Insurance Corp. of Ireland, Ltd. v. Compagnie des Bauxites de Guinee, *supra*, §88]

5. **Binding Effect:** [§119]   Once the defendant has appeared and litigated jurisdiction, she may not re-raise the issue collaterally to resist full faith and credit; she is estopped from re-litigating the issue. [Baldwin v. Iowa State Traveling Men's Association, 283 U.S. 522 (1931)]

   a. **Appellate review:** [§120]   A defendant whose jurisdictional objections are rejected can appeal that decision. However, in the federal courts and many state systems, appellate review is available only after a final decision is rendered, usually only after a trial. (*See infra*, §§1957 *et seq.*) In some state sytems, earlier review is possible. [*See* Cal. Civ. Proc. Code §418.10(e)—defendant whose motion to quash service is denied must petition for writ of mandate within 10 days or enter general appearance and waive jurisdictional objection]

E. **VENUE**

1. **Introduction:** [§121]   Venue is a statutory limitation on the geographic location of litigation designed to prevent the plaintiff from suing where it would be burdensome for the defendant to appear and defend. Venue must be considered in addition to questions of statutory authorization for exercise of jurisdiction and the constitutionality of that exercise of jurisdiction.

   a. **Federal system:** Venue statutes in the federal system limit the *federal districts* in which suit may be brought.

   b. **State courts:** Venue statutes in state court systems usually limit the *counties* in which suit may be brought.

2. **Federal Venue Limitations:** [§122]   Most suits in federal courts are considered *transitory actions* subject to the following venue rules; although some cases may be considered *local actions* subject to special venue rules (*see infra*, §140). Generally, for most federal question and diversity cases, venue is proper as follows:

   a. **Defendant's residence:** [§123]   Venue is proper in a judicial district where any defendant resides, if all defendants reside in the same state, whether federal subject matter jurisdiction is based on diversity of citizenship or federal question. [28 U.S.C. §1391(a)(1), (b)(1)]

      (1) **Residence of natural person:** [§124]   Ordinarily, residence of a natural person refers to domicile—the place she resides with intent to remain indefinitely. In this sense, it is analogous to citizenship for purposes of

jurisdiction. (*See supra,* §70.) But some cases have interpreted residence to refer also to a district in which a person has a second home. [Arley v. United Pacific Insurance Co., 379 F.2d 183 (9th Cir. 1967)]

(2) **Residence of corporation:** [§125] A corporation is deemed a resident of any judicial district in which it is subject to personal jurisdiction at the time the action is commenced. [28 U.S.C. §1391(c)] Thus, venue limitations do not pose additional hurdles (beyond those posed by limitations on personal jurisdiction) regarding corporate defendants.

(3) **Unincorporated associations:** [§126] Large unincorporated associations (*e.g.,* labor unions) normally have the capacity to sue or be sued as an entity. Venue is proper in districts in which they are ***doing business***. [Denver & Rio Grande Western Railroad v. Brotherhood of Railroad Trainmen, 387 U.S. 556 (1967)]

(4) **Partnerships:** [§127] It has been held that partnerships should be treated like unincorporated associations [Penrod Drilling Co. v. Johnson, 414 F.2d 1217 (5th Cir. 1969)], although other cases have used the residence of the partners to determine venue in such cases.

b. **Substantial part of events or omissions or of property:** [§128] Venue is proper in "a judicial district in which a substantial part of the events or omissions giving rise to the claim occurred, or a substantial part of property that is the subject of the action is situated," whether federal subject matter jurisdiction is based on diversity of citizenship or federal question. [28 U.S.C. §1391(a)(2), (b)(2)]

(1) **Rationale:** These provisions are intended to cope with the problem of ***venue gaps,*** which could arise when there are multiple defendants and there is no state that is the residence of all of them.

(2) **Compare—where claim arose:** [§129] Until 1990, venue was proper "where the claim arose." This term had generated substantial litigation over which of several districts was the single one "where the claim arose" in cases involving multiforum transactions, and received a narrow interpretation by the Supreme Court. [Leroy v. Great Western United Corp., 443 U.S. 173 (1979)] Unlike this narrow interpretation, the amended venue statute contemplates that in a number of cases venue may be proper on this ground in ***more than one district.***

(3) **Application:** [§130] Problem areas in the application of the new statutory provision include the following:

(a) **"Giving rise":** [§131] It is not clear whether Congress intended that the pertinent events be only those on which liability is predicated under the relevant substantive law. For example, in a products liability action against a manufacturer, it is likely that the retail sale of the product would not be an element of the claim (*see infra,* §609, regarding privity), but the place of retail sale may nevertheless be a proper venue even if the injury occurred in another district.

(b) **"Substantial part":** [§132]   Although the amended statute contemplates that more than one district may qualify, it is not clear how many events (or omissions) suffice as a "substantial part."

    1) **Example:** Where a creditor's demand letter was forwarded to a district by the Postal Service from plaintiff's old address, receipt of the letter in the district was held to satisfy the venue requirements for an action under the Fair Debt Collection Practices Act [15 U.S.C. §§1692 *et seq.*]. The harm Congress sought to protect against occurred when the letter was received. [Bates v. C & S Adjusters, Inc., 980 F.2d 865 (2d Cir. 1992)]

    2) **Example:** A government enforcement action against a defendant that had mailed 15 million postcards nationwide could be brought in Iowa, where 200,000 postcards were directed. [United States v. Hartbrodt, 773 F. Supp. 1240 (S.D. Iowa 1991)]

    a) **"Property present":** [§133]   The problem of location of property is similar to the question of location of property for purposes of personal jurisdiction (*see supra*, §§54-57), but turns in this instance on the intent of Congress, which may be to have the federal courts develop federal rules regarding the location of property for venue purposes.

        1/ **Property subject of the action:** The property must be the subject of the action for this venue provision to apply.

        2/ **Compare—local actions:** In some actions, the local action rule (*see infra*, §§150-153) may apply instead of the provisions of section 1391.

c. **Defendants subject to personal jurisdiction:** [§134]   Where federal subject matter jurisdiction is founded *solely on diversity of citizenship,* venue is proper in any district "in which the defendants are subject to personal jurisdiction at the time the action is commenced, if there is no district in which the action may otherwise be brought." [28 U.S.C. §1391(a)(3)]

    (1) **Service within jurisdiction:** [§135]   Personal service within the jurisdiction would not suffice to establish venue under this provision because it would not be a ground for personal jurisdiction that exists "at the time the action is commenced." Federal civil actions are "commenced by filing a complaint with the court" [Fed. R. Civ. P. 3], and the summons issues only upon "the filing of the complaint" [Fed. R. Civ. P. 4(a)].

    (2) **Unavailability of other districts:** [§136]   To use this ground for venue, plaintiff must show that venue cannot be established in any other district.

d. **Where defendant found:** [§137]   If federal jurisdiction is not based solely on diversity of citizenship, venue is proper in a "district in which any defendant may be found, if there is no district in which the action may otherwise be brought." [28 U.S.C. §1391(b)(3)]

   (1) **Meaning of "found":** [§138]   It appears that a defendant may be "found" in a district in which she *can be served with process.*

   (2) **Unavailability of other districts:** [§139]   To use this ground for venue, plaintiff must show that venue cannot be established in any other district.

e. **Special venue statutes:** [§140]   Congress has altered the general rules of venue in connection with certain types of cases:

   (1) **Additional venue options:** [§141]   In some types of cases, venue may be proper in certain locations in addition to the districts allowed under the general rules.

      (a) **Patent infringement actions:** [§142]   In *addition* to the districts specified by the general venue statutes, venue in a patent infringement action is also proper in the district where the defendant committed acts of infringement if the defendant has a "regular and established place of business in that district." [28 U.S.C. §1400(b)]

      (b) **Copyright suits:** [§143]   Similarly, in addition to the districts specified by the general venue statutes, venue in copyright suits is proper in any district in which the defendant or her agent may be found. [28 U.S.C. §1400(a)]

   (2) **Substitute venue:** [§144]   In a few types of cases, venue is proper *only* in the districts specified by the special statute.

      (a) **Federal tort claims actions:** [§145]   Venue for federal tort claims actions is proper only in the district where the plaintiff resides or where the claim arose. [28 U.S.C. §1402(b)]

      (b) **Statutory interpleader:** [§146]   In statutory interpleader actions, venue is proper only in a district where a claimant to the fund resides. [28 U.S.C. §1397]

f. **Aliens:** [§147]   In a suit against an alien, venue is proper in *any district*. [28 U.S.C. §1391(d)]

   (1) **Compare—citizenship for determination of diversity of citizenship:** [§148]   Where the residence of an alien must be considered to determine whether there is *subject matter jurisdiction* due to complete diversity of citizenship, an alien admitted to the United States for permanent residence is deemed a citizen of the state in which the alien is domiciled. (*See infra*, §299.)

g. **Removed cases:** [§149]   Where a case is removed from state court to federal court, it is assigned to the district encompassing the state court in which the action was pending, regardless of the residence of the parties. [28 U.S.C. §1441(a)] In a sense, removal creates its own venue.

h. **Local actions:** [§150] Certain types of cases involving title to property are considered "local," and venue is regarded as proper only in the district where the property is located. In effect, this is an ***unwritten limitation*** on the federal venue statutes, treating them as applicable to "transitory" actions only.

   (1) **Example:** In *Livingston v. Jefferson,* 15 Fed. Cas. 660 (C.C.D.Va. 1811), plaintiff charged former President Jefferson with trespass to plaintiff's land in Louisiana. The Court refused to proceed with the case because it was a "local action" that could be brought only in Louisiana (where personal jurisdiction could not be obtained over Jefferson).

   (2) **In rem analogy:** [§151] One court has explained that the difference between local and transitory actions is the same as that between in personam and in rem jurisdiction, and that an action is a local action only if the court needs to have jurisdiction over the real property in order to grant relief. [Raphael J. Musicus, Inc. v. Safeway Stores, Inc., 743 F.2d 503 (7th Cir. 1984)]

   (3) **Property in multiple districts:** [§152] Where the property is located in more than one district in the same state, the action may be brought in any of those districts. [28 U.S.C. §1392(b)]

   (4) **Treated as a matter of subject matter jurisdiction:** [§153] Some courts treat the local action rule as a limitation on subject matter jurisdiction. (*See infra,* §343.)

3. **State Venue Limitations:** [§154] State venue provisions involve similar considerations to federal venue rules.

   a. **Defendant's residence:** [§155] Traditionally, in personam actions can be brought in the county where the defendant resides; and where multiple defendants are sued, the action may be proper in any county where one of them resides. [*See* Cal. Civ. Proc. Code §395]

   b. **Where claim arose:** [§156] In some jurisdictions, most or some types of claims (*e.g.,* tort claims) can be brought where the claim arose. [*See* Cal. Civ. Proc. Code §395(a)—in action for personal injury, venue proper in county where injury occurs]

   c. **Actions affecting real property:** [§157] Where the action affects title to real property, venue is usually in the county where the property is located. [*See* Cal. Civ. Proc. Code §392(1)]

   d. **Nonresident defendant:** [§158] In general, nonresidents are regarded as having no venue rights, and the plaintiff may often sue them in any county. [*See* Cal. Civ. Proc. Code §395(a)]

   (1) **Equal protection challenge rejected:** [§159] A state may allow an out-of-state corporation to be sued in ***any*** county without violating the Equal Protection Clause, even when it limits suits against an in-state corporation

to the county of its principal place of business. It is rational to weight differently (i) the inconvenience of a domestic corporation in defending a suit in a forum distant from its principal place of business and (ii) the burden on an out-of-state corporation that must defend away from home in any event. [Burlington Northern Railroad v. Ford, 112 S. Ct. 2184 (1992)]

4. **Litigating Venue:** [§160]   As with personal jurisdiction, improper venue may be *waived* unless raised in the proper way. In federal court, for example, it is waived unless raised in the first Rule 12 motion or in the answer if there is no Rule 12 motion. [*See* Fed. R. Civ. P. 12(h)(1)]

   a. **Effect of timely venue objection:** [§161]   Where the defendant timely objects to venue, the court *cannot proceed* with the case. It may dismiss, but in most jurisdictions it can also transfer the case to a court that is a proper venue. (*See infra.*)

5. **Federal Transfer Provisions:** [§162]   A federal case may be transferred to another federal court in the following circumstances:

   a. **Venue or jurisdiction improper in original court:** [§163]   Where venue or jurisdiction is improper in the court selected by the plaintiff and the defendant properly objects, the court *may transfer the case to a proper court* rather than dismiss it. [28 U.S.C. §1406(a)]

      (1) **Transfer where jurisdiction also improper:** [§164]   Although the statute only talks of transfer where venue is improper, the Supreme Court has held that it authorizes transfer where both jurisdiction and venue are improper. [Goldlawr, Inc. v. Heiman, 369 U.S. 463 (1962)]

      (2) **Transfer where venue proper but jurisdiction lacking:** [§165]   Lower courts have upheld transfer where venue is proper but there is no personal jurisdiction. [Aguacate Consolidated Mines v. Deeprock, 566 F.2d 523 (5th Cir. 1978)]

   b. **Transfer for convenience:** [§166]   Where venue and jurisdiction are proper in the court selected by the plaintiff, the court can transfer the action "for the convenience of the parties and witnesses in the interests of justice." [28 U.S.C. §1404(a)]

      (1) **Compare—forum non conveniens:** [§167]   This transfer provision considers many factors that bear on the question of whether to dismiss on forum non conveniens grounds (*see infra*, §§188-191), but permits transfer on a *lesser showing of inconvenience*. [Norwood v. Kirkpatrick, 349 U.S. 29 (1955)]

      (2) **Proper transferee court:** [§168]   The statute authorizes transfer only to a district in which the action *"might have been brought."* This means that the transferee district must be a *proper venue* and have *valid personal jurisdiction*. The moving party's willingness to waive objections to venue or personal jurisdiction does not satisfy this requirement. [Hoffman v. Blaski, 363 U.S. 335 (1960)]

(3) **Procedure**

    (a) **Proper moving parties:** [§169] Either the plaintiff or the defendant can move to transfer under this section. A defendant who has removed a case from a state court can still move to transfer after removal. [Chicago Rock Island & Pacific Railway v. Igoe, 212 F.2d 378 (7th Cir. 1954)]

    (b) **Showing required:** [§170] In general, it is said that the *plaintiff's initial choice of forum should be respected*, and that transfer is proper only when the balance of conveniences *strongly favors transfer*. This showing should look to the identity and location of witnesses, access to items of real evidence, and any other factor that would make trial in the transferee forum more convenient.

(4) **Forum selection clause:** [§171] Where the parties have entered into a contract containing a forum selection clause concerning the dispute in question, the Supreme Court has stated that the presence of the clause should be "a significant factor" in determining whether to transfer the case to the forum designated. [Stewart Organization, Inc. v. Ricoh Corp., 487 U.S. 22 (1988)]

c. **Multidistrict litigation:** [§172] When cases pending in different districts raise a common question of law or fact, they can be transferred to one district. [28 U.S.C. §1407]

    (1) **Showing required:** [§173] All that need be shown is that the actions share a common question of fact or law; unlike transfers under section 1404(a) (*supra*, §170), there is no preference for plaintiff's choice of forum.

    (2) **For pretrial purposes only:** [§174] This transfer is for pretrial purposes only; the cases should be remanded to the original court for trial. [28 U.S.C. §1407(a)] The transferee court has full power to pass on any pretrial matters, however.

    (3) **Follow-up transfer for trial under section 1404(a):** [§175] Many courts hold that the transferee court can transfer these cases to itself for trial under section 1404(a).

    (4) **Procedure:** [§176] Motions for transfer are directed to the *Judicial Panel on Multidistrict Litigation*, which holds hearings and has the authority to transfer to any district *without reference to venue or jurisdiction*.

d. **Effect on choice of law:** [§177] In cases in federal court on grounds of diversity of citizenship, the transfer could affect choice of law because in such cases the federal court is required to look to the choice of law rules of the state in which it sits to determine choice of law issues. [Klaxon Co. v. Stentor Electric Manufacturing Co., 313 U.S. 487 (1941)]

    (1) **Venue and jurisdiction proper in original court:** [§178] In cases where the plaintiff sues in a court that has proper venue and jurisdiction,

a transfer for the convenience of the parties *does not affect choice of law* because the transferee court is to apply the same choice of law rules that the transferor court would have applied. [Van Dusen v. Barrack, 376 U.S. 612 (1964)] The *Van Dusen* rule applies even when the transfer is on motion of the plaintiff who chose the inconvenient forum in the first place and thus could shop for more favorable law. [Ferens v. John Deere & Co., 494 U.S. 516 (1990)]

    (2) **Venue or jurisdiction improper in original court:** [§179] If the plaintiff could not have overcome the defendant's venue or jurisdiction objections in the original court, the *choice of law rules of the transferee state should usually be applied.* [Ellis v. Great Southwestern Corp., 646 F.2d 1099 (5th Cir. 1981)]

    (3) **Federal claims:** [§180] Because the federal circuits sometimes disagree on issues of federal law, it is possible for similar choice of law problems to arise where a claim is transferred from one circuit to another. It is unclear whether the transferee or transferor interpretation applies in this circumstance. [*Compare In re* Korean Air Lines Disaster of Sept. 1, 1983, 829 F.2d 1171 (D.C. Cir. 1987), *aff'd on other grounds, sub nom.* Chan v. Korean Air Lines, 490 U.S. 122 (1989)—transferee judge need not defer to transferor interpretation—*with In re* Dow Co. "Sarabrand" Products Liability Litigation, 666 F. Supp. 1466 (D. Colo. 1987)—transferor interpretation controls]

6. **Transfer in State Court:** [§181] State courts often have transfer provisions analogous to the federal provisions. [*See, e.g.,* Cal. Civ. Proc. Code §§396—transfer where jurisdiction lacking; 397(G)—transfer for convenience of witnesses; Cal. Rules of Court 1501 *et seq.*—coordination of actions involving common questions of fact or law]

F. FORUM NON CONVENIENS

1. **Introduction:** [§182] Even when jurisdiction and venue are proper, courts may decline to exercise jurisdiction on the ground that the location the plaintiff selected for the case is grossly inconvenient. This ancient common law doctrine was endorsed by the Supreme Court as a matter of federal common law in *Gulf Oil Corp. v. Gilbert,* 330 U.S. 501 (1947), and is recognized in almost all state courts.

2. **Present Use**

    a. **Federal courts:** [§183] When the inconvenience problem can be solved by transfer to another federal district, the court may not dismiss; but if the proper forum is in another country, the federal court can dismiss. [Piper Aircraft Co. v. Reyno, 454 U.S. 235 (1981); *In re* Union Carbide Corp. Gas Plant Disaster at Bhopal, India, 809 F.2d 195 (2d Cir.), *cert. denied,* 484 U.S. 871 (1987)]

    b. **State courts:** [§184] When the more convenient court is not within the state and transfer is therefore not possible (*see supra,* §181, regarding in-state transfer) forum non conveniens remains an important device.

        (1) **Uniform Act:** [§185] The National Conference of Commissioners on Uniform State Laws has recommended a Uniform Transfer of Litigation

Act that would permit transfers similar to those between federal courts pursuant to 28 U.S.C. section 1404(a) if adopted by both the transferor and transferee states, but the uniform act has not been widely adopted.

3. **Rationale:** Courts are not required to make their jurisdiction available to parties who engage in unfair forum shopping and thereby impose substantial inconvenience on other parties and expense and burden on the courts of the forum selected by the plaintiff.

4. **Procedure:** [§186] The defendant must make a motion to dismiss on grounds of inconvenience.

   a. **Showing required:** [§187] The defendant must show that the plaintiff has selected a *grossly inconvenient* location for the suit.

      (1) **Compare—transfer:** In federal court, the showing necessary to justify transfer is not as compelling as the showing needed to justify dismissal on forum non conveniens grounds.

   b. **Factors:** [§188] The court is to consider a number of private and public factors in making a decision whether to dismiss on forum non conveniens grounds.

      (1) **Private factors:** [§189] The court should consider the following private factors:

         (a) *Relative ease of access to sources of proof*; *i.e.,* will access to needed proof be significantly easier in another forum?

         (b) *Availability of compulsory process*; *i.e.,* as to *unwilling witnesses* whose testimony is important, will there be compulsory process to compel them to attend trial in another forum that is not available in the forum chosen by the plaintiff?

         (c) *Cost of obtaining attendance of willing witnesses.*

         (d) *Need to view premises*; *i.e.,* will having the jury view the premises involved in the litigation be important at trial? If so, this weighs in favor of having the trial near the premises.

      (2) **Public factors:** [§190] The court should also consider the following public factors:

         (a) *Local interest* in having localized controversies decided at home;

         (b) *Interest in having trial in forum familiar with the law* to be applied;

         (c) *Avoiding unnecessary problems with conflict of laws*; and

         (d) *Unfairness of burdening citizens* of an unrelated forum with jury duty.

c. **Weight given plaintiff's choice:** [§191] Usually *substantial weight* is given to the plaintiff's choice to sue in a forum where venue and jurisdiction are present. When the plaintiff is foreign, however, that deference is not warranted. [Piper Aircraft Co. v. Reyno, *supra*, §183]

d. **Change in substantive law:** [§192] The fact that the law in the more convenient forum is less favorable to plaintiffs usually has no significant weight. [Piper Aircraft Co. v. Reyno, *supra*]

e. **Alternative forum available:** [§193] The court cannot dismiss unless the alternative forum is available, but problems of jurisdiction in the alternative forum can be solved by stipulation by the moving party to submit to jurisdiction there.

f. **Conditions on dismissal:** [§194] The court can condition the dismissal to protect against unfairness to the plaintiff. A common example is insistence on a stipulation by the defendant that the statute of limitations will be deemed tolled as of the time suit was filed in the inconvenient forum, so that plaintiff does not risk a limitations defense based on the delay between the filing of the original case and the filing of suit in the preferred forum.

5. **Effect on Choice of Law:** [§195] Because forum non conveniens results in a dismissal, the plaintiff must file a new suit, and the choice of law rules that apply are determined by the forum for the new suit.

6. **Compare—Contractual Limitations on Forum:** [§196] Dismissal in favor of litigation in another forum can also occur where the dispute arises out of a contract in which the parties have agreed to litigate in a specific forum, and transfer to that forum is not possible.

   a. **Federal law—generally enforceable:** [§197] The Supreme Court has declared that, as a matter of federal common law, such clauses are generally enforceable even where they result in dismissal because the forum chosen is in another country. [*See* The Bremen v. Zapata Off-Shore Co., 407 U.S. 1 (1972)—clause should be enforced absent showing that doing so "would be unreasonable and unjust, or that the clause was invalid for such reasons as fraud or overreaching"] Moreover, the Supreme Court has held that a forum selection clause on a *printed passenger ticket* is enforceable even though not the subject of bargaining, unless enforcing it would violate fundamental fairness. [Carnival Cruise Lines, Inc. v. Shute, 499 U.S. 585 (1991)] *Note:* Congress invalidated such clauses in ship passenger tickets [46 U.S.C. App. §183c], but later re-amended the statute to restore the original language, although apparently intending still to change the result in *Carnival Cruise Lines*. Such clauses may be valid in other consumer situations, however.

   b. **State law—enforcement limited:** [§198] In many states, the enforcement of such clauses is limited on the theory that the parties cannot by agreement "oust" a court with jurisdiction to decide the dispute. [*See, e.g.,* Stewart Organization, Inc. v. Ricoh Corp., *supra*, §171—"Alabama looks unfavorably upon contractual forum-selection clauses"]

   c. **Choice between state and federal rules in federal court:** [§199] Where state law claims are presented in federal court, there may be a serious problem determining whether to apply state or federal common law. The Supreme Court has not decided this question. [*See* Stewart Organization, Inc. v. Ricoh Corp., *supra*] It has, however, decided that where transfer to the selected forum is possible under 28 U.S.C. section 1404(a), the existence of such a clause is a significant factor in deciding whether to transfer.

G. NOTICE

1. **Introduction:** [§200]   In addition to personal jurisdiction and venue, one should be alert to problems of notice. Notice is not a substitute for these other factors, but is essential to a valid judgment.

2. **Constitutional Requirements:** [§201]   Due process requires that *reasonable efforts to provide notice* be made with regard to persons whose interests are to be determined. [Mullane v. Central Hanover Bank & Trust Co., *supra*, §63]

   a. **In rem cases:** [§202]   The notice requirement applies even to pure in rem actions. [Walker v. City of Hutchinson, 352 U.S. 112 (1956)]

   b. **Method:** [§203]   The method of giving notice must have a reasonable prospect of giving actual notice: "The means employed must be such as one desirous of actually informing the absentee might reasonably adopt to accomplish it." [Mullane v. Central Hanover Bank & Trust Co., *supra*]

      (1) **Personal delivery:** [§204]   Personal delivery of the notice (ordinarily the summons and complaint) is the traditional method of giving notice.

      (2) **First class mail:** [§205]   In *Mullane v. Central Hanover Bank & Trust Co., supra,* the Court required mailed notice to those whose addresses were known, reasoning that "the mails today are recognized as an efficient and inexpensive means of communication."

         (a) **Class actions:** [§206]   In class actions brought under Federal Rule 23(b)(3) (common question suits), there must be mailed notice to all identifiable class members. [Eisen v. Carlisle & Jacquelin, 417 U.S. 156 (1974)]

      (3) **Posted notice:** [§207]   Notice by posting on the defendant's residence may not be sufficient. [Greene v. Lindsey, 456 U.S. 444 (1982)—state procedure for giving notice of eviction proceedings by posting on the front door of apartment invalid in view of testimony that notices were often torn off doors; notice by mail required]

   c. **Effort to identify:** [§208]   Reasonable efforts to identify and locate affected persons are required. As to named defendants, the identification issue should not be a problem, but in other instances, such as in rem actions, it can prove more difficult.

      (1) **Example—mortgagee:** Where property was sold for nonpayment of taxes, a mortgagee with a mortgage on file with the county recorder was

held entitled to notice. [Mennonite Board of Missions v. Adams, 462 U.S. 791 (1983)]

    (2) **Example—creditor of decedent:** Application of a state requirement that claims against a decedent be presented to his executor within two months of publication of notice of the commencement of probate proceedings was held to violate due process to the extent it cut off rights of creditors whose identity was reasonably ascertainable to a decedent's executor and who were not given notice. [Tulsa Professional Collection Services, Inc. v. Pope, 485 U.S. 478 (1988)]

    (3) **Class actions:** In class actions, the Court has accepted failure to identify significant numbers of class members. [*See* Eisen v. Carlisle & Jacquelin, *supra*—inability to locate more than half of six million class members] *Rationale:* In *Mullanne v. Central Hanover Bank & Trust Co., supra,* the Court explained that "notice reasonably certain to reach most of those interested in objecting is likely to safeguard the interests of all, since any objection sustained would inure to the benefit of all."

  d. **Contents:** [§209] The notice must intelligibly advise the defendant of the nature and place of the proceeding.

  e. **Constructive notice:** [§210] In some instances where a person cannot be located after reasonable efforts, published or other constructive notice will suffice. [*See, e.g.,* Cal. Civ. Proc. Code §415.50—service by publication where party cannot by reasonable diligence be served another way]

  f. **Effect of failure to receive:** [§211] If a constitutionally valid procedure is used, the *judgment is binding* even if some interested parties do not receive notice.

3. **Service of Process:** [§212] The usual method for giving notice is service of a *summons* and complaint on the defendant directing that the defendant file an answer to the complaint or suffer a default.

  a. **Jurisdiction distinguished:** [§213] Although service of process implies an exercise of jurisdiction, the questions of jurisdiction and method of service should be kept separate. Even where the method of service is proper, the defendant can still challenge the exercise of personal jurisdiction.

  b. **Methods of service:** [§214] Service of process can be accomplished by the following methods:

    (1) **Personal delivery:** [§215] Process may be served on the person. In the case of a corporation, partnership, or unincorporated association, service may be made on an officer or managing agent, or on an agent authorized by law.

    (2) **Substituted service:** [§216] Other means of service may be authorized by statute or court rule.

      (a) **Federal Rules**

        1) **At defendant's home:** [§217] A copy of the summons and complaint can be left at the "usual place of abode" of the person

to be served with a "person of suitable age and discretion" residing therein. [Fed. R. Civ. P. 4(e)(2)]

2) **In accordance with state law:** [§218] Service may be made pursuant to the law of the *state in which the district court is located*, or pursuant to the law of the *state in which service is effected*. [Fed. R. Civ. P. 4(e)(1)]

3) **Waiver of service:** [§219] A plaintiff may ask a defendant to waive formal service by sending a request for waiver of service to the defendant by first class mail. Because a defendant has a duty to avoid unnecessary costs of service, a defendant located within the United States who fails to waive service without good cause can be liable for the costs of formal service. A defendant who waives service receives additional time to answer the complaint compared to one who is served in the usual manner. [Fed. R. Civ. P. 4(d)]

4) **On defendant in foreign country:** [§220] A defendant served in another country may be served by an internationally agreed means or, if there is not an agreed means, as directed by the law of the place of service, including, unless forbidden by the law of that country, personal delivery or any form of mail requiring a signed receipt, or as directed by the court. [Fed. R. Civ. P. 4(f)]

(b) **State law:** [§221] State law on substituted service varies. In California, for example, such service may be accomplished in the following ways:

1) **At defendant's office or home:** [§222] A copy of the summons and complaint can be left at the person's office or abode plus mailing a copy to that place. [Cal. Civ. Proc. Code §415.20]

2) **By mail within state:** [§223] A copy of the summons and complaint can also be mailed to a person within the state, if the person executes and returns an acknowledgment of service. [Cal. Civ. Proc. Code §415.30]

3) **By mail outside state:** [§224] A copy of the summons and complaint can be served on a person outside the state by using return-receipt mail. [Cal. Civ. Proc. Code §415.40]

(3) **Service in diversity cases:** [§225] In diversity cases, the service procedures of Federal Rule 4 are to be applied. [Hanna v. Plumer, 380 U.S. 460 (1965)]

c. **Immunity from service:** [§226] In some jurisdictions, there are rules that forbid service of process on a person who is in the state only to participate in a legal proceeding. *Rationale:* This immunity is designed to protect against the risk of people being unwilling to attend trials for fear of being served with process. These rules have been severely limited in recent times.

4. **Timing of Notice—Prejudgment Seizures**

   a. **Introduction:** [§227] At common law, a plaintiff could have a defendant's property seized as a method of coercing the defendant to appear for trial. Over time, this seizure—variously called replevin, attachment, garnishment, sequestration—came to be used to provide *security for any judgment* the plaintiff might obtain in the action. Very often, such prejudgment remedies were available before defendant was given notice of the action.

   b. **State law requirements:** [§228] Partly in response to constitutional decisions (*see infra*, §§230 *et seq.*), states placed *limits on such prejudgment remedies*. Thus, before considering possible constitutional objections to state procedures, one must first consider whether the prejudgment seizure sought by the plaintiff is authorized by state law.

      (1) **Example—California:** In California, attachment is available only in contract actions for more than $500 for a fixed or readily ascertainable amount. In an action against a natural person, attachment is available only if the claim arises out of the defendant's conduct of a trade, business, or profession. [Cal. Civ. Proc. Code §483.010]

      (2) **Example—New York:** Prejudgment attachment is allowed in New York only where there is a showing that the defendant has, or "is about to," assign, dispose of, or secrete property, or that the defendant is a nondomicilliary, or a resident who cannot be served in the state. [New York Civ. Prac. Law §6201]

      (3) **Federal courts:** [§229] Federal courts must apply state law concerning the availability of prejudgment remedies, unless a federal statute provides a prejudgment remedy. [Fed. R. Civ. P. 64]

   c. **Procedural due process requirements for prejudgment seizure:** [§230] In a series of cases the Supreme Court has considered the constitutional requirements for procedures attending issuance of prejudgment remedies. Because these cases are difficult to reconcile, it is worthwhile to consider them one by one.

      (1) *Sniadach*—**garnishment of wages:** [§231] In *Sniadach v. Family Finance Corp.*, 395 U.S. 337 (1969), the Court held that the state violated a defendant's due process rights by allowing prejudgment garnishment of wages. The opinion contained suggestions that wages might be viewed as a *special type of property* because they are essential to everyday life.

      (2) *Fuentes*—**seizure of chattels:** [§232] In *Fuentes v. Shevin*, 407 U.S. 67 (1972), by a 4-3 decision, the Court invalidated Florida and Pennsylvania procedures for writs of replevin that authorized the seizure of property, because there was no provision for notice and a preseizure hearing.

         (a) **Purpose of hearing:** [§233] The Court emphasized that the notice and hearing requirement ensured a "fair process of decisionmaking," but was not clear on whether this was limited to reducing the risk of erroneous issuance of writs of replevin.

(b) **Alternative safeguards against error:** [§234] The plurality viewed alternative safeguards against error as significant factors in determining the type of hearing afforded, but "far from enough by themselves to obviate the right to a prior hearing of some kind." One dissenter argued that the bond requirement, coupled with the creditor's desire to have the transaction completed, should provide sufficient protection.

(c) **Unimportance of cost of hearing:** [§235] The Court placed little importance on the possible cost of more elaborate hearing procedures, noting that "[t]he Constitution recognizes higher values than speed and efficiency."

(d) **Exception for "extraordinary situations":** [§236] The plurality recognized in dictum that the right to preseizure notice and hearing could be overcome in "extraordinary situations." It specified three factors that appeared all to be necessary:

1) Such seizures should be *directly necessary* to secure an *important governmental or general public interest*, *e.g.*, *public health* or *the war effort*.

2) Such seizures without notice may occur only where *delay would be inimical to the public interest*; and

3) Such seizures should be limited to circumstances in which the *state controlled the initiation of proceedings*.

(3) *Mitchell*: [§237] In *Mitchell v. W.T. Grant Co.,* 416 U.S. 600 (1974), the Court upheld Louisiana's sequestration procedure in a case where the seller of several household appliances obtained a writ for their seizure when the defendant missed payments.

(a) *Fuentes* **overruled?** [§238] One could argue that *Mitchell* overruled *Fuentes* since the situation was difficult to fit within the "extraordinary situations" analysis of *Fuentes*.

(b) *Mitchell's* **requirements—***Fuentes* **distinguished:** [§239] The majority in *Mitchell* said that it was applying *Fuentes*, however, and that the Louisiana procedures were different in ways that made them constitutional because:

1) They *required more than the conclusory claims of ownership* called by the state procedures at issue in *Fuentes*;

2) In the parish where this case arose, the practice was that a *judge would pass on the application* for the writ;

3) *"Narrowly confined" issues* were presented by the application for the writ in Louisiana in contrast to the broad "fault" standard applicable in the statutes at issue in *Fuentes*; and

4) The defendant in Louisiana had a *right to an immediate hearing* on whether the plaintiff was entitled to the writ, and the burden remained on the plaintiff to justify the issuance of the writ.

(c) **Explanation for shift:** [§240] The easiest explanation for the shift from *Fuentes* to *Mitchell* is that two new Justices—Powell and Rehnquist—were added to the Court in the interim.

(4) ***Di-Chem*:** [§241] In *North Georgia Finishing, Inc. v. Di-Chem, Inc.,* 419 U.S. 601 (1975), the Court struck down Georgia garnishment procedures. Its description of the distinguishing factors that made the case different from *Mitchell* provide a guide to important constitutional criteria.

   (a) **Property not subject of suit:** [§242] Unlike *Fuentes* and *Mitchell,* the property in *Di-Chem* (a bank account) had no intrinsic relation to the claim. Thus, in a sense the Court expanded the constitutional validity of seizure without notice if it had previously been limited to cases where the plaintiff had an ownership interest in the seized property.

   (b) **Purpose of due process requirements:** [§243] The majority opinion found that the procedure in *Fuentes* was unconstitutional because the seizures there were "carried out without notice and without opportunity for a hearing ***or other safeguard against mistaken repossession***." This seemed to revise the thrust of the *Fuentes* opinion, which treated the presence of safeguards as bearing on the type of hearing required, not the need for preseizure notice at all.

(5) ***Doehr*:** [§244] In *Connecticut v. Doehr,* 501 U.S. 1 (1991), the Court held Connecticut's provision for attachment of real property without prior notice and an opportunity for a hearing invalid "as applied in this case." The Court followed a three-step analysis based on *Mathews v. Eldridge,* 424 U.S. 319 (1976):

   (a) **Private interest:** [§245] The Court held that the interests of a homeowner were significantly affected by attachment even though it did not interfere with possession of the property because attachment can cloud title, impede sale, and interfere with borrowing on the property.

   (b) **Risk of erroneous deprivation:** [§246] The Court found that there was a substantial risk of an erroneous deprivation because the state practice allowed decisions based on a conclusory affidavit without prior notice and adversary hearing, and the underlying issue in the case (an alleged assault) did not lend itself to documentary proof.

   (c) **Governmental interest:** [§247] Connecticut had no significant interest in allowing a private plaintiff to attach defendant's property without notice or a showing of exigent circumstances, in view of the fact that other states have more exacting requirements for seizure without notice.

   (d) **Example—application to drug forfeiture seizure:** [§248] In *United States v. James Daniel Good Real Property,* 114 S. Ct. 492 (1993), the Court held that seizure of defendant's home after his conviction for drug trafficking there violated due process because he did not receive pre-seizure notice and an opportunity to be heard. The seizure deprived him of use of the property, created an unacceptable risk of error because owners are entitled to an affirmative defense of innocent ownership, and was unnecessary to protect the Government's interest because real property cannot abscond.

 (e) **Compare—cognovit notes:** [§249] Related issues arise in connection with cognovit notes, in which the debtor agrees that in the event of a default in payments, the creditor may immediately and without notice obtain a judgment against the debtor. The Supreme Court has held that where such arrangements are the result of arm's length negotiation between sophisticated commercial entities, they are enforceable over procedural due process objections. [D.H. Overmyer Co. v. Frick Co., 405 U.S. 174 (1972)]

(6) **Effect of *Doehr*:** [§250] *Connecticut v. Doehr, supra,* appears to have the following effects besides prescribing the three-part analysis of *Mathews v. Eldridge, supra:*

 (a) **Exigent circumstances:** [§251] The Court's opinion suggests that proof of exigent circumstances may be constitutionally necessary to permit seizure without notice. (*Compare supra,* §236, regarding "extraordinary situations" under *Fuentes.*)

 (b) **Effect of preexisting interest in property:** [§252] The Court distinguished its summary affirmance in another case involving a mechanic's lien, suggesting that less rigorous standards might apply when the plaintiff is asserting an interest in the property that *antedates the suit*.

 (c) **Type of claim:** [§253] The Court's emphasis on the difficulty of evaluating the assault claim before it on the basis of filings by plaintiff suggests that only claims that can be reliably evaluated on documentary proof may be the basis for seizure without notice.

 (d) **Due process limitations if hearing held before seizure:** [§254] Even if a hearing is held before seizure, procedural due process may limit seizure unless the above criteria are satisfied.

II. SUBJECT MATTER JURISDICTION OF THE FEDERAL COURTS

chapter approach

Subject matter jurisdiction questions are also an examination staple. When presented with litigation in federal court, remember that there must be a basis for the exercise of jurisdiction and keep in mind the following possibilities:

1. **Diversity Jurisdiction**

    a. **Complete diversity:** Are any defendants of the same citizenship as any plaintiffs? If so, complete diversity is missing.

    b. **Jurisdictional amount:** Does the plaintiff's claim in good faith put *more than $50,000* in controversy in the suit?

2. **Federal Question Jurisdiction**

    a. **Federal claim:** Is the plaintiff seeking relief on the basis of a federal claim?

    b. **Federal issue in state law claim:** If not, does the plaintiff's nonfederal claim turn on a substantial issue of federal law that is included in the *well-pleaded complaint*?

3. **Removal Jurisdiction**

    a. Was a *timely petition* for removal filed by *all* defendants?

    b. Would the case have been within the *original jurisdiction* of the federal court?

    c. If not, is the removing defendant the subject of a *separate and independent claim arising under federal law*?

    d. If the case was properly removed, should it be *remanded* because all federal claims have been dismissed, or because plaintiff in a diversity case has been allowed to amend to add nondiverse defendants?

4. **Supplemental Jurisdiction:** If there is a claim properly within federal jurisdiction, does the court have jurisdiction over other claims against existing parties or claims against additional parties as well?

    a. Would the exercise of such jurisdiction be *constitutional* because the added claim forms part of *the same constitutional case* as the claim within federal jurisdiction?

    b. If the case is in federal court *solely on grounds of diversity*, is the exercise of supplemental jurisdiction *forbidden by 28 U.S.C. section 1367(b)*?

    c. If supplemental jurisdiction is properly invoked, should the court exercise its *discretion* to dismiss the supplemental claims due to *complexity of state law*, because the *state law claim substantially predominates*, or because the court has *dismissed* the claim over which it had original jurisdiction?

Civil Procedure—41

A. INTRODUCTION

1. **Nature of Subject Matter Jurisdiction:** [§255] Historically—sometimes by mere accident—many courts obtained authority to decide only certain types of actions, *i.e.,* they had jurisdiction over only particular subject matters. Thus, whether a court has authority to hear a particular suit can depend on the subject matter involved. The most significant limitations on subject matter jurisdiction today, for purposes of this Summary, involve the subject matter limitations on the federal courts. These limitations often reflect notions of the "proper" relation between federal and state power.

2. **Territorial Jurisdiction Distinguished:** [§256] Unlike territorial jurisdiction—which provides protection for the defendant by limiting the geographic location in which the defendant can be required to defend—subject matter jurisdiction limitations focus on the *type of claim* involved and implement decisions about the allocation of authority between court systems, or among the courts of a given system. The two concepts should not be confused. It is incorrect, for example, to say that the court "has diversity jurisdiction over the defendant." To proceed with a case, the court must possess *both personal jurisdiction* over the defendant and *subject matter jurisdiction* over the claim.

3. **Defects Not Waivable:** [§257] Lack of subject matter jurisdiction is not waivable. Instead, it can lie in the background as a sort of "time bomb" in the plaintiff's lawsuit, at least until the litigation is entirely concluded. (Subject matter jurisdictional defects often can be raised on "collateral" attack, after all appeals have been exhausted or waived and the judgment has become completely final.)

    a. **Plaintiff must allege grounds:** [§258] Ordinarily, the plaintiff must include allegations in the complaint invoking the subject matter jurisdiction of the court. [*See* Fed. R. Civ. P. 8(a)(1)]

    b. **Defendant may raise at any time:** [§259] The defendant may raise lack of subject matter jurisdiction at any time during the pendency of the case, even after final judgment has been entered and the case has been appealed on other grounds. [Fed. R. Civ. P. 12(h)(3)] Indeed, the defendant may even remove the case to federal court, lose there, and then raise lack of subject matter jurisdiction as a ground for invalidating the judgment for the plaintiff. [*See* American Fire & Casualty Co v. Finn, 341 U.S. 6 (1951)]

    c. **Court to raise sua sponte:** [§260] Even if the parties do not raise the issue, the court is to raise subject matter jurisdiction on its own motion. [*See, e.g.,* Louisville & Nashville Railroad v. Mottley, 211 U.S. 149 (1908)—Court dismissed appeal for lack of subject matter jurisdiction even though neither party raised issue]

    d. **Compare—personal jurisdiction:** [§261] The defendant's failure to raise personal jurisdiction at the earliest time waives objections to personal jurisdiction. (*See supra,* §87.)

4. **State Courts:** [§262] This chapter focuses on the subject matter jurisdiction of federal courts. Except for claims within the exclusive jurisdiction of the federal courts (*infra,* §§267-270), state court systems usually exercise "general jurisdiction," *i.e.,* a

state court is available for every type of claim. Within the state court system, however, there may be subject matter jurisdiction limitations that should be kept in mind:

a. **Specialized courts:** [§263]   In many states, there are specialized courts that deal with certain types of cases. For example, probate proceedings or matrimonial disputes may have to be raised before a specialized court, or a specialized division of the court.

b. **Monetary limitations:** [§264]   In some states, there are courts that have jurisdiction over claims below a certain amount. Many states have *small claims courts* with authority to decide cases involving small sums [*see, e.g.,* Cal. Civ. Proc. Code §116.220(a)—less than $5,000], using very informal procedures that may even forbid the participation of lawyers. In addition, there may be more formal courts with jurisdiction limited to claims under a certain amount. [*See, e.g.,* Cal. Civ. Proc. Code §86(a)(1)—municipal courts with jurisdiction of claims less than $25,000]

c. **General jurisdiction:** [§265]   Each state has some court of "general jurisdiction." This means that *any type of claim* can be brought in this court, except those within the exclusive jurisdiction of the federal courts. (*See infra,* §267, regarding exclusive jurisdiction.)

d. **Concurrent jurisdiction of federal claims:** [§266]   Under the Supremacy Clause of the Constitution [U.S. Const. art. VI, §2], state courts may not refuse to enforce federal claims. Thus, even if for some reason the plaintiff may not file her entire case in federal court, she can still file it in state court.

   (1) **Exception—exclusive jurisdiction:** [§267]   As to some types of claims, Congress has granted exclusive jurisdiction to the federal courts, and state courts therefore cannot adjudicate such claims. Examples include the following:

   (a) **Patents, copyrights, and trademarks:** [§268]   Federal courts have exclusive jurisdiction when the plaintiff's patent, copyright, or trademark claim arises under a federal statute. [28 U.S.C. §1338] State courts have concurrent jurisdiction, however, to decide claims arising under the common law (*e.g.,* for unfair competition) and to decide claims for breach of contract concerning the license, sale, etc., of patents, even if the validity of the patent is challenged. [Lear, Inc. v. Adkins, 395 U.S. 653 (1969)]

   (b) **Federal antitrust regulations:** [§269]   Claims for violation of the federal antitrust laws have been held to be within the exclusive jurisdiction of the federal courts. [Freeman v. Bee Machine Co., 319 U.S. 448 (1943)] States may, however, have parallel state law antitrust provisions within the jurisdiction of the state courts.

   (c) **Federal securities acts:** [§270]   Federal jurisdiction is exclusive in actions brought under the Securities Exchange Act of 1934, including actions under *rule 10b-5* for "manipulative or deceptive conduct" in connection with the purchase or sale of securities. [15 U.S.C. §78a] States may, however, entertain claims for common law fraud arising out of the same events.

(d) **Compare—federal defense:** [§271]　When an issue of federal law arises as a defense to a state law claim, the fact that a claim for affirmative relief on the federal ground would be subject to exclusive federal jurisdiction does not prevent the state court from considering the defense. Indeed, under the Supremacy Clause, it cannot refuse to entertain the defense.

5. **Federal Courts' Jurisdiction**

    a. **Limited jurisdiction:** [§272]　Unlike state courts, federal courts are courts of limited jurisdiction.

    (1) **Constitutional grant:** [§273]　Article III, Section 1 of the United States Constitution establishes the Supreme Court and gives Congress the power to create inferior federal courts. Section 2 of Article III sets out the scope of the federal judicial power, and an exercise of jurisdiction by a federal court must be within this scope to be constitutional.

    (2) **Statutory grant:** [§274]　It is not enough that an exercise of federal jurisdiction is merely permissible under the Constitution. Because Congress had the power to decline to create the inferior federal courts, it also has power to limit the jurisdiction of the courts it creates. Thus, there must also be some statutory grant by Congress vesting the federal courts with jurisdiction. Unless Congress has done so, the fact that it might do so without violating the Constitution is irrelevant.

    (a) **Historical background:** It was uncertain at the outset whether Congress would create lower federal courts. Thus, it was also unclear whether any of the Article III jurisdiction would be used. In fact, until 1875, the primary grant of jurisdiction to the lower federal courts was authority to decide diversity cases (*i.e.*, cases in which the opposing parties were from different states).

    b. **Tactical considerations:** [§275]　Litigants with a choice between state and federal court are often moved to prefer federal court for a variety of tactical reasons.

    (1) **Location:** [§276]　Federal courts are usually located in metropolitan areas, while many state courts are in less populated areas.

    (2) **Broad discovery:** [§277]　Federal courts may afford broader opportunities for discovery (although the breadth of federal discovery has been curtailed, *see infra*, §§1310-1314).

    (3) **Speedy trial:** [§278]　In some locations, federal courts are able to offer parties shorter delays to trial, and they therefore may prefer to litigate in federal court. By the same token, where the delay is greater in federal court, a party desiring delay might want to litigate in federal court for that reason.

    (4) **Single assignment system:** [§279]　In most federal courts, cases are assigned to a single judge from the outset. Some litigants believe that this arrangement is more efficient and effective than having the case assigned

on a "master calendar" basis that assigns different aspects to different judges. Most states use the master calendar approach, although some are shifting to a single assignment system.

(5) **Source of jurors:** [§280]   Federal juries are drawn from the entire federal district, while state court juries are usually drawn from a more limited area, such as a county or part of a county.

B. DIVERSITY JURISDICTION

1. **Constitutional Authorization:** [§281]   Article III, Section 2 of the Constitution provides that the judicial power of the United States may extend to controversies between two or more states, between a state and a citizen of another state, *between citizens of different states*, or between a state (or the citizens thereof) and foreign states, citizens, or subjects.

    a. **Rationale:** The usual justification for creating diversity jurisdiction is to afford an alternative forum to those who might be victims of local prejudice against outsiders.

    b. **What constitutes diversity:** [§282]   The plaintiff and defendant have diverse citizenship if one is a citizen of one state and the other is a citizen of another state or an alien or foreign national. There is no diversity jurisdiction, however, in a suit between two aliens, even if from different countries (*e.g.*, a citizen of India and a Canadian).

       (1) **Possible constitutional challenge to statute:** [§283]   28 U.S.C. section 1332(a) provides that for purposes of diversity, permanent resident aliens shall be regarded as citizens of the states in which they are domiciled. (*See infra,* §299.) This statute could authorize jurisdiction in cases beyond the constitutional grant of federal judicial power.

           (a) **Example:** In a suit by a citizen of India, domiciled in Virginia, against a German manufacturer and its American distributor, which was a citizen of Delaware, the court upheld jurisdiction because there was citizen-vs.-alien diversity, given the presence of the Delaware citizen, but noted possible constitutional problems had that defendant not been sued. [Singh v. Daimler-Benz AG, 9 F.3d 303 (3d Cir. 1993)]

    c. **"Minimal" diversity constitutionally required:** [§284]   The Constitution requires only that one plaintiff be of different citizenship from one defendant, even if there are co-parties who are not of diverse citizenship. [State Farm Fire & Casualty Co. v. Tashire, 386 U.S. 523 (1967)] Absent minimal diversity, the federal courts are forbidden to entertain a case unless it involves a federal question (discussed *infra,* §§347 *et seq.*).

2. **Diversity Statute**

    a. **History:** [§285]   The First Congress not only created lower federal courts, but vested them with diversity jurisdiction by passing the predecessor to 28 U.S.C. section 1332. The statute closely tracks the constitutional language.

b. **Complete diversity requirement:** [§286]   In 1806, the Supreme Court interpreted the diversity statute to require complete diversity, *i.e.,* that there be no defendant having the same citizenship as any plaintiff. [Strawbridge v. Curtiss, 7 U.S. 267 (1806)] Although it has made some changes to the statute since then, Congress has not tried to change this interpretation (although the supplemental jurisdiction statute could be interpreted to weaken the complete diversity requirement, *see infra,* §§399 *et seq.*), and the section 1332 has therefore been taken to confer jurisdiction ***narrower*** than the constitutional grant.

c. **How citizenship determined**

   (1) **Natural persons:** [§287]   For United States nationals, "citizenship," in substance, has the same meaning as ***domicile***. A new citizenship may be established by physical presence in the new state and an intention to remain there—*i.e.,* no present intent to go elsewhere.

   (a) **United States national living abroad:** [§288]   An American citizen living abroad permanently has no domicile within the United States and is ***not a citizen of any state***. Such a person cannot sue or be sued in federal court on grounds of diversity of citizenship.

   (b) **Citizens of District of Columbia, Puerto Rico and U.S. territories:** [§289]   Although these persons might have suffered a similar fate to that of the expatriates, Congress provided that they should be ***treated as citizens*** of states for purposes of diversity jurisdiction, and the Supreme Court upheld this as constitutional. [28 U.S.C. §1332(d); National Mutual Insurance Co. v. Tidewater Transfer Co., 337 U.S. 582 (1949)]

   (2) **Corporations:** [§290]   For diversity purposes, a corporation is deemed to be a citizen of ***every*** state in which it is ***incorporated*** and of the state in which it has its ***principal place of business***. [28 U.S.C. §1332(c)]

   (a) **Principal place of business:** [§291]   Where the head office of the corporation and the locus of its other activities are in the same state, the concept causes no trouble. Where, however, the executive offices are in one state and principal production facilities are in another state, the courts may look to the executive offices as the ***nerve center*** of the corporation or to the ***main physical plant***.

   (b) **Compare—venue:** [§292]   For venue purposes, a corporate defendant is usually treated as a resident of every state in which it is subject to personal jurisdiction, not merely its principal place of business. (*See supra,* §125.)

   (3) **Artificial entities:** [§293]   For purposes of diversity, artificial entities created by state law ***other than*** corporations—such as ***unincorporated associations***—are viewed as citizens of ***each state in which any member is a citizen***. As a result, complete diversity is often destroyed and diversity jurisdiction is unavailable.

   (a) **Partnerships:** [§294]   A business partnership is viewed as an association for diversity purposes. Therefore, the citizenship of each partner must be considered.

1) **Limited partnerships:** [§295] In a limited partnership, in contrast to a general partnership in which the partners have full individual liability for the partnership's debts, the liability of the "limited" partners is restricted to the amount of their investment and they have negligible power to control the partnership. Nonetheless, the Supreme Court has held that the citizenships of ***all limited partners*** must be taken into account for purposes of determining complete diversity. [Carden v. Arkoma Associates, 494 U.S. 185 (1990)]

2) **Compare—professional corporation:** [§296] Some enterprises—such as law firms—that formerly operated as partnerships now operate as "professional corporations" (mainly for tax reasons). Because the "shareholder" attorneys in such corporations remain individually liable for legal malpractice, arguably their citizenship should be considered for purposes of determining complete diversity. Lower federal courts have held, though, that only the citizenship of the professional corporation should be considered. [*See, e.g.,* Coté v. Wadel, 796 F.2d 981 (7th Cir. 1986)]

(b) **Labor unions:** [§297] The Supreme Court has held that unions are unincorporated associations for purposes of diversity jurisdiction. [United Steel Workers v. R.H. Bouligny, Inc., 382 U.S. 145 (1965)]

(c) **Contrast—business trusts:** [§298] A business trust involves investments by "shareholders" who entrust their investments to trustees who control the activities of the trust. State law may give the trustees power to sue and be sued as individuals in their capacity as trustees in connection with trust affairs. When state law does so, and the trustees sue or are sued in their own right, their citizenship and not that of nonparty shareholders is to be considered in determining the existence of diversity in an action involving the trust. [Navarro Savings Association v. Lee, 446 U.S. 458 (1980)]

(4) **Permanent resident aliens:** [§299] 28 U.S.C. section 1332(a) provides that aliens admitted to the United States for permanent residence shall be deemed citizens of the states in which they are domiciled for purposes of determining diversity. Cases between resident aliens and citizens of the states in which they reside, therefore, are not within the alienage diversity jurisdiction provided by statute.

(a) **Compare—aliens generally:** [§300] Otherwise, the only persons who can become citizens of a state are United States nationals. Thus, an alien in this country for an extended stay would still be an alien for purposes of diversity jurisdiction.

(5) **Class actions:** [§301] In a class action, only the citizenship of the named representatives is considered in determining diversity. [Supreme Tribe of Ben Hur v. Cauble, 244 U.S. 356 (1921)]

(6) **Fictitious defendants**

 (a) **Removed cases:** [§302] As amended in 1988, the removal statute provides that the citizenship of fictitious defendants shall be *disregarded* in determining whether diversity jurisdiction exists, thus permitting removal despite the presence of fictitious defendants. Prior to that amendment, the presence of fictitious defendants had presented substantial difficulties, particularly in California. [*See* Bryant v. Ford Motor Co., 832 F.2d 1080 (9th Cir. 1987)—court directed that cases involving fictitious defendants be denied removal on diversity grounds until fictitious defendants are dismissed]

 (b) **Cases originally filed in federal court:** [§303] The 1988 amendment did not apply explicitly to cases originally filed in federal court in which fictitious defendants are named. Before 1988, a number of courts had held that such cases did not come within diversity jurisdiction because of uncertainty about the identity (and citizenship) of the fictitious defendants. [*See, e.g.,* Othman v. Globe Indemnity Co., 759 F.2d 1458 (9th Cir. 1985)] The treatment of these cases after the amendment is *uncertain*.

(7) **Executors, guardians, and trustees:** [§304] Under 28 U.S.C. section 1332(c)(2), the legal representative of an estate or of an infant or incompetent is deemed to be a citizen of the same state as the decedent, infant, or incompetent.

d. **Time for determination:** [§305] Diversity need only exist at the *commencement* of the action.

 (1) **Change before filing:** [§306] It is immaterial that the parties had the same citizenship when the claim arose, and a party may even move to another state to create diversity, as long as there is a genuine change of citizenship.

 (2) **Change after filing:** [§307] Similarly, a change in either party's citizenship after the filing of the suit does not deprive the court of jurisdiction.

 (3) **Removal:** [§308] Where an action is removed to federal court from state court, diversity must exist at the time of *filing of the suit* and on the date of *filing of the notice of removal*.

 (4) **Substituted party:** [§309] The post-filing substitution of a nondiverse assignee of part of a diverse plaintiff's claim pursuant to Fed. R. Civ. P. 25(c) (governing substitution of parties) does not defeat diversity jurisdiction. Diversity "is assessed at the time the action is filed." [Freeport-McMoRan, Inc. v. KN Energy, Inc., 498 U.S. 426 (1991)]

e. **Realigning parties:** [§310] In determining diversity, the court will look to the *real interests* of the parties and may realign them (as plaintiffs or defendants) according to such interests. In general, the court will look to the *ultimate interests* of the parties in realigning them.

(1) **Shareholders' derivative actions:** [§311] In a shareholder derivative action, the corporation, even though nominally joined as a plaintiff, is likely to be realigned as a defendant for diversity purposes if (as is usually the case) it is controlled by persons antagonistic to the shareholder-plaintiff. [Smith v. Sperling, 354 U.S. 91 (1957)]

f. **Efforts to create diversity:** [§312] 28 U.S.C. section 1359 provides that there shall be no jurisdiction when a person has collusively or improperly been made a party or joined in order to invoke federal jurisdiction.

(1) **Assignment of claim:** [§313] When a claim is assigned to establish diversity, or assigned without significant consideration, the assignment will not create diversity if diversity would not exist had the action been brought in the name of the assignor. [Kramer v. Caribbean Mills, Inc., 394 U.S. 823 (1969)] However, if substantial consideration is given for the assignment, jurisdiction exists even though there would be no diversity between the assignor and the defendant.

(2) **Appointment of executor:** [§314] Appointment of an out-of state executor will not create diversity, because the executor is deemed to be a citizen of the decedent's state. (*See supra*, §304.)

(3) **Compare—change of citizenship:** [§315] A genuine change of citizenship can create diversity. (*See supra*, §306.)

g. **Efforts to defeat diversity:** [§316] There is no similar statute forbidding efforts to defeat diversity, and plaintiffs have some latitude in doing so.

(1) **Joinder of nondiverse defendants:** [§317] Often the plaintiff may add claims against nondiverse defendants and thereby defeat diversity.

(a) **Limitation—valid claims:** [§318] The plaintiff must have a valid claim against the nondiverse defendant or the presence of this defendant will be disregarded in making the diversity determination.

(b) **Limitation—alternative grounds for federal jurisdiction:** [§319] Removal may be possible if nondiverse defendants are sued if federal jurisdiction can be justified on some other basis, such as federal question jurisdiction.

(2) **Appointment of nondiverse representative:** [§320] The appointment of a nondiverse executor or administrator cannot defeat diversity because the citizenship of such persons is deemed to be the same as that of the decedent. (*See supra*, §304.)

h. **Effect of lack of diversity**

(1) **Dismissal of nondiverse party:** [§321] The plaintiff often can solve the lack of diversity problem by dismissing the nondiverse party. [Newman-Green, Inc. v. Alfonzo-Larrain, 490 U.S. 826 (1989)]

(2) **Necessary party:** [§322] Where the nondiverse party is a necessary party, the plaintiff may be unable to proceed in federal court. (*See infra*,

§967—discussing decision whether to proceed with action in absence of necessary party.)

(3) **Other grounds for federal jurisdiction:** [§323] Remember to consider other grounds for federal jurisdiction if diversity is absent. For example, if a federal question is presented the case may proceed in federal court even though there is no diversity.

i. **Jurisdictional amount:** [§324] From the outset, the diversity statute limited federal jurisdiction to cases in which more than a certain *minimum amount* was *"in controversy."* Currently, diversity jurisdiction is limited to cases involving *more than $50,000.*

(1) **Rationale:** The monetary limitation seeks to ensure that only "substantial" cases will be brought in federal court.

(2) **Time for computing:** [§325] The amount is computed as of the *date of commencement* of the action. Subsequent events (*e.g.,* part payment) do not defeat jurisdiction.

(3) **Legal certainty test:** [§326] The jurisdictional amount requirement is satisfied unless the plaintiff's complaint shows to a "legal certainty" that she could not recover *more* than the minimum amount. [St. Paul Mercury Indemnity Co. v. Red Cab Co., 303 U.S. 283 (1938)]

(a) **No need to itemize damages:** [§327] The plaintiff ordinarily need not indicate in the complaint how she arrived at the amount of damages claimed.

1) **Compare—disclosure:** Rule 26(a)(1), added in 1993 and applicable only in some districts, requires a claimant to make initial disclosures, including a computation of any category of damages claimed. (*See infra,* §1192.)

(b) **Good faith limitation:** [§328] The claim for damages set forth in the complaint is determinative if made in good faith—*i.e.,* there must be some *legal possibility* of recovering the minimum amount.

1) **Removed cases:** [§329] Determination of the amount in controversy may be less strict in removed actions, since the plaintiff would presumably have no incentive to inflate her claim to satisfy federal jurisdictional requirements when filing in state court.

(c) **Effect of judgment for lesser amount:** [§330] The fact that the actual recovery does not exceed the jurisdictional amount does not affect the jurisdiction of the court, as long as the claim was made in good faith. The court may, however, deny the plaintiff costs of suit or impose them on the plaintiff. [28 U.S.C. §1332(b)] This power is rarely used.

(d) **Valuing claims for nonmonetary relief:** [§331] The courts are split on whether the relief should be valued from the *plaintiff's perspective* (value to plaintiff) or the ***defendant's perspective*** (cost to defendant) in the minority of cases in which the values would differ.

1) **Example of plaintiff's perspective:** Plaintiff sued to restrain defendant from erecting poles and wires in a way that would injure plaintiff's poles and wires. Although the cost to defendant of changing its operation would be less than the jurisdictional amount, the Supreme Court upheld jurisdiction because the value to plaintiff would exceed that amount. [Glenwood Light & Water Co. v. Mutual Light, Heat & Power Co., 239 U.S. 121 (1915)]

2) **Example of defendant's perspective:** Plaintiffs sued a railroad to quiet title to water rights that were worth far less than the jurisdictional amount to plaintiffs, but a good deal more to defendant, and the court upheld jurisdiction. [Ronzio v. Denver & Rio Grande Railroad, 116 F.2d 604 (10th Cir. 1940)]

(e) **Valuing claims for declaratory relief:** [§332] In declaratory relief actions where the plaintiff seeks a determination that he is not liable to the defendant, the amount in controversy is the amount of the claim that would be asserted by the declaratory relief defendant against the declaratory relief plaintiff. With other sorts of declaratory claims (*e.g.*, that plaintiff may continue a course of conduct defendant claims is illegal), the analysis should resemble that for nonmonetary relief.

(f) **Interest and costs:** [§333] Interest and costs are *excluded*. However, attorneys' fees that are recoverable by contract or by statute are considered part of the matter in controversy, rather than as costs, and are included.

(4) **Aggregation of claims to satisfy requirement:** [§334] Whether separate claims for less than the jurisdictional amount can be aggregated to satisfy the jurisdictional requirement depends on a number of factors.

(a) **Claims of single plaintiff against single defendant:** [§335] *All claims* of the plaintiff against the defendant, whether or not related, *can be aggregated* to meet the minimum.

(b) **Claims of single plaintiff against several defendants:** [§336] Only claims for which all defendants are *jointly liable* to the plaintiff may be combined. "Joint liability" is defined narrowly for this purpose; claims arising from closely related conduct do not satisfy the test. "Joint" liability would arise in a few situations such as co-owners of property, but ***not joint tortfeasors***.

1) **Note:** When the plaintiff alleges that the defendants inflicted separate harms on her as part of a conspiracy, allegations of conspiracy may make defendants jointly liable and therefore ***permit aggregation*** of amounts.

(c) **Claims of several plaintiffs against single defendant:** [§337] The claims of multiple plaintiffs can be aggregated only if they have a ***common undivided ownership interest*** in such claims.

(d) **Counterclaims:** [§338]   In general, the amount sought on a counterclaim cannot be aggregated with a plaintiff's small claim to satisfy the jurisdictional minimum.

   1) **Note:** A 1961 Supreme Court case [Horton v. Liberty Mutual Insurance Co., 367 U.S. 348 (1961)] appears to look to the counterclaim as the basis for jurisdiction in a case involving Texas workers' compensation. It is regarded by many as limited to its quite unusual facts.

   2) **Compare—jurisdiction over counterclaim where plaintiff has satisfied minimum:** [§339]   When the defendant's counterclaim arises out of the same transaction and is therefore *compulsory* (*see infra*, §813), it need *not* satisfy the jurisdictional minimum requirement because it is clearly within the supplemental jurisdiction of the court (*see infra*, §§400-404). With a *permissive* counterclaim (*see infra*, §812), however, there must be an *independent jurisdictional basis* and the jurisdictional minimum requirement must therefore be satisfied.

j. **Exceptions to exercise of diversity jurisdiction:** [§340]   Although the diversity statute does not limit the subject matter of cases brought in federal court, the courts decline to exercise jurisdiction in some types of cases.

   (1) **Domestic relations:** [§341]   As a matter of long-standing statutory construction, there is an exception to diversity jurisdiction that prohibits issuance by a federal court of divorce, alimony, or child custody decrees. However, the exception does not permit a federal district court to refuse to exercise diversity jurisdiction over a tort action for damages, even when the claims are brought by one divorced parent on behalf of children allegedly abused by the other parent. [Ankenbrandt v. Richards, 112 S. Ct. 2206 (1992)]

   (2) **Probate proceedings:** [§342]   Federal courts will not take jurisdiction over proceedings maintainable in probate courts, but will take jurisdiction over actions by and against fiduciaries maintainable in state courts of general jurisdiction.

   (3) **Local actions:** [§343]   Some federal courts treat the rule that actions regarding title to real property should be litigated at the location of the property (*supra*, §150) as limiting the subject matter jurisdiction of courts to entertain such actions elsewhere. [*See, e.g.,* Hayes v. Gulf Oil Corp., 821 F.2d 285 (5th Cir. 1987)—"federal and state courts lack jurisdiction over the subject matter of claims to land located outside the state in which the court sits"]

k. **Proposals to repeal diversity statute:** [§344]   For some time, there have been calls for the repeal of the diversity statute. Proponents of this move argue that any residue of prejudice against outsiders in the late 20th century is insufficient to justify imposing the burden of deciding diversity cases on the federal courts. Those who favor retaining diversity jurisdiction urge that prejudice does persist, and that it is important to preserve options for litigants. It is impossible to forecast the future of this debate.

(1) **Complex litigation:** [§345] Whatever the future of diversity jurisdiction generally, there is also sentiment favoring expanding it to cope with the demands of repeated litigation of related matters.

(2) **Increase in jurisdictional minimum:** [§346] The jurisdictional minimum was increased to $50,000 in 1988, in part as a result of a compromise of the debate over the continued existence of diversity jurisdiction.

C. FEDERAL QUESTION JURISDICTION

1. **Constitutional Grant**

   a. **Constitutional provisions:** [§347] Article III, Section 2 of the Constitution provides that federal judicial power shall extend to:

      (1) Cases in law and equity ***arising under the Constitution, the laws of the United States, and treaties*** (this is the major area of federal question jurisdiction);

      (2) Cases affecting ***ambassadors, consuls,*** etc.;

      (3) Cases involving ***admiralty*** and maritime jurisdiction; and

      (4) Cases to which the ***United States is a party***.

   b. **Broad view of federal question power:** [§348] In 1824 the Supreme Court upheld a statute that it read to grant federal courts jurisdiction over any case to which the Bank of the United States (a private bank created by Congress) was a party. It found this acceptable because, even if the suit were about a state law debt, the bank was a federal creation, and in every case there would be a question about whether it could legally sue—a federal question. The fact that this question would not be important after it was resolved did not bother the Court: "The question forms an original ingredient in every cause. Whether it be in fact relied on or not, in the defense, it is still a part of the cause, and may be relied upon [to uphold federal question jurisdiction]." [Osborn v. Bank of the United States, 22 U.S. 738 (1824)]

      (1) **Criticism:** Some have criticized this broad view of federal question power as including too many cases in which the background federal question would not really be a viable question in the case at all. Thus, it is suggested that under the broad view of *Osborn,* all land disputes in western states could be heard in federal court on the ground that the land was originally the subject of a federal land grant even though that fact had nothing to do with the dispute between the parties. Nevertheless, the *Osborn* holding stands and permits Congress to define federal question jurisdiction extremely broadly, which the courts have concluded it has ***not*** done in the ***general*** federal question statute.

      (2) **Compare—special federal question statutes:** [§349] The Supreme Court has, however, found such broad definition in some *special* "federal question" jurisdiction statutes such as the Foreign Sovereign Immunities Act, 28 U.S.C. section 1330 [Verlinden B.V. v. Central Bank of Nigeria,

461 U.S. 480 (1983)—congressional regulation of foreign sovereigns' immunity permits federal jurisdiction over alien's suit against foreign government entity even without any federal cause of action], and the federal statute chartering the American National Red Cross, 36 U.S.C. section 2 [American National Red Cross v. S.G., 112 S. Ct. 2465 (1992)—chartering statute's language confers original jurisdiction over suits involving the Red Cross, a private but federally chartered corporation, even in cases involving state law claims].

 c. **Claim based on federal substantive law:** [§350] It may be that (except where a federal creation such as the Bank of the United States is involved, *see supra*) Congress can assign to the federal courts jurisdiction over claims it creates only by promulgating or providing for a body of federal substantive law to govern the claims or delegating authority to create such substantive law to the courts.

  (1) **Example—Labor Management Relations Act:** In the Labor Management Relations Act, Congress granted the federal courts jurisdiction over suits to enforce collective bargaining agreements between employers and unions. The Court found this grant of jurisdiction valid despite lack of diversity, stressing the need for national uniformity in enforcement of such agreements and concluding that "the legislation does more than confer jurisdiction in the federal courts" because "the substantive law to apply in suits under [the Act] is federal law, which the courts must fashion from the policy of our national labor laws." [Textile Workers Union v. Lincoln Mills, 353 U.S. 448 (1957)]

2. **Federal Question Statute**

 a. **Introduction:** [§351] Congress did not grant general federal question jurisdiction to the lower federal courts (except for a brief period) until 1875, when it passed the predecessor to 28 U.S.C. section 1331, which used language very similar to that in the Constitution: "all civil actions arising under the Constitution, laws, or treaties of the United States."

  (1) **Statute interpreted more narrowly than Constitution:** [§352] Despite the similarity between the language of the statute and the Constitution, the Supreme Court has interpreted the statute more narrowly; the remainder of this section, therefore, examines the ways in which the Court has limited the reach of the statute.

  (2) **State court jurisdiction over cases raising federal questions:** [§353] Until 1875, the only courts in which federal question cases could usually be litigated, absent diversity of citizenship, were state courts. Note that as to most federal question issues, jurisdiction in such cases is now ***concurrent*** between the state and federal courts. (*See supra,* §§266-271.)

  (3) **Compare—Supreme Court jurisdiction to review state court decisions of federal questions:** [§354] Often, when the lower federal courts do not have jurisdiction under the federal question statute, the Supreme Court has jurisdiction to review decisions of state courts involving federal law issues. [*See* 28 U.S.C. §1257]

b. **Standards for determining whether a federal question is raised:** [§355] The Supreme Court's decisions under the federal question statute are sometimes difficult to reconcile, but look to two basic possibilities:

   (1) **Federal law creates claim:** [§356] There is generally no problem when federal law creates the claim sued upon. As Justice Holmes put it, "a suit arises under the law that creates the cause of action." [American Well Works Co. v. Layne & Bower Co., 241 U.S. 257 (1916)]

   (a) **Test underinclusive:** [§357] The Court has since recognized that this description is "more useful for describing the vast majority of cases that come within the district courts' original jurisdiction" than for distinguishing among cases in which jurisdiction is doubtful. [Franchise Tax Board v. Construction Laborers' Vacation Trust, 463 U.S. 1 (1983)]

   (b) **Implied claims:** [§358] Note that federal claims include claims implied by the courts in addition to private rights of action explicitly created by Congress. [See, e.g., J.I. Case Co. v. Borak, 377 U.S. 426 (1964)—implied private right of action for violation of Federal Securities Exchange Act of 1934] The Court has recently taken a cautious attitude toward implying causes of action. (For details on implied claims, see Federal Courts Summary.)

   (2) **Nonfederal claim that turns on construction of federal law:** [§359] This area presents the harder problems of application of the federal question statute. The Supreme Court has confirmed that federal question jurisdiction can be proper "where the vindication of a right under state law necessarily turned on some construction of federal law." [Merrell Dow Pharmaceuticals, Inc. v. Thompson, 478 U.S. 804 (1986)]

   (a) **Example:** A shareholder sued to enjoin a corporation in which he held stock from purchasing bonds issued by federal land banks. The shareholder asserted that under state law the corporation was forbidden to invest in bonds that were not legally issued. The only issue in the case was whether the bonds were validly issued under federal law, and the Supreme Court held that there was federal question jurisdiction. [Smith v. Kansas City Title & Trust Co., 255 U.S. 180 (1921)]

   (b) **Compare:** A railroad employee sued his employer for injuries sustained on the job, which he alleged were caused by a defective uncoupling lever that did not comply with federal standards for safety equipment. The Supreme Court held that the fact the alleged violation of the federal standard was an element of the state law tort claim did not fundamentally change the state law nature of the action and that jurisdiction was absent. [Moore v. Chesapeake & Ohio Railway, 291 U.S. 205 (1934)]

   (c) **Absence of implied federal claim:** [§360] In *Merrell Dow Pharmaceuticals, Inc. v. Thompson, supra,* the Court held that there was no federal question jurisdiction over a state tort claim for negligent manufacture of a drug, although the claim relied on the defendant's alleged violation of the Federal Food, Drug, and Cosmetic Act

("FDCA"). The parties agreed that there was no implied federal cause of action, and the Court reasoned that in that circumstance it would "flout" the will of Congress to allow federal jurisdiction over a state law claim turning on violation of the FDCA.

(d) **Substantial bearing on outcome:** [§361] Where federal law is an element of a state law claim, it suffices to support federal question jurisdiction only where it is important to the outcome of the case: "The right or immunity must be such that it will be supported if the Constitution or laws of the United States are given one construction or effect, and defeated if they receive another." [Gully v. First National Bank, 299 U.S. 109 (1936)]

1) **Compare—constitutional power:** Under *Osborn v. Bank of the United States, supra,* the unimportance of the question to the dispute before the court may not matter. (*See supra,* §348.)

(e) **Nature of federal interest:** [§362] In *Merrell Dow Pharmaceuticals, Inc. v. Thompson, supra,* the Court suggested that it would be helpful to focus on the nature of the federal issues at stake.

1) **Examples:** The Court suggested that this approach could reconcile the results in the *Moore* and *Smith* cases, *supra*. In *Smith,* jurisdiction was proper because the validity of an act of Congress was directly drawn into question, and there was a substantial federal interest in this question. On the other hand, in *Moore* the federal issue related to the employer's compliance at one place and time with one federal safety standard, and there was little federal interest in this isolated incident.

2) **Split over interpretation of *Merrell Dow*:** [§363] There is debate in the lower federal courts over whether an implied federal right of action is *necessary* for federal question jurisdiction over a state claim under *Merrell Dow,* or whether the federal interest could in other ways have the nature and importance seemingly required by the opinion. [Smith v. Industrial Valley Title Insurance Co., 957 F.2d 90 (3d Cir.), *cert. denied,* 112 S. Ct. 3034 (1992)]

c. **Well-pleaded complaint rule:** [§364] The plaintiff's federal question must appear in the properly pleaded allegations of his complaint.

(1) **Proper pleading:** [§365] When the plaintiff is not relying on a claim created by federal law (*see supra,* §356), the inclusion of references to federal law must be *required* by the rules of proper pleading and by the underlying substantive law.

(2) **Rationale:** The rule permits reliable early determinations of whether the federal court has jurisdiction, so this issue is not left to turn on later developments.

(3) **Anticipation of defense insufficient:** [§366] An allegation anticipating a defense based on federal law is not sufficient to raise a federal question.

(a) **Example:** Plaintiffs sued a railroad, alleging that it had agreed to provide them lifetime passes to settle a personal injury claim, but reneged on the basis of a federal statute forbidding such passes. Plaintiffs sought a determination that the statute was not intended to apply to them, or that it unconstitutionally deprived them of property if applied to them. The Supreme Court dismissed because plaintiffs' allegations regarding the federal statute merely anticipated a defense that the railroad would have to plead and prove. [Louisville & Nashville Railroad v. Mottley, *supra,* §260]

(b) **Rationale:** There is no way to be certain what defenses will be raised in a defendant's answer, and it, therefore, would not be possible to determine whether a case actually involved a federal question if potential defenses could be considered.

(c) **Criticism:** At least in removed cases where the defendant has filed its answer raising a federal defense, that should suffice to justify federal jurisdiction.

(d) **Preemption:** [§367] Ordinarily preemption is a defense, and the possibility that federal law preempts a state law claim does not provide a basis for federal question jurisdiction. However, Congress may so completely preempt a particular area that even a state law claim in that area is necessarily federal in character, and there is federal jurisdiction. [Metropolitan Life Insurance Co. v. Taylor, 481 U.S. 58 (1987)—state law "displaced" by Employee Retirement Security Act; Avco Corp. v. Machinists, 390 U.S. 557 (1968)—state law disputes between employers and employees displaced by §301 of Labor Management Relations Act]

(4) **Declaratory judgment:** [§368] In an action for a declaratory judgment, the court is to ask what the well-pleaded complaint would have looked like in a "coercive" action (one for an injunction or damages) and determine whether the complaint in such an action would have raised a federal question. [Skelly Oil Co. v. Phillips Petroleum Co., 339 U.S. 667 (1950)] Doing so *may*, but need *not*, involve looking to the *coercive complaint* the *defendant* would have brought had the defendant sued; the court looks to whatever would likely have been the complaint in a coercive action.

(5) **Plaintiff's election not to assert federal claim:** [§369] In general, the plaintiff may elect not to assert a valid federal claim and thereby avoid otherwise available federal question jurisdiction.

(a) **Rationale:** The plaintiff is the master of her complaint and is not compelled to assert claims she chooses not to assert.

(b) **Limitation:** In some cases, the courts may disregard such a choice and conclude that the state law claims are "federal in nature." In *Federated Department Stores, Inc. v. Moite,* 452 U.S. 394 (1981), the Court held that state court suits making claims under state antitrust law were removable because the courts would not "permit plaintiff to use artful pleading to close off defendant's right to a federal forum." The reach of this notion is difficult to determine.

    (6) **Compare—Supreme Court jurisdiction:** [§370] Federal issues that would not provide a basis for original federal question jurisdiction because they are defenses still do provide a basis for review by the Supreme Court. [28 U.S.C. §1257; *see* Louisville & Nashville Railroad v. Mottley, 219 U.S. 467 (1911)—Court reaches the Mottley's federal arguments (*compare supra,* §366) on merits on appeal from state court judgment]

  d. **Plausible assertion of federal right sufficient:** [§371] A federal claim or question is sufficient to vest the court with jurisdiction unless it "clearly appears to be immaterial or made solely for the purpose of obtaining jurisdiction, or where the claim is wholly insubstantial and frivolous." [Bell v. Hood, 327 U.S. 678 (1946)]

    (1) **Rationale:** Deciding whether the plaintiff has stated a valid claim involves a judgment about the merits.

    (2) **Dismissal on pleadings:** [§372] A dismissal for failure to state a claim is a decision about the merits and therefore not a decision that the court lacks jurisdiction.

    (3) **Example:** In *Merrell Dow Pharmaceuticals, Inc. v. Thompson, supra,* §362, the Supreme Court accepted the parties' concession that the FDCA did not give rise to an implied federal claim and, therefore, provided no basis for exercise of federal question jurisdiction. Yet when other plaintiffs sued, contending that the FDCA gave rise to implied claims, those were held sufficient to support federal question jurisdiction: "Until this court or the Supreme Court holds that there is no implied private right of action under the FDCA, the opposite position cannot be deemed either frivolous or insubstantial." [*In re* Bendectin Litigation, 857 F.2d 290 (6th Cir. 1988)]

    (4) **Significance**

      (a) **Res judicata:** [§373] If the court finds that the plaintiff has not stated a federal claim, that decision on the merits acts as res judicata. (*See infra,* §2055 for discussion of res judicata.)

      (b) **Supplemental jurisdiction:** [§374] Because the court has jurisdiction over the federal claim even if it finds that it lacks merit, it may exercise supplemental jurisdiction over related state law claims. Because state law claims should usually be dismissed as a matter of discretion if the federal claims are dismissed early in the action (*see infra,* §419), this possibility is rarely important.

  e. **Jurisdictional amount:** [§375] Where the court's federal question jurisdiction is properly invoked, there is **no minimum amount in controversy requirement** (except in a few minor categories of cases). Note that until 1980, the federal question statute contained an amount in controversy requirement.

D. SUPPLEMENTAL JURISDICTION

1. **Introduction:** [§376] From an early date, the Supreme Court recognized that federal question jurisdiction could not be limited to decision of federal issues presented in a case.

   a. **Power to decide all issues in case:** [§377] In 1824, the Court confirmed the a lower court exercising federal question jurisdiction could decide all issues in a case, not just the federal questions. [Osborn v. Bank of the United States, *supra*, §361] While jurisdiction may exist *because* of a federal claim, the jurisdiction is over *cases*, not *issues*.

   b. **Decision based on state law alone:** [§378] Federal courts exercising federal question jurisdiction can rest a decision entirely on issues of state law, without reaching issues of federal law. Where federal constitutional issues are raised, this is often the preferable approach, because it is said that courts should try to avoid unnecessary decision of matters of constitutional law. [Siler v. Louisville & Nashville Railroad, 213 U.S. 175 (1909)]

   c. **Relation to supplemental jurisdiction:** [§379] The basis for this reasoning was that the federal courts had jurisdiction over "*a whole case*, as expressed by the constitution." [Osborn v. Bank of the United States, *supra*] As joinder of claims and parties relaxed, the concept of the scope of the "constitutional case" expanded to encompass claims based on state law and claims against additional parties.

   d. **Rationale:** The goal of supplemental jurisdiction is to *promote judicial economy and consistency of decision* by removing obstacles to having all related controversies decided in one proceeding. As the Supreme Court put it, "[u]nder the [Federal] Rules [of Civil Procedure], the impulse is toward entertaining the broadest possible scope of action consistent with fairness to the parties." [United Mine Workers v. Gibbs, 383 U.S. 715 (1966)]

2. **Background of Supplemental Jurisdiction—Pendent and Ancillary Jurisdiction:** [§380] Supplemental jurisdiction, provided by statute in 1990, must be understood against the background of the preexisting doctrines of pendent and ancillary jurisdiction, which had developed in court decisions over several decades. (*Note:* Instructors have different preferences concerning the attention to be devoted to these topics. Your instructor might not emphasize these preexisting doctrines. In that case, you may find it best to skip from this point to §398, where discussion of the supplemental jurisdiction statute begins.)

   a. **Ancillary jurisdiction:** [§381] The doctrine of ancillary jurisdiction originated in cases where the federal court controlled property claimed by a litigant properly before the court. In such cases, ancillary jurisdiction allowed the court to entertain claims of others to the property even though the court had no independent basis for jurisdiction over those claims. [Freeman v. Howe, 65 U.S. 450 (1860)] Thereafter, the doctrine was expanded. Generally, ancillary jurisdiction involved assertion of a claim by a *party other than the plaintiff* that was related to the claim made by the plaintiff. The operation of ancillary jurisdiction is best understood from an examination of the various contexts in which it arose:

(1) **Counterclaims:** [§382] A counterclaim by a defendant arising from the same transaction as the plaintiff's claim fell within the ancillary jurisdiction of the court. Note that under Federal Rule 13(a), such a counterclaim is compulsory, meaning that it would be barred by res judicata unless asserted. *Compare:* For a permissive counterclaim [Fed. R. Civ. P. 13(b)], it was necessary that there be an independent basis for federal jurisdiction.

(2) **Third-party practice—impleader:** [§383] Federal Rule 14 permits the defendant to assert a claim against another person not originally a party (called the third-party defendant) to the action, seeking indemnity in whole or in part for the claim the plaintiff has asserted against the defendant. There was ancillary jurisdiction over the third-party claim.

   (a) **Compare—claim by plaintiff against third-party defendant:** [§384] If the plaintiff asserted a claim against the third-party defendant in a diversity case, however, there had to be an *independent basis for federal jurisdiction over that claim.*

   1) **Example:** Plaintiff sued a power district for causing the death of her husband when a crane hit a high tension wire. The power district impleaded the operator of the crane and later obtained summary judgment against plaintiff's claim. Plaintiff amended her complaint to assert a claim against the operator of the crane, but there was no diversity between plaintiff and the third-party defendant. The Supreme Court held that there was no jurisdiction over plaintiff's claim against the third-party defendant. [Owen Equipment & Erection Co. v. Kroger, 437 U.S. 365 (1978)] *Rationale:* If ancillary jurisdiction were permitted in such cases, plaintiff could circumvent the requirement of complete diversity by suing only diverse potential defendants and waiting for them to implead other nondiverse, potentially responsible, parties.

   (b) **Contrast—claim by third-party defendant against plaintiff:** [§385] A number of cases held that there is ancillary jurisdiction over a claim by the third-party defendant against the plaintiff. [*See, e.g.,* Revere Copper & Brass, Inc. v. Aetna Casualty & Surety Co., 426 F.2d 709 (5th Cir. 1970)]

   1) **Compulsory counterclaim by plaintiff:** [§386] If the third-party defendant filed a claim against the plaintiff, and the plaintiff had a counterclaim arising out of the same events from which the defendant's claim arose, the counterclaim would have been within the court's ancillary jurisdiction because it would be compulsory. (*See supra,* §382.)

(3) **Cross-claims:** [§387] Federal Rule 13(g) allows one defendant to assert a cross-claim against another defendant if it arises out of the transaction sued upon by the plaintiff. Because of the relation to the original claim filed by the plaintiff, there was ancillary jurisdiction over the cross-claim. [LASA per L'Industria v. Alexander, 414 F.2d 143 (6th Cir. 1969)]

(4) **Intervention:** [§388]   Federal Rule 24 allows persons who claim an interest in the litigation to intervene and become either plaintiffs or defendants in the suit. When they could intervene *of right* because of the inevitable effect of the litigation on their rights or because the present parties would otherwise be subjected to the risk of inconsistent judgments (*see infra,* §§1011 *et seq.*), **ancillary jurisdiction** covered their participation.

   (a) **Compare:** When intervention was merely *permissive,* an independent jurisdictional basis was required.

(5) **Necessary parties:** [§389]   Under Federal Rule 19, certain nonparties are considered "necessary parties" because their rights are implicated in the action or because the present parties run the risk of inconsistent or multiple liabilities if they are not joined. (*See infra,* §§1011 *et seq.*) As to such parties, an ***independent basis*** for jurisdiction is required. If there is no independent basis for jurisdiction, the court may have to dismiss the case. [*See* Fed. R. Civ. P. 19(b)—enumerating factors that affect decision whether to dismiss when necessary party cannot be joined; *see infra,* §967]

b. **Pendent jurisdiction:** [§390]   Pendent jurisdiction developed in cases where the plaintiff had both federal and nonfederal claims against a nondiverse defendant arising from the same event. The court was said to have jurisdiction over the state law claims, which are "appended" to the federal claim. Thus, it referred to the assertion of ***nonfederal claims by the plaintiff*** that are related to the plaintiff's federal claim.

   (1) **Example:** Plaintiff copyrighted a play, revised it, and submitted both versions to defendant for possible production. When defendant did not produce the play, plaintiff sued, claiming that defendant had stolen parts of both the copyrighted and uncopyrighted versions for use in a play produced by defendant. Plaintiff asserted a federal copyright claim and two state law claims of unfair competition, one for use of the copyrighted version and the other for use of the uncopyrighted version. The Supreme Court held that there was pendent jurisdiction over the unfair competition claim relating to the copyrighted version because it "results from the same acts which constitute the infringement and is inseparable therefrom." But in a narrow ruling the Court later rejected as "unecessarily grudging," it also held that there was no jurisdiction over the unfair competition claim related to the uncopyrighted version because that claim was "independent of the claim of copyright infringement." [Hurn v. Oursler, 289 U.S. 238 (1933)]

   (2) **Example:** Plaintiff claimed that defendant union violated federal labor laws and committed the state law tort of interference with contract by pressuring customers of plaintiff not to employ his services. Both federal and state claims arose from the same series of actions by defendant's agents. The federal court could grant plaintiff judgment on the state law claims even if it decided after trial that plaintiff had not established a violation of federal law. [United Mine Workers v. Gibbs, *supra,* §379]

(3) **Pendent party jurisdiction:** [§391] If plaintiff has a claim within original federal jurisdiction against D1 and a claim not within original federal jurisdiction arising out of the same event against D2, plaintiff might seek to "append" the claim against D2 to the claim against D1. Noting that "the addition of a completely new party would run counter to the well-established principle that federal courts, as opposed to state trial courts of general jurisdiction, are courts of limited jurisdiction" [Aldinger v. Howard, 427 U.S. 1 (1976)], the Supreme Court took a limited approach to pendent party jurisdiction.

(a) **Diversity claim:** [§392] The Supreme Court refused to allow a plaintiff to assert a claim against a nondiverse, third-party defendant because allowing this maneuver would enable plaintiffs to circumvent the complete-diversity requirement. [Owen Equipment & Erection Co. v. Kroger, *supra*, §384]

(b) **Federal question claim:** [§393] Even where there was exclusive federal jurisdiction over a federal claim against one defendant, the Supreme Court held that there could be no jurisdiction over a related, nonfederal claim against a nondiverse party because "a grant of jurisdiction over claims involving particular parties does not itself confer jurisdiction over additional claims by or against different parties." [Finley v. United States, 490 U.S. 545 (1989)]

(4) **Class actions:** [§394] The handling of class actions was complicated.

(a) **Existence of diversity:** [§395] For purposes of determining whether there is complete diversity, only the citizenship of the named class representative was considered. (*See supra*, §301.)

(b) **Amount in controversy:** [§396] The Supreme Court held, however, that in a class action asserting a state law claim subject to the jurisdictional minimum, it was not sufficient that the named representatives could satisfy the amount in controversy requirement. Instead, the court must satisfy itself that *each class member has a sufficient claim,* unless the claims are legally "joint." [Zahn v. International Paper Co., 414 U.S. 291 (1973)]

(c) **Contrast—federal question class action:** In a federal question class action, ordinarily there was no ancillary jurisdiction issue since each class member would have a claim within the subject matter jurisdiction of the federal court.

c. **Lack of statutory basis:** [§397] In a 1989 decision regarding pendent party jurisdiction, the Supreme Court stressed that pendent and ancillary jurisdiction appeared to contravene the principle that

> [a]s regards all courts of the United States inferior to this tribunal, two things are necessary to create jurisdiction, whether original or appellate. The Constitution must have given to the court the capacity to take it, and an act of Congress must have supplied it . . . . To the extent that such action is not taken, the power lies dormant.

[Finley v. United States, *supra*] Although *Finley* left existing pendent *claim* precedents undisturbed, it cast doubt on all extensions of ancillary jurisdiction to claims against added *parties* without express congressional authorization.

3. **Supplemental Jurisdiction Statute:** [§398] In 1990, largely to restore the law to its pre-*Finley* state, Congress enacted the supplemental jurisdiction statute. [28 U.S.C. §1367]

    a. **Jurisdictional power to limit of Constitution:** [§399] The statute grants federal courts that have original jurisdiction over a claim supplemental jurisdiction over all other claims that form part of the same case or controversy under Article III of the Constitution. [28 U.S.C. §1367(a)] The focus of the constitutional inquiry is whether the claims sought to be added to those within federal jurisdiction are part of *one constitutional case.* [United Mine Workers v. Gibbs, *supra*, §390]

        (1) **Standard for supplemental jurisdiction in federal question cases:** [§400] In *United Mine Workers v. Gibbs, supra,* the Supreme Court articulated the following three-part test to determine whether a federal court has the power to entertain pendent claims:

            (a) **Substantial federal claim:** [§401] The federal claim must be sufficiently substantial to support federal question jurisdiction. (*See supra*, §§371 *et seq.*)

            (b) **Common nucleus of operative fact:** [§402] The federal and nonfederal claims must derive from a common nucleus of operative fact.

            (c) **One judicial proceeding:** [§403] The federal and nonfederal claims must be such that the plaintiff "would ordinarily be expected to try them in one judicial proceeding."

        (2) **Diversity cases:** [§404] The Supreme Court has suggested that the same test may apply to determine the outer constitutional limits of diversity jurisdiction. [Owen Equipment & Erection Co. v. Kroger, *supra*, §392]

            (a) **Note:** Because only minimal diversity is required by the Constitution (*see supra*, §285), as long as one defendant is diverse from one plaintiff, there is no constitutional difficulty with exercise of jurisdiction over the whole case, including nondiverse parties.

        (3) **Pendent party jurisdiction:** [§405] Section (a) of the supplemental jurisdiction statute explicitly grants supplemental jurisdiction over "claims that involve the joinder or intervention of additional parties."

        (4) **Time of decision:** [§406] "The question of [constitutional] power will ordinarily be resolved on the pleadings." [United Mine Workers v. Gibbs, *supra*]

        (5) **Contrast to original jurisdiction statutes:** [§407] Unlike the statutes granting federal question and diversity jurisdiction, which have been interpreted not to go to the constitutional limit (*see supra*, §§286, 352),

subsection (a) of the supplemental jurisdiction statute *does go* to the maximum extent allowed by the Constitution.

(6) **Mandatory exercise:** [§408] It has been held that federal courts should exercise supplementary jurisdiction granted by 28 U.S.C. section 1367(a) unless a ground for declining jurisdiction exists under 28 U.S.C. section 1367(c) (*see infra,* §§416-420). [Executive Software North America, Inc. v. District Court, 24 F.3d 1545 (9th Cir. 1994)]

b. **Exception for diversity cases:** [§409] When federal subject matter jurisdiction is founded *solely on diversity of citizenship,* supplemental jurisdiction is limited. [28 U.S.C. §1367(b)] The legislative history indicates that this was done to implement the rationale of *Owen Equipment & Erection Co. v. Kroger* (*supra,* §404).

(1) **Claims by plaintiffs:** [§410] In diversity-only cases, there is no supplemental jurisdiction over claims by *plaintiffs* against persons made parties under Rule 14 (impleader), Rule 19 (necessary party joinder), Rule 20 (permissive party joinder), or Rule 24 (intervention).

(2) **Claims by parties joined as plaintiffs:** [§411] There is no supplemental jurisdiction over claims by persons *proposed to be joined* pursuant to Rule 19 or Rule 24. *Note:* This effects a change. Formerly there was thought to be jurisdiction over claims by plaintiff intervenors of right (*see supra,* §388).

(a) **Compare—Rule 20 joinder:** [§412] The supplemental jurisdiction statute makes no reference to claims by parties to be joined permissively pursuant to Rule 20, so that such additional parties might be joined under the court's supplemental jurisdiction. [Patterson Enterprises, Inc. v. Bridgestone/Firestone, Inc., 812 F. Supp. 1152 (D. Kan. 1993)—claims that fail to satisfy amount in controversy requirement are within supplemental jurisdiction in diversity case]

1) **Criticism:** Such a reading of the statute goes far toward abolishing the complete-diversity rule, and is contrary to the intent of *Owen Equipment & Erection Co. v. Kroger, supra,* to preclude devices by which plaintiffs could evade the jurisdictional requirements of the diversity statute.

(b) **Compare—class actions:** [§413] The legislative history states that the statute is not intended to affect the requirement in most state law class actions that each class member satisfy the amount in controversy requirement. (*See supra,* §395.) However, since section 1367(b) nowhere limits the use of supplemental jurisdiction under Rule 23 (class actions), and such claims could constitutionally be appended to the jurisdictionally sufficient claims of other members, the statute might not preserve this rule. [*See* Packard v. Provident National Bank, 994 F.2d 1039 (3d Cir. 1993)—discussing disagreement in cases about treatment of class actions]

(c) **Compare—compulsory counterclaims by plaintiff:** [§414] Under prior law (*see supra,* §385), there would be ancillary jurisdiction over a compulsory counterclaim by plaintiff against a third-party defendant in a diversity case. [Evra Corp. v. Swiss Bank Corp., 673 F.2d 951 (7th Cir.), *cert. denied,* 459 U.S. 1017 (1982)] It is ***unclear*** whether this rule survives the supplemental jurisdiction statute's prohibition of jurisdiction over "claims by plaintiffs" against such parties, although the legislative history's expression of intent to preserve most prior case law suggests that this form of supplemental jurisdiction may survive.

(3) **Inconsistent with jurisdictional requirements of section 1332:** [§415] The above limitations on supplemental jurisdiction apply only insofar as exercising jurisdiction "would be inconsistent with the jurisdictional requirements of section 1332." This may allow an argument that in some instances claims by plaintiffs against parties joined under Rules 14, 19, 20, or 24, and joinder of parties as plaintiffs under Rules 19 or 24 could be entertained.

(a) **Possible example:** Pre-*Finley* case law allowing ancillary jurisdiction over plaintiff's compulsory counterclaim against a third-party defendant in a diversity case (*see supra,* §386) could support an argument that despite section 1367(b)'s apparent ban on supplemental jurisdiction over some types of claims by diversity plaintiffs, such jurisdiction over the counterclaim would be permissible because exercising it would ***not*** be "inconsistent with the jurisdictional requirements of section 1332."

c. **Discretionary decline of jurisdiction:** [§416] The statute explicitly authorizes district courts to decline jurisdiction in certain circumstances that largely implement discretionary factors identified in *United Mine Workers v. Gibbs, supra,* §§400-403). [28 U.S.C. §1367(c)]

(1) **Novel or complex issue of state law:** [§417] If the law to be applied to the nonfederal claim is uncertain, the district court may decline to entertain that claim so that the parties can get a "surer-footed reading of applicable law" from a state court. [§1367(c)(1); United Mine Workers v. Gibbs, *supra*]

(2) **Nonfederal claim substantially predominates:** [§418] The federal court may conclude that the nonfederal claim is the real body of the case. [28 U.S.C. §1367(c)(2)] The court should not "tolerate a litigant's effort to impose upon it what is in effect only a state law case." [United Mine Workers v. Gibbs, *supra*]

(3) **All original jurisdiction claims dismissed:** [§419] If all claims over which the federal court had original jurisdiction are dismissed, the court may dismiss the nonfederal claims. [28 U.S.C. §1367(c)(3)] In deciding whether to do so, the court should consider the ***amount of time invested in the case by the court.***

(4) **Extraordinary circumstances:** [§420] The federal court may also decline to exercise supplementary jurisdiction in extraordinary circumstances if there are "*other compelling reasons for declining jurisdiction.*" [28 U.S.C. §1367(c)(4)]

(a) **Compare—complication of case:** [§421]   In *United Mine Workers v. Gibbs, supra*, the Supreme Court said that complication of the case in federal court would justify refusal to entertain the nonfederal claims. It has been held that this ground for decline of jurisdiction was limited by the statute to instances in which the district court finds that "exceptional circumstances" exist in the case and that these provide "compelling reasons" for decline of jurisdiction. [Executive Software North America, Inc. v. District Court, *supra*, §408]

(5) **State law tied to questions of federal policy:** [§422]   When the state claim is closely tied to a question of federal policy, this link argues in favor of exercise of supplemental jurisdiction.

   (a) **Example:** When the allowable scope of the state law claim implicates the federal doctrine of preemption, it is desirable for the federal court to employ supplemental jurisdiction. [United Mine Workers v. Gibbs, *supra*]

   (b) **Compare—preemption defense:** Preemption is usually an affirmative defense and therefore not a ground for exercise of original federal question jurisdiction under the well-pleaded complaint rule. (*See supra*, §367.)

(6) **Timing of decision:** [§423]   The question whether to decline to exercise supplemental jurisdiction remains open throughout the case, although the effort invested by the federal court may be a reason to retain jurisdiction. The court may decide, even after trial, not to entertain nonfederal claims.

d. **Tolling of limitations:** [§424]   The limitations period for any claim asserted under supplemental jurisdiction, or any other claim in the same action voluntarily dismissed at the same time or later, is tolled while the claim is pending in federal court and for 30 days after the federal court dismisses it. [28 U.S.C. §1367(d)]

(1) **Rationale:** The rationale for the tolling is that a plaintiff should not be subjected to the risk that her claim will be barred by limitations if the federal court declines to exercise supplemental jurisdiction, or if the plaintiff is mistaken about whether the claim actually falls within supplemental jurisdiction.

(2) **Voluntary dismissal of claim within original jurisdiction:** [§425]   Should a claim asserted under supplemental jurisdiction be dismissed, the tolling provision also applies to a claim properly within federal jurisdiction that plaintiff dismisses. *Rationale:* If plaintiff prefers to combine all the claims in state court, limitations should not be an obstacle.

E. REMOVAL

1. **Introduction:** [§426]   Removal allows a defendant to shift a case from state court to federal court when the plaintiff has chosen to sue in state court. Although there

is no mention of removal jurisdiction in the Constitution, some form of removal jurisdiction has existed since the federal court system was created by the first Congress in 1789.

2. **Grounds for Removal:** [§427] In general, an action that the *plaintiff could originally have filed in federal court* can be removed there by the defendant. [28 U.S.C. §1441(a)] Note that there are exceptions to this rule, such as the rule against removal on diversity grounds by a local defendant and the provision for removal of "separate and independent claims." (*See infra.*)

   a. **Federal question:** [§428] Where the plaintiff's state court complaint raises a federal question, the defendant may remove.

      (1) **Federal defenses not considered:** [§429] The *well-pleaded complaint rule* applies in the removal situation, and the fact that the defendant has raised a federal defense to the plaintiff's state law claim is not sufficient to support removal. [Oklahoma Tax Commission v. Graham, 489 U.S. 838 (1989)]

      (2) **Federal counterclaim not considered:** [§430] The fact that the defendant has interposed a counterclaim asserting a federal claim does not provide a basis for removal on federal question grounds.

      (3) **Plaintiff omits federal claim:** [§431] If the plaintiff chooses not to assert a possible federal claim, the defendant may not remove the case by citing the unasserted claim.

         (a) **Amendment to assert federal claim:** [§432] Should the plaintiff later amend to assert the federal claim in the state court action, the defendant *can then remove the case*. Note that if the plaintiff does not do so, res judicata may bar assertion of the federal claim in a later action.

         (b) **Exception—complete preemption:** [§433] If federal law completely preempts state law on the matter and converts the plaintiff's claim into one of federal law, that satisfies the well-pleaded complaint requirement and makes the case removable. [Metropolitan Life Insurance Co. v. Taylor, *supra,* §367]

      (4) **Effect of supplemental jurisdiction statute:** [§434] Under the supplemental jurisdiction statute [28 U.S.C. §1367], any case in which a federal claim is asserted in state court should be removable pursuant to section 1441(a) even though it includes defendants against whom only state law claims are asserted, as long as the claims against these defendants form part of the same federal constitutional "case."

   b. **Diversity of citizenship:** [§435] When the plaintiff could have filed the action in federal court using diversity of citizenship jurisdiction, the defendant may remove. Note that the *complete diversity* requirement applies in this situation.

      (1) **Local defendant:** [§436] However, such removal is not permitted if any defendant is a citizen of the state in which the action is brought. [28

U.S.C. §1441(b)] *Rationale:* Since diversity jurisdiction is designed to protect against local prejudice, there is no reason to invoke it on behalf of a local party. *Compare:* A local plaintiff can file an action in federal court invoking diversity jurisdiction.

(2) **Fictitious defendants:** [§437]   If the plaintiff has named fictitious "John Doe" defendants in the complaint, they are disregarded for purposes of determining whether there is complete diversity. [28 U.S.C. §1441(a)]

(3) **Fraudulent joinder:** [§438]   If the plaintiff joins a nondiverse defendant against whom he has no basis for a claim, the presence of that defendant will not defeat removal.

(4) **Jurisdictional amount:** [§439]   The jurisdictional amount requirement applies to cases removed on grounds of diversity. (*See supra,* §§324 *et seq.*) It has been held that the plaintiff can prevent removal by suing in state court for less than the jurisdictional amount, even though the claim could be for a larger sum. [Sponholz v. Stanislaus, 410 F. Supp. 286 (S.D.N.Y. 1976)]

c. **Separate and independent federal claim:** [§440]   A defendant sued on a "separate and independent claim or cause of action" within federal question jurisdiction may remove, even if the plaintiff has joined nonremovable claims. [28 U.S.C. §1441(c)]

(1) **Rationale:** The rationale is to protect the defendant's right of removal of a federal claim so that the plaintiff cannot prevent removal by joining a wholly unrelated claim.

(2) **Application:** [§441]   The cases in this area, most of which involved state law claims against some diverse and some nondiverse defendants antedated the limitation to separate federal claims (*see infra*), were very difficult to reconcile. The Supreme Court construed the provision narrowly. [*See, e.g.,* American Fire & Casualty Co. v. Finn, *supra,* §259] The difficulty in finding such claims was that, usually, state rules allowed joinder of parties only when there was some relationship between the claims asserted against them, so that it was unlikely that there would often be cases in which such claims would be separate and independent of each other. The limitation of section 1441(c) to federal question claims (*see infra*) eliminates such difficulties.

(3) **Entire action removed:** [§442]   Where the separate and independent claim requirement is satisfied, the court may retain jurisdiction over otherwise nonremovable claims or remand them to state court.

(a) **Criticism:** The retention of claims not otherwise within federal jurisdiction is anomalous, since it is premised on the relationship between those claims and the removal claim, which qualified for removal now because it was "separate and independent."

(4) **Limitation to federal question claims:** [§443]   In 1990, Congress amended section 1441(c) to permit removal on separate and independent

claim grounds only when the separate and independent claim is "within the jurisdiction conferred by section 1331" (for claims that raise a federal question).

- (a) **Possible constitutional problems:** [§444] Because section 1367(a) seems to confer supplemental jurisdiction over all claims sufficiently related to a federal question claim to permit a court to exercise jurisdiction over them, and these would seemingly be removable under 28 U.S.C. section 1441(a) and (b), it is unclear how section 1441(c) can constitutionally expand the federal court's jurisdiction.

- (b) **Power to remand matters as to which state law predominates:** [§445] The district court has discretion to remand all "matters in which state law predominates." Whether this gives the district court power to remand the federal claim as well is unsettled. [*See* Moralez v. Meat Cutters Local 536, 778 F. Supp. 368, 370 (E.D. Mich. 1991)—entire case remanded]

d. **Special removal statutes:** [§446] In certain cases, special removal statutes apply. For example, when a state court defendant in a civil or criminal case cannot adequately protect her *federal civil rights regarding racial equality* in state court, she may remove to federal court. [28 U.S.C. §1443] Also, suits against *federal officers* sued for *acts performed under color of office* are removable. [28 U.S.C. §1442]

e. **Removal forbidden in employment injury cases:** [§447] Suits brought in state court against a railroad under the *Federal Employers' Liability Act* ("FELA") or under state *workers' compensation laws* are not removable. [28 U.S.C. §1445] The rationale for this limitation is to allow injured workers to pick the court in which they wish to have their claims decided.

3. **Procedure for Removal:** [§448] A defendant seeking removal must file a notice setting forth the facts supporting removal in the federal district court and division within which the action is pending. A copy of the notice should be sent to the other parties and to the state court.

a. **Only defendant can remove:** [§449] Even if the defendant asserts a federal claim as a counterclaim, the plaintiff may not remove. [Shamrock Oil Co. v. Sheets, 313 U.S. 100 (1941)]

b. **All defendants must join:** [§450] All defendants who have been served must join in the notice of removal. [Chicago, Rock Island & Pacific Railway v. Martin, 178 U.S. 245 (1900)] However, when the ground for removal is a *separate and independent claim*, only the defendant against whom this claim is asserted need seek the removal.

c. **Timing:** [§451] The notice of removal must be filed within 30 days after the time the case becomes removable. If the action is removable as filed, the 30 days begin running from service of process on the defendant. If the action becomes removable only due to some later development (*e.g.,* amendment to add federal claim to complaint or dismissal of nondiverse defendants), the 30 days begin running from that point. However, removal on grounds of diversity is not allowed more than one year after the commencement of the action. [28 U.S.C. §1446(b)]

d. **Effect of removal:** [§452] Upon filing and service of the notice of removal, the case is considered removed, and the state court may take no further action on it. The remedy for improper removal is to seek a *remand* to state court. (*See infra,* §§455-459.)

e. **State court lack of subject matter jurisdiction:** [§453] The federal court has jurisdiction over an otherwise properly removed action even if the state court lacked jurisdiction over the claim. [28 U.S.C. §1441(e)]

   (1) **Example:** Plaintiff sues defendant in state court for violation of federal antitrust laws, a claim over which there is exclusive federal jurisdiction. Defendant may remove to federal court.

   (2) **Former law:** [§454] Before the addition of section 1441(e) in 1986, federal court removal jurisdiction was said to be "derivative," and it was held that the federal court could not have jurisdiction unless the state court also had jurisdiction.

4. **Remand**

   a. **Improper removal:** [§455] If the case was improperly removed, the federal court should remand it to state court. [28 U.S.C. §1447(c)] Remand is required whenever the court determines that removal was improper, unless final judgment has been entered.

   b. **Supplemental claims after dismissal of federal claims:** [§456] When a court would otherwise dismiss the supplemental claims after disposing of the federal claims (*see supra,* §419), it may instead remand them to state court. [Carnegie-Mellon University v. Cohill, 484 U.S. 343 (1988)]

   c. **Others grounds for remand:** [§457] The Supreme Court has indicated that remand is *usually not allowed where a case was properly removed*. [Thermtron Products, Inc. v. Hermansdorfer, 423 U.S. 336 (1976)—remand based on expectation that there would be greater delay in obtaining a trial date in federal court than in state court]

      (1) **Compare—addition of nondiverse defendants:** [§458] In 1988, Congress added 28 U.S.C. section 1447(e), providing that if the plaintiff seeks to *add additional defendants* whose addition would destroy subject matter jurisdiction, the court may *permit joinder and remand*.

   d. **Appellate review:** [§459] An order remanding a case to state court is "not reviewable on appeal or otherwise." [28 U.S.C. §1447(d)] However, the Supreme Court has upheld review via mandamus where the district court overtly remanded on a ground not authorized by the statute. [Thermtron Products, Inc. v. Hermansdorfer, *supra*]

5. **No "Reverse" Removal:** [§460] There is presently no method by which a defendant can remove a case originally filed in federal court to state court.

   a. **Compare—abstention:** [§461] Federal courts may, however, decline to proceed in certain situations where "abstention" is proper. This may be due to the presence of an uncertain issue of state law pertinent to a federal constitutional claim, or due to deference to litigation already pending in state court. (For details on abstention, *see* Federal Courts Summary.)

III. RELATION BETWEEN STATE AND FEDERAL LAW

chapter approach

1. ***Erie* Doctrine:** In a number of situations and for certain issues, the federal courts are required to apply state rather than federal law. Determining whether to apply state or federal law is known as an *Erie* problem.

   "Erie" problems are a favorite source of examination questions. In very general terms, in state law matters in the federal courts (mostly diversity cases, but not exclusively—supplemental state claims in federal question cases are analyzed similarly), **state substantive** and **federal procedural law are** followed. However, determining which law to apply is often more complex; the role and definition of the concepts of "substance" and "procedure" vary in different contexts. When either state or federal law might apply, it can help to approach the problem in two stages.

   a. *First,* ask whether there is a ***"true conflict"***—are there both federal and state rules of law that purport to apply and cannot be harmonized? No federal rule may exist, for example, or the federal and state rules—while related—might not speak to exactly the same point, or the two rules may agree. In such cases, no choice of one or the other is necessary.

   b. *Second,* if—but only if—there is a "true conflict," you need to look further. One useful approach is to ask what is the *source* of the potentially applicable *federal* rule of law; the test for the federal rule's validity and governing force varies depending on whether it derives from the Constitution, a statute enacted by Congress, a court rule promulgated under the Rules Enabling Act, or purely from decisional law (as opposed to interpretation of the Constitution, an Act of Congress, or a Federal Rule).

      (1) Is the federal rule of law grounded in the **Constitution** itself (*e.g.,* the Seventh Amendment guarantee of jury trial in actions at law in the federal courts)? If so, the federal rule governs, period, without regard to the source, importance, or substantive nature of any contrary state rule.

      (2) Is the federal rule of law found in a federal **statute** (*e.g.,* one providing for nationwide service of process)? If so, it governs as long as it is constitutional—*i.e.,* if it falls within the broad powers of Congress (which include regulation of procedure and "arguably procedural" matters in the federal courts) and does not violate any independent federal constitutional right.

      (3) Is the federal rule of law a **Federal Rule of Civil Procedure** (or Evidence or Appellate Procedure)? If so, the Rules Enabling Act [28 U.S.C. §2072] provides the principal test for its validity: It must be "arguably procedural," dealing with practice, procedure, or evidence, *and* must not "abridge, enlarge or modify any substantive right." If it passes these tests (and is constitutional, which is practically certain if it satisfies the standards of section 2072), the federal rule governs.

(4) Is the federal rule of law *judge-made* (*e.g.*, the equitable doctrine of laches)? If so, it should *not* govern in federal court if it fails the "twin-aims" test of *Erie*, as stated in *Hanna v. Plumer*: *If* the federal courts do *not* follow the state rule, will it encourage forum-shopping between state and federal courts and inequitable administration of the laws by providing different, and possibly outcome-affecting, regimes of applicable law?

2. **Federal Common Law:** Some civil procedure courses will also include coverage of "federal common law." Although in *Erie* the Supreme Court stated that "there is no federal *general* common law" (emphasis added), in several areas of special federal authority or interest the federal courts may develop federal common law by borrowing or even preempting state law. You may need to ask whether a case involves: (i) a need to borrow state law (such as a statute of limitations for a federal claim when Congress has enacted none); (ii) an express or implied authorization from Congress for the federal courts to develop federal common law; or (iii) a federal interest significant enough to call for uniform federal decisional law.

A. STATE LAW IN THE FEDERAL COURTS

1. **Rules of Decision Act:** [§462] The starting point for the applicability of state law in the federal courts is the Rules of Decision Act [28 U.S.C. §1652], originally adopted in 1789. In its present form the Act provides, "The laws of the several states, except where the Constitution or treaties of the United States or Acts of Congress otherwise require or provide, shall be regarded as rules of decision in civil actions in the courts of the United States, in cases where they apply."

2. **Former Rule—*Swift v. Tyson*:** [§463] For almost a century, the prevailing interpretation of the reference to state "laws" in the Rules of Decision Act was that it did not include state common law of a general, as opposed to local, nature. Thus, the federal courts could and did follow their own view of what the "general" common law was or should be. [Swift v. Tyson, 41 U.S. (16 Pet.) 1 (1842)] The federal courts' decisions on this "general" common law, however, were not binding precedent on the courts of the states; consequently, different rules of law could apply to the same transaction, depending on whether litigation took place in state or federal court.

   a. **Note:** Even under *Swift v. Tyson*, federal courts *were* bound by applicable state *statutes* (as long as they were constitutional) and *"local" common law* (*e.g.*, state common law regarding rights in real property within the states).

3. **Difficulties of *Swift* Regime:** [§464] The approach taken in *Swift v. Tyson* became vulnerable for several reasons.

   a. **Changing attitudes toward law:** [§465] *Swift* appeared to rest in part on a view that a "true" common law existed and could be "found" by the courts. However, many legal authorities moved away from this view and accepted the idea that each state could have its own internally authoritative common law, and that variations among states on the same point did not mean that some had to be "wrong."

b. **Failure to achieve uniformity:** [§466] *Swift* also became vulnerable because it failed to help develop a uniform common law, due to the disagreement of many state courts with the "general" common law established by the federal courts. Thus, *Swift* came to be seen as allowing the federal courts to add one more regime of common law rather than taking part in the development of one "true" set of common law doctrines.

c. **Practical difficulties and unfairness:** [§467] *Swift* led to forum shopping. Because the federal courts often applied common law rules different from the law of the states in which they sat, litigants could manipulate federal jurisdiction to gain favorable substantive law. That is unfair since parties who are similarly situated except for litigating in different court systems within the same state can be governed by different substantive rules. This undermines the ends of state common law rules and complicates private planning, because parties cannot be sure what law will govern their affairs.

   (1) **Example—*Black & White Taxicab Co.*:** The height of such manipulation came in *Black & White Taxicab Co. v. Brown & Yellow Taxicab Co.*, 276 U.S. 518 (1928), in which the plaintiff avoided a state common law anti-monopoly rule by reincorporating in another state and then bringing a diversity action in federal court, which followed a different rule.

d. **Doubts about *Swift* interpretation:** [§468] *Swift* also came into doubt because historical research on the adoption of the original Rules of Decision Act questioned whether the drafters had intended to exclude "general" common law from the term "laws of the several states" (*see supra*, §§462-463). [Warren, *New Light on the History of the Federal Judiciary Act of 1789*, 37 Harv. L. Rev. 49 (1923)]

e. **Views on the constitutional scope of federal power:** [§469] Finally, there seemed to be no constitutional basis for the federal courts' law-making authority that existed under *Swift*. The decision appeared to presume a ***general*** law-making power in the federal courts of a sort that the Constitution does not grant to Congress, and which Congress had not attempted to confer on the federal courts. (*See infra*, §478.)

4. **Overruling of *Swift* by *Erie*:** [§470] The combination of the above problems contributed to the overruling of *Swift* in *Erie Railroad v. Tompkins*, 304 U.S. 64 (1938). *Erie* held that in the absence of an Act of Congress providing governing law, a federal court should follow applicable state common law principles rather than developing and applying its own "general" common law. At issue was the liability of a railroad for injury to a person who was struck by an object protruding from a passing train. Today the issue of what substantive law governs in cases like *Erie* itself is often simple, but the decision made broad changes whose ramifications are still being worked out in the federal courts today.

   a. **Reasoning of *Erie*:** [§471] *Erie* clearly identified three distinct rationales for the decision.

      (1) **Statutory interpretation:** [§472] The Court accepted the argument that the language of the Rules of Decision Act was not intended to exclude all state "general" common law. (*See supra*, §468.) Instead, the

term "laws of the several states" includes state common law, general and local, as well as "positive" law like state constitutions, statutes, regulations, and ordinances.

(2) **Lack of uniformity and resulting discrimination:** [§473] The *Erie* majority also noted the persistence of differing views on common law questions between the state and federal courts, and the possibility this created for discrimination among litigants depending on the forum in which the case was tried.

   (a) **Note—"equal protection" red herring:** [§474] In this ***nonconstitutional*** portion of its opinion, the Court stated that the *Swift* doctrine had rendered impossible the "equal protection of the law." This misleading phrasing often makes students think that *Erie* rests on the Equal Protection Clause of the Fourteenth Amendment. This cannot be true because *Swift* was a ***federal*** law ruling; the Equal Protection Clause speaks to the ***states***, and had not yet been held applicable to the federal government at the time *Erie* was decided. Instead, "equal protection" here must refer to the serious, but nonconstitutional, problems of nonuniformity in administration of state law and unfairly disparate treatment of litigants depending on whether a case is in state or federal court.

   (b) **"Discrimination by noncitizens against citizens":** [§475] In this second part of the opinion, the *Erie* majority also said that *Swift* had "introduced grave discrimination by noncitizens against citizens," a concept repeated in some later opinions in the *Erie* line of cases. The reference is to the ability of an out-of-state party often to control the choice of federal or state forum in diversity litigation (*e.g.,* out-of-state plaintiff may decide to sue in defendant's home state court, in which case defendant cannot remove to federal court [28 U.S.C. §1441(b); *see supra,* §436]; out-of-state defendant often—but not always—has opportunity to remove case to federal court if sued in state court; *see supra,* §§426 *et seq.*). Regardless of who controls the forum choice, discrimination among litigants depending on the forum and what law it may apply remains a concern.

(3) **Unconstitutionality of *Swift* interpretation:** [§476] Whatever the persuasiveness of the above two points (erroneous statutory interpretation and resulting discrimination), the Court in *Erie* stated that it would not have been prepared to abandon the long-established *Swift* doctrine were it not convinced of *Swift's* unconstitutionality.

   (a) **Holding, not dictum:** [§477] Because the Court explicitly said that the constitutional ground was essential to the result in *Erie*, the constitutional portion of the opinion—despite some questioning—qualifies as ***holding*** rather than dictum.

   (b) **Basis of unconstitutionality:** [§478] The Court did not clearly explain why the *Swift* interpretation of the Rules of Decision Act was unconstitutional. It did not find that *Swift* violated any specific clause, but rather noted the ***absence*** of any clause in the Constitution purporting to confer upon either Congress or the federal courts a general "power to declare substantive rules of common law applicable in a state." The Court explained that the Constitution preserves the autonomy of the states, and supplanting their law with federal law is permissible only pursuant to powers specifically granted to the federal government by the Constitution.

1) **Note—Tenth Amendment alone not basis of *Erie*:** [§479] The Tenth Amendment's reservation of undelegated powers to the states or the people reinforces this argument, but by itself does not establish the unconstitutionality of *Swift*. The *Swift* interpretation probably would be unconstitutional in modern views even if there were no Tenth Amendment, because it presumes a ***general*** law-making power not granted to the federal government.

2) **Commerce power a possible basis?** [§480] Because the accident giving rise to the *Erie* litigation occurred on an interstate railroad, students sometimes wonder whether *Erie* did not overlook a possible basis for federal law in the commerce power. The Constitution does grant to Congress pervasive power over interstate commerce, pursuant to which Congress ***could have*** provided for substantive tort law to govern such accidents or perhaps authorized the federal courts to develop applicable common law in the area, but ***it had not done so*** (and still has not). Thus, the Court had to examine whether the federal courts had the power to create a "general" federal common law. It concluded that they did not, leaving state law the only law that could govern without congressional legislation.

b. ***Erie* as part of a revolution in federal court practice:** [§481] *Erie* coincided with the adoption of the Federal Rules of Civil Procedure, before which federal courts had largely followed the procedural rules of the state courts where they sat. Thus, in the same year the federal courts moved sharply in opposite directions: (i) under *Erie* toward ***more application of state substantive law*** rather than creation of federal common law and (ii) under the Federal Rules toward ***uniform federal procedural law*** in place of diverse local practice. The approach to deciding when to apply federal "procedural" law in diversity cases, however, remained problematic for some time.

c. **Principal cases developing *Erie*:** [§482] *Erie* solved many old problems but opened up new ones, especially in cases when the competing federal and state rules that might apply are in the borderland between substance and procedure. The Supreme Court has repeatedly said that in matters in the federal courts arising under state law, the ***general guideline*** is that ***state substantive law*** and ***federal procedural law*** govern. However, the distinction between substance and procedure is not always clear, unvarying, or mechanical; the role and definition of these concepts vary depending on the context. Major cases in the first decades after *Erie* dealt in differing ways with these problems; two of them—*York* and *Byrd, infra*—often receive great emphasis in teaching, but are of limited practical significance today.

(1) ***Guaranty Trust Co. v. York*:** [§483] *Guaranty Trust Co. v. York,* 326 U.S. 99 (1945), on somewhat complicated facts, presented the question

whether a state statute of limitations or the more flexible federal decisional rule of "laches"—which asks whether delay has been excessive and the other side has been prejudiced—should determine the timeliness of an equitable state law claim filed in federal court.

(a) **Specific holding:** [§484]   The Court ruled that the New York statute of limitations governed, rather than the federal laches doctrine. This makes sense because statutes of limitations, although partly reflecting procedural concerns about courts' ability to deal with "stale" claims, also have strong substantive overtones in that they provide for "repose"—when the time to sue has passed, people can stop worrying about being sued, close their books on past transactions, make plans unaffected by the possibility of litigation, and get on with their lives and businesses.

1) **Note:** Regardless of the fluctuations in the *Erie* doctrine since *York*, this holding—treating state statutes of limitations as "substantive" for *Erie* purposes—still stands.

(b) **"Outcome determination" test:** [§485]   In explaining the *York* ruling, the Court articulated what came to be regarded as a major test for whether state law should be regarded as substantive for *Erie* purposes: will application of federal law instead of the state law significantly affect the outcome of the litigation?

1) **Difficulties of the test:** [§486]   It is hard to know where to stop in applying the *York* test. If applied broadly, almost any procedural rule could qualify as substantive because (especially if disobeyed) it could affect the outcome of a case. In fact, some cases applying the test appeared to raise doubts about whether many Federal Rules of Civil Procedure could govern when state law differed, but the Supreme Court has subsequently drawn back from the most far-reaching readings of *York*.

2) **Possible overreading of test:** [§487]   It seems doubtful that the "outcome determination" test should have been read with such a vengeance, for it was contrasted with whether a state rule "concerns merely the manner or means" by which a right to recover is enforced (*i.e.*, even under *York*, if a state rule concerned only the manner or means of enforcement, federal law could govern). The opinion also pointed out that the concern was to avoid providing litigants with a second conflicting body of law. This "dual-regime" concern remains valid and is often a useful tool for discerning whether a serious *Erie* problem exists.

(2) ***Byrd* and the "interest balancing" approach:** [§488]   In *Byrd v. Blue Ridge Electric Cooperative, Inc.*, 356 U.S. 525 (1958), the Court appeared to signal another departure by at least demoting the "outcome determination" factor to one among several—to be balanced along with federal and state interests in the rules that could be applied. This came to be known as an "interest balancing" approach to *Erie* problems.

(a) **Specific holding:** [§489] The issue in *Byrd* was whether state or federal law should govern the manner of determination of an ancillary state law issue (status under workers' compensation law of an employee of an outside contractor) in a diversity case before the federal court. State practice allowed the judge to decide the issue; federal law allowed the jury to decide. The Court held in favor of the federal rule.

   1) **Note:** A federal court would probably reach the same result today (if *Byrd* arose as a case of first impression) by application of the Seventh Amendment jury trial right as it is now interpreted. At the time, though, the Court did not treat the result as required by the Seventh Amendment.

(b) **"Balancing" approach:** [§490] *Byrd* discusses three main types of factors that could bear on the choice between the state and federal rules.

   1) **Relation between state rule in question and underlying state right:** [§491] The Court first asked whether the state practice was "bound up with" the underlying state law rights and obligations being enforced, and concluded that it was not. The aim of this inquiry seems to have been to determine whether the state procedural practice was an integral part of the state substantive right, or if the state system followed it for some independent reason that might relate more to state court internal housekeeping and, therefore, have less call to be followed in federal court.

      a) **Counterexample—malpractice screening panels:** Several federal courts have followed state law requirements for screening panels in medical malpractice suits, on the theory that the procedural mechanism was adopted for purposes related to the legislature's views on the enforcement of the underlying tort claims themselves.

   2) **Countervailing interests of the federal judicial system:** [§492] The *Byrd* Court also looked to the strength of the federal policy involved—*i.e.*, the relationship between judge and jury in federal court—and the danger that following the state rule would disrupt that policy. The federal interests relevant to this inquiry fall into a narrow range; they do not pertain to the substance of the law, but rather involve the federal courts' interest in their own smooth functioning and in the uniformity and coherence of the decisional principles they have evolved to govern their procedures.

   3) **Likelihood of effect on outcome:** [§493] Finally, the Court looked to the *York* "outcome determination" test and decided that following the federal practice would not likely have an effect on the outcome of the suit.

(c) **Views on "balancing" approach:** [§494] *Byrd* drew praise for recognizing the relevance of federal as well as state concerns, for bringing to the surface factors bearing on choices between state and federal law in a complex system, and for reducing the threat that the Federal Rules of Civil Procedure would so often have to yield to state rules as to produce a patchwork and undermine the uniformity sought and achieved by adoption of the Rules. However, *Byrd* suffers from the common difficulties of multifactor balancing approaches: It has the apples-and-oranges problem, for it is hard to find a scale on which to balance state and federal interests of different types, and inconsistency in application can often result.

[handwritten margin note: adoption of Rules now seeks uniformity / Problem w/ Byrd]

(d) **Eclipsing of *Byrd* test:** [§495] Although the Supreme Court has not explicitly abandoned the *Byrd* approach, no Court majority opinion has cited the case in over 15 years. For more than a quarter of a century the Court has seemed to place its emphasis strongly on other articulations that are stated most prominently in *Hanna v. Plumer*, discussed below. *Byrd's* balancing method rarely appears in federal appellate decisions of recent years. At least outside the judge-or-jury context, it seems best regarded for present practical purposes as a transitional case, bringing *Erie* approaches back from the most extreme tilt in favor of applying state procedural rules on state law matters in federal court.

5. **Approach Under *Hanna v. Plumer*:** [§496] Until 1965, the Supreme Court treated many federal vs. state law problems as subject to a general *Erie* approach, as developed through *York* and *Byrd*. However, when Federal Rules of Civil Procedure arguably conflicted with the law that would apply in state courts, a parallel but mostly independent line of cases developed. The Court sorted out the different law choice situations and refined the approaches applicable to each in *Hanna v. Plumer*, 380 U.S. 460 (1965). It is now clear that one should not think of any *single* test or approach—substance vs. procedure, outcome determination, interest balancing—as applicable to all *Erie* situations.

   a. **Specific holding:** [§497] In *Hanna* the Supreme Court held that Federal Rule of Civil Procedure 4(d)(1), allowing "substituted" service of process on a defendant's spouse at their home, rather than the personal service required by Massachusetts law, was valid and controlling, even though the "substituted" service would not have sufficed had the same action been brought in Massachusetts state court.

      (1) **Note:** The situation incidentally illustrates the possible overextension of the "outcome determination" test, for if the state rule applied in federal court, the suit would have been dismissed because state requirements had not been met.

   b. **Two parts of *Hanna* opinion:** [§498] It is perhaps not frequently enough noticed that the majority opinion in *Hanna* has two parts: the first, technically dictum, about the *Erie* rule and the second, being the Court's holding, about the tests for the validity of a rule adopted pursuant to the Rules Enabling Act [28 U.S.C. §2072].

(1) **Erie "dictum" in *Hanna*:** [§499] The first part of the opinion confirms the scaling back of the *York* "outcome determination" test. It suggests—and later opinions appear to confirm—that while the test survives, it is to be applied in modified form in light of "the policies underlying the *Erie* rule." The Court identified these policies as the *"twin aims"* of "discouragement of forum shopping and avoidance of inequitable administration of the laws."

   (a) **Application:** Although the Court decided that *Hanna* was not the type of case to which the modified *York* test applied (*see infra*), the Court implied that if it *did* apply, the Federal Rule would govern because the different rules in federal and state court regarding service of process would neither encourage forum shopping nor cause unfair discrimination among the litigants.

   (b) **Comment on forum shopping:** Forum shopping is not always an evil; the very existence of diversity jurisdiction, concurrent with state courts' general jurisdiction, reflects an intent to let some litigants choose between forums. By itself, forum shopping seems at most a minor irritant, involving some procedural shuffling. Rather, the main difficulty appears to be with what litigants may get when they forum shop—an unfairly different rule of law from what would have governed in state court. Consequently, although Supreme Court opinions regularly mention the forum shopping concern, it seems best treated not in isolation, but in tandem with the aim of discouraging inequitable administration of the laws.

(2) **Holding with respect to validity of Federal Rules:** [§500] In the holding portion of *Hanna*, the Court found that the modified *York* approach (developed in the dictum portion of *Hanna, supra*) applied to the "typical, relatively unguided *Erie* choice," but did not apply here because Congress had provided a different standard in the Rules Enabling Act, under which the Federal Rules are promulgated. That Act gives the Supreme Court the power to adopt Federal Rules regarding practice, procedure, and evidence in the federal courts, as long as the Rules do not "abridge, enlarge or modify any substantive right." Under the Enabling Act, the *Hanna* Court ruled that the Federal Rules are to be applied in federal courts unless they violate the Constitution or the terms of the Enabling Act itself.

   (a) **Constitutional restrictions:** [§501] Recall that the power of the federal courts to create "general" common law was held unconstitutional because it did not rest on a power granted to the federal government by the Constitution. (*See supra*, §478.) The power to regulate *procedure* in the federal courts, however, has been granted to Congress under the constitutional provision establishing the federal judiciary as augmented by the Necessary and Proper Clause (*see* Constitutional Law Summary), and Congress has delegated part of this power to the Supreme Court through the Rules Enabling Act. The only *constitutional* restriction on this power is that the rules be "arguably procedural": the power to make procedural rules is broad enough to include "matters which, though falling within the uncertain area between substance and procedure, are rationally capable of classification as either." [Hanna v. Plumer, *supra*]

- (b) **Enabling Act limitations**

    1) **"Practice and procedure" requirement:** [§502] In *Hanna*, the Court reiterated that a rule passes muster under the "practice and procedure" portion of the Enabling Act if it ***"really regulates procedure***—the judicial process for enforcing rights and duties recognized by substantive law and for justly administering remedy and redress for disregard or infraction of them." It is highly unlikely that any Federal Rule the Court might conceivably promulgate could fail this test.

    2) **"Substantive rights" limitation:** [§503] The second sentence of the Rules Enabling Act requires that the Rules not "abridge, enlarge or modify any substantive right," and to be valid a rule technically must not transgress this proscription. However, in *Hanna* the Court pointed out that this limitation is not addressed to merely "incidental effects" on the rights of litigants.

- (c) **Strong presumption of validity:** [§504] The *Hanna* Court made it clear that when there is a conflict between a federal rule and state law, there is a very strong presumption in favor of the validity of the Federal Rule. It stated that the Rule is to be applied unless it appears that the Rules Advisory Committee, the Supreme Court, and Congress erred in their initial judgment that the Rule did not transgress the Enabling Act or the Constitution. Indeed, the Supreme Court has never held a Federal Rule invalid.

c. **Justice Harlan's concurrence:** [§505] Justice Harlan concurred in the *Hanna* judgment, but criticized the majority as going too far in the direction of favoring the Federal Rules. He characterized the Court's approach as: "arguably procedural, ergo constitutional." As to the Federal Rules, this characterization may understate *Hanna's* requirements, at least if the Court were to give some effect to the Enabling Act's substantive rights limitation. However, the characterization seems accurate when Congress itself has enacted legislation regulating procedure in the federal courts (*e.g.*, venue rules, *see supra*, §§121 *et seq.*), but it is unobjectionable because Congress is not bound by the Enabling Act's restriction on affecting substantive rights—that is a restriction that Congress imposed on the Supreme Court when the Court promulgates Federal Rules; Congress is restricted only by the Constitution, and "arguably procedural" is constitutionally sufficient.

(1) **"Primary private activity":** [§506] Justice Harlan also argued for an approach to federal vs. state rule choice that would have emphasized state power over "primary private activity" (*i.e.*, state rule would apply if it would affect the primary, out-of-court stages of activity from which a case arises; federal rule would apply if it affected in-court behavior following the "primary" stages). Although thoughtfully advocated, this

view has not prevailed; and if turned into a single approach, it would overlook the multiple nature of modern *Erie-Hanna* analyses.

6. **Modern Approach Under *Erie* and *Hanna*:** [§507] The *Hanna* opinion suggests an approach to analysis of many federal-state law choice issues, amplified in an important article. [Ely, *The Irrepressible Myth of Erie*, 87 Harv. L. Rev. 693 (1974)] First, it is necessary to see whether any choice is needed; there may be no conflict to resolve between federal and state rules. Second, if conflict exists, one should determine the *source* of the arguably applicable federal rule of law—the Constitution; a statute; a Federal Rule of Civil or Appellate Procedure or Evidence; or a decisional rule developed by the federal courts and not resting on interpretation of one of the foregoing sources. The *source* of the federal rule determines the *test* for its validity and governing force.

   a. **Conflict-determination stage:** [§508] For several reasons, federal and state rules of law that might apply in a situation may not conflict; *e.g.,* only one system may purport to have an applicable rule at all; or the two rules may address somewhat different, even if closely related, points and may both be applied; or the rules may agree and thus call for the same result, whichever is applied. If so, no *Erie-Hanna* choice analysis is necessary.

      (1) **Example—no federal rule:** After *Erie*, in the absence of action by Congress, there is no federal law that purports to govern in many common tort situations. The only substantive law that can govern is state law.

      (2) **Example—no direct conflict:** Federal Rule 3, which states that a "civil action is commenced by filing a complaint with the court," need not be read as speaking to when a state statute of limitations is tolled on a state cause of action. Thus, if state law provides that the action is not tolled until *process is served*—the service requirement being an integral part of the state limitations statute—the state rule applies in state law actions in federal court, without any conflict requiring the *Hanna* analysis. [Walker v. Armco Steel Corp., 446 U.S. 740 (1980); Ragan v. Merchants Transfer & Warehouse Co., 337 U.S. 530 (1949)]

      (3) **But note—no narrow construction to avoid conflict:** A Federal Rule should not be narrowly construed to avoid a "direct collision" with state law. The Federal Rules "should be given their plain meaning"; if that reading leads to a direct collision with state law, the *Hanna* analysis applies. [Walker v. Armco Steel Corp., *supra*]

         (a) **Example—*Hanna*:** In *Hanna* itself, conflict could have been avoided by reading Federal Rule 4(d)(1) to deal only with service to commence the action and not with tolling the statute of limitations. State law provided for tolling *either* by personal service *or* by filing a notice of claim in probate court; the plaintiff might thus have followed both federal and state law by using substituted service under Rule 4 and tolling the statue by filing a notice of claim. The Court did not take this course, however, saying that the Federal Rule reflected a determination that the notice purposes of state law could be achieved by "less cumbersome" means, and that the Rule implied that in-hand service was not required in federal court actions.

(4) **Example—parallel rules or borrowing:** Another reason why no conflict may exist is that many state court rules closely track the Federal Rules (and some of the Federal Rules were originally modeled on state rules), so that the two provisions may be identical in phrasing or effect. Moreover, Federal Rules, such as Federal Rule 4 on service of process, sometimes borrow certain types of state law provisions from the state in which the district court sits. This precludes the possibility of conflict to the extent that the federal rule is borrowed state law.

b. **Conflict-resolution stage:** [§509]   Only if the federal and state rules conflict is it necessary to proceed to the *Hanna* analysis. In applying that analysis, it is essential first to determine the *source* of the potentially applicable federal rule of law. The answer to that inquiry provides the approach for determining whether the federal rule is valid; if so, under the Supremacy Clause [U.S. Const. art. VI, §2] it prevails over contrary state law.

(1) **Federal Constitution:** [§510]   Some procedural rules that govern in federal court derive from the text and judicial interpretations of the United States Constitution, such as the Seventh Amendment guarantee of the right to trial by jury in suits at common law (which does not apply to state courts). Because the Constitution is our paramount law, if it speaks to a situation before a court, *it governs,* without regard to any contrary state law or practice. This situation provides a possibly oversimplified example of why one should not invariably think in the *Erie* context in terms of "substance" vs. "procedure"; such labels, about either state or federal law, are totally beside the point if the source of a rule of federal law is the Constitution itself.

(2) **Acts of Congress:** [§511]   Because of Congress's broad constitutional power over federal courts (*see supra,* §501), if Congress passes a statute governing federal court procedure, that statute is valid and prevails over any contrary state law *if* it is "arguably procedural." Thus, one should look *only* to the "procedural" nature of the *federal* statute in determining whether it is valid and governing; the substantive nature of any contrary state rule would be irrelevant, and there is no place for *Byrd's* balancing of state and federal interests, because Congress has already done the balancing.

(a) **Example—federal transfer of venue statute:** Although Alabama law that would govern in an action conducted in Alabama state court disfavored contractual forum-selection clauses, 28 U.S.C. section 1404(a) on transfer of venue between federal courts (*see supra,* §§166 *et seq.*) was sufficiently broad to cover, and governed in a state law case in Alabama federal court. Thus, the federal court could consider the effect of the parties' forum-selection clause on possible transfer to federal court in New York. [Stewart Organization v. Ricoh Corp., *supra,* §199]

(3) **Federal Rules:** [§512]   A Federal Rule promulgated pursuant to the Rules Enabling Act is judged by the standards of the Act, as reflected in the holding portion of *Hanna v. Plumer, supra.* The Rule (including court interpretations of the Rule) is to be applied instead of contrary state

law unless it appears that the relevant Advisory Committee (Advisory Committees on Civil Rules, Appellate Rules, Rules of Evidence, etc., draft proposed rules for the Judicial Conference of the United States, which recommends them for promulgation by the Supreme Court), the Supreme Court, and Congress erred in their initial judgment that the Rule did not transgress the Enabling Act or the Constitution. (Congress does not usually vote on proposed Rules, but they must be submitted to Congress at least seven months before they are to take effect. [28 U.S.C. §2074] In most cases, if Congress does not act, the rules go into effect.)

(a) **Example:** Federal Rule of Appellate Procedure 38, which allows *discretionary* penalties for frivolous appeals, prevailed in federal court over an Alabama statute *requiring* penalties for unsuccessful appeals in state court. [Burlington Northern Railroad v. Woods, 480 U.S. 1 (1987)]

(b) **Possible counterexample:** The leading case in a court of appeals declining to apply an applicable Federal Rule, because of conflict with a state rule it regarded as substantive, involved a liberal Massachusetts rule on relation back for party changes in pleading amendments. The First Circuit held that then-applicable Federal Rule 15(c)'s restrictive approach to relation back (since relaxed by amendment of the Rule, *see infra,* §858) would "defeat rights arising from state substantive law" and followed the state rule. [Marshall v. Mulrenin, 508 F.2d 39 (1st Cir. 1974)] It seems doubtful that the Supreme Court would approve the approach in *Mulrenin* if a similar case were to come before it today, because of its strong emphasis on the presumptive validity of a Federal Rule that qualifies as "procedural" and its willingness to tolerate "incidental" effects of the Rules on the enforcement of state law rights.

(c) **Rules Enabling Act's "substantive right" limitation:** [§513] Whether the Court would ever strike down a Federal Rule for violating the Enabling Act seems to depend primarily on whether it would be willing to give significant independent force to the portion of the Act that requires that the Rules "not abridge, enlarge or modify any substantive right." Most often, procedural rules will not have anything like the forbidden effect, so the problem will rarely arise.

1) **"Incidental" effects:** [§514] The Court has disregarded "incidental" effects that leave untouched the content of state substantive law, while providing a somewhat different "manner or means" to enforce it.

a) **Example:** The Court has held that any effect on substantive rights resulting from the imposition of Rule 11 (regarding improper assertion of claims or defenses, *see infra,* §§709 *et seq.*) sanctions is incidental, and that the Rule governs in diversity cases. [Business Guides, Inc. v. Chromatic Communications Enterprises, Inc., 498 U.S. 533 (1991)]

2) **Possibility of conflict with substantive right:** [§515] What the Court has not, thus far, entertained is the possibility that a generally valid Federal Rule might, in particular contexts, impermissibly conflict with a substantive right, as the First Circuit concluded had happened in *Marshall v. Mulrenin, supra.*

(4) **Judge-made federal procedural rules:** [§516] If a potentially applicable federal rule is purely *decisional*—*i.e., not* the result of an interpretation of positive law found in the Constitution, an Act of Congress, or a Federal Rule—the "twin aims" *Erie* test articulated in the dictum portion of the *Hanna* opinion governs: If applying the federal judge-made rule would counter the aims of discouraging forum-shopping and avoiding inequitable administration of the laws, the federal court should follow state law.

(a) **Example:** *Guaranty Trust Co. v. York, supra*, §483, remains a prime illustration of such a situation, although the Court's analysis when it decided *York* was somewhat different from the modern approach under *Hanna*. Today, federal courts would apply the state law rule in a case like *York* because following the federal rule would fail the "twin aims" test: a party who would be barred by a statute of limitations in state court, but might be able to argue around a more flexible federal judge-made "laches" rule, would be tempted to file in federal court; and entertaining the action in federal court, when it would be barred by limitations in state court, would also deprive the defendant of the benefits of repose meant to be conferred by the state statute.

(b) **Example—sufficiency of evidence:** In state law cases in the federal courts, the lower federal courts are divided on whether to apply state or judge-made federal standards to the issue of whether the evidence is sufficient for a case to go to the jury.

(c) **Relative infrequency of problems of this sort:** [§517] Because federal statutes and the Federal Rules cover federal procedural issues fairly broadly, and because federal decisional rules often will not conflict with potentially applicable state rules, judge-made federal law infrequently comes into play in state vs. federal law conflicts. Nevertheless, later cases discussing *Hanna* have explicitly endorsed the "twin aims" analysis for this type of situation. [*See, e.g.,* Stewart Organization v. Ricoh Corp., *supra*, §511]

1) *NASCO* **case:** In 1991, for the first time since before *Hanna*, the Supreme Court faced a case involving what it viewed as a conflict between state law and judge-made federal procedural law. [Chambers v. NASCO, Inc., 501 U.S. 32 (1991)] *NASCO* involved the inherent power of federal courts to impose sanctions for bad faith conduct in litigation before the courts, even in state law cases where the state courts would not have a similar sanctioning power. The majority opinion routinely invoked the "twin aims" approach, found no forum-shopping incentives or inequity, and upheld the federal rule.

2) **Cautionary note:** Because the two prominent intermediate cases of *York* and *Byrd* involved what the Court treated as a conflict between state law and judge-made federal law, students often mistakenly regard them as dominating the field of *Erie* problems. The Court has, however, made it clear that other tests for the validity and governing force of a federal rule apply when the rule is grounded in the Constitution itself, enacted by Congress, or promulgated pursuant to the Enabling Act.

(d) **Possible survival of interest balancing:** [§518] If *Byrd*-style interest-balancing survives at all in federal vs. state rule choice situations, it must be in this category of cases. In cases involving positive federal law, other lawmakers—the Constitution-drafters, Congress, or the Federal Rulesmakers—have already done the balancing. However, even with judge-made federal rules, the Court seems to have indicated since *Hanna* (but without ever expressly disavowing *Byrd*) that the purposive "twin aims" test, rather than interest balancing, is the approach to be followed. In *Hanna* itself, the Court stated that the "importance" of a state rule is relevant in the *Erie* context only for purposes of determining whether failing to follow the state law in federal court would disserve the "twin aims" of discouraging forum-shopping and avoiding inequitable administration of the laws. And in *NASCO, supra*, in upholding the federal courts' decisionally established inherent authority to impose sanctions for bad faith conduct in state law litigation before the courts, despite contrary state law that would govern in state court, the Court relied on *Erie, York*, and *Hanna* but ignored *Byrd*.

7. **Which State's Law Applies?** [§519] Because diversity cases—most of the state law cases in the federal courts—by definition involve parties from different states, federal courts must often decide *which* state's law is to govern.

   a. **General rule:** [§520] In diversity cases, as to matters for which the federal court is required to follow state law, it will apply the law of the state in which it sits, including that state's choice of law rules. Thus, if the state's choice of law rules require application of another state's law, the federal court will ordinarily do the same. [Klaxon Co. v. Stentor Manufacturing Co., 313 U.S. 487 (1941)]

   b. **Questionable extension of *Klaxon* to statutory interpleader:** [§521] In a companion case decided the same day as *Klaxon* [Griffin v. McCoach, 313 U.S. 498 (1941)], the Supreme Court applied the *Klaxon* rule to a case arising within federal statutory interpleader jurisdiction. (For discussion of interpleader, *see infra*, §§1036 *et seq*.) Although *Griffin* apparently remains the law for federal statutory interpleader actions, no one has defended its application of the conflicts rules of the state in which the federal court sits, since federal statutory interpleader jurisdiction was created precisely because it might not be possible to bring scattered claimants before the same state court.

   c. **Modern reaffirmance of *Klaxon*:** [§522] Despite some academic criticism of the *Klaxon* rule, the Supreme Court strongly and summarily reaffirmed it in an extreme case in which the Texas courts would have followed Cambodian law. [Day & Zimmermann, Inc. v. Challoner, 423 U.S. 3 (1975)] By contrast, the heavily criticized extension of the *Klaxon* rule to statutory interpleader in *Griffin v. McCoach, supra*, has not been relitigated at the Supreme Court level.

    d. **Exceptions:** [§523] In some instances, federal legislation may provide a *federal* choice of law rule. [Richards v. United States, 369 U.S. 1 (1962)] For example, the Federal Tort Claims Act requires courts to apply the law—including choice of law rules—"of the place where the [allegedly tortious] act or omission occurred." [28 U.S.C. §1346(b)]

8. **Determining Applicable State Law:** [§524] *Erie* referred to the law of a state as declared by the state's "highest court." Often, of course, because a state statute or supreme court decision is on point, the state substantive law to be followed by a federal court will be clear. However, in other cases, the state court system may never have faced a question, or only lower state courts may have ruled, or it may seem likely that the state supreme court would overrule an old precedent if given the opportunity.

    a. **General guideline—"proper regard" to state court rulings:** [§525] Although the Supreme Court has not recently spoken directly on how federal courts should approach the problem of determining unclear state law, it has stated that "proper regard" must be given to state court precedents. In some cases, a federal court will not be bound by the ruling of a state intermediate appellate court on a point of state law, and *a fortiori* not by a state trial court decision. Such courts' opinions are, however, relevant data for ascertaining state law. [Commissioner v. Estate of Bosch, 387 U.S. 456 (1967)]

    b. **Implementation in light of *Erie* aims:** [§526] The determination of unclear state law seems best approached with the *Erie* "twin aims" of avoiding forum-shopping and inequitable administration of the laws in mind. Adoption of simplistic or rigid tests (*e.g.,* being bound by a recent holding of a state's intermediate appellate court—even if the ruling seems contrary to what the state supreme court would probably do) could encourage forum-shopping by making available in the federal system law that would not, ultimately, govern in the state system. Therefore, many lower federal courts look to *all* relevant sources, giving due regard to the varying weights of different authorities within the state system, in an attempt to discern how the state supreme court would decide the issue. [*See, e.g.,* McKenna v. Ortho Pharmaceutical Corp., 622 F.2d 567 (3d Cir. 1980)] In any event, a federal court is supposed to ***apply*** state law and ***not*** attempt to change it to what the court thinks might be a better rule.

    c. **No deference to local federal judges:** [§527] The Supreme Court has ruled that federal appellate courts are not to defer to the interpretation of state law by federal trial judges, but must review district courts' state law determinations de novo. [Salve Regina College v. Russell, 499 U.S. 225 (1991)]

    d. **State certification laws:** [§528] Many states authorize their highest courts to answer questions of state law certified by federal courts before which cases are pending. Where this procedure is available, a federal court may seek an authoritative answer to uncertain questions about state law rather than speculating on them. [*See* Lehman Bros. v. Schein, 416 U.S. 386 (1974)]

B. FEDERAL COMMON LAW

1. **No "Federal General Common Law":** [§529] *Erie's* repudiation of *Swift v. Tyson* (*see supra*, §§470 *et seq.*) included the flat statement, "[t]here is no federal general common law." However, the very day *Erie* was decided, the Court held that federal common law governed on the specific issue of apportionment of waters in an interstate stream. [Hinderlider v. La Plata River Co., 304 U.S. 92 (1938)] The resolution to this apparent contradiction lies in the fact that the federal courts do have authority to create common law in *particular* areas of federal authority or interest, subject to overruling by Congress.

2. **Examples of Federal Common Law Areas:** [§530] The range of federal interests and grants of authority that could support federal common law is fairly broad, and the subject receives more extended treatment elsewhere. (*See* Federal Courts Summary.)

    a. **Borrowed state law:** [§531] In some cases, federal statutes may be silent as to particular issues arising under them (*e.g.*, statutes of limitations for federal claims and definitions of family status for purposes of some federal law entitlements). In such cases, the federal courts often fill the interstices in federal law by borrowing the law of the relevant state, as long as that law does not undermine the purposes of the underlying federal law.

        (1) **Example—derivative action demand requirement:** The Supreme Court has held that, in a shareholders' derivative action under the federal Investment Company Act, the scope of the "futility" exception to the requirement of a pre-complaint demand on the board of directors to take the desired action should be borrowed from state law. [Kamen v. Kemper Financial Services, Inc., 500 U.S. 90 (1991)]

    b. **Authorization by Congress:** [§532] In some areas (*e.g.*, portions of the law of labor relations), the Supreme Court has interpreted congressional legislation as intending that the federal courts develop substantive law to further national uniformity. [*See* Textile Workers Union v. Lincoln Mills, 353 U.S. 448 (1957)]

    c. **Sufficient federal interest:** [§533] The Court sometimes regards the federal government as having a strong enough interest in a transaction that it should be governed by uniform federal common law to further that interest, even in the absence of congressional authorization and despite contrary state law. [*See, e.g.*, Clearfield Trust Co. v. United States, 318 U.S. 363 (1943)—federal common law governed on issue of delay in notice of forgery of federal government check] There must, however, be a significant federal interest. [*See, e.g.*, Bank of America v. Parnell, 352 U.S. 29 (1956)—state law governed in suit between private parties on issue of good faith of holder of previously stolen government bonds; that federal government issued the paper involved in the suit does not by itself suffice to require the creation of uniform federal common law]

    d. **Interstate disputes:** [§534] In interstate disputes involving governments of or in different states, such as those over interstate pollution, it may be inappropriate for the law of one of the interested states to govern. The federal courts consequently may develop federal common law when no congressional legislation deals with the area. [Illinois v. City of Milwaukee, 406 U.S. 91 (1972)]

    e. **United States foreign relations:** [§535] When questions of American foreign relations are involved, the need for uniform federal common law may be especially clear. [*See, e.g.,* Banco Nacional de Cuba v. Sabbatino, 376 U.S. 398 (1964)]

IV. PLEADING

chapter approach

Questions on pleadings generally concern one or more of the following issues:

1. **Complaint**

   a. Does the plaintiff's complaint *state a claim upon which relief can be granted?* To do so, it must allege the *elements* required by substantive law to constitute a cause of action. If it is deficient, the complaint may be challenged by *demurrer* (in code pleading states) or by *motion to dismiss* (in Federal Rules systems.)

   b. Does the complaint make its allegations with the *specificity* required under applicable pleading rules? In code pleading systems, the complaint must include "*facts* constituting the cause of action." In the federal courts and in most state systems that are based on the Federal Rules of Civil Procedure, "*notice pleading*" suffices: In addition to any required statement of jurisdiction and a prayer for relief, the complaint need contain only a "short and plain statement of the claim showing that the pleader is entitled to relief." However, the plaintiff still needs to set forth factual matter to support each element of the claim.

2. **Answer**

   a. Does the defendant's answer *deny* the material allegations of the complaint? To the extent it does not, the allegations may be taken as *admitted.*

   b. Does the answer raise *affirmative defenses* to the complaint?

   c. Does the answer set forth *counterclaims*?

      —A counterclaim arising out of the transaction or occurrence that is the subject matter of the opposing party's claim is a *compulsory counterclaim* and should be included in the answer.

      —Any other counterclaim is *permissive* and may be included at the option of the pleader. In federal court, there generally is *no supplemental jurisdiction* over permissive counterclaims; there must be an *independent basis of federal jurisdiction.*

3. **Investigation of Claims and Defenses:** Federal Rule 11 and similar state rules require investigation of the claims and defenses made in pleadings. Be sure to consider the following:

   a. Was *reasonable inquiry* made concerning the legal and factual bases of the claim or defense?

   b. Does the claim or defense have *evidentiary support*?

   c. Is the claim or defense *warranted by existing law* or a good faith argument for extension of the law?

d. Was the claim or defense interposed for an *improper purpose*, such as to harass the opposing party?

e. If the claim or defense was improperly asserted, what *sanctions*, if any, are appropriate?

Besides these topics, be sure to review briefly the rules discussed in this chapter on amended and supplemental pleadings, default, judgment on the pleadings, and voluntary dismissal by the plaintiff.

A. INTRODUCTION

1. **In General:** [§536] The plaintiff begins a civil action by filing in a court of appropriate jurisdiction a complaint in which he seeks some sort of judicial relief against specified defendants. The court thereupon issues its process (*e.g.,* summons) directing the named defendants to appear. A defendant "appears" by filing some sort of response (*e.g.,* answer, motion, demurrer), after which other pleadings and motions may be filed until the case is "at issue."

2. **Objectives:** [§537] The basic purpose of pleadings is to give notice of the general character of the controversy between the parties. Under code pleading (*see infra,* §543; used in such states as California, Illinois, and New York), the pleadings are also intended to narrow and formulate the issues involved in the case. The pleading process thus helps to determine the scope of the action for the trial and the scope of any judgment in the action.

3. **Background:** [§538] At common law, the courts relied exclusively on the pleadings to define the issues. The result was that the pleading process was all-important and pleading rules were extremely technical. Mistakes in the pleading process often proved fatal to the pleader's case, and prevented a hearing on the merits of the case. However, under modern practice, the pleadings are merely one stage of the issue-defining process. Discovery devices and the pretrial conference (*infra,* Chapters VI and VIII) are also available. Consequently, there has been a strong trend toward liberalizing the rules of pleading and streamlining the pleading process.

B. HISTORY OF PLEADING

1. **Common Law Pleadings:** [§539] The original common law courts could grant relief only in accordance with certain recognized *forms of action,* each representing a particular theory of substantive law (*e.g.,* trespass, case, trover, assumpsit, etc.) and pleadings had to be drawn in terms of one of these recognized forms. Thus, the plaintiff was forced to fit the out-of-court transaction of which he was complaining into the mold of one of the forms. Amendments to change the form of action were not allowed, so once a plaintiff chose a particular form, he could recover—if at all—only under the substantive theory of law represented by the form; *i.e.,* if the plaintiff chose trespass, but the facts established trover, the plaintiff could not recover.

    a. **Objective:** [§540] The basic objective of pleading at common law was to narrow the issues as finely as possible (preferably to a single issue), so that the case could be determined by deciding that issue.

b. **Numerous pleadings:** [§541] For this purpose, distinct pleadings and counterpleadings were employed; *e.g.,* declaration, answer, replication, rejoinder, surrejoinder, etc. Each party was required to either demur (challenge sufficiency of the pleading responded to; *see infra,* §652) or counterplead to each pleading by his adversary. The submission of numerous pleadings was time-consuming, and a defendant could often use the pleading rules for purposes of delay.

c. **Compare—equity pleading:** [§542] The courts of equity were distinct from common law courts and were governed by different procedures. Relief was available from the equity courts only where there was no right to recover under any of the forms of action recognized in the law courts (*i.e.,* "remedy at law inadequate"). Therefore, pleaders in equity had to go outside the forms of action to state their claims; the plaintiff recited *facts* showing that he had a grievance that ought to be remedied. This concept of *fact pleading* was the basis of code pleading (below).

2. **Code Pleading:** [§543] The New York Code of 1848 (known as the Field Code) originated code pleading. This code, or adaptations thereof, was subsequently adopted in most states, and is still retained in several today. It incorporates several important departures from common law pleading rules.

   a. **Single form of action:** [§544] Unlike the rigid common law forms, the fundamental requirement of code pleading is that the plaintiff's complaint be in the form of a *statement of facts showing a right to a remedy.* This has been described as abolishing the forms of action and providing for *one form of action.* [Fed. R. Civ. P. 2; Cal. Civ. Proc. Code §307]

      (1) **Effect:** Under code pleading, the plaintiff no longer has to select and set forth in the pleadings the particular legal theory of his case. He is entitled to recover under *any* legal theory applicable to the *facts* pleaded and proved.

      (2) **Example:** P's complaint alleged that D published statements that were injurious to P's reputation (that P committed a hijacking) and that unnecessarily specified P as the person involved. The complaint failed to state a cause of action for libel because the published statements were admittedly true; but it was held sufficient to state a claim for invasion of privacy. If *any* legal theory will sustain recovery on the facts pleaded, the complaint is sufficient. [Briscoe v. Reader's Digest, 4 Cal. 3d 529 (1971)]

      (3) **Example:** P's complaint alleged that the manager of D's store had an arrangement with the local police under which the police would assist the store in refusing service to Blacks at its lunch counter. The complaint was held sufficient to state a claim for violation of P's civil rights under federal statutes, since even if the store itself was not governed by the statute, the police were so governed and the complaint alleged concerted action between D (through its manager) and the police. [Adickes v. S.H. Kress & Co., 398 U.S. 144 (1970)]

   b. **Merger of law and equity:** [§545] Another major aspect of code pleading is the elimination of separate courts of law and equity, and of the separate procedures in each court. This change has persisted under modern practice, where the same court is vested with jurisdiction to grant both equitable and legal relief. [Fed. R. Civ. P. 1]

(1) **Remedies—distinct:** [§546] Note that while the distinctions between legal and equitable *procedure* have been abolished, the distinctions between legal and equitable *remedies* remain intact. The nature of the relief available depends upon the circumstances shown (*e.g.,* whether damage has actually resulted).

   (a) **Example:** For example, equitable relief is generally available only where the legal remedy (damages) is shown to be *inadequate.*

   (b) **Example:** Similarly, various defenses are recognized where an equitable remedy is sought (laches, hardship, unclean hands, etc.), but are not recognized in actions at law.

   (c) **Jury trial:** [§547] Also note that the distinction between legal and equitable remedies is relevant to whether a jury trial is available. While a jury trial is usually available in an action at law, equitable actions are normally tried by the court alone (although the court may impanel a jury for an advisory verdict on disputed questions of fact). (*See* further discussion *infra,* §§1550 *et seq.*)

c. **Limited number of pleadings:** [§548] Far fewer pleadings are allowed under code pleading than in the old common law system, since there is no objective to reduce the case to a single issue through a pleading "dialogue."

   (1) **Types of pleadings:** [§549] The following basic pleadings are allowed under existing codes:

Plaintiff's pleadings **Defendant's pleadings**

California Civ. Proc. Code §§422.10, 430.30

Plaintiff's pleadings	Defendant's pleadings
Complaint	Demurrer to complaint; Answer
Demurrer to answer	
Demurrer to cross-complaint	Cross-complaint
Answer to cross-complaint	Demurrer to answer to cross-complaint

Plaintiff's pleadings **Defendant's pleadings**

New York Civ. Prac. Law §§3011, 3211

Plaintiff's pleadings	Defendant's pleadings
Complaint	Motion to dismiss; Answer
Motion to dismiss counterclaim; Reply to counterclaim	Counterclaim

Illinois Code Civ. Proc. §§2-602, 2-608, 2-614, 2-615

Complaint	Motion to dismiss; Answer
Reply to affirmative matter in answer	
Motion to dismiss counterclaim; Answer to counterclaim	Counterclaim

(2) **Note:** In contrast to the practices in some other code states, California and New York do not permit a reply to matters of affirmative defense in the defendant's answer. Such matter is "deemed controverted" without the necessity of a response by the plaintiff. [Cal. Civ. Proc. Code §431.20(b)]

d. **Fact pleading:** [§550] A pleading under the codes must set forth "the facts constituting *the cause of action* in ordinary and concise language." [Cal. Civ. Proc. Code §425.10(a)] This is interpreted as requiring allegation of the *"ultimate facts"* of the cause of action (or defense) involved.

(1) **"Ultimate facts":** [§551] Ultimate facts are those facts that describe *in adequate detail but without legal argument* the circumstances that the plaintiff believes entitle him to a remedy. If the allegations are too general, they are deemed "conclusions"; and if too much detail is given, it is an impermissible pleading of "evidence."

(a) **Example:** Suppose the plaintiff's complaint makes the following allegations in a negligence action:

(i) "D operated her automobile in violation of Vehicle Code section 23101, and injured P."

(ii) "D consumed one gallon of wine at the Green Frog Cafe, less than two hours before the accident in which P was injured."

(iii) "D drove her car while intoxicated and on the wrong side of the highway, causing it to strike the car in which P was riding."

Allegation (i) could be attacked as a conclusion of law. Allegation (ii) might be found to contain only "evidentiary" matter. Allegation (iii) is a sufficient statement of ultimate fact.

(2) **Consequences of improper pleading of facts:** [§552] Failure to allege ultimate facts constituting every essential element of the cause of action (or defense) involved makes the pleading insufficient and subject to a *general demurrer* or, under some codes, a motion to dismiss (which is the equivalent of a general demurrer). (*See* discussion, *infra,* §§652 *et seq.*)

(a) ***If sufficient ultimate facts are alleged,*** evidentiary allegations and conclusions of law can be treated as surplusage (but are subject to a motion to strike; *see infra,* §668).

(b) ***If the allegations are too vague*** (*i.e.,* mere conclusions), the complaint is also subject to a special demurrer (*see infra,* §§664-665).

(3) **Criticism:** Under the code pleading system, there is considerable difficulty in determining what constitutes the requisite "ultimate facts" (as opposed to "evidentiary matter" or "legal conclusions") in various situations. As a result, pleaders tend to use stereotyped allegations and form complaints that have previously been held sufficient.

3. **Pleading Under the Federal Rules:** [§553]   The Federal Rules have *further liberalized* pleading standards and have eliminated many of the technical requirements under the Field Code. Today, most states have also adopted the Federal Rules.

   a. **Pleadings permitted:** [§554]   The Federal Rules authorize even fewer pleadings than the code pleading states (above). The basic pleadings allowed by Federal Rule 7(a) are:

Plaintiff's Pleadings	**Defendant's Pleadings**
Complaint	Answer, which may contain a counterclaim against plaintiff
Reply to counterclaim	

   (1) **Note:** The ***demurrer has been eliminated*** in federal courts. In its place, the ***motion to dismiss for failure to state a claim*** is used. [Fed. R. Civ. P. 12(b)(6)]

   b. **Notice pleading:** [§555]   The Federal Rules eliminate the code requirement of pleading "facts constituting a cause of action." Instead, the Rules simply require a ***"short and plain statement of the claim showing the pleader is entitled to relief."*** [Fed. R. Civ. P. 8(a)(2)] This has been called "notice pleading."

   (1) **Rationale:** The purpose of pleading under the Federal Rules is simply to *identify* the transaction out of which the plaintiff's claim arises, so that the defendant has *notice* of the claim. Discovery and other pretrial procedures are relied on for full development of the facts. [Conley v. Gibson, 355 U.S. 41 (1957)] Under the Federal Rules, the distinctions among "ultimate facts," "evidentiary facts," and "conclusions of law" (above) are therefore unimportant. Any claim may be stated in general terms, and precision in identifying the cause of action is not required.

C. COMPLAINT

1. **In General:** [§556]   In most jurisdictions, a civil action is commenced by the filing of the plaintiff's complaint. [Fed. R. Civ. P. 3; Cal. Civ. Proc. Code §411.10] (In New

York, the action is commenced by service of process; and the complaint can be filed thereafter.)

2. **Form:** [§557] The essential parts of the complaint are: the caption, jurisdictional allegations, body, prayer for relief, and subscription.

   a. **Caption:** [§558] The complaint must set forth:

   (i) The name of the court;

   (ii) The number assigned to the action (stamped by the clerk when the action is filed);

   (iii) A designation of the pleading (*e.g.,* "Complaint for Damages"); and

   (iv) The names of the parties.

   [Fed. R. Civ. P. 10; Cal. Civ. Proc. Code §§422.30; 422.40]

   (1) **Note:** Suing "John Doe" defendants is permitted in some states if the plaintiff does not know the true names of all parties-defendant. [Cal. Civ. Proc. Code §474]

   (2) **Effect of errors:** [§559] Under modern rules, pleadings are "so construed as to do substantial justice." [Fed. R. Civ. P. 8(f)] Accordingly, the courts will disregard errors in the form or caption of the complaint that do not mislead the other party.

   (a) **Name of party wrong or incomplete:** [§560] An error or incompleteness in designating a party in the *complaint* is generally harmless error. However, if there is also error in the *summons* and as a result the intended defendant is not adequately warned that he is being sued, the action may be subject to dismissal for insufficient process.

   b. **Jurisdictional allegations:** [§561] In *federal* court, the complaint must contain allegations showing the ground (or grounds) upon which the subject matter jurisdiction of the federal court is invoked. [Fed. R. Civ. P. 8(a)(1)] Since federal courts are courts of *limited* jurisdiction, a complaint that fails to set forth the jurisdictional grounds must be dismissed unless the ground can be supplied by amendment. (*See infra,* §§841 *et seq.*)

   (1) **Example:** If jurisdiction is founded on diversity of citizenship, a sufficient statement might be: "Plaintiff is a citizen of New York and defendant is a citizen of California. The matter in controversy exceeds, exclusive of interest and costs, the sum of $50,000."

   (2) **Compare—state practice:** [§562] Jurisdictional allegations generally are *not* required in state court practice, because state courts usually have general jurisdiction.

   c. **Body:** [§563] The complaint must also contain a statement of the facts upon which recovery is sought. In code pleading states, this requires a "statement of the (ultimate) facts constituting the cause of action" (*supra,* §550); while under the Federal Rules there must be a "short and plain statement of the claim showing that the pleader is entitled to relief" (*supra,* §555).

(1) **Separate causes of action:** [§564] Each claim or cause of action should be set forth in a separate group of serially numbered paragraphs; and each paragraph should be limited to a statement of a single set of circumstances. [Fed. R. Civ. P. 10(b)]

   (a) *Under code pleading practice,* this was an essential requirement. A complaint that lumped together several causes of action was subject to demurrer.

   (b) *Under modern law,* however, failure to state separate claims separately ("First Cause of Action," "Second Cause of Action") is simply a formal defect—and is not even a basis of objection in some states (*e.g.,* California).

   (c) *Under certain circumstances,* it may be important for the defendant to know exactly the grounds on which the plaintiff is proceeding (*e.g.,* where several different claims have been lumped together and the statute of limitations is different on each claim). In such cases, the defendant's remedy is to file a demurrer for uncertainty under code pleading practice (*infra,* §654) or a motion for more definite statement under federal practice (*infra,* §687).

(2) **Direct allegations:** [§565] The allegations in the complaint should be "simple, concise and direct." [Fed. R. Civ. P. 8(e)]

   (a) **Recitals:** [§566] It is improper to allege essential facts only by way of recitals (*e.g.,* an allegation that "A, *while acting as D's agent,* executed a contract with P"). The proper form is "At all times herein, A was the agent of D. On or about _____, A made an agreement with P."

   (b) **Exhibits:** [§567] Essential allegations may appear in an exhibit attached to the complaint if *incorporated by reference* into the complaint. [Fed. R. Civ. P. 10(c)]

      1) **Example:** Where the essential allegation is that P gave D notice to quit the premises by a certain date, P can attach a copy of the written notice as an exhibit to the complaint and incorporate it by reference therein. The date can then be ascertained from the exhibit.

   (c) **Consequences of defect:** [§568] Noncompliance with these rules of form is at most the basis for a *demurrer* or *motion* objecting to the defect. In modern practice, such defects are usually disregarded.

(3) **Allegations on "information and belief":** [§569] Ordinarily, the plaintiff's allegations should be based on personal knowledge. However, if the plaintiff lacks personal knowledge of some element of his claim (*e.g.,* is relying on hearsay or conjecture), in *code pleading states* the

plaintiff may still make the allegation on "information and belief." "Information and belief" may be insufficient under the Federal Rules, however. In federal courts, allegations can be made only after reasonable inquiry and with a belief that the pleading is well grounded in fact. [Fed. R. Civ. P. 11; *see infra,* §§709 *et seq.*]

(a) **Denials:** [§570] Similarly, in code pleading states, a defendant may *deny* allegations based on "lack of information and belief." [Cal. Civ. Proc. Code §431.30] And under the Federal Rules, a statement that the defendant is "without knowledge or information sufficient to form a belief as to the truth of an averment" has the effect of a denial. [Fed. R. Civ. P. 8(b)]

(b) **Importance:** [§571] The use of allegations on information and belief is important where a pleading is to be *verified* by a party (*infra,* §590), since the plaintiff should not swear facts to be true when she has no personal knowledge thereof.

(c) **Limitation:** [§572] Allegations on information and belief are improper as to matters which the pleader obviously knows or has *reason to know* (*e.g.,* events that she witnessed), or matters as to which she has *constructive knowledge* (*e.g.,* matters of *public record*). In such cases, pleadings on information and belief will be disregarded, leaving the complaint subject to a demurrer or motion to dismiss.

(4) **Alternative and inconsistent allegations**

(a) **Inconsistent legal theories:** [§573] A plaintiff may properly allege facts based on inconsistent legal theories. Note that Federal Rule 11 may limit this latitude. (*See infra,* §§709 *et seq.*)

1) **Example:** P claims damages as the result of surgery performed on him by Dr. D. P may plead in one count that the surgery was performed without his informed consent (hence a battery) and alternatively, in a separate count, that the surgery was negligently performed. P is entitled to go to trial on *both* theories, so that if the facts do not sustain one theory, they may sustain the other.

2) **Example:** P claims that D fraudulently induced him to execute a contract. P may plead one count for damages based on the fraud and alternatively, in another count, seek rescission of the contract based on the fraud.

3) **Limitation—election of remedies:** [§574] However, while a plaintiff may go to trial on both theories and have a verdict on each, he will have to elect one theory *prior to judgment* because he cannot have two remedies (*e.g.,* duplicate damages) for the same injury. [Savage v. Van Marle, 39 Cal. App. 3d 241 (1974)]

a) **Time of election:** [§575] The plaintiff is not required to make this election until *after* a jury verdict (or fact findings by the court) and before judgment. Otherwise, the plaintiff would have to guess which version of the facts will be sustained and thereby lose the benefit of alternative pleading. [McCormick v. Kopmann, 161 N.E.2d 720 (Ill. 1959)]

(b) **Inconsistent facts:** [§576] A pleader is also permitted to plead inconsistent versions of the facts. [Fed. R. Civ. P. 8(e)] However, some jurisdictions require that the facts alleged indicate some reason why the plaintiff could not know which version was true (*e.g.,* plaintiff was unconscious at time of injury, or injury-causing events occurred outside her observation).

(c) **Alternative defendants:** [§577] The plaintiff can also plead one version of the facts against one defendant and another version against another defendant. Again, in some jurisdictions it may be necessary that there appear a reason why the plaintiff could not know which version is true.

1) **Example:** P rented a bulldozer to D-1, who used it on land in which D-2 has a subsurface gas pipe. The bulldozer operator hit the pipe, destroying the bulldozer. P could allege alternatively that the operator was negligent in hitting the pipe and that D-2 was negligent in having installed the pipe too close to the surface. [Lambert v. Southern Counties Gas Co., 52 Cal. 2d 347 (1959)]

(5) **Defenses need not be anticipated:** [§578] Ordinarily the plaintiff is not required in the complaint to anticipate any defense that the defendant may raise.

(a) **Compare—well-pleaded complaint rule:** [§579] The rule regarding anticipating defenses corresponds to the well-pleaded complaint rule for federal question subject matter jurisdiction (*supra,* §364), which provides that the existence of a federal defense is not considered in deciding whether plaintiff's claim arises under federal law.

d. **Prayer for relief:** [§580] A complaint must also contain a prayer for relief, *i.e.,* a statement of the relief sought.

(1) **In default cases:** [§581] If the defendant defaults by failing to defend, the relief granted cannot exceed what is prayed for in the complaint or differ from it in kind (*e.g.,* an injunction when the prayer was only for damages). *Rationale:* By failing to appear and contest the action, the defendant has, in effect, acquiesced in the entry of judgment against her; but the judgment entered must conform to the "consent" given. [Fed. R. Civ. P. 54(c); Cal. Civ. Proc. Code §580; *infra,* §§879 *et seq.*]

(2) **In contested cases:** [§582] In a contested case, the plaintiff is *not* limited to the relief prayed for in the complaint. The court may award *any relief to which a party is entitled* under the pleadings and proof—even if different from or greater than that prayed for in the complaint. [Fed. R. Civ. P. 54(c); Cal. Civ. Proc. Code §580]

(a) **Limitations:** [§583] In a few states, a plaintiff is not permitted to state the amount of his demand in *personal injury or wrongful death actions.* [Cal. Civ. Proc. Code §425.10(b)] *Rationale:* This rule is to prevent sensational publicity for large demands. (However, the plaintiff must provide a statement of the damages claimed on a demand by the defendant and in any event such a statement must be made before trial.)

(b) **Caution:** [§584] Some decisions hold that where the complaint alleges *specific amounts* of damages, the allegations may be treated as *binding admissions* with respect to the amount of damage sustained. Hence, it may be error to award a greater sum; and such a judgment may be reduced accordingly. [Brown v. North Ventura Road Co., 216 Cal. App. 2d 227 (1963)]

1) **Trial tactic:** [§585] Where evidence at trial indicates that the verdict may exceed the damages pleaded, the plaintiff should seek leave of court to *amend* the damage allegations and prayer upward. This may prevent the problem noted above. (Note that pleadings may be amended even after trial; *see infra,* §873.)

(3) **Other functions of prayer:** [§586] The prayer is ordinarily determinative of the *amount in controversy* for jurisdictional purposes. (*See supra,* §§324 *et seq.*) In state courts, it may also determine the nature of the action (legal or equitable), on which the *right to jury trial* depends.

e. **Subscription:** [§587] The complaint must be signed by the attorney (or by the party himself, where he is acting as his own counsel). [Fed. R. Civ. P. 11; Cal. Civ. Proc. Code §446]

(1) **Effect of signature:** [§588] In federal practice, the signature on a pleading by a party or his attorney constitutes a certification by him that to the best of his knowledge, information, and belief, formed after reasonable inquiry, the evidentiary contentions have evidentiary support or are likely to have such support after discovery and the claims or defenses are warranted by existing law or a good faith argument for change in existing law; and that it is not interposed primarily for any improper purpose such as harassment, delay, or increasing costs. [Fed. R. Civ. P. 11; *see infra,* §§709 *et seq.*]

(a) **Compare—state practice:** [§589] In state practice, subscription sometimes remains a mere formality. [Hancock v. Bowman, 49 Cal. 413 (1874)]

(2) **Verification:** [§590] A verification is an affidavit at the end of a pleading which avers that the pleading is true to the best of affiant's knowledge, information, or belief. The affidavit is made by the party, or by his attorney or other person on her behalf if the pleader cannot do so (*e.g.,* because she is incapacitated), or if another person with better knowledge of the facts is willing to make the verification for the party.

(a) **Federal practice:** [§591] In view of the importance attached to an attorney's subscription in federal practice (above), verification by a party is the exception rather than the rule in federal courts. Federal Rule 11 expressly provides that pleadings need *not* be verified except where specifically required by rule or statute.

1) **Example:** The Federal Rules specifically require verification in shareholders' derivative suits. [Fed. R. Civ. P. 23.1]

(b) **State practice:** [§592] Some code pleading rules provide that any pleading *may* be verified; and verification is frequently required by statute as to certain kinds of proceedings (*e.g.,* quiet title actions, unlawful detainer proceedings, divorce suits).

1) **Effect of verification:** [§593] If a pleading is verified, the responsive pleading must also be verified (*e.g.,* if P files a verified complaint, D's answer *must* be verified by D). Moreover, a defendant cannot use a mere general denial (*infra,* §752) in answering a verified complaint. [Cal. Civ. Proc. Code §431.30(d)]

2) **How to attack lack of verification:** [§594] If a pleading that requires verification is not verified, the pleading is subject to a *motion to strike* (*infra,* §668).

3. **Pleading Specific Claims:** [§595] As noted previously, the body of the complaint must contain allegations showing that the plaintiff has a right to recover.

    a. **In general:** [§596] The elements of any particular cause of action involve both a *substantive* and a *procedural* aspect.

    (1) **Substance:** [§597] Substantive law determines whether a specific incident or transaction *results in liability* to the plaintiff. For example, calling someone a "subversive" results in liability for defamation only if the substantive law so provides.

    (2) **Procedure:** [§598] The procedural aspect is one of *allocation:* The plaintiff must allege enough particulars about the incident to constitute a *prima facie case.* Other particulars may be relevant, but will be considered only if they are injected into the case by the *defendant,* ordinarily in an affirmative defense. *Example:* When P alleges that D called him a subversive, does P also have to allege that the statement is *false* in order to state a claim for libel? Or must defendant raise the issue by pleading truth as an *affirmative defense*? The rule varies from state to state. [*See* Brewster v. Boston Herald-Traveler, 188 F. Supp. 565 (D. Mass. 1960)]

    (a) **State pleading:** [§599] The following discussion of pleading requirements in particular causes of action is primarily important for *code pleading* states, where the general rule is that every essential element of the cause of action sued upon must be pleaded by allegations of "ultimate fact." (*See supra,* §551.)

    (b) **Federal pleading:** [§600] This is not to imply that the elements of a cause of action may be disregarded in *notice pleading* jurisdictions: Federal Rule 8(a) requires that the complaint show that the plaintiff has a "right to relief"; and Federal Rule 12(b) authorizes a motion to dismiss for "failure to state a claim upon which relief can be granted" (*see infra,* §674). However, under the Federal Rules:

1) *Less detail and specificity* are required;

2) *Omission of allegations is never fatal* (*i.e.*, they can be supplied by amendment); and

3) *Only where the allegations positively indicate that the plaintiff cannot recover* as a matter of law is the action subject to dismissal for failure to state a claim. [Conley v. Gibson, 355 U.S. 41 (1957)]

b. **Trespass to land—elements:** [§601] The essential elements in a trespass action are as follows:

(1) *Plaintiff's possession or right to possession* of the described property (as owner or otherwise) at the time of defendant's wrongful act. In most code pleading states, an allegation of "ownership" is sufficient to establish at least constructive possession, as long as there is nothing in the complaint to indicate that anyone else was in actual possession.

(2) *Defendant's wrongful intrusion* on the described property.

(3) *Damage* proximately caused by defendant's intrusion.

c. **Recovery of possession (ejectment)—elements:** [§602] In an action for ejectment, the plaintiff must allege:

(1) *Ownership* by plaintiff of some interest in the real property, adequately described. Ownership may be generally alleged; *i.e.,* "P was owner and in possession of Blackacre." This is a legal conclusion, but it is the best practical form of allegation, and hence is treated as an ultimate fact rather than a conclusion of law.

(2) *Defendant's possession and withholding.*

(3) *Damage* to plaintiff.

d. **Negligence**

(1) **Elements:** [§603] A complaint asserting negligence must contain allegations of: duty, breach of duty, damages, and causation.

(a) **Duty:** [§604] The plaintiff must allege the *specific facts from which the defendant's duty arose* (or from which it is inferred). *Examples:* Plaintiff was: "driving on public highway"; "customer in defendant's store"; "patient under defendant's care"; etc.

1) **Example:** An allegation that "the defendant owed the plaintiff a duty of care" is a conclusion of law, and the complaint would

be subject to a general demurrer. But an allegation that "the defendant was operating her automobile on Main Street near the intersection of Benton Way, and plaintiff was standing in a streetcar loading zone in the middle of that intersection" is a sufficient allegation of ultimate facts. From these facts, it can be inferred that the defendant, as a reasonable person, owed a duty of due care to the plaintiff in the operation of her automobile.

    2) **Compare:** If the duty to be inferred rests upon unusual or special circumstances, they must be specifically alleged in the complaint—*e.g.*, a landlord ordinarily owes a duty to his tenant only with respect to known, latent defects (*see* Torts Summary), so that the landlord's knowledge and the latency of the defects must be alleged.

(b) **Negligent action or omission (breach of duty):** [§605] In most code pleading states, the plaintiff can allege the defendant's breach of duty *generally*—*i.e.*, merely alleging that whatever the defendant did was "negligently" done, or that the defendant "negligently" failed to do something.

    1) **Note:** An allegation of negligence is admittedly a conclusion of law; but in most instances it is still the best way to describe how the act was done. Thus, an allegation of negligence is treated as a sufficient allegation of the ultimate fact of breach of duty—as *a rule of convenience and fairness.* [Rannard v. Lockheed Aircraft Corp., 26 Cal. 2d 149 (1945)]

    2) **Compare:** Alternatively, a general allegation of negligence may be replaced or supplemented by allegations of negligent acts showing that the defendant breached a duty of care (*e.g.*, "failed to keep a lookout"; "failed to maintain control of her car").

        a) **But note:** Ordinarily, a general allegation by itself is preferable, because it does not tie the plaintiff down to any particular set of facts he must prove on trial.

        b) **And note—res ipsa loquitur:** If the plaintiff intends to invoke the presumption of res ipsa loquitur at trial, some authorities hold that he must plead facts showing that he does not know the specific details of the defendant's negligence. In most states, however, res ipsa loquitur is no longer a matter of pleading, but one of proper instructions to the jury, to be given when the evidence of negligence is circumstantial. [Newing v. Cheatham, 15 Cal. 3d 351 (1975)]

(c) **Damages:** [§606] No cause of action in negligence will lie unless injury has been sustained. (For rules on pleading damages, *see infra*, §§623-630.)

(d) **Allegation of causation:** [§607] The courts are fairly liberal with respect to pleading causation and will allow allegations in *general terms*—*e.g.,* that plaintiff's injuries were "proximately caused" by the defendant's wrongful act.

1) **But note:** The courts insist that the *causal chain* between each step of the transaction be clearly alleged. Causation will not be inferred if there is an apparent gap between the defendant's wrongful act and the injuries to the plaintiff.

2) **Example:** P simply alleges that she suffered emotional distress "as a result" of defendant's conduct. This general statement of causation is insufficient, since P must allege facts showing the causal chain between D's conduct and P's distress—*i.e.,* the time, manner, and manifestations of the distress. [Deboe v. Horn, 16 Cal. App. 3d 221 (1971)]

(2) **Defenses need not be anticipated:** [§608] Ordinarily, the plaintiff is *not* required in the complaint to anticipate any defense that the defendant may raise (*e.g.,* assumption of risk, contributory negligence) and allege freedom from fault thereunder. Nor must the plaintiff allege facts showing that the defendant had the "last clear chance" to avoid the injury. The plaintiff can introduce such facts for the first time at trial, if the defendant has raised contributory negligence as a defense in her answer. In short, affirmative defenses in the answer are "deemed controverted." [Mahoney v. Coralejo, 36 Cal. App. 3d 966 (1974)]

e. **Products liability**

(1) **Elements:** [§609] The essential elements of a cause of action for strict liability against the manufacturer or seller of a defective product are that:

(i) *Defendant was in the business* of making or selling the product in question;

(ii) *Defendant made or sold* the product in question;

(iii) *The product was in defective condition* (unreasonably dangerous for its foreseeable use) when it left defendant's control and when plaintiff used it; *and*

(iv) *Use of the product proximately caused injury* to plaintiff.

[Read v. Safeway Stores, 264 Cal. App. 2d 404 (1968)]

(2) **Note:** Under modern cases, it is generally *not* necessary to allege or prove: (i) privity of contract between the parties (as required in a warranty action); (ii) the plaintiff's reliance as a user or consumer on the reputation, skill, or judgment of the seller; (iii) any representation or undertaking on the part of the seller; or (iv) compliance with the provisions of the Uniform Commercial Code applicable to warranty actions. (*See* Torts Summary.)

f. **Fraud**

(1) **Action at law:** [§610]   If the action for fraud is one at *law,* the necessary elements are:

   (a) *Representation;*

   (b) *Falsity;*

   (c) *Knowledge* of falsity (*scienter*);

   (d) *Intent to deceive* plaintiff;

   (e) *Justifiable reliance* by plaintiff; and

   (f) *Damages.*

(2) **Suit in equity:** [§611]   If the suit is in *equity* (*e.g.,* to rescind a contract because of a fraudulent misrepresentation), the necessary elements are the same, except that scienter and damages need *not* be shown. (*See* Remedies Summary.)

(3) **Special pleading requirement:** [§612]   In any event, the *ultimate facts* in a fraud action must always be pleaded *with particularity;* general allegations are not sufficient. [*See* Fed. R. Civ. P. 9(b); Searle & Co. v. Superior Court, 49 Cal. App. 3d 22 (1975)]

g. **Defamation:** [§613]   The elements of a defamation claim are as follows:

(1) *Publication by defendant* to third persons of specified false matter which is "of or concerning" plaintiff.

(2) *Defamatory nature* of statement.

   (a) *If the statement is defamatory per se* (*e.g.,* an assertion that plaintiff committed a felonious crime), alleging the statement is sufficient. [Megarry v. Norton, 137 Cal. App. 2d 581 (1955)]

   (b) *If the statement on its face does not appear to be defamatory,* it must be alleged that:

      (i) *Extrinsic facts* make the statement defamatory ("inducement"); and

      (ii) The statement was *understood as defaming plaintiff* ("innuendo").

   [Yorty v. Chandler, 13 Cal. App. 3d 467 (1970)]

(3) *Causation* (*i.e.,* the publication of the defamatory statement caused harm to the plaintiff's reputation).

(4) *Special damages,* where the matter:

    (i) Is not defamatory on its *face* (some jurisdictions);

    (ii) Is *oral* (slander) rather than written (libel) and does not fall into one of the slander per se categories; *or*

    (iii) Appeared in a *newspaper* or *magazine* and no timely **demand for retraction** had been made (some jurisdictions).

[Briscoe v. Reader's Digest, 4 Cal. 3d 529 (1971)] (*See* Torts Summary.)

h. **Contract actions:** [§614] A contract action should allege the following:

  (1) **Terms:** [§615] The making of the contract and its *terms,* by:

    (i) Stating the specific terms of the contract;

    (ii) Attaching and incorporating by reference a copy of the contract, if it is in writing; *or*

    (iii) Giving a general description of the terms of the agreement.

Note: In a few states, the plaintiff must also indicate whether the contract was *oral* or *in writing.* [Cal. Civ. Proc. Code §430.10(g)]

    (a) **Consideration:** [§616] Whether consideration is required to make a promise enforceable is a matter of substantive law, determined by the particular promise. If consideration is required, merely alleging that there was consideration is neither necessary nor proper.

        1) **Enforceable promise:** [§617] If the quid pro quo is specifically alleged or other allegations show the promise is enforceable (*e.g.,* because under seal), such allegations indicate consideration. Hence, a general allegation that there was consideration is a mere conclusion.

        2) **Written contract:** [§618] In some states, an allegation that the agreement is *in writing* will satisfy any requirement of pleading consideration, since a written contract is *presumed* to have been executed for sufficient consideration. [Cal. Civ. Code §1614]

        3) **Adequacy of consideration:** [§619] Adequacy of consideration may have to be alleged in suits to enforce contracts in equity (*e.g.,* specific performance), because the equitable remedy is available only if the contract is fully fair and just.

  (2) **Performance by plaintiff:** [§620] If the contract required the plaintiff to perform in whole or part before the defendant was obliged to perform, the plaintiff must allege performance on his part *or* show facts excusing his performance.

(a) **Note:** In some states, the plaintiff may allege this generally (*e.g.,* "plaintiff has performed all conditions on his part"). [Cal. Civ. Proc. Code §457]

(3) **Conditions precedent:** [§621] If some external condition must occur before the defendant's obligation arises, occurrence of the condition *or* facts constituting an *excuse* (*e.g.,* impossibility) must be alleged.

(a) **Note:** The occurrence of conditions precedent can be alleged generally. [Fed. R. Civ. P. 9(c); Cal. Civ. Proc. Code §457] If *excuse* is relied on, however, it must be specifically alleged. [Gruenberg v. Aetna Insurance Co., 9 Cal. 3d 566 (1973)]

(b) **Compare—conditions subsequent:** The plaintiff need not concern himself with alleging nonoccurrence of a condition subsequent. Occurrence of a condition subsequent is "new matter" to be raised by the defendant in the answer. (*See infra,* §778.)

(4) **Breach:** [§622] The complaint must allege that the defendant *failed to perform* her obligation. *Example:* "Defendant failed to construct the structure in a proper and professional manner"; "Defendant failed to pay the sum agreed to be paid or any part thereof."

(5) **Damages:** *See* below.

i. **Damages:** [§623] The requisite allegations concerning damages depend on whether the action is in contract or in tort and—if in tort—what kind of injury is involved.

(1) **Contract actions**

(a) **Promise to pay money:** [§624] The measure of damages for breach of a promise to pay money is the amount of money unpaid, plus interest. An allegation that no part of the sum has been paid (or "no part except $____") states the damages due.

(b) **Promise to do an act or sell a thing:** [§625] The measure of damages in this situation ordinarily is the difference between the agreed price and the price at which the plaintiff could obtain equivalent goods or services with reasonable effort at the time of breach. This difference is recoverable on a general allegation of damage in a specified amount—*i.e.,* it is *not* necessary to allege specifically the contract price "computation." [Myers v. Stephens, 233 Cal. App. 2d 104 (1965)]

(c) **"Consequential" or "special" damages:** [§626] The defendant is not liable for other damages in a contract action unless she was apprised in advance of facts indicating that they would result if she breached the contract. When such damages are sought, facts must be pleaded to show that the defendant was made aware that such losses could result. [Fed. Rule Civ. P. 9(g); Shook v. Pearson, 99 Cal. App. 2d 348 (1950)]

(2) **Tort**

(a) **Negligence and products liability:** [§627] From the fact of injury, *pain and suffering* may be inferred; and no special allegations are required for these elements of damage. However, other losses—wages, hospital expenses, etc.—must be alleged.

(b) **Defamation:** [§628] Earlier rules distinguished between damages recoverable in slander (oral defamation) and libel (written defamation). Today, allegations showing a defamatory statement are sufficient in most states to permit recovery of damages for indignation and injury to personal reputation, but *loss of income or damages to business* or profession must be specifically alleged. [Smith v. Los Angeles Bookbinders Union, 133 Cal. App. 2d 486 (1955)]

(c) **Other torts:** [§629] At common law, there were complicated distinctions between general and specific damages. In modern procedure, it is proper to describe the nature of the injuries sustained—loss of profits, shock and humiliation, etc.—and allege their monetary value.

1) *Whether a particular type of loss* (*e.g.*, loss of profit, humiliation) is *recoverable* is a matter of substantive law.

2) *Whether a particular type of loss* must be *pleaded* is a matter of *fair notice.* If the loss in question is not one that obviously would result from the conduct complained of, the facts showing the loss must be pleaded. [Continental Nut Co. v. Robert L. Berner Co., 345 F.2d 395 (7th Cir. 1965); Triodyne, Inc. v. Superior Court, 240 Cal. App. 2d 536 (1966)]

(d) **Punitive damages:** [§630] Punitive damages are allowed only in some types of intentional torts—those involving fraud or willfully inflicted injury. Even when allowed, a claim for them must be made in either the statement of the cause of action or the prayer for relief, so that the defendant is on notice that they are being sought.

j. **Pleading the "common counts"**

(1) **Definition:** [§631] A "common count" is a simple pleading form seeking contractual or quasi-contractual relief—*e.g.*, to recover the value of goods or services rendered to another, money due on a loan, a balance owing on an account, etc. [*See* Fed. R. Civ. P. Forms 4-8]

(2) **Example:** "D is indebted to P in the sum of $_____ for goods sold and delivered by P to D at D's request" is an example of the common count form. The common counts are conclusions of law, but are sufficient to state a cause of action under code pleading.

(3) **Limitation:** [§632] Pleading by means of a common count cannot overcome a substantive deficiency in the plaintiff's claim—as where the plaintiff supplied goods to the defendant in circumstances *not* reasonably

implying a duty on the defendant's part to pay for them (*e.g.,* plaintiff voluntarily sent goods to defendant through the mail and then demanded payment for them).

    (a) **Consequences**

        1) *If the plaintiff pleads a common count in this situation,* the *pleading* is sufficient; but the substantive sufficiency of the plaintiff's claim may be attacked by summary judgment (*see* Chapter VIII.). [Berk v. Alperin, 206 Cal. App. 2d 240 (1962)]

        2) *If the plaintiff pleads the common count along with an alternative count* that pleads the facts, the alternative count will be looked to in order to determine whether the underlying claim is substantively valid. [White Lighting Co. v. Wolfson, 68 Cal. 2d 336 (1968)]

        3) *In any event, where the common count leaves the defendant uncertain* as to what is being complained of, various *discovery devices* are available by which she may ascertain the facts underlying the complaint. (*See* Chapter VI.)

4. **Splitting of Claims:** [§633] A pleader cannot split a single claim or cause of action into several different parts and sue on each one. If the plaintiff sues on only part of the cause of action he has against the defendant, he is barred from suing later on the balance. This results from the doctrine of *res judicata, i.e.,* that a judgment on any portion of a single cause of action merges the cause of action into the judgment, so that there is nothing left to sue on (*see* Chapter XI.). Where judgment has not been entered, and two cases are pending, attacks on the pleadings are possible.

    a. **Obvious splitting:** [§634] If the plaintiff is proceeding in two separate actions and the splitting appears **on the face** of either complaint (unlikely), some states permit a special demurrer on the ground that "there is another action pending between the same parties for the same cause." [Cal. Civ. Proc. Code §430.10(c)]

    b. **Splitting not obvious:** [§635] More frequently, the splitting will not appear on the face of either complaint, in which case the objection must be raised by the defendant in her answer (again, on the ground that another action is pending between the same parties for the same cause).

5. **Joinder of Claims**

    a. **No compulsory joinder of claims:** [§636] While res judicata may force the plaintiff to bring suit upon her entire claim or cause of action (above), there is *no* requirement that she join in a single action what are separate and independent claims. Even where the claims are factually related, the plaintiff has the option of instituting a separate suit on each separate claim although, as a practical matter, plaintiffs usually join related claims because of the danger of *collateral estoppel.* (*See infra,* §§2074 *et seq.*)

Civil Procedure—109

b. **Permissive joinder of claims**

(1) **Early common law rules:** [§637] At common law, the joinder of separate claims was permitted only if all claims were in the same *form* of action and there was *identity* of parties to each claim.

(a) **Example:** Slander could be joined with nuisance or negligent infliction of bodily injury because both claims had the same form of action (*i.e.*, trespass on the case). Moreover, joinder was permitted regardless of whether there was any factual relationship between these claims.

(b) **Compare:** A claim for slander (trespass on the case) could not be joined with one for assault and battery (trespass)—even where both claims arose out of the same event—because the two claims involved different forms of action.

(2) **Equity rules:** [§638] In equity suits, it was generally sufficient if the claim arose out of the same transaction or transactions and involved a common question of law or fact—*i.e.*, a requirement of subject matter relationship.

(3) **Code pleading rules:** [§639] Under the original Field Code, a plaintiff was restricted as to the causes of action that could be joined in a single complaint. All causes joined had to be the *same type* of claim (*e.g.*, all for injury to person, for injury to property, or all contract claims, etc.), or at least arise out of the same transaction; all such causes had to affect all parties to the action; and no cause could require a venue different from the others.

(a) **Criticism:** These rules frequently prevented a plaintiff from settling all claims against a defendant in a single action, and drastically narrowed the rules on permissive joinder of parties (because *all* causes joined had to affect *all* parties). In effect, the rules fostered a multiplicity of suits.

(b) **Note:** To remedy this situation, many states have now adopted the more liberal Federal Rule on joinder, below. [*See* Cal. Civ. Proc. Code §427.10]

(4) **Federal Rules:** [§640] The modern viewpoint on joinder of claims is represented by Federal Rule 18(a), which *abolishes all restrictions* on the joinder of claims and provides that a party asserting a claim for relief may join as many claims as she has against an opposing party, regardless of subject matter.

(a) **Limitation in multi-party cases:** [§641] While there are no restrictions on the number or nature of claims that may be joined where a *single* plaintiff is suing a *single* defendant, the rules on joinder of parties impose limitations where there are several co-plaintiffs or co-defendants. When there are multiple parties, *at least one* of the claims by or against each party must arise out of "the same transaction or series of transactions" *and* must involve a "common question of law or fact" affecting each of the parties joined. [Fed. R. Civ. P. 20(a)]

    1) **Effect:** The joinder of parties rules thus limit the joinder of claims in multiparty cases to those among which there is a *subject matter relationship.*

    2) **Example:** P may sue D1 and D2 for personal injuries sustained in a three-car collision, asserting claims against both D1 and D2 because the same transaction is involved. P may also join a separate claim she has against D2 for nonpayment of a promissory note, even though this does not affect D1 in any way, because there are common questions of law affecting D1 and D2 in the personal injury claim.

  (b) **Separate trials:** [§642] In its discretion, the trial court may remedy any possible inconvenience or prejudice caused by the joinder of claims by ordering separate trials. [Fed. R. Civ. P. 20(b); 42(b)]

    1) **Compare:** If the claims are brought in *separate suits,* but have related subject matter, the defendant may move to have the trials *consolidated.* [Fed. R. Civ. P. 42(a), below]

6. **Consolidation of Separate Actions:** [§643] The trial judge has the power to order separate lawsuits tried together or have them consolidated into a single action, if they involve a "common question of law or fact." [Fed. R. Civ. P. 42(b); Cal. Civ. Proc. Code §1048]

  a. **Actions pending in different courts:** [§644] Where separate actions involving related facts are pending in different courts, many jurisdictions permit one or more of the actions to be *transferred* so they can be consolidated or joined for trial in the same court. The cases may be transferred in whole or in part.

    (1) **State procedure:** [§645] Transfer in state courts may be ordered where it will "promote the just and efficient control" of the various cases involved, and may involve transfer of the whole action or only certain issues (*e.g.,* liability). [Cal. Civ. Proc. Code §404]

    (2) **Federal practice:** [§646] Federal "multi-district" litigation may be consolidated in one district for all *pretrial* purposes (development of issues, discovery, pre-trial conference). [28 U.S.C. §1407] However, the parties have a right to *trial* in the district where the action was filed unless the action was transferred to another district where it "might have been brought." [28 U.S.C. §1404(a); *see supra,* §§162 *et seq.*]

D. CHALLENGES TO COMPLAINT

1. **In General:** [§647] Before responding to the factual allegations in the plaintiff's complaint (by admitting or denying them, or setting forth some defense or offset thereto), a defendant may challenge the legal sufficiency of the complaint.

2. **Common Law:** [§648] At common law, defects in the pleadings could be raised by a demurrer. There were two kinds of demurrer:

   a. **General demurrer:** [§649] A general demurrer *challenged the substantive sufficiency* of the cause or causes in the complaint. It did not specifically state the reason for demurring, but asked the court to pause (demur) and look at the complaint to see if it stated a valid case. Otherwise, why prolong the proceeding? This is still the basic idea of a general demurrer.

   b. **Special demurrer:** [§650] This common law demurrer *specially stated* a matter to be scrutinized in the complaint—*e.g.,* incapacity of plaintiff, allegations that were too vague, etc. Hence, the special demurrer challenged *matters of form.*

3. **State Practice:** [§651] The Field Code, as adopted in states such as California, preserved the demurrer. In other states, such as New York, a motion to dismiss or (when the objection is that the pleading is vague) a motion to make more definite and certain is used instead. (*See infra,* §687.) However, the functions of these challenges are similar.

   a. **Demurrer:** [§652] A demurrer is a pleading filed by one party for the purpose of challenging the *legal sufficiency* of the other party's pleading.

      (1) **Pleadings subject to demurrer:** [§653] The most frequent use of the demurrer is to challenge the plaintiff's complaint. However, the plaintiff may demur to an affirmative defense, counterclaim, or cross-complaint filed by the defendant.

      (2) **Grounds for demurrer:** [§654] The grounds for demurrer usually include the following [Cal. Civ. Proc. Code §430.10]:

         (a) *Lack of jurisdiction over the subject* of the action (note that lack of *personal* jurisdiction must be challenged by a motion to quash; a demurrer constitutes a "general appearance" and waives the defect);

         (b) *Plaintiff lacks legal capacity* to sue;

         (c) *Another action is pending* between the same parties for the same cause;

         (d) *Defect or misjoinder* of parties;

         (e) *Failure to state facts sufficient to constitute a cause of action*—the "general demurrer" (below);

         (f) *Complaint is uncertain* (ambiguous, unintelligible); *and*

         (g) In an action upon a contract, *inability to ascertain whether the contract is oral or written.*

      (3) **"General" vs. "special" demurrer:** [§655] A demurrer for failure to plead facts sufficient to constitute a cause of action is considered a "general" demurrer. A demurrer on any other ground is a "special" demurrer.

(a) **Issue:** In ruling on a general demurrer, the court must accept all facts pleaded as though they were true. The issue is whether—assuming the facts pleaded are true—*such facts would entitle the plaintiff to some form of judicial relief.*

(b) **Standard:** If the complaint alleges facts sufficient to constitute *some* valid cause of action, the general demurrer will be overruled. The test is whether the complaint sets forth *any* good cause of action.

(4) **Defect appearing on face of complaint:** [§656] The demurrer challenges only defects that appear on the face of the pleading (or matters of which the court can take *judicial notice*). A demurrer *cannot* be used to introduce facts to controvert what is alleged in the pleading; *i.e.,* "speaking demurrers" are not allowed.

(a) **Note:** For this reason, certain grounds of demurrer—*e.g.,* plaintiff's lack of legal capacity or nonjoinder of parties—are rarely sustained. Such defects rarely appear on the face of the plaintiff's complaint and thus must be raised by motion (*see* below) or by affirmative defense in the answer.

(b) **But note:** Where the plaintiff's own allegations disclose some *complete defense* (*e.g.,* running of statute of limitations) *on the face of the complaint,* a general demurrer will lie unless the plaintiff has somehow "pleaded around" the defense.

(5) **Procedure:** [§657] A demurrer normally must be filed within the time permitted to answer the complaint. (*See infra,* §796.) The defendant may choose to demur and answer at the same time—as where the demurrer goes to only one portion of the complaint.

(a) **Demurrer must specify defect:** [§658] The defendant's demurrer must be in writing and must specify the ground for objection. Unless it does so, it may be disregarded. [Cal. Civ. Proc. Code §430.60]

1) **Example:** "P's complaint fails to state a cause of action in that it does not allege what consideration, if any, was given for D's promise" is a sufficient demurrer.

(6) **Ruling on demurrer—effects**

(a) **Ruling limited to grounds raised:** [§659] Normally, the court has no power to raise grounds for demurrer on its own; its ruling must be based on the grounds raised by the demurring party.

1) **Exception:** [§660] However, the court may always raise lack of subject matter jurisdiction and the question of whether the pleading alleges facts sufficient to constitute a cause of action.

Civil Procedure—113

(b) **Where demurrer is overruled:** [§661] If the demurrer is overruled, the defendant will be ordered to answer the complaint within a period of time designated by the court. The defendant will then have to make a decision either to: (i) file an answer; or (ii) refuse to do so, allow the plaintiff to obtain a *default* judgment, and appeal the default judgment.

1) *If the defendant files an answer,* she *waives* any error in the overruling of a *special* demurrer. However, the defendant retains the right to object that the complaint does not state a cause of action.

2) *If the defendant does not file an answer* and appeals the resulting default judgment, she takes a big risk: An appellate court will not reverse unless the judgment was so plainly erroneous as to constitute an "abuse of discretion." [Bristol Convalescent Hospital v. Sone, 258 Cal. App. 2d 848 (1968)]

(c) **Where demurrer is sustained**

1) **Specify grounds:** [§662] In some states, the court must specify the particular ground or grounds upon which the demurrer is sustained. [Cal. Civ. Proc. Code §472d]

2) **Leave to amend:** [§663] Having sustained the demurrer, the court normally grants the plaintiff *leave to amend* the complaint.

   a) *If the court is convinced that the defect cannot be cured* by amendment (especially where the plaintiff has already tried unsuccessfully to amend), it may sustain the demurrer *without* leave to amend. In that event, a *judgment of dismissal* is entered (from which the plaintiff can appeal).

   b) *If the plaintiff is granted leave to amend and amends* the complaint within the time permitted, the defendant again has the choice of answering or demurring to the amended complaint.

   c) *If the plaintiff chooses not to amend* (or fails to amend within the time permitted), a judgment of dismissal will be entered. The plaintiff can then obtain appellate review; but the appellate court will affirm the dismissal if:

      1/ The complaint was *defective in substance,* even though the trial judge was incorrect as to the ground on which it was defective [Friendly Village Community Association v. Silva & Hill Construction Co., 31 Cal. App. 3d 220 (1973)]; *or*

      2/ The complaint was *defective in form and the party failed to use an opportunity* given him in the trial court *to clarify* his pleading. [Cooper v. Leslie Salt

Co., 70 Cal. 2d 627 (1969)] *Note:* Appellate courts do sometimes give plaintiffs a second chance to amend in this situation. [*See e.g.,* Gillispie v. Goodyear Service Stores, 128 S.E.2d 487 (N.C. 1963)—remand to allow plaintiff to replead]

(7) **Effect of failure to raise ground for demurrer:** [§664] Grounds for demurrer are *waived* unless raised in the defendant's *initial pleading*—demurrer *or answer*. (Where the defect does not appear on the face of the complaint—*e.g.,* plaintiff's lack of capacity to sue—it will, of course, have to be raised in the answer.) [Cal. Civ. Proc. Code §430.80]

  (a) **Exceptions:** [§665] *Failure to state facts sufficient to constitute a cause of action* and the court's *lack of subject matter jurisdiction* are never waived. These objections can be raised at any time. [Cal. Civ. Proc. Code §430.80]

  (b) **Compare—waiver of personal jurisdiction and process:** [§666] Since a general demurrer constitutes an appearance in the action, it results in a waiver of objections to *personal* jurisdiction and to sufficiency of process.

(8) **Criticism of demurrers:** [§667] Modern writers generally condemn the demurrer as encouraging dilatory tactics by the defendant. Although a general demurrer undoubtedly serves a valuable function in weeding out claims without any legal basis, demurrers that merely attack the form of the complaint can be used for the sole purpose of delay, and thus perpetuate technical objections and technical rules of pleading.

b. **Motion to strike:** [§668] The only other challenge usually permitted against the form or contents of a pleading is a motion to strike, which normally lies to reach defects not subject to demurrer. Filing a motion to strike *extends the time within which to answer* the complaint. This enables the defendant to obtain a court order striking improper allegations from the complaint before being obliged to answer them. [Cal. Civ. Proc. Code §435(c)]

  (1) **Formal defects:** [§669] The usual grounds for a motion to strike are that the pleading attacked contains *irrelevant or redundant matter* (*e.g.,* evidentiary matters or conclusions of law) or has some *defect in form* which is not a ground for demurrer (*e.g.,* lack of verification or subscription, late filing).

  (2) **Substantive defects:** [§670] A motion to strike can also be used to eliminate *part* of a claim that is otherwise valid (*e.g.,* punitive damages sought in a suit for breach of contract). [Goldman v. City Specialty Stores, Inc., 285 App. Div. 880 (1955)]

4. **Federal Practice:** [§671] The Federal Rules have deemphasized pleadings (*see supra,* §553), and accordingly limit the form and manner in which pleadings can be attacked.

  a. **Motion to dismiss:** [§672] Under the Federal Rules, the motion to dismiss is the basic challenge to the legal sufficiency of adversary pleadings. [Fed. R.

Civ. P. 12(b)] Making such a motion is *always optional* with the defendant, since he can raise the same objections in his answer (below).

(1) **Permissible grounds:** [§673]   The motion to dismiss can be made *only* on the following grounds (with any other defenses or objections raised in the answer):

(a) *Lack of jurisdiction over the subject matter;*

(b) *Lack of jurisdiction over the person;*

(c) *Improper venue;*

(d) *Insufficiency of process;*

(e) *Insufficiency of service* of process;

(f) *Failure to state a claim* upon which relief can be granted; and

(g) *Failure to join a party under Rule 19* (necessary or indispensable parties).

(2) **Failure to state a claim:** [§674]   When the motion is made under Federal Rule 12(b)(6) (failure to state a claim), its function is basically that of a general demurrer (*supra,* §655): Assuming the facts pleaded are true, do they constitute a legal claim upon which the plaintiff is entitled to judicial relief?

(a) **Test for sufficiency of complaint:** [§675]   In testing the sufficiency of the complaint in connection with a Rule 12(b)(6) motion, the following principles are generally applied.

1) **"Facts" not explicitly required:** [§676]   The complaint generally need not contain the ultimate facts; Federal Rule 8(a)(2) requires only a "short and plain statement of the claim showing that the pleader is entitled to relief."

2) **Liberal standard for sufficiency:** [§677]   The Supreme Court has stated that the complaint should not be dismissed unless the court is certain that the plaintiff cannot prove a set of facts in support of his claim that would entitle him to relief. [Conley v. Gibson, 355 U.S. 41 (1957)]

a) **Example:** A complaint charging "slanderous utterances" by defendant was held sufficient notwithstanding its failure to state, in so many words, that there had been a *publication* of the alleged defamations, because that could fairly be inferred from the allegations made. [Garcia v. Hilton Hotels, 97 F. Supp. 5 (D.P.R. 1951)]

b) **Liberal standard questioned:** Despite the Supreme Court's grand pronouncement in *Conley v. Gibson, supra,* the lower courts have continued to pay attention to whether the plaintiff indicates in the complaint that there is a factual basis for the claim. As one court put it, "although the exceedingly forgiving attitude toward pleading deficiencies that was expressed by Justice Black for the Supreme Court in *Conley v. Gibson* . . . continues to be quoted with approval, it has never been taken literally." [Sutliff, Inc. v. Donovan Companies, 727 F.2d 648 (7th Cir. 1984)]

    c) **Code pleading standard compared:** Nevertheless, the federal standard is more lenient than the requirements imposed by many state courts under code pleading. For example, Form 9 of the Federal Rules states that the following is sufficient to allege negligence: "Defendant negligently drove a motor vehicle against plaintiff." This relaxes the requirement in some code states that the plaintiff specify the underlying failure of the defendant upon which the claim of negligence is based. (*See supra,* §605.)

3) **Continuing need to set out factual matter:** [§678] Despite the absence of a specific requirement for allegations of fact in the rules, the federal courts require the plaintiff to "set out sufficient factual matter to outline the elements of his cause of action or claim, proof of which is essential to his recovery." [Daves v. Hawaiian Dredging Co., 114 F. Supp. 643 (D. Haw. 1953)]

4) **Fraud or mistake:** [§679] When claims are based on fraud or mistake, the Federal Rules require the plaintiff to plead *"with particularity."* [Fed. R. Civ. P. 9(b)]

    a) **Claims affected:** [§680] This requirement of added specificity applies only to claims where the substantive right to relief depends on proof of fraud or mistake. Examples include common law fraud, securities fraud, and actions to rescind or modify a contract for mutual mistake.

    b) **Rationale:** Courts explain that the added specificity is important to provide added notice and that it protects defendants against unfounded claims that damage their reputations.

    c) **Criticism:** It is difficult to understand why the claims covered give rise to especially troubling problems compared with other claims not covered by the rule.

    d) **Application:** Courts usually look to whether the plaintiff has provided specifics concerning the date and content of representations on which a fraud claim is based. In cases involving multiple defendants, it may be necessary for the plaintiff to specify the involvement of each one that allegedly gives rise to liability, sometimes requiring very great detail. However, some courts say that to satisfy Rule 9(b), the plaintiff need provide only "slightly more" than that which is required by Rule 8(a)(2). [*See, e.g.*, Tomera v. Galt, 511 F.2d 594 (7th Cir. 1975)]

 e) **State of mind:** [§681] Rule 9(b) also provides that "[m]alice, intent, knowledge, and other condition of mind" can be *averred generally*. This exempts all allegations on these subjects from the particularity requirement of the rule. Nevertheless, some courts apply the particularity requirement to allegations relating to state of mind. [*See, e.g.*, Ross v. A.H. Robins Co., 607 F.2d 545 (2d Cir.), *cert. denied*, 446 U.S. 946 (1980)—in securities fraud action, plaintiffs required to plead facts giving rise to a "strong inference" that defendants knew falsity of their statements]

5) **Heightened specificity for other types of claims:** [§682] With regard to certain other types of claims, some federal courts have developed pleading requirements that seem to go beyond the liberality of *Conley v. Gibson, supra.* The most prominent examples are *civil rights claims.* In such claims courts often insist that plaintiffs allege with specificity the basis for their belief that defendants acted with forbidden animus. [*See, e.g.*, Fisher v. Flynn, 598 F.2d 663 (1st Cir. 1979)—requiring employment discrimination plaintiff to plead basis for believing that firing was in retaliation for her rejection of supervisor's sexual overtures; Albany Welfare Rights Organization Day Care Center, Inc. v. Schreck, 463 F.2d 620 (2d Cir. 1972)—plaintiff required to plead basis for believing that defendant officials refused to deal with plaintiff in retaliation for plaintiff's political activities]

 a) **Stimulus for heightened pleading requirements:** [§683] The motivation for this intensification of pleadings scrutiny is *concern about the settlement value of frivolous or groundless claims.* [*See, e.g.*, Blue Chip Stamps v. Manor Drug Stores, 421 U.S. 723 (1975)—Court stated that the liberal discovery provisions can give complaints with little chance of success on the merits a disproportionately high settlement value to plaintiff, as long as he can prevent suit from being resolved against him by dismissal]

 b) **Supreme Court disapproval of heightened specificity requirements:** [§684] The Supreme Court has disapproved of heightened specificity requirements in civil rights cases, which are not governed by Rule 9(b). [Leatherman v. Tarrant County Narcotics Intelligence and Coordination Unit, 113 S. Ct. 1160 (1993)] However, it does not appear that courts need accept mere conclusions in such cases, and some lower courts have held that special pleading requirements still apply to civil rights suits against local officials entitled to claim immunity. [Branch v. Tunnell, 14 F.3d 449 (9th Cir. 1993)] The long-term impact of *Leatherman* is *unclear*.

(3) **Amendment by plaintiff if motion to dismiss is granted:** [§685] Granting or denying leave to amend rests in the discretion of the court, but leave must be liberally granted. [Foman v. Davis, 371 U.S. 178 (1962)]

   (a) *If the plaintiff amends,* he waives any error in the ruling on the original complaint, unless he can show that the outcome of the action was prejudiced by the erroneous dismissal of the original complaint.

   (b) *If the plaintiff chooses not to amend* (or if leave to amend is denied), the court will enter a judgment of dismissal. The ruling on the motion is not an appealable order, but the judgment can be appealed.

   1) *If the plaintiff appeals and wins,* the complaint is reinstated, and the defendant must answer.

   2) *If the plaintiff loses on appeal* or fails to appeal, this generally bars any further proceedings in the action. However, the appellate court has discretion to remand in order to permit an amended complaint to be filed.

(4) **Answer by defendant if motion is denied:** [§686] If the defendant's Rule 12(b) motion is denied, she must answer and proceed with the litigation—*i.e.*, the appellate court will not reexamine the denial of the defendant's motion as such. However, the defendant can raise the same issues on appeal from the final judgment and by subsequent motions (motions for judgment as a matter of law, for directed verdict, for judgment notwithstanding the verdict, etc.), which can also be reviewed on appeal from the final judgment.

b. **Motion for more definite statement:** [§687] Rule 12(e) permits a very limited attack on the *form* of the pleadings (and to this extent serves somewhat the same function as the special demurrer for uncertainty in code pleading practice). However, the motion will be granted only where the pleading under attack is *so vague and ambiguous* that it would be *unreasonable* to require the moving party to reply to it. [Fed. R. Civ. P. 12(e)]

   (1) **Note:** The motion for more definite statement is rarely granted. If the pleading is sufficiently definite that a reply *can* reasonably be made, the motion will be denied; and any vagueness or uncertainty must be overcome through discovery (*see* Chapter VI.).

   (2) **And note:** Where no response is permitted to the pleading under attack (*e.g.*, defendant's answer), the motion is *never* proper.

   (3) **As predicate for 12(b)(6) motion:** [§688] Most courts refuse to allow the motion to be used as a predicate for a 12(b)(6) motion. [United States v. Board of Harbor Commissioners, 73 F.R.D. 460 (D. Del. 1977)]

c. **Motion to strike:** [§689] Either party may move to strike an insufficient defense or any "redundant, immaterial, impertinent or scandalous" matter in the other's pleadings. [Fed. R. Civ. P. 12(f)]

   (1) **Limited use:** [§690] The motion to strike is said to be "disfavored" and generally will be denied unless the allegations attacked have absolutely *no* possible relation to the controversy (*e.g.,* allegations that a tribunal was a "kangaroo court"). [Skolnick v. Hallett, 350 F.2d 861 (7th Cir. 1965)]

   (a) **Example:** Where the alleged matter is merely of doubtful relevancy or doubtful legal value, the motion will be denied.

   (b) **Rationale:** Pleadings are not read to the jury in federal court (except in unusual circumstances where they have special relevance—*e.g.,* when they contain an admission). Consequently, it serves little purpose to strike allegations in the pleadings.

   (2) **Strike portions of complaint:** [§691] A motion to strike may also be used to attack separate portions of the complaint which are insufficient as a matter of *law*—*e.g.,* where plaintiff seeks punitive damages in a breach of contract action even though, as a matter of law, such damages are not available on such a claim.

d. **Procedure on motions under Rule 12**

   (1) **Form:** [§692] Any motion under Rule 12 must be in writing and must specify the ground (or grounds) upon which it is based. [Fed. R. Civ. P. 7(b)(1)]

   (a) **Facts:** [§693] Wherever the motion is based on asserted facts, these must be established by accompanying affidavits, depositions, or other evidence. (The opposing party may, of course, submit controverting evidence.) *Note:* On a Rule 12(b)(6) motion, scrutiny is limited to the face of the complaint. (*See infra,* §§700-701.)

   (b) **Time:** [§694] The motion must be served within the time permitted the defendant to serve the answer (normally 20 days after service of a summons and complaint; *infra,* §794). The filing of the motion operates to extend the time within which the answer is due until the court rules on the motion.

e. **Waiver of defenses:** [§695] The defendant is never compelled to file a motion under Rule 12; but if she does, she must include therein *all defenses and objections which she could then raise by motion.* If she omits an available defense or objection, she may not make a further motion on the omitted ground. [Fed. R. Civ. P. 12(g)] She will, however, be able to raise the ground in her answer, unless it is a ground that is waived by failure to raise in the first responsive pleading or motion.

   (1) **Waiver:** [§696] The following defenses are waived unless raised in the first responsive pleading:

(a) *Objections to the form* of the complaint;

(b) *Objections to venue, personal jurisdiction,* or to *sufficiency of process.*

(2) **No waiver:** [§697] However, the following basic defenses are *not* waived [Fed. R. Civ. P. 12(h)]:

(a) *Lack of subject matter jurisdiction;*

(b) *Failure to join an indispensable party;*

(c) *Failure to state a claim* upon which relief can be granted.

(3) **Rationale:** A party who invites the court to pass upon a "threshold" defense should bring forth *all* such defenses, in order to prevent waste of time by piecemeal presentation of defects.

(4) **But note:** Keep in mind that the waiver pertains only to the defenses that *could* be raised by a Rule 12 motion. Thus, there is no waiver of substantive defenses (*e.g.,* release, novation, payment, etc.), which can be raised in *only* the answer.

5. **Other Procedures:** [§698] While the demurrer (state practice) and Rule 12 motion (federal practice) are the procedures most commonly used to attack the sufficiency of a pleading, other procedures are likewise available—the most important of which is the *motion for judgment on the pleadings* (discussed *infra,* §§888-893).

6. **Additional Rules of Pleading:** [§699] In both state and federal practice, the following additional principles apply:

   a. **Materials considered**

   (1) **Pleading on its face:** [§700] In general, challenges to the sufficiency of the pleadings are limited to the allegations of the pleadings alone, and consideration of evidentiary materials, no matter how persuasive, is not allowed.

   (a) **Compare—summary judgment:** Evidentiary materials are the basis for decision of a motion for summary judgment. (*See* Chapter VII.)

   (b) **Conversion to summary judgment:** [§701] In federal court, if materials outside the complaint are submitted with a motion to dismiss for failure to state a claim and are not excluded by the court, the motion is to be considered a motion for summary judgment. [*See* Fed. R. Civ. P. 12(b); *and see* Vesely v. Sager, 5 Cal. 3d 153 (1971)—motion to strike complaint based on materials outside the complaint treated as motion for summary judgment]

   (2) **"Speaking" demurrers:** [§702] In some code pleading jurisdictions, there was once a practice of allowing "speaking" demurrers, which went

beyond the face of the complaint and called other materials to the attention of the court. This practice has generally been disapproved.

- (3) **Exhibits:** [§703] When a document is an exhibit to the complaint, it is "a part thereof for all purposes." [Fed. R. Civ. P. 10(c)] Therefore, it can be considered in connection with a motion to dismiss.

    - (a) **Caution:** The fact that the court may consider the exhibit in connection with the motion to dismiss does not mean that all assertions in the exhibit are taken as true for purposes of the motion. For example, in a defamation action based on assertions in a letter, the plaintiff might attach the letter as an exhibit to the complaint without admitting that the assertions in the letter are true.

- (4) **Superseded pleadings:** [§704] Reference to earlier pleadings filed by the same party present several kinds of problems:

    - (a) **Inconsistent allegations:** [§705] Because parties may ordinarily make inconsistent allegations within a given pleading (*see supra*, §576), the fact that the plaintiff made an inconsistent allegation in a previous complaint does not render the current complaint inadequate.

    - (b) **Omission of fatal details:** [§706] Where, however, a party has attempted to "cure" a defect simply by omitting an allegation, the court may look to the previous complaint to determine the sufficiency of the current complaint. [Lee v. Hensley, 103 Cal. App. 2d 697 (1951)—where original complaint showed that claim was barred by limitations, amendment to delete these allegations was ineffective to avoid dismissal]

- (5) **Matters judicially noticed:** [§707] Finally, a pleading is construed in light of facts that may be *judicially noticed*: historical facts, geography, etc.

b. **Anticipatory defenses:** [§708] A complaint need *not* anticipate affirmative defenses that the defendant might raise.

- (1) **Example:** P is injured, but executes a release of her claim. Later, P sues for her injuries on the premise that the release was given by mistake. P should not anticipate the defense of release, but should simply allege her claim for injury, await the defense of release, and then *avoid* it by proof at trial.

- (2) **But note:** If P *does* anticipate a defense in her complaint, the complaint must also plead facts to avoid it. *Example:* If P in the previous example alleges the release, she must also allege facts showing a mistake that would make the release ineffective. [Powell v. Lampton, 30 Cal. App. 2d 43 (1938); Hoshman v. Esso Standard Oil Co., 263 F.2d 499 (5th Cir. 1959)]

- (3) **Compare—duty to investigate:** Before filing a complaint, the plaintiff's attorney should investigate defenses. (*See* below.)

E. ATTORNEY'S DUTY TO INVESTIGATE CLAIMS AND DEFENSES

1. **Introduction:** [§709] Verification and signature requirements for pleadings have long existed. (*See supra*, §§587-594.) From 1938 through 1983, however, the original ***Rule 11*** of the Federal Rules of Civil Procedure used a ***subjective standard*** for the obligations of a lawyer signing a pleading. The Rule looked to actual bad faith of the lawyer in signing the pleading. In 1983, the Rule was amended to fortify its requirements and became a major consideration in assessing the obligations of lawyers filing suits and answers (as well as other papers). In 1993, substantial further revisions were made.

    a. **Rationale:** The rationale for enhanced scrutiny of lawyer behavior was to ***promote self-policing*** by lawyers and ***deter groundless and frivolous claims.***

    b. **Conflicting interpretations:** Under the 1983 version, courts gave the Rule conflicting interpretations on a number of key issues.

    c. **Policy concerns:** Many courts (and law professors) expressed concern that the 1983 version of the rule ***unduly constricted creative advocacy.***

2. **Certification Requirement**

    a. **Signature on paper:** [§710] Rule 11 focuses on the signature on a paper filed in court, although it may also apply to later oral argument advocating a position in a paper (*see infra*, §733).

    b. **Applicable to all filings except discovery:** [§711] The rule applies to every filing in court, but may be most important with regard to complaints and answers.

        (1) **Discovery:** [§712] With regard to discovery filings, Federal Rule 26(g) imposes similar certification requirements, and Rule 11 does not apply.

        (2) **Applicable to nonattorneys:** [§713] The rule applies to nonattorneys (*e.g.*, parties appearing pro se), as well as to attorneys.

3. **Matter Certified by Signature:** [§714] By signing a paper filed in court, a person certifies the following:

    a. **Reasonable inquiry:** [§715] With regard to the factual and legal grounds for the position taken in the paper, the person signing the paper certifies that she has made an "inquiry reasonable under the circumstances" to support that position.

        (1) **Attorney pre-filing investigation:** [§716] Ordinarily, it is expected that a lawyer will investigate factual and legal assertions before making them in a filing. This can include factual investigation of allegations and legal research regarding legal assertions.

    b. **Allegations or factual contentions have evidentiary support:** [§717] As revised in 1993, Rule 11 provides that signing a paper filed in court certifies that factual assertions "have evidentiary support." [Fed. R. Civ. P. 11(b)(3)]

(1) **Prior law:** [§718]   Under the 1983 version of Rule 11, the similar certification was that allegations were "well grounded in fact," and there was no explicit reference to evidentiary support.

(2) **Option for party lacking evidentiary support:** [§719]   The rule provides that a party may make allegations without evidentiary support for them if the allegations are *"likely to have evidentiary support after a reasonable opportunity for further investigation or discovery."* This option is available, however, only as to allegations *"specifically so identified."*

(3) **Applicable to denials:** [§720]   These certification requirements apply fully to denials of factual contentions. Denials may, however, be *based on lack of information or belief* but only if *specifically so identified*. [Fed. R. Civ. P. 11(b)(4)]

(4) **Reliance on client:** [§721]   Reliance on the client for the factual assertions may be dangerous, although prospective testimony of a client who has personal knowledge of the circumstances would seem to meet the rule's standard. [*See, e.g.,* Southern Leasing Partners, Ltd. v. McMullan, 801 F.2d 783 (5th Cir. 1986)—"blind reliance on the client is seldom a sufficient inquiry"] Where the lawyer properly relies on the client, the client can be sanctioned for signing documents filed in court even if the lawyer committed no violation of the rule. [Business Guides, Inc. v. Chromatic Communications Enterprises, 498 U.S. 4533 (1991)]

(5) **Waivable affirmative defense:** [§722]   Under the 1983 version, the courts were divided on whether a lawyer violated the rule by filing a complaint where the investigation showed that there was a valid affirmative defense that could be waived.

   (a) **Compare—burden of pleading:** [§723]   If Rule 11 forbids filing a complaint in such circumstances, it in essence has converted the affirmative defense into a part of the plaintiff's pleading burden, because the plaintiff would not be allowed to proceed despite being able to plead all the affirmative elements of his claim.

c. **Supported by law:** [§724]   The signature also certifies that the claim, defense, or other legal position taken in the paper is "warranted by existing law or by a nonfrivolous argument for the extension, modification, or reversal of existing law or the establishment of new law." [Fed. R. Civ. P. 11(b)(2)]

(1) **Need to research:** [§725]   The lawyer is expected to do research to determine whether there is a legal basis for claims or defenses that are asserted.

(2) **Objective standard:** [§726]   The rule is intended to create an objective standard. As explained under the 1983 version, it calls for sanctions "where it is patently clear that the claim has absolutely no chance of success under the existing precedents, and where no reasonable argument can be advanced to extend, modify or reverse the law as it stands." [Eastway Construction Corp. v. City of New York, 762 F.2d 243 (2d Cir. 1985)]

(a) **Conflict among district courts:** The Supreme Court has said that when there is a conflict on an issue among district courts, it is not frivolous to rely on the issue even if the position is contrary to controlling circuit precedent, where the question had not yet been decided by the Supreme Court. [McKnight v. General Motors Corp., 114 S. Ct. 1826 (1994)]

(3) **Specifying that existing law unfavorable:** [§727] The courts disagreed under the 1983 version of the rule on whether lawyers were required to state that they were arguing for an extension of existing law. [*Compare* Golden Eagle Distributing Corp. v. Burroughs Corp., 801 F.2d 1531 (9th Cir. 1986)—no need to explain that argument is for an extension of law; *with* Thornton v. Wahl, 787 F.2d 1151 (7th Cir. 1986)—failure to clarify that argument was not based on existing law can be sanctioned] The 1993 amendment does not require identification, but the Advisory Committee Notes observe that a contention so identified "should be viewed with greater tolerance under the rule." [146 F.R.D. at 587]

(4) **Concern about chilling lawyer creativity:** [§728] In scrutinizing new arguments, courts are concerned that they might "stifle the enthusiasm or chill the creativity that is the very lifeblood of the law." [Eastway Construction Corp. v. City of New York, *supra*]

d. **Improper purpose:** [§729] The signature also certifies that the paper was not filed "for an improper purpose, such as to harass or to cause unnecessary delay or needless increase in the cost of litigation."

(1) **Collateral purpose:** [§730] Some courts have focused on whether a given litigation action seemed to have a collateral purpose (*i.e.*, some objective other than relief in court), finding this to indicate improper purpose. [*See, e.g.,* Appeal of Licht & Semonoff, 796 F.2d 564 (1st Cir. 1986)—litigation used as method for obtaining information to be used in proxy battle between parties]

(2) **Purpose irrelevant if complaint not frivolous:** [§731] Other courts have decided that the improper purpose standard is satisfied as long as the complaint is not frivolous. [National Association of Government Employees, Inc. v National Federation of Federal Employees, 844 F.2d 216 (5th Cir. 1988)—"if an initial complaint passes the test of non-frivolousness, its filing does not constitute harassment for the purposes of Rule 11"]

4. **Objective Standard:** [§732] The Rule 11 standard with regard to the factual and legal basis for the claim is objective, and the actual state of mind of the lawyer is not important. "An empty head but a pure heart is no defense." [Thornton v. Wahl, *supra*]

5. **Duty to Reevaluate:** [§733] Although Rule 11 focuses on assertions in written filings with the court, it can be violated by *"later advocating"* a position previously taken in such a paper.

a. **Rationale:** Oral statements made to the court about matters arising for the first time in court may be made under circumstances where there is insufficient opportunity to investigate, but litigants' obligations with respect to assertions contained in papers should not be measured solely with regard to what they know at that time and later advocacy of those positions should be based on all information reasonably available.

b. **Compare—prior law:** Before the 1993 amendment to Rule 11, the courts were split on whether there was any ongoing obligation with respect to assertions in past filings.

c. **No requirement of formal withdrawal:** [§734] To comply with Rule 11, a party need not formally withdraw an earlier filing; the proscription applies only to later advocacy of the assertion found to be groundless after the paper was filed.

6. **Sanctions**

   a. **Discretionary:** [§735] On finding a violation of the certification requirements, a court *may* impose sanctions. [Fed. R. Civ. P. 11(c)]

      (1) **Compare—former law:** [§736] The 1983 version of Rule 11 provided that a court "shall" impose sanctions for a violation. This was read to make sanctions **mandatory**.

   b. **Nature and measure of sanction:** [§737] The court has substantial latitude in selecting the sanction, which may include directives of a monetary or nonmonetary nature. [Fed. R. Civ. P. 11(c)(2)]

      (1) **Limited to deterrence:** [§738] The sanction is to be limited to that which is *"sufficient to deter repetition of such conduct or comparable conduct by others similarly situated."*

      (2) **Ordinarily paid into court:** [§739] If the sanction is to pay money, that money ordinarily is to be paid into court and not to the opposing party. Thus, Rule 11 sanctions are *not a fee shifting device* to make the violator pay the victim's attorneys' fees or other legal costs.

         (a) **Costs of motion:** [§740] The court may, however, award the moving party the costs of making the Rule 11 motion. [Fed. R. Civ. P. 11(c)(1)(A)]

         (b) **Payment to movant warranted for deterrence:** [§741] If it is *"warranted for effective deterrence,"* however, the court may direct a payment to the moving party of some or all of its attorneys' fees and other expenses incurred as a direct result of the violation.

         (c) **Only nonmonetary sanctions against represented party regarding legal basis:** [§742] Monetary sanctions cannot be imposed on a represented party for violation of the requirement that contentions made be warranted by law. [Fed. R. Civ. P. 11(c)(2)(A)]

         (d) **Sanctions on law firm:** [§743] Ordinarily, a law firm should be held *jointly responsible* with its partners, associates, or employees for violations of Rule 11. [Fed. R. Civ. P. 11(c)(1)(A)] *Compare:* Under the 1983 version of Rule 11, it was held that only the lawyer who signed a paper, and not the law firm, could be sanctioned. [Pavelic & LeFlore v. Marvel Entertainment Group, 493 U.S. 120 (1989)]

7. **Procedure**

   a. **Separate motion:** [§744]   A motion for sanctions must be made "separately from other motions." Accordingly, parties cannot simply append a request for sanctions to other papers they file. [Fed. R. Civ. P. 11(c)(1)]

   b. **Twenty-one day "safe harbor":** [§745]   The motion is not to be filed with the court until 21 days after it is served on the opposing party, and then only if the challenged paper is not withdrawn or corrected. This provides a safe harbor for parties to reassess their filings without suffering sanctions for realizing that an earlier paper was not supported. [Fed. R. Civ. P. 11(c)(1)]

   c. **Sanctions on court's initiative:** [§746]   The court may, on its own initiative, enter an order directing an attorney or party to show cause why it has not violated Rule 11. [Fed. R. Civ. P. 11(c)(1)(B)] But monetary sanctions cannot be imposed under these circumstances unless the court issues the order to show cause before voluntary dismissal or settlement of the case. [Fed. R. Civ. P. 11(c)(2)(B)] *Compare:* Under the prior version of the rule, it was held that voluntary dismissal of the case did not deprive the court of the power to impose Rule 11 sanctions. [Cooter & Gell v. Hartmarx Corp., 496 U.S. 384 (1990)]

   d. **Sanctions order:** [§747]   If the court imposes sanctions, it should describe the conduct determined to constitute a violation of the rule and explain the basis for the sanction imposed. [Fed. R. Civ. P. 11(c)(3)]

   e. **Appellate review:** [§748]   Rule 11 orders should be reviewed under an *abuse of discretion* standard. [Cooter & Gell v. Hartmarx Corp., *supra*]

8. **Inherent Power to Sanction:** [§749]   Federal courts have inherent power to impose substantial sanctions on a party guilty of bad faith conduct not involving signing of filings even when Rule 11 does not apply. [Chambers v. NASCO, Inc., 501 U.S. 32 (1991)—repeated acts of deception of court led to imposition of almost $1 million in sanctions]

F. **ANSWER**

1. **In General:** [§750]   The function of the answer is to put at issue the factual allegations in the complaint. The answer accomplishes this by *denying* the allegations of the claim and/or by setting forth some affirmative defense ("new matter") that *avoids* the effect of the plaintiff's allegations.

2. **Denials:** [§751]   To put at issue the allegations of the complaint, the defendant's answer must contain *effective* denials. Allegations not denied are *deemed admitted* (below).

a. **Form**

(1) **General denials:** [§752] A single "general" denial will controvert all of the allegations in the complaint (*e.g.,* "D denies each and all of the allegations in P's complaint"). In most jurisdictions, this is no longer good practice.

(a) **Federal pleading:** [§753] In federal practice, the basic requirement of *good faith* based upon reasonable inquiry in pleading [Fed. R. Civ. P. 11] means that a general denial is rarely proper because there is usually *something* in the plaintiff's complaint (*e.g.,* jurisdictional allegations) which the defendant in good faith *should* admit.

(b) **State pleading:** [§754] In some states a general denial is not allowed in response to a *verified* complaint. In such a case, the answer must also be verified and *specific denials* are required. [Cal. Civ. Proc. Code §431.30(d); *and see supra,* §592]

1) **Exception:** [§755] Verified general denials to a verified complaint may be allowed where the amount in controversy is small.

(2) **Specific denials:** [§756] Anything less than a general denial can be considered a "specific" or "qualified" denial. Several different types of allegations may be used in this regard:

(a) **Specific denial by parts:** [§757] The defendant can go through the complaint, paragraph by paragraph or sentence by sentence, admitting or denying each part as appropriate. Where only part of a paragraph or allegation therein is true, the defendant should admit that which is true and deny the balance. [Fed. R. Civ. P. 8(b); Zielinski v. Philadelphia Piers, Inc., 139 F. Supp. 408 (E.D. Pa. 1956)] *Example:* "Answering paragraph 12 of plaintiff's complaint, defendant admits providing medical treatment to plaintiff on or about May 15, 1994, and, except as expressly so admitted, denies each and every allegation of paragraph 12."

(b) **Negativing plaintiff's allegations:** [§758] A denial may be effected merely by repeating the allegation but prefacing it with a word of denial.

1) **Caution—denials in the conjunctive ("negative pregnant" rule):** [§759] This type of denial, if carelessly employed, may be deemed "pregnant" with an admission of that which the defendant is attempting to deny. *Example:* P's complaint alleges that D "struck and kicked P." D's answer that "D did not strike and kick P" is pregnant with an admission that he may have struck *or* kicked P.

a) **How to avoid:** [§760] To avoid the problem, the defendant should make his denial in the *disjunctive*—i.e., "D did not strike or kick P."

2) **Denials of times, dates, or places:** [§761] Similarly, if the complaint alleges that an event occurred at a certain time, date, or place *not* material to the statement of the plaintiff's cause of action, a specific denial thereof may be held pregnant with an admission that the event occurred at some *other* time, date, or place. *Example:* P's complaint alleges "P fully and completely performed the contract *on June 1*." D's answer stating that D "denies that P fully and completely performed the contract on June 1" may be held to admit performance on another date.

   a) **How to avoid:** [§762] It is generally a good idea to add "or at any other time," "at any other place," etc., to avoid this negative pregnant problem.

3) **Ease of avoiding:** [§763] These problems can be easily avoided by denying "each and every allegation of plaintiff" except as expressly admitted, as indicated in §757, *supra.* As a result, the negative pregnant problem has virtually vanished from the scene under liberalized pleading rules.

(3) **Denial on lack of information:** [§764] If the defendant is without sufficient knowledge or information to enable her to form a belief as to the truth of allegations in the complaint, she may so state in her answer. Such a statement operates as an effective denial. [Fed. R. Civ. P. 8(b); Cal. Civ. Proc. Code §431.30]

   (a) **Information that is peculiarly within defendant's control:** [§765] Where the information of which the defendant claims ignorance is peculiarly within the defendant's control, use of the denial on information and belief may be forbidden.

      1) **Example:** Where defendant bought out the assets of the company that manufactured a product that injured plaintiff, information about the extent to which defendant assumed the tort liabilities of the manufacturer was peculiarly within defendant's control, and defendant could not claim to be ignorant of it. [David v. Crompton & Knowles Corp., 58 F.R.D. 444 (E.D. Pa. 1973)]

   (b) **Public record:** [§766] Where matters are of public record, the defendant may not deny for lack of information and belief. [Porto Transportation Co. v. Consolidated Diesel Electric Corp., 20 F.R.D. 1 (1956)]

b. **Effect of failure to deny:** [§767] Failure to make an effective denial of allegations to which a responsive pleading is required constitutes an ***admission*** of such allegations.

   (1) **Exception—damages:** [§768] Under federal practice, allegations of *damages* are deemed at issue, even if not effectively denied. [Fed. R. Civ. P. 8(d)] (State practice is generally contra—*i.e.,* allegations of damages, like any other material allegation, must be denied.)

(2) **Material vs. immaterial allegations:** [§769] Note that only *material* allegations are deemed admitted. "Material" allegations are those essential to the claim and which could not be stricken from the pleading without leaving it insufficient. [*See* Cal. Civ. Proc. Code §431.10]

   (a) **Compare:** Failure to deny *immaterial* allegations does *not* constitute an admission thereof, the immaterial allegations being treated merely as "surplusage."

   (b) **But note:** In practice, few pleaders feel confident enough to decide what is "material" and "immaterial" and hence deny *all* allegations. Alternatively, the defendant can *move to strike* from the complaint whatever she considers to be "immaterial" allegations before filing her answer (*see supra*, §668), so she will not have to admit or deny them.

3. **Affirmative Defenses:** [§770] In addition to or in lieu of a denial, the defendant in her answer must plead any defenses or objections that constitute "new matter" or an affirmative defense. Such matter is *not in issue* (and hence may not be introduced in evidence at trial) *under a simple denial.*

   a. **Definition:** Basically, "new matter" is anything that the defendant must prove in order to *avoid* the plaintiff's claim—*i.e.*, even assuming plaintiff's allegations were true, an independent reason why plaintiff cannot recover. The test usually is whether the defendant would bear the *burden of proof* on the issue at trial; if so, it is "new matter."

   b. **Federal practice:** [§771] Although burden of proof is generally deemed to be a "substantive" question for *Erie* purposes (and hence controlled by appropriate state law), pleading rules are clearly "procedural." Hence, if an affirmative defense falls within Federal Rule 8(c), below, it must *always* be specially pleaded; and this is true whether or not the defendant would have the burden of proof on this issue under state law. [Palmer v. Hoffman, 318 U.S. 109 (1943)]

   (1) **Rule 8(c):** [§772] Federal Rule 8(c) lists various defenses that must be affirmatively alleged, but this list is not all-inclusive. The Rule provides that *"any other matter constituting an avoidance or affirmative defense"* must also be specially pleaded.

   c. **Application:** [§773] The following are the most common types of "new matter" in state and federal practice:

   (1) **Tort cases:** [§774] In tort cases:

      (a) *Self-defense, consent, justification, or other privilege,* as defenses to intentional torts, are new matter and must be specially pleaded in the answer.

      (b) *Contributory negligence and assumption of the risk*, as defenses to negligence, are new matter in most jurisdictions.

      (c) *Privilege or license (as a defense to trespass); consent (as a defense to conversion)* are other examples of new matter.

(d) *But lack of causation is not new matter.* Causation is one of the ultimate facts in any tort complaint, and thus *lack* of proximate cause need not be specially pleaded. It is in issue under a general denial of an allegation that the defendant's acts "caused" plaintiff's injuries.

(2) **Contract cases:** [§775] In a contract action, new matter that must be specially pleaded (*i.e.,* not in issue under a denial) includes *fraud, mistake, duress, incapacity, release, waiver, and estoppel.*

 (a) **Illegality:** [§776] This is of course a "defense" to a contract action, but evidence of the illegality can come in even if not pleaded.

  1) **Rationale:** Public policy to nullify illegal contracts is so strong that it should not require specific pleading. Indeed, the court can raise the issue on its own motion. [Santoro v. Carbone, 22 Cal. App. 3d 721 (1972)]

 (b) **Lack of consideration:** [§777] Wherever the plaintiff has alleged consideration, lack of consideration will be in issue under a simple denial. However, consideration need not always be alleged (*see supra,* §616); and where it need not be alleged, lack of consideration is new matter which must be specially pleaded.

 (c) **Failure of conditions**

  1) **Condition subsequent:** [§778] Occurrence of a condition subsequent that the defendant claims *discharged* his duty to perform is an affirmative defense, and hence must be specially pleaded as new matter. [Pierce v. Wright, 117 Cal. App. 2d 718 (1953)]

  2) **Conditions precedent or concurrent:** [§779] However, because the plaintiff must allege the occurrence or performance of all conditions precedent or concurrent (in order to show that the defendant was under an absolute, unconditional duty to perform), a denial by the defendant sufficiently controverts the plaintiff's allegations concerning such conditions. [*See* Cal. Civ. Proc. Code §457]

   a) **But note:** Federal Rule 9(c) requires that the defendant's denial pinpoint which particular failure or condition on which she wishes to rely—in effect requiring an affirmative allegation. [Ginsburg v. Insurance Co. of North America, 427 F.2d 1318 (6th Cir. 1970)]

 (d) **Payment:** [§780] Where the plaintiff sues on an obligation for payment of money, she bears the burden of pleading and proving *nonpayment* as part of her case. However, if the defendant intends to rely on payment as a defense in the action, most jurisdictions require that she *affirmatively plead* it in her answer. [Fed. R. Civ. P. 8(c); Pastene v. Pardini, 135 Cal. 431 (1902)]

(e) **Mitigation of damages:** [§781] Although the defendant bears the burden of proof as to mitigation of damages, it does *not* always require special pleading.

   1) **Example:** Defendant may prove that plaintiff's damages have been *offset or reduced* by other income (as where a wrongfully discharged employee obtains another job) without special pleading. Such proof goes to the computation of plaintiff's damages, and is thus in issue under defendant's denial of the sum complained of. [Erler v. Five Points Motors, 249 Cal. App. 2d 560 (1967)]

   2) **Compare:** If defendant claims that plaintiff has *failed* to mitigate damages (*e.g.,* failing to seek comparable employment), this is treated as new matter in order to alert the plaintiff. [Erler v. Five Points Motors, *supra*]

(f) **Statute of Frauds:** [§782] The federal rule (also followed in most states) is that the Statute of Frauds is new matter and must be specially pleaded. [Fed. R. Civ. P. 8(c)]

   1) **Minority view:** [§783] Some code pleading states take the position that the Statute of Frauds is in issue under a simple denial of the contract. This position was originally based on the theory that noncompliance with the Statute of Frauds rendered a contract void, rather than merely voidable; although this theory is no longer recognized (*see* Contracts Summary), the pleading rule has remained. [Aero Bolt & Screw Co. v. Iaia, 180 Cal. App. 2d 728 (1960)]

(3) **Statute of limitations:** [§784] Running of the statute of limitations is new matter and must be specially pleaded.

   (a) **But note:** If it appears from the dates alleged *on the face of the complaint* that the plaintiff's action is barred, *some* courts allow the defendant to raise this defense (*e.g.,* by a motion to dismiss) even though not pleaded in the answer (*see supra,* §708).

   (b) **Title obtained by adverse possession:** [§785] Where the running of the statute of limitations establishes title in an adverse possessor and the former owner then sues for ejectment, the adverse possessor's title is in issue under a simple denial of the owner's allegations in the ejectment action—since one of the necessary allegations is a claim of title. [Denham v. Cuddeback, 311 P.2d 1014 (Or. 1957)]

(4) **Pleas in abatement (dilatory pleas):** [§786] Pleas in abatement are *not* defenses on the merits, but assert some reason why the present action should be put off or should not be heard. Matters of abatement often appear on the face of the complaint, and when they do, the complaint is subject to the demurrer or similar motion. However, where the matter of abatement does not appear on the face of the complaint—which is the

usual case—it must be raised in the answer or, in federal practice, by answer or motion; and it must be *specially pleaded* as new matter.

(a) **Grounds:** [§787]   The principal pleas in abatement are:

1) *Plaintiff lacks capacity* to sue;

2) *Nonjoinder* of parties;

3) *Another action pending* between the parties on the *same issues*;

4) *An action brought prematurely;* and

5) Lack of *personal jurisdiction* (including improper service of process) and *improper venue:*

   a) *In federal practice,* these issues may be raised by motion or answer, as long as it is in the defendant's first appearance [Fed. R. Civ. P. 12(b)];

   b) *In state practice,* lack of personal service must be raised by a motion to quash, while improper venue must be raised by motion at or before the time defendant files a demurrer or answer [Cal. Civ. Proc. Code §418.10].

(b) **Special hearing available:** [§788]   Statutes or rules often require that on motion of either party (or the court itself), matters of abatement be heard first—since they would dispense with the litigation if proved. [*See, e.g.,* Fed. R. Civ. P. 12(d)]

(c) **Pleas disfavored:** [§789]   A plea of abatement is a disfavored defense because it is generally an attempt to "put off" or "hold in abeyance" rather than to defend squarely on the merits. Accordingly, the courts require that such matters be raised *promptly* or the objection will be deemed *waived.* Thus, for example, such defenses generally cannot be raised for the first time in an amended answer. [Collins v. Rocha, 7 Cal. 3d 232 (1972)]

d. **Effect of failure to plead new matter:** [§790]   If not pleaded in the answer, new matter is not in issue and the *defendant may not offer evidence* of such defenses at the time of trial—unless the plaintiff fails to object to the introduction of such evidence or the court allows leave to **amend** (*see infra,* §860). [Jetty v. Craco, 123 Cal. App. 2d 876 (1954)]

4. **Procedure in Answering Complaint**

   a. **Form:** [§791]   The requirements for allegations in a complaint (*supra,* §§556 *et seq.*) also apply to the allegations of an answer.

   b. **Signing:** [§792]   In federal practice, the same standards apply to the answer as apply to the complaint. [Fed. R. Civ. P. 11; *see supra,* §§589, 709 *et seq.*]

(1) **Verification:** [§793]   Under state practice, an answer must be verified if the complaint is verified (otherwise, it may be striken by the court). [Cal. Civ. Proc. Code §431.30]

c. **Time limitations:** [§794]   Under federal practice, the defendant must file her answer within 20 days after being served with process, except that if she chooses during that time to file a motion under Rule 12(b), this extends the time for filing her answer until 10 days after the Rule 12(b) motion is denied. [Fed. R. Civ. P. 12(a)(1)(A)]

(1) **Service waived:** [§795]   If defendant waives service of process (*supra*, §219), the answer is not due until 60 days after the request for waiver was sent, if addressed to a defendant within the United States, or 90 days if defendant is outside the country. [Fed. R. Civ. P. 12(a)(l)(B)]

(2) **State practice:** [§796]   State practice is similar. For example, in California, the defendant must answer or demur within 30 days after service of process (although the 30-day period is measured from different dates, depending on whether defendant was served personally, by mail, or by publication). [Cal. Civ. Proc. Code §412.20(3)]

(3) **Effect of failure to file timely answer:** *See* discussion of default procedure *infra*, §§879-887.

5. **Allegations of Answer Deemed Controverted:** [§797]   Except where the answer contains a counterclaim (below), no reply to an answer is permitted in federal practice. [Fed. R. Civ. P. 7(a)] Allegations of new matter in the answer are *"deemed controverted"*—meaning that the plaintiff has the right, without further pleading, to introduce any evidence in avoidance thereof. [Fed. R. Civ. P. 8(d); Cal. Civ. Proc. Code §431.20(b)]

a. **Example:** P's complaint charges negligence. D's answer sets up the defense of contributory negligence by P. This is "deemed controverted"; and P can introduce evidence of "last clear chance" to overcome the contributory negligence defense (*see* Torts Summary) without a special pleading thereof.

6. **Challenges to Answer:** [§798]   If the plaintiff desires to challenge the legal sufficiency of an affirmative defense, he may file a *demurrer* (state practice) or a *motion to strike* "any insufficient defense" under Federal Rule 12(f).

a. **And note:** In addition, the plaintiff may employ a motion for judgment on the pleadings or motion for summary judgment to challenge such new matter. (*See infra*, §888.)

G. COUNTERCLAIMS AND CROSS-CLAIMS

1. **Federal Practice**

a. **Counterclaims:** [§799]   As part of her answer, the defendant may set forth by way of counterclaim any claims that she has *against the plaintiff.* Such claims *need not be related* to the claims set forth in the complaint. [Fed. R. Civ. P. 13(b)]

(1) **Subject matter jurisdiction**

    (a) **Compulsory counterclaim:** [§800] If the counterclaim is compulsory (*i.e.,* based on the same transaction or occurrence as the plaintiff's claim; *see* below), it is deemed *"ancillary"* to the plaintiff's claim, and therefore within supplemental jurisdiction (*see supra,* §§398 *et seq.*).

    (b) **Permissive counterclaim:** [§801] However if the counterclaim is merely permissive (below), it must ordinarily be based on some *independent ground* of federal jurisdiction (*e.g.,* if plaintiff's claim is based on a federal question, defendant's counterclaim would have to be based on some federal question or on diversity).

(2) **Venue:** [§802] Counterclaims have no effect on venue. The venue statutes regulate where the *"action* may be brought"; and this refers solely to where the plaintiff files his complaint.

(3) **Pleading:** [§803] The sufficiency of a counterclaim is tested by the same rules of pleading applicable to a complaint (*see supra,* §§671 *et seq.*).

    (a) **Form:** [§804] The counterclaim should be set forth as *part of the defendant's answer,* rather than as a separate pleading. [Fed. R. Civ. P. 13(a)]

    (b) **Caption:** [§805] A counterclaim should always be labeled as such, since a reply thereto by the plaintiff is mandatory only if it is so denominated. [Fed. R. Civ. P. 7(a)] However, failure to label a counterclaim as such has no other effect: The court may still treat it as a counterclaim and award whatever relief is appropriate. [Fed. R. Civ. P. 8(c)]

    (c) **Plaintiff's reply:** [§806] A responsive pleading by the plaintiff is required to a counterclaim labeled as such. The reply may contain denials, affirmative defenses, or even a counterclaim to the counterclaim. [Great Lakes Rubber Corp. v. Herbert Cooper Co., 286 F.2d 631 (3d Cir. 1960)]

        1) **Note:** All matters in the reply are deemed "denied or avoided" under Federal Rule 8(d).

        2) **But note:** The defendant can attack the reply by a motion for judgment on the pleadings or a motion to strike under Federal Rule 12.

(4) **Joinder of other parties:** [§807] A counterclaim lies only against the *plaintiff.* But when the presence of additional parties would facilitate a complete determination of the counterclaim, the court may order their joinder. [Fed. R. Civ. P. 13(h)]

    (a) **Necessary or proper parties:** [§808] Any third party who would be a necessary or proper party to the action if the defendant had filed an independent suit on the claim involved may thus be joined.

(b) **Caution—jurisdiction:** [§809] Note, however, that where the counterclaim is only *permissive*, it must be based on some independent ground for federal jurisdiction (*see supra*, Chapter II). If the counterclaim is based on diversity jurisdiction, additional parties cannot be joined if their citizenship would destroy diversity.

1) **Effect:** [§810] If the court determines that a third party should be joined if possible but, his joinder would destroy jurisdiction (*i.e.*, where based on diversity), the court will often dismiss the counterclaim. If the counterclaim is *compulsory*, the joinder has no effect on jurisdiction (since such counterclaims are deemed ancillary to the action; *see* above).

(5) **Dismissal:** [§811] To protect the defendant's right to relief, Federal Rule 41(a)(2) provides that once a counterclaim is asserted, the *plaintiff cannot dismiss the action without the defendant's consent* (unless the counterclaim remains pending for independent adjudication; *see infra*, §902).

(6) **Permissive vs. compulsory counterclaims**

(a) **Permissive counterclaims:** [§812] Where the defendant's claims against the plaintiff are *unrelated* to the claims set forth in the complaint, it is optional (or permissive) for the defendant to assert them by way of counterclaim; *i.e.*, the defendant may, if she chooses, assert such claims in an independent action.

(b) **Compulsory counterclaims:** [§813] However, where the defendant's claim against the plaintiff arises out of the *same transaction* as the claim set forth in the complaint, the counterclaim is *compulsory*—meaning that it must be asserted in the action or it will be barred. (This bar is implicit in Rule 13(a).)

1) **When counterclaim is "compulsory":** [§814] A counterclaim is compulsory if it:

a) *Arises out of the transaction or occurrence* that is the subject matter of the plaintiff's claim; *and*

b) *Does not require the presence of third parties* over whom the court has no jurisdiction.

2) **Scope of "transaction or occurrence":** [§815] In determining whether a counterclaim is compulsory, the phrase "transaction or occurrence" is construed in two different ways:

a) When the question is whether the counterclaim is *within the court's supplemental jurisdiction,* a *broad* definition of "transaction" is used—the object being to permit the counterclaim and thereby to avoid multiplicity of suits. [Albright v. Gates, 362 F.2d 928 (9th Cir. 1966)]

b) On the other hand, when the question is whether a defendant who *failed* to interpose a counterclaim is barred from later suing on it, a *narrower* definition may be used if it would be inequitable to bar the later suit. [LaFollette v. Herron, 211 F. Supp. 919 (E.D.Tenn. 1962)]

(7) **Statute of limitations problem:** [§816] An important issue is whether a counterclaim is barred by the statute of limitations where it is filed *after* the statute has run, but the action (plaintiff's complaint) was filed before the statute ran. The question is considered "substantive" for *Erie* doctrine purposes, and hence is resolved by appropriate state law. [Keckley v. Payton, 157 F. Supp. 820 (N.D. W. Va. 1958)]

(a) **Majority view:** [§817] The general view is that if the counterclaim arises out of the *"same transaction"* as the plaintiff's claim, it will not be barred if the plaintiff's complaint was filed before the running of the statute. *Rationale:* The plaintiff's filing of the complaint places before the court all rights and obligations of the parties to the transaction in question. [Liberty Mutual Insurance Co. v. Fales, 8 Cal. 3d 712 (1973)]

(b) **Minority view:** [§818] A minority view goes further and allows *any* counterclaim (same transaction or not) to be used *defensively*—*i.e.*, as an offset to the plaintiff's claim—even though the statute has run. [Hawkeye Security Insurance Co. v. Apodaca, 524 P.2d 874 (Wyo. 1974)]

1) **"Cross-demands deemed compensated":** [§819] Other states reach the same result via statutes that provide that where *cross-demands for money* have existed between the parties at any point in time, they are "deemed compensated"—*i.e.*, plaintiff's claim is *deemed paid* to the extent of defendant's offsetting claim. If plaintiff later sues defendant, defendant can set up her cross-demand to show payment (an affirmative defense), even though an independent action on defendant's claim would then be barred by the statute of limitations. [Cal. Civ. Proc. Code §431.70]

2) **Limitation:** [§820] Such statutes apply only where the cross-demands are *for money*. Thus, if the plaintiff is suing for recovery of property, the statute of limitations will continue to run on any cross-demand which the defendant has against the plaintiff.

b. **Cross-claims:** [§821] In federal court actions, the defendant may set forth in the answer any claims that she has against a *co-defendant* that relate to the *"transaction or occurrence"* or to any property that is the subject of the plaintiff's complaint. Such cross-claims are *not compulsory,* however. [Fed. R. Civ. P. 13(g)]

(1) **Example:** P sues D1 and D2, claiming they were jointly negligent in causing his injuries. Either defendant may cross-claim against the other on any claim arising out of the same accident. [Scott v. Fancher, 369 F.2d 842 (5th Cir. 1966)]

(a) **Contribution:** [§822] Alternatively, either defendant may file a cross-claim for *contribution* against the other, asserting that both are *jointly* liable to the plaintiff and requesting that any judgment be fashioned accordingly. (If one defendant is only secondarily liable, he may cross-claim *for indemnification* against the other who is primarily liable.) [Lumbermen's Mutual Insurance Co. v. Massachusetts Bonding and Insurance Co., 310 F.2d 627 (4th Cir. 1962)]

(2) **Jurisdiction:** [§823] Since the cross-claim must relate to the transaction in the existing action, the better view is that it is within the supplemental jurisdiction of the court, and no independent ground for federal jurisdiction is required. [LASA per L'Industria del Marmo Societa per Azioni v. Alexander, 414 F.2d 143 (6th Cir. 1969)]

(3) **Pleading**

    (a) **Form:** [§824] Like a counterclaim, the cross-claim should be set forth as *part of the defendant's answer* rather than as an independent pleading.

    (b) **Responsive pleading:** [§825] The co-defendant against whom the claim is asserted must file an *answer to cross-claim*. [Fed. R. Civ. P. 7(a)]

(4) **Parties:** [§826] The basic cross-claim must be against a co-defendant. As with counterclaims, however, the cross-claimant may add new parties against whom it has claims growing out of the same transaction. [Fed. R. Civ. P. 13(h)]

    (a) **Note:** A cross-claim is also proper in a case where there are several plaintiffs (P1 and P2) and defendant has counterclaimed against only one of them (P1). In such a case, P1 could cross-claim against his co-party (P2) for contribution or indemnification as to the claim asserted in D's counterclaim.

(5) **Other procedures compared**

    (a) **Counterclaims and cross-claims:** [§827] Counterclaims lie only against the *opposing* party (plaintiff), whereas a cross-claim lies against a *co-party* (D2).

        1) **And note:** A counterclaim is sometimes compulsory, whereas a cross-claim is always permissive. [Augustin v. Mughal, 521 F.2d 1215 (8th Cir. 1975)]

    (b) **Impleaders and cross-claims:** [§828] Impleaders are claims against a *third person* who is a stranger to the action, whereas a cross-claim lies against a *co-party* (D2). Moreover, an impleader claim is limited to a claim for indemnification or contribution, whereas a cross-claim can be asserted for *any* claim D1 has against D2 arising out of the transaction that is the basis for the plaintiff's action.

2. **State Practice—Cross-Complaint:** [§829] Most state rules governing pleading of claims by a defendant against the plaintiff or third parties follow the Federal Rules (above). However, some states (*e.g.,* California) do not recognize the counterclaim or cross-claim, but provide that a defendant's claims against *any* party (plaintiff, co-defendant, or a third person not yet a party to the action) may be asserted in a *cross-complaint.*

   a. **Form:** [§830] The cross-complaint is a *separate pleading* (*i.e.,* not a part of the answer). [Cal. Civ. Proc. Code §428.40]

      (1) **Procedure:** [§831] If the cross-complaint is filed *at the same time as the answer,* it may be filed as a matter of right. Otherwise, leave of court must first be obtained for a cross-complaint against current parties to the case. Cross-complaints against new parties can be filed without leave of court until a trial date has been set. [Cal. Civ. Proc. Code §428.50]

      (2) **Service:** [§832] The cross-complaint must be served on *every* party to the action. [Cal. Civ. Proc. Code §428.60]

   b. **Joinder of parties:** [§833] As noted above, a cross-complaint may be filed against the plaintiff, a co-defendant, *or* a third person not yet a party to the action. In the latter case, a separate summons is issued on the cross-complaint.

      (1) **Note:** The usual rules with respect to necessary and indispensable parties (*see infra,* §§961 *et seq.*) apply here as well.

   c. **Joinder of claims**

      (1) **Against plaintiff—unlimited scope:** [§834] The defendant may assert any and all claims she has against the plaintiff. There is *no* requirement of any subject matter relationship to the plaintiff's complaint. [Cal. Civ. Proc. Code §428.10(a)]

         (a) **Compulsory cross-complaints:** [§835] However if the defendant's cause of action *is* related to the subject of the plaintiff's complaint, failure to assert it constitutes a waiver thereof. [Cal. Civ. Proc. Code §426.30] Basically, the same rules apply as for federal "compulsory counterclaims." (*See supra,* §813.)

      (2) **Against other parties—subject matter relationship:** [§836] A defendant can assert a cross-complaint against a co-defendant or third party only if the cause of action sued upon is *related to the plaintiff's complaint—i.e.,* arises out of same transaction or series of transactions, or involves the same property or controversy. [Cal. Civ. Proc. Code §428.10(b)]

         (a) **Effect:** As long as there is *one* such cause of action, the defendant can join with it *any other* causes of action she has against any of the cross-defendants. [Cal. Civ. Proc. Code §428.30]

         (b) **Example:** P, while operating a car, collides with T, who is operating a car owned by O. P sues O for personal injuries. O may file a cross-complaint against P for the damages to O's car; and against T as a third-party defendant, seeking indemnity for any liability that O may be subjected to in favor of P, and also for the damages to O's car.

(c) **Note:** The California cross-complaint can thus be used to assert the claims asserted under the Federal Rules by compulsory counterclaim (same transaction), permissive counterclaim (different transaction), cross-claim (against co-party), or impleader (bringing stranger in as third-party defendant).

d. **Responsive pleading required:** [§837] Each cross-defendant must file an answer (or demurrer) to the cross-complaint. [Cal. Civ. Proc. Code §§428, 432.10] If no such response is filed, a default judgment may be entered on the cross-complaint.

(1) **Grounds for demurrer:** [§838] The grounds for demurrer to a cross-complaint are the same as for a demurrer to the original complaint.

(2) **Additional cross-complaints:** [§839] A cross-defendant, in turn, is permitted to file a cross-complaint against any other party or against any stranger to the action (just as if the cross-complaint filed against him had been the original complaint). [Cal. Civ. Proc. Code §§428, 432.10] *Note:* This means that the cross-defendant is subject to the *compulsory* cross-complaint provisions (above).

(3) **Note—indemnification:** [§840] A special statute in California allows broader defenses where the cross-complaint is for indemnification (*e.g.,* P sues D; D cross-complains against T, alleging that T is liable to indemnify D against P's claim, so that if P wins against D, T is liable to D). In such cases, the cross-defendant (T) is permitted to assert any defenses to the underlying cause of action (P vs. D) that could be asserted by the person seeking indemnification from him (D). [Cal. Civ. Proc. Code §428.70(b)]

(a) **Rationale:** The purpose of this rule is to protect against collusion on the underlying cause of action (*i.e.,* D admitting or defaulting to P's claim, in order to saddle T with the liability).

H. AMENDED AND SUPPLEMENTAL PLEADINGS

1. **In General:** [§841] Since it is the basic function of pleadings to define the issues in controversy (and thus limit the proof at trial), the rules allowing amendments and supplements to pleadings are of vital importance. The problem is the extent to which a party, by amending or supplementing pleadings, can alter or expand his case from that originally set forth in the complaint or answer. As will be seen, this depends to a significant degree on the *stage of the proceedings* at which an amendment is sought.

2. **Amendments Prior to Trial**

   a. **Amendments as a matter of right:** [§842] Either party may amend his pleading *once* as a matter of right, either (i) before a responsive pleading (as opposed to a mere motion) is served by the other party or (ii) if the pleading is one to which no responsive pleading is permitted (*e.g.,* defendant's answer) and the action has not been placed on the trial calendar, at any time within 20 days after the pleading is served. [Fed. R. Civ. P. 15(a)]

    (1) **Note:** Even though there is a right to amend, the alteration must be within the ***permissible scope*** of amendment (*see infra,* §§847 *et seq.*) or it is subject to being stricken.

b. **Amendment by permission of court:** [§843] In any other situation, a party may amend his pleading only by leave of court; however, such permission is usually granted liberally prior to trial.

    (1) **Rationale:** Modern courts stress that the primary function of the pleadings is to give ***notice*** of the pleader's claim (or defense). As long as the original pleading gave such notice, the claim may be expanded or changed in the course of litigation.

    (2) **Effect:** Leave to amend will almost always be granted, unless some ***actual prejudice*** to the other party appears. In the absence of such prejudice, refusal to permit an amendment may be an ***abuse*** of the court's discretion. [Foman v. Davis, *supra,* §685; Greenberg v. Equitable Life Assurance Society, 34 Cal. App. 3d 994 (1973)]

    (3) **Stipulation:** Ordinarily, leave of court is not required when the opposing party stipulates to the amendment.

c. **Procedure**

    (1) **Motion for leave to amend:** [§844] Unless the amendment is a matter of right or the parties consent (*supra*), the party seeking leave to amend must file a formal motion with the court, attaching a copy of the proposed amended pleading, and an appropriate showing (usually by affidavit) of the grounds upon which the amendment is sought.

    (2) **Service:** [§845] If leave to amend is granted, the amended pleading must then be filed and served in the same manner as the original pleading.

    (3) **Response to amended pleading:** [§846] If a response to the original pleading was required (*e.g.,* complaint or counterclaim), then a response to the amended pleading is required as well. The response to the pleading—be it an answer, reply, or motion—must be served within 10 days after service of the amended pleading. [Fed. R. Civ. P.15(a)]

d. **Permissible scope of amendment**

    (1) **State practice:** [§847] Under the early codes, an amendment would not be permitted if it changed the basic cause of action or defense asserted in the original pleadings. The plaintiff was not allowed to amend his complaint to set up a "wholly new and different cause of action"; nor was the defendant allowed to amend her answer to set up a "wholly new and different" defense.

(a) **Modern rule:** [§848] Even under code pleading, however, the test now employed is simply whether the proposed amended pleading is based on the *same general set of facts* as the original pleading. [Austin v. Massachusetts Bonding Co., 56 Cal. 2d 596 (1961)]

(2) **Federal practice:** [§849] Under the Federal Rules, the sole question is whether (and to what extent) the amendment results in *prejudice* to the opposing party.

(a) **Effect:** Under federal practice, therefore, it is immaterial that the proposed amendment changes the theory of the case, states a claim arising out of a transaction different from that originally sued on, or causes a change in parties. [Sherman v. Hallbauer, 455 F.2d 1236 (5th Cir. 1972)]

(b) **Amended answer:** [§850] The same liberal rules apply to the defendant's answer, *except that* defenses that are waived if not asserted in the defendant's first pleading (answer or motion)—*e.g.,* improper venue, defective service of process—cannot be revived by amendment.

e. **"Relation back doctrine"—statute of limitations problems:** [§851] Where the plaintiff seeks to amend the complaint after the statute of limitations would otherwise have run on the claim, there is a question of whether the amended claim "relates back" to the date of filing of the original complaint. *Example:* P sues D for breach of contract. Then, after the statute of limitations on an independent fraud action has run, P amends his complaint to seek damages for fraud in connection with the same contract. Should the amended claim be deemed filed at the time the original claim was filed?

(1) **"Relation back" usually permitted:** [§852] In most jurisdictions, the amended claim "relates back"—*i.e.,* is deemed filed as of the date of the original complaint—as long as the claim asserted in the amended pleading arose out of the *same conduct, transaction, or occurrence* set forth in the original pleadings. [Fed. R. Civ. P. 15(c)(2); Parrish & Sons v. County Sanitation District, 174 Cal. App. 2d 406 (1959)]

(a) **Effect:** As long as the same basic transaction is involved, the plaintiff may therefore amend his complaint to establish new theories of recovery, or even to show new facts entitling him to recover, after the statute of limitations would otherwise have run.

(b) **Rationale:** The defendant is not prejudiced because she had notice, within the limitations period, that the plaintiff was asserting *some* claim against her on the basis of the transaction involved. Consequently, a change in the nature or theory of the plaintiff's claim does not prejudice the defendant. [Tiller v. Atlantic Coast Line, 323 U.S. 574 (1945)]

(c) **Rule regarding new parties:** [§853] An amendment of the complaint cannot avoid the statute of limitations with respect to a totally new party (as plaintiff or defendant). *Rationale:* The fact that the plaintiff has filed an action against one defendant does not toll the statute of limitations on such claims as he may have against other defendants. [Anderson v. Papillion, 445 F.2d 841 (5th Cir. 1971)]

    1) **But note:** In federal courts, if the party sought to be joined (D2) has actual notice of the pendency of the action and knows or should know that, but for a mistake concerning the *identity* of the proper defendant, the action would have been brought against him, the court will order his joinder even after the statute has run (provided no other substantial prejudice is shown). [Fed. R. Civ. P. 15(c)(3)]

    2) **Time for notice:** [§854] For relation back to apply to a new defendant, the new defendant must have been on notice of the suit *within the period allowed by Rule 4(m)* for service of the complaint—120 days after the filing of the complaint.

    3) **Additional defendants:** [§855] Although Rule 15(c) speaks of changing parties, the courts have interpreted it to permit addition of parties.

  (d) **Compare—"Jane Doe" defendants named (state practice):** [§856] Some states permit the filing of a complaint against fictitious defendants ("Jane Does") where the true name of the defendant is not known when the action is filed. In such states, the complaint can be amended to name the defendant when her identity is discovered—even if the statute of limitations has then run! [Cal. Civ. Proc. Code §474; Contract Engineers, Inc. v. California-Dorian Co., 258 Cal. App. 2d 546 (1968)]

(2) **Amendments in federal diversity cases:** [§857] The Federal Rule permitting "relation back" [Fed. R. Civ. P. 15(c), *supra*] is applied by federal courts in diversity cases even if there is no similar local rule. Thus, a plaintiff may be able to assert a claim in an amended pleading that would be barred by the state court under the same circumstances. [Skidmore v. Syntex Laboratories, Inc., 529 F.2d 1244 (5th Cir. 1976)]

  (a) **Compare—state rule more liberal:** [§858] Where the state rule regarding relation back is more liberal (*e.g.,* by dispensing with the requirement of notice to the new defendant within the limitations period), it should be applied if state law provides the applicable statute of limitations. [Fed. R. Civ. P. 15(a)(1)]

f. **Amendment supersedes original pleading:** [§859] An amended pleading *supersedes* the original, and the original has no further effect as a pleading. The pleader cannot "resurrect" the original pleading by attempting to dismiss or strike the amended pleading; but she can seek leave to re-amend if she wants to return to the claim originally pleaded.

(1) **Note:** While superseded as a pleading, the original pleading can still be used *in evidence* against the pleader where appropriate—*e.g,* as an admission or prior inconsistent statement. (*See* Evidence Summary.)

(2) **And note:** In many code pleading states, if the amended pleading contains *contradictory allegations on material matters without explaining the inconsistency* from the original pleading, the adverse party may move to strike the amended pleading as sham. This applies to both verified and unverified pleadings. [Hills Transportation Co. v. Southwest Forest Industries, 266 Cal. App. 2d 702 (1968)]

3. **Amendments at Trial:** [§860] Because a basic purpose of pleading is to define the scope of the issues at trial, problems arise when a party seeks to amend the pleadings—and thus change the triable issues—during the course of the trial.

   a. **Common law background—doctrine of "variance":** [§861] At common law, a party could prevail (if at all) only on the claim stated in the pleadings. Issues outside the pleadings could not be tried; and any "variance" between the facts pleaded and those proved was often fatal to recovery. It made no difference that the other side failed to object or even *consented* to the variance.

   b. **Modern code practice:** [§862] The common law rules have been relaxed in most code pleading states today. Where the evidence offered at trial is only a *partial* variance from the pleadings, the court may grant leave to amend the pleadings at trial to conform to the proof. If the variance is prejudicial, however, no such amendment can be permitted.

      (1) **Nonprejudicial variance:** [§863] A nonprejudicial variance exists where the evidence at trial differs from the pleadings but concerns the *same transaction* as that originally alleged *and* the difference was *not prejudicial* to the opposing party (*i.e.,* did not mislead her in preparing her defense). [General Credit Corp. v. Pichel, 44 Cal. App. 3d 844 (1975)]

      (2) **Prejudicial variance:** [§864] A prejudicial variance exists where the facts proved at trial show an entirely "new and different" cause of action or theory of recovery, or otherwise differ so materially from the pleadings as to be prejudicial.

         (a) **Example:** P's complaint for malpractice alleged liability of defendant hospital by reason of the negligence of doctors who performed an operation. At trial, plaintiff sought to prove negligence on the part of members of the hospital's own staff. This was held to be a prejudicial variance, and amendment of the pleadings to assert the new theory was not permitted. [Rainer v. Community Memorial Hospital, 18 Cal. App. 3d 240 (1971)]

      (3) **Determinative factors:** [§865] Whether a variance will be deemed prejudicial depends on several factors:

         (a) *Surprise* to the opponent—*i.e.,* whether the opponent was put on notice of the new claim or defense, through discovery or pretrial disclosures;

         (b) *Whether a continuance* would enable the opponent to meet the new evidence;

(c) *Any elements of inconvenience or unfairness* in granting a continuance (prejudice from delay, extra expense in trial, etc.); and

(d) *Policy favoring amendment*—to obtain complete and final disposition on the merits.

c. **Federal practice:** [§866] The pleadings are considerably less important in federal than in code pleading practice, and amendments are therefore allowed more liberally—even during trial. The doctrine of variance is effectively *abolished* in federal practice.

(1) **Evidence received without objection:** [§867] First, any variance between the pleadings and the proof at trial is *waived* unless a specific, timely, and proper objection to the evidence is made when offered. [Fed. R. Civ. P. 15(b)—"all issues tried with the *express or implied consent* of the parties shall be treated in all respects as if they had been raised in the pleading"]

(a) **Aider by verdict:** [§868] This embodies the doctrine of "aider by verdict"; *i.e.*, that evidence received at trial without objection by the adverse party supplies the missing allegations in the pleadings, so that the defective pleadings are "aided" by the verdict.

(b) **Tactic—amend to conform to proof:** [§869] It is still sound practice to seek leave to amend to conform to proof (which can be granted even after trial and judgment)—so there will be a correlation between the judgment and pleadings. However, failure to amend to conform to proof does *not* affect the result of the trial or the validity of the judgment as entered. [Fed. R. Civ. P. 15(b)]

(c) **Problem of relevance:** [§870] The usual objection that could be made would be relevance—that the proffered evidence is not relevant to the issues made out in the pleading. In many instances, however, this may not be clear, and one can argue that evidence was relevant even without an amendment. If that is true, failure to object would not be a waiver of objections to amendment.

(2) **Amendments over objection:** [§871] Secondly, if evidence *is* objected to on the ground that it is outside the issues framed by the pleadings, the proponent of the evidence must seek leave to amend his pleadings. Federal Rule 15(b) provides that the court may allow the pleadings to be amended (during trial) and "*shall do so freely* when the presentation of the merits of the action will be subserved thereby and the objecting party fails to satisfy the court that the admission of such evidence would prejudice him in maintaining his action or defense upon the merits."

(a) **Effect:** It is up to the objecting party to show *prejudice* on the merits, or the requested amendment must be granted. Refusing leave to amend without such showing constitutes an abuse of judicial discretion and will be reversed on appeal. [Hodgson v. Colonnades, Inc., 472 F.2d 42 (5th Cir. 1973)]

(b) **Tactic—continuance:** [§872] The proper remedy for surprise resulting from a change of theory at trial is a continuance. And in granting a continuance, the court can assess *costs* against the party at fault. [Watson v. Cannon Shoe Co., 165 F.2d 311 (5th Cir. 1948)]

4. **Amendments After Trial:** [§873] In federal practice, the pleadings can be amended to conform to proof at any time, even after trial and entry of judgment (*see* above). [Fed. R. Civ. P. 15(b)] Such a motion for amendment can be made for the first time *on appeal.* However, this is subject to the general rule of appellate practice that a reviewing court will not consider grounds for appeal (other than jurisdictional) that were not reasonably raised in the trial court. (*See infra,* §§2009-2016.)

5. **Supplemental Pleadings:** [§874] The function of supplemental pleadings is to call the court's attention to material facts that have occurred *subsequent* to the filing of the original complaint. *Example:* In an action for personal injuries, a supplemental pleading might allege aggravation of injuries or increments of damage sustained after filing of the original complaint.

   a. **Discretion of court:** [§875] There is *no right* to file a supplemental pleading. The filing of such pleadings is permissive, within the sound discretion of the court. [Fed. R. Civ. P. 15(d)]

      (1) **But note:** The same policy factors favoring liberality in amendment of pleadings (above) likewise support supplemental pleadings. Indeed, there is even less chance of prejudice to the other party in this situation, since the supplemental pleading does not alter the claim or defense originally asserted.

   b. **Procedure:** [§876] The party seeking leave to supplement a pleading must file a written motion, attaching a copy of the proposed supplemental pleading.

      (1) **Response:** [§877] Whether a response to a supplemental pleading may be filed is also discretionary with the court. If the court orders a response, it will likewise set the time within which such a response must be served and filed. [Fed. R. Civ. P. 15(d)]

   c. **Effect on original pleading:** [§878] The function of a supplemental pleading is merely to *add to,* not modify, the original pleadings. If permitted, it does not replace the original pleading (as would an amended pleading), but it is a supplement to the original.

      (1) *Under state practice,* a supplemental complaint is not permitted to change the basic nature of the case by alleging what amounts to a totally different cause of action. [Flood v. Simpson, 45 Cal. App. 3d 644 (1975)]

      (2) *Federal practice* is more liberal. Federal Rule 15(d) gives the court discretion to allow supplemental pleadings despite the fact that the original pleading is defective, or that the supplement would change the nature of the relief sought.

I. DEFAULT PROCEDURE

1. **In General:** [§879]   As discussed (*supra*, §794), if a defendant fails to answer or otherwise plead within the time permitted, the clerk of the court is required to enter a default. [Fed. R. Civ. P. 55(a)]

2. **Effect of Default Entry:** [§880]   The defendant's failure to plead is regarded as an *admission* of the claim against her. So long as the default stands, any attempt by defendant to "answer" or file any other pleading in the case will be disregarded.

3. **Obtaining Judgment:** [§881]   After an entry of default, the plaintiff must proceed to obtain a default judgment. If he is suing on a promissory note or other sum certain, the judgment may be entered directly by the clerk of the court. In all other cases, the plaintiff must present his evidence to the court in order to obtain judgment. [Fed. R. Civ. P. 55(b)]

    a. **Relief limited to prayer:** [§882]   In default cases, the judgment cannot exceed the *amount or type of relief requested in the prayer of the complaint*. (*See supra*, §581.)

    b. **Defendant not entitled to appear:** [§883]   Unless she made an earlier appearance in the action, the defendant is *not* entitled to any notice of the plaintiff's application for default judgment; nor is she entitled to appear or submit evidence in opposition.

4. **Setting Aside Default:** [§884]   If the defendant's default has been entered, her remedy is to move the court to set aside the default (and any judgment entered pursuant thereto).

    a. **Time limits:** [§885]   In federal practice, a motion to set aside the default can be made at any time until judgment is entered. [Fed. R. Civ. P. 55(c)] Thereafter, a motion to set aside the judgment can be made at any time within *one year* after the judgment or order is entered. [Fed. R. Civ. P. 60(b)]

    b. **Grounds:** [§886]   Ordinarily, the defendant must show:

        (1) *That she has a valid excuse* for her default (*e.g.*, excusable neglect, fraud, inadvertence);

        (2) *That she has a meritorious defense* to the action; *and*

        (3) *That plaintiff will not be prejudiced.*

    c. **Appellate review:** [§887]   Review of a trial court's decision on a motion to set aside default is limited. Appellate courts will not overturn the trial court decision unless both of the above factors appear so clearly that the trial court ruling was an *abuse of discretion*.

J. JUDGMENT ON THE PLEADINGS

1. **Purpose:** [§888]   A motion for judgment on the pleadings is closely analogous to a demurrer or motion to dismiss under Federal Rule 12(b)(6), and is used at common

law for the same purpose—*i.e.,* to challenge the adversary's pleadings on the ground that they are *insufficient to establish any valid claim or defense*.

2. **Making of Motion:** [§889] A motion for judgment on the pleadings may be made by either party at any time after the pleadings have joined issue, but within such time as will not delay the trial. [Fed. R. Civ. P. 12(c)]

3. **Issues Raised**

   a. **Legal sufficiency of pleading:** [§890] A motion for judgment on the pleadings challenges only the sufficiency of the adversary's pleading in posing a legally meritorious contention.

   b. **Matters beyond the pleading:** [§891] Under common law and code practice, a motion for judgment on the pleadings could not raise defects that did not appear on the face of the pleadings. However, modern practice permits the moving party to present matters beyond the pleadings; and where this is done, the motion is treated as a motion for summary judgment. [Fed. R. Civ. P. 12(c)]

4. **Hearing on Motion:** [§892] As with other pretrial matters, a motion for judgment on the pleadings is generally heard before commencement of the trial (although the court may order the motion deferred until the time of trial). [Fed. R. Civ. P. 12(d)]

5. **Adversary's Right to Amend Pleadings:** [§893] Once a responsive pleading has been filed, a pleader no longer has an absolute right to amend the pleading; any amendment must be by leave of court or by written consent of the adverse party. [Fed. R. Civ. P. 15(a)] For this purpose, a motion for judgment on the pleadings is *not* a "responsive pleading" and hence does not cut off an adversary's right to amend without leave of court if no answer has been filed. [Breier v. Northern California Bowling Proprietors' Association, 316 F.2d 787 (9th Cir. 1963)]

K. **VOLUNTARY DISMISSAL BY PLAINTIFF**

1. **Common Law:** [§894] At common law, a plaintiff had the right to dismiss his own action at any time before verdict. While a dismissal ordinarily would result in an award of costs against the plaintiff, the dismissal was without prejudice to a later suit on the same claim.

2. **Code Practice:** [§895] The common law procedure was subject to some abuse by plaintiffs taking dismissals to prevent decisions on the merits favoring their adversaries. As a result, code pleading states limited the right of plaintiffs to dismiss their actions without prejudice: Such a dismissal had to occur *before* the commencement of trial; otherwise it was deemed to be with prejudice (*i.e.,* a bar to relitigation). This is still the rule in some states. [*See, e.g.,* Cal. Civ. Proc. Code §581(b)(1)]

   a. **Note:** The filing of a counterclaim or cross-demand for affirmative relief may also prevent a voluntary dismissal without prejudice. [Cal. Civ. Proc. Code §581(i)]

3. **Federal Practice—Notice of Dismissal (Voluntary)**

   a. **Filing of notice:** [§896]   Under federal practice, a plaintiff retains the right to dismiss his own action by filing a notice of dismissal. [Fed. R. Civ. P. 41(a)(1)(i)]   But the right to do so is even more narrowly limited than in code pleading states.

   b. **Time for filing:** [§897]   An effective notice of dismissal must be filed before the filing of the adversary's *answer or motion for summary judgment*. Thereafter, the plaintiff cannot dismiss without the defendant's consent or court order. [Fed. R. Civ. P. 41(a)(2)]

      (1) **Compare:** It has been held that a *motion to dismiss for failure to state a claim* is not tantamount to a motion for summary judgment, and does not terminate the plaintiff's right to file a voluntary dismissal. [Kilpatrick v. Texas & Pacific Railway, 166 F.2d 788 (2d Cir. 1948); *but see* Tele-Views News Co. v. S.R.B. TV Publishing Co., 28 F.R.D. 303 (E.D. Pa. 1961)]

   c. **Number of dismissals:** [§898]   The plaintiff is limited to one (voluntary) dismissal by notice. Thereafter, any dismissal operates as a dismissal *with prejudice.* [Fed. R. Civ. P. 41(a)]

   d. **Trial court cannot set aside proper dismissal:** [§899]   An order striking a timely notice of dismissal is reversible error, and any judgment subsequently entered against the plaintiff will be reversed on appeal after trial. [Plains Growers, Inc. v. Ickes-Braun Glasshouses, Inc., 474 F.2d 250 (5th Cir. 1973)]

   e. **Effect on power to sanction:** [§900]   Unless the court has already issued an order to show cause why sanctions should not be imposed at the time of the voluntary dismissal, it may not impose monetary sanctions on its own initiative. [Fed. R. Civ. P. 11(c)(2)(B)]

4. **Federal Practice—Dismissal by Leave of Court**

   a. **Time for motion:** [§901]   The court may grant the plaintiff's motion for leave to dismiss without prejudice at any time *prior to judgment*—*i.e.,* even after the trial has commenced. [Fed. R. Civ. P. 41(a)(2)]

   b. **Discretion of court:** [§902]   The discretion of the court to refuse a dismissal without prejudice is limited.

      (1) **Example:** A plaintiff making a good faith request based on newly discovered evidence has been held entitled to a dismissal without prejudice (to allow refiling of the action and a new trial) unless a substantial right of the defendant would be jeopardized thereby. [Durham v. Florida East Coast Railroad, 385 F.2d 366 (5th Cir. 1971)]

      (2) **Compare:** The court should not order a dismissal without prejudice merely to accommodate the plaintiff's desire to get another 10-day period within which to demand a jury trial. [Noonan v. Cunard Steamship Co., 375 F.2d 69 (2d Cir. 1967)]

(3) **Counterclaims preserved:** The court may not dismiss over the objection of a defendant who has filed a counterclaim unless the counterclaim can remain pending for independent adjudication. [Fed. R. Civ. P. 41(a)(2); *see* Chapter II regarding subject matter jurisdiction]

c. **Number of dismissals:** [§903] The court is not limited as to the number of times it may grant motions to dismiss the same action without prejudice—provided, of course, that there is a legitimate reason for the repeated requests. [American Cyanimid Co. v. McGhee, 317 F.2d 295 (5th Cir. 1963)]

d. **Conditions of dismissal:** [§904] A plaintiff seeking dismissal *without* prejudice may be required to bear the full cost of the litigation to date, including the adversary's attorneys' fees. [Fed. R. Civ. P. 41(a)(2)] But such conditions may not be imposed on a plaintiff seeking to dismiss his claim *with* prejudice. [Smoot v. Fox, 353 F.2d 830 (6th Cir. 1965)] *Note:* Under Rule 11, however, sanctions may be imposed on a plaintiff who voluntarily dismisses a groundless suit. (*See supra,* §§709 *et seq.*)

e. **Continuing jurisdiction—stipulated dismissal:** [§905] When dismissal by stipulation pursuant to Rule 41(a)(2) provides that the court shall retain jurisdiction to enforce a settlement agreement, the court has continuing jurisdiction, but otherwise dismissal terminates the court's jurisdiction. [Kokkonen v. Guardian Life Insurance Co., 114 S. Ct. 1673 (1994)—court without jurisdiction to enforce provision of parties' settlement agreement after dismissal pursuant to that agreement because the parties' obligation to comply was not made part of the order of dismissal]

V. PARTIES

chapter approach

Modern procedural rules make available several devices for joinder of parties beyond the "single plaintiff vs. single defendant" paradigm of a lawsuit. The standards for joinder vary with the functions served by the various procedural devices. When you face a problem involving more than just one plaintiff vs. one defendant, consider the following:

1. Before you even get to joinder issues, you may need to think about the requirements of *real party in interest* and *capacity to sue or be sued:*

    a. Is the action brought in the name of the *real party in interest*, *i.e.*, the party who under governing substantive law has the right to enforce the claim?

    b. Do the parties have legal competence to be parties to a lawsuit; do they have *capacity to sue or be sued?* Partnerships (as opposed to partners) and infants and incompetent persons, for example, may lack legal capacity.

2. If the situation in your question calls for joinder of someone not a party to the suit, is joinder *compulsory*?

    a. Is the absentee one whose nonjoinder would prevent the granting of *complete relief*, or *prejudice* his or the present parties' interests? Such a person should be joined if joinder is feasible. If not feasible (as when joinder would destroy complete diversity in a diversity case in federal court), the court must decide whether it can proceed with only the present parties before it.

    — If the court can proceed, the absentee is characterized as merely a *"necessary"* party, and the action can proceed in his absence.

    — If the court cannot proceed, the absentee is regarded as an *"indispensable"* party, and the action must be dismissed.

3. To determine whether *permissive* joinder is appropriate:

    a. Is the relief sought *jointly, severally, or in the alternative;*

    b. Does the claim *arise out of the same transaction* or series of transactions; and

    c. Is there a *common question of law or fact?*

4. Sometimes someone not already a party to the suit seeks to *intervene.* In that case consider:

    a. Is the case one for *intervention of right*, in which disposition in his absence could impair or impede his ability to protect an interest he claims in the property or transaction sued on, and the existing parties do not adequately represent his interest; or

    b. Is the case one in which the court may allow *permissive intervention*, with the prospective intervenor's claim or defense having a question of law or fact in common with the main action?

5. When you see facts that have two (or more) persons asserting a claim to money or property in the hands of a third party (the "stakeholder"), think of *interpleader.* The stakeholder may deposit the property with the court and seek a ruling as to which of the adverse claimants is entitled to the property.

6. A defendant in your question may seek *impleader* of a third-party defendant. If so, is the third party one (*e.g.*, an insurer) who is or may be liable to the defendant for all or part of the plaintiff's claim against defendant?

7. In federal court when an effort is made at joinder adding a party, if there is no independent basis of federal jurisdiction, think about whether there is *supplemental jurisdiction* over the added claim.

8. If the situation seems to call for a *class action*

   a. Ask:

      (1) Are the class members so *numerous* that joinder of all is impracticable;

      (2) Are there *common questions* of law or fact;

      (3) Are the representative's *claims or defenses typical* of those of the class;

      (4) Will the representative *adequately represent* the interests of the class;

   b. And in addition, ask:

      (1) Might there be *prejudice from separate actions*; or

      (2) Has the class's opponent acted or refused to act on grounds generally applicable to the class, making *class injunctive or declaratory relief* appropriate; *or*

      (3) Do *common questions predominate* over individual ones, and is a class action *superior* to other methods?

   If you find that the case may be conducted as a class action, has required *notice* been given?

A. REAL PARTY IN INTEREST RULE

1. **Background:** [§906] At common law, only the legal "owner" of a right could bring an action for infringement of that right. Since the common law did not recognize equitable interests (*e.g.*, rights of subrogees, beneficiaries of various kinds of trusts, etc.), the holder of such an interest could not sue at law for its enforcement, but instead had to rely on the legal owner to bring suit. This burdensome practice has been abolished, and today, suit can be brought only in the name of the real party in interest. [Fed. R. Civ. P. 17]

2. **Definition:** [§907] The real party in interest rule has two parts; the person who is suing must: (i) use her *own name* as plaintiff, *and* (ii) have a *legal right* to enforce the claim in question under the applicable substantive law.

a. **Burden of proof:** [§908] The plaintiff has the burden of proving that she is a real party in interest; *i.e.*, that she should be allowed to sue to protect the interest involved.

b. **Under Federal Rules and state rules:** [§909] The following parties have a right to sue as representative parties even though they may have no beneficial interest in the claims at issue [Fed. R. Civ. P. 17(a)]:

 (1) *The executor, administrator, guardian, or trustee* of an estate;

 (2) *A party to a contract made for the benefit of another party* (*e.g.*, an agent contracting on behalf of the principal or the promisee of a third-party beneficiary contract); and

 (3) *A private claimant suing in the name of the United States Government* if such a claim is expressly authorized by statute.

c. **In all other cases:** [§910] In all other cases, a determination of the real party in interest is made according to applicable substantive law. In a federal diversity action, the applicable state law is applied.

3. **Determination of Real Party in Interest:** [§911] The following situations illustrate the types of problems encountered in determining the real party in interest.

 a. **Assignments:** [§912] Whether an assignee is the real party in interest depends primarily on the nature of the assignment.

 (1) **Complete assignment:** [§913] If the assignor's entire interest has been transferred to the assignee, the assignee has become the real party in interest. The assignee may then prosecute any action to enforce the assigned right in her own name without joining the assignor.

 (a) **Gratuitous assignment:** [§914] In state and federal practice, the assignee can sue even if she paid nothing for the claim and is merely an *assignee for collection*. However, in federal court, the citizenship of the *assignor* determines whether diversity exists. (*See supra*, §313.)

 (b) **Assignment after commencement of suit:** [§915] If the assignment takes place after suit has been filed, the assignee may either continue the action in the name of the assignor or be substituted as the plaintiff. [*See* Fed. R. Civ. P. 25(c)]

 (c) **Effect of judgment:** [§916] A judgment in the assignee's action will bar any subsequent suit on the same claim by the assignor, because of the *privity* between the assignee and assignor. [Nemeth v. Hair, 146 Cal. App. 2d 405 (1956); *and see* discussion on res judicata, *infra*, §§2034 *et seq.*]

 (2) **Partial assignments:** [§917] At common law, the assignee of part of a claim could not enforce the claim at all. However, partial assignees could enforce their claims in *equity* if the assignor and all other partial assignees joined as parties in the same suit.

(a) **Modern rule:** [§918] Today, the assignor and all partial assignees are considered *"necessary parties"* in any suit to enforce the claim, and on appropriate motion, the court will order their joinder. [United States v. Aetna Casualty & Surety Co., 338 U.S. 366 (1949)]

b. **Subrogation:** [§919] Subrogation is an equitable principle through which an assignment occurs by operation of law. Under the doctrine of subrogation, the person who *pays* another for a loss or injury caused by the act of some third person is entitled to enforce whatever claim the injured person had against the third person. Most jurisdictions allow the person who paid (subrogee) to sue in his own name without joining the injured party (subrogor). [United States v. Aetna Casualty & Surety Co., *supra*]

(1) **Example:** X Insurance Co. insures P's house and pays P for damages to the house caused by D's wrongful act. X becomes subrogated to P's claim against D and is entitled to sue in its own name. [Auto Insurance Co. v. Union Oil Co., 85 Cal. App. 2d 302 (1948)]

(2) **Tactical problem:** [§920] An insurance company will usually prefer to sue in the name of its *insured*, rather than in its own name, to avoid any jury prejudice against insurers. Consequently, most insurance settlements contain provisions expressly authorizing the insurer to sue the wrongdoer "in the name of the insured."

(a) **Note:** The traditional view did not permit such suits because the insured, having been fully paid and having assigned the claim to the company, had no further interest in the matter. [*See* Sosnow v. Storatti Corp., 295 N.Y. 675 (1946)] However, most states now permit suits in the name of the insured. [*See* Anheuser-Busch, Inc. v. Starley, 28 Cal. 2d 347 (1946)]

(b) **And note:** Even states that do not permit suit in the name of the insured may recognize the "loan receipt" device. Here, the insurer—instead of paying off the insured—makes him a "loan" repayable only out of proceeds from the insured's recovery against the third person. The insured gets his money but still "owns" the claim. The insurance company then brings suit in the name of the insured, and the insurer keeps the proceeds if it wins.

c. **Trusts**

(1) **Trustee:** [§921] The trustee of a trust holds legal title to the trust estate and is therefore the real party in interest for redress of any *wrong to the trust estate.* [Fed. R. Civ. P. 17] Suit is maintained in the trustee's name as trustee (*e.g.*, "John Smith, as trustee of the Mary Doe Trust"). [*See* Powers v. Ashton, 45 Cal. App. 3d 783 (1975)]

(2) **Beneficiary:** [§922] The beneficiary of a trust may sue the trustee to protect her rights as beneficiary—*e.g.*, for an accounting, for distributions of assets, etc. [DeOlazabel v. Mix, 24 Cal. App. 2d 258 (1937)]

(a) **But note:** A beneficiary cannot sue third persons for wrongs to the trust estate unless the trustee refuses to bring suit for such injuries. In the latter situation, the beneficiary can sue the third party by joining the trustee and alleging his failure to act. [Triplett v. Williams, 269 Cal. App. 2d 135 (1969)]

d. **Executors and administrators:** [§923] Executors and administrators are the proper parties to sue on behalf of decedents' estates at law or in equity.

(1) **Note:** Problems do arise about the capacity of a representative appointed in one state to sue in another, but such problems do not result from the real party in interest provision. They concern primarily the policy of the forum state of protecting local creditors. This has led to the general rule that an executor or administrator has capacity to sue only in the state of her appointment, unless she obtains ancillary appointment in another state.

(2) **Beneficiary of an estate pursuing claims:** [§924] Ordinarily the legatee or distributee of an estate may not bring suit to pursue claims of the estate, although exceptions have been recognized in situations parallel to the exceptions for beneficiaries of a trust.

(3) **Survival statutes and wrongful death acts:** [§925] Claims under survival statutes are generally part of the decedent's estate and are to be pursued by his executor or administrator just as any other asset of the estate would be. Wrongful death acts generally specify the proper party to an action under them. Some of them name one or more of the beneficiaries, and in such a case, the party named is of course the real party in interest. Many of them require suit to be brought by the personal representative of the deceased—*i.e.*, the executor or administrator. However, when suing under such a statute, the executor or administrator is not acting as a representative of the estate but as a person designated by statute. Consequently the judgment or recovery under the statute will not be an asset of the estate at all, but will belong to the statutory beneficiaries, who may or may not be the same persons who would take as legatees or distributees of the estate.

e. **Principal and agent:** [§926] Where a contract has been executed by an agent acting for a principal, the following rules apply:

(1) *If the obligation is owed to the principal alone,* the principal is the only proper plaintiff.

(2) *If the obligation is owed to both the agent and the principal,* either party may sue (*e.g.,* where the contract was nominally with the agent—an undisclosed principal—or where there was a promise to both the agent and the principal). [Warren Insurance Agency v. Surpur Timber Co., 250 Cal. App. 2d 99 (1967)—suit by agent; Ford v. Williams, 62 U.S. 287 (1858)—suit by undisclosed principal]

f. **Third-party beneficiary:** [§927] Where a third-party beneficiary has enforceable rights under a contract, he is the real party in interest and is entitled to sue in his own name to enforce his rights. [Orcutt v. Ferranini, 237 Cal. App. 2d 216 (1965)]

(1) **Note:** The *promisee* under a contract may also be entitled to sue to enforce the promise given for the benefit of a third party. In such case, *both* the promisee and the third-party beneficiary would have enforceable rights and would be deemed real parties in interest.

4. **Attacking Violation of Real Party in Interest Rule**

   a. **Where defect apparent**

   (1) **Federal practice:** [§928]   If a violation of the real party in interest rule is apparent on the face of a complaint in federal court, the defendant should make a *motion to dismiss* for failure to state a claim upon which relief may be granted (since the plaintiff has no right to recovery). [Fed. R. Civ. P. 12(b)(6)]

   (2) **Code practice (some states):** [§929]   Under code pleading practice, a *general demurrer* is appropriate to attack defects on the face of the complaint. (*See supra*, §655.)

   b. **Where defect not apparent:** [§930]   If the defect is not apparent on the face of the complaint, the defendant may move for summary judgment (supported by appropriate affidavits to establish the defect) or may raise the matter as an affirmative defense in her answer.

5. **Nonjoinder of Necessary Party:** [§931]   If the named plaintiff has some kind of interest in the claim (assignor or assignee, principal or agent, trustee or beneficiary), and the objection is that someone else should also be the named plaintiff (another partial assignee, principal, etc.), this is an objection to nonjoinder of a *necessary party.*

   a. **When objection can be raised:** [§932]   The objection as to the named plaintiff can be raised by motion before trial or at the trial itself [Fed. R. Civ. P. 12(h)(2)], but delay may result in estoppel against raising it. If the objection is first made on appeal, it is too late unless serious injustice would inevitably result from the nonjoinder. [Provident Bank & Trust Co. v. Patterson, 390 U.S. 102 (1968)]

   b. **Compare—no cause of action:** [§933]   If the named plaintiff has *no* substantive interest in the claim being enforced, he has no cause of action. This objection is therefore proper at any time prior to judgment. Note, however, that under the usual rules governing appeal, a claim that the plaintiff has no cause of action cannot be raised on appeal for the first time, and the objection *cannot* be made in collateral attack on the judgment.

B. CAPACITY OF PARTY TO SUE OR BE SUED

1. **Definition:** [§934]   "Capacity" refers to legal competence to be a party to a lawsuit. The plaintiff must have the capacity to sue, and the defendant must have the capacity to be sued.

2. **Individuals:** [§935] The capacity of an individual to sue or be sued is determined by the law of her domicile. [Fed. R. Civ. P. 17(b)] If the plaintiff lacks capacity (as in the case of a minor or an incompetent), suit must be maintained by a duly authorized or appointed guardian. If there is none, the court must appoint one for the particular action (a "guardian ad litem"). [Fed. R. Civ. P. 17(c)]

   a. **Pleadings by guardian:** [§936] Where a guardian or conservator appears in the action, the pleadings are usually drawn in the name of the guardian "for and on behalf of" the incompetent or minor. [Fed. R. Civ. P. 17(c)] Note that state practice on such pleadings varies. For example, in California, the pleadings are drawn in the name of the minor or incompetent "by a guardian or conservator . . . ." [Cal. Civ. Proc. Code §372]

   b. **Incompetent's right to disaffirm judgment:** [§937] Where a minor (or incompetent) is a party to the action but is not represented by a guardian, any judgment rendered is *voidable by him* within a reasonable time after attaining majority (or being restored to competency) *if* it appears that his legal interests were inadequately protected in the action. [Withers v. Tucker, 145 N.W.2d 665 (Wis. 1966)—minor represented by attorney]

3. **Corporations:** [§938] The capacity of a corporation to sue (or be sued) is determined by the law of the state in which it was organized.

   a. **Example:** Statutes in some states provide for suspension of powers of a corporation that is delinquent in paying its state taxes. [*See, e.g.,* Cal. Rev. & Tax Code §23301] In such a case, the corporation would have no power to sue or defend itself or appeal from a judgment as long as it is under the suspension. [Mather Construction Co. v. United States, 475 F.2d 1152 (Ct. Cl. 1973)]

   b. **Limitation:** A state cannot impose a disability on a corporation if doing so would violate federal law.

      (1) **Example:** An attempt to deny an out-of-state corporation the right to sue in local courts to enforce a contract made in interstate commerce would violate federal law. [Allenberg Cotton Co. v. Pittman, 419 U.S. 20 (1974)]

4. **Partnerships:** [§939] Two issues arise with respect to the capacity of partnerships: (i) whether the partnership can (or must) sue as an entity, distinct from its members; and (ii) if the suit is by one or more of the members of the partnership, whether they should be named individually or should sue in the name of the partnership.

   a. **Federal practice—entity vs. aggregate:** [§940] In *federal* courts, a partnership can always sue or be sued as an entity if the litigation involves a federal question. However, in other cases—including a diversity action—the partnership's capacity to sue or be sued is determined by the law of the state in which the federal court is located. [Fed. R. Civ. P. 17(b)]

   b. **State law varies:** [§941] Most states permit a partnership to be sued, but *not* to sue, as an entity (in its common name). In those states, actions on a partnership claim must be brought in the names of the individual partners (*e.g.,* "A, B, and C, as co-partners doing business as Acme Partnership"). A few states allow the partnership to both sue *and* be sued as an entity. [*See* Cal. Civ. Proc. Code §369.5]

5. **Unincorporated Associations:** [§942] At common law, unincorporated associations were treated much like partnerships, and thus lacked capacity to sue or be sued as entities. [Ostrom v. Greene, 161 N.Y. 353 (1900)]

   a. **State practice:** [§943] Many states now treat unincorporated associations like corporations. [*See* Cal. Civ. Proc. Code §369.5; Wright v. Arkansas Activities Association, 501 F.2d 25 (8th Cir. 1974)]

   b. **Federal practice:** [§944] In federal courts, an association has capacity to sue or be sued when a *federal right* is being enforced by or against the association. But when a *state* law right is being enforced, as in a *diversity* action, the capacity of an unincorporated association is determined by the law of the state in which the federal action is brought. [Fed. R. Civ. P. 17(b)]

      (1) **Compare—existence of diversity:** [§945] For purposes of determining the existence of diversity of citizenship, the association is considered a citizen of each state of which any one of its members is a citizen. (*See supra,* §293.)

   c. **Compare—real party in interest rule:** [§946] Even where an unincorporated association has the capacity to sue, it must assert a claim that belongs to it rather than to its members individually.

      (1) **Example:** An unincorporated association of businesses has standing to seek an injunction against conduct constituting unfair competition to its members, but not to seek damages for past injury to the members, as such rights do not belong to the association. [Travel Agents Malpractice Action Corps. v. Regal Cultural Society, 287 A.2d 4 (N.J. 1972)]

6. **Attacking Lack of Capacity**

   a. **Lack of capacity on face of complaint:** [§947] If lack of capacity appears on the face of the complaint, the complaint is subject to a *motion to dismiss* (or demurrer, in some states). Usually, however, it does not appear and must be raised by motion for summary judgment or in the *answer.*

   b. **Lack of capacity not raised by time of answer:** [§948] If lack of capacity is not raised by the time of the answer, then the defect is waived. The judgment entered will determine the rights of the party despite his lack of capacity, except when he can show that he was inadequately represented (*see supra,* §937).

C. JOINDER OF PARTIES

1. **In General:** [§949] Determining which parties are to be joined as plaintiffs or defendants requires a consideration of the rules of compulsory and permissive joinder. Compulsory joinder rules cover parties who *must* be joined ("indispensable

parties") and those who *should* be joined if possible ("conditionally necessary parties"). The rules of permissive joinder apply to parties who *may* be joined ("proper parties").

2. **Permissive Joinder:** [§950] At common law and under the early codes, a plaintiff's joinder options were limited. Under the Federal Rules and modern codes, however, a plaintiff may join anyone involved in the *transaction* that is the subject matter of the suit.

   a. **Early approach:** [§951] Under the original codes, persons could be joined only if they each had "an interest" in the subject of the action *and* the relief sought. The rules governing joinder of causes of action required that causes joined "affect" *all* parties joined. These rules prevented joinder in many cases where the need was obvious. *Example:* Wife, injured by D's negligence, sues for her injuries. Husband attempts to join his claim for loss of her services. Joinder was not proper under the early approach because Husband had no "interest" in the relief sought by Wife, and vice versa. [Ryder v. Jefferson Hotel Co., 113 S.E. 474 (S.C. 1922)]

   b. **Modern approach:** [§952] Today, persons may join or be joined in one action if:

      (i) A right to relief is asserted by (or against) them *jointly, severally, or in the alternative;*

      (ii) The right to relief *arises out of the same transaction or series of transactions;* and

      (iii) There is *at least one question of law or fact common to all parties* sought to be joined.

      [Fed. R. Civ. P. 20(a)]

      (1) **Relief sought**

         (a) **Separate or joint:** [§953] Each plaintiff is not required to have an interest in *every* cause of action in all the relief prayed for. If there are several plaintiffs, they have the option to seek *separate* relief or *joint* relief. Likewise, if several defendants are joined, the relief sought may be against each separately or against them jointly.

         (b) **"In the alternative"—plaintiff "in doubt":** [§954] Sometimes, a plaintiff may be in doubt as to which of several defendants is liable for his injuries (*e.g.,* P is injured by a bullet fired by either D-1 or D-2). In such a case, it is proper for the plaintiff to set forth a claim against each defendant *in the alternative*, so that their respective liabilities can be determined.

      (2) **"Same transaction" requirement:** [§955] The requirement that the right to relief arise from the "same transaction or series of transactions" is construed very broadly. *Some causal relationship or interrelation* among the defendants' conduct, or in the interest being asserted by multiple plaintiffs, is sufficient. This tends to merge with the "common question" requirement, below.

(a) **Example:** P was permitted to join a claim against an insurance company for inducing P to refrain from suing within the statute of limitations period with a claim against his former attorney for negligently failing to file the suit on time. [Rekeweg v. Federal Mutual Insurance Co., 27 F.R.D. 431 (N.D. Ind. 1961)]

(b) **Note:** Where defendants are joined *in the alternative* because the plaintiff is "in doubt" about which one caused his injuries, the injury issue supplies the requisite relationship between the claims joined, even where the conduct of the two defendants is otherwise factually *unrelated. Example:* Where P claims permanent back injuries after involvement in two unrelated traffic accidents, alleging doubt as to whether his back injury was caused by accident 1 or accident 2, joinder of both drivers as defendants is proper. [Landau v. Salam, 4 Cal. 3d 901 (1971)]

(3) **"Common question" requirement:** [§956] It is sufficient if there is a *single* question of law or fact common to all parties joined. However, it is *not* necessary that the "common question" be in dispute.

(a) **Example:** P-1, a driver, and P-2, a passenger in the car, sue D for injuries sustained in an auto accident. The "common question" is whether D was negligent. This is sufficient for joinder purposes even though there are also many separate questions involved (*e.g.,* injuries sustained by each, any contributory negligence barring P-1's claim, etc.).

(b) **Caution:** If the common question is relatively unimportant, the court will tend to define the "transaction" somewhat more narrowly to prevent joinder of claims that have no significant *evidentiary relationship* to each other. Hence, a *practical test* for permissive joinder is applied: Are the issues in the two claims *factually intertwined* with each other in any significant way?

(4) **Additional unrelated claims:** [§957] As long as the requirements for joinder of *parties* (above) are met, each of the parties joined may assert as many *claims* as she has against any opposing party. [Fed. R. Civ. P. 18] The policy of the law is to allow *unlimited* joinder of claims as long as there is a *transactional* connection among all of the parties.

(a) **Example:** P joins D-1 against whom he claims injuries while a passenger in D-2's vehicle, and D-2 against whom he claims for the same injuries in the accident, and also for failure to pay a promissory note that D-2 executed in favor of P. This joinder is proper.

(5) **Power of court to order separate trials:** [§958] To curb expense, delay, or other prejudice that might result from the joinder of numerous parties asserting numerous separate claims against one another, the court may order separate trials for various claims joined, or otherwise regulate the proceedings to minimize the difficulties involved. [Fed. R. Civ. P. 20(b)]

(6) **Attacking improper joinder:** [§959] Under the Federal Rules, a misjoined claim may be dismissed on motion of the party against whom it is asserted; and the whole action may be dismissed as to that party if no claim for relief remains against him. [Fed. R. Civ. P. 21] Under code pleading practice, a demurrer will lie for misjoinder of claims. [Cal. Civ. Proc. Code §430.10(d)]

   (a) **Note:** Misjoinder must be raised at the outset of the litigation. Otherwise, the defect is *waived* (unless the court chooses to raise the defect on its own initiative). [Fed. R. Civ. P. 12(h)]

c. **Subject matter jurisdiction:** [§960] In addition to the requirements of personal jurisdiction over defendants, federal subject matter jurisdiction requirements must be satisfied as to all parties (whether plaintiffs or defendants) permissively joined. Supplemental jurisdiction does not extend to permissive joinder when the permissively joined matter is not part of the same case or controversy with the claim over which the federal court has original jurisdiction, or in diversity cases where banned by 28 U.S.C. section 1367(b). (*See supra*, §§398-415.)

3. **Compulsory Joinder:** [§961] Joinder is required for *any person who has a material interest in the case and whose absence would result in substantial prejudice* to the absentee or to other parties before the court. [Fed. R. Civ. P. 19]

   a. **Traditional approach—"necessary" vs. "indispensable" parties:** [§962] Historically, the statutes and cases drew a distinction between "necessary" and "indispensable" parties.

      (1) **"Necessary parties":** [§963] Necessary parties were those persons who *ought* to be joined *if possible.* However, if their interests were *"severable"* and if one or more were not joined (*e.g.,* could not be located), the court could still determine the rights and liabilities of the parties before the court.

      (2) **"Indispensable parties":** [§964] Indispensable parties, on the other hand, were those whose interests were so unavoidably involved (nonseverable) that the court could not proceed without them. Failure to join such parties meant that the action had to be dismissed. [Shields v. Barrow, 58 U.S. (17 How.) 130 (1855)]

      (3) **Criticism:** A party's interest could always be "severed" somehow, simply by leaving his interests out of the judgment and allowing them to be adjudicated later. Hence, the issue in distinguishing necessary and indispensable parties was not whether the absentee's interests *were in fact* severable (they always were), but whether they *should be* adjudicated along with those already present in the action.

   b. **Modern approach—practical considerations:** [§965] Modern rules recognize that the labels "necessary" and "indispensable" merely reflect conclusions arrived at for other reasons. Hence, these rules focus on the *practical consequences* if a party with an interest in the action is not before the court. [Provident Bank & Trust Co. v. Patterson, *supra*, §932]

(1) **Persons to be joined if feasible:** [§966] Federal Rule 19(a) provides that any person with an interest in the subject of a pending action shall be joined as a party if:

    (i) In his absence, *complete relief* cannot be accorded those already parties [Fed. R. Civ. P. 19(a)(1)]; *or*

    (ii) His interest is such that to proceed without him would be *substantially prejudicial* as a practical matter because it would:

        i. Impair his ability to protect his interest in later proceedings [Fed. R. Civ. P. 19(a)(2)(i)]; or

        ii. Expose the *parties already before the court* to the risk of double liability or inconsistent obligations [Fed. R. Civ. P. 19(a)(2)(ii)].

    (a) **Examples:** For examples, *see infra*, §§968-979.

    (b) **Caveat:** Although the modern pragmatic approach has been adopted in the federal courts and in many states, some decisions still assert that certain types of parties (*e.g.*, partial assignees, *infra*, §973) *always* must be joined—*i.e.*, that these parties are indispensable. A review of the case law, therefore, reveals two conflicting rules: (i) that compulsory joinder is a pragmatic problem, and (ii) that it is "jurisdictional" in that an action cannot proceed without an indispensable party.

(2) **Effect of nonjoinder—possible dismissal:** [§967] If a person to be joined *cannot* be made a party (*e.g.*, because he is not subject to the court's jurisdiction), the court must determine whether "in equity and in good conscience" the action can proceed without him or whether the action should be dismissed. The court's determination is based on the following practical considerations [Fed. R. Civ. P. 19(b)]:

    (a) The extent to which any judgment rendered in the action would be *prejudicial* to the interest of the absent party, or the interests of those already before the court;

    (b) The extent to which such prejudice could be *lessened or avoided* by appropriate court action;

    (c) Whether relief rendered without the absent party would be *adequate;* and

    (d) Whether the plaintiff has any *other adequate remedy* if the action is dismissed for nonjoinder of the absent party.

(3) **Application:** [§968] Situations in which compulsory joinder issues commonly arise involve:

    (a) **Joint obligors**

        1) **Parties to contract:** [§969] Joint promisors under a *contract* (and other joint debtors) should be joined as defendants

wherever possible. However, if one cannot be joined, the court can still proceed against those before the court. [Jett v. Phillips & Associates, 439 F.2d 987 (10th Cir. 1971)]

    a) **Rationale:** There is no "substantial prejudice" to the parties before the court that would justify dismissal, since an obligor held responsible on the joint debt has a *right of contribution* against the other joint obligors.

2) **Tortfeasors:** [§970] Although the plaintiff may join in one action all defendants potentially liable to her as a result of a given transaction or occurrence (*see supra*, §952), ordinarily she is not required to do so, and a joint tortfeasor is *not considered a necessary party.* [Temple v. Synthes Corp., 498 U.S. 5 (1990)—"It has long been the rule that it is not necessary for all joint tortfeasors to be named as defendants in a single lawsuit"]

    a) **Rationale:** The plaintiff is the "master of her lawsuit" and can choose to sue as many or as few potential defendants as she desires.

    b) **Compare—impleader:** [§971] Often there is a right of contribution among joint tortfeasors. Where this is so, those defendants who are sued can file third-party complaints or cross-complaints (depending on the jurisdiction) against the other tortfeasors for *indemnity* (*see infra*, §990). [American Motorcycle Association v. Superior Court, 20 Cal. 3d 578 (1978)] *Note:* This maneuver does not make the new party a defendant on the plaintiff's complaint unless the plaintiff amends to assert a claim against the new defendant. The only claim asserted against the new defendant is to indemnify the original defendant.

(b) **Joint obligees:** [§972] Where persons are jointly owed a duty under a contract, the courts have usually held that they are not only necessary, but also *indispensable* parties, and have dismissed for nonjoinder. [Jenkins v. Reneau, 697 F.2d 160 (6th Cir. 1983)]

    1) **Rationale:** A promise made to the obligees jointly should be enforced jointly since otherwise there is a risk that the right of the absent obligee to enforce the promise may be prejudiced, that the defendant might be subjected to inconsistent obligations in an action brought by the absent obligee, and that the court would be unable to afford complete relief because it could not provide in its decree for the defendant's obligations to the nonparty while enforcing the same promise for the plaintiff.

(c) **Partial assignees or subrogees:** [§973] In an action by a partial assignee or subrogee to enforce its share of a debt, all other partial owners are necessary parties who should be joined if feasible. [National American Corp. v. Federal Republic of Nigeria, 420 F. Supp. 954 (S.D.N.Y. 1976); Peerless Insurance Co. v. Superior Court, 6 Cal. App. 3d 358 (1970)—insured with claims over policy limit was necessary but not indispensable party in suit by insurer-subrogee who had paid up to policy limit]

(d) **Co-owners of property:** [§974] Co-owners of property are necessary parties in situations where the interests of all should be decided on a consistent basis (*e.g.*, rescission granted to one should be granted to all). [Worthington v. Kaiser Health Plan, 8 Cal. App. 3d 435 (1970)]

1) **Conflicting claims:** [§975] If the action seeks to determine conflicting claims between persons claiming co-ownership of property, *all co-owners* are necessary parties (*e.g.*, action for partition by one of several tenants in common, suit to fix shares of beneficiaries in a trust, suit by one of several partners to dissolve the partnership).

2) **Suits to establish adverse interest:** [§976] Similarly, in suits by a *third person* to establish or enforce an interest in the property, all co-owners must be joined if possible (*e.g.*, suits to foreclose a mortgage, remove an easement, and the like).

(e) **Third-party beneficiary suits**

1) **Original parties to contract need not be joined:** [§977] Where the third-party beneficiary sues, the federal courts have uniformly rejected the argument that the original parties to the contract must be joined. [Sandobal v. Armour & Co., 429 F.2d 249 (8th Cir. 1970)]

2) **Third-party beneficiary need not be joined:** [§978] Where the original party to the contract sues, the third-party beneficiary will not be an indispensable party. [Prudential Oil & Minerals Co. v. Hamlin, 277 F.2d 384 (10th Cir. 1960)]

(f) **Shareholder's derivative suit:** [§979] In a derivative suit by a shareholder (*i.e.*, suing on a cause of action belonging to the corporation because the corporation refuses to sue), the *corporation* is an *indispensable* party. Its rights are so inextricably involved that no complete judgment can be rendered unless it is subject to the court's jurisdiction.

c. **Procedure for compelling joinder**

(1) **Must name all necessary parties:** [§980] In the complaint, the plaintiff should set forth the names of all necessary persons who have not been joined, and the reasons for their nonjoinder. [Fed. R. Civ. P. 19(c)]

(a) **Criticism:** This provision is not effective because plaintiffs rarely concede that nonparties are necessary parties.

(2) **Failure to name all necessary parties:** [§981] If the plaintiff fails to allege the existence of such parties, the defendant can raise the matter in a motion to dismiss under Federal Rule 12 or in the answer. Failure to object may constitute *waiver.*

(3) **Joinder of necessary parties ordered if feasible:** [§982] If the plaintiff has failed to join necessary parties, the court will order that they be joined unless it is impossible to do so because their joinder would destroy subject matter jurisdiction or because the court lacks personal jurisdiction over them.

(a) **Involuntary plaintiff:** [§983] If the absentee should be aligned as a plaintiff, he may be joined as an involuntary plaintiff. [Fed. R. Civ. P. 19(a)]

(b) **Necessary parties too numerous:** [§984] Where the necessary parties are too numerous to be joined, it is possible that the case might be handled as a *class action*. (*See infra*, §§1058 *et seq.*)

(c) **Venue:** [§985] If addition of the necessary party would make venue improper, the added party must be dismissed if she objects to venue. Then the court must decide whether to dismiss.

(4) **Dismissal if joinder not feasible:** [§986] Where the court cannot order the necessary parties joined because of lack of personal jurisdiction or because their presence would destroy diversity of citizenship, it must decide whether to dismiss the action. (*See supra*, §967 for criteria used to decide whether to dismiss.)

d. **Waiver of right to compel joinder:** [§987] Nonjoinder of an absentee should be raised at the earliest possible opportunity by the parties to the action; otherwise, delay may constitute waiver of the right to compel joinder.

(1) **If absentee is indispensable:** [§988] If the absentee is determined to be indispensable, his nonjoinder can be raised at any time by pleading or motion, even at the trial of the action. [Fed. R. Civ. P. 12(h)(2)] However, delay in raising the objection is one of the factors the court will consider in exercising its *discretion* as to whether to dismiss the action (*i.e.*, in deciding whether the absentee *is* indispensable). [Provident Bank & Trust Co. v. Patterson, *supra*, §965]

(2) **No waiver by absentee:** [§989] The failure of the parties to raise the defect of nonjoinder in no way constitutes a "waiver" by the *absentee.* Since she is not a party to the action, the judgment is not legally binding on her. [Martin v. Wilks, 490 U.S. 755 (1989)]

4. **Impleader:** [§990] Impleader is a procedure that permits the defendant to bring into the lawsuit a third person who is or *may be* liable for all or part of plaintiff's claim against the defendant. [Fed. R. Civ. P. 14] In some states, the same remedy may be secured by a cross-complaint bringing in the third person. Possible

prejudice to the third party from the manner of impleader is probably adequately guarded against by: (i) allowing the third party to plead any defenses that the defendant might have against the plaintiff's claim and to participate fully in defending against it; and (ii) providing for the possibility of separate trial of any separate issues of the third-party claim if needed to prevent undue confusion or prejudice.

a. **Limited to claims for indemnification:** [§991] Impleader under the Federal Rules is confined to those situations in which the defending party has a *right to indemnity*, in whole or in part, against the impleaded third party—*i.e.*, where the defendant asserts that if he is held liable to the plaintiff, he would be entitled to collect all or some part of the judgment from the third party. This includes a claim to contribution in states where a defendant is allowed to claim contribution from a person that the plaintiff did not originally join as a defendant.

(1) **How right is determined:** [§992] Whether the defendant has any such right to indemnification, etc., is a question of substantive law, and under the *Erie* doctrine, the federal court must therefore refer to the appropriate state statutes and case law.

(a) **No right to indemnification under state law:** [§993] If the appropriate state law does not recognize such a right, the fact that the impleader procedure is available in federal court does not create one for the defendant.

(b) **Compare—liability under state law may be "accelerated":** [§994] However, federal impleader may "accelerate" liability created by state law. For example, if, under state law, the defendant can seek indemnity from a third person only *after paying* a judgment to the plaintiff, the defendant in federal court may implead the third person and assert his claim conditionally. *If* the plaintiff recovers, the defendant should get judgment—thereby closing the time gap between liability to the plaintiff and receipt of an indemnity judgment against the third party. [Glen Falls Indemnity Co. v. United States, 229 F.2d 370 (9th Cir. 1955)]

(c) **Contribution among tortfeasors:** [§995] Most states allow contribution among tortfeasors only when *judgment* is rendered against *all* of them. For federal impleader purposes, this means that the defendant in a personal injury action *cannot* implead other tortfeasors to seek contribution, because their liability arises only after the plaintiff obtains judgment against all of them. [McPherson v. Hoffman, 275 F.2d 466 (6th Cir. 1960)]

1) **But note:** If state law allows contribution where judgment is obtained against only one tortfeasor, the situation is essentially one of partial indemnity, and the tortfeasor who is sued can implead the other to recover it. [*See* American Motorcycle v. Superior Court, *supra*, §971]

(2) **Potential liability sufficient:** [§996] Rule 14 authorizes impleader of any person who is or *may be* liable for any part of the plaintiff's claim.

Thus, impleader is proper before any loss actually has been paid by the defendant.

- (a) **No direct action by plaintiff against defendant's liability insurer:** [§997] In any liability suit, a plaintiff usually would be delighted to join the defendant's insurance carrier as a co-defendant—to let the jury know that the defendant is insured. However, most states do *not* permit this, on the ground that the plaintiff has no right to relief against the defendant's insurance carrier until she has first obtained a judgment against the defendant (after which, the plaintiff would have an enforceable claim as third-party beneficiary of the insurance company's promise to indemnify the defendant).

    1) **Minority rule contra:** [§998] A *few* states are contra, with "direct action statutes" that permit joinder of the defendant's insurance carrier in the original action. [20 A.L.R. 2d 1097]

- (b) **Defendant's right to implead insurer:** [§999] It may be that the defendant himself will seek to bring his liability insurer into the action—*e.g.,* when the insurer has failed or refused to defend the action. Where this is the case, impleader may be permitted to obtain a prompt determination of the defendant's insurance coverage and avoid multiplicity of suits. [Government Employees Insurance Co. v. United States, 400 F.2d 172 (10th Cir. 1968)]

(3) **Contrast—alternative liability to plaintiff:** [§1000] It is not sufficient for impleader that the third-party defendant may be liable to the plaintiff for the plaintiff's injuries; only when the law gives the present defendant a right to relief in the form of indemnity from the third-party defendant is impleader permitted.

- (a) **Example:** Plaintiff contracted trichinosis and sued D1, which manufactured a cooker Plaintiff claimed had failed properly to cook pork she ate on July 9. D1 sought to implead the college that plaintiff attended, claiming that her trichinosis had actually resulted from eating pork in the college cafeteria on July 8. The court dismissed the third-party complaint because "[c]ontribution will not arise from distinct causes of action, regardless of how similar the events may have been or how close in time they may have occurred." [Klotz v. Superior Electric Products Corp., 498 F. Supp. 1099 (E.D. Pa. 1980)]

(4) **Supplemental jurisdiction over related claims:** [§1001] In federal court litigation, the court has supplemental jurisdiction to adjudicate a claim by the original defendant (third-party plaintiff in the impleader) for his *own* injuries when joined with a claim for indemnity.

- (a) **But note:** At least in diversity actions, there is *no* supplemental jurisdiction over a claim by the original plaintiff against the third-party plaintiff even if it arises out of the transaction originally sued on. *Example:* P sues D, who impleads T, a citizen of the same state as P. P may not assert a separate claim against T, because there is no diversity between them and ancillary jurisdiction will not be permitted. [Owen Equipment & Erection Co. v. Kroger, 437 U.S. 365 (1978); 28 U.S.C. §1367(b)]

b. **Pleadings and procedure:** [§1002] Leave of court is not required for impleader if the defendant (third-party plaintiff) files a third-party complaint of impleader not later than 10 days after he serves his original answer. Thereafter, leave of court is required, and granting of the motion is at the *discretion* of the court. [Fed. R. Civ. P. 14]

   (1) **Answer:** [§1003] The impleaded party must file an answer to the third-party complaint, and the answer may raise whatever defenses could be asserted to the *original* cause of action (P vs. D). *Rationale:* The purpose is to prevent collusion between the original parties—D admitting or defaulting to P's claim, in order to affix liability on the impleaded party.

   (2) **Counterclaim or cross-claim:** [§1004] The impleaded party may also file a *counterclaim or cross-claim* against existing parties, or may implead any person who may be liable to him, subject to the jurisdictional limits noted below. [Fed. R. Civ. P. 14(a)]

c. **Possibility of separate trials:** [§1005] The trial court has discretion to order a separate trial of the impleaded claim to avoid undue trial confusion or prejudice. [Fed. R. Civ. P. 42(b)]

d. **Effect on jurisdiction and venue:** [§1006] An impleader claim is usually deemed ancillary to the main claim and has *no* effect on jurisdictional and venue requirements. Thus, an independent ground of federal jurisdiction need not be established, and the impleaded defendant cannot object to venue. [Dery v. Wyer, 265 F.2d 804 (2d Cir. 1959); 28 U.S.C. §1367]

e. **Compare with cross-claim:** [§1007] Impleader is somewhat similar to the cross-claim procedure discussed *supra*, §§821 *et seq.* However, there are significant differences:

   (1) *An impleader can be asserted only against a person not yet a party,* whereas a cross-claim is filed by one party against another party to the action.

   (2) *Impleader must be based on a claim for indemnification* or contribution, while there is no such limitation on cross-claims.

f. **Counterclaims and cross-claims:** [§1008] Third parties also may be joined in the action where necessary for a complete determination of a claim which the defendant has against the plaintiff (counterclaim) or against a co-defendant (cross-claim). [Fed. R. Civ. P. 13(h)] Counterclaims and cross-claims are discussed in detail *supra*, §§799 *et seq.*

5. **Intervention:** [§1009] Intervention is a procedure whereby a *nonparty*, upon timely application, may become a party in a lawsuit in order to protect her interests in that action. Whether intervention is allowed depends on a balancing of *two conflicting policies:* (i) that the plaintiff should be allowed to be "master of his action," in the sense of joining such parties with him or against him as he wishes; and

(ii) that other interested parties and the court have an interest in avoiding multiplicity of litigation or inconsistency of result, which may require overriding the plaintiff's choice of parties.

a. **Types of intervention in federal cases:** [§1010]   There are several types of intervention under Federal Rule 24:

   (1) **Intervention of right—federal statute:** [§1011]   Intervention is granted as a matter of right where a federal statute confers an unconditional right to intervene (*e.g.*, 28 U.S.C. section 2323—suit to enforce an order of the Interstate Commerce Commission). [Fed. R. Civ. P. 24(a)(1)]

   (2) **Intervention of right—to protect intervenor's interest:** [§1012]   Intervention of right is also granted when the applicant claims an interest relating to the property or transaction that is the subject of the action and is so situated that the disposition of the action may, as a practical matter, impair or impede the applicant's ability to protect that interest. [Fed. R. Civ. P. 24(a)(2)]

   (a) **Nature of interest:** [§1013]   The Supreme Court has stated that only a "significantly protectible interest" suffices to support intervention of right. [Donaldson v. United States, 400 U.S. 517 (1971)] Some lower courts emphasize a direct, substantial, and legally protectible interest to satisfy this standard, while others take a more relaxed attitude.

   1) **Example:** Opponents of abortion could intervene in an action challenging a city's moratorium on abortion clinics in an area on ground that they owned houses in the area and were defending their property values, but not on ground that they were opposed to abortion. "Interests in property are the most elementary type of right that Rule 24(a) is designed to protect." [Planned Parenthood v. Citizens for Community Action, 558 F.2d 861 (8th Cir. 1977)]

   2) **Example:** Rate-payers of a utility could not intervene in a contract action between the utility and a supplier concerning the amounts the utility would have to pay for boiler fuel. Although the outcome of the litigation could affect the rates intervenors would have to pay, they had no legally protectible interest in the contract dispute. [New Orleans Public Service, Inc. v. United Gas Pipe Line Co., 732 F.2d 452 (5th Cir. 1984)]

   (b) **Outcome of litigation may impair intervenor's interests:** [§1014]   The intervenor must also show that the resolution of the litigation would impair her interest. This is not limited to legally binding effects, such as res judicata, but looks to the practical impact of resolution of the litigation on the intervenor's interest.

   1) **Example:** In an action challenging issuance of licenses to operate uranium mills without environmental impact statements,

intervenors with applications pending would be affected, as a practical matter, by the litigation's outcome if it caused defendant agency to alter its mode of operation and require more of applicants for licenses. [Natural Resources Defense Council v. United States Nuclear Regulatory Commission, 578 F.2d 1341 (10th Cir. 1978)]

2) **Example:** Where a commercial tenant of a shopping center sought to enjoin a lease to another prospective commercial tenant on the ground that plaintiff's lease limited the number of jewelry stores in the shopping center, interests of the prospective tenant might be affected if it could not compel performance of defendant's commitment to lease space to it. [*Compare* Helzberg's Diamond Shops, Inc. v. Valley West Des Moines Shopping Center, Inc., 564 F.2d 816 (8th Cir. 1977)—threat of impairing interest of prospective tenant found insufficient to make it necessary party]

3) **Stare decisis effect:** [§1015] It is sometimes argued that the stare decisis effect alone is sufficient to justify intervention of right. When a unique issue of law is involved, and there is little likelihood that it will be reconsidered after it is decided in the current litigation, that may be sufficient. [*See* Atlantis Development Corp. v. United States, 379 F.2d 818 (5th Cir. 1967)—issue of application of the Outer Continental Shelf Lands Act to specific islands that intervenor sought to develop] More generally, however, the fact that resolution of a question of law might affect cases to which the intervenor is, or may in the future be, a party would more properly be considered a ground for amicus curiae than for intervenor status.

(c) **Intervenor not adequately represented by present parties:** [§1016] Where the intervenor claims the right kind of interest and shows a threat of practical impairment, intervention could be denied on the ground that the intervenor's interest is adequately represented by the present parties.

1) **"Minimal" burden:** [§1017] The Supreme Court has said that the burden of demonstrating inadequacy of representation is "minimal." [Trbovich v. United Mine Workers, 404 U.S. 518 (1972)]

2) **Factors:** [§1018] A variety of factors can be considered in evaluating the adequacy of representation, including the amount at stake for the intervenor and the present parties, the ability and resources of the present parties to litigate effectively, and the existence of any conflicts of interest between the present party and the intervenors.

3) **Concern with complication of action:** [§1019] Although it is said that the burden of showing inadequacy is minimal, in order to avoid complication of the action due to the addition of

too many new parties, courts will resist multiple intervention applications by parties in similar situations.

(d) **Compare—compulsory joinder:** [§1020] The grounds for intervention of right are analogous to the grounds for finding nonparties to be necessary parties under Rule l9(a)(2)(i). (*See supra*, §966.) As a result, if there is a question on an examination raising issues under one of these rules, the effect of the other should be considered:

1) **Intervention more flexible:** [§1021] Even though the language is virtually the same (and may be narrower for Rule 24), it appears that courts are more willing to find that the nonparty's interests are of the protected type and are threatened where intervention is involved. This is because the nonparty intervenor has indicated a desire to participate in the litigation and the conclusion that intervention of right is proper does not mean that the litigation should not proceed unless all similarly situated nonparties are joined. Under Rule 19, the finding that a person with a certain interest should be joined means that all others with that interest should also be joined.

2) **Adequacy of representation requirement:** [§1022] This difference in treatment is confirmed by the adequacy of representation requirement for intervention. Under Rule 19, the adequacy of the present parties to protect the interests of the nonparty ordinarily does not relieve the court of the duty to add the necessary party. When Rule 19 is invoked but representation seems adequate, treatment as a class action may be in order. (*See infra*, §§1058 *et seq.*)

(e) **Conditions on intervention:** [§1023] Although this form of intervention is designated "of right," the court may nevertheless impose conditions, such as limiting the intervenor to claims already raised by other parties, or requiring that the intervenor obtain permission from one of the original parties to make motions and take discovery. This authority derives from the court's general power to control the litigation before it. [Stringfellow v. Concerned Neighbors in Action, 480 U.S. 370 (1987)]

(3) **Permissive intervention:** [§1024] The court has discretion to permit a nonparty to intervene if:

(i) *A federal statute* confers a conditional right to intervene; *or*

(ii) *A question of law or fact in common* with the main action is part of the applicant's claim or defense.

[Fed. R. Civ. P. 24(b)]

(a) **"Common question"**

1) **Example:** In a suit to set aside a zoning ordinance, adjoining property owners may intervene if their claims present common

questions of law or fact. [Wolpe v. Poretsky, 144 F.2d 505 (D.C. Cir. 1944)]

    2) **Compare—permissive joinder rules:** [§1025] Permissive intervention is the counterpart of permissive joinder under Federal Rule 20(a). The standard for permissive intervention corresponds to that for permissive joinder—*i.e.*, a common question, interpreted as claims arising from the same or a related transaction.

  (b) **Broad discretion in court:** [§1026] The trial court has very broad discretion under Federal Rule 24(b) in granting or denying permissive joinder; and a reversal on appeal is almost impossible to obtain.

  (c) **Conditions imposed by court:** [§1027] The court will often condition intervention in a lawsuit by limiting the intervenor's claims to those directly involved in the pending action.

 (4) **Timeliness of intervention:** [§1028] Whether the intervention sought is of right or permissive, the motion for leave to intervene must be made in a timely fashion. However, since a potential intervenor of right may be seriously harmed if excluded from the action, intervention motions rarely should be denied as being untimely.

b. **Effect of intervention in federal cases**

 (1) **Subject matter jurisdiction:** [§1029] If the action is in federal court solely on grounds of diversity, there is no supplemental jurisdiction over claims by intervenors or claims by plaintiff against persons who intervene. [28 U.S.C. §1367(b); *see supra*, §§398-415] In those circumstances there must be an independent basis for federal court jurisdiction to permit assertion of the claim. When federal jurisdiction does not depend solely on diversity of citizenship, there would usually be supplemental jurisdiction over claims by or against intervenors of right. [28 U.S.C. §1367(a)]

 (2) **Venue:** [§1030] The intervenor cannot question the propriety of venue in the original action, since her act of intervening is a submission to the court in question. [Trans World Airlines, Inc. v. Civil Aeronautics Board, 339 F.2d 56 (2d Cir. 1964)] Venue objections, however, may be raised by someone who is already a party to the action.

 (3) **Judgment:** [§1031] Any judgment rendered subsequent to intervention is binding on the intervening party as if she had originally been a party, and she has a similar right of appeal. [Spangler v. United States, 415 F.2d 1242 (9th Cir. 1969)]

c. **State practice:** [§1032] Most states have intervention provisions patterned on the federal rules. In other states, statutes on intervention provide that a person having an "interest in the matter in litigation *may* intervene" in an action between other parties. [*See* Cal. Civ. Proc. Code §387]

(1) **Broad discretion in court:** [§1033] The term "interest" in such statutes is very vague, but usually has been limited to a "legal" interest. The term "may" indicates that intervention is never of right. Thus, intervention in state court actions largely depends on the discretion of the trial court. Often, permission is denied on the ground that the plaintiff has the right to choose the parties to his action.

(2) **Modern trend to permit intervention:** [§1034] However, under the influence of federal intervention rules (*supra*), state courts are becoming more liberal in permitting intervention.

6. **Consolidation of Separate Actions:** [§1035] Even when joinder rules do not permit the addition of new parties to an action, the same result can be achieved by consolidating separate suits pending in the same court. The court has broad discretion, on its own motion or on the motion of a party, to consolidate actions involving **common issues** (*e.g.*, liability of common carrier in mass accident litigation). Consolidation can be complete so that the separate suits effectively become one although they are technically not merged; or it may be partial—*e.g.*, consolidation for purposes of determining liability, with separate trials on the issue of damages. [*See* Fed. R. Civ. P. 42]

7. **Interpleader:** [§1036] Interpleader is a device that enables a party against whom conflicting claims with respect to the same debt or property are asserted (the "stakeholder") to join all the adverse claimants in the same action and require them to litigate among themselves to determine which, if any, has a valid claim to the debt or property involved. Once the stakeholder's right to interplead is established and he has deposited the funds or property in court, he can be released or "discharged" from the litigation; it is up to the adverse claimants to litigate their claims to the property. (If the stakeholder denies any liability at all, or if he has a claim to the fund, he remains a party.)

   a. **Examples:** An escrow holder may interplead funds deposited with him, as to which parties are making adverse claims. Or a life insurance company, upon the death of the insured, may interplead the policy proceeds if they are claimed by both the beneficiary named and some third person.

   b. **Background:** [§1037] Interpleader originated in the equity courts as a way to protect a stakeholder from possible legally inconsistent liability, and to avoid multiplicity of actions and the risk of inconsistent results. Historically, the plaintiff had to admit liability on the obligation in question and the conflicting claims had to be mutually exclusive, but these limitations are not recognized under modern law. [*See* 28 U.S.C. §1335; Fed. R. Civ. P. 22]

   c. **Procedure:** [§1038] The party against whom claims are being made may institute the interpleader action himself (naming all claimants as defendants); or he may interplead in any action pending between the adverse claimants. If he is named as a defendant in such an action, he may interplead by filing a *counterclaim* (*see infra*, §1053).

   (1) **Deposit "stake" with court:** [§1039] To invoke *statutory* interpleader (*see infra*, §1044), the plaintiff must deposit (or give security for) the entire amount in his possession that is claimed by the claimants, and may

not hold back amounts that he claims. [Miller & Miller Auctioneers, Inc. v. G.W. Murphy Indus., Inc., 472 F.2d 893 (10th Cir. 1973)]

    (a) **No deposit required for rule interpleader:** [§1040] Where Rule 22 interpleader is properly invoked (*see infra*, §§1046 *et seq.*), there is no requirement that the stake be deposited in court.

(2) **Plaintiff may claim interest:** [§1041] As indicated above, interpleader is permitted even if the plaintiff denies *any* liability or claims some offset or defense. Such cases are often referred to as *"actions in the nature of interpleader,"* following old English practice. The difference is that classic interpleader involves a "disinterested" stakeholder, making no claim to the property, while an "action in the nature of interpleader" is brought by an "interested" stakeholder, such as an insurance company denying liability. [*See, e.g.,* State Farm Fire & Casualty Co. v. Tashire, 386 U.S. 523 (1967)]

(3) **Defendants may cross-file claims:** [§1042] Where the stakeholder initiates interpleader, the adverse claimants can—and usually do—file cross-claims (*see infra*, §1053) against each other to obtain a judicial determination of their respective rights in the fund or property interpleaded.

d. **Types of federal interpleader actions:** [§1043] In federal practice, there are two distinct interpleader remedies:

(1) **Statutory interpleader:** [§1044] Interpleader is permitted by 28 U.S.C. section 1335, which contains special provisions as to jurisdiction, venue, and service of process, if:

    (i) *Two or more claimants of diverse citizenship* are making adverse claims to the same debt, instrument, or property owed or held by the plaintiff; *and*

    (ii) *The debt, instrument, or property has a value of at least $500.*

(2) **Rule 22 interpleader:** [§1045] Federal Rule 22 permits interpleader in any action that meets the normal jurisdictional requirements in federal court—*i.e.*, a sufficient amount in controversy (if applicable) and proper diversity or federal question.

e. **Differences between statutory and Rule 22 interpleader:** [§1046] The existence of two forms of federal interpleader can be confusing, but rule interpleader is needed for cases that can properly be brought in federal court and use the device, but which do not meet the specialized requirements of statutory interpleader, which is framed to focus on situations involving scattered claimants (below). The basic differences between interpleader under section 1335 and under Rule 22 are as follows:

(1) **Requirements for diversity jurisdiction:** [§1047] Depending on the type of federal interpleader action, either minimal or complete diversity is required.

    (a) **Statutory interpleader:** [§1048] In statutory interpleader, it is sufficient that diversity of citizenship exists between *any two adverse* *claimants*, but at least two claimants must be diverse. As long as such *minimal diversity* exists, the citizenship of the plaintiff-stakeholder and any other claimants is immaterial. [State Farm Fire & Casualty Co. v. Tashire, *supra*]

　1) **Example:** I, an Illinois insurance company, is confronted by claims to insurance proceeds by A, a citizen of Illinois, B, another citizen of Illinois, and C, a citizen of Wisconsin. There is sufficient diversity for statutory interpleader even though I (as plaintiff in the action) and A and B (as defendants) are co-citizens, and A and B (as competing claimants) are co-citizens, because one of the claimants, C, is not a co-citizen of the other claimants.

(b) **Rule 22 interpleader:** [§1049] In an interpleader action under Rule 22, there must be *complete* diversity between the plaintiff-stakeholder and *all* of the adverse claimants, or a federal question must be involved.

(c) **Compare—all claimants citizens of one state:** [§1050] Where all the claimants are citizens of one state and the stakeholder is a citizen of another, the suit can be brought only under Rule 22, since statutory interpleader requires some diversity among the *claimants* (*see supra*).

(2) **Jurisdictional amount:** [§1051] Statutory interpleader requires only that the debt or property involved be valued at *$500* or more. Under Rule 22, if the case relies on diversity jurisdiction, the jurisdictional amount is the same as in any other civil action.

(3) **Limits of process:** [§1052] In *statutory* interpleader, the reach of process is nationwide. [28 U.S.C. §2361] Under **Rule 22**, service of process is the same as in any other civil action—*i.e.*, within the territorial limits of the state in which the district court is located, or by use of an applicable long arm statute.

(4) **Cross-claims and counterclaims:** [§1053] The interpleaded claimants may (and usually do) cross-claim against each other, counterclaim against the plaintiff, and implead third parties, unless jurisdictional problems prevent their doing so.

(a) **Subject matter jurisdiction:** [§1054] Such additional claims must have an independent basis of jurisdiction unless they relate to the original impleaded claim (and thus fall within supplemental jurisdiction).

(b) **Service of process:** [§1055] When a defendant is before the court only because of nationwide process under *statutory* interpleader, he is subject to additional claims through cross-claim, etc., only if they are part of "cleaning up" the original interpleader claim.

　1) **Example:** A, a driver insured by I for $20,000, injures B and C, each of whom claims more than $20,000 in damages. I

interpleads A, B, and C, contending that there is no liability on A's part, but that if there is, the claims of B and C to the insurance coverage should be interpleaded. A seeks to cross-claim against C for A's own injuries. This would be disallowed if C was before the court only through nationwide process, because it does not relate to I's interpleader claim. [*See* Allstate Insurance Co. v. McNeill, 382 F.2d 84 (4th Cir. 1967)]

(5) **Venue:** [§1056] In *statutory* interpleader, venue is proper in the district in which *any* claimant resides. [28 U.S.C. §1397] With interpleader under **Rule 22,** venue is the same as in any other civil action—*i.e.,* in the district in which a defendant resides, if all reside in the same state, or a district in which a substantial part of the events or omissions giving rise to the claim occurred. [28 U.S.C. §1391(a)(1)-(2); *see supra,* §§122-133] Alternatively, venue is proper in a district "in which a substantial part of the property that is the subject of the action is located." [28 U.S.C. §1391(a)(2)] The location of the property may be a convenient venue in many interpleader cases.

f. ***Erie* doctrine:** [§1057] The question of whether the interpleader remedy is available is a procedural matter and is decided pursuant to federal interpleader standards. To determine the law to be applied to the merits of the case, the federal court will look to appropriate state law.

D. CLASS ACTIONS

1. **In General:** [§1058] One or more members of a class of persons similarly situated may *sue or be sued* on behalf of all members of that class. Such lawsuits are permitted where considerations of *necessity or convenience* justify an action on behalf of the group rather than multiple actions by (or against) the class members individually.

2. **Background**

    a. **Original development in equity:** [§1059] Class actions originally were permitted only in equity, and then only if it was shown (i) that joinder of all parties having similar interests was *impractical* because the parties were too numerous, were presently unascertainable, or were not yet in being (*e.g.,* unborn heirs); and (ii) a few members could fairly represent all in the litigation. In such cases, the chancellors in equity permitted suit to be maintained by or against representatives of the class and, in some instances, held that the decree rendered in such an action was binding on *all* members of the class.

        (1) **Comment:** Unless the joinder of all necessary parties was not practical (usually because they were too numerous), the class action device was not needed since adequate relief could be obtained in an ordinary action.

    b. **Class actions under code pleading:** [§1060] The grounds for maintenance of class suits in equity were carried over in the Field Code, which authorized such suits wherever there were "questions of common or general interest of many persons," or when the parties were "numerous" and it would be "impracticable" to bring them all before the court. [*See* Cal. Civ. Proc. Code §382]

(1) **But note:** The courts usually limited class actions to those asserting what formerly had been equitable (as distinct from common law) claims—*e.g.*, stockholder derivative suits, creditors' bills to reach the assets of debtors, and injunction suits.

(2) **And note:** The decisions were split as to whether the judgment in a class suit was binding on the absent members of the class.

c. **Class actions under the Federal Rules**

(1) **Former Federal Rule 23:** [§1061] As originally adopted in 1938, Federal Rule 23 provided for three different kinds of class actions:

(a) *A "true class"* action was one where the rights of all members of the class were "joint" or "common," and a judgment rendered in such an action bound *all* members of the class, including absentees. *Examples:* Stockholders' suits and suits by or against the members of labor unions or other unincorporated associations were "true class" actions.

(b) *A "hybrid class"* action was one in which the subject of the action was a specific fund or property, and the members of the class had "separate" rights therein (*e.g.*, suit on behalf of numerous co-owners of an oil well against a drilling company to enforce a royalty contract). A judgment in such an action was conclusive upon the rights of all members in the specific fund or property involved, but did not otherwise affect or bind class members not before the court. [Dickinson v. Burnham, 197 F.2d 973 (2d Cir. 1952)]

(c) *A "spurious class"* action was one in which there was simply a "common question of law or fact" affecting all members of the class, and the claims of each member were separate. A judgment in such an action bound *only* those members of the class actually before the court. Accordingly, this was not really a class suit but a permissive joinder device.

(2) **Present Federal Rule 23:** [§1062] In 1966, Rule 23 was completely revised, eliminating the distinctions above and providing that members of a class can sue or be sued *with binding effect on the class as a whole.*

(3) **State courts:** [§1063] Most states have adopted the present Rule 23, sometimes with modifications. In California, the Rule has been effectively adopted by judicial decisions. [Vasquez v. Superior Court, 4 Cal. 3d 800 (1971)]

3. **Prerequisites to Class Action:** [§1064] Under Federal Rule 23(a), *all four* of the following conditions must be established in any type of class suit. All class actions must also fit into one of the categories of Rule 23(b) (*infra*, §§1084-1098).

(i) *Numerous parties*—the class must be so numerous that joinder of all members individually is impractical [Rule 23(a)(1)];

(ii) *Common question*—the action must involve questions of law or fact common to the class [Rule 23(a)(2)];

(iii) **Representative's claims typical**—the claims (or defenses) of the persons maintaining the action on behalf of the class must be typical of those of the class generally [Rule 23(a)(3)]; *and*

(iv) **Adequacy of representation**—the persons representing the class must be able fairly and adequately to protect the interests of all members of the class [Rule 23(a)(4)].

a. **Numerous parties requirement**

(1) **Rationale:** As indicated by the treatment of the real party in interest problem (*see supra*, §§906-933), ordinarily litigation is to be conducted by the persons whose rights are involved as named parties. Only where they are too numerous to be joined is class treatment considered necessary.

(2) **No fixed minimum:** [§1065] There is no fixed minimum number required to make a class "too numerous" for joinder of all members individually. Some cases have held 25 enough, while others have held that 39 is not enough. If the number is *50 or less,* whether a class will be permitted usually turns on the following factors, and note that the trial court has considerable discretion in this matter [De Marco v. Edens, 390 F.2d 836 (2d Cir. 1968)]:

(i) The *size of each member's claim* (the smaller the claim, the more likely a class suit will be allowed);

(ii) The *practical likelihood that individual suits will be brought* (the lower the likelihood, the more likely a class suit be allowed);

(iii) The *public importance of the right* being enforced (the greater the public importance, the more likely a class action will be permitted); and

(iv) The *geographic location of class members* (the more difficult the geographic location makes it for class members to intervene, the more likely a class suit will be allowed).

(a) **Example:** In a case involving a price fixing conspiracy, the Court found a proposed class of 350 members not numerous enough to justify a class action. The claims involved were large and, based on prior experience with decision of such claims, the Court found that they could best be handled by intervention and individual participation. [American Pipe & Construction Co. v. Utah, 414 U.S. 538 (1974)]

(3) **No fixed maximum:** [§1066] Similarly, there is no fixed maximum size for a class action. In *Eisen v. Carlisle & Jacquelin,* 417 U.S. 156 (1974), for example, the Court dealt with a class of six million members, and while it put severe limitations on the class action, discussed below, it did not disqualify it as a class action because of its size.

(a) **Limitation—class must be manageable:** [§1067] In actions brought under Rule 23(b)(3) (*see infra*, §§1091-1097), "difficulties likely to be encountered in management of the class" is one of the factors that the court must consider in deciding whether to permit the case to proceed as a class action: The larger the class, the greater the problems of manageability are likely to be.

(b) **Limitation—notice requirements:** [§1068] In some class suits, all identifiable members of the class must be given individual notice of the action, and the larger the class, the more cumbersome and expensive this becomes.

(4) **Need for ascertainable class:** [§1069] The class must be defined with sufficient clarity that its members can be identified. *Rationale:* If the class action is successful, it is necessary to know who is entitled to relief under the court's decree, and if the class action is not successful, it is necessary to know who is bound by the class's loss. This concern may be *less important* in actions for *injunctive relief* under Rule 23(b)(2) (*see infra*, §§1089-1090), because injunctive relief can be fashioned without knowing the identities of all class members. [Yaffe v. Powers, 454 F.2d 1362 (1st Cir. 1972)]

b. **Common question requirement:** [§1070] There must be "questions of law or fact common to the class." [Fed. R. Civ. P. 23(a)(2)]

(1) **Rationale:** Unless there is some common question, there would be no efficiencies to be achieved by adjudicating the rights of the class members in a single proceeding.

(2) **Predominance of common questions:** [§1071] In actions brought under Rule 23(b)(3) (*see infra*, §§1091-1097), there must not only be a common question, but common questions must also predominate. To satisfy Rule 23(a)(2), however, predominance is not required.

(3) **Fact question needed:** [§1072] As a practical matter, it is usually essential that the common question have factual content that would make common litigation desirable.

(4) **Compare—permissive joinder:** [§1073] Ordinarily, a closer factual connection is required to satisfy the class action common question requirement than the common question requirement for permissive joinder. (*See supra*, §956.)

(5) **Problem of individual damages:** [§1074] When class members have suffered individual damages, that presents individual questions, but this issue need not prevent a class action because there may also be common questions regarding liability.

(6) **Example:** In a securities fraud action where defendant made separate representations to various groups of investors, the common question requirement was satisfied because defendant engaged in a "common and consistent course of conduct." [Green v. Wolf Corp., 406 F.2d 291 (2d Cir. 1968)]

c. **Typical claim requirement:** [§1075] The claims of the representative suing on behalf of the class must be typical of the class generally.

(1) **Rationale:** Because the class representative acts on behalf of others, the court wishes to be assured that she will have the same objectives as the class members and sufficient motivation to protect their interests. This should flow from the fact that her claim makes her typical of the class members. [*See* Gonzales v. Cassidy, 474 F.2d 67 (5th Cir. 1973)]

(2) **Size of claim relevant:** [§1076] The size of the representative plaintiff's personal claim is relevant to the issue of whether she is properly motivated to protect the interests of the class generally. [Jenkins v. General Motors Corp., 354 F. Supp. 1040 (D. Del. 1973)]

(3) **Compare—common question requirement:** [§1077] The Supreme Court has observed that "[t]he commonality and typicality requirements of Rule 23(a) tend to merge. Both serve as guideposts for determining whether under the particular circumstances maintenance of a class action is economical and whether the named plaintiff's claim and the class claims are so interrelated that the interests of the class members will be fairly and adequately protected in their absence." [General Telephone Co. of the Southwest v. Falcon, 457 U.S. 147 (1982)]

(4) **Example:** A Mexican-American employee who challenged the denial of a promotion was not typical of a class of Mexican-American job applicants who had not been hired, even though he alleged that the job applicants had, like him, allegedly been discriminated against on grounds of national origin. His claim of denial of a promotion in a specific instance was not typical of the claims of job applicants who were not hired. [General Telephone Co. of the Southwest v. Falcon, *supra*]

(5) **Effect of mootness of representative's claim:** [§1078] When the class representative's claim becomes moot, it may be necessary to locate a new class representative who has a live claim. [*See* United States Parole Commission v. Geraghty, 445 U.S. 388 (1980)—named plaintiff whose claim expires before certification may be unable to continue as class representative; Sosna v. Iowa, 419 U.S. 393 (1975)—class representative whose claim expired allowed to continue representing class]

d. **Adequate representation requirement:** [§1079] This requirement is similar to the typical claim requirement, but also focuses on whether there is any *actual or potential conflict of interest* between the representative and the class she seeks to represent and whether the representative can prosecute or defend the suit with adequate vigor and resources.

(1) **Constitutional requirement:** [§1080] Due process requires that the class representative not have interests adverse to members of the class. *Example:* Whites seeking to enforce a racially restrictive covenant forbidding sale of houses in area to Blacks could not represent Black who desired to buy house in area. [Hansberry v. Lee, 311 U.S. 32 (1940)]

(2) **Example:** A union representing airline stewardesses in challenging the airlines' policy of discharging pregnant stewardesses could not "adequately

represent" former stewardesses who had been discharged on this ground and were seeking reinstatement because their reinstatement might harm those currently employed, thus creating a potential conflict of interest. [Air Line Stewards Association v. American Air Lines, 490 F.2d 636 (7th Cir. 1973)]

(3) **Note:** If the representative does not meet the adequate representation requirement but no one objects and the action proceeds to judgment, the judgment can be attacked by an absent member of the class on the ground that his interests were not adequately represented. [Hansberry v. Lee, *supra*] And this is true even if the court hearing the class suit expressly found the representative to be "adequate."

(4) **Time when adequate representation measured:** [§1081] The adequacy of representation is measured at two different times: (i) prior to certifying the action as a class action, the judge must believe that the named plaintiff will furnish an adequate representation of the class members; and (ii) once the suit is over, if the defendant argues that an unnamed plaintiff is bound by the result, the court in the new action by the unnamed plaintiff will evaluate whether the representation was in fact adequate in the first suit. If not, the unnamed plaintiff will not be bound. [Gonzales v. Cassidy, *supra*, §1075]

(5) **Decertification:** [§1082] Another possibility is that the court will determine, after deciding that the case is a proper class action, that the class representative is not adequate. In that situation the court can "decertify" the class and change the case back into an individual action.

(6) **Subclasses:** [§1083] If an action is otherwise properly brought as a class suit, but there is some divergence of interest among the class members, the court has authority to divide the class into *subclasses,* appoint a representative for each subclass, and allow the suit to proceed in that form. [Fed. R. Civ. P. 23(c)(4)] Each subclass must satisfy all the requirements of Rule 23.

4. **Three Grounds for Class Actions:** [§1084] If the foregoing conditions are all present, then the class suit may be based on *any one* of the following grounds. [Fed. R. Civ. P. 23(b)]

   a. **Prejudice from separate actions:** [§1085] Under Federal Rule 23(b)(1), a class suit is permitted if the prosecution of separate actions would create either of the following risks:

   (1) **Establishing incompatible standards of conduct for defendant through inconsistent adjudications:** [§1086] To justify a class suit on this ground, the court must find that a number of individual suits are otherwise likely to be filed, and that the *conduct* required of the defendant under various judgments might be inconsistent. [Fed. R. Civ. P. 23(b)(1)(A); Larionoff v. United States, 533 F.2d 1167 (D.C. Cir. 1976)]

      (a) **Examples:** Paradigm examples of proper actions under this part of the rule are actions by taxpayers to invalidate municipal action or by stockholders to compel the declaration of a dividend. In such situations, there is a risk that other similarly situated plaintiffs might sue to compel defendants to take a different course of action (*e.g.,* to proceed with the intended municipal action or to withhold a dividend).

(b) **Note:** There is no such risk of inconsistency where injured parties are simply seeking *damages* for separate tort claims arising out of a single occurrence. The fact that the defendant might be held liable in one case and not liable in another is not enough to justify a class action on this basis. [McDonnell Douglas Corp. v. District Court, 523 F.2d 1083 (9th Cir. 1975)]

(2) **Substantially impairing the interests of other members of the class:** [§1087] To permit a class action under this subsection, the court must find that separate actions would interfere with the interests of other absent persons having similar claims. [Fed. R. Civ. P. 23(b)(1)(B)]

(a) **Examples:** One of several beneficiaries of a trust sues the trustee for an accounting and distribution which would affect the interests of all the beneficiaries. [Redmond v. Commerce Trust Co., 144 F.2d 140 (8th Cir. 1944)] One of numerous claimants to a fund that is not sufficient to pay all claims seeks recovery (since satisfaction of any single claim in full would impair others). [Bradford Trust Co. v. Wright, 70 F.R.D. 323 (E.D.N.Y. 1976)]

(b) **"Limited fund" situation:** [§1088] An increasingly important occasion for invoking this part of the rule is the situation in which it is claimed that a large number of tort plaintiffs have claims exceeding the assets and insurance of the manufacturer of goods or services that injured them. In this situation, the concern is that if the first successful plaintiffs recover full damages, there will not be sufficient assets left to pay compensation to later plaintiffs. The courts have resisted allowing class actions in this situation. [*See, e.g., In re* Northern District of California "Dalkon Shield" IUD Products Liability Litigation, 693 F.2d 847 (9th Cir. 1982), *cert. denied,* 459 U.S. 1171 (1983)]

b. **Equitable relief sought as to rights held in common:** [§1089] Under Federal Rule 23(b)(2), a class action is also warranted where the basis on which the opposing party has acted is generally applicable to the class and *declaratory or injunctive relief* would benefit the class as a whole.

(1) **Example:** P sues on equal protection grounds to invalidate a statutory provision that divorce actions can be maintained only by persons who have resided in the state for at least a year. The effects on particular members of the class in question (persons who have resided less than a year) may vary; but a class action is proper because the determination will benefit the class as a whole. [Sosna v. Iowa, *supra,* §1078]

(2) **Problem of monetary relief:** [§1090] In some cases, monetary relief may be sought as well as injunctive relief. When the amounts due class

members can be calculated by a formula or on principles uniformly and easily applicable to the class, courts sometimes allow certification of *"hybrid (b)(2) classes."* When individualized determination of money damages is involved, however, this route is held improper. [Rice v. City of Philadelphia, 66 F.R.D. 17 (E.D. Pa. 1974)]

c. **Common predominant question:** [§1091] The third—and most common—basis for a class suit is under Federal Rule 23(b)(3)—the situation in which questions of law or fact common to the class *predominate* over questions affecting only individual members, *and, on balance, a class action is superior to other available methods* for adjudicating the controversy.

(1) **Relevant factors:** [§1092] In deciding whether common issues "predominate" and whether a class action is "superior" to individual litigation, the court will consider:

(i) *The interest of individual members* in personally controlling their cases;

(ii) *The nature and extent of any litigation* in progress involving the same controversy;

(iii) *The desirability of consolidating* all claims in a single action before a single court; and

(iv) *Any probable difficulties* managing a class action.

[Fed. R. Civ. P. 23(b)(3)]

(2) **Predominance of common questions:** [§1093] To find that common questions predominate, the court must *compare the relative importance* of the common questions and the individual questions presented by the case. It cannot merely compare the number of common and individual questions. Damages, for example, may present individual questions as to each class member, but may not defeat a finding that common questions predominate. Instead, the court is to determine whether the common questions are so important to the resolution of the lawsuit, and that they will occupy sufficient time and effort in the resolution of the case, that it may fairly be said that they predominate over individual questions.

(a) **Existence of common issue:** [§1094] It is important to focus carefully on whether there really is a common factual issue. For example, in many products liability cases, it may be that the common issue regarding liability can be stated only in the most general terms, because so much depends on the individual circumstances of each plaintiff. In such cases, one may conclude that there really is no common factual issue. [*See, e.g.,* Mertens v. Abbott Laboratories, 99 F.R.D. 38 (D.N.H. 1983)—in action against manufacturer of DES, allegedly common issue of defendant's knowledge of risks of DES not important, since "there is nothing to show that knowledge at a given point in time essentially settles anything with respect to liability of a particular claimant"]

(b) **Single issue certification:** [§1095] The existence of numerous and important individual issues can be partly solved by certifying the class action as to certain issues only. [Fed. R. Civ. P. 23(c)(4)(A)] However, it is unlikely that this device may properly be used to circumvent the requirement of predominance of common questions, and in most instances the court should hesitate to sidestep the problem of predominance by limiting the class action aspects to common issues.

(3) **Manageability and superiority:** [§1096] Assuming common issues predominate, the court must also ask whether a class action would be manageable, and whether it would be superior to other methods of adjudicating the case.

    (a) **Comparative analysis:** [§1097] It is important to understand that manageability is a *factor in evaluating superiority.* Accordingly, the fact that the case will be difficult to manage as a class action does not necessarily preclude a finding that handling the case as a class action is superior to other methods of adjudicating the dispute. Instead, the relevant question is whether, in view of manageability problems, using a class action is superior. Only in the most extreme instances would problems of manageability alone be decisive on this question.

    (b) **Example—class action superior:** In litigation brought on behalf of thousands of military personnel exposed to the defoliant Agent Orange in Southeast Asia, the court recognized that it confronted massive problems of manageability. Nevertheless, it compared the difficulties presented by handling the case as a class action with the enormous problems of handling the litigation as individual cases, and concluded that class action treatment had advantages over the other methods. [*In re* Agent Orange Product Liability Litigation, 506 F. Supp. 762 (E.D.N.Y. 1980)]

    (c) **Example—class action not manageable:** A suit on behalf of all residents of Los Angeles County (over 7,000,000 persons) to enjoin 293 large industrial companies from further pollution of the atmosphere was dismissed as unmanageable, because of the number of parties, the diversity of their interests, and the multiplicity of issues involved. [Diamond v. General Motors Corp., 20 Cal. App. 3d 374 (1971)]

d. **Application of different grounds to same case:** [§1098] In a given case, the plaintiff may try to satisfy different parts of Rule 23(b) in the alternative, and the case may be certified as to certain matters on one ground while certification is denied as to other parts.

(1) **Example:** Plaintiffs charged that the Philadelphia police illegally detained persons accused of crimes for as long as 20 hours without food or medical care, and sought declaratory, injunctive, and compensatory relief on behalf of a class. The court certified a class with respect to declaratory and injunctive relief under Rule 23(b)(2), but held that the action

could not be certified under Rule 23(b)(3) with respect to damages. [Rice v. City of Philadelphia, *supra*, §1090]

5. **Jurisdictional Requirements in Class Suits**

   a. **Subject matter jurisdiction:** [§1099] In class actions in federal court not involving federal claims, subject matter jurisdiction issues may arise.

      (1) **Diversity of citizenship:** [§1100] For purposes of federal diversity jurisdiction, only the citizenship of the *representative* is considered. This facilitates maintenance of a class suit in federal court. Note also that the named representatives must also meet the requirements of venue. [Supreme Tribe of Ben-Hur v. Cauble, *supra*, §301]

      (2) **Jurisdictional amount:** [§1101] However, in any class action in which the individual class members would be entitled to *separate* recoveries (rather than a recovery in common), where the amount in controversy requirement is applicable, *each* member of the class must have a claim in excess of $50,000—*i.e.*, no aggregation of claims is permitted. [Zahn v. International Paper Co., 414 U.S. 291 (1973)—refusal to permit class action where claims of representatives exceeded jurisdictional amount, but claims of unnamed members of class did not]

         (a) **Effect:** [§1102] The effect of this requirement has been to exclude most *diversity* consumer class actions from federal courts, because the claims of each member in such cases usually do not exceed $50,000.

         (b) **Compare—state courts:** [§1103] There is usually a state court of general jurisdiction, so state law class actions can be filed in that court. Where the state court of general jurisdiction has a jurisdictional minimum (*see supra*, §264), it is usually possible to aggregate claims to meet that minimum.

            1) **Possible impact of supplemental jurisdiction statute:** [§1104] 28 U.S.C. section 1367(b) does not explicitly preclude supplemental jurisdiction over the claims of class members that do not exceed $50,000, but the legislative history says the statute should not affect the rule in *Zahn, supra.* (*See supra*, §413.)

   b. **Personal jurisdiction:** [§1105] It has been held that in an action involving a nationwide class, a state court could assert personal jurisdiction over absent members of the plaintiff class when they were afforded an opportunity to opt out and chose not to do so. [Phillips Petroleum Co. v. Shutts, 472 U.S. 797 (1985)]

      (1) **Requirement of right to opt out:** [§1106] It is *unclear* whether the right to opt out is required to justify personal jurisdiction in all cases, such as actions brought under Rule 23(b)(1) or 23(b)(2). The Supreme Court reserved ruling on this point in *Shutts, supra,* and has since declined to decide whether a right to opt-out is required [Ticor Title Insurance Co. v. Brown, 114 S. Ct. 1359 (1994)—certiorari dismissed in case raising issue].

(2) **Defendant classes:** [§1107] It is also *unclear* whether the same analysis would apply to a defendant class when the right to opt out was afforded the unnamed members of the class.

6. **Procedure in Conducting Class Suits**

   a. **Certification hearing:** [§1108] As soon as practicable after commencement of an alleged class suit, a hearing should be held to decide whether the action should proceed as a class suit. If the court finds that the class action requirements (above) are met, it decides that the case can proceed as a class action. [Fed. R. Civ. P. 23(c)(1)] This is commonly called "class certification." If the court finds that no class action is possible, the suit may be continued as an individual action.

      (1) **Note:** If the trial court finds that the action should not proceed as a class action, this finding is not a final order, and consequently an immediate appeal may not be taken. (Appeal may generally be taken only from final orders; *see infra*, §§1957 *et seq*.) The named plaintiffs must try the case as a non-class action (or with a smaller class), and only on appeal from the judgment on the merits will the correctness of the trial court's refusal to certify the class be reviewed.

      (2) **Based on evidence:** [§1109] In determining whether the suit can proceed as a class action, the court can take evidence on any of the issues raised (*i.e.*, it is *not* restricted to the pleadings).

         (a) **Discovery on class certification:** [§1110] Because the class certification decision is to be based on evidentiary materials, it is said to be necessary to allow precertification discovery relevant to whether the case should be certified as a class action. [Stewart v. Winter, 669 F.2d 328 (5th Cir. 1982)] Some courts try to limit this to "class action" issues, as distinguished from "merits" issues (going to the merits of the case), but this may prove difficult since commonality and typicality are class certification issues that depend in large measure on merits information.

      (3) **Consideration of merits:** [§1111] The Supreme Court has stated that the court may not make a preliminary inquiry into the merits of the suit to decide whether it can be maintained as a class action. [Eisen v. Carlisle & Jacquelin, *supra*, §1066]

         (a) **Compare—determining whether claim satisfies Rule 23:** The court may, however, determine whether the claim is of a type that would satisfy Rule 23, and to do so it must examine the grounds for the action to identify common issues and decide whether the plaintiff has a typical claim. One court said that the court should look "between the pleading and the fruits of discovery. . . . [E]nough must be laid bare to let the judge survey the factual scene on a kind of sketchy relief map, leaving for later view the myriad of details that cover the terrain." [Sirota v. Solitron Devices, Inc., 673 F.2d 566 (2d Cir.), *cert. denied*, 459 U.S. 838 (1982)]

(4) **Precertification decision of merits:** [§1112] The premise of the 1966 amendments to Rule 23 was that the class action would be binding on all class members, whether or not it was successful. Otherwise, class members could benefit from *"one-way intervention,"* finding out how the merits were decided before they elected to remain in the action or to opt out. As a result, it was widely assumed that the court could not decide the merits until it ruled on the certification issue, but the courts have modified this view (*see* below).

   (a) **Criticism:** Where the certification process was likely to be protracted and expensive, it might give a plaintiff who added class action allegations to his groundless complaint undue settlement leverage to prevent defendants from attacking the merits of the case until certification was decided.

   (b) **Motions to dismiss:** [§1113] To counteract the risk that plaintiffs will add class action allegations to groundless complaints, courts generally will entertain motions to dismiss under Rule 12(b)(6) (*see supra*, §674) before certification is decided.

   (c) **Summary judgment motions:** [§1114] Many courts will also allow defendants to move for summary judgment. The theory to support this is that defendants can waive protection against one-way intervention by filing motions for summary judgment if they choose to. [Wright v. Schock, 742 F.2d 541 (9th Cir. 1984)]

(5) **Certification order may be modified:** [§1115] The certification order is only tentative. At any time before trial, the court may revise class certification if it decides changes are necessary, by decertifying or altering the class configuration. Indeed, it may expand class size even after judgment if this would not unfairly subject the defendant to liability. [Payne v. Travenol Laboratories, Inc., 673 F.2d 798 (5th Cir.), *cert. denied,* 459 U.S. 1038 (1982)]

b. **Statute of limitations:** [§1116] The *filing* of a suit as a class action *suspends the running of the statute of limitations* for all putative members of the class until class certification is decided. [American Pipe & Construction Co. v. Utah, *supra*, §1065]

   (1) **Rationale:** Unless they could rely on the pendency of the class action to protect their rights, unnamed members of the class would have to file their own suits to guard against the running of the limitations period. This would defeat the purpose of Rule 23 to achieve the efficient combined resolution of cases suitable for class action treatment.

   (2) **Effect:** From the date the class action is filed until class certification is decided, the running of limitations is suspended. If class certification is denied, the limitations period begins to run again, and class members have the remainder of the period to file their own actions or intervene. If class certification is granted, class members who remain in the class action are protected against a limitations defense, provided the class action was filed in time.

(3) **Opt-outs:** [§1117] Where class certification is granted and some class members opt out, the limitations period begins to run again and they must file individual actions to protect themselves against the running of limitations.

(4) **Relation to grounds for denial of certification:** [§1118] The suspension of the running of the limitations period applies even where the class certification motion is denied for lack of commonality or typicality. [Crown, Cork & Seal Co. v. Parker, 462 U.S. 345 (1983)] *Criticism:* This means that the defendant is really not on notice of the claims that are protected from the running of limitations by the filing of the defective class action.

(5) **Defendant class actions:** [§1119] The suspension of limitations has been held to apply to a defendant class action in which the unnamed member of the defendant class did not even have notice of the filing of the suit within the limitations period. [Appleton Electric Co. v. Graves Truck Line, Inc., 635 F.2d 603 (7th Cir. 1980), *cert. denied*, 451 U.S. 976 (1981)]

(6) **Successive class actions:** [§1120] The suspension of limitations has been held not to be available in a second class action that is timely only because a deficient class action earlier suspended the running of limitations. [Korwek v. Hunt, 827 F.2d 874 (2d Cir. 1987)]

c. **Notice requirements**

(1) **When notice to individual class members is discretionary:** [§1121] Where the basis for a class action is to avoid the risk of inconsistent adjudications [Fed. R. Civ. P. 23(b)(1), *supra*, §1086], or the claim is for injunctive or declaratory relief for the class as a whole [Fed. R. Civ. P. 23(b)(2)], the appropriate form of notice to class members is left to the discretion of the court. [Fed. R. Civ. P. 23(d)(2)] Individual notice to class members is not required by due process if the class representation is adequate. [Wetzel v. Liberty Mutual Insurance Co., 508 F.2d 239 (3d Cir. 1975)]

(2) **When individual notice is mandatory**

(a) **Damages class action:** [§1122] In a damages class action based on a predominant question common to the class [Fed. R. Civ. P. 23(b)(3), *supra*, §1091], members of the class must be given "the best notice practicable under the circumstances, *including individual notice to all members who can be identified through reasonable effort.*" [Eisen v. Carlisle & Jacquelin, *supra*—requiring individual notice to 2,250,000 class members; Fed. R. Civ. P. 23(c)(2)]

(b) **Settlement or dismissal:** [§1123] Once a suit has been certified as a class suit, some type of notice to the class is required before *any* type of class action may be settled or dismissed. [Fed. R. Civ. P. 23(e)]

(c) **Compare—state rules may be more flexible:** [§1124] State courts usually require individual notice only where members of the class have *"substantial" claims*, because in such cases it is essential for them to decide whether to remain in (and be bound by res judicata) or opt out and pursue their independent remedies. Where the membership of the class is large and damages to each member small, individual notice might not be required and notice by publication may be sufficient. [Cooper v. American Savings & Loan Association, 55 Cal. App. 3d 274 (1976)]

(3) **Form and content of notice:** [§1125] Federal Rule 23 does not establish any specific form or manner of giving notice.

   (a) **Form:** [§1126] Clearly, the notice itself need *not* be in the form of a complaint or summons. Letters, bulletins, or circulars mailed to members of the class are commonly used. However, when notice to each member is mandatory, it must be given at least the formality of mail. [Eisen v. Carlisle & Jacquelin, *supra*] In other instances, the court has discretion as to form. [Greenfield v. Villager Industries, Inc., 483 F.2d 824 (3d Cir. 1973)]

   (b) **Contents:** [§1127] The notice must advise the class member of the existence of the suit, the nature of the claim and relief requested, provisions for costs of maintaining the suit, and the identity of the person or persons suing on behalf of the class. When based on Rule 23(b)(3)—the predominant question ground—it must also advise each member that he will be bound by the judgment unless he opts out. [Fed. R. Civ. P. 23(c)(2)]

   (c) **Effect of notice:** [§1128] In the ordinary civil action, notice has the effect of making the notified person a *party* to the action who will be bound by any judgment in the action (including a default judgment if he does not appear). In a class suit, however, the notified person is already provisionally bound through representation by the class representative. Hence, notice has the following effects:

   1) *If accompanied by an "opt out" directive* in a Rule 23(b)(3) suit, the notice allows the notified person to terminate his involvement in the action (*see infra*, §1131.)

   2) *In other types of class suits,* the notice:

      a) Gives absent members of the class the opportunity to intervene and protect themselves; *and*

      b) Gives the opposing party more assurance that the eventual judgment cannot subsequently be attacked by an absentee claiming that the representation was inadequate (*see supra*, §1080).

(4) **Plaintiff must pay costs of notice:** [§1129] Under Rule 23(c), the plaintiff initially must pay the costs of notifying all members of the

class. [Eisen v. Carlisle & Jacquelin, *supra*] If the plaintiff **wins** the action, she can ultimately recover such expenses from the defendant as necessary court costs.

   (a) **Cost of identifying class members:** [§1130] The plaintiff must also pay the cost of identifying class members. [Oppenheimer Fund, Inc. v. Sanders, 437 U.S. 340 (1978)—$16,000 in computer costs to identify certain class members properly charged to plaintiff]

   (b) **Effect:** The cost of notice has inhibited large class actions in federal court, because the larger the class, the more unlikely it is that any single plaintiff can afford to bear the costs of notice (and thus "fairly and adequately" represent the class).

d. **Opting out by class members:** [§1131] In class actions under Rule 23(b)(3), unnamed members of the class may opt out, thereby excluding themselves from the binding effects of the class action.

   (1) **Timing:** [§1132] Usually the decision to opt out must be made before the court decides the merits, to avoid the risk of one-way intervention. (*See supra*, §1112.)

   (2) **Effect on statute of limitations:** [§1133] Once a class member opts out, she loses the class action's effect of suspending the limitations period and must file her own suit within the remainder of the limitations period to protect her rights. (*See supra*, §1116.)

   (3) **Rule 23(b)(1) and 23(b)(2) class actions:** [§1134] There is no mandatory opt-out right in the rule for these actions. In some cases, the court may, in its discretion, permit opting out, but that could undermine the purpose of certifying a case of this type in the first place. When class members have monetary claims, however, it may be an abuse of discretion to deny the right to opt out. [Holmes v. Continental Can Co., 706 F.2d 1144 (11th Cir. 1983)]

   (4) **Constitutional right argument:** [§1135] It may be argued that the Supreme Court's decision that the right to opt out permits exercise of personal jurisdiction over the claims of unnamed class members (*see supra*, §1105) means that there must always be a right to opt out where unnamed class members are not subject to the personal jurisdiction of the court.

   (5) **Right to claim collateral estoppel:** [§1136] It has been held that where class members opt out and the class action is successful, the *opt-outs may not claim collateral estoppel* from the class action victory in their individual cases, because that would be tantamount to one-way intervention. [Premier Electrical Construction Co. v. National Electrical Contractors Association, 814 F.2d 358 (7th Cir. 1987)] It is unclear whether other courts will adopt this rule.

e. **Intervention by class members:** [§1137] Intervention by class members in the class action is allowed on the same terms that govern intervention otherwise. (*See supra*, §§1009-1034.)

(1) **Adequacy of representation:** [§1138] A problem arises from this rule because intervention is not allowed where the intervenor is adequately represented by the present litigant (*see supra*, §1016), and the court must find the class representative (*i.e.*, the present litigant) adequate to certify the class (*see supra*, §1079). Some courts solve the problem by saying that the finding of adequacy under Rule 23(a) for class certification does not require a finding of adequacy under Rule 24(a) (dealing with intervention). [Woolen v. Surtran Taxicabs, Inc., 684 F.2d 324 (5th Cir. 1982)]

(2) **Role of intervenor:** [§1139] Rule 23 makes no provision for participation by a party who is not the class representative. Some courts suggest that when intervention is proper, that may suggest that the certification decision should be reconsidered, or that the intervenor should be designated a new class representative. [Lelsz v. Kavanagh, 710 F.2d 1040 (5th Cir. 1983)]

(3) **Compare—entering an appearance:** [§1140] In Rule 23(b)(3) actions, a class member may "enter an appearance through counsel." This does not entitle the class member to take an active role in the litigation, but only to receive copies of pleadings and other filings. It is, thus, a way to monitor the progress of the case.

f. **Discovery:** [§1141] Class members are treated as "quasi-parties" for discovery purposes. The opposing party is not given the full rights (*e.g.*, to depose each class member) that he ordinarily has against opposing litigants. However, he can obtain fair discovery of the "typicality" of claims, the factual basis for determining inclusion in the class, individual damages, and the like. Interrogatories for these purposes are proper, as are depositions when necessary. [Brennan v. Midwestern United Life Insurance Co., 450 F.2d 999 (7th Cir. 1971)]

g. **Communications with class members:** [§1142] Courts are concerned about the risk that unnamed members of the class may be victimized by misleading or overreaching on the part of the litigants or their lawyers, and may therefore sometimes limit contacts with class members.

(1) **Showing of need:** [§1143] The Supreme Court has held that limitations on communications with class members by class counsel may be imposed only where there is some showing of need. [Gulf Oil Corp. v. Bernard, 452 U.S. 89 (1981)] The showing should indicate a *likelihood of misleading or overreaching class members.*

(2) **Effect of certification:** [§1144] After the class is certified, class counsel is for some purposes the attorney for the class members, and the court's power to interfere with her communications is limited.

(3) **Communications by class opponent:** [§1145] After the class is certified, the court has broader authority to regulate communications by the class opponent, particularly when there is a risk that the class opponent will try to subvert the class action by pressuring class members to opt out.

(a) **Example:** In a class action against a bank alleging that it defrauded its borrowers by inflating the prime rate it charged them, the court properly punished the bank for embarking on a campaign to have loan officers call class members and pressure them to opt out of the action. [Kleiner v. First National Bank of Atlanta, 751 F.2d 1193 (11th Cir. 1985)]

(b) **Attorney contacts:** [§1146] After certification, class members should be considered "represented by counsel," and the attorney for the class opponent is therefore forbidden by ethical rules to communicate with the class members. [Resnick v. American Dental Association, 95 F.R.D. 372 (N.D. Ill. 1982)]

(4) **Remedies for violations:** [§1147] When a valid rule against communication with class members is violated, the court may hold the person who violated the rule in *contempt.* In addition, when the communication resulted in opt-outs, the court can *invalidate the opt-outs* tainted by the communication.

h. **Dismissal and compromise**

(1) **Court approval required:** [§1148] Because of the fiduciary nature of a class action, it may not be dismissed or compromised by the class representative without court approval. [Fed. R. Civ. P. 23(e)]

(2) **Notice required:** [§1149] Similarly, notice of the proposed dismissal or compromise must be given to all members of the class before the court can give its approval. [Fed. R. Civ. P. 23(e)]

(3) **Settlement before certification:** [§1150] When a class action is settled before certification, the notice and hearing requirements depend on the nature of the settlement.

(a) **Settlement of class claims:** [§1151] If the settlement purports to resolve class claims by releasing the defendant from further liability to class members, notice and a hearing are required. [Philadelphia Electric Co. v. Anaconda American Brass Co., 42 F.R.D. 324 (E.D. Pa. 1967)]

(b) **Settlement of individual claims:** [§1152] When the settlement purports only to settle the individual claims of the proposed class representatives, the court usually will determine whether there is any *indication of abuse* of the class action device or *prejudice to absent class members.* If there is, it should order notice and a hearing. [Shelton v. Pargo, Inc., 582 F.2d 1298 (4th Cir. 1978)]

i. **Distribution of proceeds of action**

(1) **Class members file individual claims:** [§1153] Ordinarily, any fund obtained by settlement or judgment in a class action will be held intact, and members of the class will be notified to file individual claims to establish their shares.

(2) **Rebate approach:** [§1154] However, when the class is numerous and the claims are small, this approach may be impractical. In this situation, some courts have adopted what amounts to a rebate approach: Where the identity of the class members at the time of the wrong cannot be determined or the amounts of their respective claims are very small, the recovery will be distributed to those persons who are *now* members of the class.

(a) **Example:** Taxi fare overcharges to former customers may be refunded by reducing fares to *future customers.* [*See* Daar v. Yellow Cab Co., 67 Cal. 2d 695 (1967)]

(b) **Criticism:** This approach may distort market structure, resulting in temporary underpricing, overuse, and competitive advantage for the wrongdoer.

j. **Award of attorneys' fees:** [§1155] Although there is no authority under the Federal Rules for awarding fees to counsel in a successful class suit, federal and state courts generally award fees out of the proceeds recovered by the class. This is based on the court's inherent equity powers under the "common fund doctrine"—*i.e.*, the plaintiff who hired the attorney should not be required to pay the entire legal fees incurred in obtaining a "common fund" benefiting all class members. [Mills v. Electric Auto Lite Co., 396 U.S. 375 (1970)] However, the fee award is carefully considered by the court on behalf of the class. [Lindy Brothers Builders, Inc. v. American Radiator Corp., 540 F.2d 102 (3d Cir. 1976)]

7. **Effect of Judgment in Class Action:** [§1156] A central issue in class actions is whether the judgment binds members of the class who were not actually before the court.

   a. **State rules:** [§1157] Some states retain the distinctions between true, hybrid, and spurious class actions (the former Federal Rule), under which the "nature" of the action determines whether the judgment is binding on absentees. (*See supra*, §1061.)

   b. **Federal Rule:** [§1158] Under Federal Rule 23, however, these distinctions are eliminated. A valid judgment in any class action (whether or not favorable to the class) *binds all members of the class who do not affirmatively request exclusion (opt out).* A person who excludes herself from the action will not be bound by an adverse judgment. Conversely, however, she may be unable to assert collateral estoppel in her own action if the judgment turns out to be favorable to the class. (*See supra*, §1136.)

8. **Defendant Class Actions:** [§1159] Rule 23 states that suits may be brought against a defendant class. For such actions, the Rule does not provide any procedures different from those for actions on behalf of a plaintiff class. Nevertheless, the *courts tend to approach defendant class actions differently* in ways that should be noted.

   a. **Adequacy of representation:** [§1160] There is a risk that plaintiff will select a weak representative for a defendant class. Adequacy of representation may therefore be *examined more closely*.

(1) **Incentive problem:** [§1161]   The defendant class representative may have less incentive to litigate vigorously, and the lawyer for the class lacks the entrepreneurial incentive of a plaintiff class lawyer, who looks forward to a large fee award if the case is successful.

(2) **Courts' attitude:** [§1162]   Despite these problems, many courts realize that defendants will try to escape service as class representative. The courts resist such efforts: "[C]ourts must not readily accede to the wishes of named defendants in this area, for to permit them to abdicate so easily would utterly vitiate the effectiveness of the defendant class action." [Marcera v. Chinlund, 595 F.2d 1231 (2d Cir.), *vacated on other grounds,* 442 U.S. 915 (1979)] Hence, when the representatives will adequately protect the class by protecting their own interests, courts will find them adequate.

b. **Qualitative differences between plaintiff and defendant postures:** [§1163] Many courts view defendants' stakes as qualitatively different. The distinction is that the unnamed plaintiff stands to gain while the unnamed defendant stands to lose. [Thillens, Inc. v. Community Currency Exchange Association, 97 F.R.D. 668 (N.D. Ill. 1983)]

(1) **Criticism:**   This represents a skewed view of litigation, because both defendants and plaintiffs stand to lose and gain. The absent plaintiff class member who has a valid claim stands to lose if the class action is decided adversely, and the absent defendant class member stands to gain res judicata protection against future suits if the defendant class is successful.

c. **Rule 23(b)(2) class actions:** [§1164]   Rule 23(b)(2) authorizes actions for injunctive or declaratory relief against "the party opposing the class," seemingly precluding a defendant class action. Nevertheless, there is a division in the courts on whether it is permissible to have a class action seeking an injunction against a defendant class. [*See* Marcera v. Chinlund, *supra*—defendant class allowed; Henson v. East Lincoln Township, 814 F.2d 410 (7th Cir. 1987)—defendant class not allowed]

d. **Personal jurisdiction:** [§1165]   In upholding the authority of a state court to exercise personal jurisdiction over absent plaintiff class members (*see supra,* §1105), the Supreme Court distinguished the situation of defendants, for "an out-of-state defendant summoned by a plaintiff is faced with the full powers of the forum state *against* it." [Phillips Petroleum Co. v. Shutts, *supra,* §1105]   It is uncertain whether this mandates granting unnamed defendant class members more than the right simply to opt out to overcome their personal jurisdiction objections.

e. **Bilateral class action:** [§1166]   Some of the most troubling class action problems involve "bilateral" class actions, *i.e.,* involving a plaintiff class suing a defendant class. One reaction of courts has been to hold that *each plaintiff class member must have a claim against each defendant class member* in such actions. [La Mar v. H & B Novelty & Loan Co., 489 F.2d 461 (9th Cir. 1973)] There are two principal ways to satisfy this requirement.

(1) **Conspiracy:** [§1167]   When it is alleged that the defendant class members conspired with each other, that provides a basis for holding each conspirator liable to each plaintiff and solves the problem.

(2) **Juridical link:** [§1168]   The courts have also allowed bilateral class actions where there is a "juridical link" among the defendants. Usually this means that defendants are officers of the same governmental unit, such as the state. [*See, e.g.*, Marcera v. Chinlund, *supra*—action against sheriffs of state for denying contact visits to pretrial detainees]

[§1169]

VI. DISCOVERY

chapter approach

Procedural rules make available several modes of discovery:

(i) *Depositions*;

(ii) *Interrogatories*;

(iii) Requests for *admissions*;

(iv) Requests for *production and inspection*;

(v) *Physical or mental examination*; and

(vi) In an increasing number of jurisdictions, *mandatory prediscovery disclosure*.

Through the use of these devices, by the time a case gets to trial, each side should know as much as possible about its own case and that of the adversary.

For examination purposes, questions most commonly center on the following issues related to discovery:

1. **Scope of discovery:** Is the matter *relevant* to the subject matter of the action and *not privileged*? If so, it is within the scope of discovery, although discovery may be limited or denied as to *work product* (trial preparation material) or *expert testimony*.

2. **Protective orders:** Is there good cause for a protective order *limiting, conditioning,* or *delaying* the discovery?

3. **Sanctions:** Has a party's resistance to discovery or *noncompliance* with discovery rules and orders been sufficient to warrant judicial imposition of sanctions?

4. **Use at trial:** Is the deposition that of a *party* or an *unavailable or distant witness*? If so, it may be introduced for *any* purpose. If it is the deposition of a witness appearing at trial, it may be used to *impeach* the witness's testimony.

A. INTRODUCTION

1. History of Discovery

a. **Common law:** [§1169] Under common law procedure, the pleadings were to disclose factual contentions and information to the adversary parties. Neither party could compel the other to disclose additional information that might support his case, even such crucial information as the identity of an eyewitness. A party was not compelled to reveal in advance the evidence he would present at trial; nor were third parties required to make disclosures except pursuant to a subpoena requiring their attendance at trial.

b. **Equity:** [§1170]   In early equity practice, a bill in equity could be used to compel the adversary to disclose information; and such bills frequently were accompanied by interrogatories which the defendant was required to answer under oath. In addition, parties or witnesses could be required to appear for depositions where interrogation through written questions could be conducted. Since answers to interrogatories and depositions were a part of the record on which the decision was made, they were really part of the trial and not merely preparatory discovery. Live testimony was usually not allowed at the hearing, so cases were decided on the basis of the material developed through discovery.

c. **Equity in aid of law:** [§1171]   A litigant in a law court could sometimes take advantage of the equitable procedures by bringing a bill in equity to compel discovery of information needed to present a claim or defense at law. Such a bill could issue if the evidence sought would be admissible in the specific legal proceeding (*i.e.,* if the moving party was not embarked on a "fishing expedition") and would be helpful to the moving party in meeting a burden of proof imposed on him.

d. **Code procedure:** [§1172]   Nineteenth-century reforms merged the bill of discovery into legal proceedings, but did not significantly enlarge its availability. Thus, heavy reliance on the pleadings continued.

e. **Federal Rules:** [§1173]   Ultimately, the Federal Rules made pretrial discovery an integral part of the process of defining the issues for trial. Similar discovery procedures have now been adopted in almost every state. However, increasing difficulty with abuse of discovery has led to repeated revision of discovery rules, as in the 1983 elimination from Rule 26(a) of a provision generally making frequency of use of discovery methods unlimited and the addition to Rule 26(b)(1) of a grant of authority to the court to limit discovery. At the same time, a new Rule 26(g) created obligations and sanctions applicable to discovery filings parallel to those for pleadings under revised Rule 11. (*See supra,* §§710-732.) Further amendments in 1993 introduced mandatory prediscovery disclosure (*see infra,* §§1183-1200), imposed numerical caps on interrogatories and depositions (*infra,* §§1207-1210, 1248), and expanded the duty to supplement prior discovery responses.

2. **Purpose and Effect of Discovery Procedures**

    a. **Obtaining factual information:** [§1174]   A party who has made effective use of discovery can go to trial with the best evidence available to prove his contentions and with a good knowledge of the presentation that his adversary will make. Surprise and delay are thus largely avoided, and the chance that the judgment will rest on accurate findings of fact is enhanced.

    b. **Narrowing the issues:** [§1175]   Discovery can help to eliminate fictitious issues, claims, or defenses by revealing overwhelming evidence on one side, thereby paving the way for stipulations, settlements, and summary disposition.

    c. **Promoting settlements:** [§1176]   It was hoped that discovery would facilitate more and earlier settlements by providing each side fuller knowledge of the strengths and weaknesses of its case.

d. **Simplification of pleading:** [§1177]   The availability of discovery makes it unnecessary to rely heavily upon the pleadings for exchanging information, narrowing issues, or disposing of untenable claims or defenses. Accordingly, where discovery is available, pleading is simplified and technical challenges to pleadings are disfavored.

e. **Costs to litigants:** [§1178]   To the extent that discovery produces settlements and stipulations, it can substantially cut down costs to one or both parties. At the same time, the discovery process itself can be very costly in terms of time spent by lawyers, parties, witnesses, and court reporters. Where the same evidence is formally discovered and then presented at trial, the expense to the parties may be almost doubled.

f. **Substantive consequences:** [§1179]   The foregoing effects of discovery can have substantive implications as well. Claims and defenses otherwise difficult to establish may be made effective by the availability of discovery. Antitrust claims, for example, are often proved with evidence discovered in the possession of the defense. And the availability of discovery may enable a tenacious and resourceful litigant to wear down one who is weaker or less energetic.

g. **Collateral purpose problem:** [§1180]   An ongoing concern with discovery is the risk that litigants may seek to obtain discovery for some *purpose other than preparation for trial*.

   (1) **Harassment:** [§1181]   Because of its cost, discovery can be used to harass an opponent or club an opponent into settlement. The court has power to limit discovery having these tendencies [Fed. R. Civ. P. 26(b)(2)] and to sanction the person who so uses it [Fed. R. Civ. P. 26(g)].

   (2) **Nonlitigation use of information:** [§1182]   Alternatively, a litigant may seek information that is pertinent to the litigation to use it for some nonlitigation purpose.

      (a) **Example:** In litigation between business competitors, one litigant may seek to force its opponent to reveal information that can be used to obtain competitive advantages in the marketplace.

      (b) **Example:** In an action between Jacqueline Kennedy Onassis and a professional photographer who specialized in unauthorized candid photos of the Kennedy family, there was concern that the photographer would use Ms. Onassis's deposition as an occasion for photographing her. [Galella v. Onassis, 487 F.2d 986 (2d Cir. 1974)—upholding protective order excluding plaintiff from defendant's deposition]

B. BASIC DISCOVERY DEVICES

1. **Prediscovery Disclosure:** [§1183]   In 1993, Federal Rule 26(a) was amended to provide for disclosure of certain information *before commencement of formal discovery* on the rationale that formal discovery is too time-consuming and expensive as to certain *core information* that will undoubtedly be revealed during the formal discovery process.

a. **Early meeting of counsel:** [§1184]   To accomplish the objectives of the disclosure provisions, counsel are to meet and confer "as soon as practicable" after the suit is filed to "discuss the *nature and basis of* their claims and defenses" and to "*develop a proposed discovery plan*" as well as to specify the materials that should be included in the prediscovery disclosures. [Fed. R. Civ. P. 26(f)]

   (1) **Presented to court:** [§1185]   The discovery plan is to be presented to the court at its initial conference pursuant to Rule 16 (*see infra,* §§1753-1757).

b. **No formal discovery until meeting of counsel:** [§1186]   Formal discovery may not be undertaken, except on stipulation or court order, until the meeting of counsel pursuant to Rule 26(f) has been completed. [Fed. R. Civ. P. 26(d)]

   (1) **Exception for witnesses leaving country:** A party may take a deposition earlier if the witness is expected to leave the country and be unavailable for deposition in this country unless examined before the meeting of counsel. [Fed. R. Civ. P. 30(a)(3)(C)]

c. **Disclosure as to disputed facts alleged with particularity:** [§1187]   As to identification of witnesses and documents (*see infra,* §§1190-1191), disclosure is required only as to information "relevant to disputed facts alleged with particularity in the pleadings."

   (1) **Rule 9(b) concept:** [§1188]   The particularity idea is borrowed from Rule 9(b)'s requirement that fraud claims be alleged with particularity (*see supra,* §§679-681). Applying this concept in other contexts where specification in pleadings is not required may lead to uncertainties in application.

   (2) **Possible motion for more definite statement:** [§1189]   Parties unable to prepare responsive pleadings due to indefiniteness in pleadings may move for a more definite statement pursuant to Rule 12(e) (*see supra,* §§687-688). But because disclosure is not a responsive pleading, and parties are free to plead generally unless the pleading rules require more particularity, it is likely that such motions should *not* be allowed.

d. **Material to be disclosed**

   (1) **Identity of witnesses:** [§1190]   Each party is to disclose the name and, if known, the address and telephone number of each person who has discoverable information relevant to disputed facts alleged with particularity. [Fed. R. Civ. P. 26(a)(1)(A)]

   (2) **Relevant documents:** [§1191]   Each party is to disclose a copy or description by category of all documents in its possession that are relevant to disputed facts alleged with particularity. [Fed. R. Civ. P. 26(a)(1)(B)]

   (3) **Damages computation:** [§1192]   Each party claiming damages should disclose a computation of those damages and *produce the documents* on which the computation is based. [Fed. R. Civ. P. 26(a)(1)(C)]

(4) **Insurance agreements:** [§1193] Each party against whom a claim has been asserted should produce for inspection and copying each insurance agreement that might cover the claim. [Fed. R. Civ. P. 26(a)(1)(D)]

    (a) **Compare—prior law:** Before 1993, insurance agreements were discoverable, but only in response to a formal discovery request.

e. **Timing of disclosures:** [§1194] These disclosures should be made at, or within 10 days after, the meeting of counsel pursuant to Rule 26(f) (*supra*, §1184) unless otherwise agreed by the parties or ordered by the court.

f. **Form of disclosures:** [§1195] Every disclosure is to be *signed* by at least one attorney of record for the disclosing party. The signature represents that to the best of the lawyer's knowledge, *formed after a reasonable inquiry*, the disclosure is complete and correct as of the time it is made. [Fed. R. Civ. P. 26(g)(1)]

g. **Duty to supplement:** [§1196] If a party learns that its disclosures were *incorrect*, or if *additional or corrective information* comes to its attention, the party is to supplement the disclosure with the added information. [Fed. R. Civ. P. 26(e)(1)]

h. **Sanctions for failure to disclose:** [§1197] A party failing to disclose as required by Rule 26(a)(1) or to supplement as required by Rule 26(e)(1) is subject to sanctions. [Fed. R. Civ. P. 37(c)(1)]

    (1) **Exclusion of evidence:** [§1198] Unless the failure to disclose was harmless, the party will not be permitted to use the material in evidence. This sanction is said to be *automatic*, and it applies not only at trial but also at motion hearings, as on a motion for summary judgment.

    (2) **Additional sanctions:** [§1199] In addition, the court may impose the sanctions authorized by Rule 37(b), which usually require an order compelling discovery as a prerequisite (*see infra*, §§1451-1456), and can *inform the jury* of the failure to make disclosure.

i. **Stipulation to limit disclosure obligation:** [§1200] The parties may stipulate to limit or alter the initial disclosure obligation.

j. **Opt-out by district or by judge:** [§1201] By general rules or orders in particular cases, local district courts, or individual judges, may choose not to adopt initial disclosure, or may decide to follow disclosure practices different from those provided in Rule 26(a)(1). A number have done so.

2. **Depositions:** [§1202] A deposition is an examination of a witness under oath in the presence of a court reporter. All parties have a right to be represented by counsel at a deposition; and counsel may examine and cross-examine the witness. The examination may be held in the presence of a judge if the witness is recalcitrant.

    a. **When timely**

        (1) **Before suit filed:** [§1203] A deposition may be taken *before* an action is filed or while an appeal is pending from a final judgment, but only by leave of court granted for the purpose of perpetuating testimony based on

a showing that the party seeking to perpetuate testimony is unable to cause the action to be brought. [Fed. R. Civ. P. 37(a)]

(2) **Moratorium after commencement of suit:** [§1204]   Since 1993, Federal Rule 26(d) has provided that formal discovery (except depositions of witnesses about to leave the country; *see supra,* §1186) must be deferred until after the parties meet and confer on a discovery plan pursuant to rule 26(f).

   (a) **Defendant's head start:** Where the moratorium does not apply, as in state court, defendants usually are protected against initiation of formal discovery by the plaintiff until a certain time after service of the complaint [*e.g.,* Cal. Code Civ. Proc. §2025(b)(2)—20-day period for noticing depositions]

(3) **Simultaneous proceedings:** [§1205]   All parties may take depositions simultaneously unless the court otherwise directs. [Fed. R. Civ. P. 26(d)] Hence, neither side is entitled to discovery "priority" before the other side can commence discovery.

b. **Optional to parties:** [§1206]   Depositions are optional. Each party has the right to take the deposition of *any* witness—without a showing of good cause—but is not required to do so. A party is also entitled to interview any willing nonparty witness without court supervision. [IBM v. Edelstein, 526 F.2d 37 (2d Cir. 1975)]

c. **Numerical cap on depositions:** [§1207]   To curb abuse, Rule 30 was amended in 1993 to impose a *10-deposition limit*. [Fed. R. Civ. P. 30(a)(2)(A)]

   (1) **Limit per "side":** [§1208]   The 10-deposition limit is not per party, but is calculated cumulatively for plaintiffs, defendants, and third-party defendants.

   (2) **One deposition per witness:** [§1209]   In addition, the rules now provide that a given witness's deposition be taken only once. [Fed. R. Civ. P. 30(a)(2)(B)]

   (3) **Change by stipulation, local rule, or order:** [§1210]   The parties may stipulate in writing to vary the deposition limitation, and the court may alter it by local rule or order.

d. **Compulsory appearance of witness**

   (1) **Issuance of subpoena:** [§1211]   At the request of a party, the court clerk will issue a subpoena commanding the named witness to appear and give testimony at the designated time and place. An attorney admitted to practice before the court may also issue a subpoena. [Fed. R. Civ. P. 45(a)]

   (2) **Service of subpoena:** [§1212]   A subpoena is served on the witness personally and must be accompanied by a tender of the fee for one day's attendance, plus reimbursement for mileage. [Fed. R. Civ. P. 45(b)]

(3) **Place of deposition:** [§1213] A witness may be required to appear at a deposition at any place within 100 miles of the place where he resides, is employed, or transacts business. [Fed. R. Civ. P. 45(c)(3)(A)(ii); *compare* Cal. Civ. Proc. Code §2025(e)(1)—75 miles]

(4) **Subpoena not necessary for party-witness:** [§1214] It is not necessary to serve a subpoena on an *adverse party*, or an officer or managing agent of a party, in order to compel attendance. [Fed. R. Civ. P. 37(d); Cal. Civ. Proc. Code §2025(h)(1)] A deposition of a party-witness may be scheduled at any reasonable place.

(5) **Deposition of corporation or organization:** [§1215] Where a corporation (or an association or governmental body) is to be deposed, the party taking the deposition need not identify the individual who is compelled to give the deposition. She need state only the *matters* on which she proposes to examine the organization, and the organization must then designate the appropriate witness. [Fed. R. Civ. P. 30(b)(6)] The adversary need not guess which employee is in possession of the required information; and the organization itself is bound by its deponent's answers.

(a) **Scope of inquiry:** [§1216] Problems can arise where the party doing discovery inquires into matters relevant to the suit but beyond the expertise of the witness. If the witness has some knowledge of the matters, she may have to answer and the organization may be bound by her testimony. *Example:* Where defendant manufacturer designated a doctor as its witness in a products liability action, the doctor could be required to answer questions about company policy as well as technical matters on which he had expertise. [Lapenna v. Upjohn Co., 110 F.R.D. 15 (E.D. Pa. 1986)]

e. **Notice to parties**

(1) **Form of notice:** [§1217] A party wishing to depose a witness must give written notice to every other *party*, identifying the deponent and the time and place of the deposition. [Fed. R. Civ. P. 30(b); Cal. Civ. Proc. Code §2025(c), (d)]

(a) **Compare:** This is a notice to the *parties* that a deposition is to be taken. A nonparty *witness* must be told to attend by means of a subpoena (*see supra,* §1211).

(2) **Time for notice:** [§1218] In federal proceedings, notice must be given a "reasonable" length of time in advance of the scheduled date for the deposition. [Fed. R. Civ. P. 30(b)] Some state codes are more explicit in regard to the time period. [*See, e.g.,* Cal. Civ. Proc. Code §2025(f)—10 days]

f. **Production of documents:** [§1219] The subpoena (when necessary) or the notice may direct the witness to bring along and produce at the deposition any documents that could properly be sought by a request for production of documents (*see infra,* §§1276-1292). [Fed. R. Civ. P. 30(b)(5); Cal. Civ. Proc. Code §2025(d)(4)]

(1) **Effect on timing:** [§1220] Where the witness is to produce documents at the deposition, more notice is required. [Fed. R. Civ. P. 30(b)(5)—time required for document production: 30 days; Cal. Civ. Proc. Code §2025(f)—20 days]

g. **Questioning of deponent**

  (1) **Oral:** [§1221] Ordinarily, the examination of deponents is conducted orally, with the examining party questioning first, and the others in turn.

   (a) **Examination by witness's attorney:** [§1222] Usually the attorney for the witness will not question the witness except to clear up important matters left uncertain by other interrogation. *Rationale:* The witness's lawyer does not wish to assist the other parties by making the content of the witness's testimony at trial more evident to them.

  (2) **Depositions in writing:** [§1223] The examining party may choose to conduct the examination in writing. If so, the questions are submitted in writing; the adversary may review the questions in advance and submit cross-questions to be answered at the same time; and the cross-questions may be followed by re-direct and re-cross-questions. Even though the *questions* are written, the answers of the deponent are given *orally*. [Fed. R. Civ. P. 31; Cal. Civ. Proc. Code §2028]

   (a) **Practicality:** [§1224] This form of deposition may be more economical because it does not require the attendance of lawyers at the place of the deposition. On the other hand, it does not give the examiner an opportunity to follow up answers effectively, and hence is not used where the witness may be evasive or where the subject under examination is complex.

  (3) **Telephone:** [§1225] In federal practice, the deposition may be taken by telephone upon leave of court or if both parties so stipulate in writing. [Fed. R. Civ. P. 30(b)(7)]

  (4) **Objections to questions:** [§1226] The lawyer for the witness may object to a question and instruct the witness not to answer.

   (a) **Limitation on instructions:** [§1227] In federal court, a witness may be instructed not to answer a question only to *preserve a privilege* (*see infra*, §§1329-1363), to *enforce a limitation on evidence imposed by the court* in the case, or to *present a motion for a protective order.* [Fed. R. Civ. P. 30(d)(1)] Furthermore, some federal courts have imposed stricter restraints on the behavior of the lawyer for the witness. [*See, e.g.,* Hall v. Clifton Precision, 150 F.R.D. 525 (E.D. Pa. 1993)—deponent's attorney forbidden to talk to deponent, except to decide whether to assert a privilege, between commencement and completion of deposition]

   (b) **Motion to compel:** [§1228] When a witness is instructed not to answer, the examining party may move for an order of the court *compelling* an answer. [Fed. R. Civ. P. 37(a); Cal. Civ. Proc. Code §2025(o)]

(c) **Failure to obey order:** [§1229] If the witness disobeys an order to answer, the witness may be held in *contempt*; and a party-witness may be subject to other sanctions as well. [Fed. R. Civ. P. 37(b); Cal. Civ. Proc. Code §2025(o)]

(d) **Protective order for witness:** [§1230] On the other hand, if questioning is conducted in an unreasonably oppressive manner, the witness may move for a protective order *limiting or terminating* the examination. [Fed. R. Civ. P. 30(d)(3)]

(e) **No waiver:** [§1231] Failure of the witness to object to a question on deposition does *not* constitute a waiver of her right to object to the same question or answer at trial. [Fed. R. Civ. P. 32(b)]

1) **Exception—matters of form:** [§1232] Errors in the taking of a deposition that *might be cured if promptly presented* but which were not, *may not be raised as grounds for exclusion* of the deposition evidence at trial. This includes objections to the form of questions or answers or in the manner of taking of the deposition. [Fed. R. Civ. P. 32(d)(3)]

h. **Transcription of deposition**

(1) **Review of transcript:** [§1233] *If requested before completion of the deposition,* a deponent is entitled to review the transcript of her testimony and make corrections in it, subject to the right of the examining party to comment on the changes if the deposition is used at trial. [Fed. R. Civ. P. 30(e)]

(2) **Videotape:** [§1234] In federal practice, a deposition may be recorded by "other than stenographic means" if the party noticing the deposition so chooses. [Fed. R. Civ. P. 30(b)(2)] Some states also permit a videotape deposition. [Cal. Civ. Proc. Code §2025(p)]

i. **Use of deposition testimony at trial**

(1) **Generally inadmissible:** [§1235] Statements in depositions are *hearsay* and thus are generally inadmissible at trial to prove the truth of statements made by deponents.

(2) **Exceptions:** [§1236] In the following circumstances, however, statements made in depositions may be admissible:

(a) **Party admissions:** [§1237] Deposition statements by party-witnesses are admissible against those parties. [Fed. R. Civ. P. 32(a)(2); Cal. Civ. Proc. Code §2025(u)(2)]

(b) **Impeachment:** [§1238] A deposition by a nonparty witness that contradicts testimony given at trial may be admitted for the purpose of impeaching the witness who has changed her story. [Fed. R. Civ. P. 32(a)(1); Cal. Civ. Proc. Code §2025(u)(1)]

(c) **Unavailability of deponent:** [§1239] If the deponent is dead, infirm, or beyond the reach of subpoena process at the time of trial, the deposition may be used in lieu of her live testimony. [Fed. R. Civ. P. 32(a)(3); Cal. Civ. Proc. Code §2025(u)(3)(B)]

1) **Note:** This rule also applies to the deposition of a party seeking to use his own deposition instead of testifying at trial, ***unless*** that party is responsible for his own absence. [Richmond v. Brooks, 227 F.2d 490 (2d Cir. 1955)]

(3) **Objectionable evidence in deposition:** [§1240] A party may object to the admission of deposition testimony on any ground that would be available if the witness were testifying in person. This is true even if the objection was not raised at the time the deposition was taken, except as to matters of form. [Fed. R. Civ. P. 32(b), (d)]

3. **Interrogatories:** [§1241] Interrogatories are written questions from one party to another party requiring written responses. [Fed. R. Civ. P. 33(a); Cal. Civ. Proc. Code §2030]

   a. **Compare—depositions:** [§1242] Be sure to distinguish interrogatories from depositions.

   (1) ***Depositions*** can be taken from a party ***or*** nonparty witness, while interrogatories may be addressed ***only to a party*** to the action.

   (2) ***Deposition*** questions may be oral or written, but the answers are ***always*** given ***orally*** before a court reporter or similar official who transcribes what is said. In contrast, answers to written interrogatories are prepared in ***writing***, usually by counsel for the answering party.

   (3) ***A deponent*** may limit her answers to matters of which she has ***personal knowledge***. Interrogatories require the party to answer not only of her own knowledge, but ***also*** on the basis of information to which she has reasonable access.

   b. **Who must answer**

   (1) **Any other party:** [§1243] A nonparty witness is not subject to interrogatories.

   (2) **Co-parties:** [§1244] Co-parties generally are obliged to respond to interrogatories (although a few states adhere to an older rule that interrogatories may be served only upon an "adverse" party).

   (3) **Corporate parties:** [§1245] Interrogatories served on a corporation may be answered by any officer or agent designated by the corporation. [Fed. R. Civ. P. 33(a)]

   c. **When served**

   (1) **Federal practice:** [§1246] In federal practice, interrogatories, like other formal discovery, may be served only after the Rule 26(f) conference on a discovery plan. [Fed. R. Civ. P. 26(d)]

(2) **State practice:** [§1247] Some state rules require the plaintiff to delay service of interrogatories for a fixed period following service of the complaint. [*See, e.g.,* Cal. Civ. Proc. Code §2030(b)—10 days]

d. **Numerical limit:** [§1248] In federal practice since 1993, interrogatories have been limited to 25, including subparts. [Fed. R. Civ. P. 33(a)] This limitation applies to each *party*, so that co-parties (such as co-plaintiffs) may *each* use 25 interrogatories even though represented by the same lawyer. The limit may be varied by stipulation or court order. Some states have similar numerical limitations. [*See, e.g.,* Cal. Civ. Proc. Code §2030(c)—35 interrogatories]

e. **Duty to respond**

(1) **Time for response:** [§1249] A party must answer or object to interrogatories within 30 days after their date of service. [Fed. R. Civ. P. 33(b)(3); Cal. Civ. Proc. Code §2030(h)]

(2) **Duty to investigate:** [§1250] A party to whom interrogatories are propounded must give all information responsive to the questions that is under her control. This generally includes all information that might be discovered in her own files or by further questioning of her agents or employees.

(3) **Option where extensive search required:** [§1251] If an answer can be supplied only by extensive search of the answering party's records and the burden of ascertaining the information is substantially the same for the inquiring and responding parties, it is sufficient to specify the pertinent records and allow the inquiring party to examine and copy them. [Fed. R. Civ. P. 33(d); *and see* Cal. Civ. Proc. Code §2030(f)(2)]

f. **Failure to make adequate response to interrogatories**

(1) **Motion to compel response:** [§1252] If an answer to interrogatories is incomplete or evasive, the court on proper motion will order the responding party to answer fully. [Fed. R. Civ. P. 37(a); Cal. Civ. Proc. Code §2030(1)] Defiance of such an order will subject the answering party to sanctions. [Fed. R. Civ. P. 37(b)(2)]

(2) **Time for motion:** [§1253] In federal proceedings, a motion to compel an answer may be made at any time. Under state rules, the motion may have to be made promptly after receipt of the unsatisfactory answer or the matter will be deemed waived. [*See, e.g.,* Cal. Civ. Proc. Code §2030(1)—45 days after response served]

(3) **Objections to interrogatories:** [§1254] A motion to compel an answer to an interrogatory will be denied if the question propounded is subject to a valid objection timely made.

(4) **Costs of proceedings:** [§1255] A party moving to compel an answer without substantial justification therefor, or a party making an objection that lacks substantiality, is subject to an award to the adversary of costs, including attorneys' fees incurred in the discovery dispute. [Fed. R. Civ. P. 37 (a)(2)]

4. **Requests for Admission**

   a. **Device to eliminate issues:** [§1256] A request for an admission imposes a duty on the party served to acknowledge the existence of facts that are not in doubt and that should not be necessary to prove at trial. [Fed. R. Civ. P. 36(a); Cal. Civ. Proc. Code §2033]

   b. **On whom served:** [§1257] A request for admission may be served by any party on any other *party*, whether or not adverse. [Fed. R. Civ. P. 36(a)]

   c. **Subject of request**

      (1) **Facts or application of law to fact:** [§1258] A request may ask the party served to admit the *genuineness* of a document, the truth of factual allegations, or the applicability of legal concepts to specified facts in issue.

      (2) **Conclusions of law:** [§1259] It is permissible to request that a party make an admission about the circumstances underlying the case that includes a legal conclusion; *e.g.*, that a person was acting as an agent, or that the speed limit at a point of impact was 50 miles per hour.

         (a) **Compare:** It is *not* proper to request an admission to an abstract statement of law (*e.g.*, that speeding constitutes negligence). [Fed. R. Civ. P. 36(a)]

      (3) **Ultimate issues:** [§1260] Under the Federal Rules, a party may be requested to admit an ultimate fact—*i.e.*, one that controls the outcome of the controversy (such as causation). [Fed. R. Civ. P. 36(a)] Not all states adhere to this rule, however.

      (4) **Opinions:** [§1261] A party may also be requested to make an admission in regard to a matter of opinion (such as the value of property or the extent of damages). A request is not improper merely because the matter to be admitted is in controversy or in doubt.

      (5) **Matters unknown to responding party:** [§1262] A party may also be requested to admit a fact that is outside his knowledge.

   d. **Time limits**

      (1) **For serving requests:** [§1263] Under the Federal Rules, a request to admit may be served at any time after the Rule 26(f) conference. [Fed. R. Civ. P. 26(d), 36(a)] In some states, leave of court is required if the plaintiff wishes to serve requests within 10 days after service of process. [Cal. Civ. Proc. Code §2033(b)]

      (2) **For responses:** [§1264] The party upon whom a request is served must file a response within 30 days. [Fed. R. Civ. P. 36(a); Cal. Civ. Proc. Code §2033(h)]

e. Appropriate responses

(1) **Admit:** [§1265] The responding party may choose to make the requested admission; and if he does so, he will not be permitted to controvert the admission at trial. But the admission is binding only in the present action; it may not be used against the party in any other proceeding. [Fed. R. Civ. P. 36(b)]

(2) **Deny:** [§1266] If the responding party chooses to deny the matter that he is asked to admit, and the matter is subsequently proved, the party may be liable for the full costs of proving that matter, unless the court finds that there were "good reasons" for the denial or that the admissions sought were of "no substantial importance." [Fed. R. Civ. P. 37(c)(2); Cal. Civ. Proc. Code §2033(o)]

  (a) **Impact:** [§1267] The matter of an award of costs is generally within the court's *discretion*. The court's power to impose sanctions is *not* affected by which party ultimately wins the lawsuit. Even the winner may end up having to pay sanctions to the loser if the winner was guilty of a "bad faith" refusal to admit (necessitating extra expenses of proof by the loser). [Smith v. Circle P Ranch Co., 87 Cal. App. 3d 267 (1978)]

  (b) **Equivocal denial:** [§1268] An equivocal denial may be treated as an admission or, on motion, the court may order a proper response. Alternatively, the court might treat an equivocal denial as a "false denial" (above) and award the full costs of proof to the requesting party.

(3) **Reasons for not admitting or denying:** [§1269] If the responding party has good reasons for objecting to the request, she may neither admit nor deny, but instead must state her refusal and the grounds therefor. However, there are few valid objections to be made.

  (a) **Nature of matter sought to be admitted:** [§1270] That the matter is one of opinion, or an ultimate issue, or a conclusion of law is *not* an adequate reason for refusing to admit or deny.

  (b) **Ignorance of matter sought to be admitted:** [§1271] However, it is sufficient for a refusal to admit that the responding party is ignorant of the matter in question, *provided she has made reasonable inquiry* and still found the information unavailable.

  (c) **Self-incrimination:** [§1272] A party can refuse to answer on the ground that her response may tend to incriminate herself.

  (d) **Consequences of giving insufficient reasons:** [§1273] The party seeking the admission may move to determine the sufficiency of any objections to his request. If the reasons are insufficient, the court may order a proper response and may impose other sanctions on the party making the inadequate response. Even if no such motion is made, the party making the request may prove the matter, in which event the court can order the objecting party to pay the full costs of proof.

  (4) **Failure to respond:** [§1274] If there is no timely response to a request, the matter is deemed *admitted*. [Fed. R. Civ. P. 36; Cal. Civ. Proc. Code §2033]

 f. **Withdrawal of admissions:** [§1275] When presentation of the merits will be served thereby, the court may allow a party to amend or withdraw an admission previously made. [Fed. R. Civ. P. 36(b); Cal. Civ. Proc. Code §2033(m)]

5. **Requests for Inspection of Documents and Other Things**

 a. **Materials discoverable:** [§1276] A party is entitled to inspect and copy a variety of items in the possession of any other party, including documents, photographs, maps, records (however kept), and correspondence.

  (1) **Computerized information:** [§1277] Included among the things that are properly subject to inspection is information stored on computers. [Fed. R. Civ. P. 34(a)—"data compilations from which information can be obtained"] To assist in this, discovery about the computer system of a party is usually permitted [Fautek v. Mongomery Ward & Co., 96 F.R.D. 141 (N.D. Ill. 1982)], and a party may be required to supply data in computer-readable form [National Union Electric Corp. v. Matsushita Electric Industrial Co., 494 F. Supp. 1257 (E.D. Pa. 1980)].

 b. **Scope of examination:** [§1278] Examination may include testing and sampling of materials, and may involve an entry onto the property of a party.

 c. **Making request for inspection**

  (1) **No court action required:** [§1279] The party seeking discovery may serve a request for inspection without prior court order or a showing of good cause.

   (a) **Inspection of premises:** [§1280] When *inspection of premises* is sought, a general showing of "relevancy" may not be enough. Since entry upon one's premises may entail greater burdens and risks than mere production of documents or other physical evidence, some degree of *necessity* is generally required for such inspection. [Belcher v. Bassett Furniture, 588 F.2d 904 (4th Cir. 1978)]

  (2) **Timing:** [§1281] Under the Federal Rules, a request for inspection may be served at any time after the Rule 26(f) conference. [Fed. R. Civ. P. 26(d), 34] Some state rules require leave of court where the request is served concurrently with the initial pleadings. [*See, e.g.,* Cal. Civ. Proc. Code §2031(b)—leave of court required if request served by plaintiff within 10 days after service of summons]

 d. **Designation of items:** [§1282] The moving party must describe the items to be produced with sufficient certainty to enable a person of ordinary intelligence to know which items are sought. Other forms of discovery are sometimes needed to identify the real evidence to be inspected.

- (1) **Designation by category:** [§1283] Often a party will request all materials that fall within a category (*e.g.,* "all documents that relate or refer to the meeting on January 1, 1994") rather than specifying individual items. This is done because the party requesting production cannot know for certain what materials the responding party possesses and wishes to avoid omitting valuable information.

- (2) **Relation to initial disclosures:** [§1284] The initial disclosures pursuant to Rule 26(a)(1)(B) (*see supra,* §1191) may enable the requesting party to be more specific in the document request.

e. **Timing of inspection:** [§1285] The request for inspection must specify the proposed time, place, and manner of making the inspection. [Fed. R. Civ. P. 34(b); Cal. Civ. Proc. Code §2031(c)]

f. **Objection to requests**

- (1) **Timing:** [§1286] In federal actions, the party receiving a request for inspection may file written objections within 30 days following service of the request. [Fed. R. Civ. P. 34(b); *compare* Cal. Civ. Proc. Code §2031(h)— 20 days]

- (2) **Motion with respect to objections:** [§1287] If objections are made, the requesting party may move for an order compelling the requested inspection; and the merits of the objections will then be determined by the court.

g. **Items in responding party's control:** [§1288] The responding party is to produce all requested items (unless objections are interposed) that are within its possession, custody, or control. Some courts hold that the "control" idea requires the responding party to make efforts to obtain documents from others if it has "influence" over the possessor. [*See, e.g.,* Cooper Industries, Inc. v. British Aerospace, Inc., 102 F.R.D. 918 (S.D.N.Y. 1984)]

h. **Organization of produced materials:** [§1289] In federal court and in some state courts, the responding party is required to produce the requested materials either as they are kept in the ordinary course of business or organized and labeled to correspond to the requests. [Fed. R. Civ. P. 34(b); Cal. Civ. Proc. Code §2031(f)(1)]

- (1) **Stimulus for requirement:** This requirement has been added because of concern that responding parties were "hiding" embarrassing materials among mounds of uninteresting materials. *Example:* Defendant's lawyer places the inculpatory memorandum among thousands of invoices instead of leaving it in the memorandum file where it is normally kept.

    - (a) **Ethical requirements:** Such conduct is probably a violation of a lawyer's ethical responsibilities, even if permitted by the discovery rules. (*See* Legal Ethics Summary.)

(2) **Course of business format usually employed:** Most responding parties will produce records in the way they are kept in the normal course of business. They do this because it is usually difficult to determine exactly which request is the pertinent one for given materials, and several requests may apply to a given item. Therefore, not only would reorganizing the files be a great deal of difficult work, it would often assist the opposing party.

i. **Failure to respond:** [§1290] Failure to respond to a request for inspection exposes the nonresponding party to sanctions, including the striking of portions of pleadings and a determination of facts on the assumption that inspection would have provided the requesting party with persuasive evidence.

j. **Materials in possession of nonparties**

(1) **Subpoena for inspection:** [§1291] Under federal practice, a subpoena can order a nonparty to permit inspection and copying of documents in its control, or to permit inspection of premises. [Fed. R. Civ. P. 45(a)(1)(C)] Some states have similar provisions. [*See, e.g.,* N.Y. Civ. Prac. Law §3120]

(a) **Compare:** Other states require a *showing of good cause* in an affidavit (usually a showing of *relevance* to the claims or defenses raised in the action) as a condition to issuance of a subpoena. [Cal. Civ. Proc. Code §1985(b)]

(2) **Independent action:** [§1292] Alternatively, real evidence not otherwise discoverable may be examined through an adequate suit in equity for discovery in aid of the original action.

6. **Medical Examinations**

a. **Court action required:** [§1293] Where the physical or mental condition of a party is in issue, in *federal court* a motion is necessary to require a party to submit to examination by experts in the service of other parties.

(1) **Compare—state practice:** In some states, prior court action is not required for the defendant to obtain a physical examination of the plaintiff in a personal injury suit. [Cal. Civ. Proc. Code §2032(b)]

b. **Condition must be in issue:** [§1294] The condition that is the subject of the examination must be raised directly by the pleadings or by the factual contentions of the parties through discovery; and the court-ordered examination must be limited to such conditions. [Schlagenhauf v. Holder, 379 U.S. 104 (1964)]

c. **Good cause:** [§1295] Where court action is required, an examination will not be ordered except upon a showing of good cause. [Fed. R. Civ. P. 35; Cal. Civ. Proc. §2032(d)] In this context, "good cause" means that the examination sought must be shown to be reasonably likely to produce information about the condition in issue.

d. **Only parties subject to examination:** [§1296] Court rules generally provide for the examination only of parties or persons in the custody or control of parties. [Fed. R. Civ. P. 35(a)] Some states also provide for the examination of agents of parties. [*See, e.g.,* Cal. Civ. Proc. Code §2032(a)(2)]

e. **Qualifications of examiner:** [§1297] Until recently, court-ordered examinations were done only by medical doctors. In federal court, however, examinations may be ordered by any *"suitably licensed or certified examiner."* [Fed. R. Civ. P. 35(a); *and see* Cal. Civ. Proc. Code §2032(b)—"licensed physician or other appropriate licensed health care professional"]

   (1) **Selected by party:** Ordinarily the courts will order examination by the examiner selected by the party wanting the examination, but where reasonable objection is made to the moving party's selection, the court has the power to appoint an "impartial examiner" of its own choosing.

f. **Place of examination:** [§1298] The examination ordinarily will be ordered at the place selected by the examining party; but the court can have the examination conducted elsewhere to diminish the burden on the examinee.

g. **Examination procedures:** [§1299] If the information sought to be obtained is important, the court may permit an examination procedure that is novel or even painful, as long as it is reasonably safe. The examinee has been held entitled to the presence of counsel at a physical examination, but *not* at a psychiatric examination. [*Compare* Sharff v. Superior Court, 44 Cal. 2d 508 (1955); Edwards v. Superior Court, 16 Cal. 3d 905 (1976)]

h. **Copies of reports**

   (1) **Examinee's right to receive copy:** [§1300] The examinee, upon request, has the right to receive a copy of the examiner's report. [Fed. R. Civ. P. 35(b); Cal. Civ. Proc. Code §2032(h)]

   (2) **Waiver of privilege:** [§1301] However, an examinee who requests a copy of the report *waives* the doctor-patient privilege with respect to any previous examinations of the same condition by his own physician [Fed. R. Civ. P. 35(b); Cal. Civ. Proc. Code §2032(i)]; any reports of such other examinations must be provided on request to the examining party. Note that the doctor-patient privilege is waived in any case by a personal injury plaintiff in regard to medical examinations of the injury for which recovery is sought.

7. **Duty to Supplement Responses:** [§1302] Until 1993, a responding party in federal court who had provided such requested information as it possessed usually had no duty to supply additional information thereafter acquired. But in 1993, the Federal Rules were amended to broaden the duty to supplement.

   a. **Federal practice—broad duty to supplement:** [§1303] Rule 26(e) requires supplementation of prior responses if *in some material respect* Rule 26(a) disclosures or discovery responses are *incomplete or incorrect* or if there is *additional or corrective information* that has been acquired since the response was made.

      (1) **Inapplicable if information otherwise made known:** [§1304] The obligation to supplement is satisfied if the additional or corrective information

has otherwise been made known during the discovery process or if it is supplied in writing.

(2) **Application to deposition testimony:** [§1305] The supplementation requirement ordinarily *does not apply to deposition answers*, but it *is* applicable to *testimony of an expert witness*.

b. **State practice compared:** [§1306] Some states have supplementation requirements similar to those in the Federal Rules, but many do not; in such states, cautious practitioners must attempt to obtain the same information by sending out *supplemental interrogatories* before the trial. Still other states use different procedures for the same purpose.

(1) **Pretrial conference orders:** [§1307] Where a pretrial conference is held, the court (on a showing of good cause) may require either side to update its responses to earlier interrogatories, particularly in connection with disclosing expert witnesses who will be called to testify at trial. A party failing to disclose an expert at this point may be barred from using that person as a witness at trial (except on such terms as the court finds appropriate). [Sanders v. Superior Court, 34 Cal. App. 3d 270 (1973); Crumpton v. Dickstein, 82 Cal. App. 3d 166 (1978)]

(2) **Demand to exchange lists of expert witnesses:** [§1308] California has a separate procedure whereby, at the time a case is set for trial, either side may serve the other with a demand to exchange information on the identity, qualifications, and expected testimony of expert witnesses. Failure to disclose such information bars the use of such experts at trial, except for purposes of impeachment or on such terms as the court may order. [Cal. Civ. Proc. Code §2034]

C. SCOPE OF DISCOVERY

1. **Relation of Discovery to Proof:** [§1309] Generally, discovery may inquire into all information not otherwise privileged that is *relevant* to the subject matter of the action, whether or not the material would be admissible as proof. It is sufficient if the information sought appears reasonably calculated to lead to the discovery of admissible evidence. [Fed. R. Civ. P. 26(b); Cal. Civ. Proc. Code §2017(a)] However, a few jurisdictions retain the old equity practice, under which discovery is limited to *admissible* evidence needed by the discovering party to bear his burden of proof.

    a. **Changing attitudes toward broad discovery:** [§1310] Starting in the 1970s, courts have become increasingly uneasy with broad discovery. As a result, open-ended invitations to use repetitive discovery contained in the Federal Rules have been eliminated, and development of a discovery plan [Fed. R. Civ. P. 26(f)], along with judicial orders regulating discovery [Fed. R. Civ. P. 16(b); *see infra*, §§1578-1580] have been used to control overbroad discovery.

    b. **Judicial limitation of discovery:** [§1311] In federal court, the court *must* limit discovery if it finds one of the following circumstances to exist [Fed. R. Civ. P. 26(b)(2)]:

(1) **Discovery unreasonably cumulative:** [§1312] If the discovery is unreasonably cumulative or duplicative, or if it is obtainable from some other source that is more convenient, less burdensome, or less expensive, the court may limit or forbid the discovery.

(2) **Party has already had opportunity for discovery:** [§1313] If the party seeking discovery has already had ample opportunity in the action to obtain discovery of the information sought, the court may limit or forbid the discovery.

(3) **Discovery unduly burdensome:** [§1314] If the discovery is unduly burdensome or expensive in view of the needs of the case, the amount in controversy, the limitations on the parties' resources, and the importance of the issues at stake in litigation, the court may limit or forbid the discovery. *Criticism:* This authority appears to permit the judge to truncate discovery in cases she does not think are "important." This is probably not what the drafters of the rule's changes had in mind.

2. **Scope of Relevant Material**

    a. **Meaning of relevance:** [§1315] Relevance describes the probative effect of a piece of information on the determination whether a given proposition is true. In federal court, "relevant evidence means evidence having any tendency to make the existence of any fact that is of consequence to the determination of the action more probable or less probable than it would be without the evidence." [Fed. R. Evid. 401; for more detail, *see* Evidence Summary]

    (1) **Fact of consequence:** [§1316] The concept of a "fact of consequence" includes all matters that are pertinent to the decision of the case. This would include all issues raised by the pleadings.

    (2) **Low threshold for relevance:** [§1317] The federal standard creates a very low threshold for relevance.

    (3) **Common sense determination:** [§1318] The determination of whether evidence is relevant depends on a common sense examination of the probative impact of the information in question on the issue it is said to bear upon.

    (4) **Compare—substantial evidence:** [§1319] A party with the burden of proof on an issue has the obligation on that issue to produce substantial evidence to justify submitting the issue to the trier of fact. (*See infra*, §1734, regarding burden to produce evidence.) The fact that such a party has some relevant evidence on the issue does not mean that she has satisfied the burden of production. Put differently, evidence may be relevant, but by itself insufficient to support a jury verdict on a given issue.

    b. **Relation to subject matter of the action:** [§1320] The requirement that the information sought be relevant to the "subject matter" of the action is interpreted broadly to facilitate discovery. Discovery may relate to the claims or defenses of either party and is not limited to information that the discovering party needs to satisfy his own burden of proof.

(1) **Comment:** This enables each party to evaluate his adversary's case as well as his own. This in turn may lead to earlier and more realistic settlement efforts—which is one of the main purposes of discovery.

c. **Matters not in dispute:** [§1321] Information may be subject to discovery even though it bears on issues that are not in dispute. Again, the test is relevancy to the subject matter rather than admissibility at trial. [Fed. R. Civ. P. 26(b)]

d. **Information about witnesses:** [§1322] The identity and location of witnesses are discoverable facts. Likewise, information bearing on the *credibility* of witnesses (*e.g.,* possible grounds for impeachment) may be discovered.

e. **Insurance coverage:** [§1323] Although not admissible as evidence, the existence and scope of insurance coverage is now discoverable in most jurisdictions. [Fed. R. Civ. P. 26(a)(1)(D); Laddon v. Superior Court, 167 Cal. App. 2d 391 (1959)] *Rationale:* Settlement negotiations are an essential part of the action, and insurance coverage is relevant at least to this aspect of the "subject matter."

f. **Financial status:** [§1324] Financial condition is generally not relevant even though the information might affect settlement negotiations.

(1) **Defendant's financial status:** [§1325] A general inquiry into the financial ability of the defendant to satisfy a judgment is usually not permitted. However, the defendant's financial condition may be pertinent in some cases, as where punitive damages are sought; and in such cases, the defendant may be required to disclose her financial condition.

(2) **Plaintiff's financial status:** [§1326] Where the plaintiff's loss of earnings is in question, he may be compelled to produce copies of his financial records, including federal income tax returns.

(3) **Bank records:** [§1327] Where pertinent, bank records may be subject to subpoena although the bank may be under a duty to notify its customer before complying, in order to give the customer an opportunity to resist disclosure. [Valley Bank v. Superior Court, 15 Cal. 3d 652 (1975)]

g. **Contentions:** [§1328] A party may be asked to particularize his contentions as to the facts (or the application of law to facts) for the purpose of narrowing the issues at trial. However, answers to such questions may be delayed by court order until pretrial, when the party can be expected to know with some precision what his contentions are.

3. **Privilege:** [§1329] Privileged material is universally excluded from obligatory disclosure through discovery. Most civil procedure courses do not examine any privilege in detail, except the *attorney-client privilege*, which will be the main focus here. It is the oldest and most frequently invoked privilege.

a. **Rationale:** The traditional rationale for the attorney-client privilege has been labeled the "*utilitarian rationale.*" It justifies the privilege on the ground that it is necessary to *promote full and frank disclosure* to the lawyer by the client. Unfortunately, there is little evidence that the existence of the privilege is necessary, or perhaps even important, to achieve that objective. Accordingly, some authorities have recently argued that the privilege is necessary to *personal autonomy* of persons faced with legal proceedings, because it ensures that there is at least one knowledgeable person from whom they can seek help with the assurance that this person will not become a witness for the other side.

b. **Requirements:** [§1330]   The widely cited definition of the requirements for application of the attorney-client privilege comes from Dean John Wigmore [8 Wigmore on Evidence §2292]:

(1) **Legal advice sought:** [§1331]   The privilege applies only to communications in which legal advice is sought. Thus, where the client is seeking *business advice*, no protection exists.

(2) **From lawyer:** [§1332]   The privilege applies only to communications seeking legal advice from a professional legal adviser acting in that capacity. In most jurisdictions, it applies whenever the client reasonably believes that the person from whom he seeks advice is a lawyer, even if the belief turns out to be wrong.

(3) **Communications relating to legal advice:** [§1333]   The privilege applies only to communications relating to obtaining legal advice; communications on entirely different subjects are not protected.

(4) **Made in confidence:** [§1334]   The privilege applies only to communications made in confidence. In general, this means that the parties must behave as though they intend the communication to be confidential.

   (a) **Presence of other people:** [§1335]   The presence of other people during the communication may indicate that the communication is *not confidential*, unless the presence of these people is *necessary* to the communication. Thus, the lawyer's secretary might be present to assist the lawyer. Similarly, a friend or close relative might properly be present if the client is unusually young or old or otherwise in need of moral support or guidance.

   (b) **Eavesdroppers:** [§1336]   Where the communication is overheard by an eavesdropper, the privilege usually is held not to preclude testimony by that eavesdropper, even if reasonable precautions were taken to protect confidentiality. Where electronic surveillance is used, however, most courts will forbid use of the fruits of that sort of eavesdropping.

(5) **By client:** [§1337]   The traditional formulation of the privilege was that the privilege protected only information communicated to the lawyer by the client. There was no need to protect the information communicated to the client by the lawyer, it was thought, except to the extent that it revealed the content of communications to the lawyer by the client.

   (a) **Criticism:** It was often difficult to distinguish communications by the lawyer that revealed client communications from others, and this limitation threatened to intrude into the relationship between the lawyer and the client.

- (b) **Modern view:** [§1338] The modern view is increasingly that *communications by the lawyer to the client* are protected also. [*See, e.g.,* Upjohn Co. v. United States, 449 U.S. 383 (1981)—privilege exists to protect "the giving of professional advice"]

- (c) **Corporate client:** *See infra,* §§1349-1355, for discussion of the problem of the corporate client.

- (d) **Compare—communication by lawyer with others:** [§1339] Where the lawyer communicates with persons other than the client, such as witnesses, the privilege does not apply. [Hickman v. Taylor, 329 U.S. 495 (1947)—interviews with witnesses]

c. **Permanently protected at client's request**

- (1) **Need to invoke:** [§1340] The privilege is not self-executing and applies only when invoked. Usually, however, the *lawyer is under a duty to invoke the privilege* on behalf of the client.

- (2) **Absolute protection:** [§1341] The protection is absolute, in the sense that it cannot be outweighed by other considerations, such as the social interest in full disclosure of relevant evidence in the case.

- (3) **Applies to disclosure by client or lawyer:** [§1342] Once invoked, the privilege precludes disclosure by the lawyer and the client (including employees of the client covered by the privilege; *see infra,* §1351, regarding corporate clients). Thus the privilege can preclude disclosure by a person who is willing to reveal privileged information.

d. **Waiver:** [§1343] Just as the client must invoke the privilege, so can the client waive it.

- (1) **Breadth of waiver:** [§1344] In general, waiver of the privilege applies to *all communications* with counsel on the subject matter regarding which the waiver has occurred. *Rationale:* If the waiver did not apply to all related communications, the client could "pick and choose" the favorable pieces of information for revelation while keeping secret unfavorable pieces of information that are necessary to make the picture whole.

- (2) **No need for intentional waiver:** [§1345] The act that constitutes a waiver need not be intentional, and in litigation unintentional disclosure of privileged material often works a waiver of the privilege.

- (3) **Application in other litigation:** [§1346] Once the privilege is waived, it cannot be revived for other litigation.

e. **Federal vs. state law**

- (1) **Federal claim or defense:** [§1347] In *federal court* the privileges available are to be determined by "principles of common law as they may be interpreted by the courts of the United States." [Fed. R. Evid. 501] Thus, the federal courts may alter the rules governing federal privilege law.

(2) **State law claim or defense:** [§1348]   In *federal court*, when state law supplies the rule of decision with respect to an element of a claim or defense, however, privilege issues are to be determined in accordance with state law. [Fed. R. Evid. 501]

f. **Corporate clients**

(1) **Privilege applicable:** [§1349]   The Supreme Court early held that the attorney-client privilege applied to corporate clients. This did not answer the question, however, of who was the client.

(2) **Control group test:** [§1350]   Many courts limited the privilege to communications between the lawyer and those persons who could be considered the "control group" of the corporation, *i.e.*, the persons who controlled the corporation and who could act on the lawyer's advice. *Criticism:* Often the members of the control group did not have the information the lawyer needed to evaluate the corporation's legal problems, and the lawyer would then be subjected to a "Hobson's choice" about whether to inquire of other employees of the corporation.

(3) *Upjohn* **test:** [§1351]   In *Upjohn Co. v. United States* (*supra*, §1338), the Supreme Court rejected the control group test as a matter of federal common law of evidence. (*See supra,* §1347.) Instead, the Court adopted a test that can extend the privilege to any employee. Although the contours of the test are unclear, it turns basically on the following factors:

(a) **Matters within scope of employment:** [§1352]   The protection extends only to communication about matters within the scope of the employee's job with the corporation.

(b) **Information not available from higher management:** [§1353] The protection is justified for "non-control group" employees when higher management cannot itself supply the information.

(c) **Other requirements satisfied:** [§1354]   In the course of its opinion, the Court emphasized the importance of other requirements of the privilege. Thus, the employee must know that the communication is designed to *obtain legal advice for the corporation* and that it is to be *held in confidence*.

(d) **Criticism:** This new formulation appears to overextend the privilege in that it provides no safeguards for the employee who makes full disclosure to the corporation's lawyer. The *corporation can waive the privilege and disclose* the employee's confidences without the permission of the employee. Thus, the employee runs a risk in disclosing to the lawyer against which the privilege provides no protection.

(4) **State law:** [§1355] At least some states have refused to follow the Supreme Court's expansion of privilege protection for corporate clients. Illinois, for example, has continued to adhere to the control group test. [*See* Consolidation Coal Co. v. Bucyrus-Erie Co., 432 N.E.2d 250 (Ill. 1982)]

g. **Other communicational privileges:** [§1356] Other privileges protect other communications from disclosure. For more information on these, *see* the Evidence Summary.

(1) **Spousal communications:** [§1357] Confidential communications between husband and wife during the marriage are privileged at the request of either spouse. [Cal. Evid. Code §980]

(a) **Compare—testimony against spouse:** [§1358] A husband or wife also has the privilege not to testify against the other spouse on any subject. [Cal. Evid. Code §§970-972; Trammel v. United States, 445 U.S. 40 (1980)] Note that no similar privilege is extended to other relatives, such as parents and children of a litigant.

(2) **Doctor/patient:** [§1359] A patient usually has a limited right to prevent disclosure of information she disclosed to her doctor in connection with medical treatment. [Cal. Evid. Code §§990-1007]

(a) **Easily waived:** [§1360] This privilege is easily waived, and is usually held waived by a plaintiff who sues for personal injuries and thereby puts her medical condition "in issue." [Cal. Evid. Code §996]

(3) **Priest/penitent:** [§1361] A priest is privileged to refuse to disclose information revealed by a penitent. [Cal. Evid. Code §§1030-1034]

(4) **Compare—tenure review materials:** [§1362] The Supreme Court has held that universities have no privilege against disclosure of confidential tenure review materials. [University of Pennsylvania v. EEOC, 493 U.S. 182 (1990)]

h. **Specificity of privilege claim:** [§1363] When a party withholds information from discovery on grounds of privilege, it should describe the materials withheld with sufficient specificity *to enable other parties to assess the applicability of the privilege*. [Fed. R. Civ. P. 26(b)(5)]

4. **Trial Preparation Materials**

a. **"Work product"—*Hickman v. Taylor* rule**

(1) **Qualified privilege:** [§1364] Materials prepared and information developed by or under the direction of a party or her attorney in anticipation of litigation are subject to discovery *only if* the discovering party can show a substantial need and an inability to obtain equivalent material by other means. [Hickman v. Taylor, *supra,* §1339; Fed. R. Civ. P. 26(b)(3); Cal. Civ. Proc. Code §2018]

(2) **Purpose:** [§1365] This qualified privilege is designed to maintain the adversary process by enabling each party to prepare her own case, with free rein to develop her own theory of the case and her own trial strategy; but this purpose must be reconciled with the overriding need to require full disclosure of the facts.

(3) **Matters protected:** [§1366] The focus of this protection is on the process of preparing for litigation. Thus, it is very broad; the Federal Rule [Fed. R. Civ. P. 26(b)(3)] covers any materials prepared *"in anticipation of litigation or for trial."*

    (a) **Possibility of litigation foreseen:** [§1367] If there is absolutely no foreseeable possibility of litigation at the time the materials are prepared, then the protection cannot apply.

    (b) **Regular reports:** [§1368] When a party makes regular reports of incidents that often lead to litigation (*e.g.,* accidents), it may be held that such reports are not prepared in anticipation of litigation, since they can be used for other purposes and are prepared in situations in which litigation is not foreseen. [*See, e.g.,* Rakus v. Erie-Lackawanna Railroad, 76 F.R.D. 145 (W.D.N.Y. 1977)—employees' accident reports to claims department are discoverable]

(4) **Showing to justify disclosure:** [§1369] To obtain production of material that is protected as work product, a party must make a showing of substantial need and undue hardship.

    (a) **Substantial need:** [§1370] The party must show that the material sought is of substantial importance to its case; courts usually do not treat minimal relevance as sufficient.

    (b) **Inability to obtain:** [§1371] The party must also show that it is unable to obtain the *substantial equivalent* without undue hardship.

(5) **Special protection for mental impressions of attorney:** [§1372] Where a showing has been made to justify disclosure, materials containing the mental impressions of an attorney are given special protection.

    (a) **Example:** A memorandum prepared by an attorney may include her observations at the scene of the accident, which would be ordinary work product. The memo could also include the attorney's theories about possible grounds of liability and promising avenues of investigation, as well as her assessments of the persuasiveness of various possible witnesses. All this material, except her observations at the scene, would be considered *opinion work product*.

    (b) **Protection under Federal Rules:** [§1373] Federal Rule 26(b)(3) says that in ordering discovery of work product, the court "shall" protect against disclosure of the mental impressions and legal theories of an attorney. This has been held to provide absolute protection to such items. [Duplan Corp. v. Moulinage et Retorderie de

Chavanoz, 509 F.2d 730 (4th Cir. 1974), *cert. denied,* 420 U.S. 997 (1975)] The Supreme Court, however, has declined to take this step: "we are not prepared at this juncture to say that such material is always protected by the work-product rule." [Upjohn Co. v. United States, *supra,* §1338] And several lower courts have denied absolute protection. [*See, e.g.,* Holmgren v. State Farm Mutual Automobile Insurance Co., 976 F.2d 573 (9th Cir. 1992)—lawyer's mental impressions a pivotal issue and need for their disclosure compelling]

    (c) **State law:** [§1374]   Under the law of some states, protection for such materials is absolute. [*See, e.g.,* Cal. Civ. Proc. Code §2018(c)—"Any writing that reflects an attorney's impressions, conclusions, opinions, or legal research or theories shall not be discoverable under any circumstances"]

    (d) **Method—redaction:** [§1375]   Where materials containing opinion work product are ordered produced, the portions containing the opinion work product may be "redacted" by covering them over in the copying process so they cannot be read.

(6) **Rule 26(b)(3) and *Hickman* contrasted:** [§1376]   In federal court, the protections of Rule 26(b)(3) and *Hickman* both continue to apply, although usually they overlap. There are significant differences, however:

    (a) **Trial preparation by nonlawyers:** [§1377]   *Hickman* protects only the work of lawyers. It applies to their assistants, and perhaps to experts hired by them or others acting at their direction. Rule 26(b)(3) is broader; it also includes trial preparation by the party's "consultant, surety, indemnitor, insurer, or agent."

    (b) **Tangible materials:** [§1378]   Rule 26(b)(3) is more limited than *Hickman,* however, in protecting only "documents and tangible things." It therefore has no application, for example, to a deposition of the attorney inquiring into her trial strategies, etc. *Hickman* would apply in such a situation, however, since it is not limited to tangible items.

(7) **Protection after litigation terminated:** [§1379]   It is not entirely clear whether work product protection endures after termination of the litigation for which the material was prepared. The Supreme Court has held in a case involving the Freedom of Information Act that the protection continues. [FTC v. Grolier, Inc., 462 U.S. 19 (1983)] It has also been held that the protection can apply in a case that was not anticipated at the time the material was prepared, as long as it was prepared in anticipation of some litigation. [Duplan Corp. v. Moulinage et Retorderie de Chavanoz, *supra,* §1373]

(8) **Compare—attorney-client privilege:** [§1380]   The work product rule must be distinguished from the absolute privilege afforded confidential communications from client to counsel.

(9) **Witness statements:** [§1381]   Because witness statements illustrate the application of work product and the attorney-client privilege, it is worthwhile to examine them in detail. Some statements of witnesses to lawyers

may be subject to the attorney-client privilege, while other communications made to lawyers or investigators may be treated as work product and thus be subject to disclosure only on a showing of substantial need.

(a) **Statements made by party to own attorney:** [§1382] If the statements were made in confidence regarding past events, the communications are privileged under the attorney-client privilege.

    1) **Attorney's employees:** [§1383] The privilege may also apply to statements made to an investigator *employed* by the party's counsel. [Brakhage v. Graff, 206 N.W.2d 45 (Neb. 1973)]

    2) **Caveat:** [§1384] Note, however, that a party cannot put documents beyond reach of discovery by turning them over to counsel. Nor can a party relieve himself of the obligation to disclose by making disclosure to his own lawyer. All that is protected is the content of the communication from client to lawyer.

(b) **Statements by employees of corporation:** [§1385] The attorney-client privilege applies to communications made in confidence by employees of a corporation, including nonsupervisory employees in many jurisdictions. (*See supra,* §1351-1354.)

    1) **Confidential reports:** [§1386] The attorney-client privilege may also apply to routine reports that are intended to be *confidential* records of the corporation, prepared for the corporation's attorney; *e.g.,* accident reports prepared by a truck driver according to company policy that such reports be submitted immediately following any accident for confidential use of the corporation's lawyers. [D.I. Chadbourne, Inc. v. Superior Court, 60 Cal. 2d 723 (1964)]

    2) **Other reports:** [§1387] Other reports of employees to corporate counsel are not covered by the attorney-client privilege, but may be subject to the qualified work product privilege *if* they were made or prepared in anticipation of litigation. [Xerox v. IBM, 64 F.R.D. 367 (1974)] However, remember that regular reports may be found to not meet the "in anticipation" requirement. (*See supra,* §1368.)

(c) **Statements of nonparty witnesses:** [§1388] Statements obtained from nonparty witnesses are usually held to be work product of the attorney, so they are not subject to discovery by an adversary unless he is not reasonably able to obtain a similar statement from the witness by his own effort.

    1) **Note:** Under federal practice, the witness himself is entitled to a copy of his statement *as a matter of right*. [Fed. R. Civ. P. 26(b)(3)]

    2) **Not covered by attorney-client privilege:** Witness interviews are not covered by the attorney-client privilege. [Hickman v. Taylor, *supra,* §1339]

(d) **Statements made by party to adversary counsel:** [§1389] Usually, no privilege (absolute or qualified) protects statements of a party made to adversary counsel. Such statements are subject to discovery without a showing of need—*i.e.,* a party-witness is entitled to a copy of statements given to adversary counsel as a matter of right. [Fed. R. Civ. P. 26(b)(3)]

b. **Expert reports:** [§1390] Lawyers are increasingly dependent on retained experts to help them prepare for trials and to testify at trials. Often the subject matter of a litigation is unfamiliar to the lawyer, and the lawyer therefore needs the assistance of a person schooled in the field to prepare adequately for trial. At trial, the technical subject matter of the litigation may make it essential that an expert testify to support the party's case. (For more detail on the rules governing the presentation of expert testimony at trial, *see* the Evidence Summary.)

(1) **Nontestifying experts**

(a) **Role:** [§1391] Where the lawyer needs the help of an expert to prepare for trial, he will often retain one to advise him on trial strategy and help develop legal and factual theories for the case. The expert can also help the lawyer prepare to cross-examine the opponent's expert.

(b) **Discoverability of facts known and opinions held:** [§1392] Under Federal Rule 26(b)(4)(B), facts known to and opinions held by nontestifying experts are discoverable only in exceptional circumstances, *e.g.,* when one party has monopolized the qualified experts. *Rationale:* Allowing discovery would give the party seeking it a *free ride* where it could hire its own expert.

1) **Reimbursement for fees:** [§1393] Where discovery is ordered, the court is to require the discovering party to reimburse the party who retained the expert for a fair portion of the fees and expenses paid for the facts and opinions developed by the expert. [Fed. R. Civ. P. 26(b)(4)(C)]

(c) **Nontestifying expert as witness for opponent:** [§1394] Experts can differ in their opinions, and when a lawyer hires an expert she will not always know the expert's opinion of her client's case. What happens if the expert develops an opinion unfavorable to the client? The opposing side will likely want to hire the expert because the circumstances tend to make her opinion very believable. At least one court has held that the opposing party may not do so in the absence of extraordinary circumstances; *i.e.,* Rule 26(b)(4)(B) (*supra,* §1392) must be satisfied [Durflinger v. Artiles, 727 F.2d 888 (10th Cir. 1984)], but other courts might not adopt this rule. The rationale is that if such use of the nontestifying expert's opinions were allowed, lawyers might be deterred from consulting experts whose opinions are unknown.

(d) **Discovery of identity of nontestifying expert:** [§1395] The courts are split on whether the identity of the nontestifying expert can be discovered. [*Compare* Ager v. Jane C. Stormmont Hospital, 622 F.2d 496 (10th Cir. 1980)—discovery not permitted because it subverts protective purposes of the rule—*with* Baki v. B.F. Diamond Construction Co., 71 F.R.D. 179 (D. Md. 1976)—discovery allowed because it does not involve disclosure of facts known or opinions held by expert]

 (e) **Informally consulted experts:** [§1396] The protections of Rule 26(b)(4)(B) apply only to experts who are "retained or specially employed" by a party. The treatment of informally consulted experts is ***unclear.***

(2) **Testifying experts:** [§1397] Since 1993, the Federal Rules have expanded discovery regarding testifying experts and imposed a requirement to provide a written report that applies to most such experts.

 (a) **Required disclosure:** [§1398] Without a formal discovery request, each party must identify each person that party will call to offer expert testimony at trial. [Fed. R. Civ. P. 26(a)(2)(A)]

 (b) **Timing of disclosure:** [§1399] In the absence of other direction from the court, this disclosure must be made at least ***90 days before trial.*** [Fed. R. Civ. P. 26(a)(2)(C)] It is anticipated, however, that the court will often stagger the disclosures and that the party with the burden of proof will often be required to disclose first.

  1) **Rebuttal:** [§1400] Within 30 days after the disclosure by an opposing party, a party may add another expert intended to offer testimony solely to rebut or contradict expert evidence identified by the opposing party.

 (c) **Required report by expert witness:** [§1401] In addition to identifying its expert witnesses, a party must ordinarily provide a detailed report from the expert. [Fed. R. Civ. P. 26(a)(2)(B)]

  1) **Experts covered:** [§1402] A report must be prepared for any specially retained expert and for any employee of a party whose duties regularly include giving expert testimony.

  2) **Signed by expert:** [§1403] The report is to be signed by the witness, although it is contemplated that counsel will assist in drafting the report.

  3) **Statement of expert's opinions:** [§1404] The report is to include a ***complete statement*** of all opinions the expert will express in testimony, along with the ***basis*** therefor and the ***data or other information*** on which they are based. This should make all materials provided the expert, including privileged materials, subject to mandatory disclosure.

  4) **Exhibits:** [§1405] Disclosure should also include all exhibits that will be used in connection with the testimony.

5) **Expert's qualifications:** [§1406] The report must include the witness's qualifications, including *all publications during the preceding 10 years* and a list of *all cases in which the expert testified during the preceding four years*.

6) **Expert's compensation:** [§1407] The report should include the compensation the expert will be paid.

7) **Supplementation:** [§1408] The report should be supplemented with new information that is developed after it is submitted. [Fed. R. Civ. P. 26(e)(1)]

(d) **Deposition of right:** [§1409] Any party has a right to take the deposition of a testifying expert. [Fed. R. Civ. P. 26(b)(4)(A)] Where a report is required, however, this deposition shall not take place until *after the report is provided*.

1) **Supplementation of expert's testimony:** [§1410] Although supplementation is not required with other deposition testimony, a party has a duty to supplement the deposition testimony of its expert witness. [Fed. R. Civ. P. 26(e)(1)]

2) **Compensation of expert for responding to discovery:** [§1411] The party taking the deposition must compensate the expert for the time spent on the deposition. *Compare:* There is no requirement to compensate the expert for the time spent on the report.

(e) **State practice compared:** [§1412] States often have similar statutory procedures for pretrial identification of expert witnesses, including provisions for pretrial depositions. [*See, e.g.,* Cal. Civ. Proc. Code §§2034(f), 2034(i)]

(3) **Unaffiliated experts:** [§1413] Rule 26(b)(4) makes no provision for a person who has expertise that may be pertinent to a lawsuit, but who has not consented to assist any party in connection with the case. On occasion, litigants subpoena such persons to compel them to testify. It has been held that they may sometimes be compelled to give such testimony, albeit perhaps only on being paid a fee for it. [*See, e.g.,* Wright v. Jeep Corp., 547 F.2d 871 (E.D. Mich. 1982)—professor who prepared report on Jeep rollover problems compelled to testify]

(a) **Rationale:** Experts should be treated like other witnesses who have information that is pertinent to the resolution of a lawsuit.

(b) **Criticism:** Society pays a price if such experts are required to spend substantial time attending depositions or trials, and they may not be adequately compensated for being required to reveal their expertise.

(c) **Protection against subpoenas:** [§1414] Rule 45 provides that if a subpoena "requires disclosure of an unretained expert's opinion or information not describing specific events or occurrences in dispute and resulting from the expert's study made not at the request of any party," the court may quash or modify the subpoena. Alternatively, "if the party in whose behalf the subpoena is issued shows a substantial need for the testimony or material that cannot be otherwise met without undue hardship and assures that the person to whom the subpoena is addressed will be reasonably compensated, the court may order appearance or production only upon specified conditions." [Fed. R. Civ. P. 45(c)(3)(B)]

(d) **Compare—expert as fact witness:** [§1415] Whether or not experts should be protected against being compelled to testify regarding matters within their expertise, they are not immune to the civic duty to testify regarding the facts of the case. Thus, if a Nobel Prize winner witnesses an accident, she must testify about what she saw just like any other witness.

D. PROTECTIVE ORDERS

1. **Introduction:** [§1416] Protective orders are designed to *prevent undue burdens* that might otherwise be imposed by discovery. The availability of protective orders recognizes both that discovery can be extremely intrusive and that parties may seek to abuse it. Both concerns can be ameliorated through protective provisions.

2. **Requirement of Good Cause:** [§1417] A protective order should be granted only on a showing of good cause by the party seeking protection. [Fed. R. Civ. P. 26(c)] Appropriate grounds include the following.

   a. **Confidential information:** [§1418] A protective order may be entered to protect "trade secret or other confidential research, development, or commercial information." [Fed. R. Civ. P. 26(c)(7)]

      (1) **Showing required**

         (a) **Confidentiality:** [§1419] Such protection is available only for information that is in fact confidential. To justify an order, the party must show that the information has been held in confidence.

         (b) **Specific harm from disclosure:** [§1420] There must also be a showing that a specific harm is likely to flow from disclosure of the information.

         (c) **Not limited to technical information:** [§1421] The protection is not limited to technical trade secret information, but may extend to wide varieties of commercial data whose disclosure could give commercial advantage to competitors. It has therefore been applied to *customer lists* [Chesa International, Ltd. v. Fashion Associates, Inc., 425 F. Supp. 234 (S.D.N.Y. 1977)], *profit and gross income data* [Corbett v. Free Press Association, 50 F.R.D. 179 (D. Vt. 1970)], and *terms of a contract* [Essex Wire Corp. v. Eastern Electric Sales Co., 48 F.R.D. 308 (E.D. Pa. 1969)].

         (d) **Privacy interests:** [§1422] Related arguments can be made to justify the protection of privacy interests of litigants because Rule

26(c)(7) allows protection against annoyance or embarrassment. [*See, e.g.,* Galella v. Onassis, *supra,* §1182—Jacqueline Onassis protected against being photographed by plaintiff during her deposition]

(2) **Stipulated orders:** [§1423] Despite the showing requirement, confidentiality orders are often entered into on stipulation. In such situations, there are *no findings* regarding either confidentiality or the risk of harm to any person.

(3) **Format—"umbrella" orders:** [§1424] Protective orders to protect confidentiality can take a number of forms. One would be to forbid discovery altogether. More often, however, the information is validly sought for trial preparation and the court places *limitations on use and dissemination* of the confidential information. Because these orders often are self-executing and apply throughout the discovery process, they are referred to as "umbrella" orders.

   (a) **Designation of confidential information:** [§1425] Usually, any person producing information is allowed to designate it as confidential and, therefore, subject to the protection of the order. Often this is done by stamping documents "Confidential."

   1) **No judicial scrutiny:** [§1426] Note that there is no judicial involvement in the designation process, which is left entirely to the parties.

   (b) **Effect of designation:** [§1427] Usually, all designated documents are to be *held in confidence* by the other parties, *used only for trial preparation*, and *disclosed only to specified persons*, usually including the client and witnesses.

   (c) **Challenges to designation:** [§1428] Any party may move the court to set aside a confidentiality designation on the ground that the material is not in fact confidential.

   1) **Burden on producing party:** [§1429] At this point, the burden is on the producing party to establish that the material is indeed entitled to protection under Rule 26(c).

   2) **Exception—blanket challenges:** [§1430] In some cases where large volumes of material have been designated confidential, however, the court may impose on the challenging party the duty to specify which confidentiality designations are challenged and why. [*See, e.g.,* Zenith Radio Corp. v. Matsushita Electric Industrial Co., 529 F. Supp. 866 (E.D. Pa. 1981)—through discovery plaintiff sought to unseal hundreds of thousands of documents designated confidential]

(4) **Public access:** [§1431] The public may have an interest in materials covered by confidentiality orders. Were the material to be offered in evidence at trial, there would be a constitutional and common law right of

public access to court trial that would enable the public to have access to the information. Before trial, there are two possible arguments:

(a) **Discovery presumptively public:** [§1432] Some courts say that discovery is presumptively public unless closed, and that orders limiting access to the public need special justification. This argument appears not to apply to material covered by proper protective orders, and the Supreme Court has stated that *there is no tradition of public access to discovery.* [Seattle Times Co. v. Rhinehart, 467 U.S. 20 (1984)]

(b) **Material involved in pretrial rulings:** [§1433] Where materials covered by a confidentiality order are involved in pretrial rulings by the court, however, the public access argument is stronger because the constitutional and common law rights are designed to allow the public meaningful access to observe judicial decision-making. The application of this concept is not always easy:

1) **Access allowed—decision on merits of case:** [§1434] When pretrial rulings resolve the merits, access to discovery materials relied on should be granted. [*See, e.g.,* Cianci v. New Times Publishing Co., 88 F.R.D. 562 (S.D.N.Y. 1980)—summary judgment granted]

2) **Access denied—decision that privileged materials should not be produced:** [§1435] When a discovery motion presents the question of whether materials sought are privileged, and, based on an in camera review of the materials, the court decides that they should not be produced, public access should not be allowed because it would undermine the privilege.

3) **Intermediate situations:** [§1436] Cases that involve neither the resolution of the merits nor non-merits decisions that would be undermined by disclosure present problems. Courts tend to deem *all materials considered in connection with a motion* to be subject to *presumptive public access.* [*See, e.g.,* Zenith Radio Corp. v. Matsushita Electric Industrial Co., *supra*, §1430—public right of access to all materials offered in good faith in connection with summary judgment motion]

(5) **Sharing with other litigants:** [§1437] An issue of growing importance is the possibility that materials covered by a confidentiality order could be shared with other litigants in similar cases. This would tend to *reduce discovery expense* for other litigants, which would be a legitimate objective. [United States v. Hooker Chemical Co., 90 F.R.D. 421 (W.D.N.Y. 1981)] Courts often allow such sharing.

(6) **First Amendment limitations on protective orders:** [§1438] Protective orders can limit expression by forbidding litigants to disclose information gained through discovery.

(a) **Prior restraint analysis:** [§1439] Some courts held that such orders could be justified under the First Amendment only where a prior restraint would be warranted, a very demanding standard. [*See, e.g., In* *re* Halkin, 598 F.2d 176 (D.C. Cir. 1979)] (For more on the prior restraint doctrine, *see* Constitutional Law Summary.)

- (b) **Supreme Court ruling:** [§1440]   The Supreme Court *rejected the prior restraint analysis* and held that a protective order supported by good cause is valid under the First Amendment. [Seattle Times Co. v. Rhinehart, *supra,* §1432]

- (c) **Continuing concern about First Amendment:** [§1441]   There is disagreement in the lower courts about whether courts should continue to consider First Amendment values in deciding whether to issue or modify protective orders. [*Compare* Cipollone v. Liggett Group, Inc., 785 F.2d 1108 (3d Cir. 1986)—First Amendment irrelevant—*with* Anderson v. Cryovac, Inc., 805 F.2d 1 (1st Cir. 1986)—First Amendment still a "presence" in protective order decisions]

b. **Inconvenient place of examination:** [§1442]   Where a deposition has been scheduled at a place that is unnecessarily inconvenient for the deponent or adversary, a protective order may issue.

(1) **Federal practice:** [§1443]   Under the Federal Rules, protective orders are the only method available for controlling the place at which the deposition of a *party* can be scheduled, since the adverse party can notice his deposition to be taken anywhere. (*Compare:* A *nonparty* witness cannot be required to appear except by subpoena, and the range of a subpoena is limited; *see supra,* §1213.)

- (a) **Nonresident defendants:** [§1444]   On applications for protective orders as to the place of deposition, courts are inclined to hold that a nonresident defendant should be deposed at his residence rather than at the place where the suit is pending.

    1) **But note:** A contrary result may be reached if the plaintiff is willing to pay the defendant's expenses to travel to the forum, or if it is shown that the defendant will be in the forum anyway.

- (b) **Nonresident plaintiff:** [§1445]   The courts appear more inclined to require a nonresident plaintiff to appear locally for his deposition, since he chose to file his action in the local forum.

(2) **State practice compared:** [§1446]   Instead of requiring a nonresident deponent to obtain a protective order, state rules frequently put the burden on the party seeking the deposition to obtain a prior court order if he wishes to compel the other party to give her deposition beyond the range of a subpoena. [Cal. Civ. Proc. Code §2025(e)]

c. **Unreasonable conduct of deposition:** [§1447]   If a deposition is conducted in a manner that is unduly annoying, embarrassing, or oppressive to a witness or party, a protective order may issue. When the court terminates a deposition for this reason, it may not be resumed or rescheduled except by court order. [Fed. R. Civ. P. 30(d)(3); Cal. Civ. Proc. Code §2025(n)]

d. **Unduly burdensome discovery:** [§1448] When discovery is unduly expensive, unnecessarily burdensome, or otherwise clearly excessive in relation to the importance of the case, a protective order may be sought to limit discovery. (*See supra*, §§1311-1314, regarding judicial limitation of discovery.)

3. **Relation Between Protective Orders and Other Discovery Orders**

   a. **Effect of prior orders:** [§1449] Protective orders are rarely appropriate in regard to discovery conducted pursuant to a prior court order. The circumstances and limitations to be imposed on a medical examination, for example, are generally determined at the time the examination is ordered. Consequently, absent some new information or a change of circumstances, there is no occasion to reconsider the initial order.

   b. **No waiver:** [§1450] A party or witness who does not seek a protective order in advance of a deposition or before the response date for interrogatories, does not thereby waive her right to make objections. She remains free to object to questioning at deposition and she may refuse answers to interrogatories, thereby forcing the discovering party to invoke the power of the court to compel answers to those questions which the court deems proper. [Fed. R. Civ. P. 37(a)]

E. **FAILURE TO DISCLOSE OR TO COMPLY WITH DISCOVERY**

   1. **Order Compelling Response—Necessary Prerequisite:** [§1451] Before discovery sanctions can be imposed, a party seeking discovery must usually obtain an order compelling discovery. [Fed. R. Civ. P. 37(a)]

      a. **Evasive or incomplete answer:** [§1452] When a motion to compel discovery is made, an evasive or incomplete answer is treated as a failure to answer. [Fed. R. Civ. P. 37(a)(3)] This means that the responding party can be ordered to provide a proper answer.

      b. **Exception—complete failure to respond:** [§1453] Where a party completely fails to file a response to a discovery request or to attend his properly noticed deposition, discovery sanctions can be sought immediately, without the need for a prior order compelling discovery. [Fed. R. Civ. P. 37(d)]

      c. **Exception—failure to make required disclosures:** [§1454] If a party fails to make disclosures required by Rule 26(a), or to supplement them as required by Rule 26(e)(1), the court should usually *exclude undisclosed materials from evidence*, and it may also *impose Rule 37(b) sanctions*, which are usually reserved for failures to comply with discovery orders. [Fed. R. Civ. P. 37(c)(1)]

         (1) **Grounds for declining to sanction nondisclosure:** [§1455] The court should not impose sanctions on a party who has *substantial justification* for its failure to disclose, or when the failure to disclose was *harmless*.

      d. **Need to meet and confer before motion:** [§1456] Before filing a motion to compel discovery, a party must attempt to meet and confer with the opposing party in an effort to secure compliance without court action. [Fed. R. Civ. P. 37(a)(2)(A), (d)]

2. **Sanctions for Failure to Comply with Order:** [§1457] Where sanctions are authorized because of disobedience of an order compelling discovery, the court has a variety of options available. [Fed. R. Civ. P. 37(b)(2)] Many of them affect the merits of the case and may therefore be called *merits sanctions*.

   a. **Order establishing facts:** [§1458] The court may order that matters pertinent to the discovery be taken as established in the favor of the party seeking discovery. [Fed. R. Civ. P. 37(b)(2)(A)]

   b. **Order disallowing claims or defenses:** [§1459] The court may deny the offending party the right to present claims or defenses raised by the pleadings, or exclude certain matters from evidence.

      (1) **Example:** When plaintiff failed to provide adequate answers to interrogatories regarding damages, the court precluded plaintiff from introducing evidence of damages, leaving it with only a claim for injunctive relief. [Cine Forty-Second Street Theatre Corp. v. Allied Artists, 602 F.2d 1062 (2d Cir. 1979)]

   c. **Dismissal or default:** [§1460] The court can use the "*litigation death penalty*" and dismiss or default the offending party, rendering judgment in favor of the party seeking discovery.

   d. **Contempt:** [§1461] The court may also impose contempt sanctions on the offending party. (*See infra,* §§1475-1478, regarding contempt.)

   e. **Discretion to select proper sanction:** [§1462] The trial court has substantial discretion to select the proper sanction. There are some guidelines in the area:

      (1) **Least severe sanction:** [§1463] Many courts hold that the least severe sanction that will undo the harm of the violation should be used. [Titus v. Mercedes Benz of North America, 695 F.2d 746 (3d Cir. 1982)]

      (2) **General deterrence:** [§1464] The Supreme Court, however, has stated that *general deterrence* can justify sanctions more severe than would be necessary to deter the offending party from future discovery misconduct. [National Hockey League v. Metropolitan Hockey Club, Inc., 427 U.S. 639 (1976); *and see* Brockton Savings Bank v. Peat, Marwick, Mitchell & Co., 771 F.2d 5 (lst Cir. 1985)— no requirement that lesser sanction first be considered]

3. **Culpability Necessary for Sanctions**

   a. **Due process requirements:** [§1465] There are due process limitations on the power of a court to impose sanctions that affect the merits.

      (1) **No merits sanctions for misconduct unrelated to merits:** [§1466] A party has a constitutional right to have her case decided on the merits, whether or not she obeys every directive of the court. Hence, it is a violation of due process for the court to enter judgment against a party merely for disobeying an order. [Hovey v. Elliott, 167 U.S. 409 (1897)] *Note:* Where the misconduct taints the merits, that is sufficient to justify

a sanction order that redresses the effects of the misconduct. Thus, the failure to comply with discovery usually will support an inference that the violator's case lacks merit and justify a merits sanction. [Hammond Packing Co. v. Arkansas, 212 U.S. 322 (1909)]

    (2) **Ability to comply:** [§1467] Even when the failure to comply relates to the merits of the case, it would violate due process to enter judgment against a party for failing to do something that he was unable to do. [Societe Internationale v. Rogers, 357 U.S. 197 (1958)]

  b. **Willfulness, bad faith, or other fault:** [§1468] The ordinary formulation looks to whether the party to be sanctioned was guilty of willfulness, bad faith, or other fault in connection with the failure to comply with the court's order. The broadest ground is "other fault," and it is unclear whether it would extend to simple negligence. [*See* Cine Forty-Second Street Theatre Corp. v. Allied Artists, *supra,* §1459—gross negligence sanctionable]

  c. **Punishing client for lawyer's misconduct:** [§1469] Often it will not be clear that the client (who is directly affected by merits sanctions) was responsible for misconduct by the lawyer.

    (1) **Lawyer as agent of client:** [§1470] The Supreme Court has said that the lawyer is the agent of the client, and that the client is therefore responsible for the conduct of the lawyer. [Link v. Wabash Railroad, 370 U.S. 626 (1962)]

    (2) **Need to show client involvement:** [§1471] Most lower courts, however, insist on some showing of client involvement before imposing harsh sanctions on the client. [*See, e.g.,* Cine Forty-Second Street Theatre Corp. v. Allied Artists, *supra*—plaintiff's principal officer "intimately involved" in litigation; Shea v. Donohoe Construction Co., 529 F.2d 1071 (3d Cir. 1986)—trial court to provide direct warning about risk of dismissal to parties before imposing ultimate sanction]

4. **Taxation of Costs of Discovery Proceedings**

  a. **Motion to compel discovery:** [§1472] Unless the court finds that the losing party on a discovery motion was substantially justified in taking the position it did, the court is to require it to pay the other side the cost of making or defending against the motion to compel. [Fed. R. Civ. P. 37(a)(4)]

  b. **Failure to obey order compelling discovery:** [§1473] The party who fails to comply with a discovery order may, in addition to other sanctions, be required to pay the moving party the cost of seeking sanctions. [Fed. R. Civ. P. 37(b)]

  c. **For failure to attend deposition:** [§1474] Federal Rule 30(g) authorizes the imposition of costs for a party's failure to attend a deposition that *he* scheduled.

5. **Contempt Power**

  a. **Defiance of prior court order:** [§1475] Failure to comply with a party-initiated discovery notice (*e.g.,* failure to answer an interrogatory to a party) is not in itself a basis for contempt. Contempt is an appropriate sanction only where the party or witness refuses to make disclosure in defiance of a *prior court order*.

    (1) **Example:** A deponent who fails to submit to a deposition after having been *ordered* to do so, or who does not comply with a subpoena, may be held in contempt of court. [Fed. R. Civ. P. 37(b)(1), 45(e)]

  b. **Civil contempt:** [§1476] The contempt sanction may be civil, and thus coercive in effect (*i.e.,* the witness may "purge" himself of the contempt at any time by providing the information sought). [International Business Machines Corp. v. United States, 493 F.2d 112 (2d Cir. 1975)]

  c. **Criminal contempt:** [§1477] In a flagrant case, it may also be proper to impose punishment on a contumacious witness, even if he is now willing to submit. [*See* Gompers v. Bucks Stove & Range Co., 221 U.S. 418 (1911)]

  d. **Limitation—no contempt to compel medical examination:** [§1478] In deference to the personal rights of parties, the contempt power may not be used to compel medical examination. [Fed. R. Civ. P. 37(b)(2)(D)]

6. **Compare—Sanctions for Improper Certification:** [§1479] Federal Rule 26(g) makes the signature of an attorney on a discovery paper a certificate with respect to the following matters, and directs that if a paper is signed in violation of this requirement the court shall impose a sanction on the person signing the paper and/or the party on whose behalf it was submitted.

  a. **Supported by law:** [§1480] The signature certifies that the request or response is consistent with the Federal Rules and warranted by existing law or a good faith argument for the extension, modification, or reversal of existing law.

  b. **Proper purpose:** [§1481] The signature also certifies that the request or response was not interposed for any improper purpose, such as to harass or to cause unnecessary delay or needless increase in the cost of litigation.

  c. **Reasonable:** [§1482] Finally, the signature certifies that the request or response is not unreasonable or unduly burdensome or expensive, given the needs of the case, the discovery already had in the case, the amount in controversy, and the importance of the issues at stake in the litigation.

F. APPELLATE REVIEW OF DISCOVERY ORDERS

1. **Orders Usually Not Appealable**

  a. **Discovery orders not final:** [§1483] Orders concerning discovery are not final judgments, and hence are not appealable in most jurisdictions.

    (1) **Not collateral:** [§1484] Nor are discovery orders regarded as "collateral" to the main action, within the principle that treats collateral dispositions as final for purposes of allowing immediate appeal. [International Business Machines Corp. v. United States, 480 F.2d 293 (2d Cir. 1973)]

b. **Not injunctions:** [§1485] Likewise, discovery orders are not injunctions within the meaning of statutes authorizing appeals from orders granting or denying injunctions. [28 U.S.C. §1292(a); International Products Corp. v. Koons, 325 F.2d 403 (2d Cir. 1963)]

c. **Appealable in some states:** [§1486] In some states, discovery orders *are* appealable orders—*i.e.,* in those states, no "final decision" requirement is imposed as a condition of appellate jurisdiction. [*See* Boser v. Uniroyal, 39 App. Div. 2d 632 (1972)]

2. **Modes of Review**

    a. **Certified appeal (federal practice):** [§1487] Where the discovery motion raises an important question about the controlling discovery rule, the trial court may *certify* the question to the appellate court if appropriate certification legislation has been enacted in the jurisdiction. [*See, e.g.,* American Express Warehousing Ltd. v. TransAmerica Insurance Co., 380 F.2d 277 (2d Cir. 1967)]

    b. **Mandamus or prohibition (state and federal practice):** [§1488] An extraordinary writ may be issued by an appellate court to correct or prevent an *abuse of discretion* by the trial judge in exercising power over the discovery process. [28 U.S.C. §1651; Schlagenhauf v. Holder, *supra,* §1294; Greyhound Corp. v. Superior Court, 56 Cal. 2d 355 (1961)] Such writs usually are issued only in *extraordinary situations.*

    c. **Review after judgment:** [§1489] The failure of the trial court to compel effective disclosure *may* be the basis for reversal of a judgment. However, the discovery ruling must be shown to have been "prejudicial" (*i.e.,* likely to have affected the *outcome* of the case), or there is little likelihood of reversal. [*See* Burns v. Thiokol Chemical Corp., 483 F.2d 300 (5th Cir. 1973)]

    d. **Sanction as final:** [§1490] Where the discovery sanction takes the form of a final disposition, such as a judgment of dismissal or any entry of judgment by default, that judgment is final and appealable. [Brennan v. Engineered Products, Inc., 506 F.2d 299 (8th Cir. 1974)]

    e. **Review of contempt order:** [§1491] An order of civil contempt is not final and hence is not generally appealable until final judgment is entered. [International Business Machines Corp. v. United States, *supra,* §1476] However, a conviction of criminal contempt is final and appealable. [Union Tool Co. v. Wilson, 259 U.S. 107 (1922)] *Caution:* Sometimes the distinction between civil and criminal contempt is difficult to discern. [*See* United Mine Workers v. Bagwell, 114 S. Ct. 2552 (1994)—for purposes of right to jury trial, contempt order was criminal, although court announced penalty for violation in advance]

G. **USE OF DISCOVERY AT TRIAL**

1. **Statements of Adversary**

    a. **Admissions:** [§1492] A party's admissions (*i.e.,* statements detrimental to his case) in a deposition or in response to an interrogatory are admissible just like any other admission. Such admissions are not conclusive, however, as they may be shown to have been inadvertent. [Fed. R. Civ. P. 32(a); Cal. Civ. Proc. Code §2025(u)]

(1) **Compare:** An admission in a response to a request for admission under Federal Rule 36 is conclusive proof of the facts admitted. [Fed. R. Civ. P. 36(b); *see supra,* §§1256-1275]

b. **Right to object:** [§1493] The party whose statement is being used may object at trial on the basis of its irrelevance or impropriety and is not barred by her failure to interpose objections at the time of discovery. [Fed. R. Civ. P. 32(b), (d)]

2. **Statements of Other Witnesses**

a. **Prior inconsistent statement:** [§1494] Depositions may be admitted at trial for impeachment—*i.e.,* to prove a prior inconsistent statement of a witness who testifies at trial. [Fed. R. Civ. P. 32(a)(1); Cal. Civ. Proc. Code §2025(u)(1)]

b. **Unavailability:** [§1495] In addition, depositions may be admitted to prove the facts testified to at the deposition if the deponent is "unavailable" at trial (*e.g.,* witness out of state, too ill to testify, deceased, etc.). [Fed. R. Civ. P. 32(a)(3); Cal. Civ. Proc. Code §2025(u)(3)]

c. **Party's own deposition:** [§1496] A party may use her own deposition in lieu of personal testimony if she is "unavailable" for trial (*see* above), ***provided*** that she has not procured her own absence (*i.e.,* leaving the jurisdiction to avoid being called as a witness by the adversary). [Fed. R. Civ. P. 32(d)(3); *see supra,* §1239]

H. PRIVATE INVESTIGATION

1. **Formal Discovery Not Obligatory:** [§1497] Civil litigants are entitled to conduct their own private investigation of the facts and are not obliged to use the discovery process to secure information. [IBM v. Edelstein, *supra,* §1206]

a. **Exception—contact with opposing party:** [§1498] However, ethical rules forbid a lawyer from contacting an opposing party known to be represented by counsel without the permission of that party's attorney.

2. **Admissibility of Proof Privately Obtained:** [§1499] Private parties are not subject to the Fourth Amendment limitations on searches or exclusionary rules intended to enforce such constitutional restraints. Thus, at least in the absence of egregious wrongdoing, civil litigants may use material as proof even if it was obtained by tortious means. [Sackler v. Sackler, 15 N.Y.2d 40 (1964)]

VII. SUMMARY JUDGMENT

chapter approach

Summary judgment is a pretrial device that permits the court to look outside of the pleadings to determine whether there is an issue of fact to be tried. In law school examinations, summary judgment issues are sometimes raised in connection with disputes about discovery that may bear on the issues raised by the summary judgment motion. When presented with a motion for summary judgment, ask yourself the following questions:

1. *Has the moving party made a sufficient initial showing*? If the moving party would have the burden of proof on the issue at trial, he must initially produce enough evidence to show that no reasonable jury could find for his opponent. If the moving party would not have the burden of proof, he still must make an initial showing of his opponent's lack of proof. If the initial showing is insufficient, the opposing party need not submit any opposing proof, and the motion should be denied.

2. *Was the opposing party given notice and an opportunity to respond*? If the initial showing was sufficient, summary judgment would still be improper unless the opposing party was given notice of the motion and an *opportunity to respond*. Note that the circumstances sometimes justify delay in the decision in order to give the opposing party an opportunity to gather evidence, especially where the motion is made early in the case or before there has been substantial discovery

3. *Is there a triable issue*? Assuming the moving party's initial burden was met and the nonmoving party was given an opportunity to respond, the court must look at the evidence in the light most favorable to the nonmoving party to determine whether there is a genuine issue of fact to be tried. If the moving party would have the burden of proof at trial, the motion should be granted only if the evidence is so strong that a reasonable jury could find only for the moving party. If the moving party would not have the burden of proof at trial, the court should grant the motion only if the opposing party fails to come forward with sufficient evidence to support a verdict in his favor.

Also note that summary judgment may be partial (*i.e.,* only as to some issues or some parties). **Denial** of summary judgment is not immediately appealable. **Grant** of summary judgment, however, may be immediately appealable if it results in a final judgment. On review the appellate court has plenary power; it need not give deference to the trial judge's decision.

A. INTRODUCTION

1. **Purpose:** [§1500] Summary judgment is a method for getting beyond the allegations of the pleadings and examining evidentiary material without holding a full-dress trial. If the evidentiary material shows that there is actually no genuine controversy that requires a trial, summary judgment can avoid unnecessary delay and expense in deciding the case.

2. **Pleadings Motions Compared:** [§1501] Summary judgment differs from pleadings motions attacking the sufficiency of a claim or defense in that *summary judgment allows the court to look at evidentiary material*. Recall that pleadings motions

look only at the face of the pleading and test only its legal sufficiency. Usually, it is said that consideration of any material beyond the face of the complaint is forbidden on a pleadings motion, or such consideration may convert the motion into a motion for summary judgment. [*See, e.g.,* Fed. R. Civ. P. 12(b)—on motion to dismiss for failure to state a claim, if materials outside pleadings are presented and not excluded by court, motion is to be treated as one for summary judgment]

    a. **Relevance of pleadings to summary judgment:** [§1502] The pleadings delineate what is in controversy in the case. Thus, if certain allegations have been admitted, those admissions may form part of the basis for summary judgment.

    b. **Reliance on pleadings in response to summary judgment motion:** [§1503] An opposing party may not rely on the allegations in her pleadings to defeat a summary judgment motion. [Fed. R. Civ. P. 56(e)]

3. **Judgment as a Matter of Law Compared:** [§1504] Judgment as a matter of law (*infra,* §§1734-1754) is similar to summary judgment in that it uses essentially the same standard to determine whether there is a triable issue. However, there are some important differences.

    a. **Timing:** [§1505] The summary judgment motion can be, and normally is, decided *before trial*. A defendant may move for summary judgment at any time and a plaintiff may do so 20 days after commencement of the action. [Fed. R. Civ. P. 56(a), (b)] A motion for judgment as a matter of law usually is made at the close of evidence at trial and it may be renewed after a verdict is returned (*see infra,* §§1830-1837).

    b. **Nature of material considered:** [§1506] The summary judgment motion is based essentially on pretrial written submissions, whereas a motion for judgment as a matter of law is based on live testimony from the trial. However, note that summary judgment may be based on live testimony from depositions, which is usually recorded in a deposition transcript.

    c. **Burden of proof—initial showing requirement:** [§1507] Summary judgment also differs from judgment as a matter of law in that on summary judgment the moving party must make an initial showing to justify scrutiny of the evidence, which is not required for the motions at or after trial if the moving party does not have the burden of proof.

        (1) **Opposing party with burden:** [§1508] Where the moving party would not have the burden of proof at trial, to obtain judgment as a matter of law, he could allow the opposing party to put on her case and then point out the insufficiencies of that case. To obtain summary judgment, such a moving party would have to make an *initial showing* of the insufficiency of the evidence of his opponent's case. (*See infra,* §§1530-1544 for discussion of the initial burden.) His opponent would then have the burden of bringing forth sufficient evidence to show that there is a genuine issue for trial.

        (2) **Compare—moving party with burden:** [§1509] Where the moving party has the burden of proof on the issue raised at the summary judgment

stage, making that showing before trial does not represent an additional burden on the party because the party would have to put on such evidence at trial to justify a directed verdict. However, such a party must make a compelling case for entry of summary judgment, because a trial should be held if a reasonable jury could disbelieve the moving party's proof.

    d. **Summary judgment traditionally more difficult to obtain:** [§1510] In many courts, it is said that summary judgment is more difficult to obtain than judgment as a matter of law—*i.e.,* it must be clearer to the court that the case can reasonably be decided only one way. However, it appears that courts are gradually becoming more accepting of summary judgment. (*See infra,* §1512.)

4. **Impact on Right to Trial:** [§1511] The traditional reluctance to grant summary judgment resulted in part from the belief that a litigant has a right to have her claims tested at trial. Nevertheless, there is no right to a trial where there is no genuine dispute about the facts, and the Supreme Court early upheld the validity of summary judgment against arguments that it violated the right to jury trial. [Fidelity & Deposit Co. v. United States, 187 U.S. 135 (1902)]

5. **Trend Favoring Use of Summary Judgment:** [§1512] Recently it has seemed that the courts have become more receptive to deciding cases on summary judgment. The Supreme Court has observed that "[s]ummary judgment is properly regarded not as a disfavored procedural shortcut, but rather as an integral part of the Federal Rules as a whole" and noted that it has an important role: "with the advent of 'notice pleading,' the motion to dismiss seldom fulfills this function [isolating factually insufficient claims or defenses] anymore, and its place must be taken by the motion for summary judgment." [Celotex Corp. v. Catrett, 477 U.S. 317 (1986)]

B. STANDARD FOR GRANT OF SUMMARY JUDGMENT [§1513]

The court is to grant summary judgment when it determines that "there is no genuine issue as to any material fact" [Fed. R. Civ. P. 56(c)], or that there is "no triable issue as to any material fact" [Cal. Civ. Proc. Code §437c(c)].

1. **Relation to Standard for Judgment as a Matter of Law:** [§1514] The United States Supreme Court has stated that in federal court the standard for entry of judgment is the same at the summary judgment stage as at the judgment as a matter of law stage. [Anderson v. Liberty Lobby, Inc., 477 U.S. 242 (1986)] This makes it appropriate to focus on whether the moving party has the burden of proof on the issue raised by the summary judgment motion.

    a. **Moving party with burden of proof:** [§1515] If the party moving for summary judgment has the burden of proof on the issue raised by the motion, summary judgment should be granted only if the evidence favoring the moving party is of such strength that the jury could not reasonably disbelieve the moving party's evidence.

    b. **Opposing party with burden:** [§1516] If the party moving for summary judgment does ***not*** have the burden of proof on the issue raised by the motion, summary judgment should be granted only if the opposing party does not present sufficient evidence to permit a jury reasonably to find for him. Put differently, unless the opposing party comes forward with sufficient evidence to support a verdict in her favor, summary judgment should be entered in favor of the moving party.

2. **Case-by-Case Determination:** [§1517] The court's evaluation process must be made on a case-by-case basis. As with judgment as a matter of law, therefore, it is difficult to generalize "rules" for making summary judgment decisions, but there are a number of general principles that are helpful in approaching problems.

   a. **All reasonable inferences indulged in favor of opposing party:** [§1518] The court is to make all reasonable inferences in favor of the opposing party, and to view the evidence in the light most favorable to that party.

   b. **Court may not "weigh" evidence:** [§1519] The court is to determine whether there is a genuine dispute; it may not choose between two versions of events and grant summary judgment to the party whose version seems more persuasive.

   c. **Role of higher burden of proof:** [§1520] The Supreme Court has held that when a party will bear a heightened burden of proof at trial, the court should use that higher standard in scrutinizing the evidence at the summary judgment stage. [Anderson v. Liberty Lobby, Inc., *supra*, §1514—"clear and convincing" required] *Criticism:* It is difficult to know how the court is to give effect to the higher standard of proof without "weighing" the evidence.

   d. **Witness credibility:** [§1521] Ordinarily, the credibility of witnesses cannot be assessed on summary judgment because that assessment is left to the jury at trial.

      (1) **Uncontradicted interested witness:** [§1522] The testimony of an uncontradicted interested witness is usually said not to be sufficient to support summary judgment in favor of a party with the burden of proof. *Rationale:* Even an uncontradicted witness might be disbelieved if he has an interest in the litigation.

      (2) **Disinterested witness:** [§1523] In some cases, courts suggest that an uncontradicted affidavit of a disinterested witness is sufficient to support summary judgment for a party with the burden of proof. [*See, e.g.,* Lundeen v. Cordner, 354 F.2d 401 (8th Cir. 1966)—affidavit of disinterested witness accepted in absence of a "positive showing that this witness's testimony could be impeached"]

      (3) **Sham affidavit doctrine:** [§1524] When the deposition of a party or an interested witness is used as the basis for a summary judgment motion by the other side, and that witness submits an affidavit in opposition to summary judgment repudiating the deposition testimony, the court may disregard the affidavit. [Perma Research & Development Co. v. Singer Co., 410 F.2d 572 (2d Cir. 1968)—"If a party who has been examined at length on deposition could raise an issue of fact simply by submitting an

affidavit contradicting his own prior testimony, this would greatly diminish the utility of summary judgment as a procedure for screening out sham issues of fact"]

e. **"Disbelief" evidence:** [§1525] Although the jury may ordinarily disbelieve even an uncontradicted witness (*see supra,* §1522), the logical possibility that this disbelief would persuade the jury that the truth is actually the opposite of what the witness claims is *irrelevant* on a motion for summary judgment or a motion for judgment as a matter of law. [*See* Dyer v. MacDougall, 201 F.2d 265 (2d Cir. 1952)] *Rationale:* Allowing such credibility determinations to satisfy the burden of proof at trial would immunize the trial court's ruling on judgment as a matter of law from appellate review since demeanor of witnesses is usually not preserved in the record on appeal, and it would also mean that summary judgment could never be granted against a party with the burden of proof if the moving party relied on a witness.

f. **Motive, intent, and state of mind:** [§1526] When issues of motive, intent, or state of mind are presented, it is said that summary judgment is peculiarly inappropriate. [Cross v. United States, 336 F.2d 431 (2d Cir. 1964)] *Rationale:* Assessments of a person's motive are best made on the basis of observing her demeanor while testifying, and the pertinent facts are peculiarly within her knowledge.

g. **Cross-motions for summary judgment:** [§1527] Where both the plaintiff and the defendant move for summary judgment, it might seem that the court should grant the motion of one or the other, but that is not so. Instead, *the showing made by each party must be evaluated independently*. It would be entirely consistent to deny both motions if neither party made a sufficient showing; that would only mean that an issue of fact remains and a trial is necessary to decide the case.

h. **Complex cases:** [§1528] For a time, a number of cases suggested that in complex cases (particularly antitrust cases) summary judgment was to be avoided. [*See, e.g.,* Poller v. Columbia Broadcasting System, Inc., 368 U.S. 464 (1962)] Recently, however, courts have evinced more willingness to entertain summary judgment in such cases. [*See, e.g.,* Matsushita Electric Industries Co. v. Zenith Radio Corp., 475 U.S. 574 (1986)]

i. **"Slightest doubt" standard contrasted:** [§1529] Under a line of Second Circuit cases, summary judgment was said to be inappropriate whenever there was the "slightest doubt" about the outcome at trial. [*See, e.g.,* Arnstein v. Porter, 154 F.2d 464 (2d Cir. 1946)] However, this approach has been repudiated. [*See, e.g.,* Heyman v. Commerce & Industry Insurance Co., 524 F.2d 1317 (2d Cir. 1975)]

C. PROCEDURE

1. **Initial Showing:** [§1530] Analytically, the court should not reach the question whether there is a genuine dispute until it has evaluated the moving party's showing to determine whether it suffices to justify pretrial scrutiny of the evidence.

   a. **Moving party's burden:** [§1531] The moving party is to demonstrate "that there is no genuine issue as to any material fact and that the moving party is entitled to judgment as a matter of law." [Fed. R. Civ. P. 56(c)]

(1) **Moving party with burden of proof:** [§1532] If the moving party has the burden of proof, he must produce evidence of such strength that *no reasonable jury could find for the opposing party*.

(2) **Moving party without burden of proof:** [§1533] If the moving party does not have the burden of proof, the matter is more complicated.

   (a) **Early view:** [§1534] Relying on a decision of the Supreme Court [Adickes v. S.H. Kress & Co., 398 U.S. 144 (1970)], some lower courts took the position that a moving party without the burden of proof had to make as strong a showing as one with the burden of proof (*supra*) to invoke summary judgment.

   (b) **Current view:** [§1535] *Celotex Corp. v. Catrett* (*supra*, §1512), rejected the early view. However, the exact requirements in this circumstance are unclear, owing to disagreement within the Court on the proper formulation.

   1) **Mere conclusory assertion:** [§1536] It appears that a bald assertion that the opposing party lacks sufficient evidence to support his case is not sufficient. [*See* Celotex Corp. v. Catrett, *supra* (White, J., concurring)—"It is not enough to move for summary judgment . . . with the conclusory assertion that the plaintiff has no evidence to prove his case"] *Rationale:* "Such a 'burden' of production is no burden at all and would simply permit summary judgment procedure to be converted into a tool for harassment." [Celotex Corp. v. Catrett, *supra* (Brennan, J., dissenting)]

   2) **Initial responsibility of informing court of basis for motion:** [§1537] The majority in *Celotex* stated that the moving party has the initial responsibility of informing the court of the basis for its motion; the party must identify those portions of the record which it believes demonstrate the absence of a genuine issue of material fact. However, it is unclear how much more than a conclusory assertion this is designed to require.

   3) **Prima facie showing:** [§1538] Justice Brennan, dissenting in *Celotex*, urged that the moving party should have to "make a prima facie showing that it is entitled to summary judgment."

   (c) **Method of making showing**

   1) **Affirmative evidence:** [§1539] The moving party can offer affirmative evidence that negates an essential element of the opposing party's case.

   2) **Preview of opposing party's case:** [§1540] Where the thrust of the motion is that the opposing party has no evidence, however, the showing should reliably indicate that. Thus, the moving party should be able to point to discovery calculated to elicit from the opposing party any evidence he had to support his case and then demonstrate that this evidence is inadequate.

Such a showing invites the argument that the opposing party needs more time to gather facts. (*See infra,* §1562.)

b. **Opposing party's burden**

(1) **Initial showing not made:** [§1541] Where the moving party has not made the required initial showing, there technically is ***no burden*** on the opposing party to make any showing in response to the motion, which should be denied.

(a) **No advance determination of sufficiency of initial showing:** [§1542] However, the opposing party is not entitled to advance notice of the court's attitude toward the sufficiency of the moving party's showing. Thus, to be prudent, the opposing party should submit opposing evidence unless he is absolutely sure of the insufficiency.

(b) **Attacking showing:** [§1543] The opposing party can call the court's attention to other material in the record that demonstrates the existence of a genuine issue.

1) **Example:** In *Celotex,* plaintiff claimed that her husband died from exposure to asbestos that defendant manufactured. Defendant moved for summary judgment on ground that there was no evidence in the record linking its products to plaintiff's husband's death. On remand, the court held that summary judgment should not be granted because plaintiff was able to point to material in the record that indicated that at trial she would have a witness to support her claim—a letter from an official of a former employer of plaintiff's husband indicating that company records showed that plaintiff's husband had been exposed to defendant's products. [Catrett v. Celotex Corp., 826 F.2d 23 (D.C. Cir. 1987)]

(2) **Initial showing made:** [§1544] Where the moving party has made the initial showing, the burden is on the opposing party to ***come forward with evidentiary material*** that establishes the existence of a triable issue, *i.e., **sufficient evidence to support a jury verdict in his favor**.*

2. **Notice:** [§1545] The opposing party is entitled to notice of the motion for summary judgment and an opportunity to submit opposing materials. [Fed. R. Civ. P. 56(c)—10 days; Cal. Civ. Proc. Code §437c(a)—28 days]

a. **Notice of summary judgment against moving party:** [§1546] The courts are divided on whether summary judgment can be entered against the ***moving*** party without prior notice that this result might occur. [*See* Procter & Gamble Independent Union v. Procter & Gamble Manufacturing Co., 312 F.2d 181 (2d Cir. 1962)—summary judgment against moving party granted by appellate court]

(1) **Compare—cross-motions for summary judgment:** [§1547] This situation is different from a case in which there are cross-motions for

summary judgment. (*See supra,* §1527.) In that situation, each side is on notice that the other side is seeking summary judgment.

- b. **Contrast—notice of need to submit opposing material:** [§1548] The opposing party is *not* entitled to notice of the need to submit opposing material to avoid summary judgment, even where there is a question about the sufficiency of the moving party's initial showing. [Jacobsen v. Filler, 790 F.2d 1362 (9th Cir. 1986)—no duty to notify pro se plaintiff of need to submit opposing material in connection with defendants' motion for summary judgment]

3. **Time for Motion:** [§1549] The earliest moment for filing motions for summary judgment varies, and some effort is made to protect defendants against having to respond to such motions before they have a reasonable time to obtain representation and investigate the case. In federal court, the plaintiff must wait until 20 days after the commencement of the action, while the defendant can move for summary judgment at any time. [Fed. R. Civ. P. 56(a), (b)] In California, by way of contrast, the motion is not allowed until 60 days after the general appearance in the action of each party against whom it is directed. [Cal. Civ. Proc. Code §437c(a)]

4. **Materials Considered on Motion**

    - a. **Pleadings:** [§1550] Admissions contained in the pleadings may be used to decide summary judgment motions, but otherwise the pleadings do not bear on the summary judgment decision except to identify the issues in contention in the lawsuit. [*See* Fed. R. Civ. P. 56(e)—opposing party may not rest on allegations of pleadings in response to motion]

    - b. **Affidavits:** [§1551] Affidavits made on *personal knowledge* of facts, showing that the affiant would be competent to testify to these facts in court, may form the basis of a ruling on a motion for summary judgment. It is probably true that affidavits are the most common materials submitted in support of (or opposition to) motions for summary judgment. However, *the moving party is not required to submit affidavits*. [Celotex Corp. v. Catrett, *supra,* §1535]

    - c. **Discovery materials:** [§1552] Material developed through discovery, whether by interrogatory, document request, deposition, or request for admissions, may be used in connection with a summary judgment motion. Often, affidavits of attorneys are used as vehicles to bring such materials to the attention of the court by "authenticating" true copies of the discovery materials.

    - d. **Oral testimony:** [§1553] Oral testimony may be heard on a motion for summary judgment, but only very rarely, since the objective is to decide the case without holding a trial, and hearing oral testimony might defeat that purpose. Moreover, the need to present matters orally may suggest that a credibility determination is necessary.

    - e. **Admissibility:** [§1554] Materials considered in connection with a motion for summary judgment must generally be capable of admission in evidence. [Fed. R. Civ. P. 56(e); Cal. Civ. Proc. Code §437c(d)]

        - (1) **Possible relaxation for opposing party:** [§1555] Although the moving party must present material that would be admissible, it may be that the opposing party is not held to such requirements, as long as it can show that it will have admissible evidence at trial. For example, after remand in *Celotex Corp. v. Catrett, supra,* a dissenting judge pointed out that the court denied summary judgment based on a letter from an official, even though there was no showing that this official had personal knowledge on the subject or that there was admissible evidence to support the assertions in the letter.

    (a) **Criticism:** Relaxing the requirement that the opposing party present admissible evidence may erode the value of summary judgment in weeding out groundless claims and defenses.

    (b) **Compare—material need not be in admissible form:** [§1556] Affidavits are usually not admissible at trial because they are hearsay, but they clearly suffice to oppose a motion for summary judgment when they indicate that the affiant would be able to testify to the facts recited. Thus, the nonmoving party need not produce evidence in a form that would be admissible at trial in order to avoid summary judgment.

(2) **Determination of admissibility:** [§1557] Before evaluating the evidentiary materials to determine whether summary judgment should be granted, the court can entertain objections to the admissibility of some of the materials and exclude them from consideration if they are not admissible. [*See, e.g., In re* Japanese Products Antitrust Litigation, 723 F.2d 238 (3d Cir. 1983), *rev'd on other grounds sub nom.* Matsushita Electric Industrial Co. v. Zenith Radio Corp., *supra*, §1528—Court commended district court's hearing on evidentiary objections because it would afford fuller consideration of them than would be possible at trial]

(3) **Waiver of evidentiary objections:** [§1558] Evidentiary objections not made in connection with summary judgment proceedings may be waived, at least as to the summary judgment proceedings. [Cal. Civ. Proc. Code §437c(b)]

5. **Partial Summary Judgment:** [§1559] When only some of the claims or defenses are ripe for summary judgment, it can be granted as to some but not all the claims or defenses before the court.

6. **Order Establishing Material Facts:** [§1560] If the summary judgment motion cannot be entirely granted, the court may enter an order determining that certain facts are established, and this order will govern the further course of the action. [Fed. R. Civ. P. 56(d); Cal. Civ. Proc. Code §427c(g)]

    a. **Statement of undisputed facts:** [§1561] In some jurisdictions, the court requires that each party to a summary judgment motion list all facts it claims are undisputed. [*See, e.g.,* Cal. Civ. Proc. Code §437c(b)]

7. **Inability to Provide Responsive Materials:** [§1562] When the opposing party is unable to provide opposing materials, ***the court may continue the hearing*** to allow materials to be obtained. [Fed. R. Civ. P. 56(f); Cal. Civ. Proc. Code §437c(h)]

a. **Rationale:** The Supreme Court identified the concerns behind this option in *Celotex Corp. v. Catrett* (*supra*, §1551): "no serious claim can be made that respondent was in any sense 'railroaded' by a premature motion for summary judgment. Any potential problem with such premature motions can be adequately dealt with under Rule 56(f)."

b. **Showing required:** [§1563]   The opposing party is said to be required to make a showing that continuance is appropriate. For example, Federal Rule 56(f) permits a continuance for "reasons stated" in the opposing party's affidavits. *Note:* In practice, courts may be liberal in treating contentions about the need for more discovery as sufficient to justify continuances.

c. **Facts material and important:** [§1564]   A continuance is appropriate only if the additional facts appear important to the disposition of the summary judgment motion.

   (1) **Example:** In an action for damages for personal injuries, defendant's need to do more discovery on the issue of damages would not be a reason for deferring ruling on plaintiff's motion for partial summary judgment on the question of liability.

d. **Facts can be obtained:** [§1565]   A continuance is appropriate only if there is some reasonable possibility that the additional facts the opposing party wishes to present can be obtained.

   (1) **Example:** In an action growing out of an accident where the issue is whether the light was red for defendant and the only two witnesses known to the parties both have testified that the light was green for defendant, plaintiff's hope that another witness will be discovered may be insufficient to justify delaying a ruling on summary judgment. [*See* Dyer v. MacDougall, *supra*, §1525—all alleged witnesses to slander assert that statement was never made by defendant]

e. **Prior opportunity:** [§1566]   When the opposing party has had a reasonable opportunity to obtain such facts but has not done so, that may cause the court to refuse the continuance.

   (1) **Example:** In an action where intervenor moved for summary judgment on the basis of affidavits by a disinterested witness, the court noted that plaintiff had not taken the opportunity to take the deposition of this witness. [Lundeen v. Cordner, *supra*, §1523]

8. **Effect of Summary Judgment Decision:** [§1567]   If the motion is granted, judgment is entered for the prevailing party. If the motion is denied, the litigation continues.

9. **Appellate Review**

   a. **Standard:** [§1568]   The appellate court uses a plenary standard of review, and gives no deference to the trial court's decision.

   b. **Timing:** [§1569]   Unless summary judgment is entered as to the entire case, appellate review of the summary judgment decision may be delayed until the final decision of the case. (*See infra*, §§1957-1985 for discussion of the final judgment rule.)

    c.   **Order denying motion:** [§1570]   If summary judgment is denied, no judgment results, so the order is not reviewable until after the trial. By that time, a mistaken denial of summary judgment may be treated as *harmless error* if the trial was properly conducted and the judgment after the trial is supported by the evidence at trial.

VIII. MANAGERIAL JUDGING, PRETRIAL CONFERENCE, AND SETTLEMENT PROMOTION

chapter approach

Until recently, pretrial conference and settlement promotion were considered beyond the scope of a first year course, and they still are more likely to be given intense attention in an advanced course on complex litigation. Nevertheless, they have increasingly been covered in the basic first year civil procedure course. Moreover, they may play an increasing role in examinations involving challenges to actions by judges that fall outside the traditional realm of judicial activity. In connection with such examination questions, there are two basic questions to be asked:

1. *Did the court have authority* to take the action it took? Except for "inherent authority," a slippery idea, courts must usually ground their right to take nontraditional actions in some statute or court rule. Many jurisdictions allow or require scheduling conferences and orders to set time limits for joining parties, amending pleadings, limiting discovery, etc. Status conferences and final pretrial conferences are also allowed to discuss issue simplification and promote settlement. Courts have also been given some power to use mandatory nonbinding arbitration and summary jury trials to promote settlement without trial.

2. *Did the court abuse its discretion*? Assuming that there was authority, an appellate court could still reverse on the ground that under the circumstances this authority was abused. The main point to remember is that the court cannot club a party into submission.

In addition, examination questions may ask for evaluation of the *policy questions* that surround the innovations that are discussed in this chapter. Indeed, an examination question may ask the student to evaluate a proposed new program of expediting litigation by comparing it to current practices and considering the arguments for and against adopting the new regime. The main arguments for most procedures are that they streamline cases by simplifying issues and make trial results less uncertain and therefore promote early settlement. The main disadvantages are that the procedures: (i) take some control away from the parties over their own cases; (ii) may force important decisions early, before the parties have had a chance to fully investigate issues; and (iii) often force judges to "prejudge" a case or issue, before all the facts are in.

A. PRETRIAL CONFERENCES AND MANAGERIAL JUDGING

1. Historical Background

   a. **Federal Rule 16:** [§1571] The original Federal Rule 16 authorized a pretrial conference to be held shortly before trial in order to organize the trial. However, concern arose that the relaxed pleading requirements and broadened discovery of the Federal Rules (and the state systems that emulated the Federal Rules) had led to amorphous lawsuits involving excessive discovery expense because they were not focused. In response, and due to rising case-load pressures, federal judges in metropolitan districts began, during the 1970s, to experiment with more active pretrial control of litigation. Sometimes this control was handled on a judge-by-judge basis, and sometimes it was implemented by district-wide local rules. This expanded judicial role in the pretrial process was explicitly built into the federal rules by amendments in 1980, 1983, and 1993. These changes provide for mandatory meet-and-confer sessions among the parties [Fed. R. Civ. P. 26(f)], numerous pretrial conferences [Fed. R. Civ. P. 16(a)-(c)], and a final pretrial conference [Fed. R. Civ. P. 16(d)].

    b. **State court practices:** [§1572] In state courts, such pretrial control was less prominent, in part because in many states, cases were not assigned to a single judge for all purposes. Nevertheless, some added emphasis on pretrial supervision has emerged. [*See, e.g.,* Cal. Civ. Proc. Code §§575-76—regarding pretrial conferences for judicial management]

2. **Scheduling:** [§1573] Under amended Rule 16, federal district court judges have an expanded pretrial role in the control and development of civil cases.

    a. **Mandatory scheduling order:** [§1574] Except in categories of cases exempted by local rule, federal district courts are ***required*** to enter a "***scheduling order***" within 90 days after a defendant's appearance and within 120 days after service of the complaint. This order is to set time limits for joining parties, amending pleadings, completing discovery, and filing motions. [Fed. R. Civ. P. 16(b)]

    b. **Conference:** [§1575] The scheduling order is to be preceded by consultation with the parties by telephone, mail, or other suitable means.

    c. **Other scheduling limitations:** [§1576] Beyond the mandatory scheduling limitations, the court may impose much more specific scheduling requirements regarding a variety of matters as part of its pretrial management of a case. These orders can come at periodic pretrial or status conferences.

    d. **Significance:** [§1577] Limitations on timing of discovery and other matters can be extremely significant to the parties, because they can no longer exercise unilateral control over the sequence and timing of pretrial litigation activities. In particular, this control may be especially significant where the parties wish to defer formal litigation activities for some reason (*e.g.,* to discuss settlement), but the court's schedule prevents this.

3. **Discovery Control:** [§1578] The federal rules affirmatively direct judges to limit discovery if it is cumulative, if the party seeking discovery has had ample opportunity already, or when the discovery sought is "unduly burdensome," given the needs of the case. [Fed. R. Civ. P. 26(b)(2)]

    a. **Meet-and-confer session by parties:** [§1579] At least 14 days before the Rule 16(b) scheduling conference or order, the parties are to meet and confer regarding "the nature and basis of their claims and defenses" and to develop a discovery plan. [Fed. R. Civ. P. 26(f)] Within 10 days after this meeting, they are to submit a written report to the court on their plan. [*See* Official Form 35]

b. **Court's pretrial order:** [§1580] Based on the parties' Rule 26(f) submission, the court is to enter an order that should limit the time to complete discovery [Fed. R. Civ. P. 16(b)(3)] and may include provisions regarding "the control and scheduling of discovery." [Fed. R. Civ. P. 16(c)(6)]

c. **Criticism:** Such precise discovery limitations further impinge on the parties' freedom to control the lawsuit. Moreover, the task of designing such limitations requires the judge to develop a much greater familiarity with the action than would otherwise be necessary, and raises the risk that the judge may misapprehend what is important (and therefore worthy of pursuit through discovery).

4. **Issue Simplification:** [§1581] At a pretrial or status conference, the court can discuss *simplification of the issues* and seek to obtain *stipulations and admissions of fact* to simplify the case.

   a. **Rationale:** By the time the matters are raised in the pretrial conference, it is said that the parties know more about their case and that, therefore, it is fair to pressure them to commit to binding positions for purpose of the litigation. *Criticism:* There is concern that early pressure toward issue simplification may undermine the supposed benefits of relaxed pleading and unduly constrict cases before the facts are out.

   b. **Compelled admissions:** [§1582] The court may not compel admissions from an unwilling party, but the court does have the right to pressure parties to abandon positions that seem unsupported. *Criticism:* Again, the court may not adequately appreciate the circumstances of the case based on the explanation given at the pretrial conference and may unjustifiably curtail legitimate litigation opportunities.

5. **Settlement Promotion:** [§1583] It has long been recognized that more active judicial involvement in pretrial activities could have an effect on settlement of cases, but for some time many judges were reluctant to become overtly involved in settlement discussions, because that might seem to erode their impartiality. This reluctance has waned, and Rule 16(c)(9) now explicitly authorizes discussion of the possibility of settlement.

   a. **Tactics:** [§1584] Judges use a variety of tactics to foster settlement, including meeting separately with each side, requiring attendance of clients at settlement conferences, and meeting with clients outside the presence of their lawyers.

   b. **Mandatory attendance:** [§1585] Rule 16(c) authorizes the court to require that a party or its representative be present or reasonably available by telephone to consider settlement.

   c. **No power to dictate terms of settlement:** [§1586] The court is not authorized to dictate the terms of the settlement. [Kothe v. Smith, 771 F.2d 667 (2d Cir. 1985)—Rule 16 "was not designed as a means for clubbing the parties— or one of them—into an involuntary compromise"] Nevertheless, the court may suggest terms for a settlement that the parties may follow.

d. **Ambiguity of judicial role:** [§1587] The judge's role in settlement is hard to square with the traditional notion that the judge decides disputed matters according to standards set out by the law.

   (1) **Evaluation of terms of settlement:** [§1588] It is unclear whether the judge should promote *any* agreement that seems likely to obtain the consent of the parties, or insist that the agreement correspond, somehow, to the strengths and weaknesses of the merits of the parties' positions.

   (2) **Absence of trial:** [§1589] The judge would usually reach conclusions about the strengths and weaknesses of the parties' positions on the merits only after a trial. To the extent that the judge is to rely on her opinion about the strength of the case in suggesting proper parameters for settlement, involvement in settlement seems to circumvent the normal decision-making process.

   (3) **Example—the weak case for plaintiff:** Where the case for the plaintiff appears weak, the judge's role becomes difficult to comprehend in traditional terms of decisions according to the law. For example, if the plaintiff has a strong case on liability, but little in the way of provable damages, the judge may be able to suggest a reasonable compromise based on the rules governing damages and her experience with awards in similar cases. However, when the plaintiff's case is weak on liability, it is hard to identify any benchmarks. There is no legal standard or reference point in decided cases for determining the "right" settlement amount in a case where the plaintiff has a small chance of success on liability, but large provable damages, since the result at trial would essentially be all or nothing for plaintiff.

e. **Promotion of alternative dispute resolution:** [§1590] The judge may also explore the "use of special procedures (*e.g.,* mini-trials, summary jury trials, mediation, etc.) to assist in resolving the dispute" during pretrial conferences. [Fed. R. Civ. P. 16(c)(9)]

6. **Final Pretrial Conference**

   a. **Purpose:** [§1591] The final pretrial conference is intended to simplify and streamline the trial and resolve as much as possible before trial. In addition, it serves to give both sides advance notice of the subjects to be covered at trial, so that they can be prepared.

   b. **Required pretrial disclosures:** [§1592] The final pretrial conference will ordinarily follow the pretrial disclosures. At least 30 days before trial, each party is to make further disclosures regarding *evidence the party may present at trial*. [Fed. R. Civ. P. 26(a)(3)]

      (1) **Matters to be disclosed:** [§1593] The following types of evidence should be disclosed, *except for evidence used solely for impeachment purposes:*

         (a) **Names of witnesses:** [§1594] The party is to identify the witnesses the party "expects to present" and those it "may call if the need arises." [Fed. R. Civ. P. 26(a)(3)(A)]

(b) **Deposition testimony:** [§1595] The party is to designate those witnesses whose testimony will be presented by deposition. [Fed. R. Civ. P. 26(a)(3)(B)]

(c) **Exhibits:** [§1596] The party is also to identify each document or other exhibit the party expects to offer or which it may offer if the need arises. [Fed. R. Civ. P. 26(a)(3)(C)]

(2) **Waiver of objections:** [§1597] As to the indicated exhibits, the other parties must object within 14 days or waive most objections to the admissibility of the exhibits or to the presentation of a witness by deposition in lieu of live testimony.

(3) **Additional local requirements:** [§1598] A number of courts, as a matter of local rule, require more detailed pretrial submissions.

c. **Topics covered:** [§1599] Local requirements vary, but courts may require delineation of a variety of matters, including the following.

(1) **Undisputed facts:** [§1600] The parties may be required to list all undisputed facts relevant to the case in pretrial filings.

(2) **Disputed facts:** [§1601] Similarly, the parties may have to list all facts that need to be resolved at the trial.

(3) **Witness lists:** [§1602] The parties are usually required to identify all witnesses they will call during their direct cases. (*See supra,* §1594.) In some instances, they are required also to provide a summary of the substance of the testimony each such witness will give.

(a) **Direct testimony in writing—court trials:** [§1603] Some courts require that in cases to be tried to the court, the entire direct testimony of witnesses be submitted in writing in advance of trial.

(4) **Legal issues:** [§1604] The parties are often required to identify and brief all legal issues that are likely to arise in the case.

d. **Final pretrial order:** [§1605] Following the final pretrial conference, the court will usually enter a final pretrial order with regard to the matters covered at the conference. This order is to control the trial, and can be *modified only "to prevent manifest injustice."* [Fed. R. Civ. P. 16(e)]

(1) **Exclusion of evidence and witnesses:** [§1606] The consequence of failure to list a witness or piece of evidence in the pretrial order can, therefore, be that the evidence will not be allowed in at the trial.

(2) **Compare—amending pleadings:** [§1607] Ordinarily, the courts take a liberal attitude toward amendment of the pleadings, and it is uncertain how much more restrictive Rule 16 is than Rule 15 (dealing with pleading amendments). [*See* Wallin v. Fuller, 476 F.2d 1204 (5th Cir. 1973)—"It is unlikely that the pretrial order under Rule 16 was intended to make the pleadings, and therefore Rule 15, obsolete"; United States v. First

National Bank of Circle, 652 F.2d 882 (9th Cir. 1981)—"Unless pretrial orders are honored and enforced, the objectives of the pretrial conference . . . will be jeopardized if not entirely nullified"]

7. **Sanctions:** [§1608]   The federal courts have explicit authority to use sanctions to enforce their authority with regard to pretrial supervision of cases. [Fed. R. Civ. P. 16(f)]

   a. **Failure to appear:** [§1609]   It a party fails to appear through counsel at a pretrial conference, sanctions may be imposed. In some instances, the court may be able to require that the party appear personally. (*See supra,* §1585.)

   b. **Appearing substantially unprepared:** [§1610]   Where a party or lawyer appears, but is not prepared to participate meaningfully in the conference, sanctions are appropriate.

   c. **Failure to participate in good faith:** [§1611]   A party can also be sanctioned for failure to participate in good faith. It is unclear whether the determination of good faith can be based on the court's disagreement with the party's views about proposed settlement terms or stipulations. (*See supra,* §§1586-1589, regarding absence of judicial power to require stipulations or impose terms of settlement.)

   d. **Sanctions available:** [§1612]   The court can impose the sanctions available for violation of discovery orders [Fed. R. Civ. P. 37(b)(2); *see supra,* §§1451-1478] and also impose expenses, including attorneys' fees, resulting from the failure to comply with responsibilities.

8. **Effect on Work Product Protection:** [§1613]   Information such as the identity of witnesses and the subject matter of their testimony would ordinarily be protected work product, yet courts routinely require revelation of this material as part of the final pretrial process. It has been held that work product protection does not limit the power of the court to require revelation of pertinent information in pretrial preparation under Rule 16. [*In re* San Juan Dupont Plaza Hotel Fire Litigation, 859 F.2d 1007 (lst Cir. 1988)]

B. COURT-ANNEXED SETTLEMENT DEVICES

1. **Introduction:** [§1614]   Because informal settlement promotion seemed not to exhaust the potential for judicial promotion of settlement, judges began to experiment with other ways of facilitating settlement. Such efforts usually involved some simulation of a trial as a method of predicting the outcome of trial.

   a. **Rationale:** A primary rationale for this form of judicial activity is that uncertainty about the outcome of a trial is a major impediment to settlement. Simulated substitutes, therefore, could erase much doubt and give the parties a more reliable format for negotiations. In addition, there are reports that such proceedings enhance litigant satisfaction and permit prompt resolution of cases.

2. **Court-Annexed Arbitration:** [§1615]   In the late 1970s, federal courts in some districts began experimenting with *mandatory nonbinding arbitration* in some

cases. In 1988, Congress expressly sanctioned these experiments in 10 districts where such experiments had begun and authorized further experiments in 10 other districts. [28 U.S.C. §§651 et seq.] This authorization has been extended until December 31, 1994 [P.L. 103-192], and may be extended further. States have authorized similar procedures in their courts. [See, e.g., Cal. Civ. Proc. Code §§1141.10 et seq.]

a. **Cases affected**

   (1) **Federal court**

       (a) **Money damages less than $100,000:** [§1616] Where only money damages are sought in an amount less than $100,000, arbitration can be ordered *in any civil action*. Note that districts can lower this amount. [28 U.S.C. §652(a)]

           1) **Relief other than money damages:** [§1617] If relief other than money damages is sought, mandatory arbitration is not allowed.

       (b) **Cases excluded:** [§1618] Cases otherwise subject to mandatory arbitration may not be referred to it if they involve the following.

           1) **Violation of Constitution or civil rights:** [§1619] If an action is for violation of a right secured by the Constitution or for violation of a civil rights statute, it may not be referred to mandatory arbitration. [28 U.S.C. §652(b)]

           2) **Complex, novel, or predominating legal issues:** [§1620] If a case involves complex or novel legal issues, or if the legal issues predominate over factual issues, the case may not be referred to mandatory arbitration. [28 U.S.C. §652(c)]

   (2) **State courts:** [§1621] In state courts where such systems exist, the criteria may turn on the amount claimed as well. In California superior courts, for example, all civil actions where the amount in controversy in the opinion of the court will not exceed $50,000 are subject to arbitration. [Cal. Civ. Proc. Code §1141.11(a)]

       (a) **Dispute about amount claimed:** [§1622] Under the California approach, there can be disputes about whether over $50,000 is really in controversy. [See Cal. Civ. Proc. Code §1141.16(a)—conference to be held to determine whether over $50,000 is actually in controversy]

       (b) **Equitable relief:** [§1623] As in federal court, in California, arbitration may not be compelled if equitable relief is sought, unless the prayer for equitable relief is frivolous. [Cal. Civ. Proc. Code §1141.13]

   (3) **Party consent:** [§1624] When the parties consent, the court may direct arbitration whether or not the case would otherwise be subject to mandatory arbitration.

b. **Timing:** [§1625] Arbitration generally occurs early in the litigation process. In federal court, the hearing is to occur within 180 days of the filing of the answer unless that time is modified by the court for good cause shown. [28 U.S.C. §653(b)]

c. **Hearing:** [§1626] The arbitration decision is based on a hearing, which resembles a trial, but may be more relaxed. The rules of evidence might not be applied with full force, and relaxed rules about the form of presentation of evidence (*e.g.,* narrative answers) may be allowed.

d. **Award:** [§1627] After the hearing, the arbitrator is to enter an award, which briefly identifies the prevailing party and (if necessary) the amount of damages. This award is filed in court and ***becomes the judgment*** of the court ***unless a trial de novo is demanded***. [28 U.S.C. §654; Cal. Civ. Proc. Code §1141.20]

e. **Trial de novo:** [§1628] On timely demand, any party may insist that the case be restored to the regular trial calendar for trial de novo, which is conducted as a regular trial, unaffected by the arbitration proceedings. [28 U.S.C. §655; Cal. Civ. Proc. Code §1141.20]

   (1) **Less favorable result:** [§1629] If the party who demands trial de novo does not obtain a more favorable result in the trial de novo, it can be required to ***reimburse the opposing party for certain costs***. [28 U.S.C. §655(e); Cal. Civ. Proc. Code §1141.21]

f. **Refusal to participate:** [§1630] If a party refuses to participate in the arbitration or fails to participate in good faith, the court may have authority to deny a trial de novo. [*Compare* New England Merchants National Bank v. Hughes, 556 F. Supp. 712 (E.D. Pa. 1983)—trial de novo denied—*with* Lyons v. Wickhorst, 42 Cal. 3d 911 (1986)—no authority to deny trial de novo under California statute]

3. **Summary Jury Trial:** [§1631] The summary jury trial ("SJT") was invented in 1980 by a federal district judge in Cleveland.

   a. **Timing:** [§1632] The SJT is normally deferred until all normal pretrial activities have been completed. All motions in limine and other similar pretrial matters should be disposed of and a final pretrial order entered.

   b. **Nature of hearing:** [§1633] The specifics on summary jury trials may vary from place to place, but generally they have similar procedures:

      (1) **In courthouse:** [§1634] The proceedings occur in the courthouse, in a regular courtroom, with a judge (or magistrate) presiding.

      (2) **Before jury:** [§1635] The case is presented to a jury summoned to appear in the normal manner for juries.

      (3) **Lawyer presentations:** [§1636] The bulk of the case is based on summaries by the lawyers of the evidence developed in the pretrial phase.

(a) **Limitations on content:** [§1637] Some guidelines will apply to limit the content of the summaries. The presentations may have to be based on material developed during discovery, or upon the attorney's professional representation that she has talked to the witness and that the witness would testify as described.

(b) **Live testimony:** [§1638] In some courts, limited live testimony may be allowed.

(4) **Instructions by court:** [§1639] After the lawyers have completed their summaries, the court gives the jury abbreviated instructions on the law applicable to the case.

(5) **Verdict:** [§1640] The jury is to render a consensus verdict, if possible, and if not, to report on reactions to the case on a juror-by-juror basis.

(6) **Effort to settle:** [§1641] With the added information provided by the jury verdict, the parties try to settle the case.

c. **Secrecy:** [§1642] Generally, the SJT is held in secret, and the public is not allowed to attend.

(1) **Example:** In a suit claiming that builders of a nuclear power plant were liable for poor design because the facility leaked radioactive steam, a newspaper was denied access to the SJT on the ground that it was merely a settlement procedure. [Cincinnati Gas & Electric Co. v. General Electric Co., 854 F.2d 900 (6th Cir. 1988)]

d. **Binding effect:** [§1643] In some instances, the parties can stipulate that the summary jury trial will be binding.

e. **Compulsory participation:** [§1644] There has been a split among the courts on whether an unwilling party can be compelled to participate in a SJT before being afforded an opportunity to have a regular trial in court. [*Compare* Strandell v. Jackson County, 838 F.2d 884 (7th Cir. 1987)—no power to compel—*with* Arabian American Oil Co. v. Scarfone, 119 F.R.D. 448 (M.D. Fla. 1988)—court has power to compel] The 1993 amendment to Rule 16, however, may signal a resolution of this split in favor of such judicial power, at least in districts that provide for summary jury trial by local rule. [Fed. R. Civ. P. 16(c)(9)—court authority at pretrial conferences to take action with respect to "the use of special procedures to assist in resolving the dispute when authorized by statute or local rule"]

IX. TRIAL

chapter approach

This chapter covers a variety of topics pertaining to a trial. Some topics are important *before* trial: disqualification of the judge, right to trial by jury, and the selection of jurors. Some topics are relevant *during* trial: presentation of evidence, motions at the close of proof, arguments and instructions to the jury, and jury deliberations. Finally, some topics become important at the *end* of the trial, such as the motions after the verdict. Of these topics, the most likely to appear on your exam are:

1. **Right to jury trial:** Consider whether there is a right to a trial by jury, normally because the case is at least in part *legal* (as opposed to equitable). If this right exists, has there been a *timely demand* for jury trial?

2. **Disqualification of the judge:** Look for facts showing *bias, personal knowledge* of the facts of the case, *financial interest* in the outcome, or a *relationship* with a party or counsel.

3. **Pre-verdict motions:** Think about whether the side with the burden of producing the evidence has shown enough to create an issue for the jury. If not, the court may grant a motion for *judgment as a matter of law.* This was formerly called "directed verdict" in federal courts, and still is in most state court systems. Remember that the judge may *reserve ruling* on the motion and, if the jury verdict is not adequately supported by the evidence, grant a *judgment as a matter of law* or *new trial*.

4. **Jury issues:** Did the judge give the jury *proper instructions* as to the applicable law? Was there any *misconduct* of the jury that may provide a basis for *impeachment of the verdict*?

5. **Post-verdict motions:** Besides *judgment n.o.v.* or post-verdict *judgment as a matter of law* in federal court (granted when the verdict is not adequately supported by the evidence), consider whether there are grounds for a *new trial* (*e.g.*, prejudicial misconduct, unfair surprise, improper evidence, etc.); a motion to *amend the judgment* (errors of law); or a motion for *relief from the judgment* (for clerical errors, fraud, newly discovered evidence).

A. RIGHT TO TRIAL BY JURY

1. Source of Right

a. Federal courts

(1) **Federal Constitution:** [§1645] The Seventh Amendment of the United States Constitution provides: "In suits at common law, where the value in controversy shall exceed twenty dollars, the right of trial by the jury shall be preserved."

(2) **Legislation:** [§1646] In matters not covered by this constitutional provision, there may also be a statutory right to trial by jury where Congress has so provided.

b. **State courts**

(1) **No federal constitutional right:** [§1647] Unlike many other Bill of Rights guarantees, the Seventh Amendment right to trial by jury in civil cases has not been held "incorporated" in the Due Process Clause of the Fourteenth Amendment. Hence, the federal Constitution does not assure such a right in state court proceedings. [Walker v. Sauvinet, 92 U.S. 90 (1875); Minneapolis & St. Louis Railroad v. Bombolis, 241 U.S. 211 (1916)]

(2) **Federal legislation:** [§1648] However, there may be a right to a jury trial in state court actions involving matters governed by federal law, where Congress has so provided. *Example:* State court civil action based on claim under Federal Employers Liability Act. [Dice v. Akron, Canton & Youngstown Railroad, 342 U.S. 359 (1952)]

(3) **State constitutions:** [§1649] Also, most state constitutions have provisions similar to the Seventh Amendment that apply to civil actions in state courts. [*See, e.g.*, Cal. Const. art. 1, §16]

2. **Cases Where Right Exists**

a. **Basic historical test:** [§1650] Because the Seventh Amendment and many state constitutional jury guarantees refer to "preserv[ing]" the right to a civil jury trial, a major factor in applying the guarantees is historical inquiry into practice at the time of their adoption. The right to jury trial existed in the English law courts but *not* in Chancery, where the system of equity was administered. Accordingly, with a traditional type of claim a federal court will consider whether the claim is *"legal"* or *"equitable"* as such terms were understood in 1791 (the year in which the Seventh Amendment became effective). [Dimick v. Schiedt, 293 U.S. 474 (1934)]

(1) **Jury right after "merger" of law and equity:** [§1651] With the abolition of separate law and equity court systems in the federal courts and nearly all states, the availability of a jury can no longer depend on the system in which a case is heard. Generally speaking (although with many qualifications), today if a claim would have gone before the law courts prior to merger, the constitutional jury right applies; if a claim would have been within equitable jurisdiction, there is no constitutional right to trial by jury.

(2) **Criticism—vague distinction:** [§1652] The line between "law" and "equity" was somewhat vague and shifting, and depended on the evolution of early English court systems. The main distinction related to the *remedy* sought. *Equity* generally afforded remedies such as *injunctions* that imposed duties directly on the parties, subjecting them to contempt sanctions in the event of disobedience. *Law courts,* on the other hand, usually afforded *monetary damages* and other remedies (*e.g.*, ejectment, replevin) that could be enforced by court officers with or without the cooperation of the parties.

b. **Present standards for right to jury trial**

(1) **Counterparts to actions at law—right to jury:** [§1653] Modern actions that are counterparts to actions at law, such as personal injury claims or claims to recover damages for breach of contract, are triable to a jury.

(2) **Counterparts to suits in equity—no right:** [§1654] However, there is no right to a jury in actions that are counterparts to suits in equity—*e.g.*, actions to foreclose mortgages, to enjoin misconduct, or for specific performance of a contract.

(3) **Statutory remedies:** [§1655] With types of claims that existed when a constitutional guarantee was adopted, the historical inquiry is usually easy and determinative. Legislatures, however, regularly redefine common law rights, replace traditional claims with new forms, and create novel statutory rights. A simple historical test usually cannot resolve the jury right question in such cases, although historical analogies to traditional claims remain a significant factor.

(a) **Statutory substitutes for actions at law:** [§1656] Legislation cannot impair the right to jury trial in federal court when the right and remedy afforded fit the historical pattern of a judicial proceeding at law.

1) **Example:** An action to evict a tenant for nonpayment of rent is triable to a jury, even where legislation has substituted a statutory remedy for the old common law remedy of ejectment. [Pernell v. Southall Realty, 416 U.S. 363 (1974)]

2) **Example:** Suits by bankruptcy trustees to recover fraudulent conveyances from parties who had not submitted claims against the bankruptcy estate are "quintessentially suits at common law" and Congress could not remove the right to jury trial by assigning jurisdiction over such actions to bankruptcy courts. [Granfinanciera, S.A. v. Nordberg, 492 U.S. 33 (1989)] *Note:* The lower federal courts are divided over whether federal bankruptcy judges (who lack Article III status) have statutory and constitutional authority to conduct jury trials, or whether bankruptcy cases in which the jury right exists must be tried in district court. [*See, e.g., In re* Grabill Corp., 967 F.2d 1152 (7th Cir. 1992)]

a) **But note:** Proceedings under the federal bankruptcy code are mostly equitable, and a creditor who files a claim against the bankruptcy estate submits to the jurisdiction of the bankruptcy court. Such a creditor cannot insist on a jury trial should the trustee assert a claim to recover a preferential transfer. [Langenkamp v. Culp, 498 U.S. 42 (1990)]

(b) **When "new right" involved:** [§1657] Congress may provide for nonjury trials when the right to be enforced is one ***not known*** at common law and practical considerations justify withholding the right to a jury in order to assure efficient disposition, especially if initial adjudication and enforcement of the right are assigned to a *federal administrative agency* rather than an Article III court. When an action on a new statutory right can be initiated in *federal court,* the approach in such cases requires examining "both the nature of the issues involved and the remedy sought." There is to be a comparison of the statutory action to 18th-century, pre-merger English actions, and an examination of whether the remedy sought is legal or equitable in nature. The second *remedial inquiry is more important.* [Chauffeurs, Teamsters & Helpers Local 391 v. Terry, 494 U.S. 558 (1990)]

1) **Example:** Congress could create new duties of employers regarding employee safety and assign disputes to an administrative agency with which a jury trial would be incompatible. [Atlas Roofing Co. v. Occupational Safety and Health Review Commission, 430 U.S. 442 (1977)]

2) **Compare:** Proceedings to enforce new statutory rights *in federal court* may be triable to a jury when the *remedy* provided is a legal remedy, such as damages (*e.g.,* claims under federal civil rights statutes). [Curtis v. Loether, 415 U.S. 189 (1974)] Similarly, an employee who seeks back wages for a union's alleged breach of its duty of fair representation has a Seventh Amendment right to trial by jury in federal court. [Chauffeurs, Teamsters & Helpers Local 391 v. Terry, *supra*]

3) **Civil penalty:** [§1658] When a statute provides a civil penalty for violation (*e.g.,* a certain amount per day of violation), that is sufficient to create a right to jury trial in an action for a civil penalty. [Tull v. United States, 481 U.S. 412 (1987)—action for civil penalties for violation of Clean Water Act]

4) **Compare—amount of penalty:** [§1659] While holding that there is a right to jury trial *with regard to liability* for a civil penalty, the Supreme Court has held that there is no right to a jury trial on the *amount* of the penalty. [Tull v. United States, *supra*]

(4) **Actions for declaratory relief:** [§1660] Actions for declaratory judgments pose special problems because declaratory relief is a *statutorily created remedy* unknown to early English law or equity and thus neither legal nor equitable in nature. In general, the federal courts look to what the underlying nondeclaratory claim would have been and determine the jury right accordingly. [*See, e.g.,* Terrell v. DeConna, 877 F.2d 1267 (5th Cir. 1989)—declaratory judgment plaintiff's insurance coverage claim if brought for nondeclaratory coercive relief would have been equitable garnishment action, so no jury trial right existed]

(a) **But note:** Issues in declaratory judgment actions will often be questions of law for the court rather than of fact for the trier of fact, so no jury right may exist whether the action would be classified as legal or equitable.

3. **Proceedings in Which Right to Jury Applies in Part**

   a. **Actions joining legal and equitable claims:** [§1661] Determining whether the right to trial by jury exists on a *claim* may be only part of the problem, for some cases involve both legal and equitable claims (*e.g.*, a contract action in which plaintiff seeks damages at law for past breach and an equitable order compelling future specific performance). In general, federal courts are to structure their proceedings to preserve a jury trial on issues common to the legal and equitable aspects of a case. [Beacon Theatres v. Westover, 359 U.S. 500 (1959)] This is usually true even if the equitable aspects of the case predominate [Dairy Queen, Inc. v. Wood, 369 U.S. 469 (1962)], which entirely or virtually eliminates in federal court any modern effect of the old equitable "clean-up" doctrine that allowed nonjury disposition of minor legal matters in a mainly equitable case. However, the clean-up doctrine survives in some states.

   (1) **Priority of issues at trial:** [§1662] It may make a great deal of difference which issues in a case are tried first, since adjudication of the equitable claim may render meaningless the claim for legal relief, or vice versa. For example, suppose the plaintiff sues for rescission of a contract for fraud, while the defendant countersues for damages for breach of contract. If the court tries the rescission claim first and holds the contract unenforceable, it thereby disposes of any claim for damages by the defendant.

   (a) **State practice:** [§1663] In state courts, the order of trial is usually within the *discretion* of the trial judge, who may order either the equitable or legal aspects tried first.

   (b) **Federal practice:** [§1664] In federal courts, however, all issues affecting the claim for legal relief must ordinarily be tried *first* to the jury. The possibility of irreparable harm to a party from delay in granting an injunction can usually be handled by grant of *interlocutory injunctive relief* (*i.e.*, a temporary restraining order ("TRO") or preliminary injunction), which requires only provisional findings that will not bind the jury or dispose formally of the legal claims.

   1) **Example:** The federal court was not to try equitable causes first in an antitrust case involving a complaint for declaratory judgment and injunction, and a counterclaim and cross-claim for antitrust treble damages, when final determination of common issues between the legal and equitable aspects of the case might prevent the jury trial of the counterclaim and cross-claim. [*See* Beacon Theatres v. Westover, *supra*]

   2) **Erroneous dismissal of legal claims:** [§1665] The Seventh Amendment bars giving preclusive effect to a district court's determinations of issues common to legal and equitable claims when the court resolves the equitable claims first solely because

it wrongly dismissed the legal claims. [Lytle v. Household Manufacturing, Inc., 494 U.S. 545 (1990)]

- b. **Equitable proceedings seeking legal relief:** [§1666] One historical role of equity was to provide procedural mechanisms for the resolution of complex disputes. Thus interpleader, class actions, and shareholder derivative suits were "inventions" of equity. However, in determining the right to jury trial, federal practice now focuses on the *nature of the underlying claim* rather than the procedural mechanism by which the claim is to be adjudicated.

    (1) **Shareholder actions:** [§1667] In a shareholder derivative action in federal court, there is a right to jury trial on all issues that would have been tried by jury if the claim had been brought by the corporation itself. [Ross v. Bernhard, 396 U.S. 531 (1970)]

    (2) **Interpleader:** [§1668] Similarly, an interpleader action would be triable to a jury when the underlying claims against the stakeholder would have been actions at law if brought by the interpleader claimants. [Hyde Properties, Inc. v. McCoy, 507 F.2d 301 (6th Cir. 1974)]

4. **Right to Jury Trial Depends on Timely Demand:** [§1669] Various rules govern the manner in which the right to jury trial must be asserted. Failure to comply with these rules operates as a waiver of the constitutional right.

    a. **State practice:** [§1670] In state court proceedings, the right to jury trial usually must be exercised by a demand in writing at the time the case is set for trial. Otherwise, the right is waived.

        (1) **Note:** If cases are set for trial by request of the parties (*e.g.*, in a motion for trial setting), the demand must be made as part of that request. Where cases are set for trial automatically by the court, the parties ordinarily have a limited period of time after receipt of the notice of trial setting within which to file the written demand for jury trial. [Cal. Civ. Proc. Code §631]

        (2) **And note:** Frequently, a deposit of jury fees is required at the time of jury trial demand. Failure to make the deposit likewise waives the right (although the other party may "pick up the tab" to preserve a jury trial).

    b. **Federal practice:** [§1671] In federal actions when the right to jury trial applies, a party must demand a jury trial in writing with regard to any issue within 10 days of the service of the last pleading directed to that issue. [Fed. R. Civ. P. 38(b)] Ordinarily, parties include the demand as an addendum to their pleadings: "Plaintiff demands a trial by jury of all issues triable by jury herein."

        (1) **Example:** If D's answer contains a counterclaim denominated as such, P must file a reply thereto. [Fed. R. Civ. P. 7(a)] If the counterclaim and reply deal with issues as to which a jury trial is available, either party has until 10 days following the filing of P's reply to demand a jury trial.

        (2) **Note:** The filing of amended or supplemental pleadings does *not* revive the right to a jury trial if no demand was made when the original pleadings

were filed (unless the amended or supplemental pleadings raise *new issues* that are triable to a jury).

  (3) **Withdrawal of demand:** [§1672] Once a party has timely demanded a jury, the case is to be tried to a jury unless all parties stipulate to trial to the court. [Fed. R. Civ. P. 39(a)]

5. **Jury Trials Discretionary with Court**

 a. **Where jury previously waived:** [§1673] The court may order a jury trial on any or all issues in a case in which the right has been waived (*e.g.*, by failure to make timely demand therefor). [Fed. R. Civ. P. 39(b)]

 b. **By consent:** [§1674] Even when no right to a jury exists, the court may order a binding jury trial with the consent of both parties. [Fed. R. Civ. P. 39(c)]

 c. **Advisory jury:** [§1675] And the judge may order a trial by jury for the purpose of obtaining an "advisory" verdict. [Fed. R. Civ. P. 39(c); *see* Cutter Labs v. R.W. Ogle & Co., 151 Cal. App. 2d 410 (1957)]

B. SELECTION OF THE JURY

1. **Summons of the Venire:** [§1676] Trial juries are selected from a larger panel of citizens, commonly known as the *venire*. Prospective jurors are summoned by the court.

 a. **Historical method of selection:** [§1677] In earlier times, the clerk or jury commissioner selected veniremen by personal contact; the officer of the court was charged with identifying citizens of good repute to serve as jurors.

  (1) **The "key man":** [§1678] Members of the clergy and other professional people known favorably to the clerk or commissioner would frequently be asked to serve as "key men" to identify appropriate prospective jurors.

  (2) **Talesmen:** [§1679] If the court was short of veniremen, the clerk or commissioner might go into the corridors of the courthouse for willing volunteers, known as *"talesmen."*

 b. **Constitutional requirements**

  (1) **Systematic exclusion:** [§1680] The systematic exclusion from jury panels of any religious, racial, ethnic, or political group is an unlawful denial of equal protection of the laws. [Eubanks v. Louisiana, 356 U.S. 584 (1957); *and see* Constitutional Law Summary]

  (2) **Cross section not required:** [§1681] On the other hand, the Constitution does *not* require that juries be strictly representative. Jury service may be confined to persons meeting certain standards of education, intelligence, judgment, and character, as long as the standards are not administered in a discriminatory manner. [Carter v. Jury Commission of Greene County, 396 U.S. 320 (1970)]

(3) **"Blue ribbon" juries:** [§1682] Nor does the Constitution proscribe the use of "blue ribbon" juries selected on the basis of special intelligence or experience to handle complicated cases. [Fay v. New York, 332 U.S. 261 (1947)]

c. **Contemporary selection practice**

(1) **Federal courts**

   (a) **Local plans:** [§1683] Jury selection methods in federal courts now conform to plans promulgated by local district courts in conformity with national standards. [28 U.S.C. §1863]

   (b) **Fair cross section required:** [§1684] The national policy requires that juries be "selected at random from a fair cross section of the community." [28 U.S.C. §1861]

   (c) **Use of voter registration lists:** [§1685] Every district uses voter registration lists as the basic source from which potential jurors are summoned. Some districts supplement these lists when necessary to foster the national policy (above). [28 U.S.C. §1863(b)(2)]

   1) **When supplementation required:** [§1686] The voter registration list *must* be supplemented if it underrepresents any group identified by race, color, religion, sex, national origin, or economic status. [28 U.S.C. §§1862, 1863(b)(2)]

   (d) **Challenge to array:** [§1687] If the venire has not been selected in strict compliance with statute and the local plan, either party may challenge the array (the whole group of prospective jurors) and require that a new venire be summoned. [28 U.S.C. §1867; *and see* Thiel v. Southern Pacific Co., 328 U.S. 217 (1946)]

   1) **Single nonrepresentative panel:** [§1688] It is not a basis for challenging the array that a single panel or venire is not cross-sectional, as long as the ***method*** by which the group was selected is random.

   2) **Nonrepresentative system:** [§1689] However, if it can be shown that the system regularly produces panels or venires that are substantially nonrepresentative in the same way, this is an adequate basis for challenge.

(2) **State courts:** [§1690] Many state courts select juries in a manner similar to the federal system, others retain vestiges of the traditional practice, and some states continue the use of "blue ribbon" jury panels (*supra*).

2. **Qualifications of Prospective Jurors**

a. **Exclusions:** [§1691] Statutes generally provide that certain classes of citizens shall be excluded from juries. Categories typically excluded include minors, felons, aliens, and illiterates. [28 U.S.C. §1865; Cal. Civ. Proc. Code §203]

b. **Excuses:** [§1692] A prospective juror may be excused for good cause, such as extraordinary financial loss from service.

c. **One-day or one-trial service:** [§1693] Some courts are now summoning jurors to serve only one day or one trial. Where this practice is used, exemptions and excuses are likely to be more sparingly recognized.

3. **Number of Jurors Required**

    a. **Typical size of venire:** [§1694] The venire usually consists of two or three times the number of persons who will be selected to serve as jurors.

    b. **Traditional jury of twelve:** [§1695] Common law juries were composed of 12 members, and for some time it was assumed that this number was required in federal courts by the Seventh Amendment. [Capital Traction Co. v. Hof, 174 U.S. 1 (1899)]

    c. **Twelve not required by due process:** [§1696] The common law requirement of 12 jurors has now been held not to be required by the Due Process Clause. [Williams v. Florida, 399 U.S. 78 (1970)—criminal case] However, due process requires at least six jurors in a criminal case. [Ballew v. Georgia, 435 U.S. 223 (1978)]

        (1) **Civil cases:** [§1697] The minimum number of jurors required in federal civil cases has not been finally resolved. Local district rules providing for *six-member* juries in civil cases have been upheld—on the rationale that the outcome of the verdict is not likely to be affected substantially by the number of jurors (at least as between 12 and six). [Colgrove v. Battin, 413 U.S. 149 (1973)]

        (2) **State practice:** [§1698] Since the U.S. Constitution does not require states to provide jury trials at all, the number of jurors in state civil trials depends entirely on state law. Many states have long used juries with fewer than 12 members in civil cases, particularly where the amount in controversy is small.

    d. **Jury size in federal civil cases:** [§1699] Federal Rule 48 provides that the court shall seat a jury of not fewer than six nor more than 12 jurors.

    e. **Appointment of alternate jurors:** [§1700] Traditionally courts have appointed alternate jurors in addition to regular jurors to provide for the possibility that a regular juror may be unable to serve for the full term of the trial. Alternates would sit through the trial, but would be excused before the commencement of jury deliberations unless needed to take the place of incapacitated jurors. However, as amended in 1991, Rule 47 *abolished* the institution of the alternate juror. Instead, the court may seat from six to 12 jurors, and may excuse some for good cause during trial or deliberations, as long as *at least six* remain (unless the parties agree otherwise).

4. **Voir Dire Examination of Jurors:** [§1701] After the venire has been screened by the court for persons who should be excluded, exempt, or excused, the prospective jurors are generally subject to further interrogation about their possible biases. This examination is known as *voir dire.*

a. **Challenge for cause:** [§1702] A party may challenge a prospective juror if it appears that the juror has a financial stake in the case or in similar litigation, if members of the juror's immediate family have such an interest, or if there is other sufficient reason to believe that the juror may be unable to render impartial service. [28 U.S.C. §1866(c)] There is *no limit* to the number of challenges for cause.

b. **Peremptory challenge:** [§1703] Each "side" is also entitled to a limited number of challenges *without* a showing of cause—*i.e.*, a peremptory challenge.

   (1) **Rationale:** The purpose of the peremptory challenge is to give each side the opportunity to act upon intimations of bias that may not be demonstrable or even rationally explainable. In this way, those persons most distrusted by either side are removed from the jury.

   (2) **Number in federal courts:** [§1704] In federal courts, each side is entitled to three peremptory challenges. [28 U.S.C. §1870]

   (3) **Number in state courts:** [§1705] The number of peremptory challenges allowed in state court proceedings varies. In California, six challenges are allowed, with more permitted in multiparty litigation. [Cal. Civ. Proc. Code §231(c)]

   (4) **Racial grounds for exercise:** [§1706] The Supreme Court has held that the equal protection component of the Fifth Amendment Due Process Clause precludes a private party in federal civil litigation from using peremptory challenges to excuse potential jurors on grounds of their race. [Edmonson v. Leesville Concrete Co., 500 U.S. 614 (1991)] The same rule would apply to state court actions under the Fourteenth Amendment's Equal Protection Clause.

   (5) **Gender grounds for exercise:** [§1707] The Supreme Court has also held that the Equal Protection Clause forbids use of peremptory strikes to remove jurors on the basis of their gender. [J.E.B. v. T.B., 114 S. Ct. 1419 (1994)]

c. **Questioning by court:** [§1708] In most jurisdictions, the judge may control the voir dire examination by asking all questions of the jurors. [Perry v. Allegheny Airlines, Inc., 489 F.2d 1349 (2d Cir. 1974)] However, the judge must ask all proper questions submitted by counsel, in order to enable them to make good use of their peremptory challenges. [Kiernan v. Van Schaik, 347 F.2d 775 (3d Cir. 1965)]

   (1) **Limited to grounds for challenge for cause:** [§1709] In most jurisdictions the inquiry on voir dire examination of jurors is limited to grounds that might provide a basis for excusing jurors for cause. (*See supra,* §1702.) In some jurisdictions, however, in criminal cases counsel are allowed to inquire into any matter that may bear on their exercise of peremptory challenges.

d. **Questioning by counsel:** [§1710] Some courts permit counsel to ask questions directly, and in some states (*e.g.*, Texas), counsel have a right to do so.

In other states (*e.g.*, New York), the examination may be conducted by counsel outside the courtroom, with the judge called in only to rule on objections.

(1) **Improper questioning:** [§1711] It is not proper to use the voir dire examination to put comments or hypothetical evidence before jurors which would not be admissible at trial. If such questioning has been allowed, a new trial should be ordered.

   (a) **Example:** Where P is not allowed to offer proof of D's insurance at trial, P's counsel should not be allowed to interrogate prospective jurors about the subject of insurance.

(2) **Tactic:** [§1712] Counsel may use the voir dire examination as an occasion to preview the case by asking prospective jurors whether they "could believe" proof of the sort described, or "could in good conscience award" damages of the amount or type being sought.

C. DISQUALIFICATION OF JUDGE

1. **Grounds for Disqualification:** [§1713] The judge assigned to a trial proceeding may be disqualified if her impartiality might reasonably be questioned. Bases for disqualification would therefore include the following. [*See generally* 28 U.S.C. §455; Cal. Civ. Proc. Code §170.1]

   a. **Personal bias:** [§1714] Where the judge has a personal bias or personal prejudice concerning a party, she may be disqualified.

   b. **Personal knowledge of the facts:** [§1715] Where the judge has personal knowledge of disputed evidentiary facts, she may be disqualified.

   c. **Previous involvement as lawyer:** [§1716] Where the judge served as counsel in connection with the controversy, or a lawyer with whom she practiced so served during the period of their association, she may be disqualified.

   d. **Financial interest:** [§1717] A judge may be disqualified where she knows that she, her spouse, or her minor child has a financial stake in the controversy or an interest that could be substantially affected by the outcome.

   e. **Family relationship:** [§1718] If the judge's spouse (or a relative of the judge or the judge's spouse) is a party, an officer of a party, or a lawyer for a party or is known to have a financial interest, or is likely to be a material witness, she may be disqualified.

   f. **Disqualification must be based on extrajudicial matters:** [§1719] The judge's adverse reaction or hostility to the parties or the evidence generally is *not* a basis for disqualification. [Liteky v. United States, 114 S. Ct. 1147 (1994)]

2. **Duty of Judge:** [§1720] The judge has a duty to be informed about possible bases for disqualification and to disqualify herself on her own motion where adequate grounds for disqualification exist.

3. **Procedure for Disqualification**

   a. **Federal practice:** [§1721] In federal court, a party seeking to disqualify a judge must do so by filing an affidavit of bias—*i.e.*, a sworn statement setting forth the facts that are the basis for disqualification. [28 U.S.C. §144] Factual averments in such an affidavit are *not* open to challenge (except in a criminal proceeding to punish the affiant for perjury). If the facts set forth are legally sufficient to disqualify the judge, she *must* excuse herself and assign the case to another judge.

   b. **State practice:** [§1722] State procedures vary greatly.

      (1) **Traditional rule:** [§1723] Most states require an actual showing by affidavit of grounds for disqualification, as in federal practice.

      (2) **Peremptory challenge:** [§1724] In some states, each party has an absolute right to disqualify *one* judge simply by filing an affidavit that he believes he cannot obtain a fair trial before that judge. As to any subsequent judge, a party may make a motion to disqualify and is entitled to a hearing on the facts in front of still another judge, who must determine whether the second should be disqualified. [*See, e.*g., Cal. Civ. Proc. Code §170.6]

         (a) **Note:** This system has been criticized as permitting too free an attack on judges and as a source of delay.

D. ORDER OF TRIAL

1. **Right to Speak First and Last**

   a. **General rule:** [§1725] Ordinarily, the party opening and closing each phase of a trial is the party who has the *burden of proof* with respect to the principal issues. This usually will be the plaintiff—but it may be the defendant if the plaintiff's prima facie case has been established by the pleadings and pretrial order.

   b. **Discretion of court:** [§1726] The decision to accord the right to speak first and last is ultimately one for the discretion of the trial judge. [Cal. Civ. Proc. Code §607]

2. **Stages of Jury Trial:** [§1727] The normal sequence of a civil jury trial is as follows:

   (i) Opening statement of plaintiff;

   (ii) Opening statement of defendant;

   (iii) Presentation of direct evidence by plaintiff, with cross-examination of each witness by defendant followed by re-direct and re-cross-examination (*plaintiff rests*);

   (iv) Presentation of direct evidence by the defendant, with cross-examination, re-direct, and re-cross-examination (*defendant rests*);

(v) Presentation of rebuttal evidence by plaintiff;

(vi) Presentation of rebuttal evidence by defendant;

(vii) Argument of plaintiff to jury;

(viii) Argument of defendant to jury;

(ix) Final closing argument of plaintiff to jury;

(x) Instructions to jury by judge;

(xi) Verdict of jury.

3. **Nonjury Trial:** [§1728] The order of a nonjury trial is essentially the same up to the point at which all evidence has been presented. Prior to the presentation of argument, or in the course of argument, the parties may propose specific findings of fact and conclusions of law to the court. At the close of arguments, the judge will render his decision, which will take the form of specific findings of fact and conclusions of law. [Fed. R. Civ. P. 52(a)]

E. **PRESENTATION OF EVIDENCE**

1. **Control Over Presentation:** [§1729] Ordinarily, presentation of the evidence at trial is the responsibility of the parties and their counsel, subject to control by the court. [Fed. R. Evid. 611(a)] Even so, most jurisdictions acknowledge the discretionary power of the trial judge to call witnesses on his own motion. [Citizens State Bank v. Castro, 105 Cal. App. 284 (1930)]

2. **Rules of Evidence:** [§1730] Proceedings in federal court are governed by the Federal Rules of Evidence. In some respects, these rules incorporate provisions of state law (*e.g.,* what privileges are recognized). Some states, like California, have evidence codes, while others rely in varying degrees on common law rules. (*See* detailed discussion in Evidence Summary.)

3. **Objections and Exceptions**

   a. **Failure to object:** [§1731] Failure to object to the admission of an item of evidence generally waives the ground for objection.

   b. **Amendment by proof:** [§1732] If no objection is made to evidence that goes beyond the pleadings or the pretrial order to raise new issues, the pleadings or the order will be treated as if they had been amended to allege the facts proved by the evidence admitted. [Fed. R. Civ. P. 15(b), 16] (*See supra,* §§860-873.)

   c. **Exceptions unnecessary:** [§1733] In modern practice, it is sufficient to state an objection to the admission of evidence and the basis for the objection. It is not necessary, in order to preserve the issue for appeal, to take exception to rulings on such objections. [Fed. R. Civ. P. 46]

4. **Burden of Producing Evidence:** [§1734] The plaintiff must produce some evidence tending to prove each element of the ***prima facie*** case. If the plaintiff fails to

do so, the defendant is entitled to a dismissal or a judgment as a matter of law at the close of the plaintiff's evidence. Similarly, if a defense is to be considered by the trier of fact, the defendant must produce some evidence tending to prove each element of his defense. *Note:* A party may be relieved of this burden by the adversary's admissions in pleadings, discovery proceedings, or at pretrial. (*See* Evidence Summary.)

5. **Judicial Notice:** [§1735] It is unnecessary to plead or prove facts that are not subject to reasonable dispute; the court must take judicial notice of such facts. (*See* Evidence Summary.)

F. MOTIONS AT CLOSE OF PROOF

1. **In General:** [§1736] At the close of proof, motions may be used to determine whether a party has carried the burden of producing evidence, *e.g.*, motion for judgment as a matter of law, for nonsuit, or for involuntary dismissal.

2. **Jury Trial—Motion for Judgment as a Matter of Law (Directed Verdict):** [§1737] In a jury trial, either party may move for judgment as a matter of law when the adversary has been fully heard with respect to the issue in question. [Fed. R. Civ. P. 50(a)]

    a. **New terminology:** [§1738] Before Federal Rule 50(a) was amended in 1991, what is now called a "motion for judgment as a matter of law" was called a "motion for a directed verdict." *State courts* usually still refer to such a motion as a *"motion for directed verdict."*

    b. **Standard for grant:** [§1739] The general standard for whether to grant a motion for judgment as a matter of law looks to whether there is a *legally sufficient evidentiary basis* on which the jury could find for the nonmoving party. The application of this standard depends on whether the moving party has the burden of proof on the issue raised.

    (1) **Moving party with burden of proof:** [§1740] If the moving party has the burden of proof, judgment as a matter of law is appropriate only if the evidence favoring the moving party is of such *compelling strength* that the jury could not reasonably find for the opposing party. Accordingly, to defeat the motion it is sufficient that the jury could reasonably disbelieve the witnesses upon whom the moving party relies.

    (a) **State court view:** [§1741] In some states, a directed verdict cannot be entered if the movant has the burden of proof unless the facts are totally uncontroverted or the parties agree to them. [Alexander v. Tingle, 30 A.2d 737 (Md. 1943)]

    (2) **Opposing party with burden:** [§1742] If the party moving for judgment as a matter of law does not have the burden of proof, the motion should be granted only where the opposing party has *no substantial evidence* to permit a jury reasonably to find in its favor.

    (a) **Scintilla rule contrasted:** [§1743] In some jurisdictions the "scintilla rule" still is invoked. Under this rule, a party with a scintilla of evidence would be allowed to have her case presented to the jury. The federal courts have rejected the scintilla rule. [Galloway v. United States, 319 U.S. 372 (1943)]

c. **Case-by-case determination:** [§1744] The court's evaluation process must be made on a case-by-case basis, and discussion of given cases should involve careful examination of the facts presented and inferences from them. As a consequence, it is difficult to present "rules" governing judgment as a matter of law. There are, however, a number of governing principles that are helpful in analysis, and these are discussed below.

(1) **All reasonable inferences indulged in favor of opposing party:** [§1745] The court is to make all reasonable inferences in favor of the opposing party, and to view the evidence *in the light most favorable to that party.*

(2) **Court may not "weigh" evidence:** [§1746] The court is to determine whether there is a genuine issue to present to the jury; it may not choose between two versions of events and grant summary judgment to the party whose version seems more persuasive.

(a) **Role of speculation:** [§1747] Within limits, the fact that the jury's decision will involve some speculation is not a ground for taking the case from the jury. If facts are in dispute or reasonable people may draw different inferences from the evidence, the jury may use speculation and conjecture to settle the dispute by choosing what seems to be the most reasonable inference. [Lavender v. Kurn, 327 U.S. 645 (1946)]

(b) **"Equal possibilities" analysis:** [§1748] It is sometimes said that the case should be taken from the jury when the evidence presented on any essential fact by the party with the burden of proof shows only an equal possibility of the existence of that fact. [*See, e.g.,* Pennsylvania Railroad v. Chamberlain, 288 U.S. 333 (1933)] This analysis has been *rejected* in most jurisdictions, as long as there is some basis on which the jury could choose between conflicting versions of events.

(3) **Evidence to be considered**

(a) **Only opposing party's evidence:** [§1749] Some courts limit their examination to the evidence offered by the opposing party, at least in cases where the opposing party has the burden of proof, and the courts may say that the moving party's evidence is irrelevant. [Lavender v. Kurn, *supra*—defendant's evidence "irrelevant upon appeal, there being a reasonable basis in the record" to support the jury's verdict for plaintiff]

(b) **All evidence presented in light most favorable to opposing party:** [§1750] The *majority rule* is that the court should "consider all of the evidence—not just that evidence which supports the non-mover's case—but in the light and with all reasonable inferences most ences most favorable to the party opposed to the motion." [Boeing Co. v. Shipman, 411 F.2d 365 (5th Cir. 1969)]

(4) **Demeanor evidence:** [§1751] The jury has observed the witnesses while testifying, and may draw conclusions about their truthfulness from their demeanor.

  (a) **Moving party with burden of proof:** [§1752] Where the moving party has the burden of proof and relies on witnesses whom the jury could disbelieve, it is not entitled to a directed verdict, even where there is no conflicting evidence offered. (*See supra*, §1740.)

   1) **Possible exception—disinterested, unimpeached witness:** [§1753] The above rule may not apply where the witness relied upon is disinterested and has not been impeached. Under these circumstances, there may be no reasonable basis for disbelieving the witness. [*See* Lundeen v. Cordner, *supra,* §1566]

    a) **Example:** Plaintiff, the executor of the estate of X, sues defendant, the executor of the estate of Y, to recover for X's injuries in the head-on automobile accident in which both were killed. The physical evidence at the scene of the accident does not show who drove over the center line and caused the accident, but Plaintiff charges that Y drove over the line and must prove this fact to collect. Plaintiff relies on the testimony of a highway patrol officer that she was driving behind Y's car and observed Y drive across the center line and collide with the car driven by X. There are no other witnesses and no other evidence, and the officer is not impeached in any way. Plaintiff should be granted a directed verdict.

   2) **Opposing party with burden of proof:** [§1754] Demeanor evidence, sometimes called ***disbelief evidence,*** is not sufficient to satisfy the opposing party's burden of producing evidence. [Dyer v. MacDougall, *supra,* §1525]

(5) **Compare—renewed motion for judgment as a matter of law (judgment n.o.v.):** [§1755] If a motion for judgment as a matter of law is made before a verdict is rendered but is denied and the verdict goes against the moving party, the party may make a "renewed motion for judgment as a matter of law" (formerly called a judgment n.o.v.). (*See infra,* §§1830-1841.) Whether resolved before or after the verdict, the motion uses the ***same standard*** and thus asks the same question at different times—whether the case should be (or should have been) submitted to the jury.

  (a) **Pre-verdict motion as predicate for renewed motion:** [§1756] In federal court, a party may not make a renewed motion unless she moved for a judgment as a matter of law at the close of all the evidence. [Fed. R. Civ. P. 50(b)]

1) **Constitutional justification:** [§1757] This requirement is a result of the Supreme Court's early decision that the judgment n.o.v. (renewed motion) violated the right to jury trial [Slocum v. New York Life Insurance Co., 228 U.S. 364 (1913)], which the Court modified to permit a renewed motion if there was first a directed verdict motion on which the judge "reserved" ruling. [Baltimore & Carolina Line v. Redman, 295 U.S. 654 (1935)] Thus, Rule 50(b) states that whenever there is a motion for judgment as a matter of law, the judge will be deemed to have reserved later ruling on it to satisfy *Redman*.

2) **Opportunity to cure deficiencies in proof:** [§1758] Some argue that the requirement of a predicate motion for a directed verdict permits parties to cure omissions from their proof before the case is submitted to the jury, and that there is good reason to give parties an incentive to call such problems to the attention of the other side.

(b) **Deferring decision until after verdict:** [§1759] Judges presented with directed verdict motions may consider a variety of factors, including the following, in deciding whether to defer decision where they find the motions persuasive.

1) **Jury will agree:** [§1760] If the judge feels that one side's case is so weak that judgment as a matter of law is proper, it is likely that the jury will also feel that way, and a jury verdict to that effect will be *harder to overturn on appeal.*

2) **Judge may be wrong:** [§1761] If the judge grants judgment as a matter of law and is reversed on appeal, it will be necessary to hold a *second trial*, whereas the appellate court may be able to reinstate the jury verdict if it reverses a post-verdict decision to grant judgment as a matter of law, and avoid thereby the need for a retrial.

3) **Time savings:** [§1762] By granting the pre-verdict motion, the judge will save the time occupied by instructions to the jury and jury deliberations. If the defendant moves for a directed verdict at the close of the plaintiff's case, the time needed for presentation of the defendant's case could also be saved.

3. **Jury Trial—Motion for Nonsuit:** [§1763] *In some states,* the defendant may move for a nonsuit at the close of the plaintiff's opening statement (or at the close of plaintiff's proof).

   a. **Test applied:** [§1764] Such a motion should be granted if the opening statement or proof reveals the plaintiff's case to be *legally insufficient.* For example, the plaintiff's failure to offer any credible evidence of damages might justify a nonsuit in a negligence case. [Seivell v. Hines, 116 A. 919 (Pa. 1922)]

   b. **Judgment on merits:** [§1765] Historically, a judgment of nonsuit was not a judgment on the merits, and thus did not bar a new action on the same cause. [Oscanyon v. Arms Co., 103 U.S. 261 (1880)] However, this rule has been changed in most states by legislation or court rule. [Cal. Civ. Proc. Code §581(e)]

4. **Nonjury Trial—Motion for Judgment as a Matter of Law:** [§1766] In a nonjury trial, after any party has been fully heard with respect to an issue, the court may enter judgment as a matter of law against that party on that issue. [Fed. R. Civ. P. 52(c)]

   a. **Early common law treatment:** [§1767] The historical analogue to this motion was a *demurrer to the evidence,* which required the trial judge to accept all of the plaintiff's evidence as true for the purpose of ruling on the demurrer.

   b. **State practice:** [§1768] Nomenclature for this motion varies among the states. In some, it is referred to as a *motion to dismiss;* while in others it is a *motion for judgment.* [Cal. Civ. Proc. Code §631.8—motion for judgment]

   c. **Test applied:** [§1769] Under modern practice, the court may grant the motion if it finds that the plaintiff's proof is *unpersuasive* on issues as to which plaintiff had the burden of persuasion. [Huber v. American President Lines, 240 F.2d 778 (2d Cir. 1957)] The rationale is that, in a nonjury trial, the judge is the ultimate trier of fact; and if she is already convinced, there is no reason to require further proof by the defendant.

G. ARGUMENT TO JURY

1. **Time for Argument:** [§1770] In federal and most state courts, counsel's argument to the jury takes place at the close of the evidence and *before* the jury is instructed by the judge (so that the last words the jurors hear are those of the judge, rather than the impassioned pleas of counsel). [Fed. R. Civ. P. 51]

2. **Right to Argue:** [§1771] Counsel have an absolute right to argument in a jury trial. [Shippy v. Peninsula Rapid Transit Co., 197 Cal. 290 (1925)]

3. **Control of Argument by Court:** [§1772] However, the trial judge in his discretion may control the duration and manner of argument.

4. **Limitations on Argument:** [§1773] In arguing to the jury, counsel is subject to the following constraints:

   a. *Comment must be based on the evidence,* and counsel may not distort the facts or assume facts not in evidence.

   b. *Argument must be within the limits of the substantive law* governing the action. Thus, for example, counsel may not argue for the use of an improper method of calculating damages (*e.g.*, to "punish" a defendant in an ordinary negligence case).

   c. *Counsel may not appeal to the passions or prejudices of the jurors.* [Pingatore v. Montgomery Ward & Co., 419 F.2d 1138 (6th Cir. 1969)] However, less restraint is imposed on counsel where the dispute is one fraught with emotion (such as a defamation trial). [Curtis Publishing Co. v. Butts, 351 F.2d 702 (5th Cir. 1965)]

5. **Effect of Improper Argument:** [§1774]   Not every improper argument requires a reversal of the judgment obtained and a new trial. A new trial is in order only if the argument is not adequately corrected by the judge, so that an incorrect verdict is likely to have resulted.

H. INSTRUCTIONS TO JURY

1. **In General:** [§1775]   Before a case is submitted to the jury for a verdict, the trial judge instructs the jury on certain relevant matters.

2. **Issues of Fact:** [§1776]   The jury's role is to decide *issues of fact* identified by the judge in the instructions, whereas the judge must decide questions of law (such as the meaning of statutes and documents).

    a. **"Law" vs. "fact":** [§1777]   Issues of law can be said to be general and to pertain to interpretation of the controlling law, while issues of fact are specific and pertain to past events. However, the boundary between the two may be unclear at times—in which case the matter must be resolved by reference to historic policy regarding the role of the jury.

       (1) **Example:** The law of negligence is usually expressed in general terms (*e.g.*, "a failure to exercise reasonable care") that minimize the role of the judge in defining the issues and maximize the role of the jury in deciding cases.

       (2) **Compare:** Where a decision necessarily requires that some additional meaning be attributed to the legal standard by the jury applying it, a law issue is inevitably intertwined with the fact issue, and such matters are sometimes said to present a *mixed issue* of law and fact. [*See* Wiener, *The Civil Jury Trial and the Law-Fact Distinction,* 54 Cal. L. Rev. 1867 (1966)]

    b. **Jury decides disputed facts only:** [§1778]   There is an issue of fact for the jury only where there is a genuine dispute about past events or the interpretation of those events.

       (1) **Facts not in dispute:** [§1779]   If only one reasonable inference can be drawn with respect to a matter, the judge should give instructions that *assume* the necessarily inferred fact. Thus, in a contract dispute in which a written contract is proved and the evidence presented by the defense bears only on the amount of damages, the court should not ask the jury to decide whether there was mutual assent.

       (2) **Disputed facts:** [§1780]   The judge may not give an instruction that assumes a fact in *dispute*. Each party is entitled to have the jury instructed to consider her version of matters that have been disputed. For example, if the defendant in a contract dispute offers proof tending to show that the written contract presented by the plaintiff was not signed by the defendant, the court must put the issue of mutual assent to the jury, however much the judge may doubt the denial.

3. **Burden of Persuasion**

    a. **Assigning the burden:** [§1781]   The judge must explain to the jury which party has the burden of persuasion in regard to each issue of fact that the jury must decide. The burden of persuasion will generally be assigned to the party having the burden of producing the evidence in regard to that issue; but this may not be the case if there is an applicable legal *presumption*. (*See* Evidence Summary.)

    b. **Degree of persuasion**

        (1) **Preponderance of the evidence:** [§1782] In a *civil* case, the trier of fact usually must be persuaded that a fact is more probable than not in order to resolve an issue in favor of the party bearing the burden of persuasion. [Sullivan v. Nesbit, 117 A. 502 (Conn. 1922)]

        (2) **Clear and convincing proof:** [§1783] In regard to issues of *fraud, duress, or undue influence,* however, the trier of fact generally is instructed to find for the party having the burden of persuasion only if the evidence is "clear and convincing."

            (a) **Comment:** This rule evolved in equity, which was said to *presume* honesty and fair dealing, thus requiring a greater amount of evidence to overcome the presumption.

            (b) **Note:** Some modern courts have rejected this principle, holding that a mere preponderance is sufficient with respect to *any* issue in a civil case. [Liodas v. Sahadi, 19 Cal. 3d 278 (1977)]

4. **Comment on the Evidence**

    a. **Majority rule:** [§1784] In most courts, the judge is allowed to comment on the quality of proof which bears on issues that the jury must decide, provided she informs the jury that it is the final decision maker. [Trezza v. Dame, 370 F.2d 1006 (5th Cir. 1967); Cal. Const. art. VI, §10]

    b. **Minority rule:** [§1785] Some states do not permit *any* comment on the evidence, on the ground that a judge's comments are too likely to prejudice the jury.

5. **Instructions Requested by Counsel**

    a. **Responsibility for preparation:** [§1786] While the ultimate responsibility for instructions rests with the judge, counsel has the duty of proposing instructions that present his theory of the case. [Willden v. Washington National Insurance Co., 18 Cal. 3d 631 (1976)]

    b. **Form of requests:** [§1787] Proposed instructions must be in writing and must be served on opposing counsel.

    c. **Time for filing:** [§1788] The Federal Rules provide that requests for instructions must be filed at the close of the evidence or at such earlier time as the court reasonably requires. [Fed. R. Civ. P. 51] In a complex case, the judge often orders such proposals to be filed before trial (at the time of pretrial conference).

(1) **State practice may vary:** [§1789]   In California, instructions covering the legal issues raised by the pleadings must be filed before the first witness is sworn. [Cal. Civ. Proc. Code §607a]

d. **Objections:** [§1790]   Each party must be given the opportunity to object to instructions proposed by his adversary. Failure to make objection before the jury retires is generally a waiver of any error not pointed out to the judge. [Fed. R. Civ. P. 51]

e. **Notice to counsel of court's action on requests:** [§1791]   Before counsel make their arguments to the jury, they are entitled to be informed of the judge's rulings on their requests for instructions. [Fed. R. Civ. P. 51] *Rationale:* Counsel need to know what the judge will say during instructions so that they can structure their closing arguments accordingly.

6. **Appellate Review of Jury Instructions**

    a. **Plain error:** [§1792]   Normally, any error in the jury instructions is waived unless timely objection was made in the trial court (*see* above). To prevent a miscarriage of justice, however, an *egregious* ("plain") error in the instructions may require a reversal even if no timely objection was made. [Mazer v. Lipschutz, 327 F.2d 42 (3d Cir. 1963)]

    b. **Harmless error:** [§1793]   On the other hand, if it appears unlikely that the jury was misled by a minor error in instructions, the error may be deemed harmless. [Fed. R. Civ. P. 61; Cal. Civ. Proc. Code §475] In applying this rule, the appellate court will consider the impact of the instructions as a whole. [Marshall v. Ford Motor Co., 446 F.2d 712 (10th Cir. 1971)]

        (1) **Note:** Where alternative theories are advanced, the instructions given are correct as to one theory but incorrect as to the other, and the jury returns a *general verdict* (with no indication as to which theory was accepted), reversal is generally required, because there is no certainty that the error was harmless. [Pacific Greyhound Lines v. Zane, 160 F.2d 731 (9th Cir. 1947)]

        (2) **But note:** A minority of courts adheres to the principle that a jury should be presumed to have based its verdict on the correct portion of the instruction. [State v. Hills, 113 N.E. 1045 (Ohio 1916)]

I. **JURY DELIBERATION AND VERDICT**

1. **Types of Verdicts:** [§1794]   Verdicts may take several forms, depending on the form of jury instructions.

    a. **General verdict:** [§1795]   The most common and traditional form of verdict is the general verdict, in which the jury simply makes a decision in favor of one party or the other. Such a verdict *implies* a finding in favor of the prevailing party *on every material issue of fact* submitted to the jury. [Cal. Civ. Proc. Code §624]

        (1) **Example:** In the typical negligence case, a general verdict for the plaintiff necessarily rests on finding that the defendant was negligent, that the

negligence proximately caused harm to the plaintiff, and that the plaintiff was free of contributory negligence. [Sassano v. Roullard, 27 Cal. App. 2d 372 (1938)]

(2) **Criticism:** At the same time, a general verdict may conceal a misunderstanding of the instructions or even a disregard of them.

b. **Special verdict:** [§1796] A special verdict consists of the jury's answers to specific factual questions that it is instructed to decide. In this situation, the jury does not decide directly which party should prevail on the law. Instead, the special verdicts should resolve all the material issues so the court can enter judgment thereon. [Fed. R. Civ. P. 49(a); Cal. Civ. Proc. Code §624]

(1) **Verdicts on all disputed issues:** [§1797] To serve their purpose, special verdicts should usually be fashioned to cover *all disputed issues,* so that the judge can determine the proper judgment from them.

(2) **Advantages:** [§1798] A special verdict reduces the burden on the judge of instructing the jury on the law and reduces the jury's need to understand the law.

(3) **Disadvantages:** [§1799] Where a special verdict is used, the jury may find it harder to reach a unanimous verdict. Moreover, *inconsistent* findings on a crucial issue may necessitate a new trial. However, the court has the power to interpret the jury's findings in order to "mold" them to a judgment. [Gallick v. Baltimore & Ohio Railroad, 372 U.S. 108 (1963)]

(4) **Disclosure to counsel:** [§1800] Some courts hold that counsel should be given access to the special verdicts and an opportunity to comment on them. [Sakamoto v. N.A.B. Trucking Co., 717 F.2d 1000 (6th Cir. 1983); Clegg v. Hardware Mutual Casualty Co., 264 F.2d 152 (5th Cir. 1959)]

(5) **Advising jury of legal consequences of answers:** [§1801] Since the judge is to draw the legal conclusions from the special verdicts, it is not necessary that the jury be instructed on them, and some courts have held that the jury should not be so instructed. [Thedorf v. Lipsey, 237 F.2d 190 (7th Cir. 1956); McCourtie v. United States Steel Corp., 93 N.W.2d 552 (Minn. 1958)] Because the use of this procedure is discretionary with the court, however, others have decided that the judge may so instruct. [Lowery v. Clouse, 348 F.2d 252 (8th Cir. 1965)] *Rationale:* The jury is likely to deduce from the lawyers' arguments which party will be benefited from a particular resolution of an issue, and so the judge should have the right to make it clear to the jury.

c. **General verdict with special interrogatories:** [§1802] The trial judge may combine the two foregoing forms of verdict by instructing the jury to return a general decision as to which party should prevail on the law, while simultaneously answering specific questions of fact posed by the evidence. [Fed. R. Civ. P. 49(b); Cal. Civ. Proc. Code §625]

(1) **Purpose:** [§1803] The idea of this combined form of verdict is to permit the jury to decide the whole case, while obtaining a "cross check" that the jury understood and adhered to the instructions on the law.

(2) **Disadvantage:** [§1804] Like special verdicts, the general instruction with special interrogatories carries the risk of inconsistency necessitating a new trial.

    (a) **Inconsistency between finding and verdict:** [§1805] If there is an inconsistency between the special finding and the general verdict, the judge in her discretion may disregard the general verdict and enter judgment according to the special findings. [Fed. R. Civ. P. 49(b); Cal. Civ. Proc. Code §625]

    (b) **Inconsistency among findings:** [§1806] However, if there are inconsistencies among *several* of the special findings, the judge must order a new trial unless she can reconcile the inconsistencies. In doing so, there is a presumption in favor of the general verdict; and special findings should be reconciled so as to support the general verdict, if possible. [Law v. Northern Assurance Co., 165 Cal. 394 (1913)]

(3) **Failure to respond:** [§1807] Failure to respond to a special interrogatory is not necessarily fatal to the verdict. The court in its discretion may assume that the missing answer would be consistent with the general verdict. [Gulf Refining Co. v. Fetschan, 130 F.2d 129 (6th Cir. 1942), *cert. denied*, 318 U.S. 764 (1943)]

(4) **Inability to agree on an issue:** [§1808] And even where the jurors announce their inability to agree on a particular issue, the verdict may be sustained if there is agreement on an alternative finding sufficient to support the general verdict (*e.g.*, jurors could not agree on which among several negligent acts by defendant caused plaintiff's injury, but agreed that one of those acts was responsible).

2. **Requirement of Unanimity**

    a. **General rule:** [§1809] In federal and most state courts, the jury must render a unanimous decision, unless the parties otherwise agree. [Fed. R. Civ. P. 48]

        (1) **Purpose:** [§1810] This requirement forces the jurors to deliberate in any case in which one of the group has serious doubt about the outcome.

        (2) **"Dynamite charge":** [§1811] Where the jurors, after deliberating, announce that they are unable to reach a verdict, it is not improper for the court to emphasize to the jury the expense of a new trial and the unlikelihood that another jury would reach a better verdict, and to ask each juror to make a renewed effort to reach unanimity. [Allen v. United States, 164 U.S. 492 (1896)] Such a charge is sometimes referred to as a "dynamite charge."

    b. **Minority rule:** [§1812] Some states permit nonunanimous verdicts. In California, for example, only three-fourths of the jury in civil cases must concur. [Cal. Civ. Proc. Code §618]

    c. **Tactic:** [§1813] The unanimity requirement generally favors the defense, at least insofar as the plaintiff has the burden of persuasion on the disputed issues.

Hence, if nonunanimous verdicts are allowed in state court, the plaintiff may prefer to litigate there, whereas the defense may seek to remove to a federal court.

3. **Jury Deliberation and Impeachment of Verdict**

   a. **Standards of jury conduct**

   (1) **Materials taken into jury room:** [§1814]   In its deliberations, a jury normally has access to exhibits or other papers received in evidence. [Cal. Civ. Proc. Code §612] The judge may allow jurors to take notes during the trial, and such notes may also be used during deliberations.

   (2) **Consideration of matters outside the record:** [§1815]   The jury is not permitted to receive any information that was not presented at trial and made a part of the record.

      (a) *Any communication from the judge* must be received in court in the *presence of counsel.* [Cal. Civ. Proc. Code §614] For example, it is error for the judge to provide the jury with a dictionary in counsel's absence, where it appears that jurors may use the dictionary definition of important terms in arriving at their verdict. [Palestroni v. Jacobs, 77 A.2d 183 (N.J. 1950)]

      (b) *It is improper for jurors to fraternize with counsel* during the trial or during deliberation.

      (c) *And it is likewise improper for the jury to conduct its own investigation* of the facts by calling experts in the absence of counsel, conducting experiments with the exhibits, or independently taking a view of the premises of an accident.

   (3) **Each juror shares in decision:** [§1816]   Consistent with the requirement of unanimity, each juror must make up her own mind on the verdict.

      (a) **Chance verdicts:** [§1817]   Accordingly, the jury may not decide by lot or other method of chance. [Cal. Civ. Proc. Code §657(2)]

      (b) **Quotient verdicts:** [§1818]   Nor may the jury reach a decision by taking an average of several awards of the jurors. Such an average *may* be computed as a means of assisting each juror to appraise the appropriate award; but the jurors may not bind themselves in advance to the result of the computation. [*See* McDonald v. Pless, 238 U.S. 264 (1915)]

      (c) **Coercion by judge:** [§1819]   The judge may not coerce the jury to agree. In this regard, it may be reversible error to *repeat* a "dynamite charge" (*see supra*, §1811) urging unanimity. [United States v. Seawell, 550 F.2d 1159 (9th Cir. 1977), *cert. denied*, 439 U.S. 991 (1978)]

b. **Impeachment of verdict for misconduct**

(1) **Common law rule:** [§1820] The traditional common law rule was that a juror could not impeach his own verdict. Thus, any misconduct in the deliberation had to be established by the testimony of someone *other than* the jurors, such as a bailiff or court attendant.

(a) **Rationale:** This rule safeguarded the secrecy of jury deliberations and protected jurors from harassment by counsel urging repudiation of verdicts. [*See* McDonald v. Pless, *supra*]

(b) **Criticism:** At the same time, the rule made enforcement of the standards of conduct described above very difficult.

(2) **Federal Rule:** [§1821] The Federal Rules of Evidence now permit a juror to testify to any *"extraneous prejudicial information"* or *"outside influence"* that may have altered the verdict. [Fed. R. Evid. 606(b)]

(a) **Note:** This rule does *not* authorize the use of juror testimony to attack the deliberative process (matters occurring *inside* the jury room), as by showing a quotient verdict. [*See* Complete Auto Transit, Inc. v. Wayne Broyles Corp., 351 F.2d 478 (5th Cir. 1965)]

(b) **Compare:** It is possible, however, to use juror testimony to show gross misconduct, such as taking of bribe or fraternizing with a party. [*See, e.g.*, Jorgensen v. York Ice Machinery Corp., 160 F.2d 432 (2d Cir. 1947)]

(c) **Example—use of intoxicants:** Where jurors drank heavily during lunch, some smoked marijuana or took cocaine during the trial, and jurors generally approached their task as "one big party," juror affidavit was inadmissible to impeach the verdict on these grounds, because they were "internal" to the verdict. [Tanner v. United States, 483 U.S. 107 (1987)]

(d) **Compare—determining what was decided for collateral estoppel purposes:** The rule of exclusion applies to challenges to the validity of a verdict, but does not forbid use of juror affidavits to determine what was actually decided in order to give proper collateral estoppel effect to verdict. (For discussion of collateral estoppel, see *infra*, §§2073 *et seq.*)

(3) **State rules:** [§1822] Some states are much more permissive than the federal courts with respect to use of juror testimony to attack verdicts. In California, for example, *any improper influence*—inside or outside the jury room—may be shown. [People v. Huchinson, 71 Cal. 2d 342 (1969)]

(a) **Example:** Juror testimony may be used to show that jurors were coerced to change their views or that improper consideration was given to the fact of insurance.

(b) **Rationale:** Assuring the "purity" of a verdict is more important than protecting its stability.

(c) **Limitation:** However, affidavits may not be used merely to show that a juror's reasoning or mental process was faulty.

c. **Impeachment of verdict for inaccurate response on voir dire:** [§1823] A juror's failure to respond correctly to voir dire may be a ground for impeaching the verdict.

(1) **Showing required:** [§1824] The party challenging the verdict must show that the juror *refused to answer honestly* a material question and that a correct response would have *provided a valid basis for challenge* for cause. [McDonough Power Equipment, Inc. v. Greenwood, 464 U.S. 548 (1984)]

(2) **Example:** A juror in a personal injury case was asked whether any member of his family had suffered "injuries . . . that resulted in any disability or prolonged pain or suffering." He failed to answer that his son had once been injured due to explosion of a truck tire, but because the juror honestly did not understand that this event was called for by the question, his failure to answer did not provide a ground to set aside the verdict. [McDonough Power Equipment, Inc. v. Greenwood, *supra*]

(3) **Compare—contempt:** [§1825] When a juror intentionally withholds disqualifying information, he may be held in contempt for doing so. [Clark v. United States, 289 U.S. 1 (1932)]

d. **Announcement of verdict:** [§1826] To help insure that deliberations were proper, the jury verdict must be announced in open court.

(1) **Polling the jury:** [§1827] At the request of either party, the jury may be "polled"—*i.e.,* each juror may be asked if he concurred in the verdict. If a juror fails to concur, the jury must continue its deliberations or a new trial must be ordered. [Fox v. United States, 417 F.2d 84 (5th Cir. 1969)]

(2) **Correction of verdict:** [§1828] Likewise, if the verdict returned is insufficient or incomplete, the court may direct the jury to continue and complete its deliberations. [Cal. Civ. Proc. Code §619]

(a) **But note:** Once the jury is discharged, however, a defect in the verdict cannot be cured. [Sparks v. Berntsen, 19 Cal. 2d 308 (1942)]

e. **Investigation of jury misconduct:** [§1829] Counsel may question jurors after they have given their verdict in order to ascertain any possible bases for impeachment.

(1) **Limitation:** However, hostile interrogation of jurors may be enjoined [Rakes v. United States, 169 F.2d 739 (4th Cir. 1948)], and some courts routinely limit post-trial interrogation of jurors.

(2) **And note:** Jurors cannot be subpoenaed unless there is some reason to expect that their testimony may reveal a ground for impeachment. The rationale is that jurors should not routinely be subject to being "placed on trial by defeated litigants." [Linhart v. Nelson, 18 Cal. 3d 641 (1976)]

J. MOTIONS AFTER VERDICT OR JUDGMENT

1. **Renewed Motion for Judgment as a Matter of Law (Judgment Notwithstanding the Verdict):** [§1830] Judgment *non obstante verdicto* ("n.o.v." or "notwithstanding the verdict") is a traditional device for nullifying a jury verdict that is not supported by the evidence. In 1991, the name was changed in federal court to renewed motion for judgment as a matter of law. [Fed. R. Civ. P. 50(b)]

    a. **Test applied:** [§1831] The standard applied for a renewed motion is the same as for such a motion at the close of all the evidence; *i.e.*, the motion should be granted only if there is **no substantial evidence to support the decision** of the jury. [Montgomery Ward & Co. v. Duncan, 311 U.S. 243 (1940)] (*See supra*, §§1739-1754, regarding standard on motion before the verdict.)

    b. **Procedural requirements**

    (1) **Motion:** [§1832] In federal court, a renewed motion for judgment as a matter of law may *not* be entered by the court on its own motion. If no motion is made, not even an appellate court has power to enter judgment for the losing party. [Cone v. West Virginia Pulp & Paper Co., 330 U.S. 212 (1946)]

    (a) **Some states contra:** [§1833] In at least some states, judgment *can* be entered *sua sponte*. [Cal. Civ. Proc. Code §629]

    (2) **Timeliness of motion**

    (a) **Federal Rule:** [§1834] In federal court, a renewed motion for judgment as a matter of law must be made within 10 days after the entry of judgment on the verdict. [Fed. R. Civ. P. 50(b)]

    (b) **State practice:** [§1835] Time limits in state practice may vary. [Cal. Civ. Proc. Code §629—15 days following notice of entry of judgment]

    (3) **Prior motion for judgment as a matter of law:** [§1836] In the federal court, a motion for renewed motion for judgment as a matter of law cannot be considered unless the moving party made a motion for directed verdict at the close of all the evidence. [Fed. R. Civ. P. 50(b)]

    (a) **Rationale:** Judgment n.o.v. was not known at common law, and hence presumably was forbidden by the Seventh Amendment. But a directed verdict *was* permitted at common law; and since the judge can reserve his ruling on that motion, a motion for judgment n.o.v. can be viewed as a renewal of the motion for a directed verdict. [Baltimore & Carolina Line v. Redman, *supra*, §1757]

    (b) **State practice contra:** [§1837] Most states do not require a prior motion for directed verdict in order to move for judgment n.o.v. [Cal. Civ. Proc. Code §629]

    (4) **Joined with motion for new trial:** [§1838] A post-verdict motion for judgment as a matter of law may be joined with a motion for new trial.

(a) **If judgment granted:** [§1839]   Where judgment as a matter of law is granted, the trial court should nevertheless rule in the alternative on the motion for new trial. In that way, if there is an appeal, the appellate court will have full knowledge of the trial judge's decision. [Fed. R. Civ. P. 50(c)]

(b) **If judgment denied**

1) **Appeal:** [§1840]   The party whose motion is denied may appeal from the judgment as entered (but not from denial of the motion, which is a nonappealable order; *see infra*, §§1957 *et seq.*).

2) **Responding party's ground for new trial:** [§1841]   If the moving party does appeal, the party seeking to preserve the verdict should assert in the alternative any grounds he may have for a new trial. Otherwise, the issues may not be preserved for consideration by the appellate court, which might reverse and order entry of judgment contrary to the verdict. [Fed. R. Civ. P. 50(d); *and see* Neely v. Martin K. Eby Construction Co., 386 U.S. 317 (1967)]

2. **Motion for New Trial:** [§1842]   The trial judge has the power to order a new trial on all or part of the factual issues in dispute. [Fed. R. Civ. P. 59(a); Cal. Civ. Proc. Code §657]

   a. **Grounds for motion—jury trial:** [§1843]   A federal court may order a new trial in a jury case "for any of the reasons for which new trials have heretofore been granted in actions at law in the courts of the United States." [Fed. R. Civ. P. 59(a)] Some state statutes are more explicit in enumerating grounds. [Cal. Civ. Proc. Code §657] In any case, appropriate grounds would include the following:

   (1) **Prejudicial misconduct:** [§1844]   A new trial may be granted if the court, the jury, or the adversary engaged in misconduct that prevented a fair trial.

      (a) **Examples**

         1) *Counsel's improper jury argument.* [Minneapolis, St. Paul & Sault Ste. Marie Railway v. Moquin, 283 U.S. 520 (1931)]

         2) *False answer by juror on voir dire examination.* [Estate of Mesner, 77 Cal. App. 2d 667 (1947)]

         3) *Improper delay* or continuance for personal convenience of the trial judge. [Citron v. Aro Corp., 377 F.2d 750 (3d Cir. 1967)]

      (b) **No new trial for harmless error:** [§1845]   A new trial should not be ordered for misconduct that was not prejudicial or was adequately corrected by appropriate instructions from the judge. [Fed. R. Civ. P. 61]

(c) **Waiver of prejudicial error:** [§1846] And a party moving for a new trial may not rely on misconduct known to him *prior* to the verdict, but which he did not point out to the court. *Rationale:* Allowing the party to gamble on the outcome of the verdict would impose an unfair risk on the adversary, who would be faced with the alternative of an adverse verdict or a new trial. [Lindemann v. San Joaquin Cotton Oil Co., 5 Cal. 2d 480 (1936)]

(2) **Accident or surprise:** [§1847] A new trial may be granted where a party is unfairly surprised by the evidence presented at trial.

  (a) **Prejudicial effect:** [§1848] The surprise must have had a *material* effect on the outcome of the trial. [Union Electric Light & Power Co. v. Snyder Estate Co., 15 F. Supp. 379 (W.D. Mo. 1936)]

  (b) **Diligence:** [§1849] The party also must have been *diligent* in guarding against the surprise.

  1) **Example:** A party who relies on a witness's promise to appear voluntarily and who fails to subpoena the witness is *not* entitled to a new trial when the witness fails to appear. [Rudin v. Luman, 53 Cal. App. 212 (1921)]

  2) **Incompetent counsel:** [§1850] A party is charged with the mistake of his counsel, so that a new trial generally will *not* be granted on the ground that counsel was negligent or incompetent. [Everett v. Everett, 29 N.W.2d 919 (Mich. 1947)]

  (c) **Timely application:** [§1851] Where surprise occurs, counsel must move for a mistrial or continuance at the earliest opportunity. [Kaufman v. DeMuths, 31 Cal. 2d 429 (1948)]

(3) **Newly discovered evidence:** [§1852] A new trial also may be granted in order to consider evidence discovered after the trial.

  (a) **Requirements**

  1) *The new proof must pertain to facts in existence at the time of trial,* not facts occurring later. [Schuyler v. United Air Lines, 94 F. Supp. 472 (M.D. Pa. 1950)]

  2) *The new proof must be highly significant,* not merely cumulative. [Wulfsohn v. Russo-Asiatic Bank, 11 F.2d 715 (9th Cir. 1926)]

  3) *And the moving party must show* that the evidence *could not have been obtained by due diligence before trial.* [Toledo Scale Co. v. Computering Scale Co., 261 U.S. 399 (1923)]

  (b) **But note:** A new trial should *not* be ordered where the "discovery" results from the failure of counsel earlier to appreciate the significance of available proof. [Slemons v. Paterson, 14 Cal. 2d 612 (1939)]

(c) **And note:** Generally, "newly discovered evidence" is a *disfavored* ground for new trial; and parties should not withhold or fail to develop proof in hopes of getting a second chance at a favorable verdict. [Estate of Emerson, 170 Cal. 81 (1915)]

(4) **Improper evidence:** [§1853] A new trial may be granted to correct an erroneous ruling on the admissibility of evidence, provided the error was prejudicial and was the subject of timely objection.

(5) **Verdict contrary to law:** [§1854] A new trial likewise may be granted where the evidence is *not legally sufficient* to support the verdict. An order granting a judgment n.o.v. may also be appropriate if the procedural requirements for such a motion were met. (*See supra*, §1836.)

(6) **Weight of the evidence:** [§1855] Finally, a new trial may be ordered if the judge finds the verdict to be contrary to the manifest weight of the evidence. [Aetna Casualty & Surety Co. v. Yeatts, 122 F.2d 350 (4th Cir. 1941)]

(a) **Standard for decision:** [§1856] The standard for decision has been expressed in different ways. An underlying policy concern is that motions for new trials on this ground not undermine the right to jury trial; if the judge can invalidate a jury decision on the ground she does not like it, the right to jury trial becomes insignificant.

1) **Directed verdict standard:** [§1857] Some courts phrase the standard in terms of whether there was substantial evidence to support the verdict—the directed verdict standard. *Criticism:* This seems overly narrow because the motion for new trial on this ground is intended as an additional safety valve in the jury system. On the other hand, when a party has failed to produce substantial evidence at the first trial, it is difficult to understand why the court should give the party a second chance and impose the cost of a second trial on the winner at the first trial.

2) **Thirteenth juror standard:** [§1858] At the opposite extreme is the thirteenth juror standard: The judge may grant a new trial whenever she disagrees with the jury. *Criticism:* This seems too easy to satisfy. It would constrict the right to jury trial because one must persuade the judge, as well as the jury, in order to prevail.

3) **Majority rule—miscarriage of justice:** [§1859] Between the thirteenth juror and directed verdict standards is the standard applied by most courts—the miscarriage of justice standard. Under this standard, the judge is to ask whether the jury has reached a seriously erroneous result. In answering this question, she may weigh the evidence, assess the credibility of witnesses, and draw inferences from the evidence.

a) **Possible exception:** It has been held that as to nontechnical matters, the court should not grant a new trial on the basis of **credibility determinations** because those are peculiarly within the province of the jury. [Lind v. Schenley Industries, Inc., 278 F.2d 79 (3d Cir.), *cert. denied*, 364 U.S. 835 (1960)]

(b) **Constitutionality:** [§1860] Because the motion for a new trial on this ground existed at common law, there has been no serious challenge to its constitutionality, even though it may seem to erode the value of the right to jury trial. [*See* Galloway v. United States, 319 U.S. 372 (1943)—discussing existence of motion for new trial at common law]

(c) **Appellate review**

1) **Traditional rule:** [§1861] The traditional rule was that the weight of the evidence was to be assessed only by the trial judge—*i.e.*, whether he granted or denied a new trial on this ground, his decision ordinarily was not reversible. The trial judge's ruling would be reversed only if a new trial was denied and there was *no* substantial evidence to support the verdict—*i.e.*, if there should have been a directed verdict. [*See* Portman v. American Home Products Corp., 201 F.2d 847 (2d Cir. 1953)]

2) **Modern rule:** [§1862] Today, appellate courts may reverse the denial of a motion for new trial if it is determined that the refusal to grant the motion was an "abuse of discretion." This means that if the evidence was seriously arguable, the trial judge should not substitute his view of the evidence for that of the jury. [Lind v. Schenley Industries, Inc., *supra*]

3) **Review of grant of new trial:** [§1863] An order granting a new trial is *not immediately appealable* because it is not a final judgment. On appeal from the final judgment following the second trial, however, the appellant may claim error in the grant of the new trial. If the appellate court agrees, it can *reinstate the verdict* from the first trial, although this rarely happens.

4) **Excessive or inadequate damages:** [§1864] The trial judge may find that the jury's award of damages is against the weight of the evidence. In such cases, a partial or conditional new trial may be ordered. (*See* discussion of remittitur and additur, *infra*, §§1883-1893.) Such rulings are generally reviewable only for abuse of discretion. [Fairmont v. Cub Fork Coal Co., 287 U.S. 474 (1933)]

b. **Grounds for motion—nonjury trial:** [§1865] Where the trial was conducted without a jury, a motion for new trial is essentially a motion for rehearing. Such a motion may be granted on the following grounds:

(1) *Newly discovered evidence;*

(2) *Erroneous findings of fact;* and/or

(3) *Error in the conduct of the trial* (*e.g.*, erroneous rulings on admissibility of evidence).

c. **Procedural requirements for new trial motion**

  (1) **Necessity for motion**

    (a) **Federal Rule:** [§1866] A federal court may grant a new trial on its own motion. [Fed. R. Civ. P. 59(d)]

    (b) **State courts:** [§1867] In some states, the court may order a new trial only on motion by a party. [Cal. Civ. Proc. Code §659]

  (2) **Timeliness of motion**

    (a) **Federal Rule:** [§1868] A motion for new trial must be served not later than 10 days after the entry of judgment. [Fed. R. Civ. P. 59(b)]

    (b) **State courts:** [§1869] State time limits may vary. In California, for example, the motion must be made within 15 days after notice of entry of judgment. [Cal. Civ. Proc. Code §659]

  (3) **Affidavits:** [§1870] A motion for new trial may be accompanied by affidavits where proof is necessary to establish the grounds.

    (a) **Time for filing:** [§1871] In federal court, the movant's affidavits must be filed at the time of filing the motion. [Fed. R. Civ. P. 59(c)] State rules may allow later filing. [Cal. Civ. Proc. Code §659a]

    (b) **No oral testimony:** [§1872] Most courts refuse to accept oral testimony in support of a motion for new trial. [Linhart v. Nelson, 18 Cal. 3d 641 (1976)]

  (4) **Hearings:** [§1873] A motion for new trial must be heard by the judge who conducted the trial, unless he is disabled.

  (5) **Time for decision:** [§1874] There is no time limit for the judge's ruling on a motion for new trial, at least in federal practice.

    (a) **State laws:** [§1875] Some state statutes impose a limit. [Cal. Civ. Proc. Code §660—failure to grant motion within 60 days after filing operates as a denial]

d. **Order**

  (1) **In nonjury cases:** [§1876] In ruling on a motion for new trial in a nonjury case, the court may order a full retrial or only *partial* new trials (*i.e.*, it

may order the reopening of the judgment for the taking of additional proof, after which it may amend its findings of fact and conclusions of law or make new findings and conclusions and direct the entry of a new judgment). [Fed. R. Civ. P. 59(a)]

(2) **In jury cases:** [§1877] In a jury case, the court must grant or deny the motion, but it may do so in parts or on conditions (*e.g.*, new trial on damages only).

   (a) **Specification of grounds**

      1) **Federal practice:** [§1878] A federal court need not specify the grounds on which new trial is granted.

      2) **State practice:** [§1879] State rules on specifications of grounds vary. In California, if the ground is *insufficiency of the proof,* the judge must specify the respect in which the proof is deficient (and this specification is reviewable on appeal). [Cal. Civ. Proc. Code §657]

   (b) **Excessive or inadequate damages:** [§1880] Where the judge finds that the jury's damage award is inappropriate, there are several alternatives:

      1) **Full new trial:** [§1881] The judge may order a full new trial. This would be the only appropriate order if the award is so excessive that the judge concludes that the verdict is the result of passion. [New York Central Railroad v. Johnson, 279 U.S. 310 (1929)]

      2) **Partial new trial:** [§1882] As a *time-saving move,* the court may order that the new trial be limited to certain issues. However, such a limited new trial may be used only when "it clearly appears that the issue to be retried is so distinct and separable from the others that a trial of it alone may be had without injustice." [Gasoline Products Co. v. Champlin Refining Co., 283 U.S. 494 (1931)] *Example:* When the low verdict for plaintiff indicates that it was a compromise verdict in which jurors who favored exonerating defendant altogether went along with a low award to plaintiff, a new trial limited to the issue of damages would be unfair to defendant.

      3) **Conditional new trial**

         a) **Remittitur:** [§1883] A remittitur is an order for a new trial, subject to recall if the plaintiff consents to *reduction* of the damage award. If the plaintiff so consents, a new trial is denied.

            1/ **Note:** Remittitur was recognized at common law and has been held consistent with the Seventh Amendment. [Northern Pacific Railroad v. Herbert, 116 U.S. 642 (1886)]

2/ **Proper sum:** [§1884] Courts vary in their approach to what is the proper sum for a remittitur.

    a/ **Fair amount:** [§1885] Many courts hold that the verdict should be reduced to whatever amount the trial judge determines to be fair and reasonable (*i.e.*, her estimate of what a properly functioning jury would have found)—on the theory that this gives the plaintiff adequate incentive to avoid the costs and risks of a retrial. [Powers v. Allstate Insurance Co., 102 N.W.2d 393 (Wis. 1960); Cal. Civ. Proc. Code §662.5(b)]

    b/ **Lowest amount:** [§1886] However, some courts reduce the verdict to the lowest amount that an impartial jury reasonably could have awarded—on the theory that this best protects the defendant from an improper award and that plaintiff can always protect himself by accepting a new trial. [Meissner v. Papas, 35 F. Supp. 676 (E.D. Wis. 1940)]

    c/ **Highest amount:** [§1887] Still other courts reduce the verdict to the *highest* amount deemed not excessive—on the theory that the jury's verdict should be upheld insofar as possible. [Gorsalitz v. Olin Mathieson Chemical Corp., 429 F.2d 1033 (5th Cir. 1970)]

    d/ **Note—effect on plaintiff's election:** [§1888] Note that remittitur gives the plaintiff the choice whether to proceed to a new trial or accept a reduced award. Using the lowest possible award standard (§1886, above) signals to the plaintiff that this amount is the worst he can do at the second trial. Using the highest possible award standard (§1887, above) signals to the plaintiff that he cannot expect to do better at the new trial and keep that result. Thus, adoption of the highest possible award standard will be more likely to induce plaintiffs to accept remittitur than the lowest possible award standard.

3/ **Waiver:** [§1889] If plaintiff agrees to a remittitur, most courts hold that he waives the right to appeal the propriety of the remittitur (except that if defendant thereafter appeals, plaintiff may cross-appeal from the reduction of damages ordered by the trial judge). [Donovan v. Penn Shipping Co., 429 U.S. 648 (1977)]

4/ **Appellate court:** [§1890] There is a split of authority as to whether an *appellate* court may make a remittitur in cases in which it finds the damages excessive. [Grunenthal v. Long Island Railway, 393 U.S. 156 (1968)] California Appellate Rule 24(c) expressly recognizes remittitur and additur by appellate courts.

    b) **Additur:** [§1891] An additur is an order granting a new trial unless the defendant consents to an *increase* in the amount of the verdict.

        1/ **Federal practice:** [§1892] Additur was not known at common law and has therefore been held forbidden in federal courts by the Seventh Amendment (*i.e.*, as violating plaintiff's right to jury trial on the issue of damages.) [Dimick v. Schiedt, *supra*, §1650]

        2/ **State practice:** [§1893] However, many state statutes and constitutions allow additur as well as remittitur. [*See, e.g.*, Cal. Civ. Proc. Code §662.5(a)]

3. **Motion to Alter or Amend Judgment:** [§1894] A motion to alter or amend judgment may be used to reopen judgments in both jury and nonjury cases. [Fed. R. Civ. P. 59(e); Cal. Civ. Proc. Code §663]

    a. **Errors of law only:** [§1895] The purpose of the motion is to correct errors of law, and it cannot be used to secure a retrial on the facts.

    b. **Examples:** Vacation of a judgment would be proper:

        (1) *Where the judgment rests on erroneous conclusions of law;*

        (2) *Where necessary conclusions of law were omitted;* or

        (3) *Where the court erroneously asserted jurisdiction.*

    c. **Time limitations:** [§1896] A motion to alter or amend judgment is subject to the same time limits as a motion for new trial. [Fed. R. Civ. P. 59(e); Cal. Civ. Proc. Code §663a; *see supra*, §§1868-1869]

4. **Motion for Relief from Judgment**

    a. **For clerical mistakes:** [§1897] If the judgment as entered by the clerk differs from that ordered by the court, the mistake can be corrected. [Fed. R. Civ. P. 60(a); Cal. Civ. Proc. Code §473]

        (1) **Procedure:** [§1898] Corrections can be made on motion or *sua sponte*.

        (2) **Timing:** [§1899] There is no time limit on the power to correct.

        (3) **"Clerical" mistake:** [§1900] Clerical mistakes subject to correction by this motion may be those of either clerk or counsel who drafted the

order or judgment, but *not* those of the judge. Judicial errors should be attacked by a motion to alter or amend (above).

b. **Other grounds:** [§1901] The court likewise may relieve a party from judgment on the following grounds:

(1) **Mistake, inadvertence, or surprise:** [§1902] A judgment may be reopened for these reasons, but the circumstances must be extraordinary. The standard of care to which the moving party is held is much higher than would be applied in a motion for new trial. [Fed. R. Civ. P. 60(b)(1); Bershad v. McDonough, 469 F.2d 1333 (7th Cir. 1972); Cal. Civ. Proc. Code §473; Martin v. Taylor, 267 Cal. App. 2d 112 (1968)]

(2) **Excusable neglect:** [§1903] The court may reopen a default judgment for excusable neglect. However, neglect of counsel is *not* a sufficient ground for relief. [Universal Film Exchanges, Inc. v. Lust, 479 F.2d 573 (4th Cir. 1973)]

(3) **Newly discovered evidence:** [§1904] The court may reopen a judgment to receive additional proof, but it must be shown that the moving party, by reasonable diligence, could not have discovered the new evidence in time to move for a new trial under Federal Rule 59. And the proof must be more than cumulative; *i.e.*, it is not enough that the moving party has now devised a new factual theory to explain the proof. [*See* Stilwell v. Travelers Insurance Co., 327 F.2d 931 (5th Cir. 1964)] The standard is essentially the same as that used on a motion for a new trial on this ground. (*See supra*, §1852.)

(4) **Fraud or misconduct:** [§1905] A judgment may be reopened for fraud or other misconduct (*e.g.*, a judgment obtained by the use of perjured testimony). [Fed. R. Civ. P. 60(b)(3); Peacock Records, Inc. v. Checker Records, Inc., 365 F.2d 145 (7th Cir. 1966)]

(a) **Burden on party guilty of fraud:** [§1906] The responding party then has the burden of showing that the fraud did not affect the outcome. [Hazel Atlas Glass Co. v. Hartford Empire Co., 322 U.S. 238 (1944)]

(b) **Example—other misconduct:** When defendant in a products liability action failed to produce a document called for by an order compelling production of documents, its failure to do so constituted misconduct. Since production of the document might materially have affected plaintiff's presentation of the case, judgment for defendant was vacated. [Rozier v. Ford Motor Co., 573 F.2d 1332 (5th Cir. 1978)]

(5) **Void judgment:** [§1907] A judgment may be reopened if it is void (as where no notice was given prior to the entry of a default). [Bass v. Hoagland, 172 F.2d 205 (5th Cir. 1949)]

(6) **Change of circumstances (equitable relief):** [§1908] Where the judgment provides for continuing equitable relief, as where an injunction

is granted, the court may reopen the proceedings to consider whether supervening events make the old decree inequitable. [Fed. R. Civ. P. 60(b)(5); De Filippis v. United States, 567 F.2d 341 (7th Cir. 1977)]

   (a) **Note:** This ground is generally not applicable in the case of money judgments. [Ryan v. United States Lines, 303 F.2d 430 (2d Cir. 1962)]

   (b) **And note:** The parties may not contract to bar the court from considering the continuing equity of a decree; it is an abuse of discretion to refuse to modify a decree that no longer fairly serves its original purpose. [System Fed. 91 Railway Employees v. Wright, 364 U.S. 642 (1961)]

(7) **Relief otherwise justified:** [§1909] Under the Federal Rules, the court may also reopen a judgment for "any other reason justifying relief." [Fed. R. Civ. P. 60(b)(6)] However, this rule has been *sparingly* applied, and the courts have frequently emphasized that it is *not* an alternative to appeal. [Ackerman v. United States, 340 U.S. 193 (1950)]

   (a) **Example:** A federal court interpreted a state law differently from the way the state supreme court subsequently interpreted the same state law in a case involving another claimant injured in the *same accident* as the plaintiff in the federal case. The need to correct the federal court's erroneous interpretation of state law was held to be sufficient to justify overriding the usual rule that mere error does not justify disturbing a final judgment. [Pierce v. Cook & Co., 518 F.2d 720 (10th Cir. 1975), *cert. denied,* 423 U.S. 1079 (1976)]

c. **Time limits**

   (1) **Federal practice:** [§1910] A motion for relief from judgment must be made within "reasonable" time.

   (a) **Note:** This cannot be more than one year from the entry of judgment if the ground asserted is mistake, inadvertence, surprise, excusable neglect, newly discovered evidence, or fraud. [Fed. R. Civ. P. 60(b)]

   (b) **Compare:** There is no outside time limit where the ground is that the judgment is void or satisfied, or that there are "other reasons justifying relief" (*see* above).

   (2) **State practice:** [§1911] Time limits in state courts vary. In California, the period is six months from the entry of judgment. [Cal. Civ. Proc. Code §473]

d. **Distinguish independent suit to set aside judgment:** [§1912] A motion for relief from a judgment must be distinguished from an independent suit in equity based on similar grounds. The motion is addressed to the court that entered the judgment; whereas the independent suit may be addressed to a different court. In addition, the grounds for an independent suit in equity tend to be narrower and more strictly scrutinized than those for a motion for relief from judgment. [Lapin v. Shulton, Inc., 333 F.2d 169 (9th Cir. 1964)]

(1) **Grounds for independent action:** [§1913]   The two basic grounds for an independent equity suit for relief from judgment are:

(a) *Jurisdictional defects;* and

(b) *Fraud*—as where plaintiff was induced not to appear or contest the case by a false promise of settlement. [*See* United States v. Throckmorton, 98 U.S. 61 (1878); Kulchar v. Kulchar, 1 Cal. 3d 467 (1969)]

1) At one time, relief through an independent suit could be obtained only if the fraud was *extrinsic,* as distinguished from fraud such as perjury. However, this distinction has now been repudiated by most courts. [Publicker v. Shallcross, 106 F.2d 949 (3d Cir. 1939)]

(2) **State-federal relations:** [§1914]   A federal court may refuse to entertain an independent action in equity to set aside a state court judgment. [Maicobo Investment Corp. v. von der Heide, 243 F. Supp. 885 (D. Md. 1965)] However, the federal court may exercise "ancillary" jurisdiction to entertain an action to set aside its own judgment. [Pacific Railroad of Missouri v. Missouri Pacific Railway, 111 U.S. 505 (1884)]

(3) **Relation to motion for relief:** [§1915]   Seeking relief by motion in the main action is *not* a prerequisite to the independent action. However, if such relief is still available in the main action, the equity court may choose not to act because there is an adequate direct remedy.

(a) **Note:** If the ground for relief asserted in the equity suit was previously presented to the court that entered judgment and was held insufficient to reopen the judgment, that decision is ***res judicata.***

5. **Coram Nobis**

a. **State practice:** [§1916]   In some states, the common law writ of coram nobis is still available. The purpose of the writ is "to declare as false a fact previously determined to be true . . ."—as where a witness recants perjury, or evidence previously concealed by a party comes to light.

(1) **Cautiously applied:** [§1917]   Writs of coram nobis are granted only where no other remedy is available and it is absolutely clear that the evidence involved was crucial to the outcome of the case. [Rollins v. City and County of San Francisco, 37 Cal. App. 3d 145 (1974)]

b. **Federal practice:** [§1918]   In federal practice, the writ of coram nobis has been ***abolished.*** [Fed. R. Civ. P. 60(b)]

X. APPEAL

chapter approach

Procedural issues in connection with appeal mostly fall under one of two headings: appealability and reviewability. **Appealability** concerns whether the action of the lower court is one that permits the case to be taken to a court of appeals *at that point*. **Reviewability** deals with *what issues*, once a case is before an appellate court, the court may consider, and what **standard of review** (de novo or deferential) governs the appellate court's consideration of the trial court's rulings.

1. **Appealability**

    a. In most court systems, the main question is whether the lower court has entered a *final judgment*. If not, a decision is usually not appealable at that time.

    b. There are *exceptions* to the final judgment rule permitting *interlocutory review*:

    — Has the lower court granted or denied a *preliminary injunction*?

    — Has the lower court *certified* a ruling for discretionary interlocutory review?

    — Has the lower court made a ruling that qualifies as a *collateral order*?

    — Is there a basis for review by *extraordinary writ*, such as mandamus or prohibition (ordinarily for serious abuse of discretion by the trial court)?

2. **Reviewability:** What may be considered by the appellate court depends on the issue involved:

    a. Was the objection *properly preserved* or was it *waived*, as by failure of counsel to make timely objection? If proper objection was not made, is there nonetheless *plain error*?

    b. Is the challenge to a ruling on a *question of law*? If so, review is *de novo*.

    c. Is the challenge to a *finding of fact*? If so, the appellate court will generally accord a degree of deference to the trier of fact.

    d. Is the action one committed to the *discretion of the trial judge*? If so, the trial court can usually be reversed *only* for abuse of discretion or failure to apply the correct legal standards.

    e. Was the alleged error one with *prejudicial effect*, or was it simply *harmless error*?

A. INTRODUCTION [§1919]

An appeal is the usual procedure for obtaining review by a higher court. The function of the appeal is to assure that the trial has been conducted in a lawful manner and that judgments conform to the law. An appeal ordinarily does not involve a retrial of the case (except in some systems that allow for "appeal" of inferior court decisions by providing trial de novo in a trial court of general jurisdiction), but is limited to a consideration of the rulings by the lower court in light of the record on which those rulings were made.

B. RIGHT TO APPEAL

1. **Status as Right:** [§1920]   The right to appeal in civil matters is a creature of statute.

    a. **Common law:** [§1921]   There was no right to an appeal at common law. A *writ of error* could issue from a higher court, but was discretionary with that court.

    b. **Constitution:** [§1922]   Similarly, the Due Process Clause does not guarantee a right of appeal—at least in civil cases. [National Union of Marine Cooks v. Arnold, 348 U.S. 37 (1954)]

    c. **Statutory foundation of right**

        (1) **State law:** [§1923]   Legislation in every state creates a civil appellate jurisdiction in some court of the state.

        (2) **Federal law:** [§1924]   There is, likewise, a statutory right of appeal in civil proceedings in federal district court. [28 U.S.C. §§1291 *et seq.*]

2. **Waiver of Right:** [§1925]   The statutory right of appeal may be lost through any of the following:

    a. *Express waiver*;

    b. *Untimely assertion*;

    c. *Voluntary compliance with judgment* (*e.g.,* a party who pays the amount of a judgment or performs the act ordered by a decree may be held to have waived the right to appeal). However, performance must be voluntary. Where a judgment is executed by officers of the court and thereby satisfied, the judgment debtor's right of appeal survives. [Reitano v. Yankwich, 38 Cal. 2d 1 (1951)]; and

    d. *Acceptance of benefits*—when the plaintiff recovers a judgment and voluntarily accepts payment of the amount recovered, he may not thereafter appeal (*e.g.,* on the ground that the award was inadequate) [Schubert v. Reich, 36 Cal. 2d 298 (1950)].

C. COURTS OF REVIEW

1. **The Federal System**

    a. **United States Courts of Appeals:** [§1926]   There are 13 United States Courts of Appeals. Twelve have a territorial jurisdiction; in addition, the Federal Circuit, seated in Washington, D.C., has subject matter appellate jurisdiction in patent cases and tort and contract claims against the United States. Appeals to the courts of appeals come from:

(1) **District courts:** [§1927]   Most appeals from district court decisions are taken to the courts of appeals.

(2) **Administrative agencies:** [§1928]   Proceedings to review decisions by many federal administrative agencies must be taken to the courts of appeals.

b. **Supreme Court of the United States:** [§1929]   The Supreme Court has a limited original jurisdiction, as authorized by Article III of the Constitution. However, the Court performs primarily an appellate function, as follows:

(1) **Direct review of district courts:** [§1930]   There is a statutory right of appeal from a district court decision *directly* to the Supreme Court when an act of Congress requires the case to be heard and determined by a *three-judge district court* (a rare thing) and the court *granted or denied injunctive relief*. [28 U.S.C. §1253]

(2) **Review of courts of appeals:** [§1931]   Decisions of the United States Courts of Appeals may be reviewed by the Supreme Court as follows:

(a) **By certiorari:** [§1932]   The Supreme Court may grant a writ of certiorari before or after judgment is entered (although review before final judgment is extremely rare). [28 U.S.C. §1254(1)] The Court has *complete discretion* to deny review without explanation.

(b) **By certification:** [§1933]   A court of appeals may certify a question of law to the Supreme Court. [28 U.S.C. §1254(2)] This route is used very rarely, the courts of appeals generally taking the view that they have the responsibility to decide issues of federal law themselves, without seeking the Supreme Court's assistance.

(3) **Review of decisions of state courts:** [§1934]   The Supreme Court may also review decisions of state courts by certiorari. [28 U.S.C. §1257]

(a) **Highest possible state court:** [§1935]   The Supreme Court will not review a state court decision while further review is still possible in the state court system. Thus, the litigant seeking Supreme Court review must first exhaust state court appeal procedures.

(b) **Involving federal law:** [§1936]   The Supreme Court can review a state court decision only to the extent that it involves issues of federal law.

(c) **Compare—state law issues:** [§1937]   The Supreme Court has *no authority* to review state court decisions of issues of state law. The state courts are the highest authorities on the meaning of state law, as long as state law does not infringe on matters protected by federal law.

2. **State Appellate Systems:** [§1938]   There are substantial differences in the organization of court systems among the various states, and no particular structure can be regarded as typical.

a. **New York:** [§1939] In New York, the principal trial court of general jurisdiction is the supreme court.

 (1) **Appeals:** There is an appellate division of the supreme court, which hears appeals of right from proceedings and orders of the trial courts. The appellate division is divided into four departments, each serving a different area of the state.

 (2) **Highest court:** The highest court is the Court of Appeals of New York. Appeals of right to this court may be taken in constitutional matters and pursuant to various statutes. In addition, the Court of Appeals has the power of discretionary review over many types of lower court decisions.

b. **California:** [§1940] In California, the trial court of general jurisdiction is the superior court, which also exercises appellate jurisdiction over the municipal courts. [Cal. Const. art. VI, §§10, 11]

 (1) **Appeals:** The courts of appeal, which are six in number, each serve a separate area of the state called a district. Three of the six are further divided into divisions, with cases randomly assigned among the divisions. The courts of appeal hear all appeals of right from superior court judgments. Also, the superior court may certify an appeal from a municipal court judgment to the court of appeal.

 (2) **Highest court:** The Supreme Court of California exercises discretionary jurisdiction over proceedings in civil cases in the courts of appeal. A hearing in the supreme court may be granted on petition for hearing by a party or by the court on its own initiative.

 (a) *If a case is heard in the supreme court*, any proceeding in the court of appeal is nullified and all orders are vacated.

 (b) *The purpose of supreme court review* is to secure uniformity of decision among the courts of appeal or to settle important questions of law. [Cal. Rules of Court 29(a)]

c. **Texas:** [§1941] The Texas courts of general civil jurisdiction are district courts.

 (1) **Appeals:** Appeals from district courts in civil cases are taken to the courts of appeals, which are 14 in number, each serving a different area and reviewing particular district courts.

 (2) **Highest court:** Review of civil decisions of the courts of appeals is by the Supreme Court of Texas, which exercises civil jurisdiction only. (Criminal appeals go to the Court of Criminal Appeals, a court of last resort, directly from trial courts in capital cases and from the courts of appeals in other cases.)

d. **Michigan:** [§1942] Michigan is typical of a number of states that have a unified intermediate court, the Court of Appeals, which is subject to review in the Supreme Court of Michigan.

e. **South Dakota:** [§1943]   South Dakota is typical of states that have only one appellate court, the supreme court, to which all appeals are taken.

D. APPELLATE PROCEDURE

1. **Filing of Appeal:** [§1944]   An appeal is commenced by filing a *notice of appeal*. The notice is filed in the appellate court or trial court, depending on the specific court rules. The notice of appeal is a written statement that the appellant invokes the jurisdiction of the appellate court to review a specified judgment from the court below. Formality in the notice is not essential; and the instrument will be liberally construed to prevent waiver. Indeed, under Federal Rule of Appellate Procedure 3(c), which provides that an appeal "shall not be dismissed for informality of form or title of the notice of appeal," a document meant as an appellate brief can qualify as the notice of appeal if it is filed within the time for filing notice and if it contains the information required in a notice of appeal. [Smith v. Barry, 112 S. Ct. 678 (1992)]

   a. **But note—need to name all appellants:** [§1945]   However, if there are multiple appellants, each one must be named in the notice of appeal. An attorney representing multiple appellants may satisfy this requirement by using such terms as "all plaintiffs" or "the plaintiffs A, B, *et al.*," but it must be clear which parties intended to appeal. [Fed. R. App. P. 3(c)] Mere use of "A *et al.*," will not suffice, and the lower court's judgment will be final as to the unspecified parties even if it is reversed as to those specified with adequate clarity. [*See* Torres v. Oakland Scavenger Co., 487 U.S. 312 (1988)]

2. **Time Limits**

   a. **Federal courts:** [§1946]   In federal court, a notice of appeal in a civil case must be filed within 30 days after entry of judgment (or within 60 days, if the United States is a party). The trial judge may extend this period for not more than 30 days, upon a showing of excusable neglect. [Fed. R. App. P. 4]

      (1) **Premature notice of appeal:** [§1947]   Under Federal Rule of Appellate Procedure 4(a)(2), a notice of appeal filed between announcement and entry of a judgment or order is treated as filed immediately after its entry. Under this rule, a premature notice of appeal ripens and becomes effective after eventual entry of judgment even if the notice is filed with respect to a ruling that is not appealable if the decision would have been appealable if followed immediately by entry of judgment, because the party filing the notice reasonably (though mistakenly) could have believed the decision to be final. [FirsTier Mortgage Co. v. Investors Mortgage Insurance Co., 498 U.S. 469 (1990)]

   b. **State practice:** [§1948]   State time limits for noticing an appeal vary. In California, the notice must be filed within 60 days after notice of entry of judgment or 180 days after actual entry, whichever is later. The court has *no* power to extend the time. [Cal. Rules of Court 2(a)]

   c. **Limits affect jurisdiction:** [§1949]   The time limits for an appeal are often jurisdictional and ordinarily cannot be waived.

3. **Appeal Bonds**

   a. **Costs:** [§1950]   To perfect an appeal, the appellant generally must file a bond to secure the payment of his adversary's costs on appeal in the event the judgment is affirmed. [Fed. R. App. P. 7]

   b. **Supersedeas:** [§1951]   If the appellant wishes to stay execution of the judgment pending appeal, he must usually assure that the judgment will be satisfied if it is ultimately affirmed. This assurance may be given in the form of a *supersedeas* bond, which is generally executed by a surety company. [Fed. R. App. P. 8]

      (1) **Possible constitutional limitations:** [§1952]   There may be a constitutional requirement that it be possible to obtain a supersedeas bond. In *Pennzoil Co. v. Texaco, Inc.,* 481 U.S. 1 (1987), Texaco argued that the Texas requirement that it post such a bond to avoid execution of a judgment for more than $10 billion violated its due process rights, because such a bond could not be obtained. The Supreme Court held that the federal courts should not intervene in this matter, which should have been handled in the state courts.

4. **Record on Appeal:** [§1953]   Review on appeal is limited to proceedings in the trial court.

   a. **Clerk's record:** [§1954]   It is the duty of the clerk of the trial court to assemble and transmit the record on appeal, which will include the pleadings, motions, orders, verdict, and judgment in the case. [Fed. R. App. P. 11]

   b. **Reporter's transcript:** [§1955]   At the request of a party, the record may also include a transcription of the testimony at trial or such portions of the testimony that the party seeks to place before the appellate court. [Fed. R. App. P. 10]

5. **Stay of Proceedings Below:** [§1956]   The taking of an appeal ousts the trial court of jurisdiction. While the appeal is pending, the trial court generally has ***no power*** to alter or vacate its judgment, and limited power to make any other order or decree affecting rights of the parties with respect to the case on appeal. [Cal. Civ. Pro. Code §916(a)]

E. **RULINGS SUBJECT TO APPEAL**

1. **Final Decision Requirement:** [§1957]   Generally speaking, only a final decision may be appealed.

   a. **General rule**

      (1) **At common law:** [§1958]   At common law, a writ of error could be taken only from a "final" judgment—*i.e.,* a written order of the trial court, which stated the outcome of its proceedings and manifested that those proceedings were complete.

         (a) **Rationale:** The purposes of the rule were:

1) *To avoid the cost and delay of multiple appeals* in the same action;

2) *To avoid needless effort by appellate courts in considering issues* that may be rendered moot by subsequent proceedings in the trial court; and

3) *To avoid the demeaning effect on the status of the trial judge* that results from excessive review of his decisions.

(2) **Modern practice:** [§1959] Today, the final decision rule is the basic rule, but it is subject to exceptions.

   (a) **Federal courts:** [§1960] Appeals to the United States Courts of Appeals may generally be taken only from final decisions of the district courts. [28 U.S.C. §1291]

   (b) **State courts:** [§1961] Similarly, all but a few states adhere to the final decision requirement (the notable exception being New York), which includes trial court actions "involv[ing] some part of the merits," or "affect[ing] a substantive right," among appealable orders. [N.Y. Civ. Proc. Law & Rules §5701(a)]

   (c) **Separate instrument rule:** [§1962] The final decision must also be embodied in a separate instrument that unequivocally manifests that the trial court proceeding is complete and that a disposition has been made. [Fed. R. Civ. P. 58]

(3) **Nonappealable orders:** [§1963] As a result of the final decision requirement, no immediate appeal may be taken from most orders of trial courts—including such important rulings as discovery orders, pretrial orders, orders denying summary judgment, and the like.

   (a) **Orders after judgment**

      1) **Orders granting new trial**

         a) **Federal practice:** [§1964] An order granting a new trial is *not* appealable in the federal courts—so that the case must proceed to retrial and a new judgment before an appeal is allowed.

         b) **State practice:** [§1965] In some states, an order granting a new trial *is* an appealable order. [Cal. Civ. Proc. Code §904.1(a)(4)]

         c) **Review after second trial:** [§1966] In those jurisdictions where an order granting a new trial is not immediately appealable, the issue may be raised on appeal after final judgment in the second trial. If the appellate court finds that the grant of new trial was improper, it can order that the first judgment be reinstated.

2) **Orders denying new trial:** [§1967] An order denying a new trial is not itself a final appealable order, but it leaves intact the final judgment from which an appeal can be taken.

3) **Appealable orders:** [§1968] An appeal may be taken from other orders made after judgment that have the effect of *vacating* the judgment or *staying* its execution.

(b) **Extraordinary review:** [§1969] In exceptional circumstances, nonappealable orders may be reviewed by means of *extraordinary writs* (see infra, §2018).

(c) **Orders not immune from review:** [§1970] The fact that an order is not immediately appealable does not mean that it is immune from review. If a judgment adverse to the party aggrieved is later entered, an appeal from the judgment can contest the correctness of the previous nonappealable order. As to some orders, such as discovery orders, it is unusual for an appellate court to find that they were sufficiently prejudicial to warrant reversal.

b. **"Jurisdictional" character of rule:** [§1971] The final decision requirement is jurisdictional in the sense that it cannot be waived by the appellee. Thus, an appeal taken from a nonappealable order will be dismissed by the appellate court *sua sponte*. [Conney v. Erickson, 317 F.2d 247 (7th Cir. 1963)]

2. **Exceptions to Final Decision Requirement**

a. **Partial final decisions:** [§1972] If multiple claims or parties are involved in the action, an order disposing of fewer than all of the claims ordinarily is not a final judgment and, hence, is not appealable until the remainder of the claims are disposed of. [Fed. R. Civ. P. 54(b)]

(1) **Appeal at discretion of trial court:** [§1973] However, if the trial judge finds that there is no just reason for delay, he may enter a partial final judgment, which is then appealable. [Fed. R. Civ. P. 54(b)] Generally, this power is exercised only when hardship would result if the appeal from the partial disposition were delayed. [Cullen v. Margiotta, 618 F.2d 226 (2d Cir. 1980)]

(2) **State practice:** [§1974] State rules often permit an appeal where the claims of a single party are severed and determined apart from the others. [Cal. Civ. Proc. Code §579]

b. **Review of equitable remedies**

(1) **In chancery:** [§1975] The final decision rule was not applied in early equity practice. One reason was that equity often used personal orders to the parties which, if erroneous, might result in consequences that could not be corrected later by review. Therefore, immediate appellate review was permitted even as to "interlocutory" orders.

(2) **Modern statutory exception:** [§1976] Modern practice generally preserves the right to interlocutory review of equitable remedies that are not

final orders but which might result in irreparable consequences. Thus, 28 U.S.C. section 1292(a) provides the following *exceptions* to the final decision requirement:

(a) Interlocutory orders *granting or denying injunctions*;

(b) Orders *appointing receivers*;

(c) Decisions in *patent infringement actions* that are final except for an *accounting*; and

(d) Certain orders in *admiralty proceedings*.

c. **Discretionary review:** [§1977] Interlocutory appeals may also be permitted by leave of court. Thus, 28 U.S.C. section 1292(b) permits an appeal if:

(i) *The trial court certifies* that a determination by the appellate court of a *controlling question of law* as to which there is *substantial ground for difference of opinion* would speed the ultimate resolution of the case; *and*

(ii) *The court of appeals grants leave to appeal*.

(1) **Entirely discretionary:** [§1978] The court of appeals may decline leave to appeal for any reason, including calendar congestion.

(2) **Reexamination of propriety of certification by district court:** [§1979] Some courts of appeals also feel bound to reexamine the determination of the district court that an immediate appeal is warranted under the statute. [*See, e.g.,* Garner v. Wolfinbarger, 433 F.2d 117 (5th Cir. 1970)]

(3) **Rationale for review:** When the district court is genuinely uncertain about the correct interpretation of the law, and it would materially advance the conclusion of the litigation to have this uncertainty cleared up, deferring appellate review would not be desirable.

d. **Collateral orders:** [§1980] A qualification established by case law in the federal courts allows an immediate appeal from orders that are final with respect to certain "collateral" matters. [Cohen v. Beneficial Industrial Loan Corp., 337 U.S. 541 (1949)] For a collateral matter to be reviewed, the following requirements must be met:

(1) **Important issue completely separate from the merits:** [§1981] The issue resolved by the court's order must be an important one that is completely separate from the merits of the underlying case. *Rationale:* The proper time to review all decisions related to the merits is after final decision of the case, and unimportant matters do not justify circumvention of the finality requirement.

(a) **Example—requiring derivative suit plaintiff to post security for expenses:** In a derivative action, the district court decided that federal rather than state law should apply to determine whether plaintiff must post a bond to secure defendant's costs of litigation. This decision was appealable because it raised issues of choice between state and federal law, which were completely separate from the merits of plaintiff's claims of misconduct by corporate officers. [Cohen v. Beneficial Industrial Loan Corp., *supra*]

    (b) **Compare—order refusing to certify class:** The decision whether to certify a class is closely tied up with the merits of the case, in the sense that the court must make a decision whether there are common questions of law and fact and whether the common questions predominate (in a Rule 23(b)(3) class action). Thus, the decision is not immediately appealable. [Coopers & Lybrand v. Livesay, 437 U.S. 463 (1978)]

(2) **Order effectively unreviewable on appeal from final judgment:** [§1982] Early review should be allowed only if deferring review until entry of final judgment would effectively destroy the appellant's claimed rights.

    (a) **Example—denial of official immunity:** An order rejecting a government official's claim of immunity from suit could not be reviewed effectively on appeal from a final judgment because the immunity is designed to protect defendant from having to stand trial. [Mitchell v. Forsyth, 472 U.S. 511 (1985)]

    (b) **Example—Eleventh Amendment objection:** An order rejecting a claim of immunity from suit under the Eleventh Amendment could not be effectively reviewed after final judgment because the value of the protection afforded by that amendment against suit in federal court would be lost if the litigation proceeded past the motion stage. [Puerto Rico Aqueduct & Sewer Authority v. Metcalf & Eddy, 113 S. Ct. 684 (1993)]

    (c) **Compare—order refusing to disqualify counsel:** An order refusing to disqualify counsel for an alleged conflict of interest can be reviewed after trial is completed, at which time the actual course of events will permit a better judgment of whether there was a conflict. [Firestone Tire & Rubber Co. v. Risjord, 449 U.S. 368 (1981)—whether counsel sacrificed interests of his client to earn business from defendant's insurer]

    (d) **Compare—refusal to enforce forum selection clause:** An order refusing to dismiss on the ground of a contractual forum selection clause could be reviewed effectively after final judgment, because defendant objected only to defending in a particular place and not to having to defend at all. [Lauro Lines, Inc. v. Chasser, 490 U.S. 495 (1989)]

(3) **Conclusively determines disputed issue:** [§1983] The collateral order rule requires that the trial court have made its final decision on the issue challenged on the appeal. *Rationale:* If the trial court has not had its final say, the appellate court should not interfere.

(a) **Example—order imposing notice costs on defendant:** In a class action, an order imposing on defendant 90% of the cost of notifying class members of their right to opt out was held to be the trial court's final determination of this issue. [Eisen v. Carlisle & Jacquelin, *supra*, §1066]

(b) **Compare—order refusing to certify class action:** Where the trial court refused to certify a case as a class action, and plaintiff claimed this signaled the "death knell" of the action, it was not a final resolution of the disputed matter by the trial court. Such orders are always subject to reconsideration at a later time, in view of later developments. [Coopers & Lybrand v. Livesay, *supra*, §1981]

(4) **Exception narrowly limited:** [§1984]   The Supreme Court has repeatedly emphasized that the collateral order exception applies to a *"small class" of cases* [Cohen v. Beneficial Industrial Loan Corp., *supra*, §1981], and it has been used in a restrictive manner.

(a) **Example—discovery orders involving privileged material:** Discovery orders compelling disclosure of allegedly privileged material seem to satisfy the requirements of the rule, because they conclusively determine claims of privilege, which are separate from the merits, and which cannot effectively be reviewed after the materials are turned over to the opposition. Nevertheless, the Court has adamantly refused to entertain appeals from such orders, noting that the party resisting discovery could refuse to comply, be held in criminal contempt, and appeal immediately from the judgment of criminal contempt. (*See supra*, §§1483-1491 for discussion of appealability of discovery rulings.)

e. **Practical construction of "finality":** [§1985]   The Supreme Court has stated that it will accord a "practical rather than a technical construction" to the finality requirement. [Gillespie v. United States Steel, 379 U.S. 148 (1964)] This does not cause a significant expansion of appealability.

(1) **Example—"death knell" doctrine:** The Supreme Court has rejected a plaintiff's argument that refusal to certify a case as a class action is final (the "death knell") where the named plaintiff cannot afford to maintain the action alone. [Coopers & Lybrand v. Livesay, *supra*]

F. **SCOPE OF APPELLATE REVIEW**

1. **In General:** [§1986]   Appellate review must be sufficiently broad to assure that the trial court properly applied the controlling substantive law and that the procedure conformed to the applicable standards. However, appellate review does not extend to retrying the facts or supplanting the trial judge's decision in matters committed to her discretion.

2. **Findings of Fact Subject to Limited Review:** [§1987]   It is not the function of an appellate court to make factual determinations; yet the appellate court must examine factual determinations to assure that the trial court has not rested its decision on insupportable factual assumptions.

a. **Jury verdicts:** [§1988] When the findings below are embodied in a jury verdict, the role of the appellate court is essentially the same as that of the trial judge—*i.e.*, to oversee the jury's adherence to the law.

  (1) **Substantial evidence test:** [§1989] The accepted test is that a jury verdict must be supported by substantial evidence, so that reasonable jurors could have found as they did—even if the reviewing judges think they would have found differently as triers of fact.

  (2) **Cases taken from jury:** [§1990] When the trial judge has taken the fact-finding function away from the jury—*e.g.*, by granting a motion for judgment as a matter of law—the appellate court must examine the record to determine whether there is any substantial evidence to support a finding contrary to that of the trial judge. If it finds such evidence, the judgment will be reversed.

b. **Judicial findings in nonjury trials**

  (1) **Explicit findings required:** [§1991] When a case is tried without a jury, the trial judge usually is required to make explicit findings of fact in order to facilitate review of her decision by the appellate court. [Fed. R. Civ. P. 52(a)]

  (2) **Clear error test:** [§1992] A judge's finding of fact may not be set aside unless the appellate court finds that it is "clearly erroneous." To find clear error, it is not enough that the appellate court is convinced that it would have decided the case differently. [Anderson v. City of Bessemer City, 470 U.S. 564 (1985)] Rather, the reviewing court must be left "on the entire evidence . . . with the definite and firm conviction that a mistake has been committed." [United States v. United States Gypsum, 333 U.S. 364 (1948)] Due regard must be given to the opportunity of the trial court to appraise the credibility of the witnesses [Fed. R. Civ. P. 52(a)], although the requirement of deference is not limited to findings that rest on credibility determinations. [Anderson v. City of Bessemer City, *supra*]

    (a) **Compare—substantial evidence test:** [§1993] The clear error test is less restrictive than the substantial evidence test, since a finding may be clearly erroneous even though there is substantial evidence to support it.

      1) **Rationale:** A jury verdict is the product of a deliberative process and reflects democratic political values that assign special worth to the participation of lay decision makers. On the other hand, the findings of a trial judge are the product of a single mind, which may be more vulnerable to bias or idiosyncrasy. Still, considerable deference to trial judges' fact findings is due because of the judges' expertise in fact determinations and the costs of extensive review to the parties and to the system. [Anderson v. City of Bessemer City, *supra*]

c. **"Fact" and "law" distinguished:** [§1994] It is only findings of fact that are entitled to deference.

(1) **Errors of law (jury trial):** [§1995] If the jury was erroneously instructed on the *law*, the verdict cannot stand, even if there is substantial evidence to support findings that could have been made pursuant to correct instructions.

(2) **Erroneous conclusions (nonjury trial)**

 (a) **Explicit conclusions required:** [§1996] In a nonjury trial, the judge must state conclusions of law, either in a recorded oral statement or in writing, in order to facilitate appellate review. [Fed. R. Civ. P. 52(a)]

 (b) **Effect of erroneous conclusions:** [§1997] If the conclusions are erroneous, so that the judge's findings rest on a false legal premise, the judgment cannot stand (even if the findings themselves are not clearly erroneous).

(3) **Mixed issues of law and fact:** [§1998] The distinction between a finding of fact and a conclusion of law is not always clear. Sophisticated observers have long noted a circularity in making this distinction for purposes of appellate review; *i.e.*, matters may tend to be treated as issues of fact where the appellate court feels less competent to resolve them and as issues of law when the court feels competent to resolve them without help from the lower court.

 (a) **Interpretation of legal documents:** [§1999] The interpretation of a contract, deed, will, or other legal document is generally regarded as a question of law if the trial court interpreted the document without judging the credibility of extrinsic evidence. If so, the appellate court may disregard any conclusions reached by the trial judge as to the meaning or effect of the document and substitute its own interpretation. [Estate of Platt, 21 Cal. 2d 343 (1942)]

  1) **Compare—findings based on documentary evidence:** [§2000] Note the difference between review of legal documents (*e.g.*, contracts, wills) and review of documentary evidence (*e.g.*, receipts, letters). Findings of fact based on documentary evidence (or on oral evidence) are reviewed under the clearly erroneous standard. [Fed. R. Civ. P. 52(a); Anderson v. City of Bessemer City, *supra*, §1993—disapproving the much-cited contrary case of Orvis v. Higgins, 180 F.2d 537 (2d Cir.), *cert. denied,* 340 U.S. 810 (1950)]

 (b) **Negligence:** [§2001] It is arguable whether a finding of negligence represents a legal or factual conclusion. (*See supra*, §605, regarding pleading of negligence.) In either event, appellate courts generally defer to a jury determination on negligence—even when there is no dispute as to the basic events.

  1) **But note:** In a nonjury trial, the judge's findings with respect to "negligence" are subject to the clear error test (*supra*).

 (c) **Other issues—suggested approach:** [§2002] In other areas, a question usually will be treated as one of fact if it:

(i) *Pertains to the occurrence or nonoccurrence of a past event*;

(ii) *Is of specific interest* to the parties to the dispute and has no bearing on the rights or liabilities of others;

(iii) *Is determined on the basis of the testimony of witnesses*;

(iv) *Is not appropriately determined by reference to general policy*;

(v) *Is determined on the basis of intuitive instinct* about the application of some general morality to a specific event.

1) **Example:** One business person transfers a new automobile to another. Whether the transfer results in taxable income to the recipient, or instead is a "gift," is an issue of fact. [Commissioner of Internal Revenue v. Duberstein, 363 U.S. 278 (1960)]

2) **Criticism:** Reliance on the "intuition" of the trier of fact in such matters is the result of judicial unwillingness or inability to formulate explicit rules of decision to govern future like cases.

3. **Review of Discretionary Rulings:** [§2003] Especially with regard to procedural matters, many decisions by trial judges are entrusted by law to their discretion. In such cases, an appellate court will not substitute its discretion for that of the trial judge in the absence of clear abuse.

   a. **Example:** Whether to *delay or continue a trial* on account of the unavailability of a witness is a matter for the discretion of the trial judge. [Napolitano v. Compania Sud Americana de Vapores, 421 F.2d 382 (2d Cir. 1970)] Likewise, *setting the amount of a security bond* to be required of a party seeking a preliminary injunction is a matter of discretion. [Fed. R. Civ. P. 65(c)] And whether to grant a new trial on the ground that the verdict is *contrary to the weight of the evidence* is within the sound discretion of the trial judge, although the modern trend is away from earlier rulings that the trial judge's discretion was virtually unlimited. [Coffran v. Hitchcock Clinic, Inc., 683 F.2d 5 (1st Cir.), *cert. denied*, 459 U.S. 1087 (1982)]

   b. **Limitation:** [§2004] The appellate court may properly review a discretionary ruling by a trial judge to determine whether he has *abused* his power. [Allis-Chalmers Corp. v. Philadelphia Electric Co., 521 F.2d 360 (3d Cir. 1975)]

4. **"Harmless Error" Standard**

   a. **General rule:** [§2005] The appellate court may not reverse a lower court judgment unless the trial court committed an error that was *prejudicial—i.e.,* one that affected the substantial rights of the parties. [Fed. R. Civ. P. 61; 28 U.S.C. §2111]

      (1) **Example—state rule:** The California Constitution provides that: "No judgment shall be set aside . . . for any error as to any matter of pleading

or procedure, unless after an examination of the entire cause, including the evidence, the appellate court shall be of the opinion that the error . . . resulted in a *miscarriage of justice*." [Cal. Const. art. VI, §4-1/2]

 (2) **Burden:** [§2006] The burden of showing prejudice is usually on the party claiming it. There is no presumption of an impairment of substantial rights merely from the fact that error occurred.

b. **Examples**

 (1) **Harmless:** Erroneous rulings on the *pleadings or on matters of discovery* will rarely be sufficiently prejudicial in their effect on the trial that a reversal would be warranted.

 (2) **Harmless:** The admission of *improper evidence* in a *nonjury* trial is generally regarded as harmless, since it is assumed that a professional trial judge will discount the improper evidence and not permit it to influence his findings of fact. [First American State Bank v. Continental Insurance Co., 897 F.2d 319 (8th Cir. 1990)]

 (3) **Compare:** The rule is to the contrary in *jury* trials: It is assumed that jurors *will* be influenced by improper evidence, at least if they are not cautioned by the trial judge to disregard it.

c. **Limitation:** [§2007] The harmless error rule will not prevent reversal where the error is "egregious." In such cases, the appellate court may reverse as a means of disciplining the trial judge, even though his error would not likely have had an adverse effect on the rights of the appellant. [Thiel v. Southern Pacific Co., 328 U.S. 217 (1946)—discrimination in selection of jury panel]

d. **Legal theory sustaining judgment:** [§2008] An appellate court may review a legal theory *not previously presented* to the trial court if considered for the purpose of sustaining the decision below. Thus, if the findings of fact below clearly support application of the correct legal principle to reach the result achieved below, the judgment will be affirmed even if the correct legal theory was never presented to the trial court. Any error in articulation of legal theory was *harmless*. [Ward v. Taggart, 51 Cal. 2d 736 (1959)]

5. **Waiver of Objections in Lower Court**

a. **General rule:** [§2009] An appellate court may not reverse a judgment below to correct an error that might have been avoided or corrected had the appellant made timely objection in the trial court. [Security Pacific National Bank v. Geernaert, 199 Cal. App. 3d 1425 (1988)] *Rationale:* The appellant should not be permitted to withhold objection and await the outcome of further proceedings before deciding whether to take advantage of a mistake by the court.

b. **Examples**

 (1) **Jury instruction:** [§2010] An error in the instruction of the jury usually will not be the basis for reversal unless the appellant made a timely objection to the charge and proposed a correct instruction. [Fed. R. Civ. P. 51]

(2) **Admission of evidence:** [§2011] Similarly, an error in the admission of evidence generally will not be grounds for reversal unless the appellant made a timely and specific objection to the admission.

(3) **Invited error:** [§2012] Where the aggrieved party *induced* the error of the trial court (*e.g.,* by proposing incorrect jury instructions or by offering inadmissible evidence), the case for waiver is strongest. [Horsemen's Benevolent Association v. Valley Racing Association, 4 Cal. App. 4th 1538 (1992)]

(4) **New matter:** [§2013] Newly discovered evidence, evidence of jury misconduct, or other matters coming to light *after trial* may not be presented directly to an appellate court. Such matters must be presented to the trial court by motion for a new trial or for relief from judgment. [*See* Fed. R. Civ. P. 60(b)(2)]

c. **Exceptions:** [§2014] An appellate court may review notwithstanding the failure of an appellant to make timely objection in the following situations:

(1) **Subject matter jurisdiction:** [§2015] When the court below lacked subject matter jurisdiction, no objection is necessary, since the jurisdictional issue can be raised belatedly or even *sua sponte*.

(2) **Clear and fundamental error:** [§2016] No objection is necessary when the error is so clear and fundamental that the trial court should have avoided it, even without timely objection, and it would be *unjust* to permit the judgment to stand.

(a) **Example:** In the course of a long trial, the judge took a long recess for his own vacation, causing a serious hiatus in the presentation of the case to the jury. Where the judge declared that under no circumstances would he consider a change in his plans, no objection was necessary to preserve the issue on appeal. [Citron v. Aro Corp., 377 F.2d 750 (3d Cir.), *cert. denied,* 389 U.S. 973 (1967)]

6. **Trial De Novo:** [§2017] Legislation may sometimes authorize a trial *de novo*, which is in effect a new trial in a higher court. This form of review is generally limited to review of trial courts that exercise minor jurisdiction (*e.g.,* small claims courts) and that make no records of their proceedings.

G. APPELLATE REVIEW BY EXTRAORDINARY WRIT

1. **Prerogative Writs:** [§2018] In exceptional cases, review of nonappealable orders may be had by means of a prerogative writ issued by the appellate court to direct the conduct of trial judges. The available writs, depending on the court system, are:

a. *Mandamus*—an order directing the judge to perform her legal duty; and

b. *Prohibition*—an order enjoining the judge from conduct that exceeds her lawful authority.

2. **Source of Power to Issue Writs**

   a. **State courts:** [§2019]   Writs in state court tend to be based on common law practice. In some states, statutes or constitutional provisions establish alternatives. In Michigan, for example, the appellate courts have power to issue "writs of superintending control."

   b. **Federal courts:** [§2020]   The United States Courts of Appeals have power to issue prerogative writs by reason of statute, which authorizes all federal courts to issue writs as necessary "in aid of their respective jurisdictions and agreeable to the usages and principles of law." [28 U.S.C. §1651(a)]

3. **Discretionary Character of Writ:** [§2021]   An important distinction between writs and an appeal is that the issuance of a prerogative writ is always discretionary with the appellate courts. The petitioner has *no right* to a hearing. [Kerr v. United States District Court, 426 U.S. 394 (1976)]

4. **Grounds for Issuance**

   a. **Conduct exceeding limits of power:** [§2022]   A prerogative writ may issue to prevent misuse of judicial power, such as:

      (1) *An abuse of discretion*;

      (2) *An excess of jurisdiction*; or

      (3) *A refusal to exercise jurisdiction*.

   b. **Necessity for immediate review:** [§2023]   Where the petitioner has no right to review by appeal at the present time, and would suffer undue hardship or substantial prejudice if appellate review was delayed until after a final judgment, a writ may properly issue.

      (1) **But note:** Extraordinary writs will not issue where adequate review by appeal is available to the petitioner. [*In re* McDonald, 489 U.S. 180 (1989)]

5. **Common Uses of Writ:** [§2024]   United States Courts of Appeals use discretionary writs:

   a. *To correct the erroneous denial of a right to jury trial* [Beacon Theatres, Inc. v. Westover, 359 U.S. 500 (1959)];

   b. *To prevent improper delegation of judicial power* with respect to special matters [LaBuy v. Howes Leather Co., 352 U.S. 249 (1957)]; and

   c. *To prevent unlawful remand to state court* of actions properly removed to federal court [Thermtron Products, Inc. v. Hermansdorfer, 423 U.S. 336 (1976)].

6. **Supervisory Mandamus:** [§2025]   In rare circumstances, mandamus may be used to resolve *issues of first impression* that may be important in a significant number of cases.

a. **Example:** Where the question of the proper treatment of physical examinations of defendants under Federal Rule 35 was presented, mandamus was available to review an order requiring defendant to submit to a physical examination, because issue had never been resolved. [Schlaugenhauf v. Holder, 379 U.S. 104 (1964)]

b. **Availability:** [§2026]   In a few jurisdictions, such as California, the grounds for issuing prerogative writs have been greatly expanded. In effect, the writ proceeding becomes a device for granting or refusing immediate appellate review of important interlocutory orders. [Abelleira v. District Court, 17 Cal. 2d 280 (1941)]

XI. PRECLUSIVE EFFECTS OF JUDGMENTS

chapter approach

After a court has entered judgment, related matters may come up in later litigation involving the same or different parties. For several reasons—including economy, prevention of harassment, and avoidance of inconsistent rulings—doctrines of former adjudication sharply limit the extent to which *relitigation* is permitted. When relitigation is not permitted, parties cannot argue in a new proceeding that the prior ruling was erroneous; the point is taken as established in accord with the prior decision.

This field of law has two main components: (i) *claim preclusion* (or, in older terminology still in widespread use, *res judicata* in its narrow sense), which bars reassertion of the same claim; and (ii) *issue preclusion* (in the older terminology, direct or collateral estoppel), which bars relitigation of the same issue, whether it arises in connection with the same claim (*direct estoppel*) or a different claim (*collateral estoppel*).

1. **Claim Preclusion:** The questions are:

    a. Is the judgment on the *same claim*? Most jurisdictions now define "claim" broadly to prevent bringing of one aspect of a related matter in one action and another aspect in a second proceeding against the same party (rule against splitting claims).

    b. Is the judgment *final*?

    c. Is it *valid*—was it rendered by a court of competent jurisdiction exercised by constitutionally adequate notice?

    d. Is it *on the merits*—did the court rule on the merits of the claim, dismiss with prejudice, or enter a default judgment?

    e. Did the plaintiff in the prior action *prevail*? If so, the doctrine of *merger* precludes a second try—the original claim is merged in the judgment.

    f. Did the plaintiff *lose* in the first action? If so, the doctrine of *bar* precludes the second suit, with the plaintiff's claim regarded as barred by the defeat.

2. **Issue Preclusion:** The questions are:

    a. Is the party against whom issue preclusion is sought to be invoked one who was a *party* to the prior litigation or *in "privity"* with such a party?

    b. Was the issue *actually litigated and determined* and *necessary* to the judgment?

    c. Can *nonmutual estoppel* be applied?

        (1) Are the *stakes* so different that it would be unfair to apply estoppel?

        (2) Could the party asserting estoppel *easily have joined* in the earlier action?

        (3) Are *procedural opportunities* available to the party against whom estoppel is asserted in this action that were not available in the earlier action?

        (4) Have there been *inconsistent determinations* of the same issue?

A. INTRODUCTION

1. **In General:** [§2027]   The res judicata doctrine has two components: (i) claim preclusion, and (ii) issue preclusion.

2. **Claim Preclusion (Also Called Res Judicata):** [§2028]   A final judgment on a claim or cause of action *precludes reassertion of that claim* or *cause of action* in a subsequent suit.

    a. **Merger:** [§2029]   If judgment was for the plaintiff on the claim, there is a *merger* of the claim in the judgment—*i.e.,* the prejudgment claim is transformed into the judgment claim.

    b. **Bar:** [§2030]   If judgment was for the defendant, it is a *bar* against the plaintiff's suing again on the claim.

3. **Issue Preclusion (Also Called Collateral Estoppel):** [§2031]   Preclusion prevents not only relitigation of a claim, but also, in some circumstances, relitigation of issues of fact resolved in a prior proceeding. A decision on an issue of fact may be binding in subsequent litigation between the same parties or, in some circumstances, between one of the parties and a different adversary.

4. **Rationale:** [§2032]   The purposes of these doctrines are twofold: (i) to avoid the time and expense of multiple litigation over the same matter; and (ii) to give stability to the results of adjudication—to prevent inconsistent results.

5. **Interjurisdictional Effect:** [§2033]   Under the Full Faith and Credit Clause, Article IV, Section 1 of the federal Constitution, the courts of one state are obligated to give effect to the judgments of courts of other states. For the law of res judicata, the import of this rule is that courts of other states generally give a judgment the same effect it would have in the courts of the state where it was rendered. A federal statute requires federal courts to follow the same rule with respect to state court judgments. [28 U.S.C. §1738]

B. CLAIM PRECLUSION

1. **In General:** [§2034]   Before any judgment can have claim preclusive effect, it must be (i) final, (ii) "on the merits," and (iii) valid.

2. **Policy Basis:** [§2035]   The basis for claim preclusion is that litigants should be compelled to litigate their entire claim on the first occasion they bring it before the courts. This can serve the following policy objectives.

    a. **Judicial efficiency:** [§2036]   Resolving all claims in a single lawsuit avoids waste of judicial resources on repeated litigation of the same claim.

    b. **Avoiding vexation of defendants:** [§2037]   To permit plaintiffs to sue defendants repeatedly on the same claim by changing their legal theories, would raise the risk of oppression to defendants. Defendants should be assured that they will not be forced to answer a given claim more than once.

    c. **Consistency:** [§2038]   Although it would often be legally consistent for a plaintiff to lose on one theory and then prevail on another with different ele-ments, requiring litigation of all theories for a claim in a single action promotes the public appearance of consistency.

d. **Effect—foreclosing matters that were never litigated:** [§2039] The net effect of claim preclusion is, therefore, often to foreclose matters that were never litigated because they were never raised in the first litigation.

(1) **Example:** Plaintiff sues defendant car salesperson for common law fraud in connection with defendant's sale of a used car to plaintiff. After judgment is entered in this action, plaintiff files a second suit against defendant, this time charging violation of the state Automobile Consumer Protection Act in connection with the sale of the same car. Even though the question of violation of the Act has never been litigated, the second suit is precluded by the first.

(2) **Compare—issue preclusion:** Estoppel (particularly collateral estoppel) applies preclusion only to matters that were actually litigated and decided in the first lawsuit.

3. **Meaning of Claim—Breadth of Preclusion:** [§2040] Determining the scope of the claim in the first lawsuit is often difficult. Unless the claim in the second lawsuit is the "same," claim preclusion does not apply (although collateral estoppel may).

a. **Traditional tests:** [§2041] The traditional tests were derived from the code pleading concept of the cause of action. The idea was that the first litigation was res judicata only as to the same cause of action. The courts developed tests to give effect to this concept:

(1) **Same primary right and duty:** [§2042] Where the plaintiff asserted a violation of the same basic right in the second case as in the first, preclusion applied. *Criticism:* Distinguishing between differences in the law that mattered (in terms of the elements of the second claim compared to those of the first claim) made it hard to determine if the second suit involved the same "primary right."

(2) **Same evidence:** [§2043] Where the second claim turned on essentially the same evidence as the first claim, preclusion was said to apply. *Criticism:* Because there was usually some difference in the evidence that could be presented, this test was also difficult to apply.

(3) **Mere change of legal theory:** [§2044] Where the second suit merely changed the legal theory upon which the earlier suit relied, preclusion applied. *Criticism:* Although this test accurately portrays one concern of preclusion doctrine, it provides little guidance in determining whether something more than the legal theory has changed.

b. **Modern approach—transactional test:** [§2045] The Restatement (Second) of Judgments adopts a transactional approach to the scope of claim preclusion: Claim preclusion applies to "all or any part of the transaction, or series of connected transactions, out of which the action arose." [Restatement (Second) of Judgments §24(1)]

(1) **Flexible definition:** [§2046] The definition is flexible: "What factual grouping constitutes a 'transaction,' and what groupings constitute a 'series,' are to be determined pragmatically, giving weight to such considerations as whether the facts are related in time, space, origin, or motivation,

whether they form a convenient trial unit, and whether their treatment as a unit conforms to the parties' expectations or business understanding or usage." [Restatement (Second) of Judgments §24(2)]

 (2) **Compare—permissive joinder of parties:** This analysis requires an examination of the facts underlying the claim similar to that called for in assessing permissive joinder of parties under Federal Rule 20. (*See supra,* §§950-960.)

4. **"Final":** [§2047] A ruling at a pretrial hearing or the determination of an issue severed for trial does not decide a claim until judgment is rendered. However, if a claim has been separately determined in the course of an action, it may be treated as the equivalent of a final judgment for res judicata purposes, even if the action is still pending. (For example, if a plaintiff sued two defendants, and one of them obtained summary judgment while the action remained pending against the other, the summary judgment, although not formally final, would be res judicata in favor of the party who obtained it.) The question is whether the claim has been *irrevocably determined for purposes of the first action*. If it has, the determination will be treated as final.

 a. **Effect of appeal:** [§2048] Whether a judgment on appeal is final for purposes of res judicata is determined by the *law of the jurisdiction in which the judgment was rendered*.

  (1) **Federal practice:** [§2049] In federal practice, once a judgment is entered it is deemed to be final even though an appeal therefrom is pending. The judgment remains final and valid until reversed or modified by the appellate court. In such jurisdictions, res judicata attaches immediately upon entry of the judgment. [United States v. Nysco Laboratories, Inc., 318 F.2d 817 (2d Cir. 1963)]

   (a) **Note:** As a practical matter, however, any suit to enforce the judgment, or in which the res judicata issue is otherwise involved, is likely to be abated or continued until the pending appeal is determined.

  (2) **State practice:** [§2050] In many states, the taking of an appeal *automatically* postpones finality until the appeal is determined. Until then, no res judicata attaches. [Anno. 9 A.L.R.2d 984]

 b. **Modifiable judgments:** [§2051] Many civil judgments are nonfinal in the sense that they are subject to modification (*e.g.,* alimony awards, child custody determination, and some kinds of injunctions). Such judgments do not prevent reconsideration of the relief granted; for example, when conditions have changed. But they are *res judicata until modified*. [Restatement (Second) of Judgments §13, comment c]

 c. **Conflicting judgments:** [§2052] Where two judgments are in conflict, the last in time controls. [Restatement (Second) of Judgments §15]

  (1) **Example:** If a judgment is rendered in action 1, but is not raised or established in action 2 (or the court in the second action holds that the earlier judgment is not entitled to res judicata), and both judgments are

Civil Procedure—315

otherwise final, the second judgment is controlling. Hence, it (rather than the earlier judgment) is entitled to res judicata in any third proceeding on the same claim. [Treinies v. Sunshine Mining Co., 308 U.S. 66 (1939)]

5. **"On the Merits"**

   a. **General rule:** [§2053] A judgment is deemed to be "on the merits" where the claim has been tried and determined—*i.e.*, where the court has ruled that the *plaintiff has (or has not) established his claim*. This includes a determination by summary judgment, judgment on the pleadings, nonsuit, and directed verdict, as well as a determination after trial and verdict.

      (1) **Note:** Rulings not on the merits generally are preclusive only as to issues. Where the court dismisses on a ground that *does not* relate to the merits (*e.g.*, for lack of jurisdiction, improper venue, or a dismissal expressly "without prejudice" to a new action), the judgment or dismissal usually does not bar a subsequent action. [Restatement (Second) of Judgments §20]

      (2) **But note:** Such a judgment is determinative of *issues decided*. *Example:* A dismissal because the defendant is not a resident of the county where sued is determinative of that *issue* in a subsequent suit (*see infra*, §§2073 et seq.). This is known as *direct estoppel*.

   b. **Meaning of "on the merits":** [§2054] If an action is dismissed on a ground closely related to the merits, the following approaches apply:

      (1) **Dismissals:** [§2055] If dismissal is for failure to state a cause of action, but it is possible that the complaint could be amended to state a valid claim, or if there was a dismissal for failure to diligently prosecute the action, earlier cases held that the judgment was not on the merits and hence not a bar.

         (a) **But note:** Today, such a dismissal *is* considered a bar—on the theory that the plaintiff had a *fair opportunity* to get to the merits (by amending his pleading, appealing, etc.). [Rinehart v. Locke, 454 F.2d 313 (7th Cir. 1971)]

      (2) **Nonsuit:** [§2056] The earlier view also held that a judgment of *nonsuit* in a jury trial was not a judgment on the merits, because a new action based on the same or new evidence could be filed. The modern rule, however, is contrary: A nonsuit *is* a determination on the merits. [Restatement (Second) of Judgments §19]

      (3) **Default and consent judgments:** [§2057] Default and consent judgments terminate the *cause* of action and hence have *claim preclusion* effect (*i.e.*, result in merger or bar of the claim). Note, however, that a default judgment may be less effective in regard to issue preclusion. (*See infra*, §2076.)

      (4) **Punitive dismissals:** [§2058] A punitive dismissal is a dismissal based on a party's refusal to obey trial court orders—*e.g.*, a dismissal of a plaintiff's action for failure to prosecute diligently, or a default judgment

against a defendant for refusal to obey a discovery order. Because such judgments terminate the cause of action, they have claim preclusion effect; but they do not involve issue preclusion.

6. **"Valid":** [§2059] The third requirement for claim preclusion is that the judgment be valid. A judgment is valid *unless*:

    (i) The court lacked *subject matter jurisdiction* of the case (*see supra*, Chapter II);

    (ii) The notice given to the defendant failed to conform to *due process requirements*, or substantially departed from the requirements of statute or court rule concerning the *form of notice* (*see supra*, §§200 *et seq.*); *or*

    (iii) The court lacked *territorial jurisdiction* of the action (*see supra*, Chapter I).

    a. **Determination of validity:** [§2060] If the question of validity was *litigated* in the original action, that determination is itself res judicata.

        (1) **Example:** A court exercises jurisdiction in an action concerning land on the basis that the land is within the state, rejecting defendant's contention that the land is across the state boundary and hence in another state. This determination of jurisdiction is conclusive, and the judgment may not thereafter be attacked as invalid. [Durfee v. Duke, 375 U.S. 106 (1963)]

        (2) **And note:** Res judicata also applies to decisions concerning the court's subject matter jurisdiction [Stoll v. Gottleib, 305 U.S. 165 (1938)] and the adequacy of notice [Gordon v. Gordon, 227 S.E.2d 53 (Ga. 1976)].

7. **Claim Preclusion When Jurisdiction Is In Rem or Quasi In Rem**

    a. **Definition:** [§2061] Jurisdiction *in rem* or *quasi in rem* is based on the presence of the property about which the lawsuit is concerned (*see supra*, §53). For example, a state can exercise jurisdiction to determine rights under a mortgage pertaining to land in that state.

    b. **Res judicata effect:** [§2062] When jurisdiction is exercised *in rem* or *quasi in rem*, the rules of claim and issue preclusion apply essentially as they do in *in personam* judgments, except that the preclusion is limited to claims in the property.

        (1) **Claim preclusion:** [§2063] Suppose A brings a suit to foreclose a mortgage on property in State X, serving notice in State X on B, the mortgagor. A judgment for or against A is res judicata as to her claim to foreclose. However, if no jurisdiction was exercised to determine B's in personam indebtedness to A, that claim is not determined and still may be sued upon by A.

        (2) **Issue preclusion:** [§2064] Any issues determined in the in rem proceeding (*e.g.*, the enforceability of the mortgage note) are conclusive in subsequent litigation.

8. **Attachment Jurisdiction:** [§2065] Attachment jurisdiction is exercised by seizing local property as a basis for collecting on an obligation allegedly due from its owner, the obligation being unrelated to the property.

a. **Res judicata effect**

(1) **Claim preclusion:** [§2066] A judgment based on attachment jurisdiction does ***not*** extinguish the claim, except to the extent of the property seized.

(2) **Issue preclusion:** [§2067] However, the issues actually litigated are conclusive on the parties if the amount of the property attached was large enough to give them a fair incentive to litigate.

b. **Restriction:** [§2068] Attachment jurisdiction has been considerably restricted by *Shaffer v. Heitner, supra,* §66, but it has not been eliminated.

9. **Exceptions to Claim Preclusion:** [§2069] Only under ***extraordinary*** circumstances may a party relitigate a claim that has been reduced to judgment. The losing party would have to establish grounds for setting aside the judgment (*e.g.,* fraud on the court) and that she has a good case on the merits. The policy is ***very strong against*** relitigation. (*See supra,* §§2034-2039.)

a. **Example:** Seven consumers brought actions under the federal antitrust laws charging defendant department stores with conspiring to fix prices of women's clothing. The actions were dismissed on the ground that consumers had no standing to sue for price fixing. Five of the plaintiffs appealed and the other two filed new actions asserting claims under state antitrust law. The Supreme Court then held that consumers did have standing to sue, and the judgments against the five plaintiffs who appealed were reversed and remanded for further proceedings. In these circumstances, the Ninth Circuit created an exception to res judicata so that the other two plaintiffs could proceed with their actions. The Supreme Court reversed, stressing that res judicata serves the vital interest "that there be an end to litigation." [*Federated Department Stores, Inc. v. Moitie,* 452 U.S. 394 (1981)]

10. **Defenses and Counterclaims**

a. **Effect of compulsory counterclaim statutes:** [§2070] A compulsory counterclaim statute or rule requires that the defendant set up any counterclaim she has against the plaintiff arising out of the same transaction as the plaintiff's claim. [Fed. R. Civ. P. 13(a)] If she fails to do so, she is barred from thereafter asserting the counterclaim, either as a defense or as the basis for affirmative relief in an independent action. Hence, the judgment in the former action is preclusive as to claims that were or should have been asserted as compulsory counterclaims in that action. [*Baker v. Gold Seal Liquors, Inc.,* 417 U.S. 467 (1974)]

b. **Where no compulsory counterclaim involved:** [§2071] In all other cases, res judicata does not prevent the defendant from asserting the same matter first as a defense to the plaintiff's action, and later as a basis for independent relief against the former plaintiff.

(1) **Example:** Contractor sues Owner for money due under a construction contract. Owner successfully defends by showing that the work was not properly done, but no counterclaim is asserted. Owner may subsequently file an independent damage action for the improper work (assuming no compulsory counterclaim statute is in effect).

(2) **But note:** The issues *actually litigated* and decided in the first action may not be relitigated, under the rule of issue preclusion (below).

(3) **Exception—nullifying initial judgment:** [§2072]   When a former defendant seeks relief in a later suit based on a claim that could have been asserted as a counterclaim, and the relief sought would nullify the judgment entered in the earlier suit, the later action is barred even if there was no applicable compulsory counterclaim rule in the earlier action. [Restatement (Second) of Judgments §22(1)(b)]

   (a) **Example:** In the first action, McDonald's sued to terminate its franchise agreement with plaintiff under a provision forbidding any member of plaintiff's family to acquire an interest in a competing fast food business. Plaintiff's son had bought a Burger Chef franchise in a nearby town. After judgment was entered in the first action finding a breach of the franchise agreement and directing sale of the franchise, plaintiff sued McDonald's, alleging that application of the noncompetition provision of the franchise agreement violated the antitrust laws. The court held the second action foreclosed because "its prosecution would nullify rights established by the prior action." [Martino v. McDonald's Systems, Inc., 598 F.2d 1079 (7th Cir. 1979)]

C. ISSUE PRECLUSION

1. **Direct Estoppel:** [§2073]   Issues actually litigated *between the parties* are binding on them in subsequent actions concerning the *same claim*. *Example:* In a child support suit, where several modification proceedings have been held, issues actually litigated and determined in an earlier proceeding (*e.g.,* legitimacy of the child) are binding on the parties in subsequent proceedings.

2. **Collateral Estoppel:** [§2074]   Where the second lawsuit involves a *different* claim (and hence no merger, bar, or direct estoppel), the first judgment may be invoked as to all matters *actually litigated and determined in the first action and essential to the judgment*. [Cromwell v. County of Sac, 94 U.S. 351 (1876); Restatement (Second) of Judgments §27] *Example:* A sues B to collect interest that has become due on a promissory note. B defends on the ground that she was induced by fraud to sign the note, and wins. If A later sues to collect the principal amount of the note after it matures, the prior determination on the question of fraud is conclusive against him.

   a. **"Actually litigated":** [§2075]   The issue preclusive effect of a prior judgment applies to issues *actually litigated* in the former action, but not to those which merely *could* have been litigated therein.

      (1) **Example:** Landlord sues and recovers judgment against Tenant for rent owed. Later, Landlord sues again for additional rent owed under the same lease. Tenant now interposes the defense that the lease was invalid at all times. The earlier judgment is *not* collateral estoppel as to this issue, since the only thing litigated in the former action was the rental claim, and the court was not called upon to determine the validity of the lease.

(2) **Default judgments:** [§2076]   There is a split of authority on whether a default judgment creates issue preclusion.

   (a) **Conclusive:** [§2077]   Many decisions hold that a default judgment is conclusive as to all issues that were necessarily involved in the former suit, even though the action went by default and there was no actual litigation thereof. [77 A.L.R.2d 1424]

   (b) **Not conclusive:** [§2078]   However, there is substantial authority contra, including Restatement (Second) of Judgments, holding that "actually litigated" requires evidence presented to, and a decision by, a trier of fact (so that default judgments do not qualify). [Restatement (Second) of Judgments §27, comment e]

   1) **Rationale:** This is believed to be the better view, because a person defaulting to a complaint may not have foreseen that the admissions created thereby would return to haunt him in a subsequent, unrelated lawsuit.

(3) **Stipulated judgments:** [§2079]   There is likewise a split of authority on whether a stipulated (consent) judgment is issue preclusive.

   (a) **Comment:** Even if an issue conceded through a default or consent judgment is not treated as within the rule of issue preclusion, it may be given conclusive effect under the law of evidence as a ***binding admission***. (*See* Evidence Summary.)

(4) **Jury vs. nonjury trial:** [§2080]   The presence or absence of a jury in the first trial is a "neutral" factor—*i.e.,* matters actually litigated in action 1 may be held collaterally estopped in action 2, even where there was no right to a jury in the earlier action (*e.g.,* a suit in equity) and the present suit is jury triable (*e.g.,* action for damages). [Parklane Hosiery v. Shore, 439 U.S. 322 (1979)]

b. **"Essential to first judgment":** [§2081]   Collateral estoppel applies only to those matters decided in the earlier lawsuit that were *essential to the court's determination*—*i.e.,* essential to the cause of action (or defense) established by the judgment therein. Other matters involved in the earlier lawsuit, even though "actually litigated," are not binding in a later action. [Restatement (Second) of Judgments §27]

   (1) **Example:** P sues D over personal injuries sustained in an auto accident. The court finds that: (i) P was contributorily negligent; and (ii) D was also negligent. The finding that D was negligent was not "necessary" (it is immaterial because P's claim is barred by his own contributory negligence). Consequently, when D later sues P for his injuries in the same accident, the finding in the earlier action that D was negligent is not binding against D.

   (2) **Test:** [§2082]   An issue is "essential" to the court's determination in the former action only if it appears that the judgment could not have been reached without determining the issue. [DeCourt v. Beckman Instruments, 32 Cal. App. 3d 628 (1973)]

(3) **Alternative findings:** [§2083]   There is a *split of authority* on whether alternative findings, either of which would have been sufficient to support the judgment, should create estoppel in other proceedings. [*Compare* Halpern v. Schwartz, 426 F.2d 102 (2d Cir. 1970) *and* Restatement (Second) of Judgments §27, comment i—no estoppel—*with* In re Westgate-California Corp., 642 F.2d 1174 (9th Cir. 1981)—estoppel allowed]

    (a) **Example:** In an action to declare involuntary bankruptcy, debtor-wife was found to have committed three acts of bankruptcy fraud, each of which would be sufficient to support the determination that involuntary bankruptcy was proper. In a subsequent action concerning her discharge, estoppel was asserted on the basis of one of the three findings because it involved fraud. The court held that estoppel should not apply because the finding was merely an alternative basis for the decision. [Halpern v. Schwartz, *supra*]

    (b) **Significance of appeal:** [§2084]   Some courts distinguish between cases in which the earlier judgment was appealed and those in which it was not. If no appeal was taken, they will hold that neither finding is preclusive. If an appeal is taken, however, there is preclusion with respect to those issues that the appellate court reaches that support its judgment. [Restatement (Second) of Judgments §27, comment o]

(4) **"Ultimate" vs. "evidentiary" facts:** [§2085]   Some cases have held that the previous determination of an issue is conclusive when the "ultimate" facts in the two actions are the same, but not when the first finding is simply a step (*i.e.,* a "mediate or evidentiary fact") toward the ultimate fact in the second action. [Evergreens v. Nunan, 141 F.2d 927 (2d Cir. 1944)]

    (a) **Example:** In a personal injury action, a finding that D was "negligent" would clearly be an ultimate fact; whereas, a specific finding that D had failed to maintain or repair her vehicle in a safe condition might be treated as "evidentiary."

    (b) **Modern approach contrary:** [§2086]   This distinction generally is *not* accepted. [*See* Synanon Church v. United States, 820 F.2d 421 (D.C. Cir. 1987)—issue preclusion applies to *any* fact determination actually litigated and essential to the judgment, without any distinction between "ultimate" and "mediate" or "evidentiary" facts]

c. **"Identical" issue:** [§2087]   The issue decided in the prior adjudication must be identical to the one presented in the instant action. Mere similarity of issues is not enough.

  (1) **Example:** When the first suit involved alleged breach of contract by defendant, there was no collateral estoppel in a second action involving securities act violations where the issues were different, even though the same conduct by defendant was involved in both actions. [Watson v. Roberts, Scott & Co., 466 F.2d 1348 (9th Cir. 1972)]

(2) **Example:** In the first action, the court held that workers could recover for injuries from defendant manufacturer of asbestos. This decision did not provide the basis for estoppel against the manufacturer in a later action brought by another worker, because issues raised in the later action were not identical and depended on circumstances under which the later plaintiff was exposed to asbestos products. [Hardy v. Johns-Manville Sales Corp., 681 F.2d 334 (5th Cir. 1982)]

d. **Exceptions:** [§2088] Issue preclusion is not as strictly applied as claim preclusion.

(1) *When the two actions involve the same parties*, the loser may be allowed to relitigate an issue in a new claim or cause of action *if*:

(a) *The stakes involved* in the second suit are *much larger* (*e.g.,* a small claims court decision of an issue will not be preclusive in a major personal injury case);

(b) *The burden of proof is lower* [People v. Cole, 10 Cal. App. 3d 332 (1970)];

(c) *The issue arises in a substantially different context* [Chern v. Bank of America, 15 Cal. 3d 866 (1976)]; *or*

(d) *Other compelling reasons* justify relitigation [Restatement (Second) of Judgments §28].

(2) *When the second action involves a different party*, all these exceptions apply and, in addition, the loser may relitigate if there are other factors that justify allowing her to do so. (*See infra,* §2106.)

D. **PERSONS PRECLUDED BY JUDGMENTS**

1. **Parties and Privies**

a. **Parties:** [§2089] A party to a judgment is bound by *claim preclusion* (so that she cannot relitigate the claim) *and issue preclusion* (so that, ordinarily, she cannot relitigate an issue determined in the first action).

b. **Privies:** [§2090] A person in "privity" with a party is usually bound to the *same extent* as the party. "Privity" is a legal conclusion, indicating that the person in question has a relationship to the party such that he should be bound. Whether "privity" exists depends in part on the type of claims involved. There are two general categories of privity:

(1) **Procedural privity:** [§2091] Where the party acted in the first action as the *representative* of the nonparty, the judgment therein binds the nonparty. [Restatement (Second) of Judgments §41]

(a) **Examples:** A party appearing as the representative of a class in a class suit [King v. International Union, 114 Cal. App. 2d 159 (1952)]; a trustee or guardian representing a beneficiary or ward [Armstrong v. Armstrong, 15 Cal. 3d 942 (1976)—parent for child]; *or* a party whose interests are represented by an executor or administrator.

(2) **Substantive privity:** [§2092]   Privity may also arise out of *substantive* legal relationships, where the nonparty is bound because of a prior legal relationship to the party. [Restatement (Second) of Judgments §41] Examples include the following:

- (a) **Bailment:** [§2093]   Either the bailee or the bailor can sue a third party for injury to the bailed chattel; and an action by one precludes an action by the other. [Anheuser-Busch, Inc. v. Starley, 28 Cal. 2d 347 (1946)]

- (b) **Medical losses of child or spouse:** [§2094]   In most states, medical expenses (*e.g.,* hospital bills) paid by a parent or spouse can be recovered either by the injured person or by the parent or spouse who paid them. Hence an action by one of those who could recover the expenses precludes an action by any of the others. [Restatement (Second) of Judgments §48]

- (c) **Successor in interest:** [§2095]   A successor in interest to property is bound by a judgment to which his predecessor was a party. [Kartheiser v. Superior Court, 174 Cal. App. 2d 617 (1959)]

    1) **Example:** A sues B, an adjoining landowner, to determine the boundary between the properties. After judgment, A transfers the property to C. C is bound by the prior determination of the boundary.

- (d) **Beneficiary of estate:** [§2096]   A beneficiary of an estate is bound by an action litigated on behalf of the estate by the trustee. [Restatement (Second) of Judgments §41(a)]

- (e) **Public official authorized by law to act on person's behalf:** [§2097]   Where a public official is authorized by law to act on a person's behalf, the person is bound by the official's litigation on his behalf. [Restatement (Second) of Judgments §41(d)]

(3) **Compare—family relationships:** [§2098]   The fact that parties have a legal relationship to each other does not of itself make them "privies." Thus, a husband's lawsuit is not binding on his wife (unless, in a community property state, the husband represents the community in maintaining the suit); nor does a parent necessarily represent a child. Whether "privity" exists depends on whether there is a *representative* capacity arising out of the relationship.

- (a) **Example:** Parent and Child are both hurt in an automobile accident with D. If Parent sues D for his injuries and loses, that does not bar Child from suing D for Child's injuries.

- (b) **Example:** In divorce action with wife, father litigated the question of whether he had given half ownership of the family farm to sons. Sons were not bound by the result, even though they testified as witnesses in the divorce action. [Searle Brothers v. Searle, 588 P.2d 689 (Utah 1978)]

(c) **Compare:** If Parent sues as Child's *guardian* for Child's injuries, that precludes a suit by Child (because she was represented in the first suit)—though it would not preclude a suit by Parent for *his own* injuries.

2. **Nonparties**

   a. **Nonparty not bound:** [§2099] In general, a nonparty is *not bound* by judgment. Such a person has not had his day in court and, as a matter of *due process*, he cannot be denied a valuable interest (his right of action) without one. [Parklane Hosiery Co. v. Shore, supra, §2080] Instances of "privity" (above) are exceptions to the rule, justified on the ground that the nonparty's interests were adequately represented by the party to the first action.

      (1) **Example—no binding effect on nonparties:** White firefighters, who had not been parties to a prior litigation between a city and civil rights claimants that resulted in consent decrees establishing minority hiring and promotion goals, were not precluded from bringing a discrimination suit against the city. It was immaterial whether the white firefighters could have intervened in the first litigation; the burden of joining additional parties to secure binding effect against them is on those already parties. [Martin v. Wilks, 490 U.S. 755 (1989)] *Note:* For cases involving federal employment discrimination claims, Congress, in the Civil Rights Act of 1991, changed the ruling of *Martin v. Wilks* to give binding effect to a litigated or consent judgment or order when the nonparty had adequate notice and opportunity to present objections, or when the nonparty's specific interests had been adequately represented by another. [42 U.S.C. §2000e-2(n)]

   b. **Nonparty may benefit:** [§2100] A nonparty may *benefit* from the judgment in an action to which he was not a party.

      (1) **Claim preclusion:** [§2101] In a number of situations, two potential defendants will have a relationship such that one is responsible for the conduct of the other. Examples include master and servant (under the principle of respondeat superior) and insurer and insured (the insurer being liable, up to the policy limits, for acts of the insured). When this relationship of vicarious responsibility exists, a judgment *exonerating either* potential defendant precludes an action on the same claim against the other.

         (a) **Example:** P claims injuries as the result of negligence by Employee, who was acting in the course and scope of his employment for Employer. If P sues either Employee or Employer alone, a judgment *exonerating* that defendant (on a finding of no negligence by Employee) will preclude a claim against the other, since Employer's liability is derivative in nature.

         (b) **Not applicable to joint or concurrent liability:** [§2102] This form of claim preclusion applies *only* in situations of *vicarious responsibility*, and not in cases of joint or concurrent tort liability. Thus, if A is injured by the *concurrent negligence* of B and C (each of whom operates his own car) and A sues B and loses, that judgment does not bar A from suing C. But if B was driving C's car, and A lost in an action against B, A could not sue C based on B's conduct.

(2) **Issue preclusion**

    (a) **Basic rule:** [§2103] A party who litigates an issue against one party and loses may not relitigate that issue with another party.

        1) **Example:** Driver A and passenger B are injured when A's car is hit by D's car. A sues D, contending that D was negligent, and wins. If B then sues D, D is bound by the first action and cannot relitigate whether he was negligent.

        2) **Rationale:** If a party has had a *full and fair opportunity to litigate an issue* in one action, there is no reason to waste the time of the court and other persons in relitigating that issue. [Blonder-Tongue Laboratories, Inc. v. University of Illinois Foundation, 402 U.S. 313 (1971); Bernhard v. Bank of America, 19 Cal. 2d 807 (1942)] The rule is often referred to as the *"Bernhard"* rule.

    (b) **Background—mutuality rule:** [§2104] Before *Bernhard, supra,* the mutuality rule prevented a nonparty from having the benefit of issue preclusion in his favor. The theory was that an estoppel should apply only if it was mutual—*i.e.,* since the nonparty would not have been bound by the issue had it been decided the *other* way (because he had not had his day in court), he should not be able to invoke an estoppel in his favor based on the earlier judgment. *Bernhard,* which rejected this mutuality rule, is now the majority view. [Restatement (Second) of Judgments §29]

    (c) **Offensive vs. defensive use of prior judgment:** [§2105] Earlier decisions held that issue preclusion could be used defensively against a plaintiff, but not offensively against a defendant (to block defendant's attempt to relitigate issues on which he had lost in the earlier trial). However, the Supreme Court has held that this is *not* a critical distinction. [Parklane Hosiery Co. v. Shore, *supra,* §2099]

        1) **Example of defensive use:** P claims to have been injured by the concurrent acts of B and C. In an action by P against B, it is found that P suffered no actual injury. If P later sues C for the same loss, C can invoke issue preclusion defensively. [Ponce v. Tractor Supply Co., 29 Cal. App. 3d 500 (1972)]

        2) **Example of offensive use:** P-1 and P-2, passengers in a bus, are hurt when the bus collides with a train. P-1 wins in his suit against the railroad. The better decisions would permit P-2 to use the earlier judgment as conclusive proof against the railroad in a suit by P-2.

        3) **Further example—offensive use:** In action 1, the SEC files suit against Corporation for false statements in a proxy solicitation in connection with a proposed merger (*i.e.,* mailings to the shareholders seeking their votes to approve the merger). Judgment is rendered against Corporation. In action 2, shareholders file suit against Corporation seeking damages as a result of their reliance

on the same proxy solicitation. The judgment rendered against Corporation in the SEC action may be held to bar Corporation from relitigating the issue of whether the solicitation was false and misleading. [*See* Parklane Hosiery Co. v. Shore, *supra*]

(d) **Limitations:** [§2106] Although issue preclusion can be used offensively or defensively, the benefits of such estoppel may be denied under certain circumstances.

1) **Issue would not be conclusive between parties:** [§2107] If the issue would not be treated as conclusive between the *parties* to the first action (*see supra,* §2088), it cannot be conclusive in *favor of a third person* not a party to the first action.

   a) **Example:** P is slightly injured while a passenger in A's car when it collides with B's car. P sues A for $300 in doctor's bills and wins on a finding that A was negligent. B then sues A for $50,000 in personal injuries. The finding in the first action does not preclude A from litigating the question of negligence against B, because the amount involved in the first case was so small that it would not be treated as conclusive even between P and A in a second action.

2) **Unjust under circumstances:** [§2108] In addition, a third person cannot have the benefit of issue preclusion against a party to the first action if it would be unjust in the circumstances. In deciding whether preclusion would be "unjust," the court may consider relevant factors such as the following: [*See* Restatement (Second) of Judgments §29]

   a) Whether the person seeking the benefit of preclusion *could have joined in the prior action*, but decided instead to "sit it out";

   b) Whether the prior determination was itself *inconsistent with an earlier determination* of the same issue;

   c) Whether the consequences in the second action are *much more serious* than those in the first action [Cochran v. Union Lumber Co., 26 Cal. App. 3d 423 (1972)];

   d) Whether the party to be estopped has *procedural opportunities* (*e.g.,* broader discovery, ability to compel live testimony of important witnesses) that were not available in the earlier action;

   e) Whether the prior finding was apparently a *compromise verdict*; and

   f) Whether the issue is one of law whose *reconsideration should not be foreclosed* [United States v. Mendoza, 464 U.S. 154 (1984)—federal government not subject to issue preclusion from prior determination in litigation with different party].

REVIEW QUESTIONS

FILL IN
ANSWER

TERRITORIAL JURISDICTION

1. P is a resident of State A. D is a resident of State B. P files suit against D in an appropriate State A court, serving D personally while D is in an airplane flying over State A. D has no other contacts with State A. Should the court grant D's motion to dismiss for want of jurisdiction over his person? _____

2. P is a resident of State A. D is a doctor in State B. P commenced an action against D in the court of State A, alleging that he had been injured in an auto collision in State A caused by a loss of consciousness in a patient of D, which in turn had resulted from an act of professional malpractice committed in State B. D moved to dismiss the action for want of jurisdiction over his person. Should the motion be granted? _____

3. P is a resident of State A. D is a drug manufacturer in State B that sells its products in State A. P commenced an action against D in the court of State A, alleging injury from a defective drug purchased by P in State A. Pursuant to the law of State A, P served D by mail at its place of business in State B. D moved to dismiss the action for want of jurisdiction over its person. Should the motion be granted? _____

4. P is a resident of State A. D is a resident of State B and is not subject to service of process in State A. P brings an action against D in the court of State A for breach of contract. Process is served on Hand, a resident of State A, who was designated as D's agent for receipt of service in the contract made between P and D. D moves to quash the service of process and to dismiss for want of jurisdiction. Should the motion be granted? _____

5. P is a resident of State A. D is a resident of State B and is not subject to service of process in State A. P commenced an action against D in the court of State A. After a contested trial, the jury rendered a verdict for P. D then raised want of jurisdiction over his person and moved to dismiss. Should the court grant the motion? _____

6. P is a resident of State A. D is a resident of State B and is not subject to service of process in State A. P writes D offering to settle a dispute on very reasonable terms if D will meet P in State A to discuss it. D arrives and is met at the appointed place by a process server in an action brought by P on the dispute. D moves to quash service of process and to dismiss for want of jurisdiction. Should the court grant the motion? _____

7. P files a diversity suit in federal court in New York, claiming damages arising out of an accident which occurred in New Jersey. P resides in Connecticut and D resides in Pennsylvania, but P chose to file in New York because most of the witnesses reside there. Is venue proper in New York? _____

8. Can the action in question 7, above, be transferred to New Jersey? If transferred to New Jersey, can the action be transferred back again to New York for the convenience of the parties and witnesses under 28 U.S.C. section 1404(a)? _____

Civil Procedure—327

9. If a transfer for convenience of witnesses was proper, could the transfer be made on the motion of *plaintiff*?

10. P, a resident of New York, wishes to sue D, a resident of New Jersey, for injuries suffered in an auto accident in Pennsylvania. Would venue be proper for a federal action in New Jersey and Pennsylvania?

11. P Co. is incorporated in Delaware and has its principal place of business there. Its employee, E, is a citizen of Pennsylvania. P and E wish to join as plaintiffs in a suit against D1 (a citizen of Florida) and D2 (a citizen of Georgia) for damage done in a ship collision which occurred in international waters. In what state would venue be proper in a federal action?

12. P and D are residents of the same state. P commenced an action against D for breach of contract. Unable to find D—who lives alone—in person, and unable to get D to waive service, P attached D's weekend cottage, recording the writ of attachment and posting notice on the door of the cottage. A default judgment was entered for P and a writ of execution issued. Before the execution sale, D moved for relief from the judgment on the ground that it is void. Should the motion be granted?

13. P is a resident of State A. D is a resident of State B. P files a diversity suit against D for $75,000 in the federal court located in State A. Copies of the summons and complaint are mailed to D in his home state of B. Has D been effectively served?

14. P is a resident of State A. D is a resident of State B. D is subject to service of process in State A and has a bank account in that state. P files an action against D in a court of State A and serves a writ of garnishment on D's bank, thereafter notifying D of the proceedings. D moves to quash the writ of garnishment and to dismiss for want of jurisdiction. Should the court grant the motion?

FEDERAL SUBJECT MATTER JURISDICTION

15. P, a citizen of Texas, files a diversity action in federal court against "XYZ, Inc."

    a. Assume that "XYZ, Inc." is in fact a partnership, having its principal place of business in Oklahoma, and consisting of three partners (X, Y, and Z), one of whom resides in Texas. Does the requisite diversity of citizenship exist?

    b. Assume that "XYZ, Inc." is a corporation incorporated in Delaware, having its principal place of business in New York with branch offices nationwide, including one in Texas. Does the requisite diversity of citizenship exist?

16. D, a citizen of Virginia, takes a vacation trip to Mexico City, where he negligently injures P. P sues D for $75,000 damages in the federal court in Virginia, claiming diversity jurisdiction. Which, if any, of the following factors would justify the court's dismissing the action for *lack* of diversity?

    (A) P is a Mexican national.

    (B) P is a U.S. citizen living permanently in Mexico City.

    (C) P is a citizen of Virginia, but has been mentally incompetent since birth; and his longtime guardian is a citizen of Maryland.

17. P files suit against D in federal court, claiming diversity of citizenship jurisdiction. Which, if any, of the following facts would justify the court's dismissal of the action for *lack* of diversity?

    (A) P and D were both citizens of State A at the time the claim arose. P moved to State B just before filing suit against D, for the apparent purpose of *creating* diversity of citizenship.

    (B) P and D were citizens of different states at the time the claim arose. Just before P filed his suit, D moved into the state where P resided, for the apparent purpose of *preventing* diversity of citizenship.

    (C) P and D were citizens of different states at the time the claim arose and at the time the suit was filed. Shortly thereafter, however, D moved into the state where P resided.

    (D) P and D are citizens of different states at all times. However, neither of them resides in the state in which the federal court is located.

    (E) P and D are citizens of different states at all times, but P is suing on a claim assigned to him for collection by a citizen of the state in which D resides.

18. P1, a citizen of State A, and P2, a citizen of State X, join in an action against D1, a citizen of State B, and D2, a citizen of State X. Federal jurisdiction is invoked on grounds of diversity of citizenship. D2 moves to dismiss for want of federal jurisdiction. Should the motion be granted?

19. P is a citizen of State A. D is a citizen of State B, but is subject to service of process in State A. P brought an action against D in the federal court in State A, alleging diversity of citizenship, and a tort claim with damages in the amount of $25,000. After trial, the jury rendered a verdict for P in the amount of $10,000. D then moved to dismiss for want of subject matter jurisdiction. Should the court grant the motion?

20. P files a diversity suit against D, alleging $125,000 damages for invasion of privacy. The jury subsequently awards P only $500 damages. Does the federal court have jurisdiction to enter such a judgment?

21. P sues B in a diversity suit for $40,000 owed on a promissory note and $15,000 in personal injuries. Has the required jurisdictional amount for diversity purposes been met?

22. P sues D1 and D2 as codefendants in a diversity suit. P alleges that D1 owes her $40,000 on one promissory note, that D2 owes her $15,000 on another promissory note, and that both promissory notes were executed at the same time and as part of the same transaction. Is the jurisdictional minimum requirement satisfied?

23. P1 and P2 join as plaintiffs to sue D in a diversity suit to recover for an auto accident in which P1 and P2 were both riding in a car hit by a car driven by D. P1 seeks to recover $40,000 and P2 seeks to recover $15,000. Is the jurisdictional minimum requirement satisfied?

24. P is a citizen of State A. D is a citizen of State B. P brought an action against D in the federal court in State B, praying for a decree of divorce. D moved to dismiss for want of federal jurisdiction. Should the motion be granted? _____

25. P and D were divorced pursuant to an agreement providing for alimony payments by D to P in fixed amounts "after taxes." P was held liable for federal income taxes on payments received. She now brings an action in federal court to recover on the promise of D to bear the income tax liability, alleging that it arises under federal law. D moves to dismiss for want of subject matter jurisdiction. Should the motion be granted? _____

26. P brought an action against D in federal court for defamation, alleging federal jurisdiction based on the federal question presented by D's defense that his speech was constitutionally protected by the First Amendment. D moved to dismiss for want of federal jurisdiction. Should the motion be granted? _____

27. P claims that his business has been damaged by monopolistic practices by D, which allegedly violate *both* the Sherman Act and a state "fair practices" act.

    a. Can P file an action asserting both claims in either state or federal court? _____

    b. If P files in federal court, can the federal court grant relief under the state act even if no violation of the Sherman Act is proved? _____

28. If there are *several* codefendants in a state court action, must they *all* join in the notice of removal to the federal court in order to confer jurisdiction on the federal court? _____

29. Smith, a citizen of Nevada, sues Jones, a citizen of California, in a California state court to enforce a promissory note for $100,000. Jones files a counterclaim against Smith for $1 million.

    a. Can Smith remove the action to the federal court in California? _____

    b. Can Jones remove the action to the federal court in California? _____

30. Black, a citizen of New York, sues Brown, a citizen of New Jersey, in a state court in New York. The claim is for copyright infringement. Can Brown remove the action to the federal court in New York? _____

31. P is a citizen of State A. D is a citizen of State B. P files an action against D for violation of the federal civil rights laws in a state court of general jurisdiction in State A. Should the court grant D's motion to dismiss for want of jurisdiction over the subject matter of the claim? _____

RELATIONSHIP BETWEEN STATE AND FEDERAL LAW

32. On July 14, P files an action against D in federal court in State X, properly invoking diversity jurisdiction, to recover for injuries sustained in an automobile accident on the previous July 15. One week after the suit was filed, D was personally served with the summons and complaint. D defends on the ground that the action is barred under the applicable one-year statute of limitations, citing a provision of State X law that the limitations period continues to run until a defendant is personally served. Is D's defense valid? _____

33. P files a diversity action against D in federal court in State X. To prove her right to recover, P must rely on certain hearsay evidence that would be inadmissible in state court in State X, but which is admissible under the Federal Rules of Evidence, which provide a number of exceptions to the hearsay rule. Should the evidence be admitted? _____

34. P sues D1 in state court in State X, and D1 properly removes to federal court on grounds of diversity. Three years later, P amends the complaint to add D2 as a defendant. D2 had no notice of the suit until it was served with the amended complaint, and it moves to dismiss on the ground the claims against it are barred by the applicable two-year statute of limitations. Under the law of State X, added defendants who are not on notice have no limitations defense if the plaintiff sues some defendant within the limitations period. Should the court grant D2's motion to dismiss? _____

35. In P's diversity suit against D in federal court in State X, D moves for judgment as a matter of law at the close of all the evidence on the ground that P has failed to produce substantial evidence as required by federal precedents. P responds by invoking the rule of the courts of State X that such a motion should be denied if plaintiff has produced a scintilla of evidence, a lower requirement. Should the court apply the federal requirement? _____

36. P files a diversity suit against D in federal court in State X. Under a 30-year-old decision of the intermediate appellate court of State X, D has an absolute defense to the case, but the more "modern" view is that this defense is no longer valid. D moves to dismiss, citing the state appellate court decision. Should the court grant the motion? _____

PLEADING

37. P files an action in a code pleading state against D Riding Stable to recover for injuries sustained when P was thrown from a horse rented from D. P's complaint is captioned "for breach of contract," and alleges that "D allowed P to ride an unruly horse without adequate warning." D moves to dismiss because the complaint nowhere alleges the existence of any contractual relationship. Should the court grant the motion? _____

38. P files a complaint against D, a restaurant owner, alleging that he suffered food poisoning as the result of consuming "improperly prepared" food in D's restaurant.

   a. Is this sufficient to state a claim for relief in federal court (apart from jurisdictional allegations)? _____

   b. Is this sufficient to state a claim for relief in a code pleading state? _____

39. P sues D to quiet title to certain real property. P alleges "on information and belief" that D has recorded a document that clouds P's title. Is such an allegation sufficient to state a claim for relief? _____

40. P files a diversity action against D in federal court, claiming $75,000 damages for a battery. In one paragraph of a verified complaint, P alleges that D himself struck

and battered P; but in a later paragraph he alleges that D did not do it personally, but rather paid a third person to batter P. D files a motion to dismiss for failure to state a claim. Should the court grant the motion?

41. P filed suit against D seeking to enjoin D's operation of an amusement park as a nuisance interfering with P's enjoyment of his property. D defaulted to P's complaint. At the hearing on entry of judgment, the court found that an injunction would be harsh and unnecessary, and instead awarded P $50,000 damages for interference with the use and enjoyment of his property. Can D successfully appeal this judgment, having defaulted in the trial court?

42. P files a personal injury action against D. P's complaint adequately pleads the elements of negligence, and then avers: "Immediately after the accident, D paid $1,000 to P in settlement of P's claim, but P was defrauded by D into accepting the settlement and thereafter returned the money to D." If the action is filed in federal court, and D moves to dismiss for failing to state a claim upon which relief can be granted, should the court grant the motion?

43. P files a defamation action against D in a code pleading state, alleging in substance the defamatory words used by D (rather than quoting them verbatim). Is the complaint subject to a demurrer for failing to state a cause of action?

44. P files suit against D for personal injuries. The complaint alleges that P "sustained personal injury to his damage in the amount of $50,000." Under such allegation, which of the following items of evidence are admissible at trial?

    (A) Proof that P broke his right arm in the accident.

    (B) Proof that P's broken arm was extremely painful.

    (C) Proof that P's broken arm will cause some permanent disability.

    (D) Proof of the hospital and medical expenses incurred in treating P's broken arm.

    (E) Proof that future medical expenses will have to be incurred in treating P's broken arm.

    (F) Proof that D acted intentionally and willfully to inflict such injury, entitling P to additional, punitive damages.

45. P has three separate and distinct claims against D: (i) for nonpayment of a promissory note; (ii) for personal injuries; and (iii) to quiet title to certain property.

    a. Can P join all three claims in a single action against D in federal court?

    b. Would the answer be the same if P named D's wife as a codefendant on the promissory note claim alone?

46. P files a breach of contract action against D. D files a general denial and also alleges, "P is a millionaire, and is bringing this suit hoping to force D into bankruptcy, so that he can pick up all of D's assets for a pittance." P moves to strike this allegation from D's answer. Should the court grant the motion?

47. P files a diversity suit in a federal court not having proper venue. D does not file a motion to dismiss, but raises the improper venue in his answer. At the time of trial, he moves for change of venue. Is D's motion timely?

48. P files a diversity suit in a federal court not having venue. D files a motion to dismiss for failure to state a claim. When this motion is denied, D files an answer in which he raises the venue objection. P moves to strike this portion of the answer because the issue was not raised in D's earlier motion to dismiss. Should the court grant the motion?

49. P files a diversity suit in a federal court. D moves to dismiss for improper venue, but his motion is denied. D then files an answer in which he raises the objection that P's complaint fails to state a claim upon which relief can be granted. P moves to strike this portion of D's answer because the issue was not raised in D's earlier motion to dismiss. Should the court grant this motion?

50. P's complaint in a federal action shows on its face that the action is barred by the statute of limitations, but otherwise sets forth all additional elements of the claim sued upon. D moves to dismiss for failure to state a claim upon which relief can be granted. P counters that the allegations of time were surplusage and asks the court to disregard them in ruling on D's motion. Should the court grant the motion?

51. P files a verified complaint in a state court action in a code pleading state. D's answer (also verified) contains a general denial. P moves to strike D's answer on the ground that a general denial to a verified complaint is improper. Should the court sustain the demurrer?

52. P sues D for nonpayment of a promissory note. D's answer contains only the following allegation: "D neither admits nor denies P's charge, and puts P to his proof at trial." P moves for a judgment on the pleadings on the ground that D has admitted liability. Should the court grant the motion?

53. P files a federal action against D for breach of contract, claiming $100,000 damages. D files an answer containing only a general denial. Is D's answer an admission that some other sum is owed P?

54. P files a defamation action against D. D's answer contains only a general denial. At trial, which, if any, of the following matters may be proved by D?

    (A) That D's utterance was true.

    (B) That no one in fact heard what D said about P.

    (C) That P and D later entered into a contract settling the matter.

    (D) That P's reputation was already so bad that no harm was done by the utterance.

55. P sues D for personal injuries in a federal action. D's answer contains only a general denial. Later, D seeks leave of court to amend his answer to object to improper venue. Does the court have the power to permit such an amendment?

Civil Procedure—333

56. In answer to P's complaint, seeking to recover for injuries allegedly caused by food improperly prepared by D's restaurant, D alleges: "Whatever food poisoning P suffered resulted from his consuming food elsewhere than at D's restaurant." What sort of pleading is now required from P in order to preserve the issue (as to where he consumed the food) for trial? _____

57. D files a counterclaim to P's complaint in a federal court action. Which, if any, of the following would be a valid ground for striking D's counterclaim? _____

    (A) The counterclaim was pleaded as part of D's answer rather than as a separate pleading.

    (B) P's complaint was for copyright infringement, while D's counterclaim was for personal injury; hence no subject matter relationship.

    (C) P's complaint was for $100,000 damages for breach of contract, with federal jurisdiction based on diversity of citizenship. D's counterclaim was for $5,000 for personal injury. Hence, no federal jurisdiction on the counterclaim.

    (D) Several other parties would have to be joined for a complete determination of D's counterclaim.

58. P filed a complaint against D on June 1 for back injuries arising out of a highway truck accident. D filed a counterclaim on July 1 for damages to his own truck arising out of the same accident. P moves to strike on the ground that the statute of limitations on D's counterclaim ran on June 15. Should the court grant the motion? _____

59. P has filed a personal injury action in federal court against D1 and D2, claiming they were jointly responsible for causing a traffic accident in which he was injured. On which, if any, of the following grounds would it be proper for D1 to *cross-claim* against D2? _____

    (A) D1 claims that the accident was entirely the fault of D2.

    (B) D1 claims that his car was damaged in the accident, and D2 was responsible therefor.

    (C) D1 claims that if P recovers a judgment against him, it should be made payable against D2 jointly.

    (D) D1 claims that D2 owes him $15,000 on a promissory note.

60. Same facts as in previous question. Suppose D2 claimed that he lost control of his car due to defective repairs made by D3. Could D2 file a cross-claim for indemnification against D3? _____

61. P sues D for personal injuries resulting from D's alleged negligence in causing an auto accident. Shortly before trial, P discovers that D had been driving under the influence of alcohol, and had been performing an errand for XYZ Co. By this time, however, the statute of limitations has run on all claims arising out of the accident.

334—Civil Procedure

a. If P seeks leave to amend his complaint to allege that D was driving while intoxicated so as to entitle P to punitive damages, should the court grant the motion? _____

b. If P seeks leave to amend his complaint to name XYZ Co. as a codefendant, asserting liability against it on respondeat superior grounds, should the court grant the motion? _____

62. P files suit against "Alfred A. Albertson," alleging that Albertson negligently operated a model airplane so as to cause it to fly through an open window of P's house, striking P in the head and causing serious injury.

    a. At trial, the evidence shows that the real name of the person sued as "Alfred A. Albertson" is "Albert T. Albrittson." P seeks leave to amend her complaint to conform to proof. D resists on the ground that the statute of limitations has run. Should the court grant the motion? _____

    b. The evidence also shows that the model airplane destroyed a valuable vase in P's home worth $10,000. P seeks leave to amend to conform to proof. D objects. What ruling? _____

    c. The evidence also shows that since the time the original complaint was filed, P's injuries have worsened, and she is now blind in one eye. P seeks leave to plead these additional facts. D objects. Should the motion be granted? _____

63. On the date set for trial in a federal diversity suit, P discovers that a crucial witness is unwilling to testify. P moves for a dismissal of the action, hoping to sue again later. D objects, wanting to obtain a judgment in his favor so as to bar any later suit. Can the court simply refuse to grant a dismissal and force P to go to trial? _____

PARTIES

64. Which of the following parties would be entitled to sue in his own name on the claim in question without joining any other party as plaintiff? _____

    (A) A collection agency on a debt assigned to it for collection.

    (B) The beneficiary of a trust on a claim against a third person for wrongs to the trust estate.

    (C) A third-party beneficiary on a contract made expressly and primarily for his benefit.

    (D) The promisee of a contract made expressly and primarily for the benefit of a third person.

    (E) The undisclosed principal on a contract entered into on his behalf by an agent.

65. If someone other than the real party in interest files suit, and the defendant fails to raise a timely objection, can the resulting judgment be attacked? _____

66. In a federal action by a partnership asserting a state law claim, does federal law determine the partnership's capacity to sue as an entity (rather than as an association of individual partners)?

67. Samantha, a minor female, wants to play baseball in the Little League system. After being refused, she files suit against Little League for injunctive relief. Little League moves to dismiss, on the ground that Samantha's father is the real party in interest. Should the motion be granted?

68. P went into the hospital for surgery. He claims that Surgeon was negligent in performing the operation, whereby he was damaged in the sum of $100,000. He also claims that the hospital was negligent in caring for him after surgery, for which he seeks $50,000 damages.

   a. Can P join both defendants in a single action?

   b. Can P join these separate claims in a single action?

   c. Assume that P cannot prove whether his injuries were attributable to improper surgery or to improper care after surgery. Is it permissible for him to join both defendants under such circumstances?

69. P brought an action against D1 and D2 alleging that each had defrauded him in separate securities transactions. D2 moves to dismiss the action for improper joinder. Should the motion be granted?

70. P brings an action against D1 on a promissory note signed by D1 and D2. D1 moves to dismiss the action for failure to join D2. Should the motion be granted?

71. P brings an action as a holder in due course against D to collect a portion of D's liability on a note. The remainder of the obligation had been assigned by the payee to A, who has not joined in the action. On motion by D, should A be joined?

72. P, a citizen of State A, brought a federal diversity action against D, a citizen of State B, to recover for alleged mismanagement of a corporation partially owned by P. The corporation is a citizen of State B. D moved to dismiss the action for failure to join the corporation. Should the motion be granted?

73. P files a diversity suit in federal court against D, claiming damages for breach of contract. D claims that he was prevented from performing the contract by reason of tortious interference by TP.

   a. Can D join TP as a party to the action?

   b. Can the federal court retain the case if it appears that TP is a resident of the same state as P?

74. P files a diversity suit against Duchess Sandwich Co., alleging that he became violently ill after consuming a sandwich purchased from Duchess which he alleges contained impure ingredients, thereby sustaining damages exceeding $50,000.

336—Civil Procedure

a. T, a co-worker in P's office, purchased a similar sandwich from Duchess on the same day as did P, and also became violently ill. If T moves to intervene in P's lawsuit against Duchess, should the court grant the motion? _____

b. XYZ is the company that furnishes Duchess with all of its ingredients, and has contracted to indemnify Duchess for any loss due to impurities in the ingredients furnished. If XYZ moves to intervene in P's lawsuit against Duchess, should the court grant the motion? _____

75. Don's life was insured for $5,000 by Apex Insurance Co., which has its principal place of business in California. Don is now dead. Apex has received conflicting claims for the insurance benefits from Don's wife, Wilma, a citizen of California, and Don's brother, Bob, a citizen of New York.

    a. If Apex pays the $5,000 into federal court, can the federal court exercise jurisdiction to determine who is entitled to it? _____

    b. Can the federal court in California exercise jurisdiction even though Bob is not subject to personal service in California? _____

76. P sues on behalf of himself "and all other students paying nonresident rate tuition at State University" to enjoin collection of the higher tuition charged nonresidents, on equal protection grounds. Approximately 500 students are affected. May the case proceed as a class action? _____

77. P, a citizen of California, files suit in federal court against Victor Vacuum Co., incorporated and having its principal place of business in New York. P sues "on behalf of himself and all other customers of Victor Vacuum Co." alleging various deceptive advertising and sales practices, causing aggregate losses exceeding $100,000. Which, if any, of the following arguments justify granting Victor's motion to dismiss the action? _____

    (A) No diversity of citizenship, because some of Victor's customers reside in New York.

    (B) No diversity jurisdiction, because the individual claims involved are not more than $50,000 each.

    (C) Improper as class suit because each customer has a separate contract with Victor, hence no common question "predominates."

78. In determining whether an action should proceed as a class action, is it proper for the court to consider the suit's likelihood of success on the merits? _____

79. Assume that federal class action status is granted on the ground that there is a "predominant common question."

    a. Is it mandatory that all members of the class who can be identified with reasonable effort be notified, no matter how many of them there are? _____

    b. Is it mandatory that the plaintiff initially pay the costs of giving such notice? _____

    c. Will a resulting judgment necessarily bind all members of the class? _____

80. P owns a Blizzo Snowmobile. P sues Blizzo in state court on behalf of herself and all other owners of Blizzo Snowmobiles, alleging that the vehicles have defective parts that make them unsafe to ride in and cause an unusually fast depreciation in value. Blizzo offers P $15,000 to settle the claim, plus putting up a fund which will assure that any other owner can recover $100 if a claim is made within one year. P then consents to entry of judgment in favor of Blizzo. Several months later, another owner, T, sues Blizzo for the same kind of damages. Is T bound by the judgment in P's action against Blizzo? _____

DISCOVERY

81. Must a party to a federal civil action disclose to an adversary, without having received any discovery request, the contents of a document in the party's possession that is harmful to its case? _____

82. P files an action against XYZ, Inc. in federal court. P wishes to conduct discovery by deposition, but is unsure which of the XYZ employees has the information he seeks, and therefore does not know whose name to put on the notice of deposition. Is it necessary for P to file interrogatories to find out the employee's name before sending out the notice of deposition? _____

83. P sues XYZ, Inc. for personal injuries sustained in a traffic accident with a truck belonging to XYZ and driven by employee E (who is not a party to the action).

   a. P took E's deposition prior to trial and obtained some admissions of negligence. Can P introduce E's deposition as substantive evidence of negligence at the time of trial? _____

   b. P also took the deposition of X, the president of XYZ, Inc., who admitted that E was driving within the course and scope of his employment. Can P introduce X's deposition testimony at trial as substantive evidence of this fact? _____

84. Which, if any, discovery procedure is available under the Federal Rules to obtain the information indicated in the following cases?

   a. P was involved in a traffic accident with D, but is in doubt whether D was at fault. Hence, *before* filing suit, she wants to obtain the testimony of eyewitness W, who has refused to talk to P about the matter. _____

   b. P sues D for personal injuries sustained in a traffic accident. P claims she was off work for several weeks. D wants to check P's time card maintained by P's employer, but the employer has refused to provide this information. _____

   c. An eyewitness to the P-D traffic accident claims to have observed the collision from his living room window. D wants to take photographs from inside the witness's living room to check the credibility of the witness's claimed observations. _____

   d. The same eyewitness was wearing thick lenses at the time in question. D has reason to doubt whether the witness's vision is sufficient to have seen what she claims to have seen. Therefore, D asks for a court order to have the witness submit to a reasonable eye examination by D's doctor. Should the court grant D's motion? _____

85. P sues D to quiet title to certain land. After considerable investigation, D's attorney obtains an old deed, which tends to support P's claim of title and to undermine D's defense. Somehow, P finds out about the deed and serves a request to produce on D. Which, if any, of the following are valid grounds for objection under the Federal Rules?

    (A) D does not have possession of the document.

    (B) The document is privileged as attorney's work product.

    (C) The request is improper because it was served without prior court order or any showing of good cause.

86. In a personal injury case, P is examined by D's doctor. P's attorney requests and obtains a copy of the report made by D's doctor. Is D now automatically entitled to copies of all medical reports by P's doctors?

87. P filed action against D Restaurant for $75,000, claiming food poisoning from impure food prepared by D. P served on D the following interrogatories, to which D objected on the grounds stated. P now moves to compel answers. How should the court rule in each case?

    a. Interrogatory: "Have you obtained statements in writing from other customers in the restaurant concerning the food served on the night in question?" Objection: Such statements are hearsay and inadmissible at trial.

    b. Interrogatory: "Do you claim that plaintiff's food poisoning resulted from consumption of food elsewhere on the date in question?" Objection: Calls for a conclusion.

    c. Interrogatory: "Has any other customer ever filed a lawsuit against you claiming food poisoning as the result of food you served?" Objection: Irrelevant.

    d. Interrogatory: "In the event P recovers a judgment for the full amount of his claim, do you have assets sufficient to pay such a judgment?" Objection: Irrelevant.

    e. Interrogatory: "Has your attorney caused any tests to be performed on the food in question to determine its purity, and if so, what are the results of the tests?" Objection: Calls for nondiscoverable expert opinion.

88. P has served and filed a set of interrogatories on D and D's wife. Which, if any, of the following are valid grounds for objection under the Federal Rules?

    (A) The interrogatories were served concurrently with the summons and complaint, and without court order authorizing such service.

    (B) D's wife is not a party to the action.

    (C) This is the third set of interrogatories served on D, and many of the questions were answered in earlier interrogatories.

    (D) The set of interrogatories includes 40 questions.

Civil Procedure—339

89. P sues D for copyright infringement of P's musical composition. P sends D a request to admit that a designated portion of a song published by D is in fact identical to a designated portion of P's song. D makes no response to this request. Which, if any, of the following statements is true?

   (A) Upon motion, the court may adjudge D in contempt and order D's answer stricken.

   (B) D's failure to respond constitutes a binding admission that the designated portions are identical.

   (C) No admission or denial was required because whether the designated portions are "identical" is the ultimate fact in issue for the trier of fact to determine.

90. P brings an action against D for personal injury. D's lawyer goes to P's place of employment, without notice to P and without permission of the employer, and interrogates P's employer and co-workers about the extent of his physical impairment. Which, if any, of the following statements are true?

   (A) The employer and co-workers may lawfully refuse to talk to D's lawyer.

   (B) On motion, the court will order D to desist from this practice because the proper way to get the information is by deposition.

   (C) On motion, the court will exclude any information secured because it was the product of an unlawful trespass.

   (D) P is at least entitled to a copy of all statements signed by the informants.

SUMMARY JUDGMENT

91. P files an action against D for personal injuries arising out of a traffic accident. D files a motion for summary judgment on the ground that he was not negligent. D's motion is supported by affidavits signed by all the other eyewitnesses, and by the police officer who investigated the accident. The only opposing affidavit is that of P, who simply controverts everything the eyewitnesses and police officer say. Does the court have the power to grant D's motion?

92. P files an action to rescind a deed for fraudulent misstatements made by D. D files a motion for summary judgment supported by his own affidavit to the effect that he believed the statements were true at the time he made them. No opposing affidavit is filed by P. Should the court grant D's motion?

93. P sues D to quiet title to property. P files a motion for summary judgment, based on an affidavit by his attorney that he has examined all pertinent land records and these records show that the chain of title is in P. D files no opposing affidavit. Should the court grant P's motion?

94. P sues D for copyright infringement of his musical composition. D's answer contains general denials of the complaint. In deposition testimony, however, D admits that a significant portion of his song is identical to P's.

a. Can the court grant P's motion for a summary judgment as to the issue of infringement only? _____

b. If D files an affidavit denying the similarity, could the court grant P's motion based on its own comparison of the songs? _____

MANAGERIAL JUDGING

95. P brings an action against D in a federal court.

   a. Thirty days after the complaint was served, the court directed the parties to appear for a pretrial conference at which it would set deadlines for completion of discovery and the filing of all motions. Does the court have authority to require the parties to attend such a conference and to impose such restrictions? _____

   b. At a later pretrial conference, the court determines that there is a possibility of settlement and orders both P and D to appear in person for a settlement conference. Are P and D required to attend if they are represented by counsel? _____

   c. At the final pretrial conference, the court directs P and D to submit their cases to a summary jury trial. P objects that such a proceeding would require revelation of trial strategy and that the parties are too far apart in their settlement negotiations to make it worthwhile. Is P required to attend and participate in the summary jury trial if the judge insists? _____

   d. After the final pretrial conference the court enters an order listing the issues in the case and witnesses for each party. At trial P calls a witness not listed in the final pretrial order. D objects. Should the court allow P's added witness to testify? _____

TRIAL

96. In which, if any, of the following cases is there a right to a jury trial in federal courts? _____

   (A) P sues D for damages for trespass to land.

   (B) P sues D to enjoin future trespasses upon her land.

   (C) P sues D to enjoin future trespasses and for damages for past trespasses.

   (D) D sues P for declaratory relief that his past entries were privileged and not actionable trespasses.

97. P files a federal suit to rescind a contract on the basis of fraudulent misrepresentations by D. D counterclaims for damages based on P's nonperformance of the same contract. P's reply alleges that D's fraud excused his performance under the contract. D demands a jury trial on the counterclaim and moves for an order that the counterclaim be tried first. Should the court grant the motion? _____

98. P sues D for medical malpractice in federal court. At the close of P's case, D moves for a judgment as a matter of law. The trial judge recognizes that P has

made out a prima facie case technically, but believes that P's witnesses are not worthy of belief and hence that the jurors should not hold D liable. Should the court grant D's motion for a judgment as a matter of law?

99. P sues D for medical malpractice in federal court. At the close of P's case, D's counsel recognizes that P's witnesses are not likely to be believed; and she rests her case without presenting evidence. P moves for a judgment as a matter of law. Should the court grant the motion?

100. The trial of P's medical malpractice lawsuit resulted in a verdict for D. Which, if any, of the following would be a valid ground for appeal?

   (A) The trial judge on her own motion called a medical witness to testify as to the standard of care in the community, which testimony hurt P's case.

   (B) At the close of the trial, the judge told the jury that while they were the triers of fact, she personally did not believe P's testimony as to damages.

   (C) In instructing the jury, the judge stated: "In determining whether D is liable, you should use your own common sense, as well as the standard of care in the community." P made no objection to this instruction in the trial court.

101. P sues D for personal injuries arising out of an auto accident. D's answer raises several affirmative defenses: contributory negligence; assumption of the risk; and P's execution of a release. The case goes to trial and there is evidence to support each of D's defenses. The judge's instructions to the jury are correct, except that he defines contributory negligence in a manner which is overly favorable to D. The jury returns a general verdict for D. P appeals on the ground that the contributory negligence instruction was incorrect, even though the instructions on the other defenses admittedly were correct. Should the appellate court reverse?

102. A jury returns a general verdict in favor of P but also answers special interrogatories which are inconsistent with a verdict for P and consistent with a verdict for D. The court thereupon enters judgment in favor of D. P appeals. Should the appellate court reverse?

103. P sues Dr. D for medical malpractice. The jury returns a verdict for D. P files a motion for new trial, claiming jury misconduct. Which of the following evidence is admissible in support of P's motion?

   (A) An affidavit by Juror 1 that Juror 2 admitted during the course of deliberations that he was a former patient of Dr. D. Juror 2 had denied knowing D during voir dire questioning.

   (B) An affidavit by Juror 3 that Juror 4 had been belligerent throughout the deliberations and had badgered and bullied him into voting for D.

   (C) An affidavit by the bailiff that he overheard the jurors say that in order to reach a unanimous verdict they would all vote for whomever the majority of them wanted.

104. P sued D for medical malpractice in a federal court action, and the jury returned a unanimous verdict for P for $100,000. D moves for a new trial. Which of the following evidence, if any, is sufficient to support the granting of D's motion?

(A) An affidavit by D's attorney that during the course of the trial, he discovered that several of the jurors had lunched and visited with P's wife, although he did not mention it to the court at the time.

(B) An affidavit by D that after the verdict had been returned, he overheard P admit that he had been faking his injuries all along.

(C) An affidavit by noted physician, W, that he had been prepared to testify as a witness for D, but had been called out of town just before the trial.

105. P sued D for medical malpractice in federal court. Although the witnesses for P gave testimony which the judge found unlikely, the judge denied D's motion for judgment as a matter of law and the jury rendered a verdict for P. D renews the motion for judgment as a matter of law and moves, in the alternative, for a new trial. What ruling should the court make?

106. The jury returned a $10,000 verdict for P in a medical malpractice case in federal court. This amount was considerably less than the special damages proved by P. P moved for a new trial on the ground of inadequate damages. Can the court grant the new trial on condition that if D consents to increase the verdict to $50,000, a new trial will be denied?

107. P filed a federal suit against D for personal injuries sustained in a traffic accident. D was ill and upset at the time and forgot to turn the pleadings over to his attorney. P obtained a default judgment against D for $60,000, but did nothing to enforce the judgment for over a year. It was only when P executed on the judgment that D remembered the matter; and he then moved promptly to set aside the judgment on the ground that he had a valid defense to P's action, and that he failed to answer only through inadvertence and excusable neglect. Should the trial court grant the motion?

108. P sues D in federal court claiming diversity of citizenship. D lacks the funds to employ an attorney, and files no answer. P obtains a default judgment against D for $55,000. Several years later, D decides he wants to attack the judgment on the ground that he and P were at all times citizens of the same state, and hence the federal court lacked jurisdiction. However, all time limits for appeal or relief in the trial court have now expired. Is there any remedy available to D?

APPEAL

109. If a party inadvertently fails to file a notice of appeal within the required time limit, can he obtain an extension of time to file from the appellate court?

110. P obtains a jury verdict for $1,000 in a medical malpractice case, in which he had proved special damages of over $5,000. If he accepts payment of the $1,000 from D, can he appeal the judgment on ground of inadequacy of damages (giving D credit for the $1,000)?

111. P sues D for personal injuries. D makes a motion to compel P to submit to a physical examination, but the trial court erroneously denies the motion. In view of the importance of the exam, can D immediately appeal the trial court's order?

112. After trial to the court, the court made findings of fact and conclusions of law, and entered judgment in favor of D. P appeals, arguing that the evidence supported findings favorable to himself. Which of the following is the appropriate standard of review? _____

    (A) The appellate court may reverse only if it finds that there is no substantial evidence to support the judgment below.

    (B) The appellate court may reverse if it finds that the findings below were clearly erroneous.

    (C) The appellate court may reverse if it determines that the findings were against the weight of the evidence.

113. P sues D for copyright infringement. At the outset of the action, the federal court grants a preliminary injunction against any further publication by D of the material that allegedly infringes P's copyright, pending trial of the case. Can D appeal the order granting this injunction? _____

114. P sues D to quiet title to certain real property. At a trial to the court, P introduces both hearsay and nonhearsay evidence to support his claim. D objects to the hearsay, but her objection is overruled. The court grants judgment for P. D appeals on the ground that the judgment rests as much on inadmissible hearsay as it does on nonhearsay. Should the appellate court reverse? _____

PRECLUSIVE EFFECTS OF JUDGMENTS

115. P unreasonably delays prosecution of his lawsuit against D, resulting in the court's dismissing his action. If the statute of limitations has not run, can P start a new action against D on the same claim and obtain a judgment? _____

116. A sued B for damages for breach of contract, and obtained a judgment. Thereafter, B sued A for damages, alleging that A had fraudulently induced him to enter into the contract sued upon in the first case. A moves for summary judgment on grounds of res judicata. Should the court grant the motion? _____

117. W sued H for installments due under their divorce property settlement agreement. H defended on the ground that W was in breach of the agreement. However, the court granted judgment for W. Later, W sues H for other installments coming due under the agreement. H now raises the defense that the agreement was void and illegal because of fraud perpetrated by W at the time it was signed. W moves to strike H's defense, claiming issue preclusion. Should the court grant the motion? _____

118. A sued B for $500 damage to his car sustained in a traffic accident. B defended on the ground that he was not negligent and that even if he were, A was contributorily negligent. The jury returned a general verdict for A. Meanwhile, B had filed a $50,000 suit against A in a superior court for personal injuries sustained in the same accident. When the judgment in the A-B action became final, A moved for summary judgment against B's suit on the ground of issue preclusion. Should the court grant the motion? _____

119. A bus owned and operated by Buslines, Inc., and driven by Driver was involved in a traffic accident. Several passengers were injured, including P and X.

a. P sued Driver for negligence, and the jury returned a verdict for Driver. P thereupon filed suit against Buslines, alleging that it was vicariously liable for Driver's negligence (respondeat superior) and was also negligent in hiring Driver. Buslines moves for summary judgment against P's suit. Should the court grant the motion? _____

b. Assume P sued Buslines first on the respondeat superior theory and lost. P then files suit against Driver for negligence. Driver claims P is precluded by the first suit. Should the court sustain the defense? _____

c. Assume P sued Driver and won a judgment. P now files suit against Buslines on a respondeat superior theory, and moves for a ruling that Buslines's liability was established by the judgment against Driver. Should the court grant the motion? _____

d. Assume P sued Buslines on a respondeat superior theory and won. Now another passenger on the same bus, X, brings suit against Buslines on the same theory and moves to establish liability on the basis of P's judgment against Buslines. Should the court grant X's motion? _____

ANSWERS TO REVIEW QUESTIONS

1. **PROBABLY NOT** — Tradition holds that personal service within the state is always adequate to sustain personal jurisdiction and the Supreme Court has recently upheld "transient jurisdiction" over a nonresident temporarily within a state (although there was no majority opinion and some Justices expressed doubt if the presence were not intentional or voluntary). [§§7, 92]

2. **PROBABLY** — The action of D's patient in driving to State A probably establishes no meaningful contact between D and State A. *See World-Wide Volkswagen v. Woodson,* in which plaintiffs drove a car purchased from one defendant in New York to Oklahoma, where they had an accident; the Supreme Court found there was no constitutional basis for jurisdiction in Oklahoma. [§29]

3. **NO** — Distribution of the drug in State A establishes a minimum contact between D and the forum state; and as long as the state has authorized such service through long arm legislation, there is no constitutional objection to the exercise of jurisdiction. [§31]

4. **PROBABLY NOT** — An agreement appointing an agent is a valid means of forum selection by contract unless perhaps the contract was an overreaching by a powerful party. [§76]

5. **NO** — Lack of jurisdiction over the person is a defense which is waived if not raised at the first opportunity. D appeared and defended at trial, and thereby waived the objection. [§§83, 87]

6. **PROBABLY YES** — If D was induced to enter the state by fraud, the service of process is invalid. [§93]

7. **NO** — Defendant does not reside there, and it is not where a substantial part of the events or omissions giving rise to the claim occurred. [§122]

8. **YES, NO** — When an action is brought in a federal district court where venue is improper, under 28 U.S.C. section 1406(a), the court may either dismiss it or transfer it to a district where the action could have been brought. [§163] Transfers for the convenience of parties or witnesses can be made only to a district in which venue *would be proper originally* (and here, venue was never proper in New York). [§168]

9. **YES** — Unlike motions for change of venue, motions for convenience transfers can be made by *either* party. [§169]

10. **YES** — In diversity suits, venue is proper *either* in the district where any defendant resides, if all defendants reside in the same state, *or* in a district where a substantial part of the acts or omissions giving rise to the claim occurred. [§122]

11. **PROBABLY NONE** — There is no state in which *all* defendants reside, nor any judicial district in which a substantial part of the acts or omissions giving rise to the claim occurred. There might, however, be venue in a district where either ship involved in the collision has its home port, or perhaps where it is located, or (lacking any other basis for venue) in a district where both defendants were subject to personal jurisdiction when the action was commenced. [§§122-139]

12.	**PROBABLY NOT**	If defendant will not waive service, does not live with anyone who can be served, and cannot be found, and if state or federal law authorizes assertion of jurisdiction by seizure of property, service by seizure is permissible. The Constitution requires reasonable efforts at providing actual notice of the action and of the opportunity to be heard, which requirements could be satisfied if D used the cottage with some frequency. [§201]
13.	**POSSIBLY**	Service may be made by any method authorized by state law where the court is located or process is served. In some states, service by mail on nonresidents is allowed. Moreover, under Federal Rule 4, plaintiff may request waiver of service by mailing the request and complaint to the defendant, and defendant has a duty to waive to avoid costs. Thus, under either approach service might be proper or waived (although if defendant refuses to waive service and state law does not allow service by mail, plaintiff must serve defendant in person or by leaving a summons and complaint with a "person of suitable age and discretion" residing at the defendant's home). [§§97, 214-225]
14.	**PROBABLY**	D was constitutionally entitled to notice and hearing before the attachment of his property. This rule generally applies even when the attachment is for the purpose of establishing jurisdiction. Once the garnishment is quashed, there is no jurisdictional basis for the proceeding, although the lack of jurisdiction could be cured by service of process. [§§245-248]
15.a.	**NO**	Diversity jurisdiction is determined by the residence of the *members* of the partnership. [§294]
b.	**YES**	A corporation is a citizen of any state where it is incorporated, *and* of the state where it has its principal place of business, but not of every state in which it operates. [§§290-291]
16.	**(B) and (C)**	Diversity can be based on *alienage*—i.e., all citizens on one side and all aliens on the other (A). [§282] (B) is correct because a U.S. citizen living abroad permanently *cannot sue or be sued* on the basis of diversity of citizenship (no U.S. domicile). [§288] On causes of action belonging to an incompetent person, diversity depends on the residence of the incompetent person. [§304]
17.	**(B) and (E)**	As long as diversity exists *at the time suit is filed,* the federal court has diversity jurisdiction. Thus, it makes no difference that P moved into the state for the purpose of creating such jurisdiction as long as P genuinely changed citizenship (A) [§306] or that once the suit was filed, diversity terminated (C) [§307]. The fact that neither party resides in the state where the court is located (D) may be relevant as to *venue* [§§122-139], but has no effect on diversity jurisdiction. [§286] Where claims are *assigned* (E), the residence of the *assignor* determines diversity. [§313]
18.	**PERHAPS**	There is diversity, but it is not complete. The jurisdictional defect might be cured by dismissal of one of the diversity-destroying parties, if he is not necessary to disposition. But if all are "indispensable," dismissal must result. [§§321-322]
19.	**YES**	The jurisdictional amount is lacking, and lack of subject matter jurisdiction can be raised at any time. [§§257, 324]

20.	**YES**	As long as the claim was filed in good faith, jurisdiction is not affected by the fact that the judgment ultimately recovered does not exceed $50,000. (But in such a case the court has discretion to deny costs to the plaintiff.) [§§326, 328, 330]
21.	**YES**	Claims by a single plaintiff against a single defendant *can* be aggregated. [§335]
22.	**NO**	Claims against several defendants can be aggregated only where it is shown that they are *jointly* liable on each claim. [§336]
23.	**NO**	Claims by multiple plaintiffs against a single defendant can be aggregated only when plaintiffs assert a *joint* right to relief. [§337]
24.	**YES**	Although there is diversity of citizenship, under a decisional exception to diversity jurisdiction, the federal courts lack jurisdiction over divorce, other domestic relations, and probate cases. [§341]
25.	**YES**	The involvement of federal law is merely incidental to the claim, which is essentially one of simple contract arising under the common law of the state. [§361]
26.	**YES**	To the extent that the federal issue is raised by the complaint, it is not "well pleaded," but anticipates a defense. Only the defense, not the claim, arises under federal law. [§§364-366]
27.a.	**NO**	Antitrust claims under the Sherman Act are within the *exclusive* jurisdiction of federal courts. [§269]
b.	**YES**	Under supplemental jurisdiction. [§§400-408]
28.	**YES**	Where the right exists, it belongs to all defendants *jointly*, except in cases in which one defendant can remove on the ground that it is the subject of a "separate and independent claim." [§450]
29.a.	**NO**	A plaintiff is *never* entitled to removal. Having filed in the state court, he must remain there. [§449]
b.	**NO**	Removal is not allowed in diversity actions in which any properly joined and served defendant is a resident of the state in which the action is filed. [§436]
30.	**YES**	On removal, the federal court has jurisdiction even if the state court lacked subject matter jurisdiction; the federal court's jurisdiction is no longer viewed as "derivative." Brown could, however, move to dismiss in state court for lack of jurisdiction rather than removing. [§453]
31.	**NO**	Unless there is statutory provision for exclusive federal jurisdiction, state courts exercise concurrent jurisdiction over claims that are within the federal jurisdiction and must accept such cases. [§§266-267]
32.	**YES**	The Supreme Court has held that, although Federal Rule 3 says that an action is commenced by the filing of a complaint, it was not intended to provide thereby for "tolling" of the limitations period in a state law action. Because the duration

of limitations is a matter of state law, the definition of the events that toll it is also governed by state law, which can coexist with Rule 3, because there is no conflict between the rule and the state law provisions. [§507]

33. **YES** There appears to be a clear conflict between the state and federal provisions. The Federal Rules of Evidence were passed by Congress, so they are valid if "arguably procedural." Determinations about the admissibility of hearsay evidence seem to be arguably procedural, so that under *Hanna* the federal rule should be applied. [§511] (Note, however, that with regard to issues of privilege, Federal Rule of Evidence 501 in fact directs that state law should be applied in federal court with regard to issues governed by state law.)

34. **NO** Federal Rule 15(c)(1) allows relation back when it is permitted by the law providing the applicable statute of limitations.

35. **PROBABLY** The federal rule is a judge-made rule, and the cases are divided on whether state or federal law governs the standard for directed verdict motions. Arguments can be made both ways. The regulation of the relations between the judge and jury seems a particularly appropriate subject for determination by federal law in federal court. On the other hand, the state's desire that these state law claims be submitted to the jury may be entitled to some weight, although it is difficult to say that it is bound up with the rights and obligations created by state law. [§516]

36. **UNCLEAR** The task for the federal court is to determine how the state supreme court would resolve the issue, not to select the "better" legal rule. But the court is not blind to trends in the law, and if there is reason to believe that the state supreme court would not adhere to the older rule the federal court should not do so. On the other hand, state appellate decisions are, in general, good indications of the content of state law, and the court should have some reason grounded in more recent, analogous state court decisions for disregarding the earlier decision squarely on point. [§§524-528]

37. **NO** The court looks to the *facts* alleged, not the caption of the complaint or even the pleader's apparent legal theory. The complaint sufficiently pleads negligence (failure to give warning of known danger), and hence sufficiently states a claim on which relief can be granted. [§544]

38.a. **PROBABLY** The allegations are sufficient if they give D *notice* of the *general nature* of the claim against him. At least after the pleading stage the federal courts do, however, demand sufficient factual matter to satisfy all elements of the claim. [§555]

b. **NO** The allegations are not of "ultimate facts"—*i.e.*, the word "improperly" does *not* present a legal issue (negligence, warranty, strict liability). [§§550-552]

39. **NO** Allegations on information or belief are proper only where the pleader lacks personal knowledge. Where, as here, he has **constructive knowledge** (*i.e.*, matters of public record), the allegation is insufficient. [§§569-572]

40. **NO** In federal courts, pleaders are entitled to state their claims or defenses "regardless of consistency." (*Compare:* The result is contra in many code pleading states, particularly when the complaint is verified.) Plaintiff might, however,

face sanctions under Federal Rule 11 if the factual allegations were made without "evidentiary support." [§§573-576, 590-594, 709-743]

41. **YES** — In a default case, the relief granted cannot exceed or differ in kind from that prayed for in the complaint. [§581]

42. **YES** — Usually, of course, P need not anticipate defenses. But when he has done so (settlement as release of claim), he must also *plead around* the defense. Allegations that the settlement was a "fraud" are not enough, because fraud must always be *pleaded with particularity*, even under the Federal Rules. [§§608, 610] Dismissal on such facts might well be with leave to amend.

43. **YES** — In most code pleading states, the defamatory words must be set forth verbatim. (The rule is contra under notice pleading.) [§613]

44. **(A), (B) and (C)** — The complaint alleges "general damages," which is sufficient to cover pain, discomfort, and disability. However, medical expenses (past or future) are *special damages* and must be specially pleaded. A fortiori, punitive damages must be specially pleaded. [§§627, 629-630]

45.a. **YES** — There is no requirement of subject matter relationship among the claims joined against a *single* defendant. (State rules are contra.) [§640]

b. **YES** — Where there are multiple parties, one claim by or against them must arise out of the same transaction and involve a common question of law or fact. [§641]

46. **PROBABLY** — Some courts deny a motion to strike where *no responsive pleading* is due. But the better view is to strike immaterial allegations to prevent such matters from being read to the jury at trial. [§§689-690]

47. **YES** — D is never compelled to file a motion to dismiss. Raising the venue objection in his answer sufficiently preserves it. [§§695-696]

48. **YES** — When the defendant *does* make a motion to dismiss, he must raise certain defenses and objections which he could raise by the motion, including venue, or he waives them. [§§695-697]

49. **NO** — Failure to state a claim can be raised at any time. [§§695, 697]

50. **YES** — A court may grant a motion to dismiss premised on a defense that appears on the face of the complaint. [§700]

51. **YES** — The rule in code pleading states is that defendant must file *specific* denials to a verified complaint, because there is usually something which ought to be admitted. (*Note:* The federal rule is contra.) [§§752-755]

52. **YES** — A failure to deny constitutes an admission. [§767]

53. **NO** — In *federal* actions, allegations of damages are deemed controverted even if not denied. *Compare:* The rule in *state* courts in code pleading states is usually contra—*i.e.*, where a sum of money is alleged to be due, it must be *specifically* denied. [§768]

54. **(B) and (D)** Truth (A) is an affirmative defense and must be specially pleaded as new matter. Likewise, as to any release or settlement (C). However, proof that no one heard (B) is admissible under the general denial, as it contradicts the element of publication, which is a part of P's case. Likewise, evidence as to the extent of damages (D) contradicts P's case and is admissible under the general denial. [§§770-774]

55. **NO** In federal actions, objections to venue are waived if not raised in the initial answer. Subsequent amendments to add such objections are *not* allowed. [§§160, 696]

56. **NONE** Allegations of D's answers are ***deemed controverted.*** No responsive pleading by P is required to preserve the issues raised thereby. [§797]

57. **ONLY (C)** (A) is wrong because the counterclaim ***should be*** a part of D's answer. [§799] (B) is wrong because no subject matter relationship is required. [§799] (C) is right because when a counterclaim is only ***permissive*** (not arising out of same transaction as complaint), there must be an independent ground for federal jurisdiction (here the parties are diverse, but the claim is for only $5,000). [§801] (D) is wrong because the court can join other parties when necessary. [§§807-808]

58. **NO** P's filing of a complaint ***tolls*** the statute of limitations for counterclaims arising out of the same transaction. For limitations purposes, D's counterclaim "relates back" to the time P filed his complaint and hence is timely. (A minority view allows ***any*** counterclaim to be used defensively, even after the statute has run.) [§§816-818]

59. **(B) and (C)** (A) is wrong because no affirmative relief is sought; D's "claim" is merely a defense. (D) is wrong because there must be a subject matter relationship to P's complaint. (B) and (C) are proper because there is the requisite subject matter relationship; claims for indemnity or contribution are permissible. [§§821-823]

60. **NO** Cross-claims lie only against codefendants. Claims against an outside party must be asserted by ***impleader***. (Most courts permit impleader only when indemnification or contribution is sought; and under this view, D2 would be permitted to implead D3 only if there were a claim for indemnification, but might then be permitted also to seek affirmative relief—*i.e.*, damages to his car.) [§991]

61.a. **YES** Amendments relating to the same transaction "relate back" for limitations purposes. A change in the nature or theory of the action does not prejudice D. [§§851-852]

b. **PROBABLY NOT** Amendments to bring in ***new parties*** after the statute of limitations has run are permitted only in limited circumstances. This amendment involves adding a party, not changing a party or the naming of a party against whom a claim is asserted, and would probably be allowed only under a liberal state policy on relation back. [§§853-854]

62.a. **PROBABLY** Here, the defendant appears to have had notice of the pendency of the action, and probably knew or should have known of the naming mistake. [§853]

b.	**DISCRE-TIONARY**	Even though such an amendment would be freely allowed *before* trial, courts are more reluctant to permit such amendments at the time of trial. In state practice, they may find a "material variance" where the relief sought by the amendment differs significantly. Federal practice is more liberal, putting the burden on the objecting party to show *prejudice* (although a continuance to enable D to prepare would usually remedy such claims). [§§860-872]
c.	**YES**	P should be permitted to file a *supplemental complaint* to allege occurrence of developments *subsequent* to the date of her original complaint, where no alteration of the basic claim is involved. [§§874-878]
63.	**PROBABLY NOT**	The federal court has *discretion* to refuse; but such a refusal here is likely to be an abuse of discretion, at least if P could not have known sooner about the witness's unwillingness. [§902]
64.	**ALL EXCEPT (B)**	The person having the *right to sue* (*i.e.*, legal title to the claim) is the "real party in interest." (B) is wrong because usually only the trustee has the right to sue third persons for wrongs to the trust estate. [§§907, 922]
65.	**PROBABLY NOT**	Unless serious injustice would result, D may be estopped to raise the issue by direct or collateral attack. [§§931-932]
66.	**NO**	In a diversity action, capacity of such a party is determined by the law of the state in which the federal court is located. [§940]
67.	**NO**	Samantha *is* the real party in interest. The correct challenge would be that she lacks capacity (as a minor). However, this challenge is *waived* if not timely made. [§§907, 934-935, 947-948]
68.a.	**YES**	Under modern rules, joinder of claims against multiple parties is proper as long as the claims arise out of the same transaction, occurrence, or series of transactions or occurrences; there is a common question of fact or law; and the defendants may be jointly or severally liable (or liable "in the alternative"). [§§952-956]
b.	**YES**	Basically, as long as the rules on joinder of *parties* are satisfied (above), so are the rules on joinder of claims. [§957]
c.	**YES**	By alleging the facts showing *why* he is "in doubt," P is entitled to join defendants and claims *in the alternative.* [§954]
69.	**NO**	But the actions should be severed because there is no connection between the transactions. If the questions of law or fact are sufficiently common to the two cases, they might be reconsolidated for the purpose of trial. [§§952, 1035]
70.	**PROBABLY NOT**	If D2 can be joined, she should be, in order to give effective protection to D1's right to contribution. However, the court can and should proceed to enforce P's right if the joinder of D2 is not feasible or if it would destroy the jurisdiction of the court. If the obstacle to joinder is incomplete diversity, some federal courts might dismiss so that P could sue both D1 and D2 in state court. [§§966-969]

71.	**YES**	In federal court, and in most states, partial assignees or subrogees are necessary but not indispensable parties who should be joined if feasible to prevent a multiplicity of actions or inconsistent results, and the court can compel joinder of A as an involuntary plaintiff. [§973]
72.	**YES**	The corporation must be joined as a plaintiff, but its joinder destroys the basis for federal jurisdiction; and the action must therefore be dismissed for want of federal jurisdiction. [§§979, 982, 986]
73.a.	**YES**	D should file a third-party complaint against TP showing why TP should be held liable on a theory of *indemnification* for whatever liability D has to P. [§§990-991]
b.	**YES**	Because the impleader claim is deemed ancillary to the P-D lawsuit. Thus TP's residence has *no* effect on jurisdiction and venue. [§1006]
74.a.	**PROBABLY NOT**	There is clearly no *right* to intervene. Permissive intervention can be granted where there is a "common question of law or fact," but here, there is only an inference that T's illness was caused by the same condition that caused P's. [§§1009, 1024]
b.	**PROBABLY NOT**	In this situation, intervention is unnecessary because a finding that Duchess is liable to P for selling a sandwich containing impure ingredients would not be binding on XYZ or affect its ability to defend against Duchess's claim for indemnification in a separate action, if Duchess fails to implead XYZ in the suit brought by P. [§§1009, 1014]
75.a.	**YES**	The Federal Interpleader Act permits a stakeholder to deposit a disputed debt with the court if the amount is at least $500, and diversity exists between the adverse *claimants*. [§1044]
b.	**YES**	Nationwide service is authorized in statutory interpleader. [§1052]
76.	**YES**	A class action is appropriate, since the issues and relief are identical for all members of the class. The number of students involved (and possibly the small amount of their individual claims) also makes a class suit the most practical way of resolving the issue, because nothing would be gained by requiring each member to litigate the same issue separately; *i.e.*, common questions *predominate*. [§§1089-1092]
77.	**(B)**	In federal class actions, *each* claim must exceed the $50,000 minimum. (A) is wrong because diversity is determined only from residence of the *representative* (P). (C) is wrong because the common sales practices, if proved, could be the requisite "common question." [§§1070-1074, 1100-1101]
78.	**NO**	It is reversible error for the court to premise its certification decision on an inquiry into the merits. [§1111]
79.a.	**YES**	*See* Fed. R. Civ. P. 23(c)(2). [§1122]
b.	**YES**	This is the impact of the *Eisen* case. [§1129]
c.	**NO**	Those who choose to opt out are not bound. [§1158]

80.	**NO**	Because (i) there is no showing that adequate *notice* of the pending settlement was given to the class members, and (ii) the special recovery obtained by P indicates that she did *not* adequately represent their interests. In federal courts, the court would have to decide whether to approve any settlement of the class suit. [§§1148-1152]
81.	**NO**	The Rule 26(a)(1) obligation of disclosure without a discovery request, if applicable, can be satisfied *either* by providing a copy of the document *or* by a "description by category and location" of the document. Also, the obligation applies only to documents *relevant to disputed facts alleged with particularity in the pleadings.* Be aware that Rule 26(a)(1) permits districts to opt out of applicability of the rule, or to adopt their own practices by local rule or orders in particular cases. [§§1187, 1191]
82.	**NO**	In federal practice, P may serve notice on a corporate party stating the *matters* upon which the deposition will be based. It is then up to the corporation to produce employees having knowledge as to such matters. [§1215]
83.a.	**DEPENDS**	If E is *unavailable* to testify, his deposition is admissible; otherwise it is not. [§1239]
b.	**YES**	The deposition of the adverse party or the officer of an adverse corporate party is admissible as substantive evidence. [§1237]
84.a.	**NONE**	Depositions to perpetuate testimony are proper before filing suit only when P can show that she is *unable* to sue now. Such depositions cannot (in federal practice) be used simply to determine the merits of P's claim. Rule 11 does not pose an obstacle to P's ability to bring suit now if she can assert that allegations against D are likely to have evidentiary support after an opportunity for discovery. [§1203]
b.	**SUBPOENA FOR PRODUCTION OR DEPOSITION**	A *nonparty* cannot be required to produce documents by a *request* to produce under Rule 34, but he can be *subpoenaed* under Rule 45 to produce them or to attend a deposition and to bring with him evidence in his control. [§1291]
c.	**SUBPOENA FOR INSPECTION**	A nonparty may be subpoenaed to permit inspection of premises in her control. [§1291]
d.	**NO**	A motion to compel a physical examination applies only to *parties*. [§1296]
85.	**NONE**	(A) is wrong because a party is deemed in control of that which is in his attorney's possession. [§1288] (B) is wrong because the work-product privilege does not apply to evidence unearthed by the attorney. [§1276] (C) is wrong because a request to produce requires neither a court order nor a showing of good cause. [§1279]
86.	**YES**	By so requesting, the examined party becomes bound to provide copies of his own medical reports on the condition at issue. [§§1300-1301]
87.a.	**MOTION GRANTED**	Discovery is proper as to information which may *lead* to admissible evidence; the information itself need not be admissible. [§1309]

b.	**MOTION GRANTED**	A party's factual contentions are usually discoverable in order to flush into the open all claims or defenses. [§1328]
c.	**MOTION DENIED**	The test of relevancy is whether the information relates to the "subject matter of the action." Unless P can somehow show that an earlier lawsuit relates to *his* claim of food poisoning, the discovery appears to be improper. [§1320]
d.	**MOTION DENIED**	Even though many courts permit discovery of insurance coverage (and the federal courts often require disclosure without a discovery request of insurance agreements), most do *not* permit discovery of a defendant's financial status except in connection with claims for punitive damages. [§§1323-1327]
e.	**MOTION DENIED**	The testing would probably be treated as opinions obtained from experts retained to advise counsel. Unless they are going to testify, discovery may be allowed only in extraordinary circumstances. No such circumstances have been stated, although it might be possible to justify discovery if the allegedly tainted food no longer exists, so that P cannot test it now. [§§1391-1396]
88.	**ALL EXCEPT (C)**	(A) is right because parties generally may not initiate discovery in federal court without meeting to discuss, among other matters, a discovery plan. [§1246] (B) is right; interrogatories can be served only on parties (though these need not be adverse parties). [§1243] (C) is not a ground for objection, although it may be grounds for a protective order. [§1448] (D) is right because interrogatories, including discrete subparts, may not exceed 25 in number without leave of court. [§1248]
89.	**(B)**	(A) is wrong because no such sanction may be imposed when there has been no prior court order to answer. [§1475] (B) is correct. [§1274] (C) is wrong because in federal practice (*e.g.*, copyright case), requests can be directed even as to the ultimate issues in the case. [§1260]
90.	**ONLY (A)**	A nonparty is not required to answer questions unless subpoenaed. [§1214] But D has the right to conduct an investigation [§1497], and the exclusionary rule has no application to this situation [§1499]. The statements are clearly work product and there is no apparent reason for requiring them to be disclosed. [§§1364, 1381] *Note:* In federal practice, the witnesses themselves have a right to a copy of their own statements. [§1388]
91.	**NO**	A motion for summary judgment must be *denied* if the essential facts are controverted by a witness competent to testify. If P claims to have seen the accident, that should suffice. Credibility cannot be determined at this stage. [§§1519, 1521]
92.	**PROBABLY NOT**	Assuming P has the burden of proving D's knowing deceit at trial (at least a debatable issue if there is no question that the statements were in fact false), it is likely that the court would find the surrounding circumstances sufficient to support the inference that D knew of their falsity, despite D's protestations of innocence. [§1522] Nevertheless, P cannot rely entirely on the jury's disbelief of D's testimony to satisfy P's burden of producing evidence of D's knowledge. [§1525]
93.	**NO**	The affidavit in support of the motion must be based on facts within the *personal knowledge* of the affiant, not hearsay or opinions. [§1551]

94.a.	**YES**	*Partial* summary judgment can be granted as to certain claims or issues, reserving the balance for trial. [§1559]
b.	**YES**	A summary judgment can be based on any admissible evidence, including comparison of the songs. [§§1552-1554]
95.a.	**YES**	The court not only has the power to set such deadlines, but under Rule 16, it is required to set such deadlines early in the action. [§1574]
b.	**YES**	If the court so orders, under its authority to require that a party or its representative be present or reasonably available by telephone to discuss settlement. [§1585]
c.	**PROBABLY**	Rule 16 authorizes trial judges to use "special procedures to assist in resolving the dispute when authorized by statute or local rule." [§1644]
d.	**PROBABLY NOT**	The final pretrial order should be amended only to avoid "manifest injustice." Unless there is some justification for P's failure to list this witness in the final pretrial order, the court would be justified in excluding the witness unless she is essential to P's case. Because the matter is discretionary, however, the court would have the power to allow the witness to testify. [§§1605-1606]
96.	**ALL EXCEPT (B)**	The right to jury trial extends to all actions "at law." Historically, (A) was "at law," while (B) was in equity. Where legal and equitable claims are joined (C), the *federal* rule is that the jury right must be preserved as to the legal claims (damages). There is a jury right in (D) because the court looks to the basic substance of the relief sought—here, to prevent tort liability (damages) for past acts. [§§1645-1661]
97.	**YES**	In federal practice, the claim for legal relief (damages) *must* be tried first, to preserve the right of jury trial on the fraud issue free of binding prior adjudication on the equitable claim. [§§1662, 1664]
98.	**NO**	As long as a prima facie case is made out, a motion for judgment as a matter of law *must* be denied. [§§1737-1762]
99.	**PROBABLY NOT**	To prevail on a motion for judgment as a matter of law, the party with the burden of proof must put on such a strong case that the jury could not reasonably disbelieve it. Ordinarily, the jury could disbelieve witnesses on the basis of their demeanor while testifying; given the fact that D's lawyer thinks the witnesses are not likely to be believed, this does not seem to be a case in which the jury would have to believe them. [§§1740, 1752]
100.	**NONE**	A trial judge may call and interrogate a witness on her own (A). [§1729] The judge may also comment on the evidence, including the credibility of a witness (B) in *most* states (minority contra). [§§1784-1785] Failure to object to a jury instruction (C) is usually considered a waiver of any objection thereto, unless the error is so fundamental that it deprives a party of a fair trial. The instruction here is somewhat confusing, but does not seem to be fundamental in the foregoing sense. [§1792]
101.	**PROBABLY**	Since the jury may have based its verdict solely on the one defense as to which the instructions were incorrect, most courts would reverse. [§§1792-1793]

102.	**NO**	When inconsistent with the verdict, the jury's answers to interrogatories may control over their general verdict. [§1805]
103.	**(A) and (C) (most courts)**	The modern rule is that concealed grounds for disqualification (A) may be proved by juror affidavit. [§§1823-1824] Few courts, however, would permit juror affidavits to attack the deliberations themselves (B). [§§1820-1821] On the other hand, affidavits by outsiders (C) are generally admissible to show improper deliberations and an agreement to be bound by majority rule when unanimity is required is clearly improper. [§§1809, 1820]
104.	**NONE**	(A) does not establish "juror misconduct" because it was known to D *during* the trial and he chose to do nothing about it (such as a motion for mistrial). [§1846] (B) might amount to fraud on the court, but usually trial verdicts may not be set aside on the basis of allegedly false testimony. [§§1844-1852] (C) does not establish "accident or surprise" because it fails to show that D had done all he could to procure W's attendance—*i.e.*, subpoenaing him. [§§1847-1852]
105.	**NEW TRIAL GRANTED**	Judgment as a matter of law cannot be granted because there is some evidence to support the verdict. [§1831] But the trial judge may order a new trial if she finds that the verdict is contrary to the weight of the evidence. [§1855]
106.	**NO**	In federal practice the trial court does *not* have the power of "additur." [§§1891-1892]
107.	**NO**	There is a *one-year limitation period* in federal practice for a motion for relief from judgment. [§1910]
108.	**YES**	D can bring a separate suit in equity to set aside the judgment. [§§1912-1913]
109.	**NO**	Time limits for filing appeals are usually jurisdictional. The Federal Rules permit the *trial* court to extend time for 30 days, but the appellate court cannot do so. [§§1946-1949]
110.	**NO**	P's voluntary acceptance of the benefits of a judgment *waives* his right to appeal therefrom. [§1925]
111.	**NO**	The final judgment rule bars any appeal of most interlocutory orders, and interlocutory review of discovery orders is especially rare. (However, appellate review by extraordinary writ may be available.) [§§1957-1970]
112.	**(B)**	Clear error is the correct test. [§§1992-1993]
113.	**YES**	Review of preliminary injunctions is one of the generally recognized "exceptions" to the final judgment rule. However, appellate review is generally limited to whether the trial court abused its *discretion* in granting the injunction. [§§1976, 2003-2004]
114.	**PROBABLY NOT**	In *nonjury* cases (quiet title) it is presumed that the trial judge considered only the legally admissible evidence in arriving at his decision. [§§2005-2006]

115.	**NO**	An involuntary dismissal is usually treated as a judgment on the merits, so as to bar any later action on the same claim. [§2056-2057]
116.	**YES**	B's fraud claim would have been a ***compulsory counterclaim*** in most jurisdictions, and since it was not raised in the first suit, it is ***barred.*** [§2070]
117.	**NO**	The first judgment is a bar with respect to the installments then in question. But it is preclusive only as to the issues ***"actually litigated."*** Since the fraud issue was not litigated, it can be raised with respect to the ***later*** installments. [§§2074-2075]
118.	**YES**	The general verdict in the A-B action necessarily found that B was negligent and A was not. The issue preclusion effect of those findings is fatal to B's claims against A in the second action. [§2082]
119.a.	**YES**	Buslines's liability, if any, is ***derivative***, *i.e.*, predicated on a showing that Driver was negligent. P litigated and lost this issue in the first action, and thus is barred from relitigating it in the second action. [§2103]
b.	**DEPENDS**	If the sole issue in the first suit was Driver's negligence, the first judgment should preclude P. However, if Buslines raised some other defense (*e.g.*, Driver was not acting in course and scope of employment), the result would be contra. [§2083]
c.	**NO**	Buslines should not be bound because it had no opportunity to litigate in the first case. Driver may or may not have defended it properly. [§2099]
d.	**PROBABLY**	Even offensive use of issue preclusion by a stranger to the prior action is usually permissible in most jurisdictions, absent any of several special circumstances (such as much smaller damage exposure in the first action) that might make it unfair to give issue preclusive effect to rulings in the first action. [§§2105-2106]

SAMPLE EXAM QUESTION I

Mitsui Machinery Co., a Japanese manufacturer, makes high-temperature ovens for heating nonferrous metals. The ovens are shipped from Japan to Mitsui-American Co., a California corporation that is a wholly owned sales subsidiary based in Los Angeles. Mitsui-American sells the ovens to various metals fabricators in the United States, including Pot Line Co., a Delaware corporation, whose principal place of business is in Utah. John Worker, a citizen of Utah, is an employee of Equipment Service Co., a Utah corporation that services manufacturing equipment, including the equipment at Pot Line.

A. Worker is injured while engaged in repairing a Mitsui oven at the Pot Line plant. Under Utah law, Worker's only remedy against Equipment Service Co. is under the workers' compensation law. Under Utah law, it is also arguable that his only remedy against Pot Line is limited to the workers' compensation law. Apart from any claim that Worker might have against Mitsui and Mitsui-American, what proceedings should he initiate? Explain.

B. Worker wishes to sue on the basis that the oven was of defective design. Can he join Mitsui Machinery and Mitsui-American, and if so, in what court or courts? Explain.

C. Assume Worker named Mitsui Machinery and Mitsui-American as defendants in an action in Utah state or federal court, and in connection with that action filed a writ of attachment upon Pot Line, asserting attachment jurisdiction over $35,000 due from Pot Line to Mitsui in payment for the oven.

   1. Assuming that Utah has state rules modeled on the Federal Rules of Civil Procedure in relevant respects, by what procedure may Mitsui Machinery and Mitsui-American challenge the attachment?

   2. Would the challenge be sustained?

D. Assume that the First National Bank of Utah had financed Pot Line's purchase of the oven and, upon learning of the attachment, is concerned that its rights under a chattel mortgage on the oven may be jeopardized by the attachment. What procedures might the bank use to protect its interest?

E. Assume that Worker sued Pot Line for damages on the theory that the oven was defective and that Pot Line impleaded Mitsui for indemnity. While discovery was being conducted, Pot Line settled with Worker for $200,000 and Worker's action against Pot Line is dismissed "with prejudice." What effect does that judgment have on Pot Line's claim against Mitsui?

SAMPLE EXAM QUESTION II

The Republican Party is an unincorporated association with headquarters in Washington, D.C. John Anderson, a member of the Party and Congressman from Illinois, decides to run as an independent for President. The National Committee of the Republican Party expels Anderson. He brings suit for reinstatement in the United States District Court for the Northern District of Illinois, alleging that the expulsion violates the First Amendment and also his rights under the common law governing unincorporated associations. He also asks for damages. Analyze whether and on what basis a damages award would be binding against the Republican Party as an organization and against individual members of the Party.

SAMPLE EXAM QUESTION III

John Moline is a citizen of Illinois; Harry Duffalo is a citizen of New York. They enter into a joint venture for buying machinery in the United States and selling it in various parts of the world, Moline being the buyer and Duffalo the seller. The venture has an office in Chicago, at which Moline works regularly and to which Duffalo checks in from time to time. After the business has been going for a while, Moline becomes suspicious that Duffalo has been cheating him by holding back payments from sales. By September 1993, Moline has collected enough evidence to convince himself of Duffalo's cheating, but on September 15, 1993, he suddenly dies of a heart attack.

On May 1, 1994, Moline's widow, as executor of his estate, commences an action in U.S. district court in Chicago against Duffalo to recover $550,000 of payments allegedly held back. Process is served on Duffalo in New York on May 5, 1994. On May 15, 1994, Duffalo commences an action in New York state court for (i) $100,000 of profits from the business that he alleges are due him but unpaid and (ii) a declaratory judgment that no sums are owing out of the joint venture accounts except the $100,000 mentioned in his first cause of action. Duffalo serves process on Mrs. Moline in Illinois and also garnishes Allstate Life Insurance Co., which had issued a life insurance policy for $250,000 on John Moline's life.

A. Does the Illinois court have jurisdiction of this action filed by Mrs. Moline?

B. Does the New York court have jurisdiction of the action filed by Duffalo?

SAMPLE EXAM QUESTION IV

Plaintiff brought an action in a federal district court for (i) specific performance of a contract and incidental damages for defendant's failure to perform on time, or (ii) full damages in case the court refused to order specific performance. Defendant filed an answer denying plaintiff's material allegations and counterclaimed for damages arising out of the same contract dispute.

A. If plaintiff demands jury trial, what issues, if any, should be tried by a jury?

B. Assume that plaintiff does not demand a jury trial, but defendant does. What issues, if any, should be tried by a jury?

C. Assume that the court strikes defendant's demand and sets all the issues of the case for a court trial. Is the order then reviewable? If so, by what means?

SAMPLE EXAM QUESTION V

The sole issue being tried by the jury in a condemnation action was the issue of just compensation. After lengthy deliberation, the jurors advised the court that they could not agree on a verdict. The judge then instructed them that each juror should write his or her valuation on a piece of paper, that they should then divide the total by 12, and that should be their verdict. After returning to the jury room, the jury shortly came in with a verdict of $37,500 in favor of the landowner. Was the instruction proper? Assume that neither the United States (the condemnor) nor the defendant landowner had objected to the court's instruction. On appeal by the defendant-landowner from the judgment entered on the verdict, may the appellant raise the giving of the instruction as error?

SAMPLE EXAM QUESTION VI

A Santa Fe railroad freight train hit a school bus at a grade crossing in Lumpe, Texas. The crossing had a sign but no light or gate. Two children were killed and three others and the bus driver were injured. The locomotive engineer was killed by flying debris. An action was brought in federal district court against Santa Fe, a Kansas corporation, on behalf of the children who were killed and injured. In discovery, the depositions were taken of the bus driver, the fireman on the locomotive, and the brakeman on the train.

The fireman said that the train was going "about normal speed, which at that place on the route would be 60 miles an hour." He said that he was at his regular seat in the front of the locomotive cab, looking ahead, when the bus "came up to the tracks and just kept going." He said there is a speedometer in the control panel at his seat but "can't recall" looking at the speedometer in the interval just before the crash.

The brakeman said the train was going "about usual speed, which is supposed to be 60 miles an hour." He did not see the bus until after the collision.

The bus driver says that he slowed down as he approached the grade crossing, did not see the train, and nearly got across the tracks before the train hit the rear of the bus. He admits he did not stop, as required by state law.

Also through discovery, the railroad was compelled to produce the paper tape from the train's speed recorder. This is an automatic device that records the speed at which the train is going at each moment of a run. The tape indicates that the train was going 80 miles per hour at the time of the collision.

Plaintiff moves for summary judgment on the issue of liability, requesting that its previous demand for jury trial be applicable only to the issue of damages. In support of the motion, plaintiff appends the depositions and speed tape described above.

The Texas constitution provides that in actions at common law, "the jury shall be the judge of the facts and the law."

Should summary judgment be granted?

SAMPLE EXAM QUESTION VII

The following is a complaint filed in United States District Court for the District of Connecticut:

1. Plaintiff Jane Smith is a citizen of Connecticut. The amount in controversy herein exceeds $50,000, exclusive of interest and costs.

2. Defendant Electronics Institute, Inc. is a Delaware corporation with its principal place of business in New York. It operates an establishment in New Haven, Connecticut.

3. Defendant advertised a course in electronics technology at a tuition of $2,500. The advertisements claimed that "completion of the course could lead to big money in electronics." Plaintiff enrolled in and completed the course and paid $2,500 in tuition therefor.

4. Plaintiff has been unable to find any employment in electronics at a wage exceeding the minimum wage. Plaintiff is informed and believes and therefore alleges that there are no jobs paying more than $5 per hour in the New Haven area for which the training provided by defendant is necessary and useful.

5. Plaintiff was induced to believe that employment at a high wage would result from taking the course provided by defendant. As a result of thus being misled by defendant, plaintiff suffered embarrassment, humiliation, and loss of self respect, to her damage of $50,000.

6. The training provided by defendant was substantially worthless.

Wherefore, plaintiff prays for restitution in the amount of $2,500; for additional damages in the amount of $50,000; and for interest and costs.

You represent the defendant. Write a memorandum for the file, analyzing motions that you might have good basis for asserting by way of attack on the complaint brought by Ms. Smith.

SAMPLE EXAM QUESTION VIII

Sierra Club, Inc. is a nonprofit corporation incorporated in California, having its headquarters in San Francisco and an office in Washington, D.C. It has 25,000 members who pay annual dues varying from $25 to $500 and who elect its board of directors. The Club organizes hikes and treks, promotes conservation through public education, and lobbies in Washington and in various state capitals for environmental regulation. In 1993 the Club discovered that persons employed by oil and coal companies were joining in large numbers and suspected an "infiltration" intended to oppose its political activism. In January 1994, Nelson Oil Bunker, a citizen of Texas and a member of the Club and president of Gusher Oil Co., sent a letter to the board demanding that the Club cease lobbying efforts because those efforts could jeopardize the Club's status as a tax exempt organization under the Internal Revenue Code. In February, the Club board adopted a resolution that no person could become or continue as a member except by subscribing to a "statement of principles" that affirmed the Club's involvement in environmental regulation. Bunker refused to sign the statement and demanded a list of Club members to contest the next election of Club directors. In April 1994, the Club board voted to cancel Bunker's membership. Litigation is imminent.

A. If the Club wishes to bring suit against Bunker individually to determine the validity of the cancellation of his membership, in what court or courts could it effectively do so? Identify court(s) and legal basis for it (their) being proper court(s).

B. Assume that on April 15, 1994, the Club brought a class suit in California Superior Court, San Francisco County, against three California members, named individually and as representatives of a class constituting those members who object to the requirement of signing the "statement of principles." The suit asks for a declaratory judgment that the requirement is valid. State a legal argument for the proposition that a judgment for the Club would be binding on Bunker.

C. Assume that, in the situation described in B., Bunker wished to become an individual party to the action. State the basis or bases upon which he could do so, with a supporting legal argument, if he acted (i) while the action was pending in state court and (ii) after the action was removed to federal court.

D. Assume that the suit mentioned in B. was removed to federal court and that the question of giving notice to the members of the class was then presented. Must notice be given to all class members? State reasons. Should Sierra Club be required to pay the cost of giving such notice? State reasons.

SAMPLE EXAM QUESTION IX

Kopp, a police officer, attempted to arrest Strong, a young man of 25, in a bar. An altercation resulted in punches; finally Kopp knocked out Strong with her blackjack. Strong subsequently sued Kopp for damages for assault. All six other persons present in the bar testified that Kopp was the aggressor and that Strong tried to avoid the altercation. The jury returned a verdict for Kopp. Within 10 days, Strong moved for a new trial but the motion papers were lost in the mail until 25 days later.

A. Under the Federal Rules, may the judge grant a new trial? Could he grant a post-verdict judgment as a matter of law in favor of Strong?

B. Is the answer different under state practice?

ANSWER TO SAMPLE EXAM QUESTION I

A. Worker should bring a workers' compensation proceeding against Equipment Service, a remedy limited in amount but very sure of recovery. Worker should also sue Pot Line on the theory that he is not an employee of Pot Line and, therefore, is not limited to a workers' compensation remedy against them. If this theory loses, he may seek a workers' compensation remedy (*see* above). The tort suit should be in Utah state court, not in federal court, because Pot Line has its principal place of business in Utah and, hence, is a co-citizen of Worker, who is also a Utah citizen. Thus, there is no diversity, so the federal court would lack subject matter jurisdiction.

B. Multiple tortfeasors may be joined as defendants under Federal Rule 20 and analogous state rules. Presumably, Utah and California have such provisions.

Subject matter jurisdiction: If the action is to be against Pot Line as well as Mitsui-American and Mitsui Machinery, Worker must proceed in Utah state court because there is no diversity with Pot Line (*see* above), and Pot Line is apparently not amenable to suit in California (there being no apparent contact between Pot Line and California). There is a question of territorial jurisdiction against the Mitsui companies (*see* below). Diversity exists between Worker and Mitsui-American, because Mitsui-American is a California corporation and its principal place of business is not in Utah. Diversity also exists with Mitsui Machinery, because it is an alien corporation.

Territorial jurisdiction: Territorial jurisdiction over Mitsui-American can be established in Utah if Utah has a typical long-arm statute. *International Shoe* contacts of Mitsui-American are plainly sufficient. Hence, Mitsui-American is amenable to suit in Utah state or federal court. Mitsui Machinery is probably subject to Utah territorial jurisdiction by its own contacts or on the theory that contacts of its wholly owned subsidiary should be attributed to it. Hence, Mitsui Machinery should be amenable to suit in Utah state or federal court if the Utah long-arm statute reaches the case. Federal venue is based on where a substantial part of the events giving rise to the claim occurred.

If jurisdiction cannot be obtained in Utah, California should be considered. Territorial jurisdiction over Mitsui-American clearly can be established in California, where it is incorporated. California territorial jurisdiction over Mitsui Machinery is more problematic: Mitsui Machinery's contacts with California are more intense than with Utah, but the tort involved here apparently did not occur in California. However, contacts seem sufficient, as Mitsui Machinery apparently ships all the ovens it exports to the United States to its California distributor. Worker could sue in California state court or in federal court in California, at least if Mitsui Machinery has no valid federal venue objection.

C. 1. Mitsui should challenge jurisdiction and service with a Rule 12(b) motion on the basis of *Shaffer v. Heitner*, the line of cases culminating in *Connecticut v. Doehr*, and the lack of necessity for using attachment procedures.

2. Generally, under *Shaffer*, attachment jurisdiction can be established only if in personam jurisdiction could be established. If analysis of territorial jurisdiction in part B. (above) is correct, the "contacts" requirement is satisfied. Hence, the motion to dismiss should be denied as far as *Shaffer* is concerned. However, that means attachment is not necessary to establish jurisdiction and hence a valid *Fuentes-Doehr* objection may exist: Seizure without notice has occurred without the possible justifying circumstance that it was necessary to establish jurisdiction, which also violates Rule 4(n)(2) on assertion of jurisdiction by seizing assets.

If "contacts" are insufficient for in personam jurisdiction, attachment is permissible only under an exception that the *Shaffer* doctrine would recognize. No such exception appears as to Mitsui-American, which is a United States corporation clearly amenable to suit in California. As to Mitsui Machinery, the doubtfulness of its amenability to suit in California (*see* above) might justify attachment jurisdiction, to give an American injured party an American forum.

D. *Intervention:* The bank might seek intervention by arguing that its interest in securing Pot Line's indebtedness is jeopardized by the attachment of the debt, because that might give Mitsui-American cause to reclaim the oven. Were that to happen, the bank's security would certainly be impaired, and it is not clear how it could protect this interest absent intervention. On the other hand, it is not clear what role it would play in the suit itself, as it has no interest in the issues being litigated at present, nor is it clear that Pot Line would fail to represent the bank's interest adequately, as it can be expected to contest tort liability to Worker vigorously.

Subject matter jurisdiction: If the case is in federal court, the bank's participation in the case might raise subject matter jurisdiction problems, depending on the identities of the other parties and how the bank is aligned as a party. If it is considered adverse to Worker, there is no diversity between them, but there is no bar to supplemental jurisdiction over the state law claims of a nondiverse intervenor-defendant in a diversity case.

E. The claim was settled without adjudication, so no issues were litigated and hence issue preclusion is inoperative. The judgment extinguishes Worker's claim against Pot Line, but not Pot Line's claim against Mitsui. Hence, there is no claim preclusion either. If Mitsui participated in the settlement or manifested acquiescence in the reasonableness of the amount, it could possibly be estopped from disputing the existence of Pot Line's liability to Worker or the amount of that liability, but that would result from Mitsui's stance in the negotiations and not from the judgment as such.

ANSWER TO SAMPLE EXAM QUESTION II

Anderson's first claim is based on federal law. Federal Rule 17 seems to say that an obligation created by federal law against an unincorporated association and members of such an association rests against the association as an entity. If so, and if the entity concept is applied consistently, Anderson's damages claim based on the First Amendment would be binding on the Republican Party as an entity if the expulsion was the act of the organization's management, as it appears to have been. The claim would not be binding on any member of the Party, except for officers or directors who might be found individually to be co-wrongdoers with the entity, in the same way that an officer of a corporation can be held personally liable for a wrong committed in the course of corporate employment.

The binding effect of the state law claim is determined by applicable state law, which could be Illinois or District of Columbia. If that law treats an unincorporated association as an entity, then the analysis above applies. Whether that law treats an association as an entity may depend on whether the claim is in tort (open-ended damages) or contract (limited damages). If the association is not treated as an entity, the situation is essentially a suit against a large number of joint wrongdoers, some of whom (the officers and board) acted personally and others of whom (the members at large) are chargeable only on principles of vicarious liability. Anderson would have to prove liability on one or the other such bases against individuals to bind them.

Procedurally Anderson should treat the "defendant" both as an entity and as an aggregate of individuals. That is, process under Federal Rule 4 and designation of the defendant under Federal Rule 23.2 should be modeled after both a suit against a corporation and a suit against a class under Federal Rule 23.

ANSWER TO SAMPLE EXAM QUESTION III

"Jurisdiction" can mean subject matter jurisdiction or jurisdiction over the person. Both will be analyzed.

A. As for subject matter jurisdiction, the federal court in Illinois appears to have such jurisdiction. The amount in controversy exceeds $50,000. There appears to be diversity of citizenship: Duffalo is a citizen of New York and Moline was an Illinois citizen. Note that it is the decedent's citizenship (Mr. Moline's), and not that of his executor (Mrs. Moline), that controls diversity. Whether the federal court in Illinois has personal jurisdiction depends on whether Duffalo has "minimum contacts" with Illinois and whether Illinois has a long-arm statute that reaches him. It appears that Duffalo's contacts with Illinois are sufficient. He had a continuous business relationship based in Illinois and the lawsuit arises out of that business. It may be assumed that Illinois has a typical long-arm statute. If so, such a statute very likely extends jurisdiction to persons "doing" or "engaging in" business in the state or entering into contracts in the state. Any such provision would be a sufficient statutory basis for asserting territorial jurisdiction over this claim arising out of Duffalo's local business.

B. As for subject matter jurisdiction of the New York state court, there is no diversity requirement. The only possible question with regard to subject matter jurisdiction is whether the suit is filed in the proper court in New York. Given the size of the claim asserted by Duffalo, that would be the trial court of general jurisdiction. [In New York that happens to be the supreme court, but this is a fact that students outside New York would not ordinarily be expected to know.]

The problem of territorial jurisdiction in New York is much more problematic. It may be assumed that New York can extend process to the decedent's representative if and only if it could extend process to the decedent himself, because there is no indication that the executor, as such, had any contacts with New York. Mr. Moline had only very tenuous connections with New York: He was a joint venturer with Duffalo and Duffalo evidently conducted much of the venture's business from New York. On that basis, it could be said that Moline himself was engaged in business in New York and hence subject to its process. On the other hand, the venture had its headquarters outside New York and Moline himself does not appear to have gone regularly to New York in the course of the business. The question could also be affected by the precise terms of the New York long-arm statute. If it required that the defendant have "done business" in New York, it might be said that Moline did not personally do business in New York and that it would be a bootstrapping maneuver to say that he did business in New York because Duffalo did. On balance, territorial jurisdiction probably would not be sustained.

As for the garnishment of Allstate, the problem is similar to, but not identical with, *Rush v. Savchuk*. In that case, the policy sought to be attached was a liability insurance policy in which the obligation of "debt" came into being only if the merits of the controversy at hand were resolved in favor of the plaintiff. Here the policy is a life insurance policy and is an existing debt, regardless of the outcome of the Duffalo-Moline litigation. Hence, the insurance proceeds can properly be considered "property" that might be subject to attachment.

However, even so, the attachment is probably improper in New York. The Allstate Company is subject to process in New York and the "debt follows the debtor," so that the property is "in" New York for purposes of attachment. Nevertheless, simple presence of property is not a sufficient basis for exercise of attachment jurisdiction, at least when the property is not real property. *Shaffer v. Heitner* requires, in general, that the principal defendant (Moline's executor in this case) have "minimum contacts" with the state in which the attachment is made. On the analysis above, such minimum contacts are missing. Other possibly justifying circumstances recognized in *Shaffer* are not present. (For example, there is no indication that Duffalo could not sue in Illinois to enforce his claim.) Thus, the attachment of the life insurance policy in New York would not meet the requirement of *Shaffer* and could not be sustained.

ANSWER TO SAMPLE EXAM QUESTION IV

A. Under *Beacon v. Westover* and related cases, for purposes of determining the right to jury trial, a pleading is read with attention to its "legal" claims and with a presumption in favor of jury trial. Viewed in this way, the complaint in this case is an action for damages (the second cause of action) with an alternative claim for specific performance (the equitable cause of action). On this analysis, plaintiff has an action for damages, which is therefore triable by jury as to all issues of liability and measures of damages. The only issue triable to the **court** would be the propriety of granting specific performance, and the terms upon which it is granted, if liability is found by the jury.

B. The foregoing applies whether the demand for jury trial is by plaintiff or by defendant. Hence, the issues of liability and damages should be tried by a jury regardless of which party made the demand for jury trial.

C. If the court rejected the defendant's demand for a jury, the order is reviewable. Most obviously, the order would be reviewable on appeal from a final judgment after the case had been tried to the court. The more important question is whether the order could be subject to appellate review before the case goes to trial. The order is not a final judgment, and hence an appeal does not lie from the order. However, the order is one that can be certified for interlocutory appellate review under 28 U.S.C. section 1292(b). To obtain review by this method, it is necessary that the trial judge certify the question as warranting immediate review and that the appellate court agree to accept the case on that basis. If the trial judge refuses to certify the order, section 1292(b) review cannot be obtained.

Furthermore, defendant may be able to obtain immediate review of the order by means of extraordinary writ, specifically, mandamus to compel the judge to put the case on the jury calendar. Review by extraordinary writ is generally disfavored in the federal courts, although the attitude varies considerably from one circuit to another. Nevertheless, where there is a plain and serious error going to important procedural rights, the writ has often been granted. In the light of *Beacon v. Westover* (itself a mandamus proceeding), the error here is serious. Hence, review by extraordinary writ might well be afforded.

ANSWER TO SAMPLE EXAM QUESTION V

The instruction was plain error. The procedure adopted is known as a quotient verdict, *i.e.*, one in which the jury sums up the jurors' individual proposed awards and then divides the total by the number of jurors. It is error for a jury to do this on its own initiative, and clearly error for the court to instruct the jury to follow such a procedure. The vice of the quotient verdict is that the process of jury discussion and mutual consideration of the issue of damages is displaced by the simple averaging of individual views.

So far as raising the objection on appeal is concerned, it is the general rule that a party may not complain on appeal of a ruling or action of the trial court unless the party raised timely objection in the trial court. The crucial questions therefore are whether the parties knew of the special instruction by the court and, if so, whether the circumstances were such that they did not have fair opportunity to object. For example, if the instruction was given without the presence of counsel, as it could have been if counsel had adjourned from court, then the party is excused from the requirement of timely objection. Similarly, if the judge had notified the parties but had made it clear that he would tolerate no objection, the "timely objection" requirement might be excused. And even if the parties had knowledge of the instruction and opportunity to object, in this exceptional case an appellate court might regard the instruction as "plain error" subject to review despite the parties' failure to object.

ANSWER TO SAMPLE EXAM QUESTION VI

The first question is whether federal law or state law should govern the question of granting or denying summary judgment. If state law is applied, it would be arguable that summary judgment should be denied. Summary judgment is proper only when there is no genuine issue of fact and, as a matter of law, the movant is entitled to judgment. Under Texas law, as stated, it would be for the jury to determine whether "as a matter of law" judgment should be granted. Hence, under state law, summary judgment could not be granted on these facts. It thus is necessary to analyze whether state law is applicable.

The argument for applying state law is as follows: This is a diversity case, governed by state law in its substantive aspects. *Erie*, as construed in such cases as *Guaranty Trust v. York*, requires that a federal court, when not applying governing federal law, apply not only state "substantive" law, but also "outcome determinative" state law. Since the Texas rule on scope of jury authority could have "outcome" effect in this case, it could be argued that the state rule should be applied in determining whether there is an issue for trial.

Although this argument has support in some of the cases, the Supreme Court in *Hanna v. Plumer* and other decisions has established approaches that make it likely federal law should govern. If the source of the potentially applicable federal rule of law is regarded as being the "no genuine issue as to any material fact" language of Federal Rule 56 itself, then the test for the validity and governing force of the federal standard is provided by the Rules Enabling Act [28 U.S.C. §2072]. The federal rule qualifies as procedural within the terms of the Act, especially give the Supreme Court's broad definition of federal court rulemaking authority as including even "arguably procedural" rules in the border area between substance and procedure. And the Court's tolerance for "incidental" substantive impacts of Federal Rules makes it highly probable that the Court would not regard the summary judgment rule here as impermissibly abridging, enlarging, or modifying any substantive right.

More likely, the federal standard for sufficiency of the evidence to go to the jury would be regarded as purely decisional, and thus subject to the "twin aims" approach articulated in *Hanna* for the "relatively unguided *Erie* choice" between a federal decisional rule affecting federal court procedure and a conflicting state rule. Lower federal courts have split over whether federal or state standards for sufficiency of the evidence to go to the jury govern on a motion for judgment as a matter of law on a state law claim, and the same problem should carry over to the summary judgment context. The question would be whether the federal court's following of the federal rule would be likely to lead to forum shopping and inequitable administration of the laws. Some forum shopping might result from plaintiffs' seeking to stay in state court for a better chance at getting to the jury in weak cases. There does not, however, appear to be great inequity or undermining of Texas policy if the federal courts in state law actions in Texas have the same substantive state law issues decided by a judge on summary judgment motion in a few cases that would get to the jury in Texas state court, and the amount of forum shopping would probably be small. The majority of federal courts that have considered the question of federal or state standard on sufficiency of the evidence have chosen the federal rule.

Applying the federal standard, a "genuine issue of fact" exists if, given the material presented in the summary judgment motion, it can be reasonably foreseen that a sufficient evidentiary basis will exist at trial for the case to go to the jury. Here the case looks very strong against the railroad, but there remains a "genuine issue." First, it has not been established in the affidavits that the speed recorder was operating properly. If it was not working properly, the indicated speed of 80 miles per hour may not have been the actual speed. Second, even if the train had been going 80, it is a question for the jury whether that speed was excessive under the circumstances. Third, even if the train was going at an excessive speed, that would not have been the proximate cause of the accident if the bus driver's conduct is regarded as a supervening cause. Although the bus driver's testimony in deposition is not contradicted, he is so situated that his testimony is self-serving. The jurors therefore could disbelieve the testimony. If they did, they could find the railroad was not responsible for the collision.

ANSWER TO SAMPLE EXAM QUESTION VII

Since the action is in federal court, the Federal Rules of Civil Procedure apply. There is no demurrer under the Federal Rules, so the question becomes what kind of motion should be prepared.

Possibly, a motion for more definite statement would be effective, but such motions are disfavored and rarely granted under the "notice pleading" approach of the Federal Rules. The complaint is very vague as to the details of the alleged advertisement. The gist of the claim seems to be fraud, which must be alleged with particularity under Rule 9. The pleading does not meet this standard. Furthermore, the allegations as to the availability of jobs in the field of electronics are also very vague. Even if a motion to make them more definite and certain were to be granted, however, it would provide only a temporary defense, because plaintiff would file a more definite pleading. The action certainly could not be dismissed on the ground that the complaint is uncertain, for under the Federal Rules an action may be dismissed only where it appears to a certainty that plaintiff could state no claim at all.

A motion to dismiss for failure to state a claim would probably not be effective. While there is grave doubt whether plaintiff states a claim entitling her to $50,000 damage, the claim for restitution of $2,500 does not seem substantively baseless. Since the plaintiff states a valid claim to this extent, the complaint would not be vulnerable to a motion to dismiss for failure to state a claim.

The most promising motion would be to dismiss for want of jurisdiction. There seems to be no basis at all for an argument on the part of plaintiff that her action is based on federal law. (If there were a valid federal claim, the amount in controversy requirement would not be applicable.) The amount in controversy in a diversity action in the federal courts must exceed $50,000. To meet the $50,000 amount in controversy requirement, the pleader must have a good faith basis upon which she might conceivably recover a judgment exceeding $50,000, exclusive of interest and costs. Although plaintiff may state a valid claim for restitution of $2,500, the defendant has a strong argument that no basis exists for recovery in excess of that amount. The allegations of fraud, which could lead to punitive damages, are insufficient. In particular, there is no allegation that defendant knew that employment of the type advertised would be virtually impossible to obtain by a graduate of the Institute. If the action is regarded as one for breach of contract, as opposed to fraud, the measure of damages under generally prevailing law does not include "embarrassment, humiliation," etc. The damage recoverable by plaintiff on a contract claim would be limited to the difference between the amount paid and the value of the education actually received. That could not exceed $2,500, and therefore the amount in controversy requirement is not met, and the court does not have jurisdiction of the action.

ANSWER TO SAMPLE EXAM QUESTION VIII

A. A suit individually against Bunker would seek to cancel his membership on the ground that he refused to abide by the rules governing membership. This claim is based essentially on the common law of unincorporated associations. A federal question might arise in the case, but it would be a defensive contention by Bunker that the Club rule requiring subscription to the "statement of principles" is a violation of his First Amendment rights. The fact that a federal question may arise defensively does not make the case one that "arises under" federal law. Therefore, the claim in an action by the Club to terminate Bunker's membership would be a state law claim.

Such a claim could be brought in federal court only if the requirements for diversity jurisdiction could be met, since the federal question basis of jurisdiction does not exist. There is diversity between the Club and Bunker. Bunker is a citizen of Texas, while Sierra Club is a citizen of California, where it is incorporated. (It does not appear that Sierra Club is also a citizen of the District of Columbia, because its principal place of business is in San Francisco.) However, diversity jurisdiction requires that the amount in controversy exceed $50,000. There is nothing to indicate that the value of the membership to Bunker is of that amount, nor that the value to the Sierra Club of excluding Bunker from membership would be in that amount. Possibly, the Club could meet the amount in controversy requirement by allegations that Bunker threatens disruption of the Club and that the disruption would damage it to the extent of more than $50,000. However, on the facts given, there seems no basis for making nonfrivolous allegations to this effect. Accordingly, the action could not be brought in federal district court.

The action could be brought in a state court where personal jurisdiction could be obtained over Bunker. That would include an appropriate state court in Texas, where presumably Bunker is subject to service of process. It seems likely that the action could also be brought in California on the ground that Bunker is subject to service of process there for any claim concerning his membership in the Club. His joining the Club was a voluntary action and he knew the Club was headquartered in California. With regard to a claim arising out of the membership activity itself, Bunker's "contact" with California seems sufficient to meet the constitutional standard applied in such cases as *International Shoe* and more recent decisions such as *Burger King Corp. v. Rudzewicz*. Because California's long arm statute goes to the limits of due process, service of process on Bunker is authorized by the statute.

There seems to be no basis upon which Bunker could be subject to process in the District of Columbia. There is no indication that he had any contact with the District or that he carried on activities relating to membership there. The simple fact that the Club has an office in the District is not a sufficient basis for subjecting members of the Club to jurisdiction.

B. The class suit names as defendants individuals who object to the requirement of signing the "statement of principles." Such individuals would adequately represent the class if they can defend the litigation with reasonable competence and diligence. On that assumption, the litigation would meet the requirements for a binding class suit: The group of affected individuals is so large that it is impractical to join all those who are similarly situated; the individuals actually named are representative of the class; they appear to be able to defend the litigation on behalf of the class. Under the principles of *Hansberry v. Lee*, they can represent the class as a whole. There does not seem to be a problem under *Phillips Petroleum Co. v. Shutts* with the California state court's exercising jurisdiction over out-of-state defendant class members, because of the members' voluntary contact with California. All this being so, the judgment would be binding on all members of the class, including Bunker.

C. If Bunker sought to become a party to the action as an individual, the proper procedure under either federal or state practice is to seek to intervene. If the action was pending in state court, his petition for intervention should state the essentials of intervention. These are that the pending action will or may determine his legal rights; that there is risk that the action will be defended by the class less effectively than Bunker could defend his own interest individually; that his petition is timely and his becoming a party will not unduly delay the progress of the litigation.

If the action were brought in federal court, the procedure would be essentially the same. However, Bunker should frame his petition in the alternative, first as a petition for intervention of right, and second as a petition for permissive intervention. There is no fundamental distinction between the two, except that intervention of right is permitted when the proposed intervenor stands in risk that his rights will be legally or practically affected by the judgment, whereas permissive intervention requires only that the petitioner show that his claim and the claims already pending in the action involve a common question of law and fact, although allowing permissive intervention is a discretionary decision for the trial court. The allegations outlined above establish that the judgment in the pending action may affect Bunker's interest. They also show that his claim involves a common question of law and fact with the claim pending in the existing action.

D. When a class action is pending in federal court, the question of notice to the class is determined under the Federal Rules. Under Rule 23, individual notice to each member of the class is required when the class suit is of the (b)(3) or damages type, where each individual member has the right to opt out. However, individual notice may not be required in other types of class suits, including those in which an injunction or declaratory judgment is sought regarding the rights and duties of the class as a whole. The present suit falls into the latter category and, therefore, individual notice is probably not required. It would be within the discretion of the court to require individual notice even in this type of class suit, but to do so might be regarded as an abuse of discretion in this case. The question involved is a legal issue common to all members of the class. Published notice to the class as a whole, plus perhaps individual notice to members known to oppose the "statement of principles," might be sufficient.

With regard to the cost of giving notice, the party opposing the class is not required to pay that cost in a "damages" type of class suit. [*See* Eisen v. Carlisle & Jacquelin] However, this is not a damages class suit so the court has broader discretion in determining whether the party opposing the class should be required to pay the cost of notice. And because this case involves a plaintiff seeking to invoke the class action procedure to sue a defendant class, it should not be a problem to make the plaintiff at least initially bear the notice costs.

ANSWER TO SAMPLE EXAM QUESTION IX

A. Following the jury verdict, Strong moved for a new trial. Apparently Strong sought to file the motion by mail rather than following the usual practice of filing the papers directly with the clerk of the court. While "service" of papers may be accomplished by depositing the papers timely in the mail, the same is not true of filing. However, filing may be accomplished by depositing papers in the mail if the mailing is actually received within the time limit. There is some possibility, therefore, that Strong's motion was timely; that is, made not later than 10 days after the entry of judgment. Timeliness on a motion for a new trial or judgment as a matter of law is strictly required under the Federal Rules. However, under the Federal Rules, the court may act on its own motion to grant a new trial if it does so not later than 10 days after the entry of the judgment. The court could not grant a judgment as a matter of law under the Federal Rules, because that relief may be granted only on motion of a party specifically requesting it, and here Strong's motion sought only a new trial.

On the merits of the motion, a new trial may be granted only if the verdict is against the weight of the evidence. The cases are divided in regard to problems of witness credibility. Some decisions suggest that the trial judge can grant a new trial even if there is some testimonial evidence to support the verdict if, in the judge's opinion, that evidence is inherently incredible. Under that interpretation, the court could grant a new trial. Otherwise, the basic issue is credibility and Kopp's testimony constitutes "substantial evidence."

B. Under state practice, in some states the judge lacks power to grant a new trial on his own motion, but has power to grant a judgment n.o.v. (the term still used in most state systems for the federal post-verdict motion for judgment as a matter of law) on his own motion. The question of timeliness under state practice depends on the time periods allowed for post-verdict motions and whether deposit in the mail constitutes "filing" for purposes of compliance with the timeliness requirement. As for the merits of the motion, the standards for post-verdict motions under state practice vary. However, in most states the judge has at least the broader authority indicated above. In some states, the judge is authorized to weigh the evidence (the "thirteenth juror" approach) in determining whether to grant a new trial. Under the latter standard, the judge would clearly have authority to grant Strong a new trial.

TABLE OF CITATIONS TO
FEDERAL RULES OF CIVIL PROCEDURE (Fed. R. Civ. P.)

Rule	Text Reference
1	§545
2	§544
3	§§135, 508, 556
4(a)	§135
4(d)	§219
4(d)(1)	§508
4(e)(1)	§218
4(e)(2)	§217
4(f)	§220
4(k)(1)(A)	§108
4(k)(1)(B)	§109
4(k)(1)(C)	§110
4(k)(1)(D)	§110
4(k)(2)	§111
4(n)(2)	§114
7(a)	§§805, 825, 1671
7(b)(1)	§692
8(a)	§600
8(a)(1)	§§258, 561
8(a)(2)	§§555, 676
8(b)	§§570, 764
8(c)	§§771, 772, 780, 782, 805
8(d)	§§768, 797, 806
8(e)	§§565, 576
8(f)	§559
9(b)	§§612, 679, 680, 681, 684, 1188
9(c)	§§621, 779
9(g)	§626
10	§558
10(b)	§564
10(c)	§§567, 703
11	§§514, 709, 710, 712, 718, 723, 731-734, 736, 739, 748, 753, 792, 1173
11(b)(2)	§724
11(b)(3)	§717
11(b)(4)	§720
11(c)	§735
11(c)(1)	§§744, 745
11(c)(1)(A)	§§740, 743
11(c)(1)(B)	§746
11(c)(2)	§737
11(c)(2)(A)	§742
11(c)(2)(B)	§§746, 900
11(c)(3)	§747
12(a)(1)(B)	§795
12(b)	§§86, 600, 686, 701, 787, 794, 1501
12(b)(6)	§§554, 674, 675, 688, 693, 888, 928, 1113
12(c)	§§889, 891
12(d)	§§788, 892
12(e)	§§687, 1189
12(f)	§§689, 798
12(g)	§695
12(h)	§§697, 959
12(h)(1)	§§87, 160
12(h)(2)	§987
13(a)	§§804, 813, 2070
13(b)	§§382, 799
13(g)	§§387, 821
13(h)	§§807, 826
14	§§109, 411, 416, 990, 996, 1002
14(a)	§1004
15	§1607
15(a)	§§842, 846, 893, 1728
15(a)(1)	§858
15(b)	§§867, 869, 873, 1732
15(c)	§§855, 857
15(c)(2)	§852
15(c)(3)	§853
15(d)	§§875, 877
16	§§1185, 1571, 1573, 1586, 1607, 1613, 1732
16(a)	§1571
16(b)	§§1310, 1574
16(b)(3)	§1580
16(c)	§§1571, 1585
16(c)(6)	§1580
16(c)(9)	§§1583, 1590, 1644
16(d)	§1571
16(e)	§1605
16(f)	§1608
17	§§906, 921
17(a)	§909
17(b)	§§935, 940, 944
17(c)	§§935, 936
18(a)	§640
19	§§109, 389, 411, 412, 416, 673, 961
19(a)	§983
19(a)(1)	§966
19(a)(2)(i)	§§966, 1020
19(a)(2)(ii)	§966
19(b)	§§389, 967

Rule	Text Reference
19(c)	§980
20	§§413, 416, 2046
20(a)	§§601, 952, 1025
20(b)	§§642, 958
21	§959
22	§§1037, 1045, 1046, 1049-1052, 1056
23	§§1061-1063, 1111, 1112, 1116, 1125, 1139, 1158, 1159
23(a)	§§1064, 1077, 1138
23(a)(1)	§1064
23(a)(2)	§§1064, 1070, 1071
23(a)(3)	§§1064, 1071
23(a)(4)	§1064
23(b)	§§1064, 1084, 1098
23(b)(1)	§§1085, 1106, 1121, 1134
23(b)(1)(A)	§1086
23(b)(1)(B)	§1087
23(b)(2)	§§1069, 1089, 1090, 1098, 1106, 1121, 1127, 1134, 1164
23(b)(3)	§§1067, 1091, 1092, 1098, 1122, 1127, 1128, 1131, 1140
23(c)	§1129
23(c)(1)	§1108
23(c)(2)	§1122
23(c)(4)	§1083
23(c)(4)(A)	§1095
23(d)(2)	§1121
23(e)	§§1123, 1148, 1149
23.1	§591
24	§§388, 411, 412, 416, 1021
24(a)	§1013
24(a)(1)	§1011
24(a)(2)	§1012
24(b)	§1024
25(c)	§915
26(a)	§§1173, 1183, 1454
26(a)(1)	§§327, 1201
26(a)(1)(A)	§1190
26(a)(1)(B)	§§1191, 1284
26(a)(1)(C)	§1192
26(a)(1)(D)	§§1193, 1323
26(a)(2)(A)	§1398
26(a)(2)(B)	§1401
26(a)(2)(C)	§1399
26(a)(3)	§1592
26(a)(3)(A)	§1594
26(a)(3)(B)	§1595
26(a)(3)(C)	§1596
26(b)	§§1309, 1321
26(b)(1)	§1173
26(b)(2)	§§1181, 1311, 1578
26(b)(3)	§§1364, 1366, 1376, 1378, 1388, 1389
26(b)(4)	§1413
26(b)(4)(A)	§1409
26(b)(4)(B)	§§1392, 1394, 1396
26(b)(4)(C)	§1393
26(c)	§§1417, 1429
26(c)(7)	§§1418, 1422
26(d)	§§1186, 1204, 1205, 1246, 1281
26(e)	§1303
26(e)(1)	§§1196, 1408, 1410, 1454
26(f)	§§1184, 1186, 1194, 1246, 1263, 1281, 1310, 1571, 1579, 1580
26(g)	§§712, 1173, 1181, 1479
26(g)(1)	§1195
30(a)(2)(B)	§1209
30(a)(3)(C)	§1186
30(b)	§§1217, 1218
30(b)(2)	§1234
30(b)(5)	§§1219, 1220
30(b)(6)	§1215
30(b)(7)	§1225
30(d)(1)	§1227
30(d)(3)	§§1230, 1447
30(e)	§1233
30(g)	§1474
31	§1223
32(a)(1)	§§1238, 1494
32(a)(2)	§1237
32(a)(3)	§§1239, 1495
32(b)	§§1231, 1240, 1493
32(d)	§§1240, 1493
32(d)(3)	§1496
33(a)	§§1241, 1245, 1248
33(b)(3)	§1249
33(d)	§1251
34(a)	§1277
34(b)	§§1286, 1289
35	§1295
35(a)	§1296
35(b)	§1300
36	§1274
36(a)	§§1256-1260, 1263, 1264
36(b)	§§1265, 1275
37(a)	§§1228, 1252, 1450, 1451
37(a)(2)	§1255
37(a)(2)(A)	§1456

Rule	Text Reference
37(a)(3)	§1452
37(a)(4)	§1472
37(b)	§§1199, 1229, 1454, 1473
37(b)(1)	§1475
37(b)(2)	§§1252, 1457, 1612
37(b)(2)(A)	§1458
37(b)(2)(D)	§1478
37(c)(1)	§§1197, 1454
37(c)(2)	§1266
37(d)	§§1214, 1453, 1456
38(b)	§1671
39(a)	§1672
39(b)	§1673
39(c)	§1674
41(a)	§898
41(a)(1)(i)	§896
41(a)(2)	§§811, 897, 901, 904, 905
42	§1035
42(a)	§642
42(b)	§§642, 643, 1005
45	§1414
45(a)(1)(C)	§1291
45(c)(3)(B)	§1414
45(b)	§1212
45(c)(3)(A)	§1213
46	§1733
47	§1700
48	§§1699, 1809
49(a)	§1796
49(b)	§§1802, 1805
50(a)	§§1737, 1738
50(b)	§§1756, 1757, 1830, 1834, 1836
50(c)	§1839
51	§§1770, 1788, 1790, 1791, 2010
52(a)	§§1991-1992, 1996, 2000
52(c)	§1766
54(b)	§§1972-1973
54(c)	§§581, 582
55(a)	§§879, 881
55(c)	§885
56(a)	§§1505, 1549
56(b)	§§1505, 1549
56(c)	§§1513, 1531, 1545
56(d)	§1560
56(e)	§§1503, 1550, 1554
56(f)	§§1562, 1563
58	§1963
59	§1904
59(a)	§§1842-1843, 1876
59(b)	§1868
59(c)	§1871
59(d)	§1866
59(e)	§§1894, 1896
60(b)	§§885, 1910, 1918
60(b)(1)	§1902
60(b)(2)	§2013
60(b)(3)	§1905
60(b)(6)	§1909
61	§§1793, 2005
64	§229
65(c)	§2003

TABLE OF CASES

Abelleira v. District Court - §2026
Ackerman v. United States - §1909
Adam v. Saenger - §81
Adickes v. S.H. Kress & Co. - §§544, 1534
Aero Bolt & Screw Co. v. Iaia - §783
Aetna Casualty & Surety Co. v. Yeatts - §1855
Aetna Casualty & Surety Co., United States v. - §§918, 919
Agent Orange Product Liability Litigation, In re - §1097
Ager v. Jane C. Stormmant Hospital - §1395
Aguacate Consolidated Mines v. Deeprock - §156
Airline Stewards Association v. American Air Lines - §1080
Albany Welfare Rights Organization Day Care Center, Inc. v. Schreck - §682
Albright v. Gates - §815
Aldinger v. Howard - §391
Alexander v. Tingle - §1741
Allen v. United States - §1811
Allenberg Cotton Co. v. Pittman - §938
Allis-Chalmers Corp. v. Philadelphia Electric Co. - §2004
Allstate Insurance Co. v. McNeill - §1055
American Cyanimid Co. v. McGhee - §903
American Express Warehousing Ltd. v. Trans-America Insurance Co. - §1487
American Fire & Casualty Co. v. Finn - §§259, 442
American Motorcycle v. Superior Court - §§971, 995
American National Red Cross v. S.G. - §349
American Pipe and Construction Co. v. Utah - §§1065, 1116
American Well Works Co. v. Layne & Bower Co. - §356
Anderson v. City of Bessemer City - §§1992, 1993, 2000
Anderson v. Cryovac, Inc. - §1441
Anderson v. Liberty Lobby, Inc. - §§1514, 1520
Anderson v. Papillion - §853
Anheuser-Busch, Inc. v. Starley - §§920, 2093
Ankenbrandt v. Richards - §341
Appeal of - see name of party
Appleton Electronics Co. v. Graves Truck Line, Inc. - §1119
Arabian American Oil Co. v. Scarfone - §1644

Arley v. United Pacific Insurance Co. - §124
Armstrong v. Armstrong - §2091
Armstrong v. Pomerance - §§30, 68
Arndt v. Griggs - §2
Arnstein v. Porter - §1529
Asahi Metal Industries Co. v. Superior Court - §§35, 51
Atlantis Development Corp. v. United States - §1015
Atlas Roofing Co. v. Occupational Safety and Health Review Commission - §1657
Augustin v. Mughal - §827
Austin v. Massachusetts Bonding Co. - §848
Auto Insurance Co. v. Union Oil Co. - §919
Avco Corp. v. Machinists - §367

Baker v. Gold Seal Liquors, Inc. - §2070
Baki v. B.F. Diamond Construction Co. - §1395
Baldwin v. Iowa State Traveling Men's Association - §119
Ballew v. Georgia - §1696
Baltimore & Carolina Line v. Redman - §§1757, 1836
Banco Nacional de Cuba v. Sabbatino - §535
Bank of America v. Parnell - §533
Bass v. Hoagland - §1907
Bates v. C & S Adjusters, Inc. - §132
Beacon Theatres, Inc. v. Westover - §§1661, 1664, 2024
Belcher v. Bassett Furniture - §1280
Bell v. Hood - §371
Bendictin Litigation, In re - §372
Bendix Autolite Corp. v. Midwesco Enterprises - §78
Berk v. Alperin - §632
Bernhard v. Bank of America - §§2103, 2104
Bershad v. McDonough - §1902
Black & White Taxicab Co. v. Brown & Yellow Taxicab Co. - §467
Blackstone v. Miller - §56
Blonder-Tongue Laboratories, Inc. v. University of Illinois Foundation - §2103
Blue Chip Stamps v. Manor Drug Stores - §683
Board of Harbor Commissioners, United States v. - §688
Boeing Co. v. Shipman - §1750
Bosch, Estate of, v. Commissioner - §525
Boser v. Uniroyal - §1486

Bradford Trust Co. v. Wright - §1087
Brakhage v. Graff - §1383
Branch v. Tunnell - §684
Breier v. Northern California Bowling Proprietors' Association - §893
Bremen, The v. Zapata Offshore Co. - §197
Brennan v. Engineered Products, Inc. - §1490
Brennan v. Midwestern United Life Insurance Co. - §1141
Brewster v. Boston Herald-Traveler - §598
Brisco v. Reader's Digest - §§544, 613
Bristol Convalescent Hospital v. Sone - §661
Brockton Savings Bank v. Peat, Marwick, Mitchell & Co. - §1464
Bryant v. Finnish National Airline - §73
Bryant v. Ford Motor Co. - §302
Buckeye Boiler Co. v. Superior Court - §39
Burger King Corp. v. Rudzewicz - §§27, 30, 39, 41, 43, 50, 69
Burlington Northern Railroad v. Ford - §159
Burlington Northern Railroad v. Woods - §512
Burnham v. Superior Court - §§9, 57
Burns v. Thiokol Chemical Corp. - §1489
Business Guides, Inc. v. Chromatic Communications Enterprises, Inc. - §§514, 721
Byrd v. Blue Ridge Electric Cooperative, Inc. - §§482, 488-490, 492-496

Calder v. Jones - §§36, 52
Capital Traction Co. v. Hof - §1695
Carden v. Arkoma Associates - §295
Carnegie-Mellon University v. Cohill - §457
Carnival Cruise Lines, Inc. v. Shute - §197
Carolina Power & Light Co. v. Uranex - §64
Carter v. Jury Commissioner of Green County - §1681
Catrett v. Celotex Corp. (1987) - §1543
Celotex Corp. v. Catrett (1986) - §§1512, 1535-1538, 1543, 1551, 1555, 1562
Chambers v. NASCO, Inc. - §§517, 518, 749
Chauffeurs, Teamsters & Helpers Local 391 v. Terry - §1657
Chern v. Bank of America - §2088
Chesa International, Ltd. v. Fashion Associates, Inc. - §1421
Chicago Rock Island & Pacific Railroad v. Igoe - §169
Chicago Rock Island & Pacific Railroad v. Martin - §451
Cianci v. New Times Publishing Co. - §1434
Cincinnati Gas & Electric Co. v. General Electric Co. - §1642

Cine Forty-Second Street Theatre Corp. v. Allied Artists - §§1459, 1468, 1471
Cipollone v. Ligget Group, Inc. - §1441
Citizens State Bank v. Castro - §1729
Citron v. Aro Corp. - §§1844, 2016
Clark v. United States - §1825
Clearfield Trust Co. v. United States - §533
Clegg v. Hardward Mutual Casualty Co. - §1800
Cochran v. Union Lumber Co. - §2108
Coffran v. Hitchcock Clinic, Inc. - §2003
Cohen v. Beneficial Industrial Loan Corp. - §§1980, 1981, 1984
Cole, People v. - §2088
Colgrove v. Battin - §1697
Collins v. Rocha - §789
Commercial Air Charters v. Sundorph - §95
Commissioner v. Estate of Bosch - §525
Commissioner of Internal Revenue v. Duberstein - §2002
Complete Auto Transit, Inc. v. Wayne Broyles Corp. - §1821
Cone v. West Virginia Pulp & Paper Co. - §1832
Conley v. Gibson - §§555, 600, 677, 682
Connecticut v. Doehr - §§244, 250
Conney v. Erickson - §1971
Consolidation Coal Co. v. Bucyrus-Erie Co. - §1355
Continental Nut Co. v. Robert L. Berner Co. - §629
Contract Engineers, Inc. v. California-Dorian Co. - §856
Cooper v. American Savings & Loan Association - §1124
Cooper v. Leslie Salt Co. - §663
Cooper Industries, Inc. v. British Aerospace, Inc. - §1288
Coopers & Lybrand v. Lindsay - §§1981, 1983, 1985
Cooter & Gell v. Hartmarx Corp. - §§746, 748
Corbett v. Free Press Association - §1421
Coté v. Wadel - §296
Cromwell v. County of Sacramento - §2074
Cross v. United States - §1526
Crown, Cork & Seal Co. v. Parker - §1118
Crumpton v. Dickstein - §1307
Cullen v. Margiotta - §1973
Curtis Publishing Co. v. Butts - §1773
Cutter Labs v. R.W. Ogle & Co. - §1675

D.H. Overmeyer Co. v. Frick Co. - §249
D.I. Chadbourne, Inc. v. Superior Court - §1386
Daar v. Yellow Cab Co. - §1154

Dairy Queen, Inc. v. Wood - §1661
Daves v. Hawaiian Dredging Co. - §678
David v. Crompton & Knowles Corp. - §765
Day & Zimmermann, Inc. v. Challoner - §522
Deboe v. Horn - §607
DeCourt v. Beckman Instruments - §2082
De Filippis v. United States - §1908
DeMarco v. Edens - §1065
Denham v. Cuddeback - §785
Denver & Rio Grande Western Railroad v. Brotherhood of Railroad Trainmen - §126
DeOlazabel v. Mix - §922
Dery v. Wyer - §1006
Diamond v. General Motors Corp. - §1097
Dice v. Akron, Canton & Youngstown Railroad - §1648
Dickinson v. Burnham - §1061
Dimick v. Schiedt - §§1650, 1892
Donaldson v. United States - §1013
Donovan v. Penn Shipping Co. - §1889
Dow Co. "Sarabrand" Products Liability Litigation, *In re* - §180
Dubin v. Philadelphia - §61
Duplan Corp. v. Moulinage et Retorderie de Chavanoz - §§1373, 1379
Durfee v. Duke - §2060
Durflinger v. Artiles - §1394
Durham v. Florida East Coast Railroad - §902
Dyer v. MacDougall - §§1525, 1565, 1754

Eastway Construction Corp. v. City of New York - §§726, 728
Edmonson v. Leesville Concrete Co. - §1706
Edwards v. Superior Court - §1299
Eisen v. Carlisle & Jacquelin - §§206, 1066, 1111, 1122, 1126, 1129, 1983
Ellis v. Great Southwestern Corp. - §179
Emerson, Estate of - §1852
Erie Railroad v. Tompkins - §§470, 471, 474, 477, 480-482, 506, 508, 510, 516, 518, 529, 771, 816
Erler v. Five Points Motors - §781
Essex Wire Corp. v. Eastern Electric Sales Co. - §1421
Estate of - *see* name of party
Eubanks v. Louisiana - §1680
Everett v. Everett - §1850
Evergreens v. Nunan - §2085
Evra Corp. v. Swiss Bank Corp. - §415
Executive Software North America, Inc. v. District Court - §§408, 422

FTC v. Grolier, Inc. - §1379
Fairmount v. Cub Fork Coal Co. - §1864
Fautek v. Montgomery Ward & Co. - §1277
Fay v. New York - §1682
Feathers v. McLucas - §102
Federated Department Stores, Inc. v. Moitie - §§369, 2069
Ferens v. John Deere & Co. - §178
Fidelity & Deposit Co. v. United States - §1511
Finley v. United States - §§393, 397, 398
Firestone Tire & Rubber Co. v. Risjord - §1982
First American State Bank v. Continental Insurance Co. - §2006
First National Bank of Circle, United States v. - §1607
FirsTier Mortgage Co. v. Investors' Mortgage Insurance Co. - §1947
Fisher v. Flynn - §682
Flood v. Simpson - §878
Foman v. Davis - §§685, 843
Ford v. Williams - §926
Fox v. United States - §1827
Franchise Tax Board v. Construction Laborers' Vacation Trust - §357
Freeman v. Bee Machine Co. - §269
Freeman v. Howe - §381
Freeport-McMoRan, Inc. v. KN Energy, Inc. - §309
Friendly Village Community Association v. Silva & Hill Construction Co. - §663
Fuentes v. Shevin - §§232, 239, 240, 242, 251

Galella v. Onassis - §§1182, 1422
Gallick v. Baltimore & Ohio Railroad - §1799
Galloway v. United States - §§1743, 1860
Garcia v. Hilton Hotels - §677
Garner v. Wolfinbarger - §1979
Gasoline Products Co. v. Champlin Refining Co. - §1882
General Credit Corp. v. Pichel - §863
General Telephone Co. of the Southwest v. Falcon - §1077
Gillespie v. United States Steel - §1985
Gillispie v. Goodyear Service Stores - §663
Ginsburg v. Insurance Co. of North America - §779
Glen Falls Indemnity Co. v. United States - §994
Glenwood Light & Water Co. v. Mutual Light, Heat & Power Co. - §331
Golden Eagle Distributing Corp. v. Burroughs Corp. - §727
Goldlawr, Inc. v. Heiman - §164

Goldman v. City Specialty Stores, Inc. - §670
Gompers v. Bucks Stove & Range Co. - §1477
Gonzales v. Cassidy - §§1075, 1081
Gordon v. Gordon - §2060
Gorsalitz v. Olin Mathieson Chemical Corp. - §1887
Government Employees Insurance Co. v. United States - §999
Go-Video v. Akai Electric Co. - §112
Grace v. McArthur - §7
Granfinanciera, S.A. v. Nordberg - §1656
Gray v. American Radiator Standard Sanitary Co. - §§35, 102
Great Lakes Rubber Corp. v. Herbert Cooper Co. - §806
Green v. Advance Ross Electronics Corp. - §106
Green v. Wolf Corp. - §1074
Greenberg v. Equitable Life Assurance Society - §843
Greene v. Lindsey - §207
Greenfield v. Villager Industries, Inc. - §1126
Greyhound Corp. v. Superior Court - §1488
Griffin v. McCoach - §§521, 522
Gruenberg v. Aetna Insurance Co. - §621
Grunenthal v. Long Island Railway - §1890
Guaranty Trust Co. v. York - §§482-487, 493, 496, 499, 516-518
Gulf Oil Corp. v. Bernard - §1143
Gulf Oil Corp. v. Gilbert - §182
Gulf Refining Co. v. Fetschan - §1807
Gully v. First National Bank - §361

Halkin, *In re* - §1439
Hall v. Clifton Precision - §1227
Halpern v. Schwartz - §2083
Hammond Packing Co. v. Arkansas - §1466
Hancock v. Bowman - §550
Hanna v. Plumer - §§225, 497, 509, 512, 516, 518
Hansberry v. Lee - §1080
Hanson v. Denckla - §§24, 26, 29
Hardy v. Johns-Manville Sales Corp. - §2087
Harris v. Balk - §§12, 53, 66
Hartbrodt, United States v. - §132
Hawkeye Security Insurance Co. v. Apodaca - §818
Hayes v. Gulf Oil Corp. - §343
Hazel Atlas Glass Co. v. Hartford Empire Co. - §1906
Helicopteros Nacionales de Colombia, S.A. v. Hall - §73, 74
Helzberg's Diamond Shops, Inc. v. Valley West Des Moines Shopping Center, Inc. - §1014

Henry L. Doherty & Co. v. Goodman - §17
Henson v. East Lincoln Township - §1164
Hess v. Pawlowski - §17
Heyman v. Commerce & Industry Insurance Co. - §1529
Hickman v. Taylor - §§1339, 1364, 1376-1378
Hills Transportation Co. v. Southwest Forest Industries - §859
Hinderlider v. La Plata River Co. - §529
Hodgson v. Colonnades, Inc. - §870
Hoffman v. Blaski - §168
Holmes v. Continental Can Co. - §1134
Holmgren v. State Farm Mutual Automobile Insurance Co. - §1373
Hooker Chemical Co., United States v. - §1437
Horsemen's Benevolent Association v. Valley Racing Association - §2012
Horton v. Liberty Mutual Insurance Co. - §338
Hoshman v. Esso Standard Oil Co. - §708
Hovey v. Elliott - §1466
Huber v. American President Lines - §1769
Hurn v. Oursler - §390
Hutchinson, People v. - §1822
Hyde Properties, Inc. v. McCoy - §1668

IBM v. Edelstein - §§1206, 1497
Illinois v. City of Milwaukee - §534
In re - see name of party
Insurance Corp. of Ireland v. Compagnie des Bauxites de Guinee - §§44, 88, 118
International Business Machines Corp. v. United States (1973) - §1484
International Business Machines Corp. v. United States (1975) - §§1476, 1491
International Products Corp. v. Koons - §1485
International Shoe v. Washington - §§21, 22, 25, 26, 57, 68, 69, 92, 100

J.I. Case v. Borak - §358
Jacobsen v. Filler - §1548
James Daniel Good Real Property, United States v. - §248
Japanese Products Antitrust Litigation, *In re* - §1557
Jenkins v. General Motors Corp. - §1076
Jenkins v. Reneau - §972
Jett v. Phillips & Associates - §969
Jetty v. Craco - §790
Jorgensen v. York Ice Machinery Corp. - §1821

Kamen v. Kemper Financial Services, Inc. - §531
Kaufman v. DeMuths - §1851

Keckley v. Payton - §816
Keeton v. Hustler Magazine, Inc. - §§49, 50
Kerr v. United States District Court - §2121
Kiernan v. Van Schaik - §1708
Kilpatrick v. Texas & Pacific Railway - §897
Klaxon Co. v. Stentor Electric Manufacturing Co. - §§177, 520, 522
Kleiner v. First National Bank of Atlanta - §1145
Klotz v. Superior Electric Products Corp. - §1000
Kokkonen v. Guardian Life Insurance Co. - §905
Korean Air Lines Disaster of Sept. 1, 1983, *In re* - §180
Korwek v. Hunt - §1120
Kothe v. Smith - §1586
Kramer v. Caribbean Mills, Inc. - §313
Kulchar v. Kulchar - §1913
Kulko v. Superior Court - §§37, 41, 42

LASA Per L'Industria v. Alexander - §§387, 823
LaBuy v. Howes Leather Co. - §2024
Laddon v. Superior Court - §1323
LaFollette v. Herron - §815
LaMar v. H & B Novelty & Loan Co. - §1166
Lambert v. Southern Counties Gas Co. - §577
Landau v. Salam - §955
Langenkamp v. Culp - §1656
Lapenna v. Upjohn Co. - §1216
Lapin v. Shulton - §1912
Larionoff v. United States - §1086
Lauro Lines, Inc. v. Chasser - §1982
Lavender v. Kurn - §§1747, 1749
Law v. Northern Assurance Co. - §1806
Lear, Inc. v. Adkins - §268
Leatherman v. Tarrant County Narcotics Intelligence and Coordination Unit - §684
Lee v. Hensley - §706
Lehman Bros. v. Schein - §528
Lelsz v. Kavanagh - §1139
Leroy v. Great Western United Corp. - §129
Liberty Mutual Insurance Co. v. Fales - §817
Licht & Semonoff, Appeal of - §730
Lind v. Schenley Industries, Inc. - §§1859, 1862
Lindemann v. San Joaquin Cotton Oil Co. - §1846
Lindy Brothers Builders, Inc. v. American Radiator Corp. - §1155
Linhart v. Nelson - §§1829, 1872
Link v. Wabash Railroad - §1470
Liodas v. Sahadi - §1782
Liteky v. United States - §1719
Livingston v. Jefferson - §150

Louisville & Nashville Railroad v. Mottley - §§260, 366, 370
Lowery v. Clouse - §1801
Lumbermen's Mutual Insurance Co. v. Massachusetts Bonding and Insurance Co. - §822
Lundeen v. Cordner - §§1523, 1566, 1753
Lyons v. Wickhorst - §1630
Lytle v. Household Manufacturing, Inc. - §1665

McCormick v. Kopmann - §575
McCourtie v. United States Steel Corp. - §1801
McDonald v. Pless - §§1818, 1820
McDonald, *In re* - §2023
McDonnell Douglas Corp. v. District Court - §1086
McDonough Power Equipment, Inc. v. Greenwood - §1824
McGee v. International Life Insurance Co. - §§23, 32, 49
McKenna v. Ortho Pharmaceutical Corp. - §526
McPherson v. Hoffman - §995
Mack Trucks, Inc. v. Arrow Aluminum Castings Co. - §103
Mahoney v. Coralejo - §608
Maicobo Investment Corp. v. von der Heide - §1914
Marcera v. Chinlund - §§1162, 1164, 1168
Marshall v. Ford Motor Co. - §1793
Marshall v. Mulrenin - §§512, 515
Martin v. Taylor - §1902
Martin v. Wilks - §§989, 2099
Martino v. McDonald's Systems, Inc. - §2072
Mather Construction Co. v. United States - §938
Mathews v. Eldridge - §§244, 250
Matsushita Electric Industries Co. v. Zenith Radio Corp. - §§1528, 1557
Mazer v. Lipschutz - §1792
Megarry v. Norton - §613
Meissner v. Papas - §1886
Mendoza, United States v. - §2108
Mennonite Board of Missions v. Adams - §208
Merrell Dow Pharmaceuticals, Inc. v. Thompson - §§359, 360, 362, 363, 372
Mertens v. Abbott Laboratories - §1094
Mesner, Estate of - §1844
Metropolitan Life Insurance Co. v. Taylor - §§367, 434
Miller & Miller Auctioneers, Inc. v. G.W. Murphy Industries, Inc. - §1039
Milliken v. Meyer - §70
Mills v. Electric Auto Lite Co. - §1155

Minneapolis & St. Louis Railroad v. Bombalis - §1647
Minneapolis, St. Paul & Sault Ste. Marie Railway v. Moquin - §1844
Mitchell v. Forsyth - §1982
Mitchell v. W.T. Grant Co. - §§237, 240-242
Montgomery Ward & Co. v. Duncan - §1831
Moore v. Chesapeake & Ohio Railway - §359, 362
Moralez v. Meat Cutters Local 536 - §445
Mullane v. Central Hanover Bank & Trust Co. - §§63, 201, 203, 205, 208
Myers v. Stephens - §625

Napolitano v. Compania Sud Americana de Vapores - §2003
National American Corp. v. Federal Republic of Nigeria - §973
National Association of Government Employees, Inc. v. National Federation of Federal Employees - §731
National Equipment Rental Co. v. Szukhent - §76
National Hockey League v. Metropolitan Hockey Club, Inc. - §1464
National Mutual Insurance Co. v. Tidewater Transfer Co. - §289
National Union Electric Co. v. Matsushita Electric Industrial Co. - §1277
National Union of Marine Cooks v. Arnold - §1922
Natural Resources Defense Council v. United States Nuclear Regulatory Commission - §1014
Navarro Savings Association v. Lee - §298
Neely v. Martin K. Eby Construction Co. - §1841
Nelson v. Miller - §§105, 106
Nemeth v. Hair - §916
New England Merchants National Bank v. Hughes - §1630
New Orleans Public Service, Inc. v. United Gas Pipe Line Co. - §1013
New York Central Railroad v. Johnson - §1881
Newing v. Cheatham - §605
Newman-Green, Inc. v. Alfonzo-Larrain - §321
Noonan v. Cunard Steamship Co. - §902
North Georgia Finishing, Inc. v. Di-Chem, Inc. - §§241, 242
Northern District of California "Dalkon Shield" IUD Products Liability Litigation, *In re* - §1088
Northern Pacific Railroad v. Herbert - §1883
Norwood v. Kirkpatrick - §167

Nysco Laboratories, Inc., United States v. - §2049

Oklahoma Tax Commission v. Graham - §430
Omni Capital International v. Rudolf Wolff & Co., Ltd. - §98
Oppenheimer Fund, Inc. v. Sanders - §1130
Orcutt v. Ferranini - §927
Orris v. Higgins - §2000
Osborn v. Bank of the United States - §§348, 377, 379
Oscanyon v. Arms Co. - §1765
Ostrom v. Greene - §942
Othman v. Globe Indemnity Co. - §303
Owen Equipment & Erection Co. v. Kroger - §§384, 392, 405, 410, 413, 1001
Oxford First Corp. v. PNC Liquidating Corp. - §97

Pacific Greyhound Lines v. Zane - §1793
Pacific Railroad of Missouri v. Missouri Pacific Railway - §1914
Packard v. Provident National Bank - §414
Palestroni v. Jacobs - §1815
Palmer v. Hoffman - §771
Parklane Hosiery v. Shore - §§2080, 2099, 2105
Parrish & Sons v. County Sanitation District - §852
Pastene v. Pardini - §780
Patterson Enterprises, Inc. v. Bridgestone/Firestone, Inc. - §413
Pavelic & LeFlore v. Marvel Entertainment Group - §743
Payne v. Travenol Laboratories, Inc. - §1115
Peacock Records, Inc. v. Checker Records, Inc. - §1905
Peerless Insurance Co. v. Superior Court - §973
Pennoyer v. Neff - §§4-7, 10, 11, 14-16, 18-21, 91
Pennsylvania Fire Insurance Co. v. Gold Issue Mining & Milling Co. - §78
Pennsylvania Railroad v. Chamberlin - §1748
Pennzoil Co. v. Texaco, Inc. - §1952
Penrod Drilling Co. v. Johnson - §127
People v. - *see* name of party
Perkins v. Benguet Consolidated Mining Co. - §73
Perma Research & Development Co. v. Singer Co. - §1524
Pernell v. Southall Realty - §1656
Perry v. Allegheny Airlines, Inc. - §1708

Philadelphia Electric Co. v. Anaconda American Brass Co. - §1151
Phillips Petroleum Co. v. Shutts - §§82, 1105, 1106, 1165
Pierce v. Cook & Co. - §1909
Pierce v. Wright - §728
Pingatore v. Montgomery Ward & Co. - §1773
Piper Aircraft Co. v. Reyno - §§183, 191, 192
Plains Growers, Inc. v. Ickes Braun Glasshouses, Inc. - §899
Planned Parenthood v. Citizens of Community Action - §1013
Platt, Estate of - §1999
Poller v. Columbia Broadcasting System, Inc. - §1528
Ponce v. Tractor Supply Co. - §2105
Portman v. American Home Products Corp. - §1861
Porto Transportation Co. v. Consolidated Diesel Electric Corp. - §766
Powell v. Lampton - §708
Powers v. Allstate Insurance Co. - §1885
Powers v. Ashton - §921
Premier Electrical Construction Co. v. National Electrical Contractors Association - §1136
Proctor & Gamble Independent Union v. Proctor & Gamble Manufacturing Co. - §1546
Provident Bank & Trust Co. v. Patterson - §§965, 988
Prudential Oil & Materials Co. v. Hamlin - §978
Publicker v. Shallcross - §1913
Puerto Rico Aqueduct & Sewer Authority v. Metcalf & Eddy - §1982

Ragan v. Merchants Transfer & Warehouse Co. - §508
Rainer v. Community Memorial Hospital - §864
Rakes v. United States - §1829
Rakus v. Erie-Lackawanna Railroad - §1368
Rannard v. Lockheed Aircraft Corp. - §605
Raphael J. Musicus, Inc. v. Safeway Stores, Inc. - §151
Read v. Safeway Stores - §609
Redmond v. Commerce Trust Co. - §1087
Reitano v. Yankwich - §1925
Rekeweg v. Federal Mutual Insurance Co. - §955
Resnick v. American Dental Association - §1146
Revere Copper & Brass, Inc. v. Aetna Casualty & Surety Co. - §385
Rice v. City of Philadelphia - §§1090, 1098
Richards v. United States - §523
Richmond v. Brooks - §1239

Rinehart v. Locke - §2055
Rollins v. City & County of San Francisco - §1917
Ronzio v. Denver & Rio Grande Railroad - §331
Rosado v. Wyman - §372
Rosenberg Bros. & Co. v. Curtis Brown Co. - §73
Ross v. A.H. Robins Co. - §681
Ross v. Bernhard - §1667
Rozier v. Ford Motor Co. - §1906
Rudin v. Luman - §1849
Rush v. Savchuk - §§13, 56, 61, 67
Ryan v. United States Lines - §1908
Ryder v. Jefferson Hotel Co. - §951

Sackler v. Sackler - §1499
St. Paul Mercury Indemnity Co. v. Red Cab Co. - §326
Sakamoto v. N.A.B. Trucking Co. - §1800
Salve Regina College v. Russell - §527
San Juan Dupont Plaza Hotel Fire Litigation, *In re* - §1613
Sanders v. Superior Court - §1307
Sandobal v. Armour & Co. - §977
Santoro v. Carbone - §776
Sartheiser v. Superior Court - §2095
Sassano v. Roullard - §1795
Savage v. Van Marle - §547
Schlagenhauf v. Holder - §§1294, 1488, 2025
Schubert v. Reich - §1925
Schuyler v. United Air Lines - §1852
Scott v. Fancher - §821
Searle & Co. v. Superior Court - §612
Searle Brothers v. Searle - §2098
Seattle Times Co. v. Rhinehart - §§1432, 1440
Seawell, United States v. - §1819
Security Pacific National Bank v. Geernaert - §2009
Seider v. Roth - §13
Seivell v. Hines - §1764
Shaffer v. Heitner - §§8, 12, 56-58, 62-66, 68, 92, 114, 2068
Shamrock Oil Co. v. Sheets - §450
Sharff v. Superior Court - §1299
Shea v. Donohoe Construction Co. - §1471
Shelton v. Pargo, Inc. - §1152
Sherman v. Hallbauer - §849
Shields v. Barrow - §964
Shippy v. Peninsula Rapid Transit Co. - §1771
Shook v. Pearson - §626
Siler v. Louisville & Nashville Railroad - §378
Sing v. International Union - §209
Singh v. Daimler-Benz AG - §283

Civil Procedure—387

Sirota v. Solitron Devices, Inc. - §1111
Skelly Oil Co. v. Phillips Petroleum Co. - §368
Skidmore v. Syntex Laboratories, Inc. - §857
Skolnick v. Hallett - §690
Slemons v. Paterson - §1852
Slocum v. New York Life Insurance Co. - §1757
Smith v. Barry - §1944
Smith v. Circle P Ranch Co. - §1267
Smith v. Industrial Valley Title Insurance Co. - §363
Smith v. Kansas City Title & Trust Co. - §§359, 362
Smith v. Los Angeles Bookbinders Union - §628
Smith v. Sperling - §311
Smoot v. Fox - §904
Sniadach v. Family Finance Corp. - §231
Societe Internationale v. Rogers - §1467
Sosna v. Iowa - §§1078, 1089
Sosnow v. Storatti Corp. - §920
Southern Leasing Partners, Ltd v. McMullan - §721
Spangler v. United States - §1031
Sparks v. Berntsen - §1828
Sponholz v. Stanislaus - §440
State v. Hills - §1793
State Farm Fire & Casualty Co. v. Tashire - §§284, 1041, 1048
Stewart v. Winter - §1110
Stewart Organization, Inc. v. Ricoh Corp. - §§171, 198, 199, 511, 517
Stilwell v. Travelers Insurance Co. - §1904
Stoll v. Gottleib - §2060
Strandell v. Jackson County - §1644
Strawbridge v. Curtiss - §286
Stringfellow v. Concerned Neighbors in Action - §1023
Sullivan v. Nesbit - §1782
Supreme Tribe of Ben-Hur v. Cauble - §§301, 1100
Sutliff, Inc. v. Donovan Companies - §677
Swift v. Tyson - §§463-470, 474, 476, 478, 479, 529
Synanon Church v. United States - §2086
System Fed. 91 Railway Employees v. Wright - §1908

Tanner v. United States - §1821
Tele-Views News Co. v. S.R.B. TV Publishing Co. - §897
Temple v. Synthes Corp. - §970
Terrell v. DeConna - §1660

Textile Workers Union v. Lincoln Mills - §§350, 532
Theodorf v. Lipsey - §1801
Thermtron Products, Inc. v. Hermansdorfer - §§458, 460, 2024
Thiel v. Southern Pacific Co. - §§1687, 2002
Thillens, Inc. v. Community Currency Exchange Association - §1163
Thorton v. Wahl - §§727, 732
Throckmorton, United States v. - §1913
Ticor Title Insurance Co. v. Brown - §1106
Tiller v. Atlantic Coast Line - §852
Titus v. Mercedes Benz of North America - §1463
Toledo Scale v. Computering Scale - §1852
Tomera v. Galt - §680
Torres v. Oakland Scavenger Co. - §1945
Trammel v. United States - §1358
Trans World Airlines, Inc. v. Civil Aeronautics Board - §1030
Travel Agents Malpractice Action Corps v. Regal Cultural Society - §946
Trbovich v. United Mine Workers - §1017
Treinies v. Sunshine Mining Co. - §2052
Trezza v. Dame - §1784
Triodyne, Inc. v. Superior Court - §629
Triplett v. Williams - §922
Tull v. United States - §§1658, 1659
Tulsa Professional Collection Services, Inc. v. Pope, §208

Union Carbide Corp. Gas Plant Disaster at Bhopal, India, *In re* - §183
Union Electric Light & Power Co. v. Snyder Estate Co. - §1848
Union Pacific Railroad, United States v. - §97
Union Tool Co. v. Wilson - §1491
United Mine Workers v. Gibbs - §§379, 390, 399, 407, 417, 418, 419, 422, 423
United States v. - *see* name of party
United States Gypsum, United States v. - §1992
United States Parole Commission v. Geraghty - §1078
United Steelworkers v. R.H. Bouligny, Inc. - §297
Universal Film Exchanges, Inc. v. Lust - §1903
University of Pennsylvania v. E.E.O.C. - §1362
Upjohn Co. v. United States - §§1338, 1351, 1373

Valley Bank v. Superior Court - §1327
Van Dusen v. Barrack - §178

Vasquez v. Superior Court - §1063
Verlinden B.V. v. Central Bank of Nigeria - §349
Vesley v. Sager - §701

Walker v. Armco Steel Co. - §508
Walker v. City of Hutchinson - §202
Walker v. Sauvinet - §1647
Wallace v. Herron - §38
Wallin v. Fuller - §1607
Ward v. Taggart - §2008
Warren Insurance Agency v. Surpur Timber Co. - §926
Watson v. Cannon Shoe Co. - §872
Watson v. Roberts, Scott & Co. - §2087
Western Union Telegraph Co. v. Pennsylvania - §56
Westgate-California Corp., *In re* - §2083
Wetzel v. Liberty Mutual Insurance Co. - §1121
White Lighting Co. v. Wolfson - §632
Willden v. Washington National Insurance Co. - §1786
Williams v. Florida - §1696

Withers v. Tucker - §937
Wolpe v. Poretsky - §1024
Woolen v. Surtran Taxicabs, Inc. - §1138
World-Wide Volkswagen Corp. v. Woodson - §§27-29, 31, 33-35, 39, 44, 45, 106
Worthington v. Kaiser Health Plan - §974
Wright v. Arkansas Activities Association - §943
Wright v. Jeep Corp. - §1413
Wright v. Schock - §1114
Wulfsohn v. Russo-Asiatic Bank - §1852
Wyman v. Newhouse - §93

Xerox v. IBM - §1387

Yaffe v. Powers - §1069
Yorty v. Chandler - §613

Zahn v. International Paper Co. - §96, 1101
Zenith Radio Corp. v. Matsushita Electric Industrial Co. - §§1430, 1436
Zielinski v. Philadelphia Piers, Inc. - §757

Civil Procedure—389

INDEX

A

ABATEMENT, PLEAS IN
    See Answer
ADDITUR, §§1891-1893
ADMISSIONS
    See Discovery; Requests for admission
ADVISORY JURY, §1675
    See also Jury
AFFIRMATIVE DEFENSES
    See Answer
ALTERNATIVE DISPUTE RESOLUTION, §1590
    See also Pretrial conferences and managerial judging
ALTERNATIVE FINDINGS, §§2083-2084
    See also Res Judicata
ANCILLARY JURISDICTION
    See Supplemental jurisdiction
ANSWER, §§750-798
    See also Complaint; Pleadings
    affirmative defenses, §§770-790
        contract cases, §§775-783
        defined, §770
        dilatory pleas, §§786-789
        federal practice, §§771-772
        new matter, failure to plead, §790
        pleas in abatement, §§786-789
        statute of limitations, §§784-785
        tort cases, §774
    amended, §850
    denials, §§751-769
        equivocal. *See* Requests for admission
        failure to deny, §§767-769
        general, §752
        material allegations, §769
        negative pregnant rule, §§759-763
        on lack of information, §§764-766
        special denial by parts, §757
        specific, §§756-769
        times, dates, places, §761
    procedure, §§791-796
ANTICIPATORY DEFENSES, §708
    See also Complaint
ANTITRUST CASES, §269
APPEAL, §§1919-2026
    appeal bonds, §§1950-1952
    appealable orders, §1968
    certified question, §1487
    "clear error" test, §§1992-1993
    courts of, §§1926-1943
        federal, §§1926-1937
        state, §§1938-1943
    discovery orders, §§1483-1491
    discretionary rulings, §§2003-2004
    extraordinary writs, §§2018-2026
        mandamus, §2018
        prohibition, §2018
    fact and law, §§1994-2002
    final decision rule, §§1957-1985. *See also* Final decision rule
    harmless error, §§2005-2008
    invited error, §2012
    judgment n.o.v., §§1840-1841
    jury instructions, §§1792-1793, 2010
    jury verdicts, §§1988-1990
    mandamus, §§2018-2026
    motion for new trial, §§1861-1864
    nonappealable orders, §§1963-1970
    nonjury trials, §§1991-1993
    notice of appeal, §1944
        premature, §1947
    orders granting new trial, §§1861-1864, 1964-1966
    procedure, §§1944-1956
    record, §§1953-1955
    res judicata, §§2048-2050
    right to appeal, §§1920-1924
        waiver of, §1925
    separate instrument rule, §1962
    stay of proceedings below, §1956
    summary judgment, §§1568-1570
    time limits, §§1946-1949
    trial de novo, §2017
    waiver of objections, §§2009-2016
    weight of evidence, §§1855-1864
APPEARANCE
    in personam jurisdiction, §§83-90
    limited, §117
    special appearance rule, §§85-88
APPELLATE PROCEDURE
    See Appeal
ARBITRATION, §§1615-1630
    See also Pretrial conferences and managerial judging
ARGUMENT TO JURY
    See Jury
ASSIGNMENT OF CLAIM
    diversity jurisdiction, §313
ASSIGNMENTS
    partial, §§917-918, 973
    real party in interest rule, §§912-918. *See also* Real party in interest rule
ATTACHMENT JURISDICTION, §§227-254, 2065-2068
ATTORNEYS' FEES
    class actions, §1155

B

"BLUE RIBBON" JURY, §1682
    See also Jury

C

CAPACITY TO BE SUED
    corporations, §938
    guardian, §936
    incompetents, §§936-937
    individuals, §§935-937
    lack of, §§947-948

partnerships, §§939-941
unincorporated associations, §§942-946
CERTIFICATION BY ATTORNEYS, §§709-749, 1479-1482
See also Pleadings
CERTIFIED FINALITY, §§1973, 1977
See also Final decision rule
CHOICE OF LAW, §§519-528
See also Erie doctrine
venue and, §§177-180
CITIZENS LIVING ABROAD, §288
CITIZENSHIP
See Diversity jurisdiction; Territorial jurisdiction
CLAIM PRECLUSION, §§2028-2030, 2034-2072
See also Res judicata
CLAIMS, JOINDER OF
See Class actions; Joinder
CLAIMS, SPLITTING OF, §§633-635
CLASS ACTIONS
adequate representation, §§1079-1083
attorneys' fees, §1155
bilateral class action, §§1166-1168
certification, §§1108-1115
common predominant question, §§1091-1097
common question, §§1070-1074
communications with class members, §§1142-1147
consent to class, §82
decertification, §1082
defendant class actions, §§1159-1168
discovery, §1141
dismissal and compromise, §§1148-1152
distribution of proceeds, §§1153-1154
diversity jurisdiction, §§301, 395, 1100
effect of judgment, §§1156-1158
Federal Rules, §§1062-1064
grounds for, §§1084-1098
historical background, §§1058-1061
"hybrid," §1061
intervention, §§1137-1140
joinder, §§1058-1059, 1064, 1073
jurisdictional amount, §§396, 1101-1103
manageability, §§1096-1097
notice requirements, §§1068, 1121-1130
opting out, §§1131-1136
pendent jurisdiction, §§394-396
personal jurisdiction, §§1105-1107, 1165
representative's claim, §§1075-1078
requirements for, §§1064-1083
settlement before certification, §§1150-1152
shareholders' derivative actions. *See* Shareholders' derivative actions
size of claim, §1076
"spurious," §1061
state courts, §1063
statute of limitations, §§1116-1120
subclasses, §1083
supplemental jurisdiction, §§394-396, 413
"true," §§1061-1063
typical claim, §§1075-1078
"CLEAR ERROR" TEST, §§1992-1993
See also Appeal
CODE PLEADING, §§543-552, 862-864

COLLATERAL ESTOPPEL, §§2074-2088
See also Res judicata
COLLUSIVE JOINDER
See Joinder
COMMON COUNTS
See Compalint
COMMON LAW PLEADINGS, §§539-542
COMMON QUESTIONS
class actions, §§1070-1074, 1091-1097
permissive joinder, §956
COMPLAINT, §§556-646
See also Answer; Pleadings
allegations
alternate and inconsistent, §§573-577
anticipating defenses, §578
direct, §§565-568
information and belief, §§569-572
jurisdictional, §§561-562
anticipatory defenses, §708
challenges to, §§647-708
anticipatory defenses, §708
demurrer, §§648-670. *See also* Demurrer
federal practice, §§671-708
judgment on the pleadings, §§888-893
motion for more definite statement, §§687-688
motion procedure, §§692-698
motion to dismiss, §§672-686
amendment, §685
sufficiency of complaint, §§675-684
motion to strike, §§668-670, 689-691
other rules, §§699-708
common counts, §§631-632
consolidation of separate actions, §§643-646
contract actions, §§614-622
damages, §§623-630
contract, §§624-626
defamation, §628
tort, §§627-630
defamation, §§613, 628
ejectment, §602
errors, §§559-560
form of, §§557-594
fraud, §§610-612
joinder of claims, §§636-642
jurisdictional allegations, §§561-562
negligence, §§603-608
prayer for relief, §§580-586
products liability, §609
separate causes of action, §564
splitting of claims, §§633-635
subscription, §§587-594, 709-749
substance and procedure, §§596-600
sufficiency of, §§675-684
trespass to land, §601
verification, §§590-594
voluntary dismissal, §§894-905
CONFLICTING JUDGMENTS, §2052
See also Res Judicata
CONSOLIDATION OF ACTIONS, §1035
CO-OWNERS
See Joinder

COPYRIGHTS, §268
CORAM NOBIS, §§1916-1918
CORPORATIONS
    capacity to be sued, §938
    depositions, §§1215-1216
    diversity jurisdiction, §§290-292
    interrogatories, §1245
    venue, §§125, 292
COUNTERCLAIMS, §§799-820
    compulsory, §§414, 813-815
    cross-complaints compared, §827
    "cross-demands deemed compensated," §819
    dismissal, §811
    joinder, §§807-810
    jurisdiction, §§800-801, 809-810
    permissive, §812
    pleading, §§803-806
    statute of limitations, §§816-820
    supplemental jurisdiction, §§382, 386, 414
    venue, §802
CROSS-CLAIMS, §§821-828
    counterclaims compared, §827
    generally, §821
    impleader compared, §§387, 828, 952
    jurisdiction, §823
    parties, §826
    pleading, §§824-825
    supplemental jurisdiction, §387
CROSS-COMPLAINTS, §§829-840
    form, §§830-832
    generally, §829
    indemnification, §840
    joinder of claims, §§834-836
    joinder of parties, §833
    pleading, §§837-840
CROSS-DEMANDS
    See Counterclaims

D

DAMAGES
    See Complaint
DECLARATORY RELIEF
    amount in diversity cases, §332
    class actions, §1164
    federal question, §368
    right to jury trial, §1660
DEFAMATION ACTIONS
    See Complaint
DEFAULT
    See Pleadings; Res judicata
DEFENSES, AFFIRMATIVE
    See Answer
DEFENSES, ANTICIPATORY
    See Anticipatory defenses
DEMEANOR EVIDENCE, §§1751-1754
DEMURRER
    common law, §§648-650
    criticism of, §667
    failure to raise grounds for, §664
    general, §§649, 655

    grounds for, §654
    overruled, §661
    rulings on, §§659-663
    special, §§650, 655
    state practice, §§651-670
    sustained, §§662-663
DENIALS
    See Answer
DEPOSITIONS, §§1202-1240
    See also Discovery
    compulsory, §§1211-1216
    corporations, §§1215-1216
    defined, §1202
    interrogatories compared, §1242. *See also* Interrogatories
    notice, §§1217-1220
    numerical limits, §1207-1210
    optional, §1206
    place of, §§1213, 1442-1446
    questioning, §§1221-1232
    real evidence, subpoena for inspection of, §§1291-1292
    timeliness, §§1203-1205
    transcription, §§1233-1234
    unnecessary, §1448
    unreasonably conducted, §1447
    use at trial, §§1235-1240
    videotape, §1234
DILATORY PLEAS
    See also Answer
DIRECT ESTOPPEL, §2073
    See also Res judicata
DIRECT VERDICT, §§1737-1762, 1836-1837
    See also Judgment as a matter of law
DISCOVERY
    appellate review of discovery orders, §§1483-1491
    bank records, §1327
    class actions, §1141
    collateral purpose, §§1180-1182
    common law, §1169
    contentions, §1328
    cost to litigants, §1178
    depositions, §§1202-1240. *See also* Depositions
    documents, §§1219-1220, 1276-1292
    duty to supplement, §§1302-1308
    expert reports, §§1390-1415
    Federal Rules, §1173
    financial status, §§1324-1327
    history, §§1169-1173
    insurance coverage, §1323
    interrogatories, §§1241-1255. *See also* Interrogatories
    judicial limitations, §§1311-1314
    medical examination, §§1293-1301, 1478
    pretrial conference, §§1578-1580
    private investigation, §§1497-1499
    privilege, §§1329-1363
    protective orders, §§1416-1450
        confidential information, §§1418-1441
        depositions, §§1442-1447
        First Amendment limitations, §§1438-1441
        good cause requirement, §§1416-1448
        inconvenience, §§1442-1446
        no waiver, §1450

prior orders, §1449
privacy interests, §1422
public access, §§1431-1436
stipulated orders, §1423
"umbrella" orders, §§1424-1430
unduly burdensome, §1448
relation to proof, §§1309-1314
relevancy, §§1315-1328
requests for admission, §§1256-1275. *See also* Requests for admission
requests for inspection of documents, §§1276-1292. *See also* Requests for documents and other things
required disclosures, §§1592-1599
Rule 16(b) meeting, §1579
sanctions for noncompliance, §§1451-1482
   contempt, §§1475-1478
   costs award, §§1472-1474
   review of contempt citation, §1491
scope of, §§1309-1328
trial preparation materials, §§1364-1415
use at trial, §§1235-1240, 1492-1496
witness's statements, §§1381-1388, 1494-1496
witnesses, §1327. *See also* Interrogatories
work product, §§1364-1389

DISMISSAL
by lease of court, §§901-905
involuntary
   disciplinary device, §§1460, 2058
   motion for judgment as a matter of law, §§1766-1769
   res judicata, §§2053, 2058
notice of, §§896-899
voluntary, §§894-905
   code practice, §895
   common law, §894
   federal practice, §§896-905

DISQUALIFICATION OF JUDGE, §§1713-1724

DIVERSITY JURISDICTION, §§281-346
See also Supplemental jurisdiction
assignment of claim, §313
choice of law, §§519-528
citizenship, §§287-304
   artificial entities, §§293-298
   business trusts, §298
   class actions, §§301, 395, 1100
   corporations, §§290-292
   executors, §304
   fictitious defendants, §§302-303
   guardians, §304
   labor unions, §297
   natural persons, §§287-289
   partnerships, §§294-295
   professional corporations, §296
   resident aliens, §§299-300
      constitutional question, §283
   trustees, §304
   unincorporated associations, §§293-298
collusive appointments, §§314, 320
complete diversity requirement, §286
constitutional authority, §§281-284
diversity statute, §§285-330
   arguments for repeal, §§344-346
   constitutional question, §283
   fictitious defendants, §§302-303
   joinder, §§317-319
   jurisdictional amount, §§324-339
      aggregation of claims, §§334-339
      counterclaims, §§338-339
      declaratory relief, §332
      in general, §§324-329
      interest and costs, §333
      judgment for lesser amount, §330
      nonmonetary relief, §331
   lack of diversity, §§321-323
   minimal diversity requirement, §346
   nondiverse party, §§312-323
      appointment of representative, §320
      collusive joinder, §§312-315
      dismissal of, §321
      necessary party, §322
      valid joinder, §§317-319
   realigning parties, §§310-311
   shareholders' derivative suits, §311
   subject matter discretionary jurisdiction, §§340-343
      domestic relations, §341
      local actions, §343
      probate proceedings, §342
   substituted party, §309
   supplemental jurisdiction, §§392, 404, 409-415
   time for determining, §§305-309

DOMICILE
See Diversity jurisdiction, citizenship

DUE PROCESS
See Jurisdiction; Minimum contacts

"DYNAMITE CHARGE," §1811
See also Jury

E

EJECTMENT
See complaint

EQUITY RULES, §§542, 1654-1665

EQUIVOCAL DENIAL
See Requests for admission

***ERIE* DOCTRINE**
See also Jurisdiction
choice of state law, §§519-528
   determining applicable law, §§524-528
   Erie principles, §§526-528
   existence of conflict, §§507-518
   federal choice of law exception, §523
   general rule, §520
   statutory interpleader, §521
Erie Railroad v. Tompkins, §§470-480
Erie rule, §470
Federal Rules vs. state law, §§496-518
   arguably procedural, §501
   Enabling Act limitations, §§502-506
   modern approach, §§507-518
   no federal general common law, §§501, 508
   practice and procedure requirement, §502
   presumption of validity, §504
   substantive rights limitation, §§503, 513

historical development, §§462-469
interest balancing approach, §§488-495, 518
interpleader, §§521, 1057
modern approach, §§507-518
    Acts of Congress, §511
    determining if conflict exists, §508
    Federal Constitution, §510
    Federal Rules, §§512-515
    judge-made procedural rules, §§516-518
    resolution of conflict, §§509-518
"no federal general common law" dichotomy, §§529-535
    borrowed state law, §531
    congressional authorization, §532
    foreign relations, §535
    general rule, §529
    interstate disputes, §534
    sufficient federal interest, §533
outcome determination test, §§485-487
Rules Enabling Act, §§502-515
Rules of Decision Act, §462
sources of federal law, §§500-518
state substantive and federal procedural rule, §482
underlying policies, §499
validity of Federal rules, §§496-518

ESTOPPEL, COLLATERAL
See Collateral estoppel

ESTOPPEL, DIRECT
See Direct estoppel

EVIDENCE, PRESENTATION OF, §§1729-1735

EVIDENCE, REQUESTS FOR INSPECTION OF REAL
See Requests for inspection of real evidence

EXECUTORS, §§304, 314, 320, 923-925

EXPERT REPORTS
See Discovery

EXPERT WITNESS LISTS
See Interrogatories

EXTRAORDINARY WRITS
See Appeal

F

FAILURE TO STATE CLAIM, §§372, 674-683

FEDERAL JURISDICTION
See Jurisdiction

FEDERAL LAW, SOURCES OF, §§500-518
See also Erie doctrine
Acts of Congress, §511
Federal Constitution, §510
Federal Rules, §§500-504, 512-515
judge-made procedural rules, §§516-518

FEDERAL QUESTION JURISDICTION, §§347-378
"arising under" federal law, §§356-358
assertion of federal right, §§359-363
constitutional provisions, §§347-350
no jurisdictional amount, §375
special federal question statutes, §349
statutory authorization, §§351-354
sufficiency of assertion, §§371-374
    dismissal on pleadings, §372
    res judicata, §373
    supplemental jurisdiction, §§374, 393, 400-403

well-pleaded complaint rule, §§364-370
    declaratory judgment, §368
    election not to assert claim, §369
    preemption, §367
    Supreme Court jurisdiction compared, §370

FEDERAL RULES OF CIVIL PROCEDURE, §§500-504, 512-515
See also Erie doctrine

FICTITIOUS DEFENDANTS, §§302-303, 437

FINAL DECISION RULE, §§1957-1985
See also Appeal
certified finality, §§1973, 1977
common law, §1958
exceptions, §§1972-1985
    collateral orders, §§1980-1985
    discretionary review, §§1977-1979
    equity, §§1975-1976
federal courts, §1960
jurisdictional character, §1971
nonappealable orders, §§1963-1970
partial final decisions, §§1972-1974
practical finality, §1985
separate instrument rule, §1962
state courts, §1961

FORUM NON CONVENIENS, §§182-199
choice of law, §195
contractual limitations, §§196-199
federal court, §183
forum shopping, §185
in general, §182
procedure, §§186-194
state court, §184
uniform acts, §185

G

GENERAL DEMURRER
See Demurrer

GENERAL DENIAL
See Answer

GENERAL JURISDICTION, §§69-74
See also Territorial jursidiction

GOVERNMENT RECORDS
See Discovery

GUARDIANS
capacity to be sued, §936
diversity jurisdiction, §304

H

HARMLESS ERROR, §§2005-2008
See also Appeal

"HYBRID" CLASS ACTIONS
See Class actions

I

IDENTICAL ISSUES, §§2087-2088
See also Res judicata

IMPLEADER, §§990-1008
cross-claims compared, §§387, 828

indemnification, §§991-1001
jurisdiction, §1006
pleadings, §§1002-1004
potential liability, §§996-1000
separate trials, §1005
supplemental jurisdiction, §§383, 386
venue, §1006
IN PERSONAM JURISDICTION
See Territorial jurisdiction
IN REM JURISDICTION
See Territorial jurisdiction
INCOMPETENTS
capacity to be sued, §§936-937
right to disaffirm judgment, §937
INDEMNIFICATION, §§911-1001
INDEPENDENT SUIT TO SET ASIDE JUDGMENT, §§1912-1915
INDISPENSABLE PARTY
ancillary jurisdiction, §§389, 409
joinder, §964
INSURANCE
discovery, §1323
impleading insurer, §999
in rem, §§13, 56, 67
INTERPLEADER
See also Joinder
cross-claims and counterclaims, §§1053-1055
diversity jurisdiction, §§1047-1050
Erie doctrine, §1057
federal, §§1043-1045
jurisdictional amount, §1051
jury trial, §1668
procedural matter, §1057
process, §§1052, 1055
Rule 22, §§1045-1056
statutory
diversity jurisdiction, §§1047-1050
generally, §1044
venue, §1056
INTERROGATORIES
See also Discovery
burdensome, §1448. *See also* Discovery, protective orders
corporations, §1245
costs, §1255
defined, §1241
depositions compared, §1242
duty to investigate, §1250
duty to respond, §§1249-1251
expert witness lists, §1308
extensive search, §1251
failure to respond, §§1252-1255
motion to compel response, §§1252-1253
numerical limit, §1248
objections to, §1254
time for response, §1249
when served, §§1246-1247
who must answer, §§1243-1245
INTERVENTION
See also Supplemental jurisdiction
by right, §§1011-1023
effect of, §1029

generally, §1009
permissive
generally, §§1024-1027
supplemental jurisdiction, §384
supplemental jurisdiction, §§388, 409
timeliness, §1028
venue, §1030
INVESTIGATION, PRIVATE, §§1497-1499
See also Discovery
INVITED ERROR, §2012
See also Appeal
ISSUE PRECLUSION, §§2031, 2073-2088
See also Res judicata

J

JOINDER
claims, §§636-642, 834-836
class actions, §§1058-1059, 1064, 1073
collusive, §§312-315
compulsory, §§961-989
dismissal, §986
diversity jurisdiction, §986
modern approach, §§965-979
nonjoinder, effect of, §967
procedure, §§980-986
venue, §985
waiver of, §§987-989
consolidation, §1035
co-owners of property, §§974-976
counterclaims, §§807-810, 1008
cross-complaints, §§833, 836, 1008
diversity jurisdiction
collusive joinder, §§312-315
impleader, §§971, 990-1008
improper, §959
indispensable parties, §964
interpleader, §§1036-1057. *See also* Interpleader
intervention, §§1009-1034. *See also* Intervention
joint obligees, §972
joint obligors, §§969-971
necessary parties, §963
partial assignees, §973
permissive, §§950-960
additional unrelated claims, §957
common question, §956
improper joinder, §959
same transaction, §955
subject matter jurisdiction, §960
procedure for compelling, §§980-986
shareholders' derivative suits, §979
subrogees, §973
supplemental jurisdiction, §960
third party beneficiaries, §§977-978
tortfeasors, §§970-971
JOINT OBLIGEES, §972
JOINT OBLIGORS, §§969-971
JUDGE, DISQUALIFICATION OF, §§1713-1724
JUDGMENT AS A MATTER OF LAW, §§1737-1762, 1766-1769, 1836-1837
and renewed motion, §§1755-1762, 1836-1837

396—Civil Procedure

burden of proof, §§1739-1743
case-by-case determination, §§1744-1754
demeanor evidence, §§1751-1754
nonjury trial, §§1766-1769
renewed motion, §§1830-1841
    joined with motion for new trial, §§1838-1841
    procedure, §§1832-1841
    test, §1831
    timeliness, §§1834-1835
scintilla rule, §1743
standard for grant, §§1739-1743
terminology, §1748

JUDGMENT N.O.V., §§1830-1841. *See also* Judgment as a matter of law
and motion for directed verdict, §§1836-1837
and motion for new trial, §§1838-1841
timeliness, §§1834-1835

JUDGMENT NOTWITHSTANDING THE VERDICT
See Judgment n.o.v.

JUDGMENTS
alternative. *See* Res judicata
modifiable. *See* Res judicata
on pleadings, §§888-893
relief from. *See* Motions
stipulated. *See* Res judicata

JUDICIAL NOTICE, §1735

JURISDICTION
See Diversity jurisdiction; Federal question jurisdiction; Subject matter jurisdiction; Territorial jurisdiction

JURISDICTIONAL AMOUNT
aggregation of claims, §§334-339
class actions, §§1101-1103
determination of, §§324-339
diversity jurisdiction, §§324-339
federal question jurisdiction, §375
"good faith" limitation, §328
interpleader, §1051
removed actions, §§329, 439

JURY
advisory, §1675
alternate jurors, §1700
argument to, §§1770-1774
"blue-ribbon," §1682
coercion by judge, §1819
instructions, §§1775-1793, 2010
    appellate review, §§1792-1793
    burden of persuasion, §§1781-1783
    clear and convincing proof, §1783
    comment on evidence, §§1784-1785
    "dynamite charge," §1811
    issues of fact, §§1776-1780
    objections to, §§1790-1791
    preponderance of evidence, §1782
    requested by counsel, §§1786-1791
materials allowed in jury room, §1814
misconduct, §§1820-1829. *See also* Verdict polling, §1827
qualifications of jurors, §§1691-1693
right to trial by, §§1645-1675
    advisory jury, §1675
    civil penalties, §§1658-1659
    constitutional right, §§1645, 1647, 1649
    declaratory relief, actions for, §1660
    discretionary jury trials, §§1673-1675
    historical test, §§1650-1659
    interpleader, §1668
    law and equity, §§1650-1654, 1661-1665
    shareholder actions, §1667
    statutory remedy actions, §§1656-1659
    statutory right, §§1646, 1648
    timely demand for, §§1669-1672
selection of, §§1676-1712
    constitutional requirements for, §§1680-1682
    federal courts, §§280, 1683-1689
    "key man," §1678
    qualifications of jurors, §§1691-1693
    state courts, §1690
    talesmen, §1679
    venire, §§1676-1690, 1694
size of, §§1695-1700
source of, §280
stages of jury trial, §1727
summary jury trial, §§1631-1644
unanimity requirement, §§1809-1813, 1816
venire, §§1676-1690
    size of, §1694
verdict. *See* Verdict
voir dire, §§1701-1712
    challenge for cause, §1702
    fraud, §§1823-1825
    peremptory challenge, §§1703-1707
    questioning by counsel, §§1710-1712
    questioning by court, §§1708-1709

K

"KEY MAN," §1678
See also Jury

L

LIMITED APPEARANCE, §117
LONG ARM LEGISLATION, §§100-106
See also Jurisdiction
specific acts, §§102-106

M

MANAGERIAL JUDGING
See Pretrial conferences and managerial judging
MANDAMUS, §§2018-2026
See also Appeal
MEDICAL EXAMINATION, §§1293-1301, 1478
See also Discovery
MERITS
See Res judicata
MINIMUM CONTACTS, §§21-52
See also Territorial jurisdiction
and First Amendment, §52
domicile, §70
in rem jurisdiction, §57
purposeful availment, §§24, 27-45

reasonableness requirement, §§46-53
transacting business, §102
MODIFIABLE JUDGMENTS, §2051
See also Res judicata
MOTIONS
    after verdict or judgment, §§1830-1918
    at close of proof, §§1736-1769
    for directed verdict, §§1737-1762, 1836-1837
    for failure to state claim, §§674-684
    for judgment as a matter of law, §§1737-1762, 1766-1769, 1836-1837
    for judgment n.o.v., §§1830-1841
    for judgment on the pleadings, §§698, 888-893
    for leave to amend pleadings, §844
    for more definite statement, §§687-688
    for new trial, §§1842-1893. *See also* New trial
    for nonsuit, §§1763-1765
    for relief from judgment, §§1897-1911
    for summary judgment, §§1530-1549
    renewed, for judgment as a matter of law, §§1830-1841
    Rule 12 procedure, §§692-694
    to alter or amend judgment, §§1894-1896
    to compel response, §§1252-1255
    to dismiss, §§672-686
    to strike
        federal, §§689-691
        state, §§668-670
    waiver of defenses, §§695-697
MULTIPLE DEFENDANTS
    jurisdictional amount, §336
    removal, §149
    venue, §123
MULTIPLE PLAINTIFFS
    jurisdictional amount, §338
MUTUALITY RULE, §2104
See also Res judicta

N

NECESSARY PARTIES, §§389, 963
See also Joinder
NEGATIVE PREGNANT RULE, §§759-763
See also Answer
NEW MATTER, FAILURE TO PLEAD
See Answer
NEW TRIAL, MOTION FOR, §§1842-1893
    additur, §§1891-1893
    and judgment n.o.v., §§1838-1841
    and renewed motion for judgment as a matter of law, §§1838-1841
    grounds for, §§1843-1865
    jury trial, §§1843-1864
    nonjury trial, §1865
    order, §§1876-1893
    procedure requirement, §§1866-1875
    remittitur, §§1883-1890
    standard for ruling on, §§1856-1859
    timeliness, §§1874-1875
NONSUIT, §§1763-1765
NOTICE, §§200-254
    See also Service of process; Territorial jurisdiction
    constructive, §210
    contents, §209
    depositions, §§1217-1220
    due process requirements, §201
    failure to receive, §211
    identification efforts, §208
    methods of, §§203-207
    service of process, §§212-254
NOTICE OF APPEAL
See Appeal
NUMEROUS PARTIES REQUIREMENT
See Class actions

O

OBJECTIONS AND EXCEPTIONS, §§1731-1733
OBJECTIONS TO JURISDICTION, §§116-120, 257-261
See also Territorial jurisdiction
ON THE MERITS
See Res judicata

P

PARTIAL FINAL DECISIONS, §§1972-1974
See also Final decision rule
PARTIES AND PRIVIES, §§2089-2098
See also Res judicata
PARTNERSHIPS
    capacity to be sued, §§939-941
    diversity jurisdiction, §§294-295
    venue, §127
PATENTS, §268
    venue, §142
PENDENT AND ANCILLARY JURISDICTION
See Supplemental jurisdiction
PENDENT CLAIM JURISDICTION
See Supplemental jurisdiction
PENDENT PARTY JURISDICTION
See Supplemental jurisdiction
***PENNOYER* DOCTRINE,** §§4-20
PLEADINGS
    amended
        after trial, §873
        answer, §850
        at trial, §§860-872
            code practice, §§862-865
            federal practice, §§866-872
            nonprejudicial variance, §863
            prejudicial variance, §864
        by permission, §843
        by right, §842
        judgment on pleadings, §§888-893
        procedure, §§844-846
        "relation back" doctrine, §§851-858
        scope of, §§847-850
        statute of limitations, §§851-858
        supersede original pleadings, §859
    answer. *See* Answer
    certification by attorney, §§709-749, 1479-1492
        sanctions, §§735-749
    code pleading, §§543-552

common law pleadings, §§539-542
complaint, §§556-646
counterclaims, §§799-820. *See also* Counterclaims
cross-claims, §§821-828
cross-complaints, §829-840
default procedure, §§879-887
    res judicata, §§2057, 2076-2078
demurrer. *See* Demurrer
denials. *See* Answer
equity pleading, §542
fact pleading, §§550-552
federal question jurisdiction, §§364-370
Federal Rules, §§553-555
impleader, §§387, 828
joinder of claims. *See* Joinder
judgment on the pleadings, §§888-893
notice pleading, §555
specific claims, §§595-632
    common counts, §§631-632
    contracts, §§614-622
    damages, §§623-630
    defamation, §613
    ejectment, §602
    fraud, §§610-612
    in general, §§596-600
    negligence, §§603-608
    products liability, §609
    trespass, §601
summary judgment, §§1501-1503, 1550
supplemental, §§874-878

PLEAS IN ABATEMENT
See Answer

PRAYER FOR RELIEF
See Complaint

PRETRIAL CONFERENCES AND MANAGERIAL JUDGING, §§1571-1644
arbitration, §§1615-1630
    award, §1627
    cases affected, §§1616-1624
    hearing, §§1626
    refusal to participate, §1630
    timing, §1625
    trial de novo, §§1628-1629
discovery control, §§1578-1580
final conference, §§1591-1607
final pretrial order, §§1605-1607
history, §§1571-1572
informal settlements, §1614
issue simplification, §§1581-1582
sanctions, §§1608-1612
scheduling, §§1573-1577
settlement promotion, §§1583-1590
    alternative dispute resolution, §1590
    judge's role, §§1586-1589
    mandatory attendance, §1585
    tactics, §1584
summary jury trial, §§1631-1644
topics covered, §§1599-1604
work product, effect on, §1613

PRIVATE INVESTIGATION, §§1497-1499
See also Discovery

PRIVILEGE
See Discovery

PROCEDURAL PRIVITY, §2091

PRODUCTS LIABILITY, §609

PROHIBITION, WRIT OF, §§2018-2026
See also Appeal

PROTECTIVE ORDERS
See Discovery

PUNITIVE DISMISSAL
See Dismissal

PURPOSEFUL AVAILMENT, §§24, 27-45
See also Minimum contacts

Q

QUALIFIED DENIAL, §§756-763
See also Answer

QUASI IN REM JURISDICTION
See Jurisdiction

QUESTIONING
See Depositions; Jury

R

REAL EVIDENCE
See Requests for inspection of real evidence

REAL PARTY IN INTEREST RULE, §§906-933
assignments, §§912-918
definition, §§907-910
determination of real party in interest, §§911-927
executors and administrators, §923
nonjoinder, §§931-932
principal and agent, §926
subrogation, §§919-920
third party beneficiaries, §927
trusts, §§921-922
violations of, §§928-930

REALIGNMENT OF PARTIES, §§310-311

"RELATION BACK" DOCTRINE, §§851-858

RELIEF FROM JUDGMENT
See Motions

REMAND
See Removal

REMITTITUR, §§1883-1890

REMOVAL, §§426-461
See also Jurisdiction
diversity of citizenship, §§435-439
    fictitious defendants, §§302-303, 437
    fraudulent joinder, §438
    jurisdictional amount, §§329, 439
    local defendant, §436
effect of removal, §452
federal question, §§428-434, 443-444
grounds for, §§427-447
in general, §426
procedure, §§448-454
    all defendants must join, §450
    defendant's right, §449
    timing, §451
remand, §§455-461
    abstention compared, §461

improper removal, §455
joinder and, §458
no reverse removal, §460
nonappealable, §459
supplemental claims, §456
separate and independent claim, §§319, 440-445
special removal statutes, §§446-447
supplemental jurisdiction, §434
where state court lacks jurisdiction, §§453-454

RENEWED MOTION FOR JUDGMENT AS A MATTER OF LAW
See Judgment as a matter of law; Judgment n.o.v.

REQUESTS FOR ADMISSION, §§1256-1275
See also Discovery
denial, §§1266-1268
equivocal, §1268
false, §§1266-1267
failure to respond, §1274
no response, §§1269-1274
on whom served, §1257
purpose, §1256
subject of
conclusions of law, §1259
facts, §1258
opinions, §1261
ultimate issues, §1260
unknown matters, §1262
time limits, §§1263-1264
use at trial, §§1492-1493
withdrawal of admission, §1275

REQUESTS FOR DOCUMENTS AND OTHER THINGS, §§1276-1292
See also Discovery
computerized information, §1277
designation, §§1282-1284
failure to respond, §1290
objection to, §§1286-1287
subpoena for inspection, §1291
scope of, §§1276-1278
timing, §§1281, 1285

RES JUDICATA
alternative findings, §§2083-2084
appeal, effect of, §§2048-2050
attachment jurisdiction, §§2065-2068
claim preclusion, §§2028-2030, 2034-2072
exceptions, §2069
collateral estoppel, §§2074-2088
conflicting judgments, §2052
default judgments, §§2057, 2076-2078
direct estoppel, §2073
family relationships, §2098
identical issue, §§2087-2088
in rem jurisdiction, §§2061-2064
issue preclusion, §§2031, 2073-2088
exceptions, §2088
modifiable judgments, §2051
mutuality rule, §2104
nonparties, §§2099-2108
"on the merits," §§2053-2058
parties and privies, §§2089-2098
procedural privity, §2091

punitive dismissals, §2058
stipulated judgments, §2079
substantive privity, §§2092-2098
validity of judgment, §§2059-2060

RULE 12
See Motions

RULE 22
See Interpleader

RULES ENABLING ACT, §§502-515
See also Erie doctrine
Federal Rules, §§512-515
limitations, §§502-503, 513
presumption of validity, §504

RULES OF DECISION ACT, §462

S

"SAME TRANSACTION," §955
See also Joinder

SANCTIONS
discovery violations, §§1451-1482
improper certification by attorney, §§735-749, 1479-1482
pretrial orders, §§1608-1612

SCINTILLA RULE, §1743

SECURITIES ACTS, §270

SEPARATE INSTRUMENT RULE, §1962
See also Appeal; Final decision rule

SERVICE OF PROCESS, §§212-254
See also Notice; Territorial jurisdiction
immunity from, §226
in general, §212
jurisdiction distinguished, §213
methods of, §§214-225
prejudgment seizures, §§227-254
within jurisdiction, §§91-95

SETTLEMENTS, §§1583-1590, 1614
See also Diversity jurisdiction; Pretrial conferences and managerial judging

SHAREHOLDERS' DERIVATIVE ACTIONS
diversity, §311
joinder, §979
jury trial, §1667

SPECIAL APPEARANCE RULE, §§85-86

SPECIAL DENIAL BY PARTS
See Answers

SPECIFIC ACTS
See Long arm legislation; Minimum contacts

SPECIFIC DENIAL
See Answer

"SPURIOUS" CLASS ACTIONS
See Class actions

STATE LAW IN FEDERAL COURTS
See Erie doctrine; Subject matter jurisdiction

STATUTE OF FRAUDS, §§782-783

STATUTE OF LIMITATIONS
affirmative defense, §§784-785
amended pleadings, §§851-858
as substantive law, §§512, 531
counterclaims, §§816-820
"relation back" doctrine, §§851-858
supplemental jurisdiction, §§424-425

STAY OF PROCEEDINGS BELOW, §1956
    See also Appeal
STIPULATED JUDGMENTS, §2079
    See also Res judicata
SUBJECT MATTER JURISDICTION, §§255-280
    See also Diversity jurisdiction; Federal question jurisdiction; Pendent and ancillary jurisdiction; Removal
    choice of state vs. federal court, §§275-280
    diversity cases, §§340-343
    in general, §255
    interpleader, §1054
    intervention, §1029
    joinder, §960
    limited federal jurisdiction, §§272-274
    not waivable, §§257-261
    source of, §§272-274
    state courts, §§262-271
        concurrent with federal claims, §§266-271
            exceptions, §§267-270
        general jurisdiction, §265
        monetary limitations, §264
        specialized courts, §263
    territorial jurisdiction distinguished, §256
SUBROGATION, §§919-920, 973
SUBSCRIPTION
    See Complaint
SUBSTANCE AND PROCEDURE, §§482-518
    pleadings, §§597-600
    statute of limitations, §§512, 531
SUBSTANTIVE PRIVITY, §§2092-2098
    See also Res judicata
SUMMARY JUDGMENT, §§1500-1570
    appellate review, §§1568-1570
    burden of proof, §§1531-1544
        opponent, §§1541-1544
        proponent, §§1531-1540
    class actions, §1114
    cross-motions for, §1527
    effect of decision, §1567
    initial showing requirement, §§1507-1508, 1530-1540
    judgment as a matter of law compared, §§1504-1510
    materials considered, §§1550-1558
    modern use, §1512
    motion procedure, §§1530-1549
    notice, §§1545-1548
    partial summary judgment, §§1559-1561
    pleadings motions compared, §§1501-1503
    purpose, §1500
    sham affidavit doctrine, §1524
    standard for granting, §§1513-1529
    timing of motion, §§1505, 1549
SUMMARY JURY TRIAL, §§1631-1644
    See also Jury
SUPPLEMENTAL JURISDICTION
    ancillary jurisdiction, §§381-389
        counterclaims, §§382, 386
        cross-claims, §387
        definition, §381
        impleader, §§383-386
        intervention, §388
        necessary parties, §389
    basis for, §§376-379, 397
    constitutional limits, §§379-408
    discretionary decline, §§416-423
        dismissals, §419
        extraordinary cases, §§420-421
        federal policy, §422
        nonfederal claim predominates, §418
        novel or complex state law, §417
        timing, §423
    diversity, §§392, 404, 409-415
        class actions, §413
        compulsory counterclaims, §414
        plaintiffs' claims, §§410-411
        Rule 20 joinder, §412
    federal question cases, §§392, 393, 400-403
    historical background, §§380-396
    pendent jurisdiction, §§390-415
        class actions, §§394-396
        defined, §390
    pendent party jurisdiction, §§391-393, 405
        diversity, §392
        federal question, §393
    tolling of limitations, §§424-425

T

TALESMEN, §1679
    See also Jury
TERMINATION WITHOUT TRIAL
    See Dismissal; Judgments; Motions; Summary Judgment
TERRITORIAL JURISDICTION
    See also Forum non conveniens; Notice; Service of process; Venue
    consent, §§75-90
        appearance as, §§83-90
            default, §90
            effect on jurisdictional objections, §§85-90
            extent of jurisdiction conferred, §89
        class actions, §82
        implied, §§79, 81-82
        local actions excepted, §80
        objections to, §§83-90, 116-120
        registration as, §§77-79
    due process requirements, §§21-25
    federal courts, §§96-98
    general jurisdiction, §§69-74
        corporations, §§71-73
        natural persons, §70
        vs. specific, §69
        when used, §74
    in personam,
        appearance, §§83-90
        class actions, §§1105-1107, 1165
        consent, §§75-90
        definition, §1
        due process requirements, §§21-25
        historical development, §§4-20
            consent, §16
            notice, §§18-20
            process within state, §§6-7
            status, §15

territorial limits, §§6-20
transient jurisdiction, §§7-9
long arm statutes, §§100-106
minimum contacts, §§21-52
due process requirements, §§21-25
purposeful availment, §§24, 27-45
choice of law distinguished, §§42-43
commercial vs. noncommercial activities, §41
component supplier, §35
effect in forum, §§36-38
foreseeability, §§28-38
similar claims, §§39-40
single act, §32
specific jurisdiction, §§39-40
stream of commerce, §§33-35
reasonableness factor, §§45-52
factors, §47
First Amendment concerns, §52
foreign country defendants, §51
plaintiff's interests, §46
notice. *See* Notice
service of process. *See* Service of process
in rem, §§2, 53-68
claims related to ownership, §61
definition, §2
enforcement of judgments, §65
in personam alternative, §68
insufficient contacts, §66
insurance obligations, §§13, 56, 67
intangibles, §§55-56
jurisdiction by necessity, §63
minimum contacts test, §57
notice, §202
preexisting claim, §60
prejudgment seizures, §§10-13, 232-254
presence of property in forum, §§53, 58-66
quasi in rem, §§3-20, 53, 64
real property, §62
tangible property, §54
traditional jurisdiction, §§4-20
limited appearance, §117
litigation of, §§116-120
binding effect, §§119-120
appealability, §120
default, §116
discovery rules, §118
limited appearance, §117
long arm statutes, §§100-106
minimum contacts, §§21-52
nonresident motorists, §17
notice. *See* Notice
objections to, §§83-90, 116-120
pendent. *See* Pendent and ancillary jurisdiction
quasi in rem, §§3-20, 53, 64
service of process, §§6-9, 91-95
See also Service of process
fraudulent inducement, §§93-95
modern standard, §92
traditional rule, §§7-9, 91
special appearance, §§85-86
specific jurisdiction, §69

statutory authorization, §§99-114
federal courts jurisdiction, §§107-114
in personam, §§108-113
in rem, §114
in general, §99
long arm statutes, §§100-106
full power, §101
specific acts, §§102-106
venue. *See* Venue

THIRD PARTIES
real party in interest rule, §927

TORT CASES
See Answer; Complaint

TORT CLAIMS, FEDERAL
venue, §145

TORTFEASORS, JOINDER OF, §§970-971

TRADEMARKS, §268

TRANSACTING BUSINESS
See Territorial jurisdiction

TRANSFER OF ACTIONS
See Forum non conveniens; Removal; Venue

TRANSITORY ACTIONS
See Venue

TRESPASS TO LAND
See Complaint

TRIAL DE NOVO, §2017

TRIAL, ORDER OF, §§1725-1728

TRIAL, RIGHT TO JURY
See Jury

"TRUE" CLASS ACTIONS
See Class actions

TRUSTEES
collusive appointments, §314
diversity jurisdiction, §304
real party in interest rule, §921

TYPICAL CLAIM
See Class actions

U

UNANIMITY REQUIREMENT
See Jury

UNINCORPORATED ASSOCIATIONS
capacity to be sued, §§942-946
diversity jurisdiction, §§293-298
venue, §126

V

VALIDITY OF JUDGMENT, §§2059-2060
See also Res judicata

VENIRE
See Jury

VENUE, §§121-181
aliens, §§147-148
corporations, §§125, 292
counterclaims, §802
diversity cases, §§128-133
federal courts, §§121-153
federal question, §§128-133
impleader, §1006

improper
    choice of law, §179
    objection to, §161
    waiver, §160
in general, §121
interpleader, §1056
intervention, §1030
local actions, §§150-153
natural persons, §124
partnerships, §127
"property present," §133
removal, §149
special venue statutes, §§140-146
    copyrights, §143
    federal tort claims, §145
    patent infringement, §142
    statutory interpleader, §146
state courts, §§121, 154-158, 181
substantial part of events, §§128-133
transfer provisions, §§162-181
    convenience, §§166-171
    effect of choice of law, §§177-180
    forum non conveniens compared, §167
    forum selection clause, §171
    multidistrict litigation, §§172-176
    state provisions, §181
    transferee court, §168
transitory actions, §122
unincorporated associations, §126
where claim arose, §129

VERDICT
    announcement of, §§1826-1828
    appeal, §§1988-1990
    chance, §1817
    contrary to law, §1854
    correction of, §1828
    general, §1795
    general with special interrogatories, §§1802-1808
    impeachment of, §§1820-1829
    judicially coerced, §1819
    quotient, §1818
    special, §§1796-1801
    unanimity requirement, §§1809-1813, 1816

VERIFICATION
    See Complaint; Pleadings

VIDEOTAPE DEPOSITION, §1234

VOIR DIRE
    See Jury

WXYZ

WITNESS'S STATEMENTS
    See Discovery

WITNESSES
    See Discovery; Interrogatories

WORK PRODUCT
    See Discovery